Woodworking with the Router

Professional Router Techniques and Jigs Any Woodworker Can Use

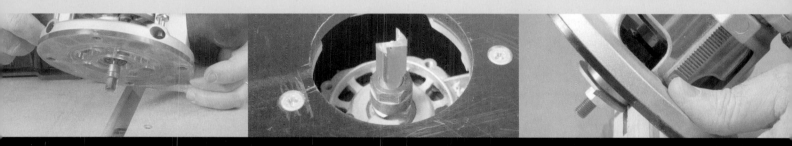

Completely Revised and Updated

Bill Hylton

Reader's Digest

The Reader's Digest Association, Inc.
Pleasantville, New York/Montreal

This revised edition is dedicated to my friend and woodworking mentor, Fred Matlack, who co-authored the original edition.

A READER'S DIGEST BOOK

Copyright © 2006 by The Reader's Digest Association, Inc.

All rights reserved. Unauthorized reproduction, in any manner, is prohibited.

Reader's Digest is a registered trademark of The Reader's Digest Association, Inc.

American Woodworker is a registered trademark of The Reader's Digest Association, Inc.

Design and layout: Jerry O'Brien
Photography: Donna Chiarelli
Illustrations: Frank Rohrbach

Copy Editor: Barbara McIntosh Webb
Project Designer: Nick Anderson
Cover Designer: George McKeon
Indexer: Nan Badgett

Reader's Digest Trade Publishing
        Executive Editor: Dolores York
        Canadian Project Editor: Pamela Johnson
        Associate Art Director: George McKeon
        Manufacturing Manager: John L. Cassidy
        Director of Production: Michael Braunschweiger
        President and Publisher, Trade Publishing: Harold Clarke

Library of Congress Cataloging-in-Publication Data

Hylton, William H.
  Woodworking with the router : professional router techniques and jigs any woodworker can use / Bill Hylton ; [photography, Donna Chiarelli ; illustrations, Frank Rohrbach].
    p. cm.
  Includes index.
  ISBN 0-7621-0800-2
  1. Routers (Tools) 2. Woodwork. I. Title.
TT203.5.H95 2006
684'.083--dc22

                2006042231

Address any comments about *Woodworking with the Router* to:
        The Reader's Digest Association, Inc.
        Adult Trade Publishing
        Reader's Digest Road
        Pleasantville, NY 10570-7000

For more Reader's Digest products and information, visit our website:
        www.rd.com (in the United States)
        www.readersdigest.ca (in Canada)

A NOTE TO OUR READERS
All do-it-yourself activities involve a degree of risk. Skills, materials, tools, and site conditions vary widely. Although the author and editors have made every effort to ensure accuracy, the reader remains responsible for the selection and use of tools, materials, and methods. Always follow manufacturers' operating instructions and observe safety precautions.

Printed in China
1 3 5 7 9 10 8 6 4 2

Acknowledgments

I want to invest a few paragraphs up front to acknowledge help I was given in revising this book. Big help and long-suffering support.

Revising the book was the idea of Dolores York of Reader's Digest Books. She got the router powered up, so to speak, then let me guide it through the job. Without her steadfast support throughout, you wouldn't be reading this. "Brisk" is the appropriate feed rate on a job like this, but I'm afraid "brisk" is not a dynamic I've ever mastered. Assuming that you share my belief that "there's a *lot* of good stuff in here!" then we both owe Dolores. Big time.

Three of the four people most involved in the project reprised roles played in the development of the original edition. They knew what they were getting into, and yet they signed on! I am grateful for that.

Frank Rohrbach produced all the illustrations. For the original book, Frank literally worked with pencil on paper to outline and label the drawings. Nowadays, he uses the computer. His work appears in books, including several other Reader's Digest woodworking titles, and magazines, including *American Woodworker*.

Donna Chiarelli spent many, many days in my basement workshop, producing the hundreds of photos for the book. She didn't get to work on the original edition, but she and I have worked together on several books and many magazine articles. She's a great photographer and a good friend.

Barbara Webb was the copy editor for both the original and this revised edition. The copy editor ensures that what you've written is what you actually *meant*. Sure, the copy editor deals with spelling and punctuation, but the substance of what a writer writes is also under scrutiny. Barb and I have worked on several books together, and I've come to trust her good judgment, value her great patience, and expect the well-timed nudge. I hope I get to work on more book projects with her in the future.

Jerry O'Brien did the last big job: combining the words, photos, and drawings on the page. Laying out the book. That job is a jigsaw puzzle, one in which the puzzle pieces have some elasticity. The job demands creativity, problem-solving skill, attention to zillions of niggling details, and unflappable composure. That's Jerry.

Many other people contributed to the revision. In the years since the first edition was published, I've been accumulating techniques and ideas and equipment and jigs contributed by woodworking compatriots, readers, and tool manufacturers. But without the contribution of the five individuals I've named, the accumulated know-how would still be only in my head.

Contents

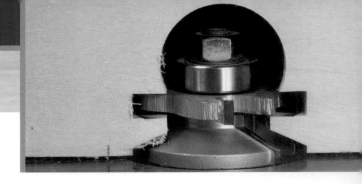

Introduction

Welcome to the second edition of *Woodworking with the Router*—bigger and more colorful than the original, but just as focused and practical. This book is your comprehensive router woodworking manual. It tells how to do all sorts of woodworking operations using the router.

We all understand that the router is woodworking's most versatile power tool, right?

That was true more than a decade ago, when *Woodworking with the Router* was originally published, and it is still true. You can use a router in just about every aspect of a job but assembly (it won't drive nails or screws). In the extreme, used creatively, it'll do almost any kind of cutting and shaping of wood. You can use it to prepare rough-cut lumber for a project, shape the pieces, cut the joinery, and embellish the finished assembly with decorative edge profiles.

But finding out how to do all those operations hasn't always been easy. Despite all the books and all the magazine articles that have been published in the last decade, *Woodworking with the Router* stands as the single most comprehensive and practical book on the subject.

And that's not just an author hyping his book. If you have the means and the interest, do a search on the World Wide Web, and you'll turn up comments from readers like: "This may be the only router book you will need." "Great book for learning about the router." "This book will tell you everything you need to know."

Now the book is better, even if I do say so myself.

When we put together the original edition, Fred Matlack and I spent nearly two years compiling and shop-testing router techniques. (Fred was the co-author of the original edition.)

There are jobs that can be done *only* with a router—edge treatments and template-guided work, to name two. Other jobs—cutting curves and cutting joints, for example—can be done exceptionally well with a router, though there are other options. And finally, there are jobs the router can do, even though it wouldn't be your first-choice tool. We tried 'em all.

Because there's always more than one way to do a thing, we conscientiously looked for more than one router-oriented approach. For example, a plunge router may make an operation simple. We explained how. But not everyone has a plunge router, so we explained how to do the job with a fixed-base router, too (if possible). And finally, we covered doing the operation on a router table.

Revising the book has taken more than a year. I revisited every topic, every technique, every sentence. The good stuff is still here, and I've added to it. Because this edition is in full color, all the photographs and drawings had to be redone, and that afforded the opportunity to look at each with a fresh eye. In color the illustrations are clearer and easier to understand. I weeded out those that didn't stand the test of time, but added new ones. This edition has more photos.

All the jigs and fixtures were similarly reevaluated. Sure, I still use some of the jigs shown in the original edition. But many I've replaced with improved versions. And over the years, I've discovered better ways of doing some jobs, often with a totally new jig. On top of that, manufacturers have introduced better routers, a broader array of bits, and lots of interesting and useful accessories.

Though the opening chapter is on routers, and it's followed by one on bits, *Woodworking with the Router* isn't really a shopping guide. These opening chapters remind you of all the routers available and expose you to features and configurations that you may not know about. Seldom in the book will you read about jigs to buy. Instead, I'll show you jigs to *make*. Sure, you can open your wallet and buy a lot of them, but why buy a jig if you can make it? (It's always struck me as odd that folks who consider themselves to be woodworkers would buy items they can easily—and more economically—make themselves.)

Router tables get more attention in this edition. New router models and new accessories like router lifts have enticed more and more woodworkers to use their routers in a table mounting. So I've expanded the chapters on designing and using router tables. You'll see different configurations of tables, including one in which the router is mounted horizontally. It offers an "angle of attack" that makes some jobs easier to perform than they would be on a regular router table. To increase the value of any router table you make, we have a range of accessories—bit guards, fences, sleds (which are like your table saw's miter gauge), and a variety of hold-downs and guides. Most are surprisingly easy to make.

Is all this information original? Of course not. Cutting a dado is cutting a dado. Sometimes the best techniques are the tried and true ones.

What is original, both in the original and now in the revised edition, is the logical, thorough, in-depth presentation. For this to be a basic operating manual, it's got

to cover those solid, traditional techniques, as well as the exciting, new derivations. Likewise, the information must be easy-to-find, complete, and clearly presented. It's got to be down-to-earth and practical. When you've got a question, when you can't remember an operation's exact sequence of steps, you want to be able to flip to the proper page without thumbing through the entire book. You need to be confident that the operation is covered, and that it's covered thoroughly and understandably, and that what's being presented isn't some speculation, however well-intentioned.

All these criteria are met. So a basic operating manual is exactly what you hold in your hands. It's a systematic, thorough guidebook to router woodworking. There's an index so you can find information quickly. Cross-references link you from an operation to similar or related ones elsewhere in the book.

Whether or not a technique is one we invented, I've tried it in my own shop. Thanks to the generosity of router, bit, and accessory manufacturers, I was able to prove out techniques using a simply capital assortment of equipment.

There's nothing in here that I'm not confident about, nothing that I haven't successfully done. What's here is not the sum total of what I tried, of course. Techniques that proved problematic, excessively involved, too specialized, or simply hazardous simply weren't included.

What you will find is the distillation: the most excellent router techniques.

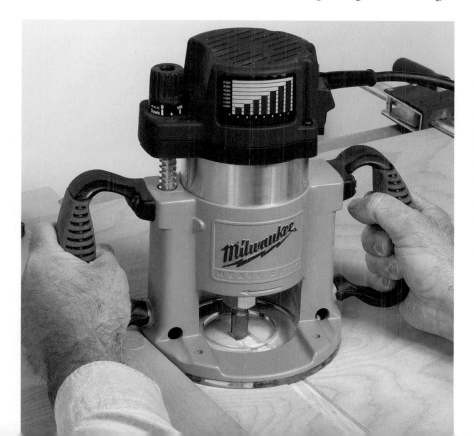

Routers

The basic router is an extremely simple piece of equipment. In general terms, it's a motor and several crucial controls. A rotary cutter is fitted into the collet on the lower end of the motor. It's direct drive in the purest form. The cutters largely determine what you can do with the router.

There are three main parts to a router: the motor, the collet, and the base.

The motor is the universal type, used in portable power tools. (Your table saw, jointer, and other stationary tools use a different kind of motor called an induction motor.) The power ratings of the motors used in routers range from $3/4$ horsepower up to about $3 1/2$ horsepower. The more power the motor has, the bigger the router is.

The collet is a simple but accurate chuck. Attached to the end of the motor armature, it holds the bit so the motor can make it spin. Designs vary, and some collets are intrinsically better than others. All collets, however, allow you to change bits.

The base holds the motor, posi-

The controls on a fixed-base router typically are divided between the motor and the base. The switch is on the motor, the handles on the base. The vertical adjustment system is shared between motor and base. The motor and base are easily separated for unrestricted access to the collet for bit changes.

The base of a dedicated plunge router is spare—a roughly donut-shaped casing with two smooth posts, long springs inside, rising from it. The bulky motor head contains the motor and virtually all the controls—handles, switch, plunge-depth adjuster, plunge lock. The motor head and base aren't intended to be separated, so collet access is somewhat restricted.

tioning it in relation to the work. It usually incorporates handles so the operator can hold and control the tool. The base's most critical feature is its depth-of-cut adjustment mechanism. There are two fundamental types of bases: the fixed base and the plunge base. The type of base your router has is pivotal to what your router does, how it handles, and what it costs.

Let's take a closer look.

Because the motor in a multi-base set is for a fixed-base router, most of the controls—handles, base latch, vertical adjustment—must be centralized on the plunge base. Access to the collet is improved, since the motor can be pulled from the base. But the assembled router is still top-heavy.

The Motor

Here's a curiosity. What is the measure of utility or capacity commonly used with tools? Other than the router, does any tool use its horsepower rating as the primary measure?

You talk of your table saw, circular saw, chop saw, or radial-arm saw in terms of the blade diameter first. Drills? Chuck capacity for portables, measure from chuck to column for drill presses. Band saw? Depth of the throat. Planer or jointer? Length of the cutting knives. Sanders? Size of the sanding area or belt.

But with the router, it's the horsepower rating that you mention first. That's because the power rating conveys the size of the bits it will drive, and suggests the tool's size and weight.

Power Ratings

The industry convention is to report *peak* horsepower on a universal motor, the type that drives a router, and *continuous* horsepower on an induction motor, the type used in stationary power tools. The universal (brush-type) motor is used primarily for intermittent, variable-speed operation. The induction (brushless) motor is used primarily for long-

term, fixed-speed operation. These differences will help explain why a 1 1/2-horsepower router is so much smaller than the 1 1/2-horsepower motor on your table saw. The big

table saw motor will deliver its rated power for hours on end, while the router motor will squeeze it out for about 30 seconds—under very special circumstances—and then die.

Which of these three motors is really most powerful? The largest is an induction motor that will run all day, continuously producing its rated 3/4 horsepower. The two router motors are the universal type. Neither the smaller, rated 7/8 hp, nor the larger, rated 2 1/4 hp, can produce its rated power under normal operating conditions.

I'd advise you not to put too much stock in horsepower ratings. The ratings are based on the manufacturer's dynamometer tests, so they are legitimate. But the tests are run with the motors wired up to draw amperage without limit. America is wired with 15-amp outlets, so portable power tools are rated at—and thus corded for—a maximum of 15 amps. With that 15-amp limitation, the motor in your router can't produce 3 horsepower even if it *is* rated for that.

You may have been advised to look at amperage ratings instead of horsepower. An amperage rating is assigned by Underwriters Laboratories (UL) to motors, and it's specified on every tool. It is the maximum amount of current the tool can draw for a protracted period without overheating and, potentially, starting a fire. The UL rating isn't the maximum amperage the motor can *use*, mind you, nor is it related directly to its potential power output. The UL rating has to do with fire safety.

Promotional hyperbole aside, and technical details notwithstanding, the links between amperage ratings

Speed Control

Most routers are equipped with an electronics package that's commonly dubbed EVS, which is short for electronic variable speed. You probably can't find a new 3-plus-horsepower router without it. It's an option—a very popular option—on most mid-power models, too.

Being able to vary the router's speed is the obvious benefit of EVS, but an intriguing aspect of the option is that it generally adds to the horsepower rating, as much as 1/2 horse.

Routers cruise at 22,000 rpm, a speed that's fine for bits less than 1 inch in diameter. But a 3-inch cutter spinning that fast is moving more than 260 feet per second at the cutter tips. That's about the length of a football field in the time it takes to say, "Oops." EVS allows you to dial back the router's rpm, making it safer to use large-diameter bits.

Variable speed is accompanied by what's called "soft start." A non-EVS router will have what amounts to "instant on." Flick the switch and in a nanosecond, it's running at 22,000 rpm.

Getting a router up to speed takes quite a bit of force. As Sir Isaac Newton might have put it, "When you hit the switch on your router, the handles want to turn counterclockwise

just as much as the bit wants to turn clockwise." That power-on jerk is startling, particularly with the more powerful routers; but more than that, the sudden torque is hard on the router's bearings. Soft start tempers the startup by easing the motor up to speed over a period of a second or so. Though "a period of a second or so" sounds awfully short, there is a distinct difference between a soft start and what I guess you'd have to call a hard start.

Another valuable benefit integral to EVS is a feedback system that enables the motor to maintain speed under varying loads. Some systems monitor motor current, while others monitor rpms. Either way, the electronics feed the motor the electricity that it needs to maintain the speed you've set. This prevents the router from bogging down as you feed it into a cut. (Nevertheless, you *can* bog down any router with an excessive cut or an overly aggressive feed.)

The feedback loop is the reason for the boosted power ratings. A motor with feedback electronics is able to keep running longer under load than the same motor without it. Since the peak horsepower tends to be delivered just before the motor stalls, that extra running time keeps the power curve rising.

A tiny thumbwheel on the motor—rotate it to change motor speed—is the only outward evidence of the electronics available on most contemporary routers (including at least two laminate trimmers).

The electronics are increasingly sophisticated, and the manufacturers are finding ways to make them more robust. The electronics can be expensive to replace, and when they fail, the router can be sidelined completely. So packaging them to withstand the vibration and dust that routing entails is essential.

and advertised horsepower are consistent industry-wide. A 5- or 6-amp motor has a $7/8$- to 1-hp rating, 7 to 9 amps is $1\,1/4$- to $1\,5/8$-hp, 10 to 11 is $1\,3/4$-hp, 12 is 2- to $2\,1/4$-hp, 15 amps is $3\,1/4$- to $3\,1/2$-hp. Is anybody claiming $2\,1/4$ hp out of a 9-amp motor? I don't think so. Or $3\,1/2$ hp out of 12 amps? Of course not.

What's important to you, the router user, is whether your router has enough moxie to power a particular bit through the cut that you need to make.

The Collet

The collet is a tiny, but vital, part of the router. Though it weighs only an ounce or two, this is the part that holds the cutter on the end of the motor's armature shaft.

Here's how the job is done. The typical collet is a tapered cylinder with a precisely sized, perfectly round, perfectly concentric hole

Common Collet Designs

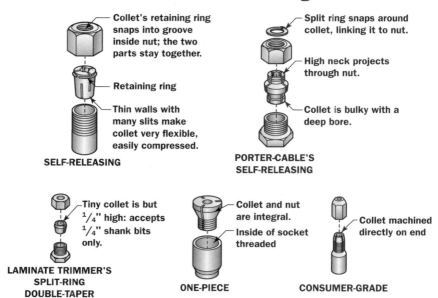

Collet's retaining ring snaps into groove inside nut; the two parts stay together.

— Retaining ring

— Thin walls with many slits make collet very flexible, easily compressed.

SELF-RELEASING

Split ring snaps around collet, linking it to nut.

— High neck projects through nut.

— Collet is bulky with a deep bore.

PORTER-CABLE'S SELF-RELEASING

— Tiny collet is but $1/4$" high: accepts $1/4$" shank bits only.

LAMINATE TRIMMER'S SPLIT-RING DOUBLE-TAPER

— Collet and nut are integral.
— Inside of socket threaded

ONE-PIECE

— Collet machined directly on end

CONSUMER-GRADE

through the center. It has at least one slit through its wall, from top to bottom. It fits into a conical socket in the end of the motor's armature. When the collet nut is turned onto threads on the armature, it forces the collet down into the socket. The slit

is forced closed, which reduces the diameter of the collet's bore. If a bit of the proper shank size is in the bore, an even pressure is exerted on that shank.

Of the types in use, the best is called the self-releasing collet. The

The self-releasing collet is the industry standard, used on all but a few routers. Designs vary. Some are slender and flexible (left), while others are quite bulky and stiff (right). All self-releasing collets are linked to the collet nut. Those on the left snap onto a retaining ring machined inside the nut. The collets on the right are secured with a separate split ring. Unthreading the nut pulls the collet from the socket, freeing the bit without a tussle.

The super-simple one-piece collet integrates the collet and nut. The part has threads at its base and a pair of wrench-flats at the top. While the collet isn't markedly shorter than other styles, its socket is. Made only with a 1/2-inch bore, you need a sleeve-type reducer to fit 1/4-inch-shank bits in it.

collet and the nut are connected. As you loosen the nut with a wrench, the collet is drawn out of the socket, releasing the bit. You should know that varying amounts of slack are inherent in this system. You usually have to use the wrench twice, first to "crack" the nut, then to actually pull the collet so it releases its grip on the bit.

All the professional-grade routers,

excepting Hitachi and Triton, use the self-releasing style of collet.

The bulk of such collets varies from brand to brand. DeWalt, Fein, and Festool use a slender, flexible collet that you can squeeze and deform with your fingers, while Porter-Cable and Milwaukee use a thick, stiff collet. All are more than an inch long and fit in sockets 2 or more inches deep.

The least-acceptable collet is what I call a split-arbor. This collet is integral to the motor's armature, and if the collet gets damaged or worn, you can fix it only by replacing the armature. It'll be cheaper to buy a whole new router.

A different design is the one-piece collet, found on several Hitachi models and the Triton. The collet and nut are integral, with the threads on the inside of the socket and the outside of the collet—just the opposite of the usual arrangement. The collet is heavy and thick, with one slit through to the bore, and two partial slits. The socket for it is less than an inch deep.

It's best if you focus on routers that have both 1/2-inch and 1/4-inch col-

lets, in my opinion. Large-diameter and very long cutters especially should have 1/2-inch shanks, and you need to get a router that will take them. At the same time, avoid models that don't provide a true 1/4-inch collet, instead forcing you to use a sleeve to fit 1/4-inch shanks in the 1/2-inch collet.

The Router Base

With a router, you have some pretty impressive power at your fingertips and the ability to make it go or stop. To use this power effectively, you need to have a base to hold the motor in a controlled relationship to the work. There are two general types: fixed and plunge.

With a fixed-base router, you set the depth-of-cut and don't change it while the router is running. The plunge router allows on-the-fly cutting-depth changes.

The fixed-base model is less glitzy, perhaps, than a plunge model; but it is the first you should buy. And if you feel you can buy only one router, make it a fixed-base model.

Putting the Squeeze On
How collets work

Tightening the nut drives the collet into the socket; collet compresses around and grips the bit shank.

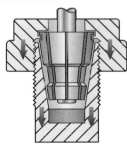

Collet is long enough to hug almost entire length of shank.

Crack nut with wrench, then turn to take up slack until it binds against collet.

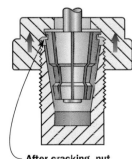

After cracking, nut turns freely until it bears against collet.

Unscrewing the nut pulls the collet from the socket, freeing the shank.

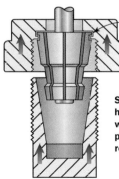

Collet is linked to the collet nut.

Shallow taper holds collet tight, won't allow it to pop free if nut is removed.

The fixed-base router generally is compact, with a low center of gravity, making it the more stable tool for the majority of the routing you'll do. Its handles are low enough that you can grip them firmly and still have the heels of your hands braced against the work.

The plunge router enables you to lower the spinning bit into the work in a controlled manner, so you can begin and end a cut almost anywhere on a board. Ideal for cutting stopped grooves and for inside work with templates, it's essential for cutting mortises.

The trade-off is balance. The motor rides up and down on a pair of spring-loaded posts rising from the router base. To plunge the router, you release a lock and conscientiously push down on both handles. At rest,

Balance is the trade-off in choosing between fixed-base and plunge routers. Compare the handle positions on these two routers, versions of the Bosch 1617. Both have the same-length bit bottomed against the benchtop. The plunger's handles are substantially higher than those of the fixed-base router.

Multi-Base Router Sets

If you are shopping for your first router, a multi-base set is the ideal purchase. It costs more than either a fixed-base or a plunge router, but it's cheaper than one of each. Yet one of each is effectively what you get.

The routers are mainstream, workhorse models. The typical package includes a 2 1/4-horsepower motor with EVS and both 1/4-inch and 1/2-inch collets, a fixed base, a plunge base, and a plastic case. The motor will fit either base, of course, and the change from one to the other is fast and easy. Use the plunge base for mortising and other operations that require on-the-fly cutting-depth changes. Switch the motor to the fixed-base for edge-profiling, dadoing, and similar operations.

The multi-base router package was pioneered by Porter-Cable more than a decade ago, and it had the

Multi-base sets are among the best buys available. You get a single motor and both a fixed base and a plunge base. You can switch the motor from one base to the other quickly. You concede nothing in terms of capabilities, accuracy, or durability in opting for such a package.

niche to itself for a surprisingly long time. In recent years, Makita, Bosch, DeWalt, and Hitachi elbowed into the niche, and PC introduced a new model. Bosch even makes a version of its package for Sears Craftsman.

The bulk of a plunge router and especially the larger base opening make the tool tricky to steady at a corner. The base is mostly unsupported, and the whole router wants to tumble off the work. If it does, the bit will gouge the work.

A fixed-base router, with its lower center of gravity, is easier to manage in the edge cuts. The modest-sized baseplate opening common to fixed-base routers improves support for the router at corners.

The D-handle base has several practical benefits. The handle is easy to grip firmly and gives you good directional control of the router, even with one hand. The on-off trigger is under your index finger—as with a circular saw or belt sander—which allows you to switch the motor on and off without lessening your hold on the router. Not to be overlooked is the fact that you can unplug the motor at the switch, making it easy to disconnect the power every time you change bits. The D-handle is supplemented by a knob on the opposite side of the base.

the handles are 4 to 6 inches above the work. Even with the router plunged to the max, you may have difficulty bracing the machine because the handles are a little too high above the work.

In my opinion, any work that does not require those on-the-fly changes in cutting depth should be done with a fixed-base router. This includes edge-profiling and cutting dadoes, grooves, and rabbets. In my shop, fixed-base routers do the wide majority of the work.

The Assembled Package

Your first reaction to any router probably isn't based on individual parts. You look at the handles, gauge the size, and judge the router's stance. You pick it up, heft it, think about how comfortable it "feels." It's largely a tactile evaluation. You may never look at the collet or try to find out how well the motor is constructed.

As you shop, know all the options. The broad options extend beyond plunge versus fixed-base.

Two Grades: Consumer and Professional

There are two grades of routers, just as there are of other portable power tools. They are professional and consumer. You can choose from fixed-base and plunge models in both grades.

The obvious difference is cost. You can pick up a consumer-grade router for $60 to $100. Professional-grade routers run between $140 and $325.

Underlying the cost differences are, of course, significant differences in design and manufacture, predicated on anticipated uses. A professional tool is designed to weather the workaday uses and abuses of the job site and commercial shop. Long running times, incessant on-off cycling, heavy cuts—often with massive bits—and cumulatively, hundreds and hundreds of hours of use.

The consumer tool, on the other hand, is expected to be used for brief periods. Think about it. A hobby woodworker who averages 10 hours of shop time a week over the course of a year will have about 500 hours invested. If his (or her) router is actually *running* for a tenth of that time,

The differences between a consumer-grade router (left) and a professional-grade model (right) might not be immediately obvious, though prices may tip you off. Disparities in motor construct are hidden. Compare the controls carefully for differences in refinement, precision, and durability.

it'll have 50 hours on it. A tradesman or cabinetmaker can log that in a month or two.

The upshot is that the designer of a consumer-grade tool can compromise on almost every aspect of it. The motor need not be as robust as a pro-grade motor. Aluminum might be used in the windings rather than copper. The bearings will be a lower grade. It may tend to run hotter, and heat kills motors. Running it for protracted periods can shorten its life.

There're more trade-offs than longevity, though. The controls on the consumer-grade router will be less sophisticated. You'll find plastic levers and knobs used instead of metal ones. Fine-adjustment features will be absent. The tool will be harder to set up precisely. Some setups are outside its capability.

Fit and finish won't be as good. Castings will be low-quality "pot metal," with rough edges and little refinement. Consumer models "feel" more like toys than precision tools.

Two Sizes: Medium and Large

Routers are clustered in two sizes characterized primarily by amperage and horsepower ratings. The dimensions and weights of the routers parallel the power ratings.

The largest number of brands and models, both fixed-base and plunge types, are rated between 1 3/4- and 2 1/4-horsepower. These are often called mid-sized or mid-powered routers, but the truth is, these are the baseline models. Aside from consumer-grade brands and models, you'll find only three routers rated at less than 1 3/4-horsepower. Those are Porter-Cable's venerable Model 100, Festool's unique plunge router, and

Makita's fixed-base 3606, which crowds the line between consumer and production routers.

The second cluster is the 15-amp, 3- to 3 1/2-horsepower club, which currently includes two fixed-base routers and 11 plungers. All are professional-grade tools.

You'll find that the medium-sized routers weigh between 7 and 9 pounds, while the big ones weigh between 12 and 14 pounds. Interestingly, the consumer models tend to be heavier than the pro ones. Dedicated plunge routers tend to be a little heavier than comparable fixed-base machines. The plungers *feel* substantially larger than fixed-base machines.

Choosing a router size is largely a matter of use. The big routers are dedicated to table use 90 percent of the time. For most of us, they are

Though the marketplace is chockablock with 3-plus-horsepower plunge routers (left), the really practical model is a middleweight (right). For handheld work that requires on-the-fly changes in cutting depth, a mid-sized plunger is nimble and easy to manage. Most woodworkers who buy the heavyweight gorillas dedicate them to use in a table mounting.

unmanageable as portable tools. The mid-sized routers are versatile, great for handheld operations and service-able as table routers.

As you sort through the candi-dates, assess the characteristics that are vital. Don't get sidetracked by bells, whistles, and non-essentials. Things like switch location and spindle locks can be tie-breakers, if they enter at all into the choice.

Manageability

Manageability is essential. You need to be able to lift your router easily and handle it with confidence. If it is too big or too heavy, if the knobs or handles don't fit your hands, you will have a difficult time using it effectively.

In the fixed-base marketplace, the middleweight 1 3/4- to 2 1/4-horsepower models (right) dominate. At least nine brands have contenders in this division, so you have an inter-esting assortment of configurations to consider. These are the most manageable, most versatile, and thus most popular of the routers. Jump to the bigger 3+ hp size (left), and you have but two models to look at. Both are first-rate table routers.

Compact routers have largely disappeared from the market, but short, lightweight routers are really handy for most common operations. Bosch aimed its diminutive 1-horsepower "palm router" at this niche. Slightly larger than a laminate trimmer, you grip it in one hand. It takes only 1/4-inch shanks, and the base opening restricts you to bits 1 1/4 inches or less in diameter.

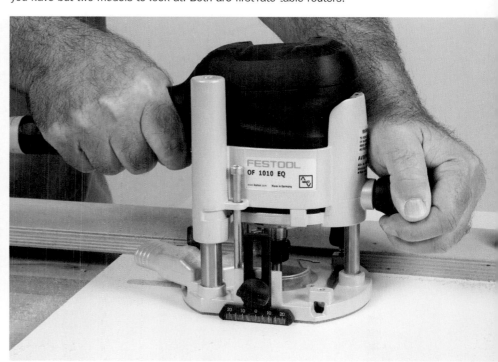

Festool, a German manufacturer, makes two routers that stand apart, refusing to conform to router design dogma. Both are short, with a knob at one end and a pistol-grip-style handle at the other. Routing with either mimics working with a hand plane or a circular saw or belt sander. You can actually plunge them smoothly with one hand. I see them as D-handled plunge routers. Both have plenty of moxie for common hand-guided cuts.

Versatility notwithstanding, no single router can do it all. You need a mid-sized model (or two or three) for routine joinery cuts and decorative profiling, and a big one for your router table.

You also need a mini-router to fit into spots too tight for a full-sized tool, a router you can grasp in one hand. This router is called a laminate trimmer. It can't spin BIG bits, but boy! can it plow an inlay groove or hollow out a hinge mortise.

Originally designed for trimming plastic laminate after it is cemented to its substrate (hence the name), it was quickly adopted by woodworkers who make the cabinets and counter-tops that lie beneath the laminate. Trimmers are great for:

- Rounding-over, chamfering, or profiling edges

- Inlay work

- Mortising for hinges

- Trimming plugs, through tenons, and edge bands

- Sign making

Don't think of trimmers as wimpy. Today's trim routers pack as much power as the full-sized routers of 30 years ago. But use discretion: You can overtax a trimmer's bearings and motor, causing it to overheat.

Two base styles dominate; one I call the sleeve-type, the other I call a two-piece. The sleeve-type base is common to regular-sized fixed-base routers. The sleeve is split, but it has a bolt that spans the split. Tighten the bolt, and it pulls the split closed, tightening the sleeve around the motor and preventing it from moving. Loosen the bolt to move the motor.

The specifics of the two-piece base design vary from one trimmer to

A trimmer can be held in one hand and guided confidently around the edges of a workpiece to cut a round-over or other small profile.

A trimmer with a sleeve-type base that surrounds the motor is likely to hold the bit square to the base. This is important for accurate joinery cuts and problem-free profiling. The vertical adjustment range is usually wider than with a two-piece base, another feature valuable in woodworking more than in laminate work.

another. Generally one of the pieces is a split-ring clamp with a post. The clamp holds the motor. The other piece is the base itself, and it also has a post rising from it. The posts overlap and are bolted together. To adjust how much the bit extends from the base, you loosen the bolt and slide the posts past each other. A jack screw controls the movement, making it a micro-adjustment from one end of the range to the other.

A common problem with the two-piece base is vertical alignment. You want the bit axis perpendicular to the baseplate. But with the two-piece base, the motor can be slightly cocked in the clamp, the assembly bolt can be insufficiently tightened, or wear can introduce a misalignment between the base parts. In my experience, these trimmers aren't reliably accurate for some common operations. Twist the tool as you round-over

edges, for example, and you can introduce a hairline fillet to the shape. Just here and there. Just enough to make you nuts. And it is because the base surface isn't square to the bit axis.

Make your selection based on what you plan to do with the trimmer. A set with a motor and three or four different bases is *so seductive!* All those accessories! A set makes good sense if you are in the counter biz, trimming odd angles and around backsplashes and scribing laminate edges to fit a wall. But if you are doing general woodworking, the extra bases will see little if any use. Another expensive bargain.

If you will be using the trimmer for edge detailing or any operations that demand that the bit axis be absolutely perpendicular to the trimmer's base, get one with a sleeve-type base. The other designs aren't accurate in this regard.

Switch position doesn't have to be a big issue. You prevent mishaps by resting the router on the work with the bit clear. When it's steady and you are ready, turn on the router. If you have to release one handle to reach the switch, you don't relinquish control of the tool.

Get a router that doesn't intimidate you. Switch it on—with it plugged in, of course, so you experience the motor screaming—and maneuver it around a workpiece, real or imaginary. If you have an opportunity to actually cut with the router, jump at it.

Above all, don't be reluctant to start small. Get experience. You'll probably find that you can do a lot of practical work with a relatively small machine. And when the time is right, buy up, getting a larger, more powerful machine.

Adjustability

Adjustability covers the range, simplicity, and accuracy of setups, particularly the depth-of-cut. Obviously, this is vital. You want to be able to set the

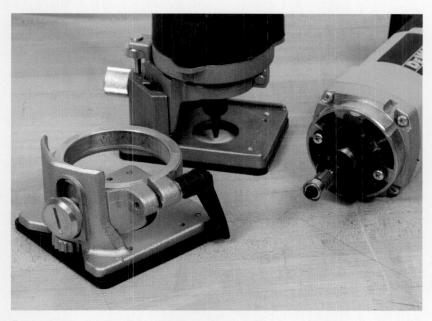

For laminate work in all its variety, a trimmer with a two-piece base is ideal. Bit adjustments are infrequent and modest in range. Swapping the standard base for an offset or tilting model is easy. And if the bit's a degree or two shy of square to the base, it won't show in the cut.

cutting depth quickly, yet have it be accurate. The best systems provide both coarse and fine adjustment capabilities, so you can make an initial setting easily and quickly, followed by infinitesimal adjustments. And of course, you need to be able to lock in the setting securely, without wrenches or pliers, so your setting doesn't very subtly drift as you make cuts.

With all routers, the cutting depth is governed by the vertical position of the motor in the base.

Plunge routers: The motor of a plunge router is mounted on posts, of course, and what you set is a stop to limit how close to the base the motor can descend. Release the plunge lock and the motor—spring-loaded—bounces up the posts, away from the base and thus from the work. The cutting depth diminishes.

While the details vary from brand to brand and model to model, the cutting depth of a plunge router is established by the gap between the depth-stop rod and a pad or turret on the base. You install the bit, then plunge the router, bottoming the bit against the work (so the bit's tip is flush with the bottom surface of the baseplate). Drop the rod against the turret, then back it away—a distance equal to the desired cutting depth—and lock it.

To refine a coarse setup, most systems incorporate a means to alter the length of the rod. On several models, for example, the depth rod is actually a tube with a threaded shaft penetrating it. Without moving the tube, you can extend or retract the threaded shaft, which alters the distance between its end and the turret. Regardless of the exact mechanism, you can increase or decrease the depth in increments as miniscule as 1/128 inch.

This adjustment paradigm works when the plunge router is held in your hands but doesn't when the router is hung upside down in a table. Used that way, the router needs some sort of "height stop" to control the motor's movement away from the base. A router without this can be maddening to adjust in a router table. See the sidebar "Table-Friendly," page 14.

Fixed-base routers: Viewed broadly, the adjustment dynamic is the same on all fixed-base routers. The base is simply a big sleeve-type clamp around the motor. Loosen it, and you can slide the motor in and out, altering the distance that the bit extends beyond the base (or removing the motor completely to change bits). Tighten the clamp, and the position is locked.

The toggle latch is the state-of-the-art lock, with only a couple of models still using a wing nut to cinch the clamp/base. A wing nut has nothing to recommend it, and manufacturers are abandoning it as they introduce new models.

To better illuminate the variations in adjustment schemes, let's look at some specific brands and models.

Plunge-stop systems don't get much simpler than the threaded rod on the Makita 3618C. Push and hold the spring-loaded release button to slide the rod up or down. Turn the plastic knob on top to dial in micro-adjustments of 1/16 inch or less. The gap between the rod's tip and the base is the plunge depth.

Some plunge-stop systems are sophisticated. DeWalt's DW621 has a tubular stop with a fine-pitch screw inside. Turn the winder (with zero-able graduated ring) on the router's front to move the entire rod up or down, roughly setting a plunge depth. With the rod locked at the coarse position, turn the knob on top to extend or retract the tip, micro-adjusting the plunge depth.

■ Bosch uses a two-stage system. You choose one of three positions—$1/2$ inch apart—as a coarse setting, then turn a threaded rod to dial in a precise setting. Each rotation moves the bit $1/16$ inch. The system is easy to use and accurate. But if you get to the end of the adjuster's range without reaching your setting, you have to shift to the next coarse position and turn the adjuster all the way to the opposite end of its range to pick up where you left off. Irksome.

■ Porter-Cable (except for the new 890), Makita, and Hitachi use pins registering in a spiral ramp for vertical adjustments. PC has the ramp cast into the base, while Makita and Hitachi have incorporated it into the motor housing. To extend or retract the bit, you twist the motor clockwise or counterclockwise, respectively. A by-product is that the switch moves, something many complain about, though users seem to be able to deal with.

For controlled adjustments, these routers have a graduated ring attached to the base. You zero out the ring by rotating the "zero" to align with an indicator on the motor. Then you twist the motor (without moving the ring) till the indicator aligns with the desired fraction on the ring. Fine adjustment is all in your wrist.

A three-stage, screw-based vertical adjustment system is used on the Bosch's 1617 (and the Craftsman version of it). The finger projecting into the base (right) engages a recess on the motor. Turn the knob to wind the finger up or down a 16-threads-per-inch adjuster screw, taking the motor with it. The system is accurate but not fast. Jumping from the top of one stage to the bottom of the next requires winding the finger from one end of the screw to the other.

■ DeWalt also uses the spiral ramp, but its approach keeps the motor from rotating. The graduated ring is turned onto the motor. When the motor is dropped into the base, two latches on the ring grab the base, locking the ring and the base together. Turn the ring, and the motor rises or falls without rotating. Very fine adjustments are as

Here's the nut-and-bolt approach to depth adjustment. Thanks to spiral ramps cast into the base (think of them as threads) and a few pins on the outside of the motor, the motor screws into the base, just like a bolt into a nut. A scribe-line on the motor tracks depth changes on the graduated ring encircling the base. Porter-Cable has used this system for decades, and Makita and Hitachi adopted it for its newest fixed-base models.

The ring-and-spiral ramp functions like the nut-and-bolt, but neither the motor nor the base turns. Only the ring does. The spiral ramp is integrated into the motor housing. Turn the ring that's clipped to the base and the motor rises or falls. The zero-able scale on the ring allows you to make micro-fine tweaks to the vertical setting. DeWalt uses this system on its DW618 router.

A router frequently is hung in a table to create a stationary tool. If this is your intention, then fold table-friendliness into your primary selection criteria. Following are things I consider important in a *dedicated* table router.

1. Power. If you are buying a router strictly for a workhorse router table, then buy one that will spin the largest bits. That requires power and speed control. Don't be chintzy.

2. Base opening. Bit manufacturers insist that their largest bits—horizontal panel-raisers, for example—be run only in a router table. Consequently, it's essential that a table router be able to accommodate them, and to me, "accommodate" means the opening in the base must provide unobstructed passage for the bit from one end of the vertical adjustment range to the other.

That makes it easier to access the collet nut for bit changes, allows you to back the bit down into the table to make a shallow cut, and eliminates the inadvertent, unexpected collision between bit and base casting.

3. Bit changing. The key issue is how you get to the collet nut when the router is mounted in a table.

As I write this, you can buy a few routers—the Triton, the Freud FT3000VCE, and the PC 890—that can plunge their collets through the base (and thus through a tabletop) for bit changes. More routers with this capability are on the way, I am sure. This capability mimics the premium router lifts.

Changing bits above the table is also possible with fixed-base routers. You simply drop the motor out of the base, bring it out from under the table, and set it on the tabletop.

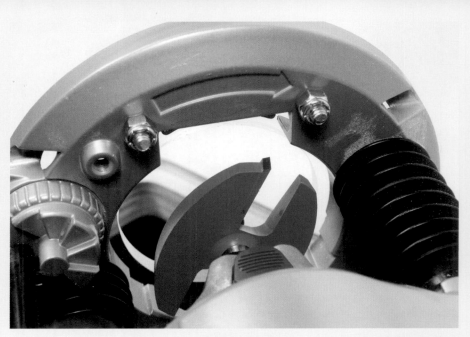

The best table routers allow you to retract a 3 1/2-inch bit completely through the base. But on most routers the opening is too small. The bit will smash against the rim or mounting tabs for template guides. The Bosch 1619EVS shown here is one of the few with a base opening large enough for the biggest bits on the market.

Triton was the first production router designed to push its collet through the base for bit changes. When it's mounted in a table, this capability allows you to change bits "above the table." Several other manufacturers have incorporated this feature into their routers, and others surely will follow.

With other plunge routers, the common routine is to pull the tool out of the table, and lay it on the tabletop for bit changes. This routine requires you to hang the router on a mounting plate (oftentimes called an insert). The Triton, the Freud, and all the fixed-base machines can be mounted directly to the underside of the table, leaving your tabletop seam-free.

Though it isn't what most woodworkers think of when you say "above-the-table bit changes," what you see here is just that. With a fixed-base router, you can change bits most easily by dropping the motor out of its base and standing it on the tabletop.

4. Bit-height adjustments. Evidence of how important this is to woodworkers is their willingness to spend as much for a router lift as they do for a router. (Personally, I'd rather buy two routers than one router and a lift.)

Speed of adjustment is as important to me as accuracy. Virtually *every* router can give you accurate adjustments, even in fine increments, though none give you a direct readout. Very few give you speed as well.

With most plunge routers, you use a knob or crank threaded into the router's height-stop rod to drive the motor toward the base (or allow it to rise away from the base). Typically, the thread pitch gives you an adjustment on the order of 1/16 inch per rotation. This is great for fine adjustments, but a larger move—retracting the bit through the base so you can replace it, for example—translates into 20 to 30 wrist-wrenching revolutions. And that's followed by a similar number of

turns to wind the new bit up into cutting position. This is exactly why two-stage adjustment is so desirable.

Of the current plunge routers, only Triton and the Bosch 1619EVS have two-stage coarse-fine adjustment. Of the fixed-base models, all Milwaukees and PC's 890 offer two-stage adjustments, but as a practical matter most fixed-base routers adjust quickly.

5. Switch. If I intend to use the router's switch as the primary on-off control, then I prefer one that snaps on and snaps off. That leaves out triggers. But this facet of switch design isn't a deal breaker. If I like other aspects of the router, I'll deal with a trigger, even one that's difficult to lock.

A separate, exposed switch is an

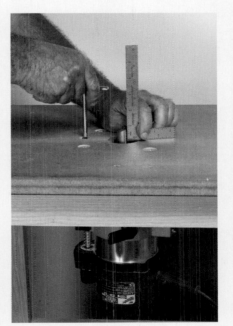

Milwaukee supplies a T-handle wrench with its routers so the vertical adjuster can be accessed through a hole in the base. Several other router models have similar features. With one of these routers hung under a table, you can adjust the bit height from topside (a highly overrated feature, in my opinion).

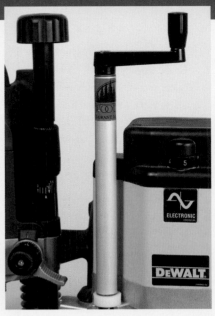

Many plunge routers can be modified for easy, precise height adjustments with the addition of a knob or crank. Knobs are cheap, and often are supplied with the router. The crank works far faster, but it's available for a limited number of models.

important router-table feature to me. I don't think any switch you can't see is going to be easy to find in a panic situation. Ergo, the separate switch. So the router's switch must be one that can be locked on and left on as long as it's in the table.

Price and compromise. The routers I prefer, based on my interpretations of the criteria, are high-priced. But for many woodworkers, price is the pivotal criterion. Compromise on the features as you deem necessary and appropriate to get the best table router you can afford.

Oftentimes you can make a router more table-friendly with an aftermarket accessory or some modifications. If that router is a low-cost one, so much the better. But don't let price hijack the evaluation process. Do your homework first, *then* compromise to fit your budget.

easy to achieve as with the threaded-rod-based approaches.

If there's a hitch here, it's that gross adjustment is only possible with the motor out of the base. Then you can spin the ring quickly. Once the base and motor are assembled, all vertical adjustments are slow and steady.

■ Milwaukee routers have continuous adjustment from top to bottom, using an Acme-thread screw. The screw is mounted on the motor and engages in

An Acme-thread screw is the heart of Milwaukee's vertical adjuster. Pushing the black release button enables you to insert and remove the motor from the base without touching the screw. The release also enables you to make a coarse cutting-depth setting quickly. To make very fine adjustments, you turn the screw. Either adjustment must be made with the toggle latch open.

the base. Push a release on the base to slide the motor quickly in or out of the base. You can make a gross movement to any point along the threaded adjuster. Let go of the button, then turn the screw for a niggling little alteration. Using the screw adjuster to move the motor from one end of the range to the other isn't necessary.

Moreover, the screw adjuster can be accessed using a special wrench (it's supplied) through the baseplate.

Smoothness

In a plunge router, quality number one is how well it plunges. In my opinion, the only reason to buy a plunger is to make plunge cuts. Make sure the one you buy does that well. The movement should be smooth. No stickiness at any place along the continuum.

Bear in mind that none plunge smoothly when only part of the base is supported, which is to say, when routing along an edge. The router needs support beneath both posts. Likewise, you can't plunge a router smoothly with one hand. You need equal pressure on both handles.

You have to try different brands and models of plunge routers to assess the effort required to make a plunge cut. Some are very stiff, demanding a surprising amount of effort to plunge. Others have low spring rates, and seem more buoyant. You've got to try them and judge which you prefer.

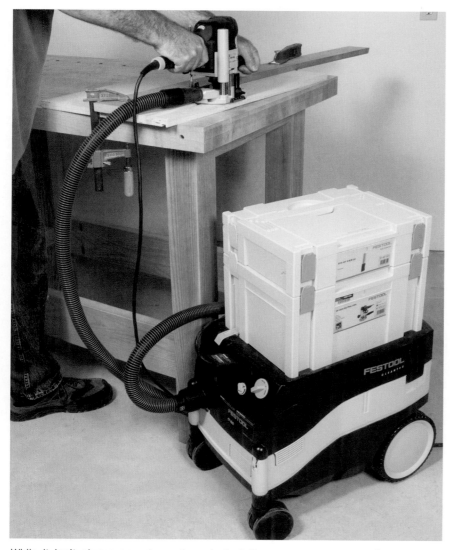

While it isn't always easy to capture dust at the source, router manufacturers are increasing their efforts to design-in dust pickups. To take advantage of them, you must tether the router to a shop vacuum and maneuver the tool around the workpiece without tangling either the cord or the hose. The benefits make the effort worthwhile.

Bits

You are bent over your workbench, a brand new router at your side. It's your first router, and you are really itching to put it to work. Instead of working wood, though, you're flipping through a big fat catalog of router bits.

You have this much figured out: Without a bit, the router's just an expensive, noisy motor.

In woodworking with a router, there are three essential components to success. One is the router itself. Another is the woodworker—you. The last is the bit. A savvy woodworker using good bits can do a lot with a lousy router. But the best woodworker with the greatest router will be stymied by a dull, poorly balanced bit.

So the bit is easily the most important part of the whole routing operation.

The thing about woodworking with a router is that the more bits you have, the more different jobs you can do with the basic machine. That's not really true of other woodworking machines.

A bit catalog is the right place to start. Get them from several different manufacturers; look at everything available. Note how remarkably similar every manufacturer's "library" of cutters is. Read what each maker has to say about bits. Note that some talk mostly about low prices, and others emphasize their high-tech manufacturing process and boast about their carbide formulations, steel quality, and protective coatings.

As you page through, keep asking yourself what you are going to do with your router. Do you want to profile edges and make moldings? Cut joints? Duplicate parts? Make frame-and-panel doors? These intentions should direct you to particular bits (or at least categories of bits).

Not sure? Look *seriously* at a starter set, which will give you the chance to sample the router's capabilities.

What Do You Need to Know?

Sooner or later you're going to wonder what differentiates one line of bits from another. Prices vary widely, first of all. Are the low-cost bits junk? Are the expensive ones way overpriced? Then there're coatings. Some bits are colored and others are not; is that just for show? Finally, there's the question of choice. In certain categories, some manufacturers have *so* many options, it seems impossible to figure out which one is right for your job.

Virtually all router bits made and sold these days are carbide or carbide-tipped. Carbide is an extremely hard material, close to the hardness of diamonds. While it can't be honed as sharp as high-speed steel (HSS), it holds its edge far, far longer than HSS. That enduring edge is the reason carbide reigns.

The main weakness of carbide is brittleness. It chips easily. While it comfortably cuts wood of all sorts, plastics, and even brass and aluminum, hitting any ferrous metal debris—a nail or screw buried in a board—will chip it.

Carbide is also expensive. That, coupled with its brittleness, is why more bits aren't solid carbide. The shank and body of most bits are machined from steel, and then slips of carbide—the cutting edges—are

Catalogs from a cross-section of bit vendors are invaluable in choosing bits. Whenever you tackle a new project, you can flip through the pages and look for bits that will make the job easier, the results better. The more bits you have, the more work your router will do for you.

brazed to the bit. This is an economical means of putting the carbide where it will do the most good.

Bit prices range widely. A particular profile made by one manufacturer may cost 2 or 3 times that made by another. The cost difference may stem from where the bits are made (the U.S. or Europe versus the Far East, for example). It may stem from *how* they're made. It may stem from the design.

The usual advice is to examine a bit for visible signs of quality: the thickness of the carbide, how evenly it is brazed to the bit body, and the

Chip the carbide cutting tip—by hitting a hidden fastener, for example—and the bit may be scrap. Only one of two cutting edges is chipped, but it's evident in the cut itself. Impossible to determine is whether the carbide is fractured. Grinding out the damage without compromising either the cut dimension or the profile is difficult.

Bit Dimensions
Here's what you need to know

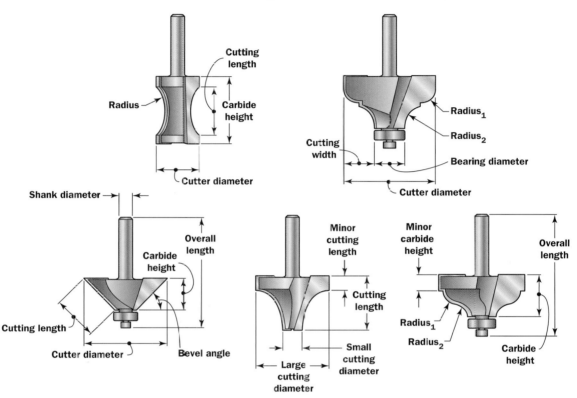

smoothness of the cutting edge. These aren't necessarily the most important aspects of bit quality, but they are things you can see. If they're poor, the likelihood is that the invisible aspects will also be poor.

The carbide's thickness suggests the ultimate lifespan of the bit. A skinny strip of carbide will disappear after a couple of sharpenings. (Whether or not you ever will have it resharpened is immaterial.) A fat carbide tip indicates that the maker expects it to last a good many years, even if you are a pro and will have the bit resharpened a half-dozen times.

A corollary to thickness is support. The carbide tip should be supported along its full length. It's brittle, remember, and if it isn't fully supported, and especially if it's not too thick, the carbide may break. That could be dangerous! The steel behind the tip shouldn't be visibly pitted.

Finally, check the quality of the edge ground on the carbide. You may want serrations on a knife edge. But a router bit doesn't cut wood the way a knife slices bread or cheese. If you can see grinding marks, the edge has been ground only roughly. If the bit's cutting edges look under magnification like a serrated knife, pass it by; that bit will leave a serrated finish. Better bits will appear and feel smooth.

Of the quality aspects you *can't* see, the most critical is the roundness of the shank and the overall balance of the bit. You can't tell about the bit's balance until you use it. *Then you'll know!* If the bit's shank isn't perfectly rounded, or if the bit isn't perfectly balanced, it will vibrate. When you cut with it, it'll chatter.

Compare a low-priced bit (left) with a comparable higher-priced one (right). You'll often find that the body of the lower-priced bit is slightly smaller in diameter and the carbide slips are thinner. Less obvious are compromises that may have been made in the geometry—hook angle, clearance, and shear angle. Any compromises made in the carbide grade or the steel used are completely invisible.

Bit Geometry

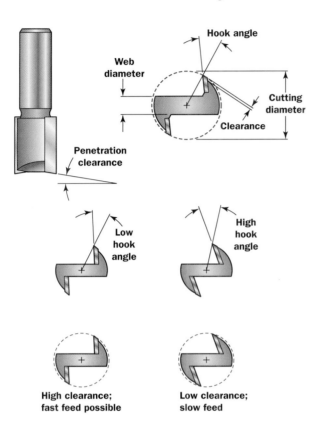

Vibration is hard on the router, the bit, and the cut.

Marketing plays a big role in the cost difference, in my opinion. The costlier bit is targeted to the worldwide industrial and professional market, with the hobby market as a tag-along. Cost is important, of course, but an industrial customer requires a bit made to tight tolerances and designed to endure hours and hours of sustained use and repeated resharpenings.

The cheaper bit is sold primarily to the hobby market, with sales to professionals coming as a fortuity. In this marketplace, low cost usually is paramount. But the bit doesn't have to withstand hours of use and repeated resharpenings.

So the market focuses the manufacturing. Simplistically, one bit is designed and spec'ed to do a job and is priced according to its manufacturing cost. The other bit is designed and spec'ed to be produced at a given cost. Is one bit overpriced? No. Is the other shoddy? Probably not.

Color-Coated Bits

Why are router bits colored? Depends on whom you ask.

Colored bits first appeared, I believe, in the early 1990s. The color was a byproduct of coating the bits with heat-resistant, nonstick poly-tetrafluoroethylene (PTFE), such as DuPont's Teflon. Those manufacturers using PTFE coatings contend that it diminishes friction and drag, reduces pitch buildup, and prevents rusting. These are significant benefits, though perhaps less for a hobby woodworker than for an industrial operation.

But some, primarily manufacturers who don't use the coatings, argue vehemently that PTFE coatings are ineffective. The colored coatings, they insist, are all a marketing scam.

Scam is an ugly word, of course, but it is true that marketing is behind the color. Though it didn't have to be, the coating *could* be colored, and whatever color a manufacturer chose would become its trademark. Orange for CMT, red for Freud, and so on. Nowadays, very few bit brands are without a color. A woodworker who isn't brand-loyal has bits in red, several shades of green and of blue, as well as orange, yellow, white, and silver. But not all those colors mean that the coating is PTFE. In most cases, it's a powder coating—better than paint on

the one hand, but less high-tech than PTFE on the other.

If you accept the contention that PTFE is beneficial, seek out the brands that use the coating. Color alone is no guarantee that that's what you are getting.

A flute is the opening in front of a bit's cutting edge, which provides clearance for the wood chips. The vast majority of bits have at least two, and a small number have three or even four. Only straight bits are made in the single-flute configuration (left). A single-flute bit allows a higher feed rate but makes a cut with a rougher finish. Because it cuts twice in each revolution, a double-flute bit (right) can't be fed as fast as a single-flute bit. But those two cuts yield a smoother finish.

The overwhelming majority of straight bits have the cutting edges parallel to the bit axis (left). Placing the cutting edge at a slight angle—a shear—reduces the power needed to make the cut and produces a better finish (center). Only a few manufacturers make straight bits with shear angles, though many use them on profile cutters. Spiral bits—the ones that resemble twist-drill bits—take the shearing action further, combining it with chip augering (right). The quality of the cut is improved, but the cutting action is slowed. Spirals are either solid HSS or solid carbide.

Up or Down?

Shear angles are either down-cut—sometimes called negative-shear—or up-cut or positive-shear.

Downward slicing action leaves a clean, generally fuzz-free edge, which is particularly beneficial when working plywood or melamine. But it tends to drive the router and the workpiece apart, so a secure grip or the use of hold-downs is important. In addition, it tends to push chips to the bottom of the cut, rather than clearing them from it. Of course, on a through cut, it does move chips away from the router and onto the floor.

Down-shear is used on spiral bits, a few straight bits, and (hinge) mortising bits (left). Look down on a bit's tip. It's down-shear if the flutes descend in a counterclockwise spiral.

An upward slicing action is favored for deep grooves and mortising, where the upward spiral helps clear chips from the cut. It also augers the bit into the workpiece, thus pulling work and router together. A disadvantage is that the upward slice tends to lift the wood fibers at the edge of the cut.

In addition to spirals and some straights, up-shear is used on almost all profile-cutting bits, whether edge-forming or groove-forming (right). You can identify an up-shear by looking down on a bit's tip. If the flutes descend in a clockwise spiral, they're up-shear.

Just Starting?

Whittling the possibilities down to the affordable and versatile few—the ones you need to start a router bit collection—can be overwhelming. If you have no bits at all, try to match your dollar investment in a router with a dollar investment in bits. Put $200 into a router, $200 into bits.

Unless you know exactly what you are going to be doing, it's a good idea—and good economy—to begin with a "set." The economy is in the price. The set's cost is always lower than the aggregate cost of the individual bits.

Every bit manufacturer, importer, or vendor that I can think of packages bits in sets, and invariably, one is a "starter set." This 12- or 13-bit assortment includes joinery and profiling bits, all in a handy box. The specific selection may vary, but the typical set includes three or four straight bits, a rabbet bit, three or four edge-profile bits, a V-groover, a dovetail bit, and a flush-trimming bit. This assortment allows you to sample the primary categories of router operations. *You don't need a set substantially larger than 12 bits.*

Don't overstretch the "economy" aspect by buying a cheap set at a home center. Remember what I said at the outset: "The bit is easily the most important part of the whole routing operation." Good bits give good results, and good results are always encouraging and rewarding. You'll have the core of your collection, and subsequent purchases will merely expand it. Buy a cheap set, though, and you'll end up replacing every one.

One thing about sets I want to address here. You may find that you seldom—if ever—use a couple of the bits. And some folks dwell on that: "Don't buy a set. It'll have bits

The router is a crackerjack joint-cutter, and for the majority of joinery cuts—dadoes and grooves, mortises, tenons, laps and half-laps, even rabbets if you've got an edge guide—you need straight bits. Begin with the basics, and add those special-application straights as the *need* for them in your work dictates. To me, the basics are 1/4-inch, 3/8-inch, 1/2-inch, and 3/4-inch bits, with cutting edges between 3/4 inch and 1 1/4 inches long. They'll do a good range of jobs, from 1/8-inch-deep dadoes to 1-plus-inch-deep mortises.

Your joint-cutting capabilities can be enhanced with the addition of only a few bits to the four basic straights. A 1/2-inch 14° dovetail bit (on a 1/4-inch shank) is essential for routing half-blind dovetails, but it also cuts sliding dovetails. A slot cutter set makes tongue-and-groove joints and forms grooves for splined joints of all sorts. An upspiral or two improves your mortising, and straights sized for plywood produce tight dadoes and grooves.

The rabbet bit (left) is often touted as essential, but I don't agree. Yes, you'll find one in every starter set. But all it'll ever cut is rabbets. I recommend you invest first in a mortising bit (right), which cuts any width rabbet, plus tenons and laps. In addition, it's ideal for surfacing stock.

you don't use. Just buy 'em as you need 'em."

Bah! I say. *Most* bits are seldom used. I've got dozens and dozens of those bits. But when a job requires a specific bit, then that bit becomes *essential.* Too often you don't realize how useful a particular bit is until you have it. I'll repeat: A starter set gives you the means to sample the primary categories of router operations.

Shopping for Bits

Bits are sold in hardware stores and building centers everywhere, though the selection usually is limited. You'll probably find better brands and a wider selection at a woodworking retail store or a tool dealer. To get what I *really* want, I usually buy bits through mail-order catalogs (or on the Internet). Yes, it requires a bit of self-control, since as much as a week passes

Almost all bits today are anti-kickback. With a router bit, kickback stems from slicing a chip big enough to jam the router's advance. Unless the motor stalls, it'll kick the tool back at you. The body of an anti-kickback bit is configured to be just 1/16 inch smaller than the cutting diameter. In addition, it has a gullet ahead of the cutting edge that limits the size of chip that can be sliced from the work. These features

between my phone call or mouse-click and the bit's delivery. I've survived.

While shopping by mail prevents me from examining the bit before I buy it, the fact is that critical characteristics aren't visible to the naked eye anyway. You can't assess the hardness and quality of the carbide, or the bit's overall balance, simply by looking at it.

How do you decide what brand to buy? I go by reputation, price, and

prevent you from feeding the router too aggressively, thus preventing kickback. The features are most obvious in large-diameter cutters.

my own experience. Buy a brand that you see advertised regularly and that comes at a price you can manage. You'll do fine. I've sampled well over a dozen brands, and the truth is that I've gotten very few absolute lemons over the years—and most of those were replaced by the supplier. So don't procrastinate, don't agonize. Buy some bits and make that new router sing you a woodworking song.

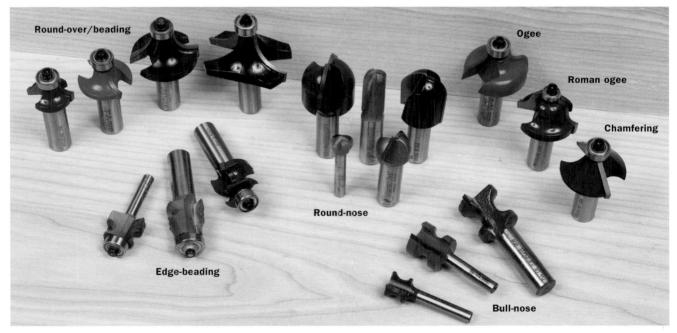

The array of bits made for decorative profiling is astonishing. But as you'll see in the chapter "Decorative Treatments," page 139, simple bits used in two- and three-step operations can produce complex molding. Start simple and expand into the complex bits as your interest and finances dictate. A good collection consists of several sizes of round-over bits (with alternative bearings that convert them to beading bits) and round-noses (for cutting flutes and coves), plus an ogee and a Roman ogee, a chamfering bit, and bull-nose and edge-beading bits in one or two sizes.

A first-time router buyer can easily do worse than investing in a modest (10- to 15-bit) set. The bits in the typical starter set enable you to cut practical joints, decorate edges, and do simple template work. Virtually every vendor packages such sets, pricing them at a distinct savings over the aggregate cost of the individual bits, and packaging them in a useful storage box.

Template work often involves either a flush-trimming bit or a pattern bit. The flush-trimmer's pilot bearing is on the tip, and the pattern bit's is on the shank. The flush-trimmer is safer because you expose only enough of the cutting edges to do the work. With the pattern bit, the entire cutting length must be exposed so the bearing can reference the template. Both come in a variety of diameters and lengths. To start, buy a 1/2-inch-diameter flush-trimmer with 1-inch-long cutting edges or a 3/4-inch pattern bit of the same length.

Using Bits

There is a little more to using a router bit than slipping it into the router collet and cinching down the collet nut. You've got to match the bit to the cut and the router. You've got to balance the bit speed with the feed rate. Here are some pointers for using your bits to their best advantage.

Bit selection. Always use the bit with the shortest cutting edge that will do the job. Excessive length amplifies vibration and deflection, which degrade the cut and can lead to tool breakage. If you are cutting a 3/8-inch-deep dado, use your dado bit with the 5/8-inch-long cutting edges, rather than your straight bit with the 1 1/2-inch-long cutting edges.

Always use the bit with the largest-diameter shank you can. See "Shank Size" on page 26 for the rationale.

Pilots. Each time you fit a bearing-piloted bit in your router, give the bearing a flick to ensure that it spins freely and that its rim is smooth and clean. The prime cause of tracks and scorch marks on the workpiece edge is a frozen bearing.

The purpose of the pilot is to guide the cut and to control its width. The bearing is supposed to roll along the workpiece edge at the feed rate, while the bit spins inside it at the router's speed. But if you don't put enough pressure on that bearing, it can spin along with the bit and really stink up the edge, if you know what I mean. (On the other hand, press that bearing too hard against a soft wood, and you crush the wood fibers, leaving a different sort of track along the edge.)

Dirt or grit stuck on the bearing's rim can cause a wavy or choppy cut. The dirty pilot acts like a kind of cam, lifting the cutting edge infinitesimally away from the work each time the dirt speck hits the guiding edge. (The same unsatisfactory finish

Using a bit that's overly long for the job can lead to a broken bit. A 2-inch-long straight may be just right for tenoning, but it's way too long for a 3/8-inch dado. Most of us have a limited selection and use a midlength cutter—3/4 to 1 inch long—for both jobs.

Getting a Firm Grip
Fitting a bit in a collet

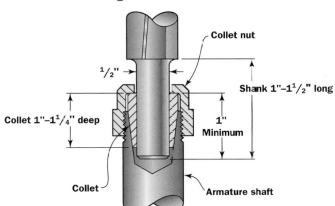

Collet nut

1/2"

Shank 1"–1½" long

Collet 1"–1¼" deep

1"
Minimum

Collet

Armature shaft

SOME PROBLEMS

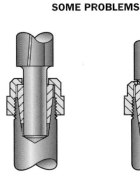

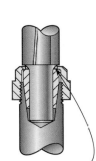

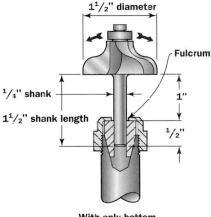

1½" diameter

Fulcrum

1/4" shank

1"

1½" shank length

1/2"

Collet pulls shank down into socket as nut tightens. That jams a bit that bottoms when it's inserted.

Collet catches transition fillet, doesn't seat against shank. Bit is thus not secured.

With only bottom 1/2" of shank in collet, leverage amplifies forces trying to break the shank.

can be achieved by running a clean pilot along a dirty, chipped work edge, by the way.)

The collet. Always use the correct collet for your router, and avoid using sleeves or bushings to make a 1/4-inch-shank bit fit in a 1/2-inch collet. These reducers add to vibration and run-out, and they generally don't hold the bit as well as a collet alone. (A number of router manufacturers don't make separate 1/4-inch collets for their 1/2-inch-collet machines, and if you've got one of them, using a bushing is unavoidable.)

When you tighten the collet nut, it pulls the collet and the bit shank down into the socket. If the shank is bottomed, it can jam, perhaps preventing the collet from seating tight, perhaps forcing the bit off-center by a thousandth or two. That's enough to cause pretty severe vibration.

How deep the bit shank must be inserted in the collet is not something all bit manufacturers agree on. Most urge you to avoid cheating the bit out of the collet to extend its reach. But that *is* occasionally a tempting idea. You need to cut juuusssst a little deeper, so you back the bit out of the collet an extra 1/4 inch or an extra 1/2 inch. One old rule of thumb says the minimum insertion is twice the shank diameter. As a practical matter, you don't always have a lot more length than that on 1/2-inch-shank cutters. But having a hefty cutter on a 1/4-inch shank inserted only 1/2 inch into the collet seems excessively venturesome to me.

Feed rate. The rate at which the router is fed along the work (or the work is fed across a router table) is very important to the overall quality of the cut and to the longevity of the bit. You should feel a constant, even pressure when the work meets the cutter. Feed rate ultimately depends on the type of material being cut, the amount of material being removed, and the type of bit being used.

The most common feed rate mistake is excessive restraint. And feeding too slowly is a quick way to ruin a bit. Letting the bit "dwell" in the cut will lead to a burned cut, caused by the bit heating up, which in turn reduces the bit's life immensely. Remember, heat can ruin a sharp tool. So keep the router (or the work) moving.

If you are concerned about bogging the router down, make several light passes to complete the cut instead of trying to hog away too much material in one pass. This is especially true if you are using a large-diameter bit. This will reduce the stress on the bit and will generally be a safer practice.

Router speed. The speed at which the bit turns can be important. The typical router runs at somewhere between 20,000 rpm and 24,000 rpm, depending upon the brand and model. Router bits cut fine at this operating speed.

But as the diameter of the bit increases, the router's high operating speed becomes a problem. The issue isn't cut quality, it's safety. The explanation is shown in the drawing *Tip Speeds.* At 22,000 rpm, the tips of a 3/4-inch-diameter bit are traveling 49 mph. But the tips of a 3 1/2-inch-diameter horizontal panel-raiser have much farther to go per revolution, so at the same rpm, they're traveling 228 mph!

There's general agreement among manufacturers of routers and bits that large-diameter bits—3- to 3 1/2-inch-diameter panel-raisers, for example—should be spun at no more than 12,000 rpm. (At that speed, the tip of the bit would be traveling at just under 130 mph.) But the recommended speed settings for other sizes of bits aren't so uniform:

■ One bit maker recommends operating any bit larger in diameter than 1/2 inch at no more than 17,000 rpm, and dropping that speed to no more than 14,000 rpm when the diameter exceeds 1 inch.

■ A couple of others recommend slowing the router to 18,000 rpm when the bit diameter exceeds 1 1/4 inches, to 16,000 rpm when the bit diameter tops 2 1/2 inches.

If the 130-mph tip speed is appropriate for a 3 1/2-inch bit, why wouldn't that be the speed limit for all bits? If it is, then you can run a 2-inch-diameter bit at 22,000 rpm; its tip speed at that rpm setting is 131 mph. On the other hand, if a lower tip speed—say, 105 mph—is safer, then you can run bits up

Shank Size

The majority of router bits made today have either 1/4-inch or 1/2-inch shanks. Prices are about the same. Which size should you buy?

Just look at the difference in girth. Is there any question as to which is stronger? Compared to the 1/4-inch shank, the 1/2-inch shank has the following:

■ 4 times the surface area of the smaller, so the collet has more to grip

■ increased heat dissipation

■ greater stiffness so it is less prone to deflect; deflection degrades the cut

■ greater mass to absorb vibration

Nevertheless, there are reasons for buying *some* 1/4-inch-shank bits. Some routers, notably laminate trimmers, don't have 1/2-inch collets. Some bits are available only on 1/4-inch shanks. Sometimes, as when routing mortises, for example, it's advisable to work with a shank the same size or smaller than the bit's cutting diameter.

Tip Speeds
From short track
to super speedway

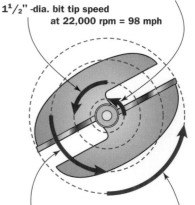

3/4"- dia. bit tip speed
at 22,000 rpm = 49 mph

1 1/2"-dia. bit tip speed
at 22,000 rpm = 98 mph

2 1/2"-dia. bit tip speed
at 22,000 rpm = 164 mph
at 17,500 rpm = 130 mph
at 14,000 rpm = 104 mph

3 1/2"-dia. bit tip speed
at 22,000 rpm = 228 mph
at 12,500 rpm = 130 mph
at 10,000 rpm = 104 mph

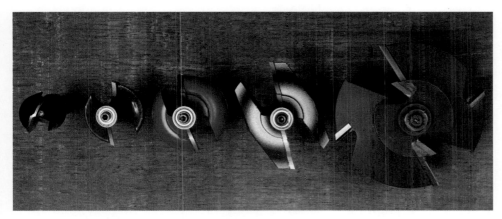

The speed at which you spin a bit should be reduced as its diameter expands. Dial back your router's speed as you switch from bit to bit, left to right. I think you can safely run the 1- and 1 1/2-inch bits at full tilt. Chuck a 2-inch bit in the router, and reduce the speed to 17,500. Switch to a 2 1/2-inch bit and shave the rpm to 16,000. And run that horizontal panel-raiser at only 10,000 rpm.

to 2 inches in diameter at full speed. But at 2 inches, you reduce the router speed to 17,500 rpm, at 2 1/2 inches to 16,000 rpm, and at 3 1/2 inches to 10,000 rpm.

I should add that most variable-speed routers have an rpm range from 10,000 to 22,000 rpm. A few run as slow as 8,000 rpm.

Balancing speed and feed. We slow down big bits simply because it's unsafe to run them at "full router speed." Do we ever slow down smaller bits? Sure. We do it so that a workable balance can be struck between bit rpm and feed rate. As I mentioned before, a feed rate that's too slow is common. If the bit moves too slowly through the cut, the heat builds up. Sometimes the wood scorches, and all too often the bit dies.

The prevalence of plunging operations fuels this problem. You have a short slot to cut, for example. Each time you want to plunge the bit deeper, you tend to pause, allowing the spinning bit to dwell in the cut. You can just smell the wood scorching. The cut is short, and each change in direction brings another slowing of

the feed rate, another pause. One way to mollify the problem is to slow down the bit's revs. Even when the cutter is relatively small in diameter.

Bit Care

Keeping your bits in good condition starts with appropriate storage. The last thing you want is to have them scattered around the shop or tossed in a drawer. Loose in a drawer, they clatter into one another each time you pull it open. The sound of bits clinking together is also the sound of carbide chipping.

Whatever storage method you adopt should not be *dead* storage. Assuming your bits are being used, they'll get dirty, collecting deposits of pitch and resin. After all, tremendous heat builds up in the bit as it spins at 22,000 rpm. The heat transfers to the wood, cooking the oil from it—especially from gummy woods. The oil fuses onto the bit.

One of the worst things you can do is to leave that buildup on the bit. When you use the bit, its cutting action is impeded. If you pause or even

slow the feed rate, the cut can burn. That turns up the heat. Even a tough carbide bit can feel this kind of stress!

To remove the pitch from a router bit, remove the pilot bearing (if it has one), then soak the bit in one of several solvents. Lacquer thinner works fine. If you have gum and pitch remover, that will work. Give the solvent a moment or two to work, then wipe off the bit with fine (#0000) steel wool. Polish the shaft with a piece of steel wool or a Scotch-Brite pad.

Ball bearings are usually packed with a special grease, and though they are supposed to be sealed, solvents can seep in and break down the grease. This is why you remove the bearing before solvent-cleaning a bit. Use an air gun to blow dust or dirt off the bearing. Frozen bearings—those that don't spin freely—should be tossed, as should those that are loose. A new bearing is a lot less dear than time wasted on sanding away burn marks. Worn or damaged hardware—the nuts, screws, and/or washers used to assemble the bit or mount the pilot—should be replaced, too.

If you feel the need to lube the bearing—it's sealed, remember—use a dry lubricant like Drycote.

Check the shank after each use. If there are any burrs or galling (rough spots) on the shank, sand them smooth with emery cloth. Then immediately check the collet carefully for dust or wear. Burrs and galling are a sure sign that the bit slipped while you were cutting. If the collet is bad, every bit you use can be damaged. And you know now how these things go: The collet damages the shank, then the shank damage exacerbates the collet damage. The old downspiral. Replace that collet!

Most manufacturers suggest lightly coating the bit with machine oil or

To prevent carbide-chipping collisions between loose bits, store them in some orderly fashion. A drawer in a router table holds frequently used bits. A block with a few 1/2-inch holes secures three or four bits for a trip across the shop or to a job site. I store seldom-used bits in a large drawer (standing on end here) fitted with perforated and grooved strips so the bits can be labeled.

WD-40 to prevent rust. Most new bits, in fact, are so coated. Wipe off the oil before using the bit, of course. Oil left on the bit can stain the wood, as well as attract sawdust and turn it into paste.

Should you hone your bits between uses? Most manufacturers advise against it. When the bit starts getting dull—when it resists, when it burns the wood—take it to a professional shop to have it sharpened. You'll be charged somewhere around $5 to $8 to sharpen a carbide-tipped bit, but the job will be done right. Bits coming off a 400-grit diamond wheel are extremely sharp.

If you are determined, however, you can probably touch up a carbide bit with a diamond-impegnated sharpening stone. Rub the cutting surfaces of the flutes back and forth a few times along the corner of the stone. Count the strokes, sharpening each flute an equal amount. This will keep the bit balanced. Sharpen only the inside (flat) surfaces of the flutes. Leave the outside (curved) surfaces alone. If you try to sharpen these, you might change the diameter or the profile of the bit.

See Also...

"Decorative Edge Treatments," page 139, for bits that produce coves, ogees, beads, and other profiles used for furniture, architectural molding, picture-frame stock, and similar work.

"Template-Guided Work," page 155, for pattern bits.

"Frame-and-Panel Construction," page 209, for rail-and-stile cutters and for panel-raising bits, both horizontal and vertical.

"Dadoing and Grooving," page 235, for various dado- and groove-cutting bits.

"Edge Joints," page 259, for joinery bits like tongue-and-groove sets, finger-joint cutters, and glue-joint bits.

Cleaning a bit is largely a matter of softening the gunk that builds up, then rubbing it off. Special pitch solvents are available, and you can use lacquer thinner if you have it. Using oven cleaner is inadvisable, since it attacks and degrades the cobalt binder in carbide. Soak the bit in the cleaner for a few minutes, then scrub off stubborn dirt with an abrasive pad (like Scotch-Brite) or a brass-bristle brush.

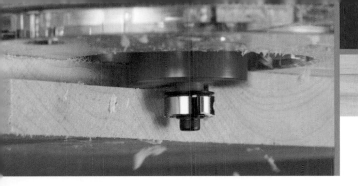

Router 101

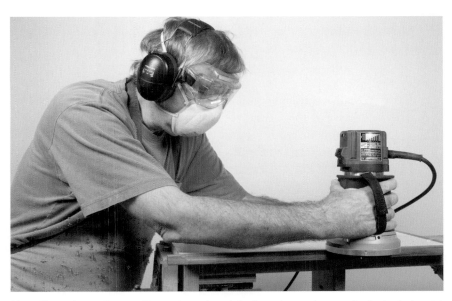

Versatile and easy to use, the router gets a lot of use in most power-tool-oriented wood shops. Injuries are uncommon, but the risk of debilitating injury is real over the long term. Reduce the risk by wearing hearing, vision, and respiratory protection each time you use your router.

You've got a router and some bits. It's a versatile machine, and it can be used in a vast assortment of woodworking operations. You're itching to put it to work.

But hold on! Before you plunge into router woodworking, there are some basics you should know that will make your endeavors safer, easier, altogether more satisfying.

Safety

Address your own safety first. The router is an intimidating tool. Oh, it's just a little package, but when you switch it on, it gives that startling jerk. And it runs 6 times faster than your power saw or your drill. Hold it in your hands, motor shrieking, and wobble it; you can feel the dynamic power.

More than anything, that noise gets you. Not only is it LOUD, the sound has a frantic urgency. The router just plain *sounds* dangerous. Nevertheless, the *gruesome* router injury is atypical. It's the long-term, debilitating injuries that are the router's primary threats.

Most people know that extended exposure to loud noise will permanently impair hearing. Of two sounds of equal intensity, the higher-frequency sound is more likely to cause hearing damage. So a router cutting at high speed, emitting its characteristic high-pitched whine, produces exactly the sort of sound that damages hearing.

Be smart. Wear your hearing protection.

Dust and chips are hazards, too.

The barrage of particles the router spews makes eye protection a must.

The dust that accompanies the chips is another risk factor because it hangs in the air for a long time. Dust collection has become more prevalent on routers. But if you are still using a decade-old tool (It works, so why toss it?), the best available protection is a dust mask, or better still, a respirator to capture the microscopic particles that cause the most damage in your lungs.

▰▰▰▰▰▰▰

Safety First!

Along with a router and bits, you must buy and use accessories for your protection. What you need isn't pricey. Get muffs, eyewear, and serviceable dust masks at a home center or hardware store.

Hearing protection: Passive muffs are the most common hearing protectors in woodworking shops. It's all the protection that you'll need.

Alternatives include plugs and canal caps. Plugs of various kinds are available, including disposable foam plugs that are cheap and are actually washable and thus reuseable (well, for a time). You insert plugs in your ear canals when you go into the shop and don't remove them until the work's done. Canal caps are ear plugs on a headband. The pads fit into the ear canal, but not as far as traditional plugs, and the band keeps them in place.

Vision protection: All sorts of protective eyewear is available, and not all styles emphasize dorkiness. You can find wrap-around styles that look cool—if that's important to you—and offer excellent protection. If you wear glasses, you can find styles that fit over them.

Respiratory protection: Everyone is familiar with nuisance dust masks. Cheap and readily available, they're better than nothing. But at the hardware store, you should be able to find a wider selection of masks, including some with a vent intended to prevent the air that escapes around the mask's margins from fogging your glasses. The best I've found are pleated.

Don't be a cheapskate on this. If you're willing to spend $200 to $300 for a router and hundreds more for bits and maybe a router table, invest in top-quality eye and hearing protection.

Stock

Although there are exceptions, you usually rest the router on the work itself to cut into the face or edge. The movement of the router and the location and depth of the cut are affected by the condition of the stock. If it's bowed, crooked, twisted, tapered, or rough, you can't be confident that you'll get the desired or required cut.

And mounting the router in a table won't circumvent this essential.

If you expect to get accurate cuts from your router, the stock you work has to be properly prepared. Simply put, the stock has to be flat in length and width, and free of twist. The faces must be parallel to each other, the edges likewise, and the faces and edges must be square to each other.

I'm not going to dwell on this. If you have a jointer and a planer, make sure you follow the conventional sequence in preparing the stock that you work. If you are buying surfaced stock, choose individual boards with care, selecting only the flattest ones in the stack.

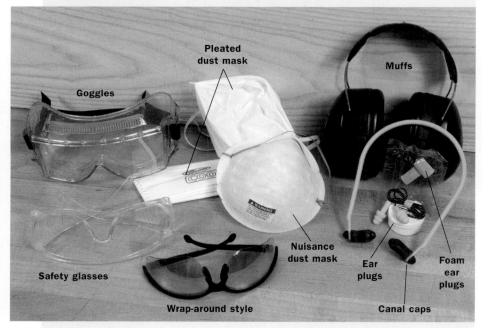

A cut that's inexplicably errant can oftimes be traced to the stock itself. Accurate stock preparation to flatten, true up, and square the workpieces is essential when the joinery cuts are registered off the faces and edges and ends of the board. Check the boards with squares that you know are accurate.

(image labels: Goggles, Pleated dust mask, Muffs, Safety glasses, Nuisance dust mask, Ear plugs, Foam ear plugs, Wrap-around style, Canal caps)

Problem Solver

Using a Guide

Routing is seldom done freehand. The rotation of the cutter tends to steer the tool, and variations in wood density and grain direction easily deflect its course, making a freehand cut unpredictable and difficult to control.

Forget freehand. Use a guide for every router cut.

Pilot Bearings

Pilot bearings are mounted on the bit, usually on the tip or the shank. Occasionally the bearing is sandwiched between elements of the cutting profile (cutters used for cope-and-stick joinery are like this). The bearing rides along the edge of the workpiece or a template to control both the width of the cut and its path.

Nothing is foolproof, but it *is* hard to go wrong using a piloted bit.

Piloted bits may be the first ones you use in your router. They are simple to master since the bearing is already on the bit. You just switch on the power, pull the router so the bearing contacts the edge, and then advance the router through the cut.

A few caveats apply.

Pilots are sensitive to edge defects. Dents or nicks in an edge will telegraph into the cut. So will a rough or rippled edge. Be sure the edge is smooth and true before you rout.

An edge can be burnished or otherwise marred by the pilot. Apply too much pressure and you can leave a bearing track on a soft wood. Conversely, apply too little pressure, and the bearing can spin and scorch the edge. A scorched edge is more commonly the mark of a frozen bearing.

One of the most important things you can do to improve the accuracy of your router woodworking is to mill the working stock properly. The router is capable of incredible accuracy and precision, but it's usually dependent upon the surfaces and edges of the workpiece for guidance.

In handheld operations, the router slides across the surface of the work. If the workpiece is bowed or twisted, if its surface is rough or rippled, the router won't be able to even them out. The cut may be of uneven depth, it may be choppy. When you're using a piloted bit, the pilot will telegraph any imperfections in the edge very visibly into the cut.

Make sure the stock is smooth, flat, and square.

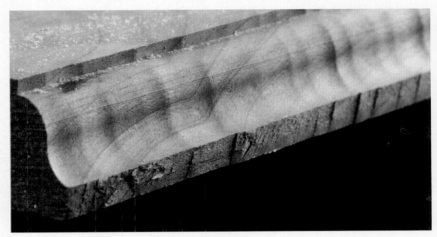

Neglect to joint an edge before routing a profile, and you'll discover that the cut finish reflects the edge's roughness. Every bump and ridge that the pilot bearing encounters will telegraph into the profile.

Tiny as it is, the pilot bearing on the tip of a bit controls both the cut and the router's movement. Many woodworkers do little with a router that's outside the realm of pilot-guided cuts. Keep pilot bearings clean, and make sure they spin freely before each use.

Fences

The obvious example of a fence is a straight board clamped to the work. You place the router base against this fence and maintain that contact as you move the router across the work, making a controlled, perfectly placed cut.

You'll find specific examples of such fences scattered throughout the remaining chapters. But also you'll find variations: T-squares that can quickly be set perpendicular to an edge for guiding a dado cut, for example. You'll see the occasional setup that traps a router between two fences.

Not all fences are planted directly on the work, of course. Jigs and fixtures for specific operations often have fences incorporated into them. And not all fences guide the base. A template that controls the course of a router through a guide bushing or pattern bit is also a fence.

While many of us grab a couple of clamps and whatever straight board is available when the need for a fence arises, you can find a variety of aluminum extrusions, complete with adjustable clamps and accessory stops and auxiliary baseplates, in woodworking tool catalogs.

Edge Guides

The edge guide is a fence that attaches to the router base. It can be adjusted from a position surrounding the bit to one about 8 to 10 inches away. The guide slides along the edge of the work and ensures that the router's cut is parallel to it.

With most edge guides, you make coarse adjustments by sliding the guide body along the mounting rods. Then you make fine adjustments with a vernier screw. A good guide locks securely on the rods, and fine adjustments are both possible and precise.

Every router manufacturer makes edge guides specifically for its models. Many are quite good, although some are overlarge and awkward to

Festool sells a track system for several of its portable tools, including the routers. A guide that mounts on the edge-guide rods hooks over a ridge on the track, so the router won't drift off line regardless of feed direction.

Edge guides vary in design, size, and quality. The rudimentary guide at right, which comes with Makita's RF1101 router kit, is functional but has no provision for precise adjustments. The Freud model (left) is appropriately sturdy for its 3-plus-horsepower router, but has only limited range. Festool's edge guide has range and the semblance of micro-adjustability; backlash and slop in the adjuster reduce its precision.

maneuver. Most lack realistic fine adjustment. There is a "micro-adjuster," of course, but it's loose and sloppy and is by no means precise. A few guides are downright cheesy: a metal stamping secured to mounting rods with metal wing nuts—hard on your fingers and just about impossible to tighten securely without pliers.

My advice? If a guide comes with your router, try it out, evaluate how well it works, and if you're satisfied, use it. The two essentials are that the guide must slide easily and that the setscrews must really set. If the guide fails on these points, toss it.

You can purchase an excellent edge guide from MicroFence (see "Sources," page 367). It's the only after-market guide I know of, and this one guide fits most any router you own, including some laminate trimmers.

An alternative approach is to make your own. See the chapter "Jigmaking," page 43.

Setting Up

To avoid problems, be as methodical as you can in setting up a cut. The process includes installing a bit in the router, making a vertical adjustment on the router, positioning a guide, and securing the workpiece. The trick in routing—as in all woodworking—is to get the setup right. If not

Measuring and Layout Tools

Although the unstable nature of wood makes the pursuit of machine-like precision quixotic, using precision tools for measuring and layout will have a major positive impact on your work. Only a few are essential, and you ought to buy top quality.

The best rules are etched rather than printed and have graduations as fine as 64ths. Squares are useful for layout and checking setups and assemblies. Calipers help you accurately measure thicknesses, diameters (inside and outside), and even depths. The sliding bevel and accompanying gauge enable you to set and measure angles. Thought it isn't precise, a pocket-friendly tape measure is very practical.

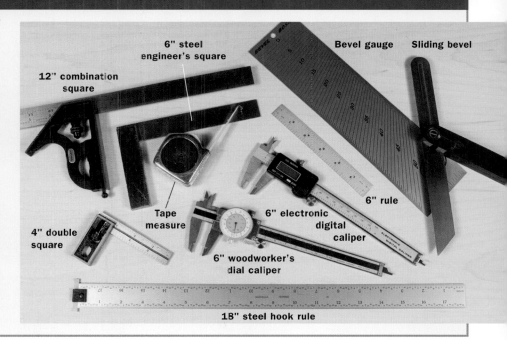

12" combination square · 6" steel engineer's square · Bevel gauge · Sliding bevel · 4" double square · Tape measure · 6" woodworker's dial caliper · 6" electronic digital caliper · 6" rule · 18" steel hook rule

the first time, at least before you actually cut the good wood.

The first decision is whether you're doing the job with the router handheld or mounted in a table. While the following is directed primarily at handheld operations, you follow the same sequence in setting up a router table operation. More detail on the latter is in the chapter "Router Table Savvy," page 119.

Chucking the Bit

Read over the section on *using* bits in the previous chapter ("Bits"). Match the cutter to the cut as well as possible. You will get best results if the bit is sharp, the pilot bearing clean and free-spinning, and the shank clean and smooth—no scoring, no rust.

Check over the bit before inserting it into the collet. If it's really spoiled goods—chipped carbide, shank scored beyond repair—chuck it. Meaning throw it away.

Look over the collet periodically, too. Like the bit shank, it should be clean and smooth. No rust, no galls, no deformities. Inspect the collet socket and the collet nut, too.

Sleeves that adapt a small-diameter shank to a larger collet are common, but double the potential for an imprecise match between inside and outside diameters. To maximize the grip, align at least one slit in the sleeve with a slit in the collet.

How easy it is to actually "chuck" the bit in the router depends a lot upon the router design, as explained in the "Routers" chapter, page 1. I like to separate the motor from the base to change bits. Obviously, you can't do this with a dedicated plunge router. Sometimes you just have to rest the router on its side, and work within the confines of the base.

Insert the bit at least 3/4 inch into the collet, and further if the collet depth and shank length allow. If the shank bottoms, withdraw it slightly. Tightening the collet nut draws the collet and shank down into the collet socket, and having the shank against the socket bottom before tightening the nut can be trouble.

While it isn't a *good* idea to use a reducer or sleeve to adapt a small shank to a large collet, sometimes it is unavoidable. (Some routers don't have 1/4-inch collets, and almost none have 3/8-inch collets.) Align slits in the sleeve with slits in the collet to get the best possible grip.

You shouldn't have to be an arm-wrestling champ to tighten the collet. A one-handed squeeze—both wrenches gripped in one hand—is tight enough.

Bits are easier to slip in and out of the collet if their shanks are clean and polished to a shine. Use an ordinary abrasive kitchen pad to shine up a bit shank after each use. Keeping after it is the best way to prevent rust and tarnish from forming.

How tight should the collet nut be? Offset the collet wrenches, hold both handles in one hand, and squeeze. That one-handed squeeze should do the trick. To loosen the nut, just reverse the offset of the wrenches and repeat the squeeze.

Setting the Cut Depth

Techniques for setting the cut depth vary with the type of router.

Fixed-base router. When a specific, measurable depth is desired, use a 6-inch rule or a small square to measure how far the bit extends beyond the base. Then make a short test cut in scrap and measure the cut itself.

The proof is always in a test cut, and sometimes it takes three or more such cuts to zero in on a precise setting. But take your time, analyze your setup, and *know* it's right before cutting the good stuff. You can't put the wood back once it's routed away.

Fine-tuning the depth-of-cut is fairly easy with some routers, a trial with others. On a good router, the motor won't shift or move when you loosen the base clamp. A good router will have a screw-type adjuster or a ring on the motor, enabling you to move it up or down in increments as fine as 1/64 inch. You do have to contend with backlash in these adjusters, and the graduations are often hard to decipher.

If yours isn't so refined, you have to use the rule. If the motor has a flat top, stand it on its top and gingerly move the base as required to make whatever niggling adjustment is necessary.

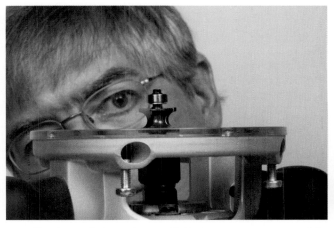

A profile bit usually is set by eye. Hold the router so you can sight across the base to the bit. Profile bits typically have a landmark feature to help you set the bit's projection. To bead an edge, for example, you want the cutting edge's arc tangent to the base surface. Turn the bit to view the profile squarely.

The universal setup method for fixed-base routers is to adjust the bit projection against a rule. Hold the body of a small square flat on the baseplate with its rule right beside the cutting edge. How good is your eyesight? This edge of the rule is graduated in 16ths, the back in 32ths and 64ths.

Screw adjusters are used on a number of fixed-base routers. On Milwaukee's routers (this is the 5616-29), a full turn of the Acme-thread screw raises or lowers the motor 3/16 inch. The knob has a zero-able graduated ring to guide fine adjustments. The marks are 1/4 inch apart and represent a vertical adjustment of 1/64 inch.

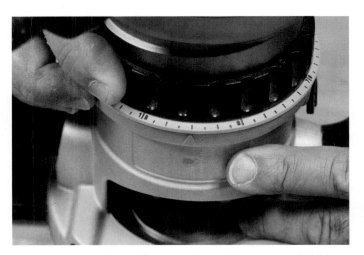

The large scale of an adjustment ring—this one on a DeWalt DW618 router—allows miniscule adjustments to be made with ease. A complete rotation of the ring moves the motor up or down 1 inch. The yellow ring is graduated in 64ths, with those marks 3/16 inch apart.

Plunge router. All plunge routers have the same fundamental design for controlling the plunge depth. There's an adjustable rod on the motor that hits a stop on the base. The plunge/cut depth equals the space between the stop rod and the stop when the bit is bottomed. What can be confusing, if only briefly, is that each model seems to have a slightly different depth-adjustment system. Some have a stop rod that you can wind up and down, while others depend on gravity to move the rod down and you to move the rod up.

Most do have a graduated rule behind the rod or a graduated band on the winding knob to enable you to set the plunge to a precise measurement, but the accuracy of most, in my experience, is iffy.

The universal setup technique, which is precise even when the router's controls are suspect, is to use shims or spacers to set the gap between stop and stop rod. You can buy setup blocks made of brass or aluminum, or you can make them from a stable hardwood by planing strips to precise thicknesses. Typically a set of blocks range from 1/16 inch to 3/4 inch in thickness, and you use them individually or in combinations. To further fine-tune a setting, you can use feeler gauges.

Bottom the bit against the benchtop. Rest the appropriate spacer on the stop. Drop the stop rod onto it, and lock the rod. Remove the spacer, and the router is set for a test cut.

Securing the Workpiece

A vital part of setting up for a cut is anchoring the workpiece. The last thing you need is for the work to shift or slide away from you as you feed the router. Not only can it screw up

Regardless of the plunge router make and model, this setup technique works. Bottom the bit against the work surface. Unlock the stop rod, letting it drop onto a precision-thickness setup gauge you hold on top of the stop. Relock the rod. The resulting gap between rod and stop is the distance the router can plunge, and thus the depth to which it will cut.

your cut and ruin the work, it can put you at risk.

Ideally, you just fix the work to a bench with at least two clamps. But handheld routing is full of challenges, not the least of which is contriving methods of holding the work. You don't want to move the clamps three times in a course of a single pass.

Here are some examples of measures you might take.

■ To slot a narrow workpiece, sandwich it between two wider boards that will provide additional bearing for the router.

■ To rout an edge treatment on a circular or oval blank, try "dogging"

A three-point bench-dog system (two on the vise, one on the benchtop) makes securing odd-shaped workpieces a cinch. Profiling the edge of an oval tabletop? You'll only have to shift it once to rout the entire edge. And that shift is as easy as opening and closing the vise. No clamps to take off and put back on.

it on a narrow workbench, so the maximum amount of edge is overhanging the bench. After routing as much of the edge as possible, one shift of the workpiece exposes the remaining uncut edge.

■ Clamps that secure a T-square can also secure the work to the bench. They serve double-duty.

■ Hot-melt glue has enough strength to bond a template to a workpiece, or a workpiece to a bench. Yet it's too weak to resist a sharp mallet blow or a little prying with a chisel.

■ A shop-made fixture with toggle clamps can expedite repetitive routing by making it easy to switch workpieces. Clamp or dog the fixture to a bench, then switch work by flipping the toggles open and closed.

After you position and clamp the work, make a dry run through the cut with the unplugged router. Are the clamps clear of the router's path? Is the work (and the bench) solid and steady? Sometimes you have to devise a two-stage process. Rout about halfway, stop and shift clamps, then complete the cut. In any event, you want to *know* before you begin that you can complete the cut without a hitch.

Feed Direction

All routers spin the bit in the same direction: clockwise. Knowing this allows us to make sensible rules about how to control the router.

Think of the router bit as a tire. Imagine that as you touch the spinning bit/tire to the edge of the workpiece, it smokes like a dragster and takes off along the edge of the work, with you along for the ride. That's

Cutting Action

HOUSED CUTS

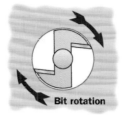

As the bit plunges into the work, all cutting edges are engaged and forces are balanced. Bit exerts no lateral pull.

Move the router laterally, and bit cuts through half of each revolution. The equal and opposite reaction to clockwise cutting sweep is counterclockwise.

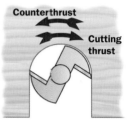

So when grooving and unrestrained, a router will move generally counterclockwise.

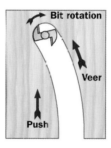 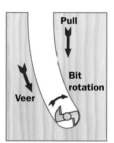

Push and the router veers to the left.

Pull and the router veers to the right.

EDGE CUTS

The bit cuts on only a quarter of each revolution. Cutting edges dig into edge and pull router same direction as bit rotation – clockwise. Equal and opposite reaction pushes bit away from edge. This is a climb cut.

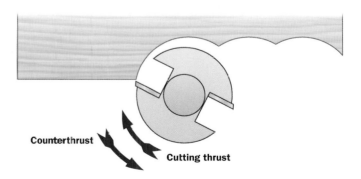

Feed Direction
Feed router so its counterclockwise veer keeps it tight against its guide

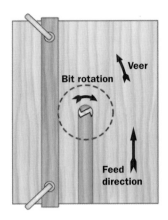

WITH CLAMPED-ON FENCE

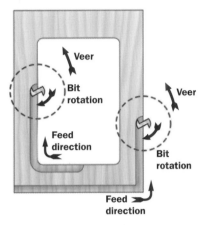

WITH EDGE GUIDE

WITH PILOTED BIT OR GUIDE BUSHING

what would happen if you let it. But you seldom want that.

The direction the *router* wants to go when you are routing an edge is universally called a "climb cut," because of the bit's tendency to climb out of the cut if given its druthers.

You want to move the router *counter* to the rotation of the bit. The bit is spinning clockwise, so you move the router counterclockwise. Knowing that enables you to begin a cut in the right place so you can move the router in the direction YOU want to go, and not the direction it wants to go.

The direction *you* want to go has no universal name. Some call it an "anti-climb cut" and others an "aggressive cut." I've always referred to it as "the correct feed," though that's not particularly catchy.

The main reasons you feed the router this way are safety and control. The router doesn't automatically take a break every time your human concentration does. If you feed the contrary way I suggest, you'll notice that when you slip, lose

concentration, or get a little off balance, the router will minutely back up into an area that has already been cut. This allows the cutter to spin freely while you regain your balance and poise.

When you're routing a groove, you don't have "climb cut" issues. Stand a plunge router on a board, switch it on, and plunge the bit into the wood, then let go of the handles. It will just stand there, wailing, perhaps lazily rotating (clockwise, of course!), thanks to the dynamics of the motor running.

Grasp the handles again and start feeding the router. The hole will elongate into a groove as the bit cuts a path. But the router won't move in a straight line, your best efforts notwithstanding. Rather, the path will veer counterclockwise.

That counterclockwise veer is what we are exploiting in feed-direction rules. You move the router generally counterclockwise and position whatever guide you are using where the router will bear against it.

A drawing is far better at explaining feed direction, so look carefully at it.

Splintering

Anytime you rout across a board's grain, you're going to get some degree of splintering. Most troublesome is the splintering as you break through the board's edge at the end of the cut.

If you're profiling the edges routing all around a piece—something like a plaque, for example—you can rout the ends first, letting the corners blow away. Then rout the long-grain sides, which will, in most cases, clean up the blown-out corners.

If you're not routing the long-grain sides—let's say you're cutting shelf dadoes in a cabinet side—you can't get away with the previous strategy. Here you need to clamp pieces of scrap stock to the edges where your cuts will exit. Cut right into the scrap, and let it support the good edges of the project to prevent blowout.

You often will get splintery fringes along the surface edges of the entire cut—I call 'em "fuzzies." A few swipes with sandpaper is the remedy. Don't view fuzzies as a symptom of a

Rout across the grain, and the wood fibers right at the surface tend to shred and lift, leaving a fuzzy arris along each side of the cut. Light sanding removes these fuzzies. While a down-shear cutter can minimize fuzzies, the cutting forces can literally push the router up off the work. Avoid that risk. Sanding is safer.

dull bit. They are symptomatic of cross-grain cuts, period.

Here's another common splintering problem. Sometimes, when you're routing the long-grain edge, the cutter will pull out a splinter from the area ahead of the cut. That's always annoying, but it becomes a real problem when the grain "runs in" so that the split extends into the area that isn't supposed to be cut.

What's making the splinters? As the cutter arcs into the wood, it's cutting nearly parallel with the grain. But as it swings to the edge of the stock, it's cutting almost perpendicular to it. This is the most difficult direction for the cutting action, as well as the weakest situation for the wood to resist splitting. The cutter passes a point where it takes less force to split the wood than to cut through it.

So what can we change to prevent splitting? Either make the bit cut better or make the wood stronger! Don't laugh; we can do both. Obviously, a sharp bit will cut more easily than a dull one. In many cases a shear or spiral bit will cut more easily than a straight one. And anything you can do to "back up" the wood will help it to stay together.

Bear in mind that the problem is the wood. When the grain is twisty and convoluted, especially when it runs out the long-grain edge rather than running parallel to it, you can have splintering.

A shallow climb cut, known as a scoring cut, often helps. The cutting edges are chopping in on the surface fibers, severing them cleanly and leaving a crisp arris. Once that shoulder is established, subsequent passes to widen the cut won't pull out splinters except in extreme cases.

Though the scoring cut is by definition very shallow, the unpredictable dynamic of climb-cutting suggests you try it with trepidation. You need experience in cutting in the correct direction, and it's a good idea to practice on some scraps before trying a climb cut on an essential project part.

Eliminate End-Grain Tearout
Three options

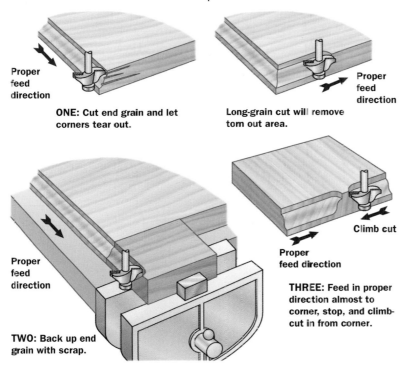

ONE: Cut end grain and let corners tear out.

Long-grain cut will remove torn out area.

TWO: Back up end grain with scrap.

THREE: Feed in proper direction almost to corner, stop, and climb-cut in from corner.

Chipping at the arrises of an edge cut (left) is one of the major banes of routing. A very shallow pass in the climb-cut direction, usually called a scoring cut, often circumvents the problem (center). Subsequent cuts in the proper direction complete a clean, chip-free cut (right).

Some suggest routing in the correct direction to within a 16th of the final depth, then making the climb cut as a shallow cleanup pass. But if the grain is really troublesome, the damage will be done on those first passes, and it just may be too severe to rectify with a shallow climb cut.

How do you actually do it? You can skim essentially freehand along the edge with the router, trying to achieve a shallow cut. You'll probably find that this technique yields a wavering cut, deep at spots where the router dug in and took off, shallow where you maintained control. As a practical matter, this achieves the goal, so it's fine.

If you are determined to maintain control, clamp a fence to the work to prevent a cut deeper than you want. Or switch to a larger bearing on a piloted bit. Or use an edge guide.

Thwarting Tearout
Eliminate splintering on long-grain edge cuts

Bit rotation

Outward push of bit's cutting edge splinters wood at edge.

Correct feed direction

THE CAUSE OF SPLINTERING

Complete cut with final pass in correct feed direction.

Bit rotation

Cutting edge leaves wood at shallow angle.

Shoulder is formed in first pass.

Correct feed direction

CORRECT FEED SECOND

No splintering, cutting edge chops in.

Bit rotation

Climb cut generally leaves uneven shoulder.

Climb cut

CLIMB CUT FIRST
Shallow pass removes waste without splintering.

Climb cuts tend to be unpredictable and wavering in their width (bottom). As the cutter pushes off the work's edge, the cut narrows, then abruptly widens again as you react. Set an edge guide to override the pilot bearing (right), and it can help you produce a more consistent width on a scoring pass (top).

Dust Control

Routers throw chips everywhere. Where they go depends in part upon the bit and the cut. Rout a groove with a straight bit, for example, and the chips shoot out the already-cut channel. Rout an edge profile, and the chips spray on your pants and on the floor.

Here's a two-tier plan: Get an accessory or two to capture dust at the source, and a couple designed to deal with the mess on the bench and floor.

A very few routers have a dust pickup integrated into them (DeWalt's DW621 is the prime example). Most others have dust pickups as accessories. You need a shop vacuum to extract the dust through these pickups. Use them whenever possible.

A practical accessory, which fits many but not all routers, is Leigh's vacuum attachment. This spring-loaded chip pickup is mounted like an edge guide, and has a port for vacuum hoses up to 1 1/2 inches in diameter. It sucks up all the chips generated when routing dovetails or rabbets or profiling edges. These are some of the messiest operations.

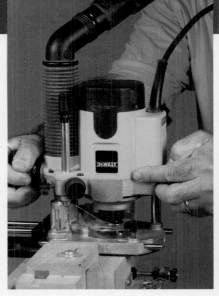

DeWalt's DW621 was the first router to have a designed-in system for capturing chips and dust at the bit and channeling them to a shop vac. The system works great for surface cuts, less well on edge cuts.

You do more jobs with a router than these, of course, and as often as not at the end of a shop session, you've got chips all over the floor. Worse, the finest particles are floating in the shop air and infiltrating your lungs with every breath.

Deal with it! Get a big ol' dustpan and brush and sweep up after every session. Address the secondary dust, the fine stuff floating in the air, with an air cleaner that circulates the shop air, pulling it through pleated filters and a filter bag.

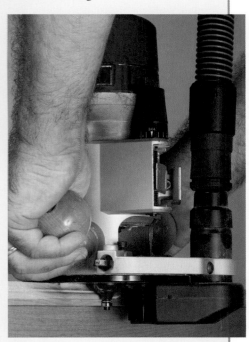

Leigh designed and sells this accessory dust pickup for capturing the chips generated when cutting dovetails with their jig. The accessory fits many routers and works on all sorts of edge cuts.

Workloads

Like every other power tool in your shop, the router does have limits. Just because your bit has a 1-inch-long cutting edge doesn't mean the router will make a 1-inch-deep cut in a single pass. Try it. Your router will probably tell you it's overloaded. It will start to bog down, losing speed sharply. If you persist, it will probably stall completely, maybe trip the breaker, maybe burn up.

The conventional wisdom is that the router is a trimming machine. If you have a heavy cut to make, nibble at it. Make a sequence of light cuts. If you can, remove waste with a cut on a table saw or band saw, then finish up with a precise router cut.

The conventional rule of thumb is to cut about 1/4 inch deep at a pass. This is safe and reasonable.

But as you get more experience in router work, you probably will come to view that rule of thumb as a little wimpy in many situations. If you are using a sharp, 1/2-inch-shank bit, even a 2-horsepower router can hog away more than a 1/4 inch of material. You have to listen to the router. Is it running free or starting to bog down? Is the bit whizzing through the wood, or is it chattering? Do you have to feed so slowly that the wood burns?

Feed rate is significant. Beginners tend to move the router much too slowly. That prolongs the operation and degrades the cutter quickly. If the wood is being scorched, the cutter is been dulled prematurely. While you don't want to degrade the cut quality by feeding too fast, you don't want to dawdle, either.

The goal is to get a good-quality cut without overtaxing the router and the bit. With experience you develop a "feel" for pacing and loading.

A plunge router's depth-stop system allows you to make a full-depth cut in several passes, each cutting progressively deeper. Using the turret stop allows you to control exactly how deep each pass cuts.

Without conscious thought, you weigh the power of the router, the configuration of the bit, and even the hardness of the stock. Hard maple? Lighten up. Pine? Hog away. Using a 1/4-inch straight bit? Take it easy, even if it's on a 1/2-inch shank.

Your First Cuts

Practice is appropriate, for woodworkers new to routers as well as new woodworkers. I suggest you buy an 8-foot 1×10 "whitewood" board at the home center, or if you've got the equipment, mill a similar-sized poplar board. This is your practice stock. Once you've reduced it to scrap and chips, you'll be pretty proficient with your new power tool.

Cut some dadoes first, since the router will be fully supported, rather than teetering on an edge. Follow the step-up sequence, installing a bit and adjusting it for cut depth. Clamp a fence to the stock. Do a dry run. Then cut a dado.

Unplug the router and think over the exercise. Run through the whole routine a second time. Cut some more dadoes. Experiment with different cut depths, different feed rates. Get a feel for the sounds that the router and the bit make, for the feel of the router while it's cutting.

Beginners tend to be hesitant about moving the router through a cut, feeding it haltingly along the fence. What you want to achieve is a smooth, steady feed. With experience, you develop a feel for how fast you can go. It does vary with the density of the stock, the condition of the cutter, and the power of the router.

Once you're (reasonably) comfortable routing dadoes and grooves, try working the edge. Again, begin with some dry runs, perhaps with just the pilot of a profile cutter protruding below the base. As you move the router with the pilot riding along the edge, you'll get a largely risk-free feel for balancing and supporting a tool that's more than halfway off the work.

Readjust the bit, plug in the router, and make an actual cut.

Even with experience, it's a good idea to practice with every new router you buy, every new bit, every new accessory. You can call it testing. But it'll really just be practice. And practice makes perfect, doesn't it?

Jigmaking

"**H**ow do I get the job done with the router I have in my shop?" That's the big question you have, and the one I try to answer throughout this book.

And in every chapter, the answers involve jigs and fixtures that *you can make yourself*. In a few cases, you can *buy* a jig that does much the same thing. But why would you buy a commercial jig when you can realize twice the satisfaction by making it yourself? First, there's the joy of having successfully built it. Then there's the joy of having saved some money.

When the jig is completed, your payoff is that it helps you do better woodworking and thus improves your skill level and, yes, your *satisfaction*.

I should point out that the difference between a jig and a fixture is purely technical. A *fixture* is something that "fixes" the work, holding it securely so the router can be moved over it. A vise is a fixture. A *jig* (going along with the dance known as the jig) puts the work or the router through controlled movements. It guides the cut, by guiding either the work or the router. A trammel is a jig. (A jig can have fixtures on it. A sled

Doing accurate, efficient work with a router requires jigs and fixtures. The more you use your router, the more jigs and fixtures you'll make. Like the featherboards, coping sled, and trammel, some you'll use frequently. Others, like the flush-trimming jig and surfacing platform, will see limited use. Most templates are used once and then tossed.

for the router table is a jig, and the toggle clamp on it is a fixture.)

One of the things that makes woodworking so interesting is that there usually are several ways to accomplish the same task. For example, if you page through the chapter "Dadoing and Grooving," on page 235, you'll find several different jigs and fixtures that'll enable you to cut accurate, consistent dadoes. There are several different fences (jigs) to use if you have a bit of the correct size for the dado you want to cut. There's one jig—the adjustable-width dadoing guide—to use if you

43

want to cut the dado—say it is 5/8 inch wide—with a 1/2-inch bit. And there's another—the fractionating baseplate—to use in conjunction with a fence to cut that same dado with that same bit.

There are some jigs and fixtures you'll build without a specific task in mind. Maybe you'll build a router table, knowing it will expand your router woodworking horizons, yet without knowing just how extensive the payoff will be. If you are like me, you'll soon wonder why you waited so long to get it built.

Design

Jigmaking can be very creative and spontaneous. Solving problems is definitely an eclectic process. Most of the router jigs and fixtures in this book came into being because some woodworker faced a problem and found a way to solve it. He shared his solution with others, some of whom adopted his solution, but more of whom adapted it.

That's the evolutionary part of woodworking! You confront problems and struggle to find solutions. The more you read—in magazines, in books like this one—the better prepared you are to solve those woodworking problems. You've seen similar problems solved, you know the parameters of your particular problem, then one day, Pow! it hits you. An adaptation is what you need.

In this book, you'll find plans for making and using many different router jigs and fixtures. If a jig suits your needs, follow the directions to make it. But if, after reading about the jig or fixture, you say to yourself, "This jig would work better for me if I...," make it your own way! We've

Building precision jigs and fixtures is abetted by a small selection of precision layout and setup tools. The essentials include a steel rule with etched graduations, an engineer's square (or two), a ground straightedge, and dial calipers. A set of setup blocks improve the accuracy of your machine setups, and a selection of transfer punches enable you to transfer precise hole locations from a pattern to a part, or from one part to another.

given you an idea, and goaded you into creating your own design that'll solve your particular problem.

As you tackle the design and construction of jigs and fixtures, keep some basic principles in mind.

"Keep It Simple, Stupid" (K.I.S.S.) is the most important principle in jigmaking. Direct it at three aspects of the jigmaking process.

First, focus on one process. Loading up a jig or fixture with lots of features is not good. Yes, that arguably makes it more versatile, but you risk compromising one or all of those features. Think about the job at hand, not about potential jobs or future jobs.

As you focus on the job at hand, parse the steps. Be sure you don't expect too much of the jig. Perhaps you should divide the process across two or even more jigs, so that each is simple and effective.

Second, pare down the design so there are as few parts to the jig as possible. The more parts the jig has, the more opportunities there are

for dimension and alignment errors to creep in. Accuracy is vital, and simplicity enhances accuracy. So keep it simple.

Third, simplify the construction as much as possible. If it's going to be a success, you must be able to make the jig, simple as it might be in concept and design.

Accuracy is a primary reason for making and using jigs. You want to be able to make a cut with confidence, knowing the outcome will be accurate. You also want to be able to repeat the cut again and again and have it be the same each time. For this to happen, the jig must be made accurately and must be robust enough that repeated use—or simply the passage of time—does not degrade its precision.

So you must use good materials. Your workmanship must be precise. Building a jig for a one-time use may moderate the need for top-quality materials, but won't diminish the need for good workmanship.

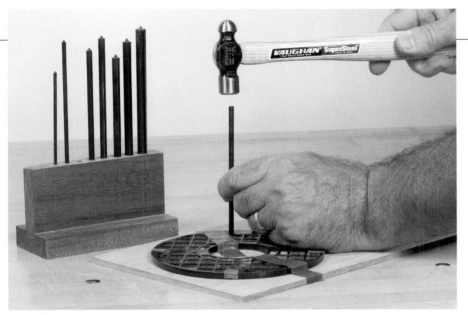

Tuning and retuning are essential in good tool design. To establish accuracy and then maintain it, you may need to square and occasionally re-square a fence or stop.

Why? Many of the materials you are likely to use will expand and contract over time. Also, the impacts of use—the stresses of clamping and unclamping, for example—may dislodge or displace parts, however slightly. Recognize the reality, and design in the ability to tune and retune the jig.

Fixturing any jig that you attach to a workpiece or that holds a workpiece (and that covers them all, doesn't it?) is essential. "Fixturing" includes fences and stops to position the work, clamps to secure the work, and clamps (or space for clamps) to secure the jig.

Using a factory baseplate as a pattern for making jigs and fixtures that attach to a router's base is a common practice. The machinist's transfer punch, sometimes called a spotter punch, is the most accurate tool for transferring the hole locations in the baseplate to the jig stock. Punches to match every drill diameter—fractional and metric, even letter and number sizes—are available. The tip of the punch is pointed to produce a starting dimple for the drill bit.

A ground straightedge is the tool to confirm the flatness of surfaces and straightness of edges. Use it, too, to align surfaces, such as the infeed and outfeed faces of a router-table fence. While it may look like an ordinary steel strip, this 24-inch-long tool has its edges ground flat to within 0.001 inch over its length, then heat-treated to remove residual stresses and ensure that it remains true.

Even plywood moves a little seasonally, so you must incorporate modest adjustability so you can keep a jig or fixture in perfect working tune. One good way to ensure that parts stay square is to add shims under braces. Use machines screws—but no glue—to assemble such devices.

Design

It's possible to get by with your eyes and fingers as your means of aligning a jig and workpiece with one another. So, too, with carpet tape or hot-melt glue as your clamps. I do both from time to time. But your results will be far more accurate and consistent if you use fixed stops and fences to align your jig and workpiece, and if you use clamps to secure the work.

Safety is as important in jigmaking as simplicity and accuracy. It should go without saying—but nevertheless I *will* say it—that any jig or fixture you use should make the job safer to do. If guarding is appropriate, design it into the jig. Don't overextend the tool or tooling.

Prototyping is an often-overlooked aspect of the design process. You design something on paper,

Fences attached to a template ensure that the workpieces are positioned consistently, so after the routing is done, each will be identical. However, fences that trap the ends of the workpiece will also trap sawdust accumulations. Substituting pins for one or more of the fences allows that sawdust to escape.

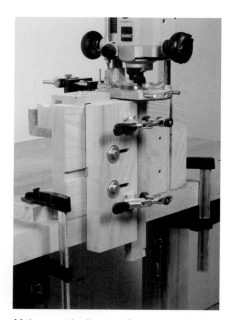

Make sure the jigs and fixtures you design and build will account for the need to fix them to a workbench. The mortising fixture that I use most must be clamped to the bench so it doesn't slide around. A strip glued to the fixture extends beyond each end of the block, providing out-of-the-way spots for two clamps.

build the jig to the plan, then discover that it doesn't function as well as you imagined. Often, the scale of your investment—in both time and money—prompts you to ignore the shortcomings.

The truth is that you sometimes need to cobble together a working model that you can try out. Be judgmental as you test it. Be willing to modify it, and even to try out alternatives that you are skeptical of. When you have a model that proves itself, make a neat, precise keeper.

Materials

Router jigs don't have to be fancy. Some are made as one-use throwaway items. These are the jigs you probably will cobble up using materials from the scrap bin. If you ordinarily work with decent materials, then your scraps will make good jigs. But scraps being scraps, you won't regret tossing the jig when its job is done.

The majority of the jigs included in this book are designed to be used again and again—a flush-trimming baseplate, for example, or a trammel, a mortising jig, or a T-square. For these, you just might want to invest in new, specialized materials and hardware.

Wood

We're all woodworkers here, so wood should be the primary material used in our jigs and fixtures, right? Nope.

While wood is strong and durable and available in every woodshop, it's also unstable. It's continually expanding and contracting with changes in temperature and humidity. This is okay in furniture, but not in a precision tool like a jig or fixture. Instead of building an entire jig from wood, use it selectively for fences and stops.

Sheet Goods

Depending upon your experience level and the nature of the woodworking you do, you may be thoroughly familiar with sheet goods. Surely, every router woodworker has worked with plywood and hardboard, which are stocked by home centers as well as lumberyards. For making jigs, especially, you ought to venture beyond the common construction sheet goods.

Medium-density fiberboard (MDF) is my top choice for making jigs and fixtures. It's dense, homogeneous, flat, and stable. Oh, and relatively inexpensive. It's particularly fine for templates. A router bit's pilot bearing won't compress its edge (or

Though it's our favorite material, both strong and beautiful, wood isn't always the ideal material for jigs and fixtures. Use it selectively. It's good for fences and stops on templates and sleds, but avoid using it where its instability would compromise the jig's accuracy.

Sheet goods like MDF, hardboard, and hardwood plywood usually are first choices for making router jigs and fixtures both large and small. In general, all sheet goods are relatively inexpensive, flat, and stable. Most active woodworkers have lots of scraps.

dive into a void between plies). Its flat, uniform surface makes it an excellent substrate for laminates. Routing its edges produces sharp, crisp profiles.

MDF thicknesses are very precise: A 3/4-inch-thick panel is right on the money. A home center may stock 1/2-inch and 3/4-inch MDF, but wholesale suppliers stock sheets in a range of thicknesses from 1/4-inch to

more than 1-inch. The standard panel size is an inch over 4 feet by 8 feet. MDF is heavy, about half again as heavy as a comparable piece of plywood.

But MDF isn't a problem-free material. If it gets wet, it wicks up moisture and swells, causing permanent changes in dimension. Another hitch is that large MDF panels have a tendency to sag under load, even

under their own weight, because the material has no grain to provide stiffness. In the typical jig or fixture, this isn't a problem: Covering both faces with plastic laminate will stiffen an MDF panel. A third problem also stems from MDF's grainlessness: Regular wood screws strip out. Use deep-threaded screws for good grab. For even better holding power, drill and tap holes for machine screws.

Plywood is a common choice for jigs, and it is a reasonable one. But avoid the construction grades stocked in home centers. Birch plywood is far better. It is fairly smooth and can be sanded, sealed, and waxed to provide a durable, smooth-sliding surface.

Typically, a 3/4-inch-thick sheet of veneer-core plywood has 7 plies—5 core plies and 2 face veneers. Higher-grade plywood has a greater number of plies (usually 13 in a 3/4-inch-thick panel), which makes the panel stiffer and more stable. This is important in the typical jig. With a high-quality plywood such as Baltic Birch or ApplyPly, a raw edge can be sanded and polished for a decorative effect.

Full sheets of plywood are seldom flat (certainly not as flat as MDF), but the impact is reduced when you cut the sheet into the small panels that most jigs and fixtures require. Plywood's worst problem may be the edges, which tend to get splintery and lose their accuracy. And, of course, 1/4-inch plywood can have an annoying amount of flex in some applications.

Particleboard is widely available and cheap, so it is attractive to many woodworkers. It is considered an excellent substrate for plastic laminates, and thus is widely used for countertops and cabinetry.

Materials

Often called flakeboard or chipboard, particleboard is made from chips that are compressed under heat and pressure. Its internal density is low, and it has rough edges that result from the large chips used to make it. The upshot is that particleboard is not a great choice for most jigs.

Tempered hardboard is a decent choice for quickie baseplates and templates. It is quite uniform with no voids or splinters, but you may have to apply several coats of sealer to prevent the edges from getting fuzzy. There are several grades of hardboard available, and for this purpose, the harder the better. Quarter-inch hardboard is suitable for many custom baseplates, though it may be a bit limber for some applications.

Plastics

Plastics are useful in making many different jigs and fixtures. Clear baseplates, for example, make it easier to see what the router is doing as you work. So if an offset baseplate is what

As easy as it is to apply, plastic laminate is underused in jigmaking. It's most commonly used for router table tops, but consider using it on any surface that needs to be slick and long-wearing. Beyond a few router bits, the only tools you need for laminate work are a disposable brush to spread contact cement and a J-roller to seal the bond.

you need, make it of a clear plastic, like acrylic or polycarbonate.

You won't find plastics—other than plastic laminate—at the local building center, but there's probably a plastics dealer near you. Your woodworking power tools will cut and bore and shape plastic as well as they do wood.

Plastic laminate is a great material for hardworking surfaces because it wears well, slides easily on wood, and

is easily machineable. By itself, it has little utility; you have to back it up with plywood or some other material to make it structural. For a low-cost, durable surface that you'll use again and again, it's worth the bother to cover it with plastic laminate. If you know anyone who does any counter or cabinet work, scraps of the material are easily available. (More information is in the chapter "Working Laminates," page 229.)

Sources for Jigmaking Materials and Hardware

Finding good materials for making jigs is a challenge for many woodworkers, especially hobbyists, who aren't always welcome as customers at wholesalers.

The national home centers—who welcome everyone—generally stock construction-grade materials only. High-quality hardwood plywood and MDF aren't what they sell. The same is true of plastics and specialized hardware.

But every urban center has a sheet-goods wholesaler or two that sell to cabinet shops and other businesses. A

"trade-only" sign may dissuade you from inquiring, but cash often talks. If the sheet you want is in stock, you can often buy it on a cash-and-carry basis. Look in the Yellow Pages under Lumber and under Plywood, and make some exploratory calls. Ask for suggestions at the home center or at cabinetmaking businesses.

The same is true for plastics. Most regions will have a choice of suppliers; again, look in the Yellow Pages and call around. Some are adamant about selling only to businesses; others will sell you a full sheet. But there *are*

vendors around that will sell you odds-and-ends and partial sheets.

My locale has a few good hardware stores and a bunch of so-so stores. For the hardware oddments I can't find locally, I turn to catalog and online retailers. Most diversified woodworking catalogs, for example, list jigmaking plastics and hardware. Firms that cater to machinists have tools, materials, and hardware that you didn't even know existed, much less that you needed. Check "Sources" in the back of this book (page 367).

Plastics have characteristics that are valuable in jigs and fixtures. The clear plastic used in the router table bit guard and dust pickup allows you to see what's happening at the cutter without exposing you to a shower of chips. The same is true in a flush-trimming baseplate. Though the material is easily worked with woodworking tools, some types have the strength and rigidity needed for mounting a router in a table.

Acrylic and polycarbonate are useful in jigmaking. You can usually buy odds-and-ends. If you can't find what you want locally, try shopping through catalogs or online.

Bit Drawer

For fast cuts in soft plastics, look for a single-flute, solid-carbide bit with an "O" flute. They are made by a number of manufacturers, including Amana and Bosch. The unique curved flute contour is designed specifically to eject plastic chips more easily. The geometry reduces heat buildup, thus helping to prevent "welding in the cut," and gives a surprisingly smooth finish.

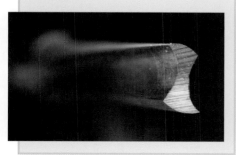

What is the practical difference between the two types of plastic? The acrylic is crystal-clear, rigid, and quite strong, and as such is well regarded as a less-fragile glass substitute. Nevertheless, it is possible to break. Polycarbonate, conversely, is very hard to break (it's the stuff safety glasses are made of), but it is less rigid than acrylic. Under stress, polycarb will tend give.

Both materials are quite easily worked with carbide-tipped woodworking tools. These plastics are popular primarily because they are available in clear sheets. But both plastics scratch easily, so after being used a while, they become webbed with scratches and thus fairly opaque.

Phenolic plastic is gaining popularity in jigmaking. It wears and slides extremely well, it's heat-resistant, and, depending on a particular phenolic's composition, it can be very rigid and strong. It machines well and doesn't tend to melt and stick like the other plastics. Typically, phenolic plastic is brown or black.

The range of grades is bewildering, and it's difficult to know whether a particular piece will be suitable for your purpose. Try NEMA XX, the lowest grade.

The problem with phenolics is availability. The plastics dealer who sells you scraps of acrylic and polycarb may not even carry phenolic. It is available through national catalog-based retailers and online retailers.

Polyethylene is a lubricious white plastic that can be used to make accessories for baseplates and router tables. Because it is pretty soft and very limber, it isn't a great material for a baseplate. But for add-on guide strips, it's great. Credit that primarily to its inherent slipperiness. It's easily worked with woodworking cutters.

Hardware

Almost every woodworking jig or fixture has some hardware in it. Well, okay, templates probably don't have hardware, and various positioning gauges don't have hardware. But even custom baseplates need mounting screws.

Just the right piece of hardware can simplify a jig, make it work better, more efficiently, even more safely. How to secure a fence or stop? How to speed an adjustment or setup? How to hold the work? How to ensure accuracy?

The answers to all these jig-design questions just may be readily available hardware. When trying to work out a jig design, it's a great resource. I roam the aisles, looking at the fasteners and fittings and gewgaws and widgits. And sometimes the answer is there.

I don't think that I need to list

Materials

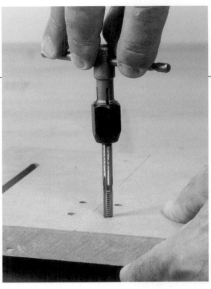

Drywall screws are ubiquitous in woodshops, but for jigs and fixtures, sheet-metal and machine screws are better choices. Because they are heat-treated to harden them, sheet-metal screws are stronger than wood screws. In addition, they are threaded from end to end. Machine screws have more threads per inch than either of the tapered screws. You do have to tap holes for them, but this is a minor job that pays dividends in the strength and accuracy of your jigs and fixtures.

You can cut threads in wood and plastic as easily as you can in aluminum, brass, or steel. Every tap is marked with the size of hole you need to drill. Insert the tap in a tap wrench, drop the end into the hole, and begin turning clockwise. The first few threads you cut determine the course that the tap will follow, so align the tap carefully as you start. You must use an oil-based cutting fluid when tapping metals, but plain soap-and-water works fine for plastics. No fluid is needed for tapping wood.

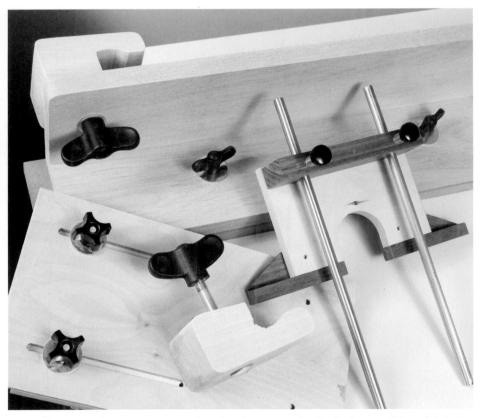

If you are a turner, you can produce handsome wooden knobs for your jigs and fixtures. The rest of us benefit from the ready availability of a wide variety of plastic knobs, wing nuts, and cranks. They are easier on your hands and fingers than metal wing nuts and thumbscrews, and they tighten securely without tools.

Toggle clamps are excellent for gripping work in a fixture. A quick flick opens the clamp; a second flick closes it. That's a big time-saver in an operation like cutting tenons with the right-angle jig. With the jig held in your bench vise, you can switch workpieces quickly and rotate them expeditiously.

So many router operations involve shaping an edge. You perch the machine on the work, but more than half of it is unsupported. Okay, maybe you keep the handles aligned with the edge of the cut. But as often as not, you've got one handle over the work, the other out there in "unsupported" territory. It's a balancing act.

So is it any wonder that you occasionally bobble, tipping the router and sniping the edge?

An offset baseplate like this can help you prevent those bobbles. Its oblong shape changes a router's balance. It has a hefty knob at its farthest reach, so you can outleverage the bobble.

The baseplate is a fairly simple project. Copy the layout from the drawing, duplicating it on your choice of materials. (I used a piece of 3/8-inch

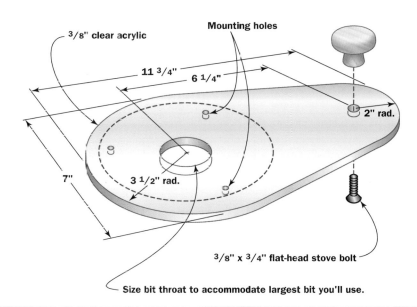

Offset Baseplate
Keep your router upright

3/8" clear acrylic

Mounting holes

11 3/4"

6 1/4"

2" rad.

7"

3 1/2" rad.

3/8" x 3/4" flat-head stove bolt

Size bit throat to accommodate largest bit you'll use.

acrylic.) Cut it out. Using the factory baseplate as a template, mark the locations of the mounting-screw holes and the bit orifice. Drill and countersink the holes. Cut the bit hole.

Install the knob next. Look at some hardware catalogs. Reid Tool Supply (see "Sources," page 367) sells a 1 7/8-inch-diameter black plastic knob (catalog number DK320) that looks perfect. Mount the knob, then mount the baseplate on your router.

Are you a turner? If you are, you can turn a knob, patterning it—roughly, anyway—on those used on hand planes. Install a threaded insert in your blank, then use it to mount the blank on the lathe. After turning and finishing the knob, drive a flat-head machine screw through the baseplate into the threaded insert.

An offset baseplate is easily made and eminently useful for edge-routing. Hold down on the offset knob to keep the router from tipping, and push or pull the router along the edge with one of its knobs.

all the fasteners that might be useful in making jigs. You know about and use drywall screws, machine screws, stove bolts, carriage bolts, hex-head bolts, washers and fender washers, stop nuts and wing nuts. As you tackle the various jig projects in this book, you'll run across the less commonplace hardware items that solved problems for me—nylon washers, plastic sleeves, bronze bushings, coupling nuts, threaded rod, compression springs, T-nuts, threaded inserts, and the like.

Making an Edge Guide

An edge guide is a practical router accessory, useful when making a variety of joinery cuts, as well as decorative cuts. Typically, you use an edge guide made for your router by its manufacturer. The guide may be part of its standard equipment, but most often, it costs extra. Frankly, not all edge guides are worth a whole lot.

You can make a pretty good edge guide using small wood scraps and some commonplace hardware. Making your own gives you an opportunity to practice a few precision techniques that are so useful in making jigs: step-and-repeat drilling, for example.

The drawing shows two versions of the edge guide. The simple guide requires three pieces of wood, two steel rods, seven screws, and two thumbscrews. You can take the dimensions from the drawing, then scale the guide to fit your router.

To use the completed guide, you'd lay out the cut, set the router on the work, and align the bit on the layout. Then slide the edge guide on its rods until the fence contacts the reference edge of the work. Tighten the thumbscrews, and you are ready to rout.

Edge Guide

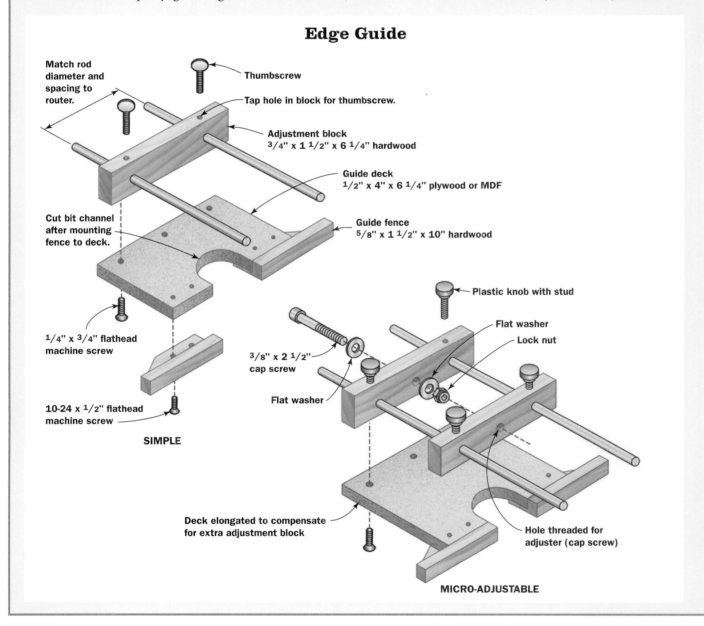

Match rod diameter and spacing to router.

Thumbscrew

Tap hole in block for thumbscrew.

Adjustment block
3/4" x 1 1/2" x 6 1/4" hardwood

Guide deck
1/2" x 4" x 6 1/4" plywood or MDF

Cut bit channel after mounting fence to deck.

Guide fence
5/8" x 1 1/2" x 10" hardwood

1/4" x 3/4" flathead machine screw

10-24 x 1/2" flathead machine screw

SIMPLE

Plastic knob with stud

Flat washer

Lock nut

3/8" x 2 1/2" cap screw

Flat washer

Deck elongated to compensate for extra adjustment block

Hole threaded for adjuster (cap screw)

MICRO-ADJUSTABLE

Making an edge guide for your router is not difficult, doesn't require a lot of materials, and pays dividends in simplifying a variety of operations. To set up and subsequently adjust the simple guide, you loosen the thumbscrews and slide the guide along the rods.

The more sophisticated model has a micro-adjustment block in addition to the basic block. A $3/8$-16 screw passes through the basic block and threads into the micro-adjustment one. Loosen all four thumbscrews to make a coarse adjustment, but only the thumbscrews on the basic block to make a fine adjustment.

Construction

The primary difference between building a jig or fixture and building a stool or bookcase or cabinet is the degree of precision required in layout, in cuts, in assembly. Sure, a jig usually is assembled of only a few parts, using fastened butt joints. But you have little room for error. Those parts must be made from stable materials, to precise dimensions and angles, and assembled so that the finished jig is flat, straight, and square.

Following are some tips and tricks for improving your layout, cutting, and assembly techniques so that your work will be precise and accurate. The result will be better jigs and fixtures. The byproduct is that all your work will be improved. You'll end up doing a better job on that stool or bookcase or cabinet.

The micro-adjustable guide has an extra adjustment block and some extra hardware. With it, you do the basic setup the same as with the simple guide. But after a test cut, you can adjust the position of the guide in fractions as small as $1/64$ inch.

In constructing either guide, two measurements are critical, and both are best made using dial calipers. The first is to measure the router base for the diameter of rod used for the edge guide. The second is to measure the center-to-center spacing of the rods on the router. Knowing those dimensions, you can buy the rod and dimension the adjustment block.

Make the block first, drilling the holes for the rods and for the thumbscrews. If possible, make the rod holes $1/64$ inch larger than the rods so the completed edge guide will slide freely on the rods. Assuming you'll tap the thumbscrew holes, make them $15/64$ inch. Use a $1/4$-inch 20-tpi tap to cut the threads.

Mount the deck to the block and fit it to the router. You want it to extend past the bit axis so that you can override the pilot bearing on a bit. Attach the fence, then cut the bit clearance notch in both fence and deck at the same time.

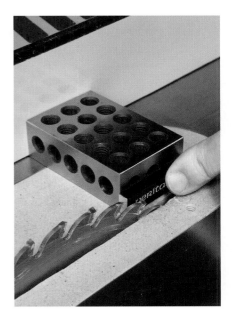

Setup blocks eliminate errors caused by misreading a rule or the scale on a tool. The perforated block is precisely 1 inch thick, 2 inches wide, and 3 inches long. The five black slips range in thickness from $1/16$ inch to $3/4$ inch. Use them individually or in combinations to set stops or fences to precise cuts.

Construction

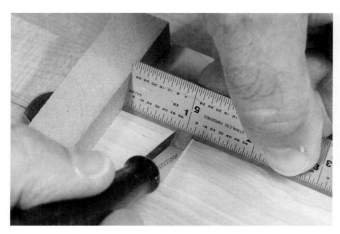

Accurate measurement requires something more than a tape measure and a pencil. Use a quality rule with etched markings and a marking knife. To measure from an edge, butt a block to the edge, then set the rule's end against it. Slide the knife down the etched line to the wood to achieve a precise layout.

Step-and-repeat is a process used by tool-and-die workers to accurately space holes. First cut blocks equal to the desired spacing between two or more holes. Set a stop block to locate the first hole, then insert a spacing block between the stop and the workpiece to shift the work for the next hole. This is the ideal way of accurately locating the rod holes in the body for a shop-made edge guide.

■ Acclimate the materials to your shop environment. It's well understood that wood should be brought into the shop a couple of weeks before use, but so too should sheet goods and even plastics.

■ Make sure your machines are tuned up and properly aligned. Typically, you set up a tool like your table saw when you first get it. You align the blade, miter-gauge slots, and rip fence so they're parallel to each other. You square the blade to the tabletop and calibrate the tilt scale.

What you need to do now is check these settings with reliable, accurate measuring tools. If necessary, retune the settings. Do this for all the machines you'll use in making the jig or fixture.

■ Eliminate the variables in layout and cutting. For example, use a high-quality steel rule and marking knife for layout instead of a tape measure and pencil. Use a stop to position stock for a cut, and measure a test cut to ensure that the stop's position is accurate. Cutting to a line, even a knife line, is too iffy.

Dial calipers are accurate to the thousandth of an inch. With its capacity— 6 inches is a common size—you can measure inside and outside dimensions, as well as depths. To make an edge guide, you must determine the center-to-center spacing of your router's mounting-rod holes. Measure from rod to rod, as shown here, then subtract the rod diameter.

■ Rely on test cuts and measurements of the actual cuts to "prove" your setups. It's an extra step, perhaps, but it's worth it to eliminate an error that otherwise would cascade through your jigmaking endeavor and on into your final project.

■ Use temporary fences, corner blocks, and other helpers to keep parts square and properly aligned when fitting them and/or drilling screw or bolt holes.

■ Dry-assemble the jig to assess the fit and alignment of all the parts.

Remake any that won't align or fit. And remember that a jig that's a "keeper" should have adjustability incorporated so that you can keep it square and true. Sometimes it's better to use fasteners without glue.

■ Apply a finish to jigs you're making for long-term use—T-squares, mortising fixtures, box-joint jigs, and the like. My propensity is to use something (like shellac) that dries quickly. Brush on a couple of coats, then rub out the finish with fine-grit sandpaper and paste wax.

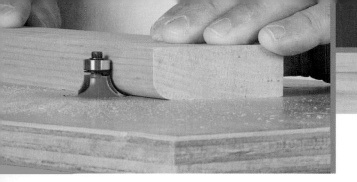

Router Table Design

Of all the accessories made to use with a router, the router table is easily the most useful. It turns the portable router into a precision stationary machine. What other portable power tool can you transform into a precision machine by mounting in a table? None that I can think of.

Moreover, a router table can be a very inexpensive piece of equipment.

You can construct a workable table in an hour, and you don't need to spend more than $25 on it. You can use almost any router, and you won't be giving it up as a portable tool. Use it in a table for one operation, then pop it out to use handheld for the next.

That doesn't mean that we don't spend lavishly to create eye-popping examples, or that we don't buy routers especially for a table. In today's marketplace, it is easy to drop a grand into a router table with an expansive top, a sophisticated fence with micrometer adjusters and lots of attachments, and a cabinet replete with bit and accessory storage, dust collection, and its own electrical system. Combined with today's sophisticated bits and cutters, the router table functions like a small shaper, and though it doesn't have to, it can cost as much as or more than a midsized shaper.

What are the benefits of this small-shop powerhouse?

■ It allows operations and a level of precision that are difficult, if not impossible, to achieve with the router handheld.

■ It allows you to rout workpieces that are too small or too oddly proportioned to be conveniently secured for handheld routing.

■ It allows you to use the biggest bits available, as well as the smallest.

■ It takes a lot of the intimidation out of the router. You don't actually hold the tool in your hands.

A router table is on standby for all sorts of jobs, especially those requiring the biggest of bits. You can improve the accuracy of your work without a lot of folderol. Just install the bit, set the fence, and start routing.

- It reduces the tool's noise and improves the level of dust collection that's possible.

- It puts the router on standby for work, just the way your table saw, band saw, jointer, and other shop tools are. Just install the bit, adjust the fence, hit the power, and cut.

Router Table Architecture

There are many router table variants—stand-alone constructions, based on either an open stand or a cabinet; benchtop models; table-saw extension-wing or outfeed-table mounts; even rudimentary contraptions supported on sawhorses, or held in a Workmate, or plopped on top of an open trash can. The most elaborate router tables are the creations of hobby woodworkers, who lavish hours of planning on their designs, use only the finest materials, and invest endless hours of shop time in the construction.

It's interesting (to me, anyway) how router table design and construction has evolved. If you were following woodworking periodicals twenty or twenty-five years ago, you saw plans for smallish benchtop units: maybe a three-sided plywood box with a 3/4-inch plywood table-top, or something with short legs. Then a crafty soul modified a sink cutout, acquired as a castoff, and captured the slickness and durability of plastic laminate for the router tabletop. With this sort of tabletop, a mounting plate was needed.

Eventually, woodworkers began making custom tabletops, applying plastic laminate to both sides of a ply-

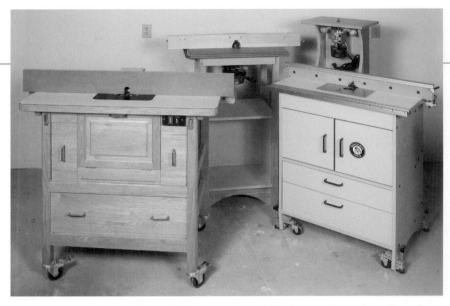

Router tables are manufactured by many companies in a variety of configurations, including cabinet-based and stand-based styles. But the router table is one of the few shop tools you can build yourself, and the most satisfying-to-use table is the one you do build for yourself.

Bit Storage

In, on, or near your router table is a logical place to store your bits, accessories, and other routers. If you build a permanent router table, be sure to include the storage space you'll need. Avoid the common tendency to throw your bits into a box or drawer. Not only are they hard to keep track of that way, but they're hard to keep clean, sharp, and undamaged.

Even carbide edges will be quickly destroyed if they knock together.

Make a drawer, a box, or just a block of wood and drill 9/32-inch (for 1/4-inch shanks) and/or 17/32-inch (for 1/2-inch shanks) holes about 3/4 inch deep. Insert the bit shanks. The bits will be held securely (so their cutting edges don't bang together) and openly (so you can easily see what you have).

Po' Boy Router Table

This is the only complete plan for a router table in this chapter. Novice woodworkers often fret about whether to buy or build a router table. It is not a big deal.

On Saturday morning, drive down to the local home center, and buy a quarter-sheet of 3/4-inch plywood (be extravagant and get birch plywood!) and a handful of 2 1/2-inch drywall screws. Also buy new, longer screws to replace those that attach the baseplate to your router. Shouldn't cost you more than 15 bucks, total.

Head home. In your shop, cut the plywood into a 12-inch by 16-inch top, two 6-inch by 13-inch sides, and a 6-inch by 12 1/2-inch stretcher. You'll have more than half the plywood left, so you'll be able to make a suitable fence.

Mount your router base to the top. To do this, set the base on the plywood, orient the handles with the long dimension, and by eye, center it. Trace around it. Then remove the baseplate, relocate it inside the traced lines, and drill holes for the mounting screws through the plywood. Flip the plywood over and countersink the holes. Turn it back and attach the router's base, sans plate, using the long screws you bought.

Assemble the base next. Drill and countersink pilot holes and screw the stretcher to the edges of the sides. You want the stretcher to hang below the sides so you can capture it in the bench vise. Set the base up, set the top in place, drill and countersink pilots, then screw the top to the base.

Install a big straight bit in the router, and fit the motor into the base so the bit is just shy of the top's underside. With the table securely clamped in your bench vise, turn on the router and run the bit through the top, forming the bit opening. Don't immediately ream out the opening and make it any bigger than you have to.

For a fence, cut a 3- to 5-inch-wide by 16- to 24-inch-long strip of the plywood. Use clamps to secure it to the tabletop.

Shazam! You have a router table, and it isn't even time for lunch.

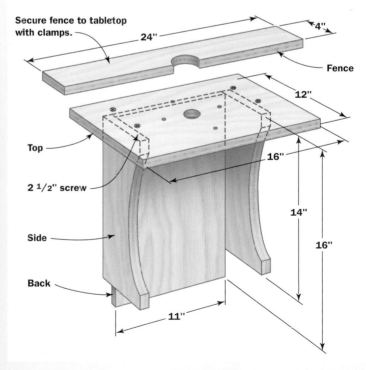

Po' Boy Router Table
Simple and cheap, use it as a first table or a handy auxiliary

Secure fence to tabletop with clamps.
24"
4"
Fence
12"
Top
16"
2 1/2" screw
14"
16"
Side
Back
11"

Here's an ideal table for routing small pieces. It stands on the workbench, so it is higher than the usual router table. Because it has a tail to clamp in the bench's vise, it is quick to set up and very steady.

wood, particleboard, or medium-density fiberboard (MDF) substrate, then cutting a hole in it and suspending the router from a mounting plate of acrylic, polycarbonate, or even phenolic plastic.

Nowadays, the marketplace is abuzz with router tables, made with tops of laminate-covered 1- to 1 1/4-inch-thick MDF or 3/4-inch-thick phenolic clad with laminate, lightweight cast aluminum, or stiff steel plate. I guess there are dozens of manufacturers, and easily hundreds of sources.

The availability of good tabletops notwithstanding, I remain as convinced today as I did a dozen years ago that every router woodworker should build his or her own router table(s), top and all.

When first you think about a router table, think about what you are going to rout on it, and about what router you are going to use. Ask yourself where you are going to put it. (Do you have a spacious shop, or only a tight corner?) The answer to this—along with your thoughts on what work you'll be doing and what router you'll be using to do it—may help you determine how big the tabletop will be. A foot square? One foot by 2 feet? Two feet by 3 feet?

And how will that tabletop be supported? Short pedestal legs to clamp to a benchtop? A small plywood box for benchtop use? Trestle legs of some sort, or a leg-and-apron structure? How about a full cabinet, with storage for bits and accessories?

Height should be decided thoughtfully. Table-saw height is a typical standard, but you don't have to follow it. I've found that a 38- to 42-inch height for a router table suits me much better than my table saw's 34-inch height.

No one router-table height is right for every woodworker. It's common for a router table to match table-saw height. But a benchtop table invariably ends up a foot or more higher than that, elevating the work to band-saw level. The router table that I built for myself stands midway between these extremes.

But before you go too far with your planning and design work, consider the router you will use in the table. Is it one you already own? Or one you will buy for it? The router has an impact on how you mount it and how you make adjustments, and of course both these considerations impact the design.

What Router?

Power and adjustability are the primary considerations in choosing a router for a table.

You probably wouldn't buy a router of less than 3+ horsepower specifically for table mounting. You might buy a lower-power router if you want one router for both hand and table use.

Power, coupled with speed control, is important if you expect to use the largest-diameter bits in your router table. I'm reluctant to say it is essential, because you can usually work around a power limitation. But it sure is nice to have a router with the moxie to handle any bit you put in it. If your budget is limited, if you aren't sure what projects you'll tackle with the router table, bear in mind that you can start with a mid-power router, then move up without rebuilding the table.

As I write this, there are only two 3+ hp fixed-base routers available—the Porter-Cable 7518 and the Milwaukee 5625. There are more plunge routers in that power range, but not all are easily adjustable if mounted under a table.

Make the short step down to the mid-power routers, and you find more than a half-dozen fixed-base routers to chose from.

The fixed-base router is the most flexible model to use in a table, but plunge routers have their advantages. Before committing to a particular brand and model, think how you will mount it and how, given that mounting, you will change bits and adjust the bit height. You do have options, but not all routers lend themselves well to each option.

You may be predisposed to buy a router lift because you've heard that these accessories make bit changes convenient and bit elevation adjustments simple and super-accurate. While I wouldn't dispute either contention, I would say there are less costly ways to achieve that end. And you wouldn't be quite so limited in the routers you could use.

The next logical step is to look at tabletops and at mounting systems. Then we'll revisit the router choice question.

The Tabletop

The tabletop is *the* critical component. In some router table–construction accounts, the tabletop seems to be the last element considered, after a stand or cabinet is designed and constructed, a router and lift selected, a high-ticket fence purchased. The top is key; a poorly considered design can lead to no end of trouble.

The design and construction of the top is impacted by the router you use, the way it's mounted to the top, how the top is supported, and to a degree by the accessories you use with it. It's not surprising then that the process of designing a tabletop is looping rather than linear. Each new choice prompts a review of previous choices.

First and most important, your tabletop should be flat, smooth, and free of obstructions. What it is made of, what the surface covering is, where the router is—those are choices. But having a flat, smooth, obstruction-free top is not a choice, it is an essential.

The very worst is to have the bit in the center of a saucer, which is what you get when a tabletop sags. This definitely will lead to inaccurate cuts, and the little inaccuracies may be hard to trace. Not only will joinery cuts be inconsistent and slightly out of square, so will profiles.

Sag is surprisingly common, even in manufactured tops. (If you buy a tabletop, check it with a straightedge as soon as you get it out of the packaging. If it is not flat, arrange to ship it back and get a new one.)

As to smoothness, that just makes it easier and safer to slide work across the top. To me, it means that the surface is reasonably slick, that it's free of catches and obstructions. This is not the exclusive province of any particular material or surface coating.

The paradigm for a router table top is this: flat, smooth, and uncluttered. This homemade top has a router mounted directly to the underside. There are no seams or slots—only four router mounting-screws set as close to flush as possible.

Router tables typically have a 2-foot by 3-foot top. But the top of a table you make for yourself doesn't have to fit the norm. A smaller top may be easier to make and keep flat, saves a bit on materials, takes up less space, and works just as well in all but a few job situations.

Size

What size should your router table's top be? In my experience, it doesn't make a lot of difference in terms of utility.

The idea that you *need* an expansive surface to support big workpieces is largely a mental thing. Raising a long panel, say for a door for a 42-inch wall cabinet? You don't need 18 or 20 inches of tabletop under that panel to rout it. You'd do fine on all but the smallest table with a pair of featherboards on the fence holding the panel firmly against the tabletop.

The standard commercial tabletop is roughly 24 inches by 32 inches. That's giving the manufacturer a yield of six tabletops from a 4-foot by 8-foot sheet of MDF, a common tabletop material. That's roughly the size of the cabinet router table on page 81. But the benchtop model on page 60 has a roughly 16-inch by 20-inch tabletop. And that Po' Boy benchtop special on page 57 has a 12-inch by 16-inch top.

Don't feel constrained by the top dimensions. Whatever you want to do, you can find a way to do, regardless of the tabletop dimensions.

One unrecognized aspect of tabletop size is its impact on flatness. I think that a smaller top is easier to keep flat. A really big top is more likely—in my mind—to develop sags.

Gallery: Benchtop Router Table

For the small shop, for the remote job site, or as an extra in the busy shop, this little router table is just the ticket. It sets up on a workbench, a couple of sawhorses, or some other multipurpose work surface, and it allows you to do all sorts of router-table jobs, from profiling edges to cutting joints to raising panels (see page 219). It holds a midsized router, but isn't possessive about it. In just seconds—literally seconds!—you can pop the router out of the table and have it ready to use handheld. Full plans for this table are in my book *Router Magic* (Reader's Digest, 1996; see "Sources," page 367).

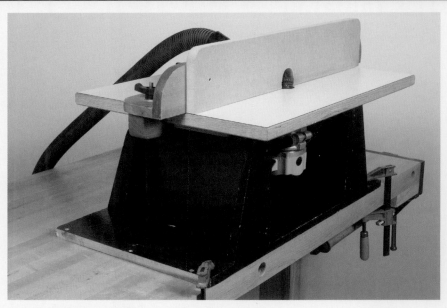

This benchtop router table is compact and uncomplicated. Its small size doesn't restrict the work you can do on it, but that size and light weight make it easy to move around and to stow in an out-of-the-way corner when it isn't in active use.

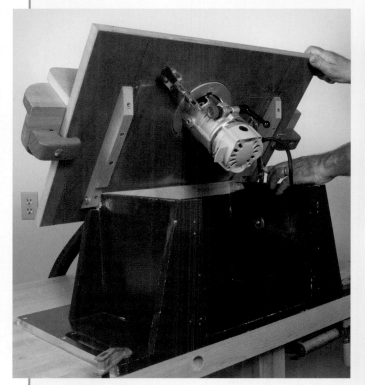

This benchtop table only *borrows* the router. To reclaim it for a handheld operation, just lift the tabletop until the lid stay locks (above). Grasp the router with one hand, and pop open the two toggle clamps with the other (center). The router then virtually falls out of its mounting recess. Note that its stock baseplate is still in place (bottom).

Router-Mounting Options

Before wrapping up the design and engineering of your tabletop, decide how you will mount the router to it. That choice will have a big impact on the tabletop.

Two options for mounting your router in a table dominate. The use of a mounting plate is surely the most common. But you can also mount the router directly to the tabletop. Both of these approaches have advantages and both have disadvantages. Neither is just right.

Router lifts are variants of the mounting plate system.

Router Placement

Before jumping into the *how* of mounting the router, let's look at the *where*. Here is a recommendation for you to consider:

Offset the router toward the front of the tabletop. Don't plop it in the center.

Offsetting the router does several things. It makes the router table more

comfortable to use, by locating the center of the action—the router bit—close to you. You don't have to bend and reach. For most operations, you need support on the left and right, not between the bit and the table's edge. For those occasional operations that do need broad support, address the table from the back.

Keeping the router close to one edge allows you to use a sled rather than a miter gauge (see "Router Table Accessories," page 101). A sled does the same work as a miter gauge, but it rides against the table's edge rather than requiring a slot in the table. Slots are a nuisance: They gather dirt, they catch your work and cause mistakes, and they sometimes cause your table to sag or warp.

With the router offset, you can run a support under the center of the table to ensure that it stays straight.

Finally, if the router is close to the front edge, it is accessible. It's easier to adjust. You can even change bits without taking the router out of the table, a real handy feature. Even if you use a drop-in mounting plate, even if you routinely pop the machine up out of the table to

Offsetting the router toward the tabletop's front edge moves the bit closer to you, so common operations are more comfortable to perform (top). You spend less time leaning awkwardly over the table. Moreover, when you have a broad panel to feed across the table (bottom), you can turn the fence around and work from the back, and the panel will have more support than if the bit was dead-center in the tabletop.

Work Sectors
Offsetting the router gives you options

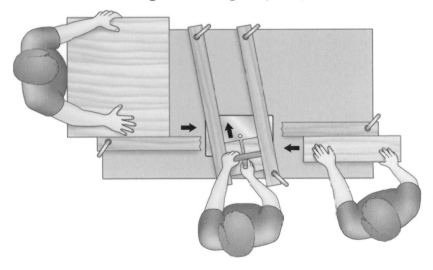

change bits, there will be times when you'll want to adjust the router without moving it. For example, say you want to hog out a groove with a straight bit, then switch to a dovetail cutter for a final pass. If you leave your fence set up, you know that the final pass will center up on the groove cut by the first pass. But nine times out of ten, the fence is across the mounting plate. If you're going to save your setup, the router has to be accessible.

Mounting Plates

Let's look at the plate system first. Some call it an insert or an insert plate; I've always called it a mounting plate. Regardless of the name, it's plastic or metal, between 1/4 inch and 3/8 inch thick, measuring roughly 6 inches by 9 inches, and it is screwed to the base of the router. An opening the same size as the plate is cut in the tabletop. Usually, a rabbet is cut around the opening so there's a ledge to support the plate. Often, blunt-tipped screws are driven through the ledge so the plate can be aligned flush with the top's surface. (An alternative is setscrews in the plate that serve the same purpose.) Gravity holds the plate and router in place.

This mounting allows you to remove the router from the table quickly. You can pop it out to change bits, to use it for a hand-guided operation (with the plate still mounted on it), or to substitute a different router. You can attach any sort of router to a plate—fixed-base or plunge, large or small. You can even attach another tool, like a jigsaw, to a plate and use it in a table.

Commercial mounting plates often have snap-in rings to adjust the size of the bit opening. You keep the

rings in place when using small-diameter bits, but you can remove them to get an opening large enough for a large-diameter bit. This is an important safety feature.

The plates are widely available. You can buy them blank or with holes drilled for attaching your router—you even get the correct screws to use! Plates configured to accept template guides are available. As I mentioned, you can get them in acrylic plastic, polycarbonate, phenolic, and aluminum. You can make your own from scratch, or you can buy one and use your router and a flush-trimming bit to produce duplicates.

Is there a drawback to this mounting system? Critics of it cite at least two. One is that the required opening weakens the tabletop, inviting sagging, twisting, and cupping. The second is that the seam between the tabletop and the plate is problematic. As you feed your workpiece across the table, the transition from tabletop to plate (and then back) must be perfectly smooth. A slight mismatch can cause a slight hesitation in the work's movement, which can result in a "dwell" mark in the cut. If the mismatch is bad enough, it can stall the cut completely. A third shortcoming is that, if you use polycarbonate, the plate itself can sag.

The plate system is the most common means of mounting a router in a table. Dozens of brands and models are on the market. Most have interchangeable reducers that adjust the diameter of the bit opening. They are made of acrylic plastic, polycarbonate, phenolic, even aluminum or steel. Exact dimensions vary. But it is easy—and cheap!—to make your own.

I've used mounting plates, both purchased and homemade, for years. In my opinion, these shortcomings are real but somewhat overstated.

If the tabletop is well braced and the edges of the opening are sealed, the tabletop is unlikely to deform. And keeping the plate flush is a matter of occasional maintenance, not one of adjusting each time you use the table.

Direct Mounting

The direct-mount approach has the router attached to the underside of the tabletop itself. This isn't by any means a common approach, and only a few commercial setups accommodate it. Typically, it's used on shop-made tables.

This mounting eliminates the need for a *large* opening—a 6 inch by 9 inch one, specifically—and it eliminates any transition seams from the tabletop.

But it doesn't eliminate problems, by any means. It simply presents a new batch of them.

Reduced cutting-depth capacity. Most tops are 1 to 1 1/2 inches thick. Unless you are willing to sacrifice that much from your total depth-of-cut capacity, you need to reduce the top's thickness at the mounting point.

For the direct-mount setups I've made, I laminated two 1/2-inch-thick panels. Before the glue-up, I cut a hole in one panel for the router. The tops combined that panel with an uncompromised one, and the thickness of the uncompromised panel is what supported the router. The typical mounting plate is 3/8 inch thick, so I sacrificed that plus an additional 1/8 inch from the maximum possible cutting depth.

Router choice, as a practical

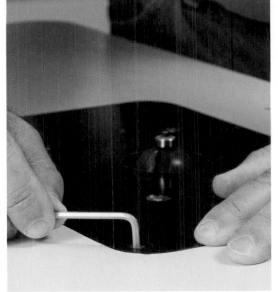

Keeping the mounting plate flush with the tabletop surface is important. The most common installation has a rabbeted opening cut in the tabletop for the plate. Screws that run up through the base of the rabbet support the plate, and by raising or lowering individual screws, you alter the plate's alignment. Bench Dog uses flat-tipped Conformat screws driven up though the rabbet (top left). I've used drywall screws driven down into the rabbet (top right). You can drill and tap the plate for setscrews (left). This approach allows you to adjust the plate from the top of the table.

matter, is limited because your access to the router is limited.

Here's what this means. The router is screwed to the table and can't be removed for any reason—to change bits, for example—without removing the screws.

If you mount a dedicated plunge router directly to the table, you'll have a devil of a time changing bits. You won't be able to reach the collet

very easily, and you won't be able to see it well. The tabletop is opaque, and the router is in the dark.

If you use a router that allows the motor to be easily separated from the base, this is much less of a problem. (Most fixed-base routers, and a few plungers, fall into this category.) You can drop the motor free of the base and change bits with it on top of the table.

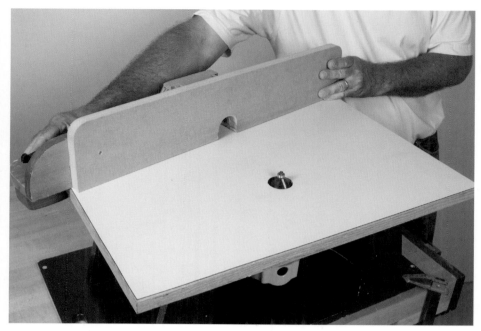

Mounting the router directly to the tabletop yields a smooth, obstruction-free path for the work. The surface is flush all the way across, so bit-height setups are accurate in relation to the tabletop edges as well as the area immediately around the bit. There are no seams to interrupt the movement of the work across the top.

supplement the large one in the tabletop itself. The overlays are secured with the fence and, if needed, some spring clamps or carpet tape at the corners.

A third option is to make your own insert rings of the sort that mounting plates have. The commercial tops configured for direct mounting have them. This introduces a seam in the table surface, which counters a reason for using a direct mount. But it is an option.

Cut disks from 1/8-inch hardboard or plastic (acrylic, for example). Rout a circular recess in the tabletop, centered on the bit axis. When the bit opening needs to be altered, press a new disk into the recess and rout a zero-clearance hole in it. If necessary, use a screw or two to secure the insert disk.

A very important exception here is a tilting top, which is an optional feature of the cabinet router table presented in the next chapter. You have plenty of access to the router for changing bits when the top is tilted up, even if it is a plunge router and you've mounted it directly to the top.

The bit opening is tough to close down. Use your direct-mount setup once to raise panels with a large bit, and you've got a major opening to contend with. It's unsafe for any operation that requires a smaller bit.

If you've made your own direct-mount top, you can do what one router expert does. Make two or three tops, each with a different bit-opening size.

I'm too lazy to change tops, I'm afraid, so I've made auxiliary tops of 1/8-inch hardboard. Because my router is offset, two such overlays give me four different opening sizes to

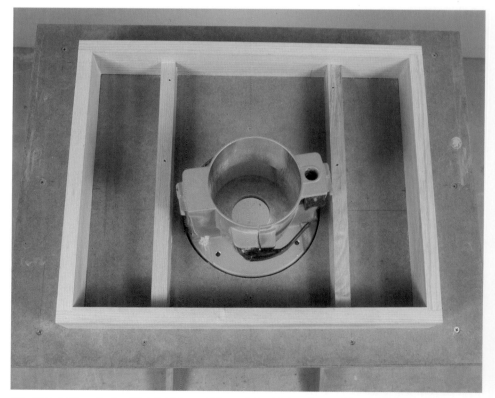

We often believe that a thick tabletop will be a flat tabletop. But a thin top with a frame attached to its underside may be a better bet in that regard. This frame incorporates support immediately beside the router to combat sag.

Gallery: A Stand-Type Table

Built just to try out a few things, this rudimentary router table lives on and on because it works. I wanted to try a taller-than-average table, a direct mounting for the router, and a laminate-free tabletop.

Mounting the router directly to the tabletop means the support structure must be open sufficiently that the tool is readily accessible. Using a smallish top and requiring overhang all around (to allow clamping of the fence and featherboards and reference blocks and other accessories) means the support structure's footprint must be small.

Because it was just an exercise, I used a simple construction approach, biscuiting legs and panels together to form the stand. The top rails are joined to the legs with connector bolts and cross-dowels. Feet screwed to the legs and each other reduce the table's tippiness. Were I to build this now, I'd use full-height panels, so the stand would be more like a lectern, enclosing the router on three sides.

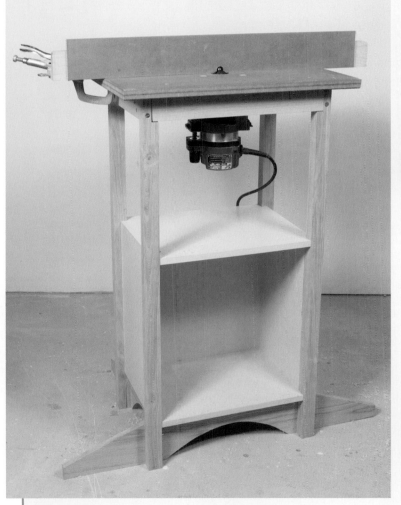

Built primarily as an experiment, this stand-type router table is pure function. Except for storage, it has everything you want in a router table—even good shop-vac-based dust collection. A modest redesign of the stand would provide that storage.

The bit opening accommodates under-2-inch-diameter bits, and I close it down using an auxiliary top. The top is dotted with the heads of screws used to mount the router and the support frame, but it has no seams or slots. The edges are chamfered to prevent chipping, but aren't banded. The laminate-free top is slick and durable, but applying the oil finish took longer than applying laminate would have.

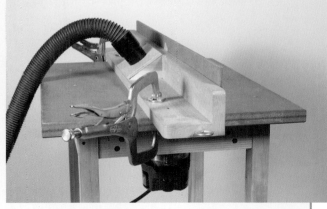

The General-Purpose Fence (see pages 104–105 for plans) is secured to the tabletop with Vise-Grip C-clamps, which you can apply with one hand.

What Router, Revisited

Back in the late 20th century, when I worked on a router table for the first time, you could change bits by pulling the whole router (or just the motor), and working on the table-top. Or you could leave the router in the table and peer through the clear mounting plate to see what you were doing.

Adjusting the bit height could be a bit dodgy. Refining a setup with some routers was frustrating because the motor would plunge to the floor as soon as the clamp locking the motor in the base was loosened. With others, the bit axis would wobble as you screwed the motor into the base to elevate the bit.

These are problems that a router lift fixes.

Router Lifts

Currently, the top-of-the-line lifts have two splendid capabilities. They enable you to:

■ Adjust the bit up and down from the top of the table, using a removable crank and monitoring the adjustment on an indicator.

■ Raise the collet above the tabletop for bit changes.

For a lot of woodworkers, these are must-have capabilities in a router table setup. They don't want to deal with anything less, and they'll pay any price to get these features.

Bear in mind that not all lifts have these capabilities—just the premium models, at $250 and up. Bear in mind, too, that you can't use just any router in one of the top-end lifts.

All consist of a flat metal plate

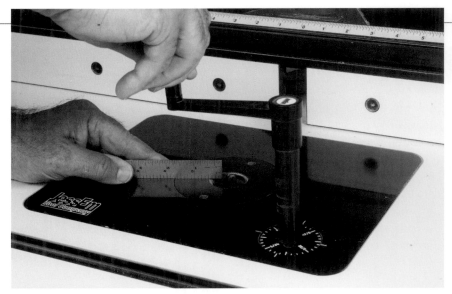

Above-the-table adjustments are what router lifts are all about. To adjust the bit elevation (top), you plug a crank into a socket on the lift's surface and wind the bit up or down. Make the initial setting against a rule held beside the bit. All lifts have a dial for gauging subsequent fine adjustments—up or down ¹/128 inch, for example. To change a bit (bottom), you crank the lift until the router collet is above the table surface.

(comparable to a regular-mounting or insert plate) that drops into an opening in the tabletop. Attached to its underside is a pair of posts on which a mount for the router itself rides. A screw or threaded rod drives the mount up and down the posts, raising or lowering the router. The screw is operated from above the plate, usually with a removable crank. As the crank is turned, an indicator dial spins, seemingly giving you a readout on the bit's elevation.

Two basic mount designs are used in the lifts. With the top-of-the-line lifts, you remove the router motor from its base and clamp it in the lift's mounting block. This arrangement provides the best vertical adjustment range, and enables you to raise the router so its collet projects through the bit opening in the lift's surface plate. Bit changing is a snap.

Three top-end lifts accept the same router motors and share a design concept. But the differences among them abound, from materials to drive mechanisms. The Precision Router Lift from Woodpecker (left) features a roller chain linking the crank sprocket to the twin drive screws. Bench Dog's cast-iron ProLift Ni (center) has an Acme-thread drive screw and precision-ground guide posts in bronze bushings joining the router mount to the top plate. Jessem's Mast-R-Lift has extended sockets for the guide posts and a drive screw with a cogged-belt-and-pulley transmission.

The top lifts were designed specifically for the Porter-Cable 7518 motor, but some will also accept the Milwaukee 5625. All will also accept a modest selection of mid-power (1¹⁄₂- to 2¹⁄₄-hp) router motors through the use of sleeves.

The second tier of lift design has a mount with a plate to which you attach the router's base. You can use virtually *any* router with these lifts, including plunge models. The combination of the router base and the mount's plate, however, restricts the elevation that's possible. You simply can't raise the router enough to have the collet extend above the tabletop. So these two lifts give you above-the-table fine adjustment of the bit position, but not above-the-tabletop bit changing. (In fact, depending upon the router you use, bit changes with these lifts may actually be more difficult than with a conventional insert-plate mounting.)

I should add that some enterprising woodworkers have cobbled up mounting blocks—used instead of the router's base—to install routers in these second-tier lifts. The blocks allow the motor to be positioned higher, so the lift can jack the collet above the table surface.

All the lifts are excellent products: well designed and well manufactured. The key features are worthwhile, saving you a little time and improving the precision of your router table cuts.

But—and this is a *big* but—are the two primary features worth more than $250? The fact is, there are other ways to achieve fast, convenient, accurate bit adjustments and changes. They expand your router choices, and they don't cost nearly as much.

Transform a less-expensive second-tier router lift by making a mounting block for the router motor, replacing the router base. You'll be able to position the motor higher in the lift, thus allowing it to raise the collet above the tabletop for bit changes.

Plunge-Router Adjusters

Before the woodworking world had router lifts, it had plunge routers. A lot of us have viewed plunge routers as a natural choice for use in a table mounting, simply because their basic design lends itself well to easy, accurate bit-height adjustment.

Many plunge routers, in fact, are factory-equipped with a simple depth-of-cut adjuster for router table use. Turn a big knob and the router motor moves up and down the plunge posts. Reach the bit setting you want and stop turning. You don't get a continuous readout on a dial, but you can monitor the rise and fall of the bit with a rule.

Such adjusters are widely available for most plunge routers, and generally cost about $25. To make the adjustment even easier, you can get after-market adjusters with a crank in place of the knob. The cranks cost more, about $35.

The simplicity and effectiveness of this system haven't kept other plunge-router adjusters off the market.

An excellent add-on is the Router Raizer, which can be mounted on virtually any plunge router. It costs about $90. Remarkably flexible, it allows you to adjust the bit height manually from either the top or the bottom of the router, using a removable crank. But it doesn't prevent the router from being used for regular plunge operations.

With the router hung in a table, you insert the end of the Router Raizer's crank into the bottom-end socket—the one right beside the bit—and wind the bit up or down. Each full rotation changes the bit elevation 1/16 inch, so a quarter turn equals 1/64 inch (about 0.015 inch).

Neither approach can elevate the collet through the base and proud of

the tabletop. The design of the routers simply won't allow it.

A fairly common solution to this vexation is the bent wrench. After-market bent wrenches are available for selected routers (typically those—like Porter-Cable and Hitachi—that come with stamped-steel wrenches). A step is bent into the wrench handle right at the working end. With the collet raised as high as possible, you can dip the end into a large tabletop bit opening and engage the collet nut while still having a good grasp on the handle.

Not the perfect solution, perhaps, but a darn serviceable one.

My low-rent solution to bit changes and height adjustments is to hinge the tabletop to the stand. To change bits and dial in my initial bit setting, I tip the tabletop up. The router is held at an angle at about waist height, where it's easy for me to see the collet and to get the wrench on it. With the bit secured, I can reach across the tilted tabletop, hold a rule beside the bit, and use the crank

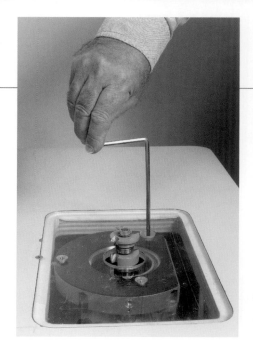

A relatively inexpensive adjuster for table-mounted plunge routers is the Router Raizer. With the unit installed on the router, you use a separate crank to manually and progressively alter the depth-of-cut. You insert the crank through a hole drilled in the base and wind the motor up or down the plunge posts.

to adjust the height. Drop the top and I'm ready to rout.

Does it match a high-end router-lift setup? Pretty close, I say. And best of all, my investment, beyond the router and the table, is a mere $35.

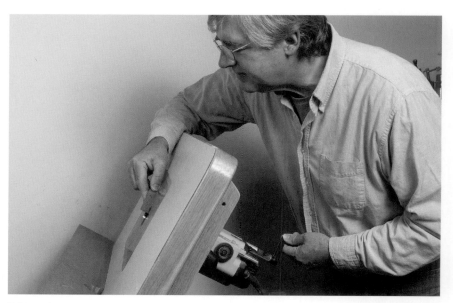

With a tilting-top router table, you can adjust the bit elevation while standing bolt upright. Use the router's adjuster to raise or lower the bit while you peer down across the slanted tabletop at a rule held beside the bit. Lock up the router, lower the top, and you are ready for a test cut.

This modular router table displays the features that most woodworkers want. It has a big uncluttered top, a solid, easily set fence, and a powerful router with its own precise-adjustment capabilities. While not unique, the tilt-up tabletop is unusual. With the top up, you have excellent access to the router for changing bits and setting the bit elevation. These working parts are supported by a post-and-rail stand mounted on locking casters. A separate, removable cabinet houses the router, containing the noise and collecting the chips, and providing some bit storage as well. Full plans for this table are in my book *Router Magic* (Reader's Digest, 1996; see "Sources," page 367).

This may not be the most beautiful router table you've ever seen, but it isn't bad for a hardworking piece of shop furniture. It's been my principal router table for a decade. It's on its third router, but with the exception of the casters, the table is unchanged since it was built.

With the tabletop tilted up, it's surprisingly easy to change bits and adjust the bit elevation. The router is suspended at a convenient height, and you can use both hands to loosen and tighten the collet. This design predated router lifts, and though I've used lifts, I'm not a convert. I prefer the lift-top approach to bit changes and adjustments.

The table is modular to the extent that the upper cabinet—which houses the router, the electrics, the primary dust collection, and the bit storage—and the big lower drawer can be removed. You still have a fully functioning router table. The modularity enables you to use the tool even while constructing it, and eases the chore of moving it from shop to remote job site.

Fences

The most-used guide system on a router table is the fence. You need a good one.

The primary characteristics of a good fence are these:

- It is perfectly straight from end to end.

- The face is perpendicular to the tabletop surface.

- It has a cutout equidistant from the ends to house whatever bit you are using.

- It is unfettered—meaning that it can be moved freely around the tabletop and can be removed completely without undue fuss.

- It can be fixed securely at any position, again without undue fuss.

Secondarily, a good fence should have a dust pickup, and it should be free of frivolous accessories and adjustability.

Whether you buy a fence or make one is up to you, of course. As with a table, you can invest heavily and be no better off than your buddy who made his own fence from project leftovers. I'd suggest you begin with a straight, true board and a pair of C-clamps. Let your fence evolve as your skills do. If you are like me, you'll eventually have a general-purpose fence along with a special-purpose fence or two (one for jointing and tapering, for example).

Though the clamps that fix this manufactured fence to the tabletop are simple—in a sophisticated sort of way—they are vexing to use. Because the fence base is so narrow and the clamp stem so close to the fence upright, a knob or wing nut can't be used. The lever seldom works reliably with one hand.

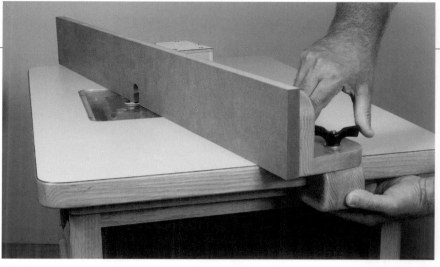

The features you need in a router-table fence include a broad base, changeable facings, a dust pickup, and integral clamps to grip the tabletop edges. The clamp system allows you to move and remove the fence quickly, leaving no trace behind. A separate micro-adjuster can provide precision when you need it.

This manufactured fence is colorful and functional, with a dust pickup and individually adjustable facings. Though the actual purpose of the measuring tape along the top edge is a mystery, it does lend an air of precision. The fence mounts to tracks, each with its own zero-able rule, that flank the tabletop. Easy to adjust, tough to remove quickly.

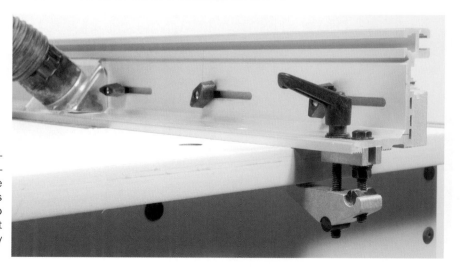

"Repeatability" and "micro-adjustment" are awfully seductive concepts. There are some super-sophisticated commercial fences available that give you the ability to adjust the fence in thousandths of an inch. They consume a great deal of tabletop space, and they cost a lot. I believe they work as advertised, but I've personally never felt the need for one.

Plans for three different fixed fences are in the chapter "Router Table Accessories," page 101. You can adapt them to fit virtually any router table. One is little more than a straight board that you set and lock with a pair of clamps. At the opposite end of the spectrum is the fence with adjustable split facings, integral clamps, and a dust pickup.

The Underpinnings: Stand or Cabinet

The underpinnings of your tabletop and fence can be just about anything you want them to be. What you choose will probably have an impact on the tabletop construction you need.

I see two main options: a leg-and-apron stand (a *table,* in other words) or a cabinet. The stand may go together faster, but the cabinet provides more benefits; compromises abound. Look at the "gallery" tables (pages 60, 65, and 69), the Cabinet Router Table (page 81), and the table-saw extension-wing mounting on page 74.

Stand: Light weight and speed of construction are the primary benefits of a stand. You don't need a great deal of material to make a rigid stand. The joinery need not be sophisticated, but it does need to be sound and tight. The typical stand-type router table can be picked up and moved as easily as a household occasional table.

Commercial models are widely available and aren't expensive. You can bolt one together in less than a hour.

The router isn't housed in a little compartment and hidden away behind a door, so it's easy to access from any side. But because the router is out in the open, its noise is unabated. Dust collection tends to be overlooked or ignored, so the mess goes all over the floor, your pants, and your shoes. But dust collection—

Built quickly of low-cost materials and using very basic joints, this stand provides good support for the top. The box frame at the top will prevent the top from sagging under the router's weight. The frame would bear up well even supporting the heaviest lift. The slightly splayed legs help resist racking.

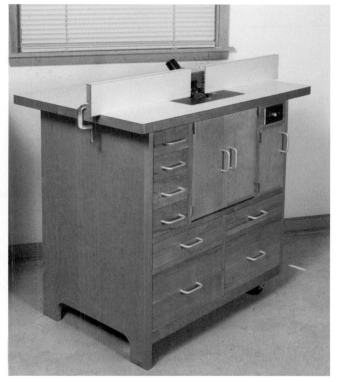

Building your own router table allows you to design the setup that satisfies you. This table couples a shop-made tabletop with a manufactured mounting plate. The manufactured fence is secured with commonplace C-clamps. All the storage is customized for the woodworker's collection of routers, accessories, and bits. The materials, fit, and finish reflect the builder's woodworking sensibility.

Electrifying!

Put some power in that router table. Yes, a killer router is nice; but unless it's cordless, it needs some 110.

The advantages are several. You can position an outlet next to the router, making it convenient to unplug when changing bits. (The main reason woodworkers fail to take this simple safety step is that it's inconvenient.) You can position an on-off switch where it's easy to find. (This is especially appealing when you need to kill the router *fast*.) You can add an outlet for something like a small dust collector or a shop vac, making it switch-controlled. When the router goes on, so does the dust collector. (This works if your router has the "soft-start" feature, or if both router and dust collector are relatively low-amperage. But two high-amperage motors—say, a 15-amp router and a 12-amp dust collector—kicking on at the same instant can overload a 20-amp circuit, tripping the breaker.)

To start, get some electrical supplies. You'll need a couple of receptacle boxes, a duplex receptacle, a single-pole switch, a few feet of type NM cable (12/2 with ground), a few wire nuts, a receptacle plate, a switch plate, a length of type SJT appliance cable (again, 12/2 with ground), and a ground plug rated at 20 amps.

Begin by attaching the receptacle boxes to the router table. Place the "outlet" box close to the router, and the "switch" box where you can find it without fumbling, without looking. Run the type NM cable from one box to the other. Install the plug on one end of the appliance cable, and insert the other end into the switch box. Wire the switch following the wiring diagram, and install the

A switched outlet strip can be screwed to the underside of the tabletop or to a leg. Such strips often have two or three outlets controlled by a switch, plus one or two that are always hot. Plug the router and dust collector into the switched outlets, and plug a worklight into the unswitched outlet.

switch plate. Likewise, wire the receptacle and install the receptacle plate.

Plug everything in, and you're ready to go.

Some will quibble about that single-pole switch. The reason we use that switch is because it's available everywhere and costs only a buck or two. But it isn't without its drawbacks. If you brush against it—without meaning to—the power comes on.

Safer switches intended for router tables are available through some woodworking-tool retailers, but they are far more costly. I've used a two-button switch intended for a stationary power tool. Check the manufacturer's online parts list for a jointer or band saw or drill press, get the number for the switch, and order it as a replacement part. Depending upon the brand, the cost may be reasonable.

In the woodshop, the two-button on-off switch is the benchmark. The "on" button is slightly recessed and surrounded by a raised rim, so bumping it with a hip or brushing it won't turn on the power unexpectedly. You have to poke the "on" button deliberately. The "off" button, however, is larger and slightly raised. A slap with your palm kills the power.

Router Table Wiring

Both halves of receptacle are switch-controlled

White (neutral) conductors (Never break neutral side of circuit with switch.)

12/2 cable

Black (hot) conductors

Receptacle boxes; metal or plastic okay

Ground metal box with green grounding screw.

20-amp single-pole switch

Connect hot (black) conductor to brass-colored terminals.

Ground (bare) conductor from receptacle's (green) grounding screw.

Ground (bare) conductors

Incoming power

20-amp receptacle

Connect neutral (white) conductor to silver-colored terminals.

One outlet switch-controlled, one outlet always hot

Incoming power

Red (hot) conductor carries current to outlet that's always hot.

White (neutral) conductor always is connected to silver-colored terminals. Leave tab intact and one conductor will serve both outlets.

Black (hot) conductor to brass terminal.

20-amp single-pole switch

Break off tab to separate the outlets.

Black (hot) conductor carries current to switch-controlled outlet.

12/3 with ground type NM cable

This outlet controlled by switch.

Red (hot) conductor to brass terminal

This outlet is always hot, even when switch is off!

Crimp ring (used only on ground conductors)

20-amp receptacle

good dust collection—is possible, as you'll see on page 75.

Most vexing to me is that the typical stand provides no storage. You've always got a few items to keep handy—wrenches, extra collet, featherboards, pusher, bits, starting pin, setup gauge or small square. Without a drawer or bin for these things in the stand, they tend to get scattered around the shop.

Cabinet: All the shortcomings of the stand are addressed in a cabinet-style router table. Yes, it usually takes longer to build and involves more expense. And unless you mount it on casters, it's more difficult to move.

But with the router in a compartment, the majority of the chip-storm is contained, making dust collection relatively easy. If the compartment has a door, the router's noise is significantly reduced.

The router table will have more mass, be less top-heavy, and probably be less prone to slide away from you as you work.

Best of all, you'll have a place to stow all your router table gear and accessories.

Mounting the tabletop: The biggest structural issue is whether the stand or cabinet will stiffen the tabletop and help keep it flat. If it will, the tabletop often can be thinner, even if you are using a heavy router or a lift.

In general, a rigid cabinet does a better job of supporting the tabletop than an open stand. Often, you'll have attachment points close to the router mounting, as well as near the perimeter of the top.

Generally, a stand is less likely to contribute to the overall strength and rigidity of the tabletop. If the stand design lacks a rigid frame at the top, you ought to incorporate one into the tabletop.

Mounting a router in the extension wing (or outfeed table) of a table saw is a favorite space-saver. You gain a router table without sacrificing precious shop space. Though good in concept, it can be sunk by an ill-conceived setup.

I think you must position the router at the end of the wing, so you can access it from three sides. That way, you can follow the work. No awkward stretches. Obviously, you have to keep the end of the extension clear so you can move around and maneuver a workpiece. Most frequently, you'll approach the router from what is the saw's right rear corner.

This position also makes the router accessible for adjustments and bit changes.

Because it's there on the saw, the rip fence often doubles as the router-table fence. You can slide it into position quickly and set it. No

clamps to fiddle with. And it won't shift out of position, either.

The disadvantage crops up when you are switching back and forth between the router table and the table saw. When I had an extension-wing

setup, I regularly discovered a need to rip one more piece just after having tweaked the fence setup for the router operation. One solution here is to get organized. Another is to make and use a separate router-table fence.

Need to conserve space in a small shop? Hang a router from your table saw's extension wing. This homemade table extends the saw's capacity to accommodate full-sized sheet goods, and it doubles as a router table. The saw's rip fence doubles as a router table fence. Substantial hardwood blocks serve as facings, protecting the fence itself from the bit.

Extension-Wing Router Table Savvy

Router table feed direction

Table saw feed direction

When using the table saw's rip fence to guide a router cut, the feed direction is exactly opposite that for a saw cut. So the optimal post for a router woodworker is facing the right end of the saw.

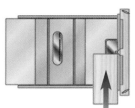

With the split fence positioned outboard of the bit, the feed direction mimics that of a saw cut. Stand in front of the saw and push the work, just as in making a saw cut.

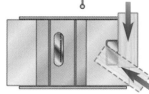

When using a bit's pilot to guide a cut, your working post is more flexible. The feed direction "rotates" clockwise around the bit.

A long straightedge can be clamped across the saw table to guide a cut in an especially long or wide workpiece. This approach provides the best support for the workpiece. Position the fence "behind" the bit, and feed from the saw's right to its left.

Dust Collection

Routers make dirt. Most cuts create handfuls of chips and lungfuls of fine dust, and the cutting action disperses the mess everywhere. When you mount the router in a table, you don't diminish the dust, but you do change the distribution of it. It becomes considerably easier to capture at the point of origin.

While it's common to use a fence with a port for a shop-vac hose, that's only partly effective. On edge-forming cuts, a lot of chips and dust can be captured with the fence-mounted pickup. But the fact is, when you work on a router table, most of the dirt goes straight to the floor (or into the router compartment).

This is inexorable, a function of bit design. Bits are designed first to cut, then to excavate the waste from the cut. This means that, when chucked in a table-mounted router, the bit pulls the waste out of the cut and blows it down over the router. A pickup mounted on the table surface isn't going to capture this dirt.

An open-legged design—a router table that's really a table, in other words—doesn't typically provide a means for capturing any of the dirt blown below the table. (When you're done, you capture it with a broom.) In a cabinet-style table, the compartment in which the router hangs *will* capture this dirt. If the compartment is open—no door, or a door that's left open—it will hold the chips until they spill onto the floor. A closed one will hold the chips until they smother the router.

These days, woodworkers are more aware of the impact of dust on their health, and dust collection is much improved. We've advanced from a shop-vac pickup on the fence to two-level collection—from fence

This simple dust-collection setup takes advantage of the containment offered by the frame supporting the tabletop and the fixed base of the router. Semicircular baffles at the ends of the frame eliminate corners in which chips can collect, and the plywood panels close off the frame, transforming it into a channel. A little duct tape seals the gaps around the router base—inelegant, perhaps, but effective.

and router compartment—using 4-inch ducting and a real collector with a high-filtration cartridge. Even those open stands can be fitted with good under-the-table collection—and I don't mean that broom!

The point here is to urge you to incorporate good dust collection into your router table design. The system used in the Cabinet Router Table (page 81) can be a good starting point when you design your own cabinet-style table. Or try a form of the under-the-table pickup shown above on the open-leg stand.

Engineering the Tabletop

Having worked through the router-mounting options, the fence options, and the structural options, go back to the tabletop. Engineering the top goes beyond appearances and delves into the practicalities of producing a flat, durable surface that supports the weight of the router. You must design something you can make, using materials you can both obtain and afford. It doesn't mean reinvention, although if that's your bent, go ahead and be innovative.

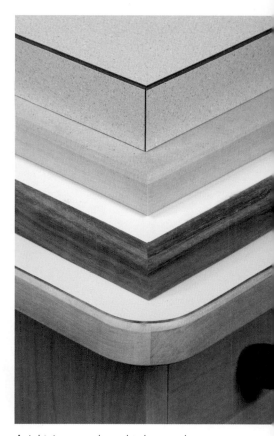

A tabletop can be edged several ways. You can carefully square the top before applying the laminate, then laminate the edges as well as the faces (top). If you've opted to use a penetrating oil finish instead of plastic laminate, you can simply chamfer the top's edges (second from top). You can apply the plastic laminate, then glue on $1/2$- to 1-inch-thick hardwood edge bands (third from top). Or you can edge-band the substrate before applying the laminate (bottom).

Anatomy of a Router Table Top

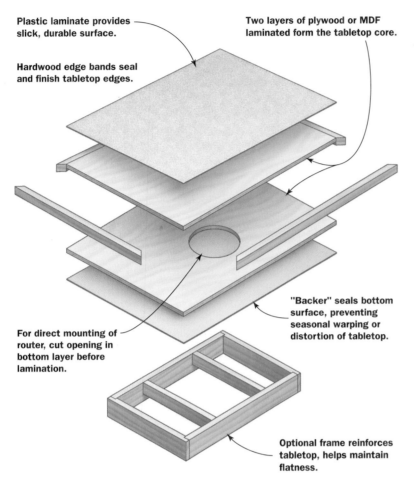

Plastic laminate provides slick, durable surface.

Hardwood edge bands seal and finish tabletop edges.

Two layers of plywood or MDF laminated form the tabletop core.

"Backer" seals bottom surface, preventing seasonal warping or distortion of tabletop.

For direct mounting of router, cut opening in bottom layer before lamination.

Optional frame reinforces tabletop, helps maintain flatness.

There are a couple of proven ways to engineer your top. For years, woodworkers have been gluing two pieces of plywood or MDF face-to-face to bolster the thickness. The result is usually a top that's 1 1/2 inches thick. Thinner material can be used to produce a thinner top.

Often, the edges of the top are banded with hardwood, either before or after laminate is applied. The corners may be rounded off. Commercial tops usually have a rubbery T-molding banding the edges.

Depending upon the way the top is mounted, a support frame may be beneficial. If your top is fixed to a rigid cabinet with a flat top, the frame isn't necessary, even if the tabletop is only an inch thick. But if it's mounted to a stand, or especially if it is to be hinged, make and attach a frame to the underside.

Materials

Consider the criteria for a good router table top. It must be flat, strong, and stable, must both withstand and dampen vibration, and must have a hard, tough, slick surface. It must also be made of fairly commonplace materials that can be worked in the typical home woodworking shop.

Particleboard is probably okay as a core for your tabletop. Particleboard is a sheet product composed primarily of sawdust and glue. It has no grain structure, so it lacks

The tabletop core is usually a stable material such as MDF, particleboard, or birch plywood. These substrates are almost always edge-banded with hardwood, then clad with plastic laminate. Melamine-coated particleboard, known simply as melamine, is a reasonable alternative for a table that's not heavily used.

plywood's strength. It's made in a variety of grades for a variety of purposes, and it surely is the most common substrate for laminate-covered kitchen counters. Thus, the sink cutouts I mentioned are likely to be particleboard.

Melamine is an attractive form of particleboard for router table tops because it already has a slick coating. While I'm not completely sold on the coating's durability for a heavily used table, I think it would be a reasonable choice for a hobbyist's occasional-use router table. Bear in mind that laminating two pieces face-to-face to increase the thickness is problematic because of the melamine coating.

Plywood is a good substrate. Not construction plywood, of course, but good hardwood plywood. Because its individual veneers have grain direction and strength, and because these veneers crisscross in layers, plywood has great strength that the other sheet goods don't. The big shortcoming of plywood is that it isn't always perfectly flat. You can compensate for this, however, if you glue up a substrate from two pieces of the plywood. You will probably do this, since in most instances you'll want a tabletop at least 1 inch thick.

MDF (medium-density fiberboard) is a excellent core material, and in fact, it's the most commonplace constituent of commercial tabletops. Made up of very fine particles, it is very dense, stable, and dead-flat. That last characteristic is what makes it so good for router table tops: flatness.

The drawbacks are several. It is *heavy*. A standard-sized sheet (which measures 49 inches by 97 inches, by the way) of 3/4-inch MDF weighs about 100 pounds. The sawdust isn't dust, it is extraordinarily fine *powder*. Finally, though it is manufactured in a wide range of thicknesses and grades, it isn't as readily available as plywood. The "big box" home centers in my locale stock a low-grade 3/4-inch sheet, and occasionally 1/2-inch sheets. (Read some shopping tips in the "Jigmaking" chapter, page 43.)

Assembling and clamping the multi-ply substrate on a surface you *know* is flat is the key to making a flat tabletop. I do the job on my table saw, covering the cast iron with kraft paper to protect it from glue. Spread ordinary yellow glue on one ply with a printmaker's brayer (top), then place the second ply on top. Work the top piece on the bottom one to improve the tack, then apply clamps. Lay cauls across the top, clamping the ends to the saw table (bottom).

Tabletop Surface

Because it is slick, wears well, and is easily machinable, plastic laminate is a great material to use in making a router table and accessories, and in making router jigs and custom baseplates. It is readily available and is easy to bond to wood. (Some of it is even supposed to *look* like wood, though we all know it doesn't even come close.)

Installing a Mounting Plate

Cutting a rabbeted opening for a mounting plate in a router table top is a bit of a challenge. The possibility that you'll screw up your pristine top is daunting for even experienced woodworkers. And knowing that a perfect fit is essential adds to the mental burden.

One of the best ways to do it uses the plate itself as the pattern. Guided by the plate, you rout an internal template. Then you use the template to guide the routing of the opening. It's the same sequence you'd follow to do an inlay. The opening in the template is larger than the plate itself, but by using the correct combination of bit and guide bushing, you offset the cut into the tabletop and produce an opening that exactly matches the plate. See the chapter "Template-Guided Work," page 155, for more information on "offset" and inlay routines.

Use the mounting plate itself to guide the routing of a template. Bond the plate to the template stock, and rout counterclockwise around it. Keep the guide bushing tight against the plate throughout the cut. A scrap the same thickness as the plate, stuck to the router's base with carpet tape, keeps the router from tipping.

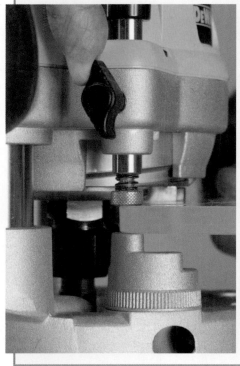

Set the plunge depth using the mounting plate. First stand the router on the template and bottom the bit against the tabletop. Then slip a corner of the plate between the router's depth-stop rod and its stop. With the rod tight against the plate, lock the rod. You are ready to rout a groove of the exact depth you need.

Grooving the tabletop is a less ticklish operation than routing the template. Stand the router on the template, bushing tight against the template edge. (A scrap block stuck to the base stabilizes the router here, too.) Guide the router clockwise through the cut. If the router does drift away from the template edge, it'll just be cutting into the waste.

An advantage of this approach is that you can test the template by cutting a test opening in scrap.

To make the template, bond the mounting plate to the template stock with carpet tape. Outfit a plunge router with a 3/8-inch-O.D. guide bushing and a 1/4-inch straight bit. Keeping the guide bushing tight against the mounting plate, rout around it in the direction indicated in the drawing. Make several passes, plunging a little deeper on each circuit, until the waste is cut free.

The router cut you make in the tabletop guided by the template is a groove. After it is cut, you saw out the waste with a jigsaw, completing the opening and converting the groove into a rabbet.

To make the template-guided cut, position the template on the router table top and clamp it.

Switch to a 5/8-inch straight bit in the collet, and install a 1 1/4-inch-O.D. guide bushing. Porter-Cable makes this guide; it's part number 42021. (You can also use a 3/8-inch straight bit in a 1-inch-O.D. template guide. This combination, obviously, will yield a narrower groove.) Set the plunge depth to match the thickness of the mounting plate and account for the thickness of the template as well.

Rout around the inner perimeter in the direction indicated in the drawing. Make several passes, plunging a little deeper for each circuit, until the maximum depth is achieved. That done, cut the waste out of the tabletop opening. You'll get a clean cut if you drill 3/4-inch-diameter holes at each corner, as shown in the drawing. This way, you can insert the jigsaw's blade into the hole and make a straight cut from one corner to another.

With the waste removed, the mounting plate should fit perfectly, which is to say, just a bit hard. You will be able to set it into the opening, but you'll probably have to smack it with your fist to seat it.

Routing Tabletop Opening
Making and using a guide-bushing template

A. MAKE AN INTERNAL TEMPLATE

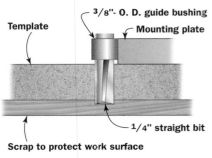

- Template
- 3/8"- O. D. guide bushing
- Mounting plate
- 1/4" straight bit
- Scrap to protect work surface

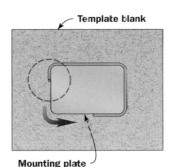

- Template blank
- Mounting plate

B. ROUT THE PLATE SUPPORT RABBET

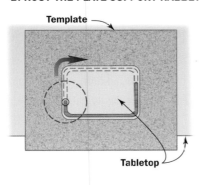

- Template
- Tabletop

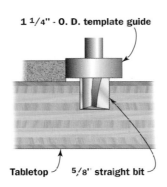

- 1 1/4" - O. D. template guide
- Tabletop
- 5/8" straight bit

C. CUT THE INTERNAL WASTE FREE

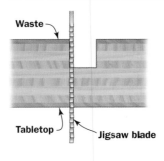

- Waste
- Tabletop
- Jigsaw blade

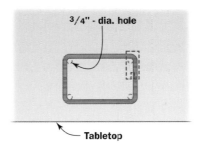

- 3/4" - dia. hole
- Tabletop

The material is made by impregnating several layers of kraft paper with phenolic plastic resin. The color and pattern is in a separate sheet of paper, impregnated with melamine plastic resin, which covers the core. The surface can be embossed with a design or texture. The paper layers and the plastics are bonded together under high heat and pressure. The resulting material is hard and durable—easily cleaned, and scratch- and wear-resistant. For all this, it isn't expensive.

In the router workshop, plastic laminate can be used to cover anything that needs a wear-resistant, slick, easily cleaned surface. Router table tops. Fence facings. You can use it to advantage on the base of a sled or the edges of a straightedge. If a stable, flat surface is needed, the laminate should be applied to both sides of the core to prevent warping. In some instances, it's appropriate to apply laminate to both surfaces, but where one will be hidden from view, money can be saved by using what's called backer to the hidden side. Backer is laminate without the color layer.

Sold in several grades, the most commonly used is the horizontal grade, which is about 1/16 inch thick. Many sheet sizes are available, ranging in width from 30 inches up to 60 inches, and in length from 8 to 12 feet. Most lumberyards sell several different brands, and will have an incredible assortment of 1- by 2-inch samples to choose from. Order the color and finish you want, select the sheet size, and in a few days—most likely—your plastic laminate will be ready for you to pick up, tied up in a 2- to 3-foot-diameter roll.

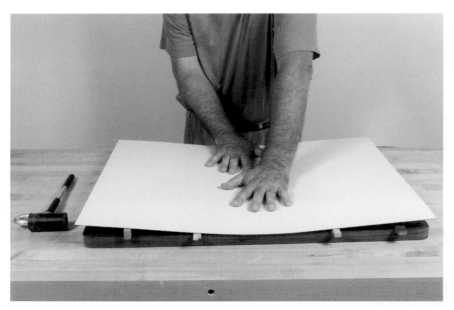

Applying laminate to a tabletop takes about half an hour per side. Brush or roll contact cement on the substrate and the underside of the plastic laminate. Allow it to dry; it usually takes 15 to 20 minutes. Lay four or five scrap strips across the substrate, and place the laminate on top of them. Make sure the laminate is aligned so it overhangs the substrate all around. Press the center section of the laminate against the substrate, as shown, and it will immediately bond. Pull out the strips and rub down the laminate from the center to the edges. Use a J-roller to burnish the laminate to the substrate.

In a nutshell, the procedure for working with laminates is: Cut a piece of plastic laminate to a size just a fraction of an inch larger than the plywood, MDF, or other substrate it is to cover. Bond it to the substrate; contact cement is the most popular glue for this. The laminate is positioned so its edges overhang those of the substrate just a little. With your router or laminate trimmer and a flush-trimming bit, zip around the edges, trimming away the excess laminate, and making it flush with the substrate's edges. Perfect!

There's a little more to working with plastic laminates than that, but the router is the key trimming tool used throughout the process. In addition to trimming the edges to finish a laminate project, you can also use the router to cut the pieces you need from the laminate sheets to start the project.

Despite all I've just said, be assured that you don't *have* to sheath the top in laminate. A tabletop made of melamine, for example, already has a reasonable surface coating. And a Po' Boy–type table may not need any coating other than wax.

Penetrating oil is a great finish for an MDF tabletop. The hitch, to me, is that the application process drags on for days. You want to apply two or three coats, and you have to allow a day or more for each to dry before applying the next. On the other hand, you can assemble a tabletop on a Saturday morning, apply laminate after lunch, and be using the table before supper.

Cabinet Router Table

The Cabinet Router Table has a generously proportioned tabletop, kept flat by a solid frame mounted to its underside. The router's housed in a noise-muffling, dust-capturing compartment flanked by bit drawers and a small odds 'n' ends closet below the two-button switch. Drawers in the lower half of the cabinet store bit sets and router table accessories.

If you are going to build a router table—and why in the woodworking world wouldn't you *build* your router table—here's an excellent model.

It's basically simple, it's sturdy, it's practical, and it's versatile. It'll handle any job you'd want to do on a router table. While the example shown wasn't *cheap,* the cost was reasonable. Construction is not complicated (some of it is unusual), but it isn't something you can complete in just a weekend or two.

As shop furniture goes, it's even pretty attractive.

The tabletop is composed of two layers of 1/2-inch MDF with hardwood edge bands and is covered top and bottom with plastic laminate. This is pretty commonplace. What's unusual is the 2 1/2-inch-high hardwood frame screwed to the underside. The frame stiffens the top and keeps it flat.

The frame is particularly important because the tabletop is hinged to the cabinet so it can be tilted up, providing access to the router for changing bits. And the access is important because the router is mounted directly to the tabletop. The direct mounting eliminates a common speed-bump: the seam between the table and mounting plate.

Tilting the top up offers the additional benefit of raising the router to a height convenient for bit changes (even though the change isn't taking place "above the table") and for setting the initial bit elevation for a cut (see a photo of this on page 68). You don't have to bend or stoop, and you don't have to remove the router. And you save the cost of a router lift.

Absent are slots for a miter gauge (a table saw accessory) and crisscrossing tracks for mounting a fence or plastic featherboards or other widgets. They're dust-catching obstacles that weaken the tabletop, as far as I'm concerned.

But the tabletop does have generous overhangs so you can clamp practical shop-made accessories anywhere around the perimeter.

The cabinet is birch plywood with birch edge bands, drawer fronts, and doors. (I used birch for the tabletop edge bands and support frame, too.) The parts thus are in visual harmony. Birch plywood is readily available, even in home centers; and at least in my locale, birch lumber is less expensive than maple and oak.

The cabinet configuration is conventional. A center compartment housing the router is flanked on the left by narrow drawers for bits and on the right by a compartment with the wiring and electrical boxes for the two-button switch and a duplex

The tabletop is hinged to the cabinet, so you can easily access the router to change bits, adjust the cut depth, change the speed setting, and make other adjustments. A stout steel prop (at right) has several notches that catch on a bolt screwed into the cabinet side, holding the tabletop securely.

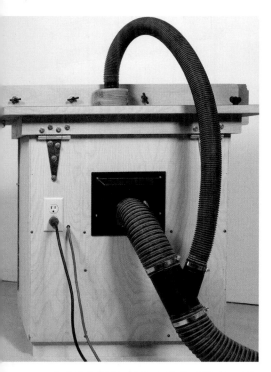

A 4-inch hose from a dust collector connects to a jointer hood screwed to the cabinet back. The collector pulls air through a tiny slot under the router compartment doors, which sweeps across the compartment floor, carrying dust and chips into the hood. A Y-fitting enables the collector to also pull dust from a fence-mounted pickup.

receptacle facing out the back and another facing the router.

Below these compartments is a pair of half-width drawers and below them one deep, full-width drawer. In these drawers I keep boxed sets of bits, featherboards, the plesiosaur, a coping sled, the bit guard–dust pickup, and other router table accessories. These accessories, by the way, are shown in the chapter "Router Table Accessories," which begins on page 101.

Because the tabletop frame drops over the cabinet's top, you have two compartments that are hidden when the top is down but exposed when the top is tilted up. I call them "tills," after the small compartments in six-board chests. In them I keep the extra collet, the collet wrenches, perhaps an abrasive pad for buffing bit shanks, and a short rule or small square for setups. These are tools and accessories I want at hand when I'm changing a bit, then setting it for an initial cut.

The top is hinged to the cabinet with ordinary T-hinges. The prop is made from a stout steel flat.

The cabinet is mounted on a rectangular base. Its height is tailored to place the tabletop surface at the same level as the typical table saw. If

you want to adjust that height without completely resizing the cabinet, just alter the base. If you want mobility, replace the base with casters.

Dust collection is always problematic with a router, even when it's mounted in a table. Where the dust spews varies with the operation.

The router table's system centers around a plenum partitioned off in the router compartment. A dust collector—rather than a shop vac—is connected to the plenum, and its suction draws air from the router compartment through a narrow slot in the dust baffle at the compartment's floor. If you run a dust hose between the fence-mounted pickup and the plenum, the suction will also pull dust captured at the fence into the plenum.

This system depends upon a venturi effect in two places. One is the air intake at the bottom of the router compartment doors. As air is pulled through the narrow gap, it speeds up, sweeping across the compartment floor toward the dust collector port, carrying dust along. The slot at the bottom of the dust baffle is the second venturi. It rushes the dust-laden air through the plenum and into the collector hose.

Construction

Construction of the router table breaks down into three stages. The first is to build the tabletop, the second to build the cabinet, and the third to kit out the cabinet with wiring, drawers, trays, and doors.

Once the tabletop is constructed, you can mount your router and use the tabletop simply by resting it on a pair of sawhorses or shop trestles, or by cantilevering it off the edge of your workbench with a couple of clamps at the back corners.

Build the cabinet next, but leave the back off until after you've completed the wiring, followed by the bit tray construction, making and fitting the drawers, and finally making and mounting the doors.

Construct the Tabletop

Before tackling the tabletop's construction, read (or re-read) pages 75–80, which address tabletop design and construction. *Anatomy of the Tabletop* (page 76) illustrates the tabletop you are building, and photos show a couple of the steps.

1. Glue up the substrate. Cut two pieces of 1/2-inch MDF to size; see the cutting list. Cut a hole for the base of the router you're going to mount through one piece. See the drawing *Tabletop and Frame Layout* for the location of the hole's center. Glue the two pieces of MDF face to face. After the glue dries, trim and square the substrate.

2. Apply the edge-banding. Use hardwood for the bands, cutting four strips to the specified thickness and width, but leave them overlong. One by one, fit the bands to the substrate, mitering the ends. Glue

them in place. Trim the bands flush with the top and bottom surfaces of the substrate. You can leave the corners square, or round them off.

3. Make the support frame. First establish how far apart the frame braces must be to accommodate your router. You want them as close to the router as possible, without having them interfere with the handles.

Cut the frame parts. Rabbet the ends of the front and back for the ends. Rout dadoes for the braces and the crossbrace.

Assemble the frame carefully. Most important is for it to be flat-

edged so that it keeps the tabletop flat. Assemble the frame on a surface you know is flat, and clamp it down to the assembly surface.

4. Mount the frame on the underside of the substrate. Begin by applying plastic laminate to the underside of the tabletop. I used "backer" on the underside, but you can use regular laminate. Trim it flush around the edges and cut it away from the router recess.

Lay out connector-bolt locations on the frame edges, as shown below. With a 3/4-inch Forstner bit, drill a counterbore for a bolt head at each

Connector bolts, used to mount the support frame to the tabletop, are available in a limited number of lengths. Measure the bolts you have and drill counterbores in the frame so the bolt extends about 3/4 inch into the tabletop core.

Tabletop and Frame Layout

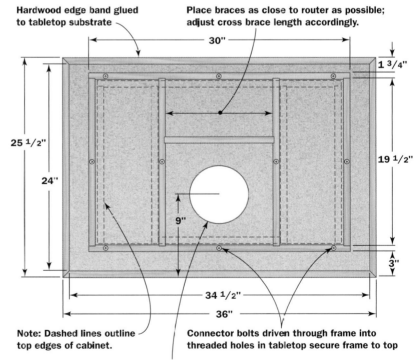

Hardwood edge band glued to tabletop substrate

Place braces as close to router as possible; adjust cross brace length accordingly.

30"

1 3/4"

25 1/2"

24"

19 1/2"

9"

3"

34 1/2"

36"

Note: Dashed lines outline top edges of cabinet.

Connector bolts driven through frame into threaded holes in tabletop secure frame to top

Cut hole to match router base diameter in 1 tabletop ply.

Cutting List: Cabinet Router Table

Part	Number	Thickness	Width	Length	Material
Tabletop					
Top plies	2	1/2"	24"	36"	MDF
Edge banding	2	3/4"	1 1/4"	36"	Birch
Edge banding	2	3/4"	1 1/4"	25 1/2"	Birch
Frame, front/back	2	3/4"	2 1/2"	30"	Birch
Frame ends	2	3/4"	2 1/2"	19 1/2"	Birch
Frame braces	2	3/4"	1 3/4"	19 1/2"	Birch
Cross brace	1	3/4"	1 3/4"	12 1/2"	Birch
Top surface	1		26 1/2"	37"	Plastic laminate
Bottom surface	1		26 1/2"	37"	Backer
Cabinet					
Sides	2	3/4"	19"	30 3/8"	Birch plywood
Middle panels	2	3/4"	18 1/4"	26 3/4"	Birch plywood
Bottom	1	3/4"	17 1/2"	26 3/4"	Birch plywood
Middle divider	1	3/4"	18 1/4"	4 3/4"	Birch plywood
Router compartment sides	2	3/4"	18 1/4"	15 1/8"	Birch plywood
Bit drawer runners	2	1/4"	3 1/2"	17 1/2"	Plywood
Bit drawer runners	4	1/4"	3 3/4"	17 1/2"	Plywood
Till bottoms	2	3/4"	5 3/4"	18 1/4"	Birch plywood
Switch front	1	3/4"	3 1/2"	5 1/2"	Birch
Bottom rail	1	3/4"	1"	26 1/2"	Birch
Dust baffle	1	3/4"	14"	13"	Birch plywood
Splines	2	1/4"	1/2"	12 1/2"	Plywood
Deflectors	2	3/4"	6 7/8"	13"	Birch plywood
Dust box top	1	1/4"	8"	14"	Plywood
Back	1	3/4"	27 1/2"	30 3/8"	Birch plywood
Base front/back	2	3/4"	2 3/4"	26 1/2"	Birch plywood
Base sides	2	3/4"	2 3/4"	17"	Birch plywood
Corner braces	4	1 1/2"	5"	5"	Birch plywood

NOTE: Exposed plywood edges should be banded, either with edge-banding tape or with solid birch strips.

Part	Number	Thickness	Width	Length	Material
Bit Drawers					
Top bit drawer front	1	3/4"	3 3/4"	5 1/2"	Birch
Middle/bottom bit drawer front	2	3/4"	4"	5 1/2"	Birch
Bit drawer bottoms	3	1/4"	5 1/2"	18"	Birch plywood
Bit holders	3	3/4"	5"	18"	Birch plywood
Drawers					
Half-width fronts	2	3/4"	4 1/2"	12 7/8"	Birch
Half-width sides	4	5/8"	4 1/2"	17 3/4"	Poplar
Half-width backs	2	5/8"	4"	12"	Poplar
Half-width bottoms	2	1/4"	12"	17 3/4"	Birch plywood
Full-width front	1	3/4"	8 3/8"	26 1/2"	Birch
Full-width sides	2	5/8"	8 3/8"	17 3/4"	Poplar
Full-width back	1	5/8"	7 7/8"	25 3/4"	Poplar
Full-width bottom	1	1/4"	25 3/4"	17 3/4"	Birch plywood
Doors					
Utility compartment	1	3/4"	8 1/4"	5 1/2"	Birch
Router compartment	2	3/4"	12 1/2"	7"	Birch

Hardware

8 connector bolts, 1/4"-20, 2 3/4"

3 connector bolts, 1/4"-20, 2"

Pan-head sheet-metal screws (back to cabinet) as needed, #8, 1 1/2"

Flathead wood screws (base to cabinet) as needed, #8, 2"

10 pulls, red oval-tapered plastic knobs; Reid Tool # ROA-4

10 round-head machine screws, 1/4"-20, 1 1/4"

10 flat washer, 1/4" I.D.

10 star washer, 1/4" I.D.

3 pr. hinges, 2" × 1 3/16", with screws

Wiring

3 receptacle boxes

1 two-button switch and switch plate

2 duplex receptacles, 15-amp

2 receptacle plates

3' Romex cable, 12-2 with ground

1 power cord, 10'–20', 14/3 type SJ

1 plug

Tilting Tabletop Hardware

2 T-hinges

16 flathead machine screws, 1/4"-20, 1 1/4"

16 flat washers, 1/4" I.D.

16 star washers, 1/4" I.D.

1 flat (prop), 1/16" × 1 1/4" × 36", steel

1 flathead machine screw (prop to support frame), 1/4"-20, 3/4"

1 machine screw (catch bolt for prop on cabinet), 1/4"-20, 1"

Cabinet Router Table
A shop tool with all the frills

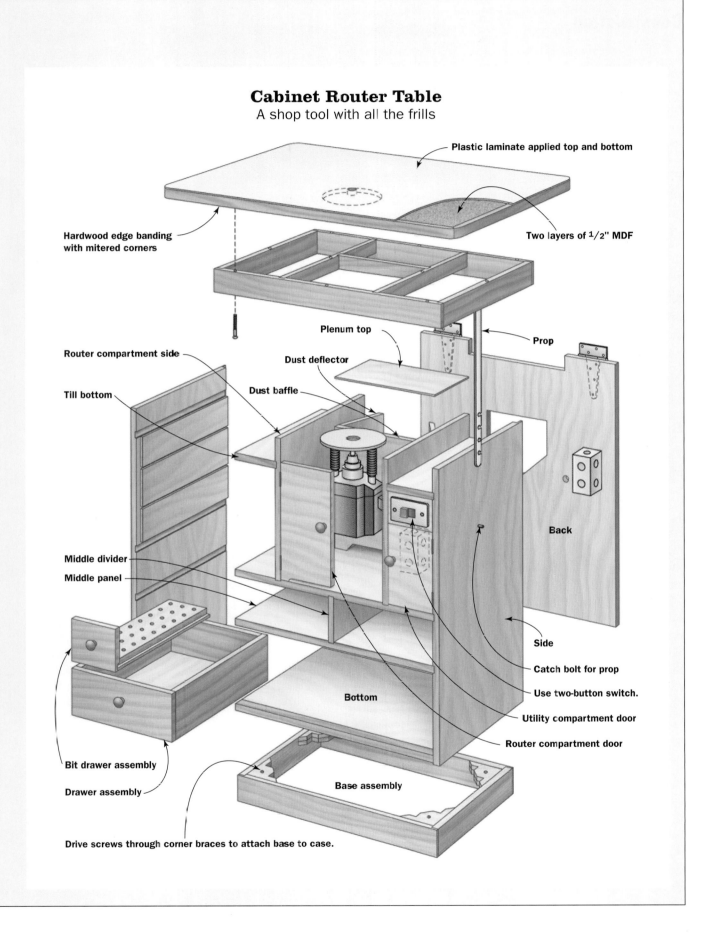

Plastic laminate applied top and bottom

Two layers of 1/2" MDF

Hardwood edge banding with mitered corners

Prop

Plenum top

Router compartment side

Dust deflector

Till bottom

Dust baffle

Back

Middle divider

Middle panel

Side

Catch bolt for prop

Use two-button switch.

Bottom

Utility compartment door

Router compartment door

Bit drawer assembly

Drawer assembly

Base assembly

Drive screws through corner braces to attach base to case.

spot. Then drill 1/4-inch shank holes, centered in the counterbores, through the frame. Transfer the bolt-hole locations to the tabletop. Drill a 13/64-inch hole through the tabletop at each spot. Use a 1/4-20 tap to cut threads in these holes. Bolt the frame to the tabletop with the connector bolts.

5. Apply plastic laminate to the tabletop. The laminate will cover the mounting-bolt holes. Trim it flush around the edges, then bevel trim it.

6. Mount the router (if only temporarily). Set the router (or just the router base) in the recess and decide how you want it oriented. Transfer the mounting bolt hole locations to the tabletop. Drill and countersink the holes.

Build the Cabinet

The cabinet is made of 3/4-inch birch plywood, and it is assembled primarily with 1/8-inch-deep dadoes.

1. Cut parts and the principle joinery. The primary cabinet parts are 3/4-inch plywood. Apply banding to the edges that will be exposed in the assembled cabinet.

Lay out and rout dadoes in the sides, middle panels, and router compartment sides. Cut a rabbet in each side for the back. The back fits into the rabbets, flat against the back edges of the bottom, panels, and divider, and flush with the top and bottom edges of the sides. In the final assembly, it is secured only with screws, not glue.

2. Assemble the basic cabinet. Begin by dry-assembling the sides, bottom, middle panels, middle divider, and back. Apply clamps. Check the cabinet methodically with a square and straightedge to ensure that it's square. If everything is square and fits as

To transfer the hole locations, align the frame on the underside of the core. Insert a 1/4-inch spotter (a.k.a. a transfer punch) into each bolt hole and hit it with a hammer, marking the centerpoint of the hole. Drill and tap each hole.

intended, glue up the basic cabinet. The back is not glued in place, remember. Attach it temporarily with a few screws to help square the assembly. Cut and attach the bottom rail.

3. Make the bit storage compartment. Set the left-hand router compartment side and till bottom into place, and clamp them temporarily.

Install the 1/4-inch plywood

pieces that form the bit-drawer runners. Remove the cabinet back to get access. Use a bit-drawer bottom as a positioning gauge. Lay the gauge between the cabinet side and the compartment side. Apply glue to the two runners and set them on the gauge and against the sides. Apply clamps at front and back. Pull out the gauge, rest it on top of the runners, and position two more run-

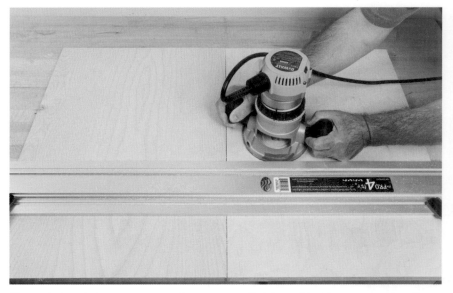

Where dadoes in two parts must align to ensure that the cabinet is square, set up those parts edge-to-edge and cut the dadoes by guiding a router along a straightedge that spans both parts.

ners. Repeat to mount the upper-most runners. Remove the compart-ment side and drive some brads into each runner.

4. Make the utility compartment. Dry-assemble the right-hand com-partment side and till bottom. Locate the receptacle into which you'll plug the router; trace around a receptacle box on the compartment side. Re-mount the cabinet back temporarily. Scribe around the inside of the utility

Elevations

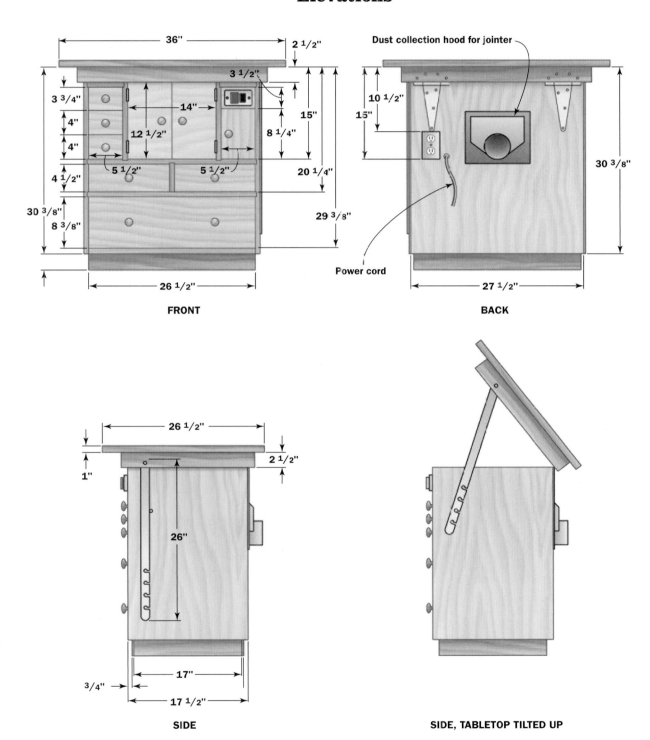

Construction

compartment on the cabinet back to help locate the receptacle-box cutout and the hole for the power cord.

Cut and fit the switch blank. Trace around a receptacle box on it, then cut the opening. Measure and mark the locations of the hinges for the utility door.

5. Cut parts and joinery for the dust plenum. To begin, measure the contour of the dust hood, transfer it to the cabinet back, and saw the opening. Lay out and cut the clearance notch for the tabletop frame. While you have the saw out, lay out and cut the opening for the rear-facing receptacle box. Drill a hole for the power cord.

Remount the back, both compartment sides, and the till bottoms, and

The bit drawers fit in slots created by attaching pieces of 1/4-inch plywood to the cabinet sides. Work with the cabinet back removed and the compartment side merely clamped in place. Tape some shims—to provide sliding clearance—to a drawer bottom and lay it in place. Drop the runners onto it and clamp them to the cabinet sides. Move the bottom up and set the next pair of runners in place.

Installing a Lift

Gotta have a lift in your router table? The sturdy tabletop construction of the Cabinet Router Table is exactly what you need, and the project's design accommodates almost any premium lift easily.

Here's how to modify the project.

First of all, glue up two solid MDF plies to form the tabletop core; you don't need a recess for the base. When it's time to cut the tabletop opening for the lift, follow the directions on pages 78–79.

Next, make sure the braces of the tabletop support frame won't interfere with the lift. But a lift adds to the weight dangling from the tabletop, so the support frame is essential. Keep those braces as close to the lift as possible. If you can position them directly under the rabbet in the tabletop opening, that would be ideal. Incorporating a second cross brace, so you have one on either side of the lift, is advisable.

A lift counters the need for the tilt-top feature, of course. The hinges and prop aren't needed. Screw the top to the cabinet; drive two screws through each support frame end into the cabinet side— that's all you'll need.

check the fit and determine the exact location of the dust baffle. Pull the sides and baffle to rout stopped slots in the compartment sides and the edges of the baffle for the splines used to secure it. Rout the air notch across the bottom of the baffle. Then reassemble these parts.

Determine the dimensions and bevel angles for the angled dust deflectors, and cut them to fit. Cut the plenum top and make sure it fits.

Lay out the locations of the hinges for the doors on the router compartment sides. Disassemble the compartments and plenum. Using the actual hinges, lay out the

mortises in the compartment sides and in the right-hand cabinet side. Cut these mortises.

6. Assemble the upper cabinet, and use glue this time. Don't glue the cabinet back. You'll find it helpful to have access to the cabinet from the back for fitting the drawers and wiring the receptacles and switch.

7. Make the base. Cut the front, back, and ends, and rabbet the ends of the front and the back. Assemble the base frame.

Cut each corner brace blank in half, cut two notches in each on the band saw, and mount them as shown

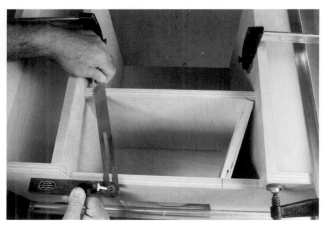

Use a sliding bevel to determine the angle of the dust baffles. Align the blade with the cutout in the cabinet back and swing its tip toward the compartment side. Tilt the table saw blade to that angle to bevel the edges of the deflectors.

on page 85. Glue the braces to the frame, and apply clamps to pull the braces tight into the corners.

Mount the base to the underside of the cabinet by driving screws through each brace into the cabinet bottom.

Make the Bit Drawers

Each bit drawer consists of a hardwood front, a 1/4-inch plywood bottom, and a 3/4-inch plywood (or MDF) bit holder. The bottom and the bit holder are the same length, but the holder is 1/2 inch narrower than the bottom. The holder and the bottom are glued face to face, then glued into a 1-inch-wide by 1/2-inch-deep rabbet in the front.

1. Cut the plywood parts. Stack the bit holders with a backup scrap on the bottom, tape them together with packing or masking tape, then drill 1/2-inch holes through the stack, as shown in the drawing *Bit Drawer Construction*. Then glue the holders to the drawer bottoms.

2. Make the drawer fronts next. Cut a piece of hardwood to 4 1/8 inches by 17 or 18 inches. Rabbet one edge for the holder-and-bottom units. Crosscut the piece into three drawer fronts to fit the cabinet.

3. Fit each drawer to the cabinet. Trim the length of the holder-bottom as necessary, and plane the edges of the front for clearance. Locate and drill a hole in the front for the pull's mounting screw. Then glue the front to the holder-bottom.

Make the Drawers

The three drawers in the cabinet are constructed with hardwood fronts, to match the rest of the cabinet, and sides and backs of a secondary wood.

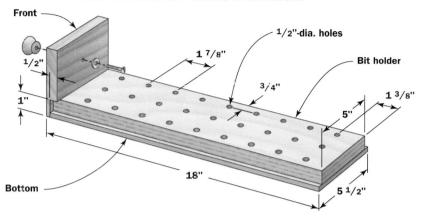

Bit Drawer Construction

Front
1/2"-dia. holes
1/2"
1"
Bottom
1 7/8"
3/4"
Bit holder
1 3/8"
5"
18"
5 1/2"

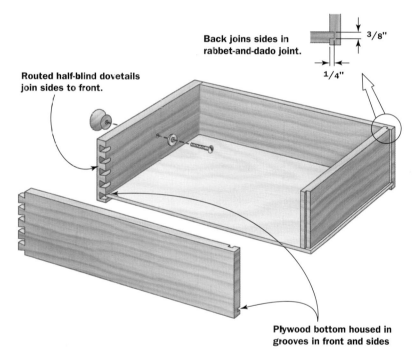

Drawer Construction

Back joins sides in rabbet-and-dado joint.
3/8"
1/4"
Routed half-blind dovetails join sides to front.
Plywood bottom housed in grooves in front and sides

The bottoms are 1/4-inch plywood. Routed half-blind dovetails join the front and sides, and dado-and-rabbets join the sides and back. The bottoms fit beneath the back and are housed in grooves in the fronts and sides.

1. Rip and crosscut all the parts to the dimensions specified on the cutting list.

2. Set up your router and half-blind dovetail jig and rout the joinery for the fronts and sides. (Specific information on this operation is in the chapter "Dovetail Joints," beginning on page 305.)

The height of the half-width drawers will allow you to begin and end each run of dovetails with a half-pin. The dovetails on the full-width drawer will begin with a half-pin, but end with a half-tail. This won't affect the strength of the assembled joints.

3. Cut the rest of the joinery. Groove the front and sides for the drawer bottoms. Dado the sides for the back, then rabbet the back to fit the dado.

4. Assemble the drawers, and install the pulls.

Make the Doors

The cabinet has three doors—a pair enclosing the router compartment, and a single one on what I call the utility compartment. All are hardwood, to match the drawer fronts, and have their grain oriented to match that of the drawer fronts. This is unusual, but to me it looks better than having some elements with horizontal grain and some with vertical grain.

1. Prepare the stock for the doors. If necessary, edge-glue narrow pieces to produce boards of the needed width.

The utility-compartment door is relatively easy to fit, since the opening for it is well-defined top, bottom,

and sides. Rip and crosscut the door to fit.

The top of the router compartment is open, so you measure from the compartment floor to the top of the till bottom. Rip the door blank width to match that measurement. Crosscut a single blank to fit between the compartment sides.

2. Transfer the hinge-mortise locations from the cabinet to the doors. Then lay out and cut the mortises on the door edges. Mount the hinges on the utility door, and mount the door on the cabinet. Install the pull.

3. Complete the router compartment doors. Rout a narrow notch into the bottom edges of the two doors, which haven't yet been cut apart. The cut, which is like the one cut into the dust baffle's bottom edge, begins and ends about 1 inch short of the ends of the blank and is about 1/4 inch wide.

Cut the door blank into two halves, and mount them to the cabinet. Install the pulls.

Mount the Tabletop

The final job is to mount the tabletop. Use large T-hinges. Mount them first to the tabletop support frame, then set the tabletop in place, and bolt them to the cabinet back.

The prop is a steel flat. Cut the steel to length. Drill and countersink a mounting-bolt hole at one end, then round off that end on a grinding wheel. Lay out the four notch locations. Drill a 3/8-inch hole through the steel about 1/2 inch from one edge. With a hacksaw, cut from the edge into the hole. File away burrs.

Lay out, drill, and tap a mounting-bolt hole in the support frame and in the cabinet side. Attach the prop to the frame with a flathead machine screw. Use a hex-head bolt for the prop pin.

The support frame is a fairly tight fit on the cabinet. To provide clearance, sand back the top front edges of the cabinet and router compartment sides, using a belt sander.

Customize This Router Table!

The Cabinet Router Table needs to be customized. It's a *tool*, dagnabbit. If it's going to work hard for you, you have to be comfortable with it.

My *working* version of the CRT is shown at right. It's obviously taller, with an extra pair of half-width drawers and casters instead of a fixed base. For my comfort, I want a table that's higher than the norm. For the conditions in my shop, I need a table that I can move around easily. (Don't be distracted by the lack of router compartment doors; you're looking at a work in progress.)

Fulfilling my needs wasn't difficult. After all, I'd fulfilled my top

priorities—tilting, obstruction-free top, two-level dust collection—in my basic design. So I bought the casters I wanted to use (Lee Valley's 4-inch locking swivelers; see "Sources," page 367), then determined how much using them instead of the base would raise the tabletop. To stretch the cabinet higher, I simply added drawers. I could have extended the height of the router compartment, instead, but I value the extra drawers.

What do you want that this design doesn't provide? Tracks in the tabletop? A lift? A storage compartment with doors instead of those drawers? Change the plan!

Horizontal Router Table

Brought to life as a mortising machine, this router table does a whole lot more than mortising. The router is mounted horizontally, so the bit's axis is parallel to the table surface. It's good for *any* operation that on an ordinary router table would require you to balance the workpiece on edge.

- Mortising is one, yes.

- Cutting tenons, too.

- Cutting the tails for sliding dovetails.

- Grooving the edges of straight, flat boards.

- Raising panels with a vertical bit.

- Cutting wide rabbets.

- Routing architectural molding with tall face-molding bits.

Stable, easy to adjust accurately, and very flexible, it is effectively two tables.

One is a conventional horizontal router table, in which the tabletop is fixed. You feed the work across the table. The router is mounted on the

horizontal and can be adjusted up and down, controlling the point at which it contacts the work.

But the sliding tables go beyond

The horizontal router table—shown here without tables—holds a router horizontally. The router mounting is precise and easily raised and lowered, yet it's simple and relatively inexpensive to build. The router-mounting board is MDF and rides a pair of T-track rails attached to a stout upright support. The support has an oblong port for the router. A threaded rod with a crank on the end winds the mount up and down.

conventional. They are the linchpin of this horizontal router table, mimicking the operation of a multi-axis slot mortiser, an expensive industrial power tool

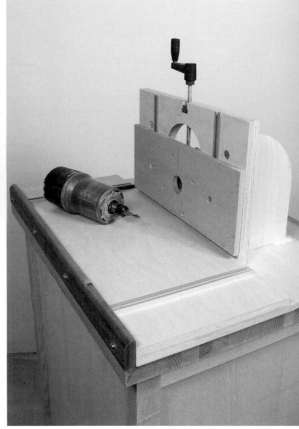

for cutting slots and mortises. One table moves along the axis of the bit (the Y axis). The other moves across the bit axis (the X axis). Used together, the movements allow you to plunge a workpiece onto a bit, then move the piece laterally to form a groove.

The "tables" are double-thick pieces of MDF (medium-density fiberboard). The smaller X table rests on top of the Y table, which in turn rests on the base of the router mount. The only contact either table has with the surface beneath it is on two strips of 3/4-inch-wide extruded aluminum T-track. The narrow, slick tracks minimize friction, allowing the tables to be moved almost effortlessly. To reiterate, the bottom table moves only forward and back (toward the router and away from it). The upper table moves only side to side (or across the axis of the router). You can immobilize either table (or both) by trapping it between stops fastened to the tracks.

I've seen plans for all sorts of sliding tables, using precision-ground rods and linear-motion bearings, drawer-slide hardware, wooden slides, dovetail ways, and more. Each woodworker's goal was an inexpensive, shop-built device to replicate the slot mortiser.

This one really works, in my estimation. It was conceived by Gregory Paolini, a small-shop professional in upstate New York. I adapted his setup after reading his description of it in a woodworking magazine.

Both sliding tables are inexpensive and simple to make. There are no moving parts, other than the tables themselves. You use 3/4-inch MDF and extruded aluminum T-track to make the tables, and you need a few oval nuts (designed to slide in the track), 1/4-inch bolts or machine screws, and a couple of toggle clamps

With the sliding tables in place, the horizontal router table functions like a slot mortiser. The bottom table slides toward the mounting board and back, while the table resting atop it slides side to side, parallel to the mounting board. Stops can limit the travel of either table.

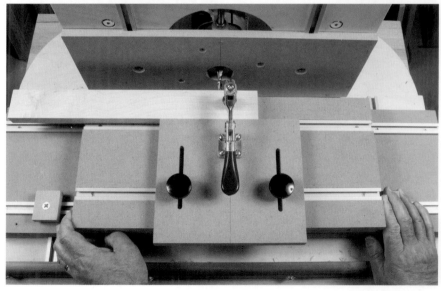

Backstops bolted to the tracks secure your workpieces with toggle clamps. Make cuts by moving the tables, rather than sliding the work across a fixed table. The rail backstop (top) mounts to both tracks, and its big toggle clamp captures a rail for mortising, tenoning, lapping, and dovetailing. Once the table is set up, you can cut piece after like piece without layout. The stile backstop (bottom) mounts to a single track and adjusts in and out to accommodate all sizes of stiles and legs and posts for controlled mortising or slotting. The red lines scribed on the mounting board, X table, and backstop simplify table setup and workpiece alignment.

to outfit the unit with stops and backstops.

The router mount has a progressive adjustment system that allows you to drop the bit below the tables or raise its axis 2 inches above the tables. The adjuster is built around a threaded rod with 16 threads per inch, which translates into a 1/16-inch movement per rotation. The mounting board rides on a pair of T-tracks partially recessed into the vertical support, so it moves vertically, not rocking or twisting. A vertical setting can be secured by locking the mounting board on the tracks with a pair of screws and oval nuts.

The router itself controls the bit projection. You can use most any router, fixed-base or plunge, large or midsized. Bit changes will be easier with a fixed-base router, because you can quickly remove the motor.

Construction

The entire project has three modules: the router mounting, the fixed table, and the sliding tables. The mounting is an essential, but you can make one of the table setups and not the other. The parts and hardware are listed on page 94.

Get all the hardware together before starting on the device (a good general rule to follow in building any project). You won't find all of it at your local hardware store.

T-track is an essential part of the package. It's the basis of the sliding table design but is also used to maintain vertical alignment of the mounting board. Check several woodworking catalogs, and you'll find that it isn't uniform in dimension and profile. I bought T-track (and complementary oval nuts) from Woodhaven (see "Sources" on page 367). It's 3/4 inch wide and 3/8 inch deep, sold in 48-inch lengths, and devoid of

Router Mount

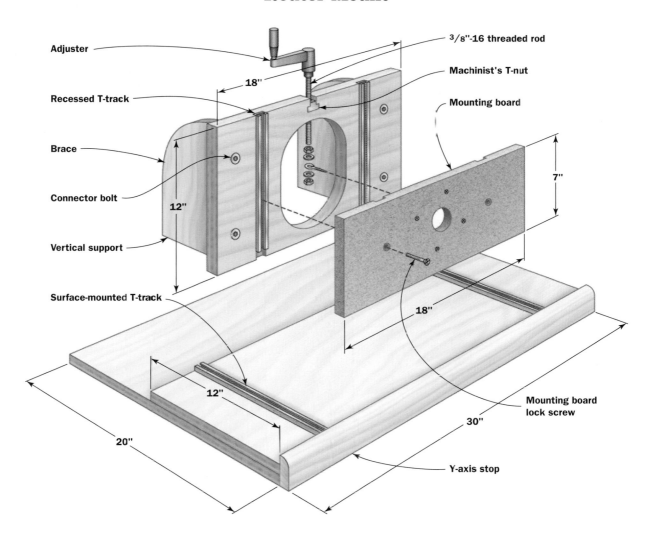

Adjuster

Recessed T-track

Brace

Connector bolt

Vertical support

Surface-mounted T-track

3/8"-16 threaded rod

Machinist's T-nut

Mounting board

18"

12"

7"

18"

12"

30"

20"

Mounting board lock screw

Y-axis stop

Cutting List: Router Mount

Part	Number	Thickness	Width	Length	Material
Base	1	$3/4$"	20"	30"	Baltic Birch plywood
Track base	1	$3/4$"	12"	30"	Baltic Birch plywood
Vertical support plies	2	$1/2$"	12"	18"	Baltic Birch plywood
Brace plies	4	$1/2$"	6"	9"	Baltic Birch plywood
Mounting board	1	$1/2$"	7 $1/4$"	18"	MDF
Y-axis stop	1	$7/8$"	2"	30"	Hardwood

Hardware

T-track	2 pcs.	$3/8$" × $3/4$" × 12" Woodhaven*
Flathead wood screws	as needed to attach tracks to support; $3/4$" #6	
Connector bolt	8 pcs.	$1/4$"-20 × $2 3/4$"
Cross dowels	8 pcs.	$1/4$"-20 bore, 3 $3/4$" long
Machinist's T-Nut	1 pc.	$3/8$"-16 Reid Tool # TN-19
Threaded rod	1 pc.	$3/8$"-16 × 6"+
Stop nuts	2 pcs.	$3/8$"-16
Nylon washers	2 pcs.	$3/8$" I.D.
Eyebolt with nut	1 pc.	$1/4$"-20 × 1"
Crank	1 pc.	Reid Tool # JCL-575
Stop-mounting screws	4 pcs.	$1/4$"-20 × $1 1/2$" machine screws with washers
Mounting board lock screws	2 pcs.	$1/4$"-20 × $5/8$" flathead machine screws with oval nuts†
Router-mounting screws	number and size as required to mount router to mounting board	

*Woodhaven catalog # 4248 is a 48" strip of T-track. Three pieces are sufficient for the mounting and the sliding tables.

†Woodhaven catalog # 5760 is a package of 10 oval nuts. Ten should be sufficient for the project, though extras are always handy.

mounting-screw holes. I didn't want to compromise the various panels by using $1/2$-inch-deep track, which would require deeper dadoes and grooves. A plus for the deeper track is that the heads of commonplace hex bolts fit into it, eliminating the need to use special nuts to secure the stops and backstops.

A critical part of the router height adjustment mechanism is a machinist's T-nut, which I got from Reid Tool Supply (see "Sources" on page 367). In the assembly, it is captured in the vertical support, and the adjustment rod threads through it. The nut is fixed, so the rod rises or descends as you rotate it, in turn raising or lowering the mounting board.

The crank also came from Reid, which has a wide assortment of knobs and cranks that could be substituted.

Build the Router Mount

Regardless of which table configuration you intend to use, the router mount—the base for either table—is the first component to build.

1. Cut to rough size the parts that must be glue-laminated (that is, glued face to face to yield a thick blank). Rough size means about $1/2$ inch wider and longer than the size of the final blank. The parts make up the base, the vertical support, and the braces.

Glue-laminate the parts. When

the glue is dry, set the vertical support aside until you cut the mounting board. Clean the dried glue off one edge of the other three parts, then rip and crosscut the blanks to square them and true all the edges.

2. Cut the mounting board and the vertical support to final size. Cut both to exactly the same width, by cutting both on the table saw at the same setting, one right after the other.

3. Cut the T-track into the various lengths needed (see the cutting list). Remove rough edges with a file or emery cloth.

Dill and countersink mounting holes. Because of the track configuration, you can't use a standard countersink. Instead, use a 1/4-inch twist bit as a countersink. Set the drill-press depth stop to prevent you from inadvertently boring completely through the track.

4. Cut dadoes for the T-track in the support and the mounting board. The goal is to size the dadoes to exactly house the track, and position it exactly the same in both parts, so the plate will slide smoothly and unhesitatingly along the track, but without slop.

Cut these dadoes with a 3/4-inch straight bit, either in a portable router with an edge guide or in a router table with a fence. Make a fairly long test cut and fit the track to the cut to ensure that you have a good fit. That confirmed, cut a 3/16- to 1/4-inch-deep dado parallel to each end of the vertical support. Then lower the bit and cut matching 1/16-inch-deep dadoes parallel to the ends of the mounting board. When assembled with the tracks, you want no more than 1/16 inch clearance between the upright and the plate, with the deeper cut in the upright.

Check your work by setting pieces of the T-track in the support's dadoes, fitting the mounting board on the tracks, and sliding the board back and forth. You want smooth action with no slop. If the dadoes don't line up, if the action is sloppy, you have no recourse but to start over.

5. Complete the vertical support. The first step to that end is to lay out the vertical centerline on the support and the mounting board. Capture the T-track between the two parts and mark the center on the top ends of both at the same time. Then carry the line down the faces of both. Set aside the mounting board and tracks.

Use a router and trammel to cut

Cut the top and bottom arcs for the vertical support's oblong "router port" using a router and trammel. The medium-range trammel shown on page 178 is ideal for this job. Stick the support to a sacrificial panel (to protect your benchtop) and rout. Swinging more than 180° isn't a problem because you are cutting into the waste. Once both arcs penetrate the support, free the waste by cutting the port's straight side with a jigsaw.

the oblong opening for the router in the support. Using two different pivot points on the centerline, rout the top and bottom arches. Then cut the vertical sections with a jigsaw to remove the waste.

Drill holes for the connector bolts and cross-dowels that join the support and the base. To make a drill guide, square up the waste from the router opening and, at the drill press, drill a 1/4-inch-diameter hole into the edge and on through the guide. Clamp the guide to the edge of the support and use a long bit to bore the bolt holes. Lay out the locations of the cross-dowels, and drill them. Finally, use dowel centers in the bolt holes to transfer their locations to the base. Drill holes through the base and counterbore recesses for the bolt

heads in the underside. Make sure everything lines up by bolting the support to the base.

Drill the hole for the adjuster rod next. Center it on the top edge of the support and be sure it is vertical. You can use the same type of guide for this operation as you did to bore the connector-bolt holes.

The best way to bore the connector-bolt holes in the support (and the braces) is with a long bit in a portable drill. Use a shop-made guide block to locate the holes and keep the drill perpendicular to the work's edge. Make the guide from a scrap of the laminated stock, marking across the edge and face and then boring the guide hole on the drill press. Clamp the guide to the workpiece.

Insert the drill bit in the connector-bolt hole and use it to indicate the hole's axis. Measure along that axis and mark the locations for the cross-dowels.

Bore the cross-dowel holes on the drill press. A stop collar on the bit is a sure way to prevent the hole from completely penetrating the part.

Cut a slot for the T-nut. Lay out the bottom of the slot, the width of the shoulders, and the width of the neck. Stand the support on edge, braced by the miter gauge, and saw the neck-width slot on the table saw. Then nibble out the shoulders on the band saw. Make sure the nut fits the slot, of course.

Finally, fasten the T-track to the support.

6. Make the braces. Begin by drilling the holes for connector bolts and cross-dowels in the braces, just as you did in the vertical support.

Now bolt the support to the base temporarily. Use the dowel centers, and transfer the bolt-hole locations to the support. Drill and counterbore holes in the support. In the same manner, temporarily bolt the braces to the support and the support to the base, so you can transfer the bolt-hole locations in the braces to the base. Bore and counterbore the holes in the base.

Finally, round off the outside corners of braces. I used a router and template to refine a band-sawn curve.

7. Complete the mounting board. First, mark centerpoints for the adjuster eyebolt and for the bit axis on the centerline drawn across the board's face. With the baseplate removed, align the router on the line (use a V-groover to spot the router's bit axis on the line) and transfer mounting-screw locations to the mounting board. Drill and countersink the holes.

Drill and tap the hole for the eyebolt.

Lay out, drill, and countersink the holes for the locking screws. When assembled, these screws thread into oval nuts captured in the tracks, keeping the mounting board in place. Loosen them to allow vertical adjustment, then tighten them to hold a particular setting.

Finally, open up the hole for the bit.

8. Assemble the table base. First, bolt the support to the base and the braces to the support and the base. Add the mounting plate. Fit flathead machine screws through the holes in the board and turn oval nuts onto them. Slide

the board from the top down on the tracks, and catch the oval nuts inside the track as you do. Settle it all the way to the bottom.

Check the base-to-support alignment for square. The face of the mounting board must be perpendicular to the base surface. If necessary, insert shims—plain card stock is good—under the braces.

Turn a nut onto the eyebolt, then thread it into its tapped hole. After the adjustment rod is in place, you can jam the nut against the inside face of the board to lock the eyebolt.

Now assemble the adjuster. Slip the T-nut into its slot. Thread the rod through the T-nut and on through the support. And keep on turning. When the end of the rod approaches the mounting board, thread a stop nut onto it. Just before the end enters the eye, fit a nylon washer onto the rod. After it penetrates the eye, add a second nylon washer and a stop nut. Close the stop nuts on either side of the eyebolt to minimize backlash. Thread the crank onto the rod.

Finally, fasten the Y-axis stop to the front edge of the base. This strip prevents the Y table from sliding off the tracks (and likely down off the bench and onto your toes).

Build the Sliding Tables

The sliding tables are very simple to make. The critical operation is cutting the grooves and dadoes for the tracks. The cuts in the Y table must perfectly match those in the X table if the movement is to be smooth and free. Too, the cut widths must match the track width, so there's no slop in the action.

Make a test cut and check how the track fits. You can make the cuts on the router table or with a portable router fitted with an edge guide. Set the distance from bit to either the guide or the fence and make all four cuts (two in each table) at that setting, before altering the setup for other cuts.

Here, step by step, is the sequence for making the sliding tables.

1. Cut individual plies about 1/2 inch longer and wider than the final dimensions, then glue-laminate the two plies forming the X and the Y tables.

2. Trim each table to final size. Make sure it is square.

3. Rout or saw the grooves for the T-track.

■ Cut 3/4-inch-wide by 1/4-inch-deep dadoes into the underside of the Y table, 3 1/2 inches in from each end. These parallel the short dimension, of course.

■ Cut 3/4-inch-wide by 1/8-inch-deep grooves in the top of the Y table and the underside of the X table. These are 1 1/8 inches in from the edge and parallel to the long dimension. The grooves in one table must perfectly align with those in the other.

Sliding Tables

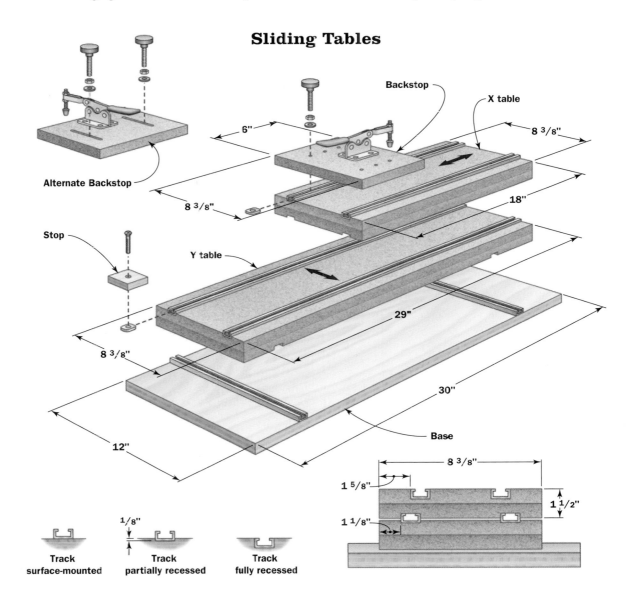

Alternate Backstop

Backstop

X table

Stop

Y table

Base

6"

8 3/8"

8 3/8"

18"

29"

30"

8 3/8"

12"

Track surface-mounted

Track partially recessed

1/8"

Track fully recessed

8 3/8"

1 5/8"

1 1/8"

1 1/2"

Cutting List: Sliding Tables

Part	Number	Thickness	Width	Length	Material
Y-platform plies	2	3/4"	8 3/8"	29"	MDF
X-platform plies	2	3/4"	8 3/8"	18"	MDF
Backstop	1	3/4"	8 3/8"	5"	MDF
Backstop	1	3/4"	8 3/8"	5"	MDF
Stops	2–4	1/2"	1 1/2"	1 1/2"	MDF
Hardware					
Base tracks	2 pcs.	3/8" × 3/4" × 11 5/8"		Woodhaven*	
Y-Platform tracks	2 pcs.	3/8" × 3/4" × 29"		Woodhaven*	
X-Platform tracks	2 pcs.	3/8" × 3/4" × 18"		Woodhaven*	
Studded knobs	4 pcs.	1/4"-20 × 1 1/4"		Reid Tool # DK-20	
Hex nuts	4 pcs.	1/4"-20 [use as spacer on stud]			
Flat washers	4 pcs.	1/4" I.D. [use as spacer on stud]			
Oval nuts	8 pcs.	1/4"-20		Woodhaven†	
DeStaCo clamps	2 pcs.			Reid Tool # TC-225-U	
Clamp-mounting screws	8 pcs.	1/4"-20 × 3/4"		Roundhead machine screws	

*Woodhaven catalog # 4248 is a 48" strip of T-track. Three pieces are sufficient for the mounting and the sliding tables.

†Woodhaven catalog # 5760 is a package of 10 oval nuts. Ten should be sufficient for the project, though extras are always handy.

■ Cut 3/4-inch-wide by 3/8-inch-deep grooves in the top of the X table, 1 9/16 inches in from the edges and parallel to the long dimension.

4. Attach the T-track strips. The long track pieces set into the grooves on the top surface of each table. Fasten them to the table with flathead screws; be sure to set the heads flush so they won't interfere with the oval nuts securing the stops and the workrests.

Lay the two short T-track strips on the base, and put the Y table on top of them. Shift the table and tracks to align it equidistant from the ends of the base, and square against the mounting board. Drive screws through the exposed ends of the tracks into the base. Slide the table away from the mounting board to expose the other ends of the tracks and screw them to the base. The table should slide in and out on the tracks smoothly and without hesitation or binding. Remove the table and drive an additional screw or two through each track.

5. Make the backstops. One, used for working rails, has mounting-bolt holes spaced to line up with the X-table tracks. Use bolts or studded knobs with oval nuts to secure this backstop to the X-table tracks. The second, which you use for mortising stiles, has slots for the mounting bolts, so it can be adjusted in and out in relation to the mounting board. This backstop attaches to one of the two X-table tracks.

The backstops are single pieces of 3/4-inch MDF. Cut each to size, being sure it is square. Lay out and bore the mounting-bolt holes (or rout the slots). Fasten a toggle clamp to each.

Build the Fixed Table

The fixed table is almost crude in its construction, but the work goes quickly, the structure is sound, and the table works fine. I didn't use glue in the assembly, only biscuits for alignment and screws to hold things together.

Odds and ends were the principal components of the fixed table shown in the photos. I used a piece of melamine for the tabletop, and an assortment of plywoods for the other parts. MDF is completely satisfactory,

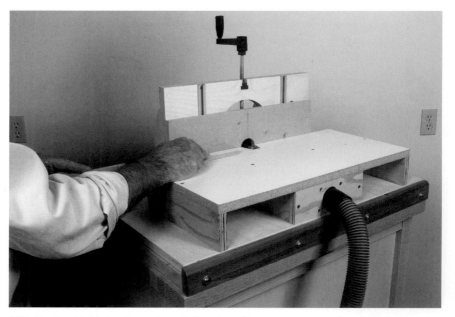

With the fixed table in place, the unit functions like more commonplace horizontal router tables. You feed the work across the bit, from left to right. With the bit lowered partially into the table, you can rout moldings, cut rabbets, raise panels. The dust box incorporated into the table is very effective, even with a mere shop vac providing the suction.

Horizontal Savvy

With the router's orientation changed from vertical to horizontal, you must change your setup and feed orientation.

Your terminology should change, first of all. The adjustment you make on the router itself is for bit extension. It governs how far out from the mounting board the bit extends. Bit height, when we're talking about the horizontal router table, refers to the height of the bit in relation to the plane of the tabletop.

In addition, feed direction is turned around. You feed from left to right. But let's not get ahead of ourselves. Do the adjustments first.

Bit-extension adjustment. Easy to do. The router is hanging out in the open, readily visible and accessible. No stooping is necessary to see what you're doing. Hold a rule next to the bit and adjust the router.

Bit-height adjustment. The mounting board's adjustment system is straightforward. Turn the crank counterclockwise and the mounting board rises, elevating the bit. Turn it clockwise and it descends, lowering the bit. One full revolution moves the bit 1/16 inch. A half-turn moves it 1/32 inch; a quarter-turn, 1/64 inch.

In practice, the most productive routine is to set a coarse position with reference blocks or a setup gauge. The blocks come into play for slots and mortises, where the bit is completely above the table. Lay the block (or combination of blocks) of the precise thickness on the tabletop and lower the bit against it. Make a test cut and use the adjuster's thread pitch to fine-tune the bit elevation.

For operations like tenoning or raising panels, the bit is largely housed in the table. Here you use a setup gauge like the one on page 121. Again, make a test cut and adjust the bit elevation.

For mortising and slotting, use setup blocks to set the initial bit elevation. Setup blocks are small spacers of precise dimensions that you place between the table and the bit. Raise the mounting and bit, place the block or combination of blocks representing the shoulder width, then lower the bit until its cutting edges just kiss the block. Use a test cut to serve as the basis for fine adjustments.

Use a setup gauge (or a similar device) to establish the initial bit elevation for a rabbet-like cut. Establish how deep the cut is to be, set that on the gauge, and position the gauge over the bit, as shown. Using the router mount's vertical adjuster, move the bit as necessary until its cutting edge just grazes the gauge's slide.

Feed direction is from left to right, the opposite of the feed on a regular router table. This is because you're using what would be, on a regular router table, the back of the bit.

It's easy to figure out. Look at the bit as it extends into the tabletop bit opening. Look at the cutting edge. Does it remind you of the cutters on a jointer, the way they are pitched into the cut? It does to me. I look at that router bit and I just can see it's going to spin toward the left. Counterclockwise.

And because you always feed against the cutter rotation, I know I'm going to feed the stock from left to right.

Here's the Essential Horizontal Savvy

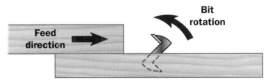

Feed against rotation of the bit.

Construction

if that's what you have. If you don't have offcuts and scraps large enough, buy a quarter-sheet of melamine. You can make all the parts from it, and have some left over.

Here's a step by step:

1. Cut the parts to the dimensions specified by the cutting list.

2. Rout dadoes across the bottom for the Y-axis tracks. The table isn't intended to move, of course. It is trapped between the Y-axis stop and the mounting board, and the dadoes fit over the tracks and keep the table from shifting side to side. (The table I made is a snug fit and I never fasten or clamp it to the base; switching from fixed to sliding tables is quick.)

3. Assemble the bottom and risers. First, lay out the locations of the risers on both the bottom and the tabletop. Cut biscuit slots in the risers, bottom, and tabletop. Stand the risers on the bench, with biscuits in the exposed slots. Set the bottom in place, then drive a couple of screws through the bottom into each riser.

4. Make the dust-collection box next. Bore a hole matching the size of your shop-vac hose in the box front. Then attach the front to the risers with screws. Cut a U-shaped notch for the bit in the box back, then screw it to the risers. Finally, bevel the ends of the baffles and attach them inside the box. A couple of screws through the front and the back into the baffle ends will hold them.

5. Install the top last. Fit biscuits in the slots in the risers, then fit the top in place. One screw through the top into each riser holds the top. The bit notch can be cut with a jigsaw before assembly, or with a large bit afterwards. I would scale the notch to the bit you'll use immediately, then enlarge it as projects dictate.

Cutting List: Fixed Table

Part	Number	Thickness	Width	Length	Material
Bottom	1	3/4"	11 1/2"	29"	Melamine or similar
Outside risers	2	3/4"	3"	11 1/2"	Melamine or similar
Dust box risers	3	3/4"	3"	10 3/4"	Melamine or similar
Dust box front	1	3/4"	3"	8 1/2"	Melamine or similar
Dust box back	1	3/4"	3"	7"	Melamine or similar
Baffles	2	3/4"	3"	12"	Melamine or similar
Tabletop	1	3/4"	11 1/2"	24"	Melamine or similar
Hardware					
Biscuits	#20		as required		
Drywall screws	2"		as required		

Fixed Table

Tabletop — 24" — 11 1/2"

Baffle
Dust box back
Dust box riser

3"

Outside riser
Bottom

Dust box front

11 1/2" — 2 1/2" — 29" — 8 1/2"

Router Table
Accessories

Your router table is only as versatile as the collection of accessories you have for it. In this chapter, you'll find a basic selection, to which you can add a dozen more by simply paging through the rest of the book. Most of the accessories here are scaled to the cabinet table, which is the most used of the several in my shop.

Altering the dimensions to suit *your* router table should be easy.

The basic list of accessories isn't long: a bit guard, a fence, feather-boards, a pusher.

Starting Pin

With a handheld router, a piloted bit is used without a guide or fence. Some woodworkers do the same on a router table. This is usually okay.

But once in a while, at the start of a cut, the cutter will catch the wood and rip it out of your grasp. For the pilot to control things, it has to contact the wood. But because the cutter usually is larger than the pilot, it engages the wood first. If the circumstances are just a wee bit wrong, the cutter can flick the workpiece

aside before it touches the pilot. The workpiece gets a gouge, you get a surprise, and usually, that's the end of it. But you can be injured if you're startled enough that your fingers get into the bit.

A starting pin is the best way to avoid this. It's a fixed shaft or edge, $1^{1}/2$ to 4 inches from the bit, against which you brace the work as you "lever" it into the bit. It controls things until the stock gets to the pilot.

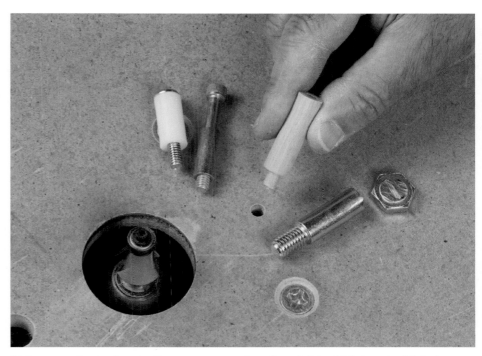

Make yourself a starting pin. Here are some options (from left to right). Insert a $1/4$-inch machine screw or cap screw through a nylon or bronze bushing; the screw turns into a hole in the tabletop, and the bushing is the reference surface for the work. Or make a one-piece pin by turning a tenon on a piece of dowel. Or buy a shoulder bolt and cut off the hex head with a hacksaw.

A commercial mounting plate will come with a starting pin. A shop-made plate needs a shop-made pin. You have several options:

■ Rout a 3/8- to 1/2-inch tenon on a length of dowel, then cut the dowel so you have a pin about 1 to 1 1/2 inches long. Drill a hole for the tenon in the plate or in the tabletop.

■ Cut the head off a shoulder bolt. Make the cut with a hacksaw, then file any raw edges smooth. This bolt, commonly used to mount wheels on lawn mowers, has a solid shank of one diameter, and a short threaded stem of a smaller diameter. Drill and tap a hole in your shop-made plate (or in your tabletop) to accommodate the bolt's thread.

■ Use a round-head machine screw and bushing as a pin. A well-stocked hardware store will have an assortment of short tube-like sleeves or bushings

made of steel, bronze, and plastic. Choose one of a suitable length— maybe 1 inch—and a 1/4-inch inside diameter. Insert a screw through the bushing and turn it into that tapped hole in your plate or tabletop.

Bit Guards

You should guard your hands from the bit when working at the router table. Perhaps this goes without saying.

The typical guard is a small, clear shield of acrylic or polycarbonate suspended just above the bit. The shield deflects chips arcing up off the bit and serves as a physical deflector for your fingers, while nonetheless allowing the workpiece access to the bit. Tips on working with acrylic and polycarbonate can be found in the chapter "Jigmaking," page 43.

Three-in-One Guard

More than a bit guard, this accessory is a starting pin–dust pickup–bit guard. You use it when the fence is not being used—when raising a curved-edge panel, for example. It's designed to be placed almost anywhere on the top of the table. When routing with a piloted bit and no fence, you locate the pickup where it can collect the stream of chips coming off the bit. What's more, this dust pickup has a rounded front edge on the right that, like a starting pin, supports the work as you begin the cut.

To use it, position the guard and pickup at the bit and clamp the base at the tabletop edge. Use two clamps to keep the unit from shifting as you address the starting "nose" with the workpiece. Plug in the hose from your shop vac.

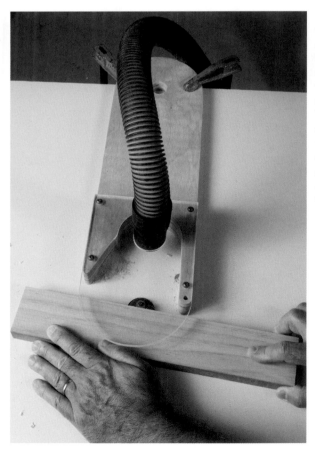

For pilot-controlled cuts, this guard–dust pickup accessory is invaluable. Position it at the bit, and clamp it at the edge of the table. The leading edge serves as a starting pin. The clear top cantilevers over the bit to keep your hands out of danger without obscuring the action, and the contour of the inside corrals the majority of the chips and dust.

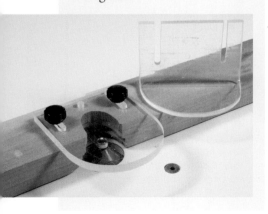

Safety First!

Don't neglect safety when making any fence for your router table. Include a bit guard. You can screw a clear plastic visor to a flat fence. A high fence may need an L-shaped guard. Don't let an odd configuration deter you—include a bit guard.

Bit Guard–Dust Pickup

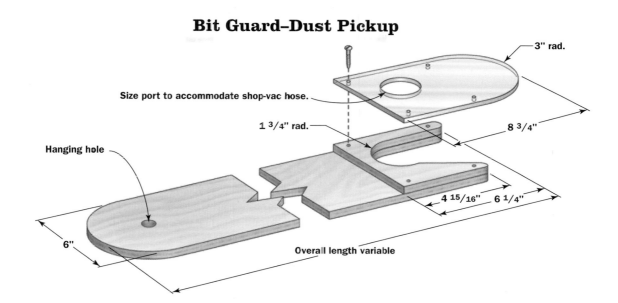

Size port to accommodate shop-vac hose.

Hanging hole

3" rad.

1 3/4" rad.

8 3/4"

4 15/16"

6 1/4"

6"

Overall length variable

Cutting List

Piece	Number	Thickness	Width	Length	Material
Base	1	3/4"	6"	34"	Plywood
Riser	1	3/4"	6"	6 1/4"	Plywood
Guard	1	1/4"	6"	8 3/4"	Clear acrylic
Hardware					
4 screws, 1" × #6					

1. Cut the base and the riser. The base length should be scaled to your router table. Glue them together, face to face.

2. Lay out the contour of the pickup. Begin shaping it by boring a 3 1/2-inch-diameter hole, using either a hole saw or a router and trammel. Saw into the hole to form the pickup. Round the noses and smooth the inside of the contour with a sanding drum.

3. With a router and trammel, round off the end of the base.

4. Make the guard from acrylic or polycarbonate. Cut the blank to size, then bond it to a scrap of plywood with carpet tape. Lay out the arc, drill a pivot in the plywood, then rout the arc through both the materials.

5. Measure the diameter of your shop-vac hose, and drill a hole that size in the guard.

6. Fasten the guard to the pickup with four screws.

Fence

A router table without a fence is like a table saw without a fence. You can do some work, but not a whole lot. Just as the router table is shop-built, so too is the fence. I've got three fences here, each a little more sophisticated than the last. Besides these three, there are a few others scattered throughout the book. Like the jointing fence (see the chapter "Edge Joints," page 259), these tend to be designed for one specific operation and nothing more, so they're presented in conjunction with the appropriate operation.

The Basic Fence

The fence you'll use foremost is also the most simple. It's a straight, knot-free, hardwood board.

A lot of router users (primarily me) perceive such fences as disposable. Rather than set a fence board aside, they clamp whatever straight piece is at hand to the tabletop. When the operation is done, the "fence" goes back onto the wood rack or into the scrap bin.

Here's a "keeper" fence of this sort. It's been worked a bit, so it *is* something more than just a "board."

The principal requirement is that the fence be perfectly straight, flat, and square—and so it won't warp, straight-grained. It ought to be just a little longer than your table is wide,

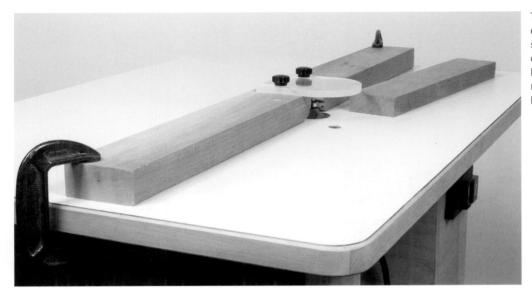

This one-board fence is obviously a keeper. It's notched so it can house the bit, it's chamfered so dust doesn't keep the work from accurately referencing the fence, and it has an adjustable bit guard.

Basic Fence
Just a little more than a straight, true board

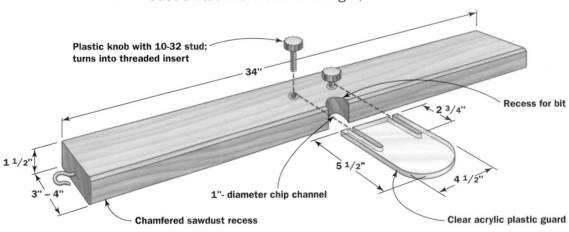

Plastic knob with 10-32 stud; turns into threaded insert

34"

Recess for bit

2 3/4"

1 1/2"

5 1/2"

3" – 4"

1"- diameter chip channel

4 1/2"

Chamfered sawdust recess

Clear acrylic plastic guard

but other than that, the dimensions are up to you. Make it of 5/4 or 8/4 stock, and rip it 3 or 4 inches wide.

The next thing to do is rout a channel across the front edge for the bit. The fence then can fit around most bits. A similar—though shallower—channel across the bottom face allows chips to blow under the fence, rather than collecting around the bit.

Finally, don't forget the guard. Install a couple of threaded inserts in the top face of the fence. Then you can attach a flat, clear plastic

bit guard to the fence with plastic thumbscrews.

General-Purpose Fence

The improvements this fence offers over the Basic Fence are support and dust collection. It's got a tall face (well, at 3 inches high, it's *relatively* tall) attached at right angles to the base. Of course, there's a cutout for the bit, and the configuration allows you to add a dust pickup.

The fence is reversible: You can rest

the 4 1/2-inch-wide base on the table-top and have a 3-inch-high support, or you can get a 4 1/2-inch-high support by resting the 3-inch-wide face on the tabletop. Either way, the fence provides better support for work that has to be presented to the bit on edge or on end, rather than flat on the table. Either way, the dust pickup works.

Like the basic fence, this general-purpose fence is designed to be secured to the router table with separate clamps.

As with any router table fence, this

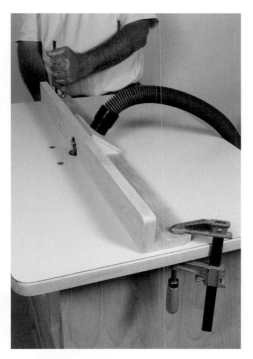

This fence offers more vertical support than a basic one-board fence. Because it is unfettered by built-on clamps, it can be rolled to present either a 3-inch-high face or a 4 1/2-inch-high face to the work. The dust pickup works in either orientation.

Cutting List

Piece	Number	Thickness	Width	Length	Material
Fence base	1	1"	3"	34"	Hardwood
Fence face	1	1"	3"	34"	Hardwood
Dust pickup sides	2	1/2"	3"	34"	Hardwood
Dust pickup cap	1	1/2"	3"	34"	Plywood
Bit guard	1	1/4"	6"	7"	Clear acrylic

Hardware

4 threaded inserts, 8-32

2 studded knobs, 8-32 × 1/2"

one can—and should—be equipped with a guard. Bend a scrap of acrylic into an L-shape—to match the fence—and secure it to the fence with studded knobs turned into threaded inserts.

1. Joint and plane stock for the fence base and face to the dimensions specified in the cutting list. The exact width and thickness of these pieces is not critical.

2. Cut the fence and fence back to the lengths specified in the cutting list.

3. Bore holes in the base and the face, then cut from an edge to these holes, forming U-shaped cutouts. When the base and face are glued up, these cutouts house the bit.

4. With a belt sander, round off the top corners of the fence, as shown in the drawing.

General-Purpose Fence
More support for your workpieces

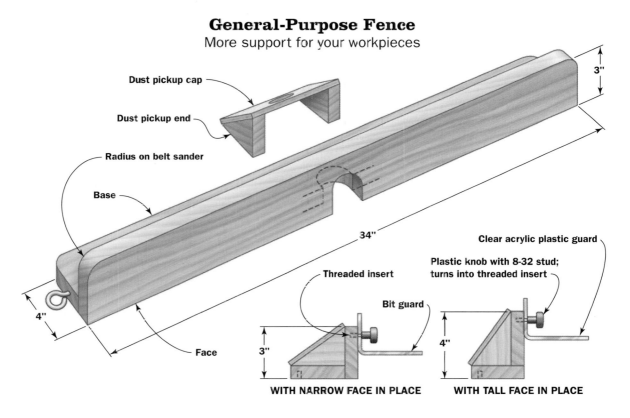

Fence

5. Glue and clamp the two fence parts together.

6. Remove the clamps from the fence, and true the fence on the jointer. Take a light cut from the bottom. Then, holding the bottom firmly to the jointer fence, take however many cuts are required to make the fence face absolutely square to the fence base.

7. Cut and glue the triangular dust pickup ends to the back of the fence, flanking the bit cutout. Bore a hole matching the diameter of your shop-vac hose in the pickup top. Attach the top to the pickup ends with glue and brads.

Clamps are the most straightforward way to secure a fence to the router table. I like the ease of application of Vise-Grip C-clamps. Once set to the thickness of material being clamped, these plier-like clamps lock in place with the squeeze of one hand. You can hold the fence with one hand and snap the clamp in place with the other.

Try This!

You can't build a router table and a lot of accessories for it without also making a set of stop blocks. Sure, you can fetch stop blocks out of the scrap bin anytime. But these, as you can see, are custom-tailored to fit over the L-shaped fence. The stop block itself is long enough to reach all the way to the router table top, while the shorter cinch block carries the means for securing the assembly to the fence. To make them, you need some hardwood scraps, a couple of T-nuts or threaded inserts, two carriage bolts with nuts, and two wing nuts. The dimensions are shown in the drawing. Construction is evident. One important tip: Be sure you turn the carriage bolts into the T-nuts *before* you glue the pieces together.

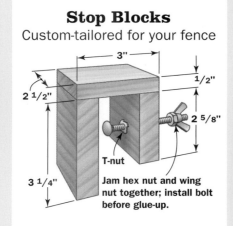

Stop Blocks
Custom-tailored for your fence

3"
2 1/2"
1/2"
2 5/8"
3 1/4"

T-nut

Jam hex nut and wing nut together; install bolt before glue-up.

Deluxe Fence

This fence has three features worth talking about:

- Integral, adjustable clamps

- Adjustable, replaceable split facings

- A good dust pickup

The broad base and the integral clamps work together to provide solid clamping, regardless of the fence orientation. There's plenty of clearance around the large plastic wing nuts that tighten the clamp blocks against the underside of the tabletop, so you won't scrape your knuckles on the facing.

You can remove the fence easily from the table. Just loosen the clamp knobs and slide it off the table. No loose parts to deal with. The clamps and knobs stay connected to the fence, whether it's on the table or off.

The dust pickup is made for a shop-vac-sized hose, which you can run directly to a shop vacuum, or connect to a table-wide dust collector with a short length of hose routed to a Y-fitting.

1. Cut the parts. Select dry, straight-grained, defect-free stock for the base and back. Joint, plane, rip, and cross-cut the stock to size. The blank for the clamps and the dust pickup housing is formed by face-gluing three layers of 3/4- to 7/8-inch hardwood stock.

2. Shape the fence parts. Begin by cutting the notches for the bit as shown in the drawing. The arcs are formed by boring holes with hole saws or Fortsner bits. Then you saw from the edge into the hole. Radius the corners, as shown in the drawing on page 108. Finally, lay out and drill the four mounting holes for the facings in the fence back.

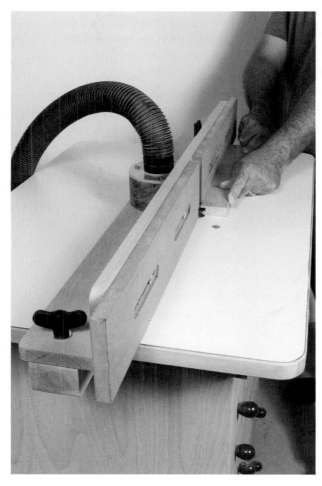

Here's a first-class fence for any router table. Its integral clamps make positioning and repositioning it fast. Its separate faces adjust laterally to create zero-clearance around a bit, and one can be shimmed to offset it for jointing. The dust pickup can be used with a shop vac or tied into a table-wide dust collection system.

The integral clamps are among the best features of the deluxe fence. You can hold your rule in one hand and loosen and tighten the fence with the other. A long carriage bolt fitted with a large plastic wing nut secures the clamping bolt to the fence, while the small screw projecting from the block catches in a stopped hole in the fence to keep the clamping block from twisting.

Deluxe Fence
Adjustable, strong, flexible, yet simple

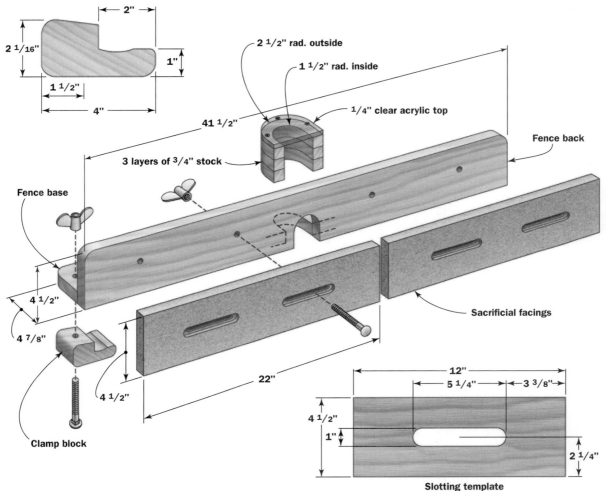

2"

2 1/16"

1"

1 1/2"

4"

2 1/2" rad. outside

1 1/2" rad. inside

1/4" clear acrylic top

41 1/2"

Fence back

3 layers of 3/4" stock

Fence base

4 1/2"

4 7/8"

4 1/2"

Clamp block

22"

Sacrificial facings

12"

5 1/4"

3 3/8"

4 1/2"

1"

2 1/4"

Slotting template
Use with 1" OD guide and 1/4" bit for through slot
Use with 1" OD guide and 3/4" bit for counterbore

3. Assemble the fence with glue only. After the glue has set, joint the bottom surface while holding the face tight to the jointer fence. This ensures that the base is perfectly square to the face.

4. Cut the clamp blocks to shape. The contour and dimensions are shown in the drawing. The clamps are easiest to form with a sequence of table saw cuts, but you may prefer to cut them on a band saw. Radius the corners if desired.

5. Each clamp block is hung on the base with a 3/8-inch carriage bolt. To keep the block from twisting out of position, it has an alignment screw projecting into a stopped hole in the fence base. Drill the mounting-bolt hole and a pilot hole for the screw. Drive a 3/4-inch #8 screw into the pilot, letting it protrude about 3/8 inch.

6. Lay out and bore both the clamp-bolt holes and the alignment-screw holes on the fence base. Make the bolt holes 3/8 inch, but elongate them

by rocking the drill; this allows the clamps to pivot slightly as they are tightened and loosened. Make the alignment holes somewhat larger than the screw-head diameter.

7. Shape the dust pickup and glue it to the fence. Bore a 3-inch-diameter hole though the block (use a hole saw), forming the curved inside wall, then saw into the hole to complete the internal contour. Shape the outside contour and sand the edges smooth and fair.

Cutting List

Piece	Number	Thickness	Width	Length	Material
Fence base	1	$7/8$"	4"	$41 1/2$"	Hardwood
Fence back	1	$7/8$"	$4 1/2$"	$41 1/2$"	Hardwood
Split facing plies	2	$3/4$'	$4 1/2$"	22"	MDF
Dust pickup housing	1	$2 1/4$"*	4"	5"	Hardwood
Dust pickup top	1	$1/4$"	4"	5'	Clear acrylic plastic
Clamp blocks	2	$2 1/4$"*	$2 1/8$"	4"	hardwood

Hardware

2 carriage bolts, $3/8$"-16 × $3 1/2$"

2 pan-head sheet-metal screws, $3/4$" #8

2 plastic wing nuts with $3/8$"-16 through insert (Reid # ESP-608)

2 flat washers, $3/8$" I.D.

3 round-head screws, $1 1/4$" # 8

4 connector bolts, $1/4$"-20 × 50 mm

4 plastic wing nuts with $1/4$"-20 through insert (Reid # ESP-600)

*Laminate three pieces of $3/4$" stock to form the blocks.

8. Make the pickup top from clear acrylic plastic. Saw a blank to size. Trace the contour of the pickup housing onto the plastic and saw off the back corners on the band saw. Bond the top to the housing with carpet tape, and flush-trim the top to match the housing's contour.

9. Lay out and bore the hole for the shop-vac hose.

10. Glue the housing to the fence. Mount the top with three round-head screws.

11. Cut the two facings for the fence. Rout the slots for the connector bolts in the facings. Mount the facings to the fence with connector bolts and plastic wing nuts.

Fence Micro-Adjuster

This simple accessory enables you to make tiny but accurate adjustments in the fence position. You can use it with any router table fence, whether commercial or shop-made. It works the same way that a reference block with shims does.

Typically, a router table fence is fixed at the ends. To make a small adjustment in fence position, you free one end and swing the fence with the fixed end as the pivot. The movement at the middle of the fence, where the bit is, is half that at the free end. Move the fence $1/16$ inch out at the end, and the change will be $1/32$ inch at the bit.

The micro-adjuster has both $3/8$-inch and $1/4$-inch screws as the adjusters.

One rotation of the $3/8$-inch screw, which has 16 threads per inch, moves the end $1/16$ inch. A quarter-turn moves the end $1/64$ inch. Halve that

The fence micro-adjuster clamps to the tabletop right behind the fence. To make it easier to track the rotations, use a cap screw for the adjuster, which is turned with an Allen wrench. The L-shaped wrench will serve as a pointer, making it easy to segment rotations into halves, quarters, and even eighths.

and you have an adjustment of $1/128$ inch at the bit.

One rotation of the $1/4$-inch screw, which has 20 threads per inch, moves the end 50 thousandths of a inch. A quarter-turn moves the end just under 13 thousandths. Halve that and you have an adjustment of less than 7 thousandths. (Curiously enough, $1/128$ inch is between 7 and 8 thousandths. So either adjustment screw yields about the same results.)

The micro-adjuster is a wooden C-clamp with either a $1/4$-inch or a $3/8$-inch machine screw (or both) passing through it. You fit the block onto the edge of the tabletop, just a fraction of an inch behind the fence, and tighten the screw knob. Turn the adjuster screw until it contacts the fence.

■ To move the fence closer to the bit, you loosen the fence clamp and turn the adjustment screw clockwise. That will extend the screw, pushing the fence.

■ To move the fence away from the bit, you zero the adjuster against the fence. Then turn the screw counterclockwise, backing the end away from the fence. Loosen the fence clamp, push the fence back against the screw, and retighten the fence clamp.

1. Glue two pieces of $1/2$-inch plywood face-to-face to form the blank for the adjuster body. It's best to begin with an oversized blank, because that will make it easier and safer to cut the notch in the body.

2. Cut the blank to shape, beginning with the notch. Raise the table saw blade to $2 1/2$ inches, stand the blank against the miter gauge, and form the notch with a series of through cuts. That done, lay out the body and cut it to shape using a cutoff box on the table saw.

3. Soften the corners and edges of the body. Use a belt sander to round off the outside corners, then round-over the outside edges with a $1/4$-inch round-over bit on the router table.

4. Bore the holes for the clamp and the adjusters. The hole for the clamp gets a $5/16$-inch brass threaded insert; size the hole for the insert you use. Drive the insert. The two adjuster holes are tapped. Use a $13/64$-inch bit for the $1/4$-inch adjuster and an "O"-gauge bit for the $3/8$-inch adjuster. Tap the holes.

5. Assemble the body and attach the hardware.

Fence Micro-Adjuster

Precise but simple, this accessory works with any router table fence

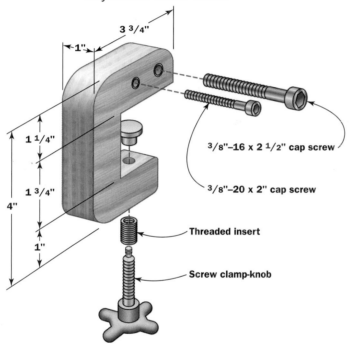

3 3/4"
1"
1 1/4"
1 3/4"
4"
1"

$3/8$"–16 x $2 1/2$" cap screw
$3/8$"–20 x 2" cap screw
Threaded insert
Screw clamp-knob

Cutting List

Piece	Number	Thickness	Width	Length	Material
Body	1	1"	4"	$3 3/4$"	$1/2$" plywood*

Hardware

1 cap screw, $1/4$"-20 x 2"

1 cap screw, $3/8$"-16 x $2 1/2$"

1 screw clamp knob, $5/16$"-18 x $2 15/32$" (Reid # SSC-1133)

1 large pad for screw clamp (Reid # SSC-1602)

1 brass threaded insert, $5/16$"

*Glue two pieces face-to-face to form the body blank. Listed dimensions are the final size; begin with a blank both wider and longer than specified.

Sliding Fence

When you are using it to guide a cut, a router table fence is fixed, right?

It doesn't have to be. This fence adapts the table-saw cutoff box concept to the router table. Designed to move as you cut, it straddles the tabletop from front to back and has guides hugging the tabletop edges. It includes an adjustable backup facing with a stop.

The latter feature is essential on a router table. When you move a workpiece from right to left across the bit, the rotation of the cutter pulls the work toward the back of the table. In the typical setup, the fence guides the work's movement, and that rotational force serves to keep the work against the fence. But if you borrow the miter gauge from your table saw and use it alone to feed the work, that rotational force is going to pull the work and leave you with an out-of-square cut. With the end of the work against this fence's stop, however, the bit can't move it.

An additional benefit of the adjustable facing is that it backs up the work as the bit plows through it, preventing blowout.

The adjustable facing can be secured to the sliding fence in either of two ways: bolts or clamps. With flat-head stove bolts or connector bolts extending through slots in the fence, the facing can be shifted side to side about 3 inches. The face that supports the work is unobstructed. But the adjustment range is a bit meager.

Clamping the adjustable facing to

Cutting List

Piece	Number	Thickness	Width	Length	Material
Fence base	1	3/4"	3 1/4"	29 1/2"	Hardwood
Vertical facing	1	3/4"	4"	29 1/2"	Hardwood
Table-edge guides	2	3/4"	2"	20 3/4"	Hardwood
Rear fence	1	3/4"	2 1/2"	29 1/2"	Hardwood
Adjustable stop	1	3/4"	4"	36"	Plywood
Stop block	1	3/4"	4"	2"	Plywood

Hardware

1 1/4" # 8 screws

2 flat-head stove bolts, 1/4" × 2 1/2"

2 plastic knobs with 1/4" through inserts (Reid # DK-54)

Sliding Fence
A miter gauge explicitly designed for the router table

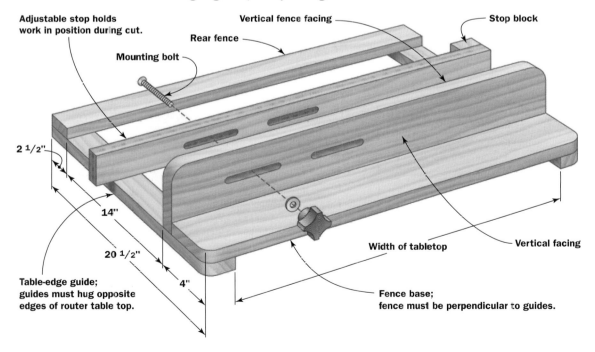

Adjustable stop holds work in position during cut.

Vertical fence facing

Stop block

Rear fence

Mounting bolt

2 1/2"

14"

20 1/2"

4"

Table-edge guide; guides must hug opposite edges of router table top.

Width of tabletop

Fence base; fence must be perpendicular to guides.

Vertical facing

Sliding Fence

Instead of borrowing your table saw's miter gauge for router table use, make a sliding fence. It supports and guides a workpiece through a cross-grain cut, and its adjustable stop prevents the bit rotation from pulling the work as it cuts.

the fence allows faster setups and provides a continuous adjustment range. But the clamps might be in the way on certain jobs.

While it isn't an accessory that sees everyday use, the sliding fence is invaluable for cutting dadoes, lap joints, tenons, various sliding dovetails (including French-dovetailed drawers), and box joints.

1. Begin by establishing the maximum length for the table-edge guides. You want the rear fence to still be on the tabletop when the bit is cutting into the main fence. Cut the guides to that length or less.

2. Clamp the guides against opposite edges of the tabletop. Use a bar clamp or pipe clamp. To ensure that you have

sliding clearance, insert a sheet of paper between each guide and the table's edge before applying the clamp.

3. Cut the fence base, vertical facing, and rear fence to length (measure from guide to guide to determine what the required length is).

4. Cut the stop-bar mounting-bolt slots in the vertical facing. Locate the spot on the vertical facing that the bit will contact as you cut. Lay out 3- to 4-inch-long slots on the centerline of the facing, locating them an equal distance from the bit. Rout the slots with a plunge router and edge guide.

5. Glue the facing to the base, face to edge. After the glue sets, scrape off any squeeze-out, then joint the fence

to ensure that the face is perpendicular to the base. Round off the outside corners with a belt sander.

6. Screw the fences—both main and rear—to the guides. Be sure they are perpendicular to the guides. Remove the clamp from the guides (and the paper shims) and test the unit's action.

7. Cut a stop bar and fasten a stop block at one end. The bar can be mounted on the fence in either of two ways. You can use the slots in the vertical facing as guides to drill mounting-bolt holes in the bar. Thanks to the slots, you'll have a couple inches of adjustment leeway. Or you can simply slide the stop into position, then clamp the bar to the vertical facing.

Workpiece Controllers

Holding the work on the router table and simultaneously feeding it into the bit is fraught with difficulties. Especially if the piece is outsized, it's easy for it to drift away from the fence, tip up off the bit, or chatter and shake.

Following are several shop-made accessories that solve a lot of these problems. The featherboards, spring-board, and hold-down will keep the work tight against the table and firmly against the fence. Use them individually or in pairs.

In addition, the pusher—and in special cases the sled—keeps the workpiece moving and your fingers clear of danger.

Featherboards

In router table work, you clamp featherboards on the fence and/or the tabletop, one on either side of the bit, to ensure that the work doesn't drift or bow away from the bit. More important, the featherboards prevent the work from kicking back.

1. Select a scrap of hardwood, such oak or ash, for the featherboard.

2. Miter the end, then scribe a line, parallel to the mitered end, but offset about 3 to 6 inches. This line marks the base of the feathers.

3. Cut the feathers. No layout—beyond the baseline—is necessary. Set the rip fence about 1/8 inch from the blade. Feed the blank into the blade, cutting as far as the baseline. Pull the work back. Move the fence 1/4 inch away from the blade. Make another cut. Keep up this routine until you run out of featherboard width.

A Basic Featherboard
Simple to make, crucial to use

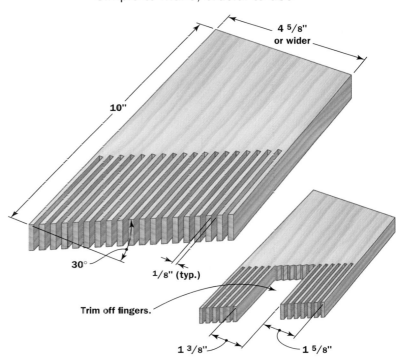

Featherboard with Thumbs

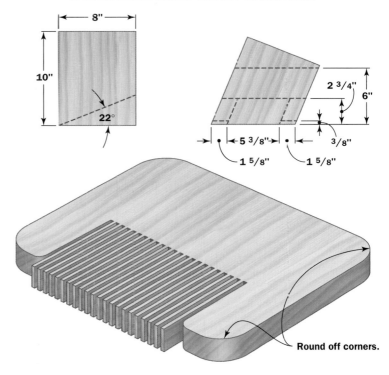

Is there a typical featherboard? I doubt it. Make the featherboard you need for the job at hand—narrow, wide, thick, or thin. Knock a few feathers out of the middle of a wide board so it can straddle the bit. They are easy to make and important to use.

A tandem featherboard cuts down on the number of clamps required. It speeds up setup, too, because if one featherboard is positioned properly, the second also will be. Join two 'boards with a cleat to make a tandem.

With its pads for clamps flanking the feathers, this featherboard is a little different. It's short enough for you to clamp it to the front of any router table as well as to the fence, and the thumbs eliminate the need to place the clamp jaws on some of the feathers, thus limiting their flexibility.

A **"thumbed" featherboard** can be secured by applying clamps to the 1- to 2-inch-wide sections on one or both sides of the feathers.

As you can see from the layout drawing (page 113), the thumbs are 3/8 inch or so shorter than the feathers. While the particular version shown in the drawing, with its radiused corners, is a band-saw project, you can easily produce a workable model on the table saw.

The tandem featherboard saves clamps. Typically, a featherboard needs two clamps to keep it from pivoting out of position. And usually you need two featherboards to keep the work in line.

So tie two featherboards together with a cleat. One clamp applied to each 'board in the tandem will suffice. Set a tandem on the tabletop or fence so it straddles the bit.

Springboard

The springboard is a bowlike affair with a clamp pad at each end. To use it, clamp one end to either the fence or the tabletop—depending upon whether it is to hold *down* or *in*. Flex the other end to bow the springboard

and create pressure against the work, then clamp the second end.

For this straightforward band-saw project, you should use a springy wood like oak, ash, or hickory. Enlarge the

pattern, sketch it on the stock, then saw to the line. The edge that bears against the work should, of course, be smooth. Whether you opt to sand the rest of it smooth is up to you.

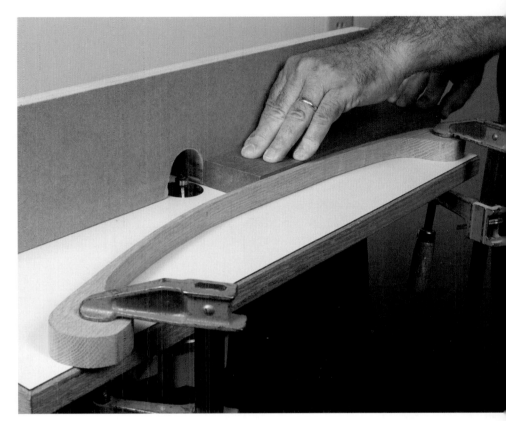

The springboard is an alternative hold-down/hold-in that uses the natural springiness of woods like oak, ash, and hickory. You clamp one end to either the table or fence and bow it as you plant and clamp the other end.

Springboard

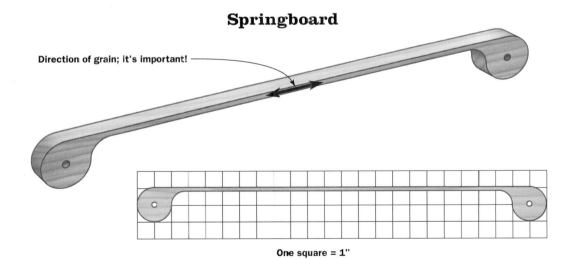

Direction of grain; it's important!

One square = 1"

Hold-Down

Plesiosaur is what I've always called this hold-down, designed and built years ago by my friend and former colleague Fred Matlack. Like a dinosaur, it cranes its long neck over the fence and presses its outsized head against the work, pinning it against the tabletop.

The brains are in the tail end; a wedge cut from the base lets you adjust the head position. With the wedge removed, the head is suspended about $2\,5/8$ inches above the tabletop. With it driven completely into place, the head rests against the tabletop. What you do is adjust the wedge so the head is a tad below the top surface of the workpiece. Apply a clamp holding both the hold-down and the wedge. A second clamp locks the plesiosaur, preventing it from pivoting on the first clamp as you force the work under the head.

Pushing the workpiece under the

Plesiosaur Hold-Down
No place to clamp a featherboard? Use this instead

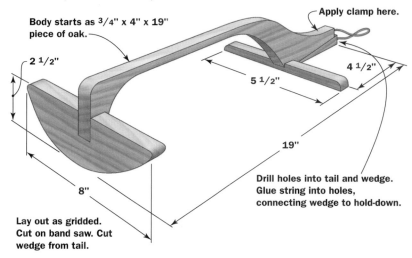

Body starts as $3/4$" x 4" x 19" piece of oak.

$2\,1/2$"

$5\,1/2$"

$4\,1/2$"

Apply clamp here.

19"

8"

Lay out as gridded. Cut on band saw. Cut wedge from tail.

Drill holes into tail and wedge. Glue string into holes, connecting wedge to hold-down.

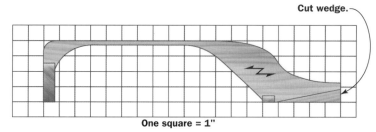

Cut wedge.

One square = 1"

The plesiosaur applies downward force on a workpiece. You set it so the pressure on the work is not directly over the bit, but just to the side. It's most useful for operations like raising curved-edge panels, where the bit's pilot controls the cut and there's nothing to which you can clamp a featherboard to hold the work down on the tabletop. Nevertheless, you can use it with a fence, as shown here, because the contour of the neck allows it to reach over the fence.

head should take a bit of effort; that's a sign that it's doing its job of holding the work down against the tabletop.

Sled

The sled combines the roles of miter gauge, push block, and chip breaker. Use it when doing end-grain cuts. Because it hooks over the table edge, it doesn't need to be used with the fence, nor does it require a slot.

When the sled is serving as a chip breaker, the bit cuts through the work and into the sled itself. It gets chewed up in this kind of use, so the sled is, in a strong sense, a consumable. It's easy to make another, so you can make special sleds for different cuts. The sled shown has been used exclusively for cope-and-stick work, and was made of scrap-bin materials.

The toggle clamp is a practical feature. It keeps your work firmly in place, freeing both hands to guide the sled. Its position is designed to keep the end of the work from bowing up away from the bit, which could give you an irregular cut.

1. Cut the parts to the sizes specified in the cutting list. The parts need to be flat and square. Cut the handle to shape on the band saw or with a jigsaw. The exact shape is less important than whether it fits in your hand; achieve the latter.

2. Cut a rabbet for the base in the flange, then glue and screw the two parts together.

3. Glue and screw the brace in place. Be sure it is at right angles to the edge of the flange. Keep the screws back from the edge where the bit might hit them.

4. Screw the toggle clamp to the brace.

5. Glue and screw the handle to the sled.

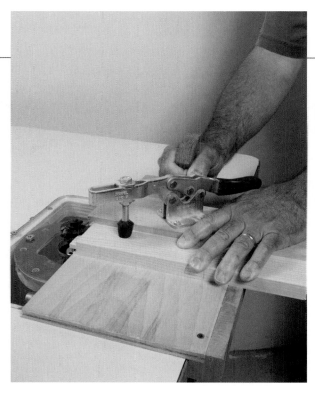

You can have a miter gauge for your router table without having a tabletop slot to guide it. A fence attached to the bottom of the sled slides along the tabletop edge and maintains the sled's position vis-à-vis the bit. It's just what you need for the cope-and-stick work being done here, as well as for many other router-table operations.

Sled
Reference the router table edge for end-grain cuts

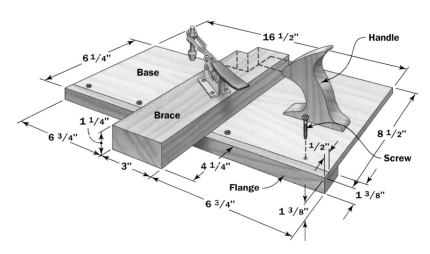

Cutting List

Piece	Number	Thickness	Width	Length	Material
Base	1	$1/2$"	8"	$16 1/2$"	Plywood
Flange	1	$1 3/8$"	$1 3/8$"	$16 1/2$"	Hardwood
Brace	1	$1 1/4$"	3"	11"	Hardwood
Handle	1	1"	$4 1/2$"	$4 1/2$"	Hardwood

Hardware

6 drywall-type screws, 1" #6
1 quick-release toggle clamp

Pusher

For the router table, you want a pusher like this one.

Using the heel to hook the work puts the sole of the pusher flat on the workpiece. That way you can apply some downward force on the work at the same time you are feeding it forward. This is a definite plus on the router table.

Using the V-groove in the sole allows you to hold the work down, but also forces it against the fence as you feed it. To do this, you tilt the pusher and catch the edge of the work in the groove. The heel hooks the end of the work. This is the most useful aspect of the pusher on the router table, especially when shaping the edges of relatively narrow sticks.

Given the versatility of the pusher, you want it to feel good in the hand. So the saw-handle grip is perfect.

1. Make a template by tracing a saw handle on a piece of hardboard, and extend lines from the handle to connect it to the body layout taken from the pattern. Pushing on the

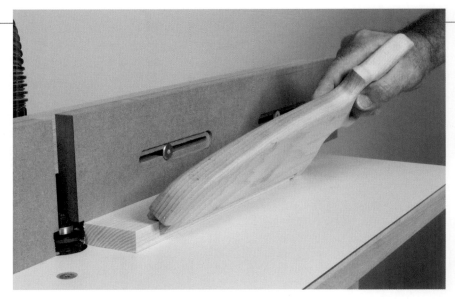

With a V-groove in its sole, this pusher is perfect for router-table work. Tilt the pusher so that the edge of the work nestles into the groove. The heel hooks the end and allows you to feed the work while simultaneously holding it down on the tabletop and in against the fence.

router table is a slightly different action than sawing. So rotate the handle up about 20°. Cut out the template.

2. Stick the template to your blank and the blank to an expendable piece of plywood. Use a guide bushing–equipped plunge router to rout around the template and cut the pusher to shape.

3. Rout the stopped V-groove with a V-grooving bit on the router table.

4. Glue on the heel, a 1/2-inch by 1-inch bit of the working stock. Then notch the toe, as shown in the drawing.

5. Round-over the edges, using a 5/16-inch round-over bit on the router table.

Pusher

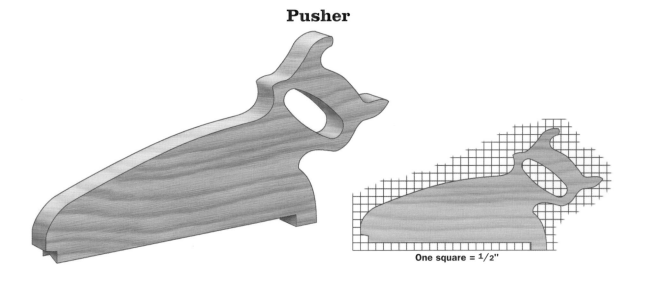

One square = 1/2"

Router Table Savvy

Using a router table effectively—and safely—takes some study and practice. The study ought to begin *before* you spend a lot of money on a table setup. The practice should begin just as soon as you can set something up to practice on.

It's all too easy to find yourself with a table that makes setups and adjustments and commonplace operations a real pain in the behind. Because you can drop a pretty startling sum on a router-table setup, you want to be sure *before* you invest that what you buy or build will be easy to use, accurate, and practical.

Begin with a rudimentary table—like that $25, 1-hour Po' Boy shown in the chapter "Router Table Design" beginning on page 55. Use whatever router you've got. Use it for weeks or months. It's your router table—put it to work! Any experience you gain will expand the frame of reference in which to evaluate table plans or to scrutinize commercial tables.

If you have experience with a router, you can "hack" your way through lots of router-table operations. But there's lots to absorb, and

there are lots of options, good and bad. You need more than a superficial understanding of general procedures.

The best way to learn is to watch a savvy hand at work. Next best is to read up—starting here, of course!—and to experiment. Work with the fence. Do some cuts with a piloted bit and the starting pin. Pay close attention to feed direction.

As you progress, you'll master the tricks, starting with changing bits, and progressing through setting the bit height and positioning the fence. You'll learn the safe ways—and safe directions—to move the workpiece.

Changing Bits

A decade ago, when Fred Matlack and I wrote the first edition of *Woodworking with the Router,* there were two ways of getting at a table-mounted router's collet to change bits.

■ You could fumble around under the table with the wrench or wrenches.

■ You could remove the router (or just the motor, if you were dealing

with a fixed-base router) from the table and make the change on the table or benchtop.

Both of those approaches still work, of course. But now you have additional options, thanks to routers and after-market accessories that weren't available 10 years ago. And thanks as well to some plain old ingenuity.

■ At least one router, the Triton, can plunge its collet through its base. When hung in a table, this feature allows bit changes from above the table.

■ Premium router lifts elevate the collet above the tabletop for bit changes. (Be aware that not all lifts, expensive though they may be, have this capacity.)

■ Using a bent wrench on a router with a spindle lock enables you to change bits from above the table, even when the collet itself is below the table surface. A big bit opening in the table is required, of course.

■ A lift-top table exposes the router, giving you easy access to the router without having to remove it from its mounting.

Changing bits is incontestably the most-complained-about router-table routine. It is easy when you have unrestricted access to the collet. Pulling the router from the table (left) or elevating the collet above the tabletop (above) relieves you of the need to fumble under the table as you peer through the mounting plate. Tilting the tabletop up (lower left) gives you easy access to drop the motor out of a fixed base. You can even work a collet wrench between the posts of a plunge model (see photo on page 69).

As you sort through your options, don't lose sight of what you are trying to accomplish. You can easily spend $300+ on something (okay, on a router lift) that's designed primarily to make bit changes easier. I can think of dozens of better investments. You can simplify bit changes for a whole lot less.

Setting the Bit Extension

After installing the bit in the collet, you need to set its height for whatever cut you want to make. Your bit-changing system is a harbinger of what's involved in adjusting the bit height.

Setting the height of the bit is sometimes an "eyeball" proposition, sometimes a measuring task. However you go about it, a test cut is almost always in order. That way you can assess *the result* and make any adjustment that might be necessary.

In either situation, you need to hunker down and sight across the tabletop to the bit. Yes, there are some measuring devices that help you set the bit without bending or stooping. But getting your line of sight even with the bit is the most consistently accurate way to do it.

Use a practical measuring device like a 6-inch steel rule or a small square. These devices have a variety of graduations—eighths, sixteenths, thirty-seconds—and one is certain to suit your purpose. I have a 6-inch square that I use more often than any other rule or adjustable square with my routers.

An alternative measurement approach is to use a setup gauge. Several different devices are on the market, and I've included a plan for a simple one you can make. You set the adjuster so the distance between the base and the gauge post match the bit extension you want. Position the gauge beside the bit, and raise the bit until its tip bumps the post.

Adjustable Depth Gauge

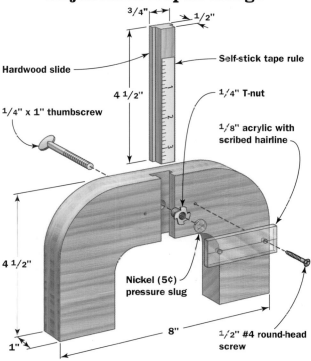

- 3/4"
- 1/2"
- Hardwood slide
- Self-stick tape rule
- 4 1/2"
- 1/4" T-nut
- 1/4" x 1" thumbscrew
- 1/8" acrylic with scribed hairline
- 4 1/2"
- Nickel (5¢) pressure slug
- 8"
- 1"
- 1/2" #4 round-head screw

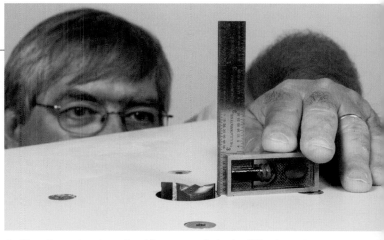

Setting the extension of a bit accurately isn't difficult or time-consuming. Hold a small square or a rule right beside the bit. Hunker down and sight across the tabletop as you adjust the tip of the bit to align with the appropriate graduation on the rule.

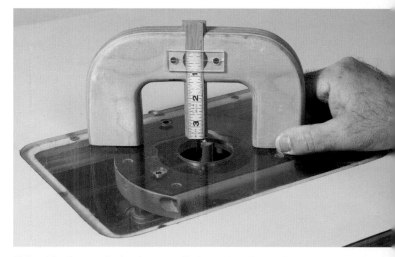

Using this shop-made depth gauge eliminates bending and squinting. Set it to the height you want, then place it over the bit. Crank the bit up until it touches the end of the slide. With a piloted bit, make sure the slide clears the pilot and touches only the cutting edge.

There's a different sort of gauge you might find useful. It's usually called a setup block. A few specialized joint-cutting bits—cope-and-stick cutters or lock-miter bits, for example—can be very frustrating to set. Your initial elevation is set by eye. Then you cut some test pieces, join them, and make adjustments based on how they fit. Eventually, you get the setup dialed in.

At that point, you make a setup block for the next time you use the bit. It's simply a sample cut. To use it, you elevate the bit and adjust it up or down until the block nestles comfortably into the profile.

A setup block is a sample cut made with the bit, and sometimes the fence, at the optimal setting. You use the block to return the bit to that setting each time you use it, avoiding a protracted sequence of adjustments and test cuts. Slide the block's profile through the cutter as you inch the bit up and down. When it passes through without drag, the bit's set.

Choking Up on the Bit

This is safety as much as savvy. You should have the bit opening in the mounting plate or tabletop closed down around the bit just as closely as possible. This prevents the workpiece from dipping into the bit opening, snagging the edge, maybe stalling the cut.

If you've opened up the bit hole to accommodate a 3-inch (or larger) panel-raising bit, don't then fit a 1/2-inch dovetail bit or 1/4-inch straight bit in the router and expect to rout a groove without hazard or hangup. You don't necessarily need zero clearance, but a big reduction in the size of the opening will make setup easier and operation safer.

Most commercial mounting plates have nesting reducer rings. So do router lifts. Use those rings.

If you are using a shop-built plate or direct-mount tabletop, you can make auxiliary tops for the table using 1/8-inch hardboard. With the router offset, just two of these tops will give you four different opening sizes (two in each top).

When you need to close down that throat, make one by first

An auxiliary top is a first-rate way of closing down the bit opening (left), and it transforms any router tabletop. It bridges miter-gauge slots, countersunk screw heads, and seams between top and mounting plate, providing a surface interrupted only by the projecting bit. Made of thin hardboard, the top shown matches the tabletop in size and, because the router is offset, provides two different bit-opening sizes.

On the router table, this sort of bit-to-plate-opening mismatch is trouble. The work can catch the far side of the bit opening and tip into the void. If you are lucky, it will only ruin the workpiece.

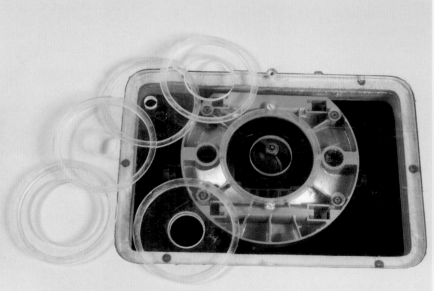

Reducer rings for a mounting plate with a large bit opening are as easy to make as the plate itself. Use a couple of small machine screws to hold a reducer in place. Drill and tap holes in the plastic for the screws, positioning them in the seam between plate and ring.

dropping the router so the bit's below the table. Then lay a piece of hardboard over the tabletop. Stick it in place with double-stick tape or a couple of spring clamps. The fence will help hold it, too. Turn on the router and run your bit up through the hardboard. The bit hole will perfectly match the bit. You can set this auxiliary top aside and use it again and again, every time you use that bit. Just center it by fitting it over the bit, stick it down, set the fence, and rout your work.

An alternative is to make a mounting plate with a set of reducing rings. I made such a set from 3/8-inch clear acrylic. The basic bit opening in the mounting plate is 3 1/2 inches in diameter, large enough to accommodate the largest panel-raiser in my collection. It has a 1/4-inch-wide by 3/16-inch-deep rabbet around it. The reducers are 4 inches in diameter and are similarly rabbeted, so the reducer fits into the bit opening and rests flush. The bit openings in the reducers are matched to different, commonly used bit sizes—1/4 inch, 1/2 inch, 3/4 inch, 1 inch, and so on. I even made one that's bored out and rabbeted for template guides. There's more information on making and using templates for this application in the chapter "Template-Guided Work," page 155.

The mounting plate's bit opening can be cut with a commonplace up-spiral bit, using a template guide to follow a circle template. Routing the rabbet is simple with a rabbet bit. Cut the reducers on the router table, using a flush-trimming bit and a template.

Controlling the Workpiece

To get work done on the router table, you must be in control. Remember: The router is simply a powerful, fast-spinning motor with a sharp cutter on the end. To be productive with it, you need to establish control over the tool and the workpiece.

Always use some mechanical device to control the work. It could be the pilot bearing on the bit, the fence, a sled of some sort, a template guide, a starting pin.

An absolute essential here is having internalized feed-direction savvy. It's important to position the fence so the work has adequate support through-out a cut, or so the fence isn't in your way. One of the biggest factors in controlling the workpiece during a cut is getting the bit's energy working in your favor. Equally important is knowing when that energy can't be harnessed and thus being able to take appropriate measures—setting hold-downs, for example.

Feed-Direction Savvy

Feed-direction savvy is simply knowing which way to feed the workpiece, regardless of the particular setup. It's really not difficult to master. Push the work *against* the rotation of the cutter.

You want the bit to be pushing the work back, whether you are pushing

Try This!

Need three hands to change bits? When you do this with the router in "table position," it often seems that way, especially if you want to avoid bottoming the bit (meaning, letting the bit rest against the collet bottom). And all bit makers entreat you to avoid bottoming the bit (the drawing *Getting a Firm Grip,* on page 25, shows why).

Here's a trick to try:

Fit an O-ring—buy 'em at an auto-parts store—on the shank of each bit you have. The rubber ring will catch on the collet and limit the shank's penetration into it. In most cases, you'll position the ring to keep the bit from bottoming. On short-shanked bits, this will be near the cutter.

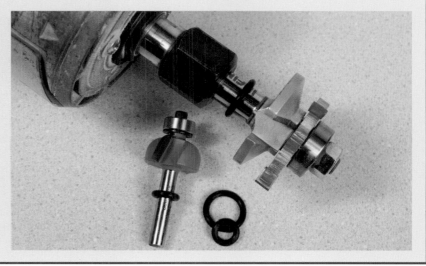

Router Table Feed Direction

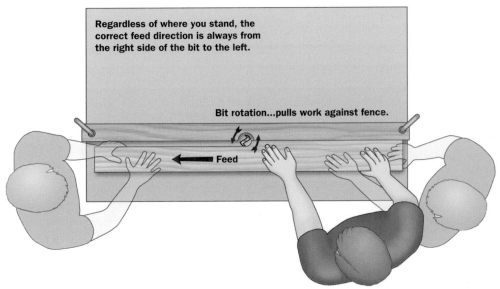

Regardless of where you stand, the correct feed direction is always from the right side of the bit to the left.

Bit rotation...pulls work against fence.

← Feed

CORRECT FEED DIRECTION ALONG FENCE

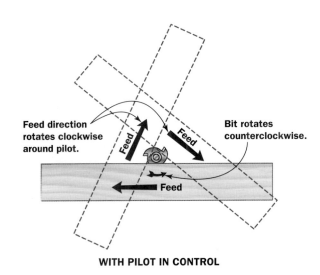

Feed direction rotates clockwise around pilot.

Bit rotates counterclockwise.

Feed

Feed

← Feed

WITH PILOT IN CONTROL

Feed Direction for Widening a Groove

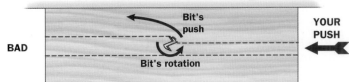

BAD

Bit's push

Bit's rotation

YOUR PUSH

Cutting on fence side of groove; feeding right to left is a climb cut.

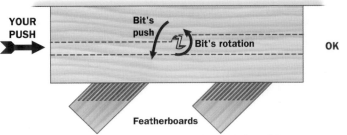

YOUR PUSH

Bit's push

Bit's rotation

OK

Featherboards

Cutting on fence side of groove; feeding left to right; not a climb cut, but bit pushes work away from fence.

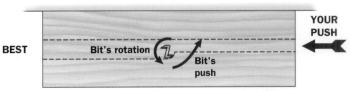

BEST

Bit's rotation

Bit's push

YOUR PUSH

Cutting on side of groove away from fence; feed right to left; not a climb cut, and bit pushes work against fence.

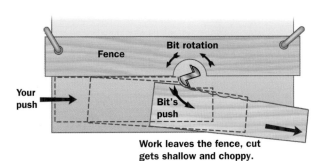

Fence

Bit rotation

Your push

Bit's push

Work leaves the fence, cut gets shallow and choppy.

CLIMB CUT DANGER!

it side to side or away from you. If you are pulling the work, you want the bit to be pulling back. An ancillary result of feeding against the bit rotation is that the force generated by the rotation helps drive the work against whatever guide that you're using—the pilot bearing or the fence.

Feeding the work *with* the cutter's rotation—a process called climb-cutting—gives the bit the opportunity to take control. It'll *help* you move that work. Spinning at 22,000 rpm, it's going to hurry things along, even if it has to pull the work right out of your hands to do it. Believe me, you don't want this.

My advice is this: At the router table, *never climb-cut*.

When it is upended in a table mounting, a router motor spins *counterclockwise*. If you can't remember, just look at the bit. The angle of the cutting edges will make it clear which way it has to turn to cut. Seeing that, and knowing that you feed the work *against* the cutter's rotation, should tell you which way to feed the work, regardless of where you stand and regardless of whether you are pushing the stock away from you, pulling it into you, or shoving it from one side to the other.

In most router operations, you feed the work from right to left across the cutter. You stand at the right front corner of the table, with the workpiece on the table, typically against the fence. With the router running, you push the workpiece along the fence into the cutter, and you keep on pushing until it has cleared the bit to the left. You may move your body to the left as you feed the work.

If you use the pilot on a bit to control the cut, the feed direction is basically the same. But note in the drawing that you can safely profile all four edges of a workpiece by maneu-

Trapping the work between the fence and the cutter is trouble, an invitation to unpleasant surprise and potentially to injury. If you feed the work right to left, it's a climb cut, and you may lose control of the workpiece unexpectedly. Feeding left to right is correct, but hardly any better. If the workpiece edges aren't parallel, if the cutter hits a knot or convoluted grain, if the wood begins to break up and splinter, the feed could be stalled and the cutter could fire the work back at you.

vering the work clockwise around a piloted bit. The bit, remember, is spinning counterclockwise; so by advancing the work clockwise, you are feeding it against the bit rotation.

Special Hazards

A couple of setups deserve special attention, because you may not recognize them as hazardous. But you want to avoid them.

The first is where the setup places the workpiece between the fence and the cutter. This is a hazard in two different ways. Hypothetically, you set the fence one board's width away from the bit, then feed the board along the fence, routing the exposed edge. Feeding the board from right to left along the fence with the cutter addressing the near edge is a climb cut. Bad.

It is a generally accepted rule that you never trap the work between the fence and the cutter.

The other hazard can occur if you are cutting a groove in two passes—that is, you make a groove and with a second pass you widen it. The second cut may be a climb cut.

The first pass is made right to left, and the bit's rotational forces are contained, resisting the feed and pressing the stock against the fence. As you shift the fence to widen the cut, you can move it toward you or away from you.

If you move it toward you, the bit will be cutting the side of the groove closest to the fence. If you feed right to left, the cutting edges will be helping the feed. It'll be a climb cut. It's an easy mistake to make, and it's a breathtaking surprise when that workpiece suddenly leaves your control and shoots off the table.

Can you safely cut on that side if you feed left to right? Probably—you are no longer making a climb cut. You'll be feeding against the cutter's rotation. But, once *almost* bitten, twice shy.

What you should always do in this situation is to back the fence away from the bit. Then the bit will be working the side of the cut closest to you (rather than to the fence). And you still feed right to left.

Chipping, Splintering, Tearout, and Blowout

Here's another aspect of control: dealing with and—as much as possible—preventing splintering.

Whenever you rout across end grain, you'll get some degree of splintering as the bit exits the cut. This usually isn't a problem when you're routing all around a piece. You rout across the ends first, letting the two exit corners blow away. Then you rout the long-grain sides. In most cases, this will clean up the splintering.

Suppose you're not routing the long-grain sides. Here you need to clamp scrap stock to the edges where the cuts will exit. You cut right into the scrap, and *it* splinters rather than the good stuff.

More vexing, and harder to contend with, is when the long-grain edge of your workpiece chips and splinters. You're routing along an edge and you can see the wood splitting ahead of the cut. It becomes a real problem when the grain "runs in" so the split extends into the area that isn't supposed to be cut.

This takes more imagination to remedy.

Anything you can do to "back up" the wood will help it stay together. Holding the wood tight against the fence backs it up. The split begins where the cutting tip clears the wood. Usually, there's a gap in the fence at

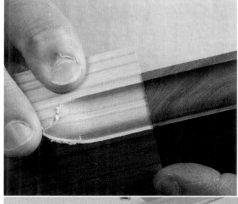

On the router table, cross-grain cuts usually involve guiding the narrow end of an oblong workpiece along the fence. A clean cut is tough to achieve because the piece tends to "walk." On top of that, the cut usually ends with splinters being torn out of the long grain as the cutter exits. The solution to both these problems is a square pusher—a piece of scrap will do. The pusher stabilizes the work as you advance it along the fence, and it prevents the exit tearout (inset).

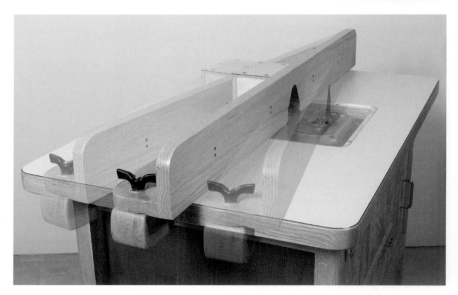

A router-table fence doesn't have to be parallel to the edge of the table. It just has to be the proper distance from the bit. So the easiest way to set the fence is to move it into approximate position and lock down one end. Swing the free end back and forth as you measure between fence and bit. When the position is right, secure the free end, too.

that very spot. In other words, right at the most vulnerable spot, the wood has no backing. So creating a zero-clearance housing for the bit will help immensely (see "Zero-Clearance Tactics" on page 129).

Many veteran router woodworkers suggest staging your cut so you can finish off with a light pass in the wrong direction—a climb cut. That's okay, perhaps, when you're hand-holding the router, but not, as we've seen, when you're working on the router table.

Using the Fence

The most frequently used router-table guidance system is the fence. You use the fence to direct the movement of the workpiece to and across the bit. You use the fence to position the cut. Sometimes you use the fence to control how deep the cut is or what its profile will be. You use it with piloted bits as well as unpiloted bits.

So on a router table, you can set the fence pretty much willy-nilly across the tabletop—side to side, front to back, diagonally corner to corner. The only critical matter is the distance between the bit and the fence.

Setting the fence: My usual fence-setting procedure is to position the fence by eye, then clamp one end. Then I get out a rule or a square and measure between the bit and fence as I swing the free end back and forth. When I've captured the desired distance, I clamp the second end of the fence.

At this point, you make a test cut on a smallish piece of the working stock. Measure the cut if need be, to determine how wide or deep it is, or where it is. Perhaps it is something

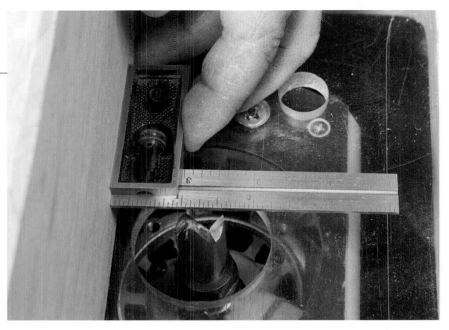

Set the handle of a square against the fence's face. The blade will jut away from it at a right angle. Slide the tool up to the bit and measure to either the cutting edges or the axis of the bit. Rotate the bit a little with your fingers to align the cutting edges, and get the rule as close as possible to the appropriate edge. Pinpointing the axis? Good luck! It's tough to estimate accurately where the exact center of the bit is.

you need to fit to an already-cut part, like a tenon to a mortise. Maybe you need simply to assess what it looks like.

Based on your assessment, you want to slightly shift the fence position.

Micro-adjustment tactics: You've done a quick positioning. You've made a test cut. You are *really* close, but need to shift something about 1/32 inch, maybe only 1/64 inch.

Commercial tables and fences often have scales that enable adjustments that are quite fine. Shop-made fences don't have to be any less precise.

In making a fine adjustment, put geometry to work for you. Did you know that moving only one end of your fence gives you adjustment leverage? The distance you move the end of the fence is halved at the center.

Here's what that means in practical terms. If you want to shift the cut 1/32 inch, you leave one end of the fence fixed and move the other end 1/16 inch. That 1/16 inch is easier to see on a rule.

You can make a pretty fine adjustment simply by measuring from a pencil line. Trace along either the front or back edge of the fence, right at the edge of the table. Shift the fence away from the line as you monitor the distance with a rule.

As the desired adjustment gets *really* fine, use shims and a block to make adjustments. Put a shim

Setting the Fence
How to measure from bit to fence

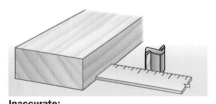

Inaccurate:
Cutting edges turned; rule in wrong place.

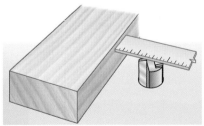

Accurate:
Cutting edges properly aligned; rule placed where marking is next to cutting edge.

Controlling the Workpiece

between the fence and a stop block you clamp to the router table. Unclamp the fence, remove the shim, and set the fence against the stop block. Reclamp the fence. You've moved it the thickness of the shim.

This trick works going either way. You "open up" the fence setting by putting the shim in when you set the block. But you could also set the block right against the fence, then close the fence by putting in the shim to move the fence away from the block.

Use cards for shims—business cards, playing cards, index cards. If you are a tool junkie, this is a good excuse for buying feeler gauges. You can buy a set with 16 to 20 thicknesses for about $20. A good alterna-

To adjust a fence a small amount, scribe a pencil line along the fence—where the fence will be moving away from it—and measure with your rule from that line to the fence. Remember that the distance you move one end of the fence will be halved at the bit.

Shift the fence a controlled distance using shims and a reference block. Shims can range from playing cards and scraps of plastic laminate to precision-thickness gauge blocks (the brass bars in the photo) and feeler gauges. Set a shim against the fence, set the block against the shim, and clamp the block. Loosen the fence, remove the shim, and shift the fence against the block. The movement at the bit will be half the shim's thickness.

tive is the Fence Micro-Adjuster on page 109. This simple gadget helps you achieve the same fine adjustments to the fence without the scrap, clamp, and other paraphernalia.

Fence plus piloted bit: More often than not, when working with a piloted bit, you use the fence.

The fence gives you better control of the work and the workpiece. You can reduce the workload for the router and bit by adjusting the fence forward of your final setting. You move the fence back in stages, so it takes three passes—or more—to achieve the full profile. A light final pass can skim minor chipping out of the cut, without introducing new imperfections.

Not to be overlooked is the safety factor. The fence houses the bit, concealing most of it, thus serving as a guard.

In addition, most fences have a built-in dust-collection pickup. It works best with edge-forming bits, which, in the main, are piloted. If for no other reason than managing the dust generated by a cut, you ought to use the fence.

Positioning the fence properly is simple. Bring the fence up around the bit so that most of it is inside the cutout. Use a straightedge to align the fence face tangent to the bearing. Slide the straightedge back and forth a little as you move the fence, watching the bearing. Just where the

straightedge loses contact and the bearing stops turning is your spot. That's where you lock down the free end of the fence.

Zero-clearance tactics: Cut quality and your personal safety are both good reasons to try to zero out the clearance around bits that are partially housed in the fence.

You'll get cleaner cuts with profile-cutters, rabbet bits, cope-and-stick bits, panel-raisers, and many other bits if you close the fence opening as close as possible around the cutter. In addition, you eliminate the feed hesitations that result from the work momentarily hanging up on the outfeed edge of the fence opening.

To set the fence for use with a piloted bit, clamp one end and swing it up to the bit, housing it enough that the pilot is "inside" the fence. Set the edge of a steel rule against the fence so it bridges the cutout, and shift the fence so the pilot just touches the rule, as shown here.

Controlling
the Workpiece

To form a true zero-clearance fit, you just slide the facings, one at a time, against the bit as it spins. When you switch bits, slide the facings off the fence and trim off the end. Eventually, the strips will become too short to be of much use, and you'll have to replace them.

Here's a good zero-clearance tactic that should work on any fence.

Cut a strip of 1/4-inch hardboard or plywood to match the height and length of the fence. Both materials are cheap, flat, and easy to cut. Attach the strip to one end of the fence with a spring clamp or the like. Either material is flexible in that thickness, so you flex it so it's bowed away from the bit. Switch on the router and bring the strip back against the fence. The bit will cut through the strip, of course, and you will have a true zero-clearance fit.

The free end of the strip can be

Fences, both purchased and shop-made, often have two facings, one on each side of the bit. These adjust so you can crowd them in on a small bit, or spread apart to accommodate a large one. To form a zero-clearance fit, you just slide the facings, one at a time, against the bit as it spins.

held to the fence with an additional clamp or two. If the clamps will interfere with the work, use carpet tape or hot-melt glue to attach the strip to the fence temporarily.

To deal with the pilot bearing (if the bit has one), cut a clearance hole for it or remove the bearing from the bit. (Remount the bearing when the cut's done, so you don't misplace it.)

Make a one-piece zero-clearance facing from thin plywood or hardboard. Create an undersized opening for the bit and its pilot bearing by boring a hole at rough bearing height and cutting from the edge to the hole. Attach the facing to the fence, and swing the fence onto the spinning bit to enlarge the cutout, cutting the exact bit profile (above). The outfeed side of the cutout may be chipped and ragged, but the infeed side, which is the critical one, will be clean.

Problem Solver

A pilot bearing *can* burn the edge of the work. The operating theory is this: When in contact with the work, the bearing's outer surface doesn't move. But the bit spins freely inside it. Now if the contact with the work isn't sufficiently firm, the bearing spins with the bit, and when that happens, the friction can either scorch or burnish the work. What really aggravates the problem is a dirty or gummed-up bearing that won't spin freely.

Using such a bit with a fence presents a prime opportunity for this problem. To avoid it, just make sure you set the fence so the pilot doesn't touch the workpiece. All the support and guidance you need can be provided by the fence. And, of course, keep the bearing clean!

Starting Pins and Alternatives

It isn't at all uncommon to make a cut on the router table guided by the pilot bearing on the bit. There's a hazard associated with this, but it can be eliminated through the use of a starting pin.

Here's the problem: No matter how you come at the bit, the cutting edges engage the wood before the pilot does. What can happen is that the cutting edges flick the workpiece aside before it can contact the pilot. There you are, inching the wood into the bit, when *SUDDENLY!* it exits right.

I don't want to overstate the hazard here. The most common result is a workpiece that has a bit of a profile across an end, when what you wanted was a profile only along its edge. But it would be cavalier to ignore the potential for injury.

A starting pin is usually a wooden, plastic, or metal pin standing about 2 to 4 inches from the bit. It is a fulcrum: You brace the work against it, then "lever" it into the bit. The pin is stationary, so you can brace the work securely. By giving you leverage, it multiplies the strength of your hold on the wood.

It's called a *starting* pin because it helps at the beginning of a cut. It is superfluous once the work is in firm contact with the pilot; so if the work comes off it, that's okay.

A starting pin is the fulcrum for beginning a cut with a piloted bit. Brace the work against the stationary pin, then pivot it until it contacts the bit. Even if the cutter grabs the work, the pin's position prevents it from shooting the piece to the right, or worse, snatching it from your grasp.

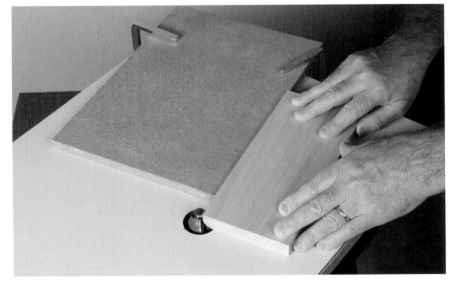

A starting pin doesn't have to be a "pin." This scrap, clamped to the router table, is as good a fulcrum as a more elaborate, handcrafted accessory. It is particularly easy, with this approach, to vary the distance between the "pin" and the bit.

The pin is most important when you need to begin a cut at the end of the piece. When you're routing all around a workpiece, you can sweep in on a long-grain side, rather than starting at a corner. You work your way around the piece, and end in the middle of the side, where you began. But you don't want to begin in the middle and back out to the end. That would be a climb cut, something you should never do on the router table.

Stopping Cuts

Stopped and blind cuts take a little more setting up than do through cuts. A stopped cut is one that begins or ends shy of one end of the work but is through at the other end. A blind cut begins and ends shy of the ends.

You first have to set the bit and the fence. Beyond that, you have to figure out where to begin and end the cut, then either put temporary marks on the table or clamp stops to it so you can produce the cut you desire.

The first step, beyond the initial setup, is to lay out the extent of the cut on a sample workpiece. The next step is to mark where the bit is and how big it is, either on the tabletop or on the fence, whichever place will be visible as you make the cut. I usually put the marks on masking tape so that I can remove them when the job is done simply by peeling off the tape.

The proper feed direction is right to left, so line up the starting mark on the work with the mark for the outfeed side of the bit (the one on the left). Plunge the stock onto the spinning bit. (Depending on the cut, the plunging action either lowers the work onto the bit or slides it across the tabletop against the bit.) Feed the work. As the end-of-cut mark on the

Using a Starting Pin

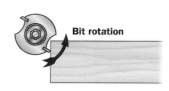

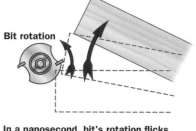

Bit rotation

Workpiece is caught by cutting tip of spinning bit before it reaches the pilot bearing.
WITHOUT STARTING PIN

Bit rotation

In a nanosecond, bit's rotation flicks work aside.

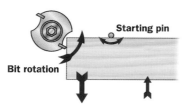

Starting pin

Bit rotation

Starting pin gives leverage to counter rotational force of bit.
WITH STARTING PIN

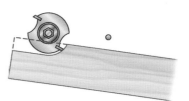

Maintaining contact with starting pin isn't necessary once work contacts pilot bearing.

Making an accurate stopped or blind cut depends on being able to tell where the bit is when the workpiece is concealing it. Apply some tape to the tabletop (or to the fence), and transfer the bit tangents to it using a block of wood and a pencil. Make sure you are referencing the cutting edges and not the bit body.

stock comes up to the mark at the *right* of the bit, carefully lift or pull the end of the workpiece off the bit.

For stopped cuts, begin feeding the

work as though making a through cut, but halt the feed and remove the work when the marks align. Or you can plunge the work onto the bit to

Stop blocks are time-savers when you have a large number of identical pieces to work. The easiest way to set stops accurately is to use an already-cut workpiece. With the router switched off, set the piece on the bit, at the beginning of the cut. Set and clamp a stop against its back end. Slide the piece to the cut's end point and set a stop against its front end. Now you can cut the remaining pieces and have them all be identical.

Stopped Cuts without Workpiece Layout

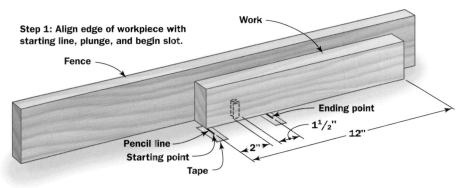

Step 1: Align edge of workpiece with starting line, plunge, and begin slot.

Fence

Work

Ending point

1¹/₂"

12"

Pencil line

Starting point

Tape

2"

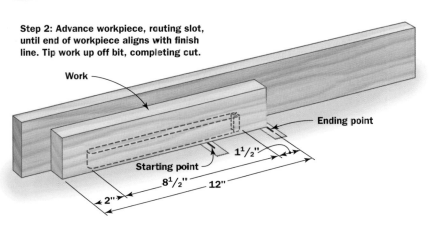

Step 2: Advance workpiece, routing slot, until end of workpiece aligns with finish line. Tip work up off bit, completing cut.

Work

Ending point

1¹/₂"

Starting point

8¹/₂"

12"

2"

begin the cut, then feed through the end. Depending on the specifics of the job, you may do some parts one way, and others the second way.

An alternative to marking each workpiece is to place marks on the table (or fence) with which to align the *ends* of the workpiece as you begin and end the cut. This works if all the parts have the cut beginning or ending the same distance from the work's end.

If you have many pieces to rout, you can clamp stop blocks to the fence or tabletop. You then can skip the layout marks on the workpieces, and you won't have minor variations from piece to piece. Most commercial fences have T-slots for mounting things like stops, and the manufacturer will be glad to sell you a pair of them. I just clamp scraps to my shop-made fences.

Making the Cut

Before making the chips fly, ask yourself: How much work am I expecting the router to do? How can I make the cut manageable for it? Do I need to alter the router speed? Should I plant some featherboards on the table or fence? Do I have the proper safety gear on? How about a pusher?

Let's start this final checklist with the workload that the cut represents.

Workload

The router is a trimming machine. It works best when it's kinda nibbling at the stock.

Need a ¹/₂-inch-deep by ³/₄-inch-wide dado? What you *should* do is set the bit extension at ³/₁₆ inch and make a cut. Then increase the extension to ³/₈ inch and cut again.

Increase the extension again, taking it to the full 1/2-inch cut depth that you want. Make one more cut to finish the dado.

There are two approaches to staging a cut so that you can make it in manageable increments. Sometimes you have no options; it's one approach and no other. In other situations, you can do one OR the other.

The first option, already explained, is to elevate the bit in stages, beginning with a shallow cut and making it progressively deeper through one, two, or more additional passes.

The second option has you stage the fence position. Obviously, this can be used only on edge-forming operations, where the fence plays a role in scaling the cut, not simply in placing it.

I prefer to get everything set up so that I can make and evaluate a full cut before starting to cut the real workpieces. I've got some procedures that allow me to do that. After my final test cut, I can back away from one aspect of the setup or the other, but still get back to that final perfect setup.

The shim is my first workaround. I can use one or two or three, either on the tabletop to elevate the workpiece or on the face of the fence to house more of the bit. In either case, less of the bit is exposed with the shims in place, so its cut is reduced.

I use hardboard or MDF (or both) for shims. Use a 1/8-inch and a 1/4-inch hardboard shim to stage a cut in 1/8-inch increments. Use both to reduce the bite by 3/8 inch, then pull the thin one for another pass, then substitute the thin for the thick for a third pass. The final pass is made without the shims entirely.

You do need a cutout for the bit, and the shim must be large enough to support the work properly. Secure

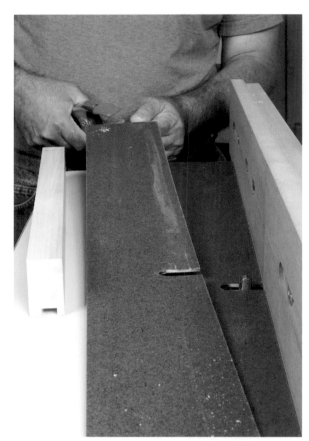

Stage a cut by way of depth changes using shims on the tabletop. You can accurately set a cut depth that's critical before working the good stock. Lay strips of hardboard on the tabletop and secure them with a spring clamp. The workpiece rides on these shims, and effectively reduces the cut depth so the router and bit don't have to work so hard. Remove a shim and cut again, penetrating a little deeper into the workpiece. The deeper the full cut, the more shims you should use.

You can stage a cut using the fence position in most instances. Move the fence into position for the final cut, then clamp stops against the back edge. They'll "remember" the position, so you can go back to it without measuring or making test cuts. Pull the fence away from the stops, reducing the bite on the first pass. Make incremental moves back toward the stops between subsequent passes.

them with spring clamps, carpet tape, even hot-melt glue.

The stop block is my second workaround. It works only with the fence. The procedure here is to butt a block against the back edge of the fence—preferably one on each side—and clamp it to the tabletop. You've captured the fence position. Loosen the fence clamps, edge it forward, then reset the fence clamps. You've reduced the cut for a light first pass. Edge it back in stages, and you can increase the overall cut incrementally.

A very light final pass is often desired to produce the smoothest possible surface, right off the cutter. Insert shims between the fence and

the stops on the penultimate pass, then remove them and reset the fence for the final "buffing."

Featherboards and Other Controllers

Before switching on the router, there are some additional controls you should consider for your setup.

The most familiar device is the featherboard (sometimes called a fingerboard). Properly positioned and adjusted, featherboards keep the work erect and tight to the fence or flat and tight to the tabletop. They free you to simply push the work through the cut. The angled fingers

flex to allow the work to advance, but they jam against the work should you try to pull it back toward you. And the bit can't kick it back, either.

You can make your own from scraps, customizing them for particular applications. (Patterns for different styles are shown on pages 113–115.) A couple of clamps on each featherboard hold them in place.

Trap fence: A secondary guide strip that you mount on the tabletop, parallel to the main fence, to form a channel to confine the workpiece's movement, is called a trap fence. It seldom needs to be anything more than a straight strip of wood held in place with a couple of clamps.

A good way to set a featherboard for stock of commonplace 3/4-inch thickness is with a scrap of plywood. Set the featherboard so all the fingers rest against the plywood, as shown, and clamp the featherboard to the fence. Since the plywood is slightly less than 3/4 inch thick, the featherboard will apply pressure to stock that really is 3/4 inch thick.

The trap fence provides much the same guidance as a featherboard, but it won't provide kickback protection. What you avoid with a trap fence is having the bottom edge of a tall workpiece skid away from the fence.

In a slightly different form, you can set trap fences on the tabletop to guide a jig like a box-joint cutter (see page 341). You place a trap fence on either side of the jig so its movement is confined.

Template guides: Yes, a template guide is in the same bailiwick as a pilot bearing, but it can do some things on a router table that a bearing can't. I'll get into its value in template-guided work in the chapter of that name (page 155). But let me note here that you can use a template guide to locate a jig so you don't need trap fences.

Miter Gauge Alternatives

It's common for a router table top to have a miter gauge slot so you can use a table saw accessory on the router table. Since the miter gauge is the primary guide for crosscutting on a table saw, it seems right to use it on the router table for similar operations. But as much as you need a device to guide cross-grain cuts, you need a means to prevent blowout as the cutter emerges from the workpiece and to prevent self-feeding.

Look at blowout. If you are cutting from edge to edge across the grain—whether making a dado across the face of the stock or a rabbet across the end of it—the outermost wood fibers won't be cut cleanly by the bit as it emerges from the wood. These fibers may simply curl back; but most often, the bit blows long splinters out of the edge, defacing it.

The most reliable preventive is backup material tucked tight against the workpiece edge. The bit never really emerges from the good wood. It passes from it into the backup.

And what is self-feeding? It's the same dynamic that's experienced in a climb cut. The bit pulls the work as it cuts. When you use the router table fence and feed the workpiece from right to left, you are enlisting this dynamic to help you maintain control of the work and keep it against the fence.

When you're using something like a miter gauge, however, the dynamic can be your foe. If your attention wanders or your grip isn't tight, it will pull the work and give you a less than square cut.

Rout a dado across a board using the sliding fence. The bit wants to pull the work to the right as it cuts. You may be able to grip the board firmly enough to resist, but if you fail, the cut (top) will be out of square. The solution to this problem is to use a stop clamped to the sliding fence to immobilize the workpiece.

What's the alternative to a miter gauge? Actually, there are several.

For some jobs I use the sliding fence. This is presented in the previous chapter, "Router Table Accessories." But for a great many jobs, I use the fence as the guide and a scrap block as a pusher.

Pacing the Cut

The pace at which you feed work is critical to the overall cut quality. There are a lot of variables in determining the right feed rate in each situation: the material being cut, the amount of material being removed, and the type of bit being used.

Excessive restraint is a very common problem. Unsure of how fast to feed the stock, and perhaps a little intimidated by the frenzied sound of the router, a woodworker will cautiously inch the workpiece through the cut. Because the feed is too slow, the cut surface is scorched and burnished.

A secondary penalty for a too-slow feed rate is a dull bit. Letting the bit "dwell" in the cut causes it to heat up, and heat will quickly dull even carbide. A couple of relatively short cuts at a very slow feed can toast a brand new bit. Once the bit is dull, of course, it won't cut well at any feed rate.

Too fast a feed rate, on the other hand, usually leads to roughness in the cut surface and lots of chipping and splintering on the margins.

What you have to do is develop a sense for feed rate that you can apply from job to job, situation to situation. You develop it through experience.

Router speed: A second aspect of pace is the speed at which the router spins the bit. While the need to slow large bits is commonly understood, many router users don't recognize the balance between bit speed and feed rate. To a degree, you can offset the effects of a slow feed by also slowing down the router's rpm.

If you want to make a stopped or blind slot, for example, you can dial back the rpm a little to compensate for the halting pace of such cuts. You don't just push the work through the cut, of course. Instead, you have to plunge it onto the bit to get the cut started, then begin advancing it. You get to the end, and you have to tip it up off the bit. The average feed rate is reduced, so to moderate the effects of dwell, back off on the rpm.

Routing Small Parts

Small workpieces are a challenge to rout. Right up front here, I want to emphasize the hazards. Maneuvering small pieces is tricky. Contact with the spinning bit can demolish them. Bad things can happen. If you are intent on working a small part, take all the precautions you can.

The *very first* thing is to assess, then reassess, the size of the work. Often, you can do the router cuts on an oversized piece, and then reduce its size. In terms of table-routing, a 6-inch-square part can seem awfully small for certain operations. Can you

A halting feed is sometimes the consequence of taking too big a bite. Trying to raise a panel in one pass, for example, can bog down a router pretty quickly. So you back off on your feed rate, and maybe even stop momentarily. As the rpm picks up, so does your feed rate. When you are done with the pass, you've got scorched spots, maybe a dwell mark or two. Balance the bite, the router speed, and the feed rate to get a quality cut.

make the required cuts in a 6-inch by 12-inch board, then cut it?

Assess your setup next. Be sure your bit has a zero-clearance housing.

Next, get yourself a work holder. Try gripping the workpiece with a wooden hand screw. Or attach a handle of some sort to the work with hot-melt glue. Use a grout trowel or a foam-bottomed stock pusher. Either will grip the part well enough to slide it around the cutter while absorbing the vibration. Your fingers will thank you.

Finally, let me remind you about "sweaty palms syndrome." Working with small pieces often triggers it in me. As I said before, when I hear that whisper in my ear—"Are you SURE you want to do this?!?"—I make it a point to listen.

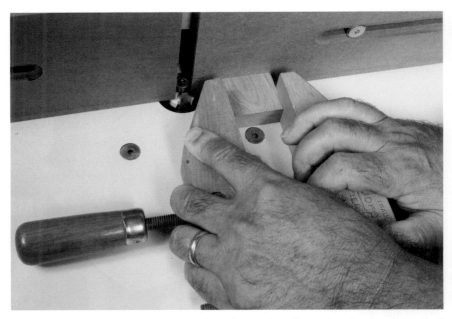

Here's a way to grasp a small workpiece for routing: Use a hand screw instead of your hand. The hand screw is big enough to hold and provides some mass to the piece being routed. Should it inadvertently contact the bit, the wooden jaw will be marked but certainly not ruined, and the bit will be fine.

Decorative Treatments

Decorative edge treatments are the most elementary router operations there are. Choose a piloted cutter, tighten it in the collet, set the desired cutting depth, and you can run all around your project with a design-unifying, aesthetically pleasing, decorative edge. It's that simple.

Though a fair number of woodworkers never get beyond this use of the router, the natural extension is to use the router to cut design-unifying, aesthetically pleasing decorative *grooves* on the work. And to use the router to produce moldings to trim furniture, frame pictures, and finish off a room. The techniques used go beyond edge treatments. But once mastered, they apply to all sorts of other decorative and functional router operations—even cutting joinery.

Profile Bits

There are two sorts of molding profiles: simple and complex. A simple molding is composed of a single basic shape. A complex molding combines two or more of the basic shapes. You can vary the size of the

The router is the ideal small-shop power tool for making moldings for picture frames, furniture, and even architecture. A vast array of cutters are available and economical. The tool can be used handheld on big work, and in a table for everything else.

Molding Profiles

Simple bits produce a wide variety of molding profiles

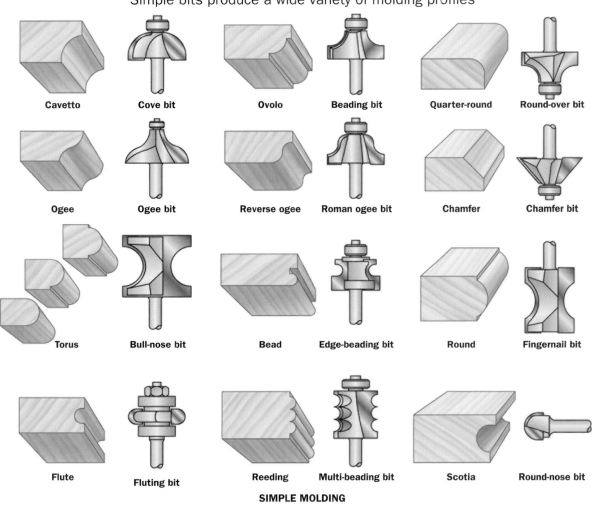

| Cavetto | Cove bit | Ovolo | Beading bit | Quarter-round | Round-over bit |

| Ogee | Ogee bit | Reverse ogee | Roman ogee bit | Chamfer | Chamfer bit |

| Torus | Bull-nose bit | Bead | Edge-beading bit | Round | Fingernail bit |

| Flute | Fluting bit | Reeding | Multi-beading bit | Scotia | Round-nose bit |

SIMPLE MOLDING

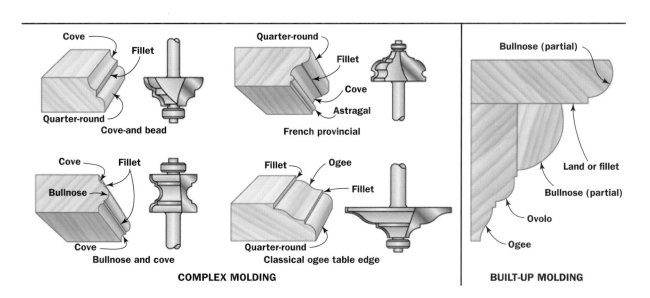

COMPLEX MOLDING   **BUILT-UP MOLDING**

Edge-profiling bits are made in an almost bewildering array of contours and sizes. This sampling includes matching multi-flute and multi-beading bits, ogee and Roman ogee bits, round-overs, coves, and chamfering bits, even a couple of multi-profile cutters. All of these have pilot bearings to control the cut. The bull-nose bits are among the few edge-profilers that lack pilots; use any of them in a router table, the smaller ones with an edge guide.

basic shapes, you can vary the way they are arranged, and you can vary the proportion of one shape to another.

As you devise a molding, remember first that it need not be a separate strip of wood in all situations. Quite often, a profile is cut directly on a furniture component—a tabletop or countertop, a drawer front, a case edge, a table leg, a base. The basic shapes can usually be produced with a single cutter, and there are cutters available to produce many complex shapes.

A molding with just one of the simple shapes can be very effective. Starting with a square edge, for example, you can knock off the corner, or arris, to create a chamfer. You can round the edge to make a quarter-round, or, going a bit further, make an ovolo, which is a quarter-round with a flat at each end of the arc.

On the other hand, a molding sometimes needs to be so big and have so many elements that it can't be cut on a single piece of wood. In this situation, it is created from several separate strips that are joined together.

Some examples of these constructions are shown in the drawing.

Take a look at the range of decorative bits on the market. Page through a well-illustrated bit catalog. Many decorative profile bits are available, including those that create complex profiles.

In making complex-profile moldings, you'll save some time if you use one of the latter bits. But you won't be able to customize the proportions of the individual forms. Too often, these combination bits blind us to many of our options. When I first started in woodworking, I'd look for a single bit that would cut a profile *close* to what I had in mind, rather than focusing on how I could produce the *specific* profile with commonplace single-form bits.

To make a specific profile may require passes with two or more cutters. You need to choose these cutters carefully, plan the order of cuts, and determine how you're going to support either the router or the work. Yeah, there are a few tricks here, but mostly it's straightforward routing.

I hope this chapter will serve as a jumping-off point for you in developing your own special patterns, or simply in using the basic bits you have to produce more complex combinations.

Most profiling bits can be sorted into one of two catagories: edge-forming bits and groove-forming bits.

Edge-Forming Bits

These bits are intended to shape the edges of boards, forming one of, or combinations of, the eight basic molding shapes.

In general, edge-forming bits are characterized by the presence of a pilot on the end of the bit. The pilot catches on the edge of the work and prevents the bit from setting out across the face of a board, forming a groove in the process. With a piloted bit, setup is pretty much limited to establishing the bit height. The width of the cut is governed by the pilot, and you can change bearing sizes or work with a fence or edge guide to reduce that.

Decorative Treatments   **141**

A very few bits in this category, such as the bull-nose bit, don't have a pilot bearing. These bits cut the entire workpiece edge, so there's no surface that a pilot could reference. While smaller sizes can be used in an edge-guide-equipped router, these bits usually are used in the router table.

Groove-Forming Bits

Odd as it may seem, the groove-forming profile bits, which are unfettered by pilots, are usually more versatile and flexible in routing trim and moldings. The truth is, the pilot is sometimes a hindrance.

For example, suppose you want to create a cove-and-bead profile of your own proportion on a board's edge. You rout the bead right along the board's edge with a beading or round-over bit. Now you are ready to nestle the cove in next to it. But the cove bit's pilot won't let you position the cove wherever you want. In this situation, the pilot's an impediment.

Bit Drawer

Furniture crafted in the late 17th century and on through the 18th century has some of the finest carved, shaped, and molded decoration. Think of cabriole legs, scalloped aprons, scrolled pediments, carved shells, and yes, multiform moldings. Though the original pieces were made entirely with hand tools, craftsmen of today who reproduce this period's furniture often work with power tools. Accurately reproducing the moldings has often required them to have cutters custom-ground.

Infinity Cutting Tools now has a collection of 11 bits that produce shapes common to William and Mary furniture. The style originated in England, then became popular in the American colonies. In particular, the Infinity bits cut the cornice, drawer divider, and waist moldings found on a highboy of the period.

Though based on furniture moldings, the bits collectively are called the Architectural Profile Set. You can buy them individually or as a set. Three of the bits have ball-bearing pilots, but the rest lack them. All have 1/2-inch shanks. Use them in a powerful, variable-speed, table-mounted router.

I like "country" furniture from the 18th and early 19th centuries, which borrowed freely from the formal styles—William and Mary, Queen Anne, and the like—but wasn't constrained by the their rigid patterns and order. For me, these bits are great for decorating all sorts of tables, cabinets, cupboards, and other pieces.

The selection of profiled grooving bits is somewhat limited. The size and proportion of profiles used for moldings range from very small on jewelry and keepsake boxes to very large in architectural applications. In contrast, profiled grooves tend to be intimate in size and proportion. Most common are core-box/round-nose bits and V-groovers. Some beading and ogee cutters are made without pilot bearings, allowing them to cut grooves.

You need a groove-forming bit, which doesn't have a pilot. You control the bit using a fence or an edge-guide or a template. The bit forms a groove with a profile.

Edge-Routing Techniques

Routing the edge of a board is pretty straightforward stuff. In most cases, you'll use a piloted bit. The pilot will control the cut width, and it will keep the router from drifting too far into the board. This doesn't mean that you can't go wrong.

Your success will be enhanced by your grasp of the fundamentals. And knowing some tricks can help you deal with unusual situations and problems.

Once you know what profile you want to use, you have to choose a router setup. The rule of thumb on this, articulated throughout this book, is that if you can manipulate the work comfortably on a table, use

the router table. But if the work is too large or too heavy or too awkward, clamp it down and move the router over it.

Which way do we go? Direction of feed is important when routing edge treatments. Look at the drawing *Feed Direction and Sequence.* It depicts the general-purpose feed direction. Move the tool counterclockwise around a board.

If you are unclear on this, just a little uncertain as to why you should do it this way, take a moment to page back to the section on feed direction, in the chapter "Router 101," page 29. The full explanation is there, complete with drawings.

Recall that when the router is held in its conventional orientation, the bit spins clockwise. If you let the router go its own way, the bit's rotation will drag the tool generally clockwise. The movement will be

Feed Direction and Sequence
Route your router correctly

Around the workpiece

Grain direction

Sweep in along end grain to start cut.

Feed counterclockwise...

Then sweep out of end grain, completing cut.

Edge-Routing Techniques

herky-jerky. As the cutting edges dig in, the router will gallop ahead but veer away from the guiding edge. As the cutting edges drift away from the edge, they'll lose traction and the router's advance will slow. You'll probably end up with an uneven or scalloped line of cut.

This is a "climb cut." The cutter wants to climb along the edge, out of the cut. In general, this is the wrong way to do it. The general rule is that you feed against the cutter's rotation. The bit wants to drive the router to the right, so you push or pull it toward the left. That way, the bit rotation forces the tool against the guide—be that a pilot on the bit (or a template guide bushing surrounding the bit), the edge guide mounted on the router, or a fence clamped to the workpiece. The operation is controllable: no jerks, no unexpected acceleration, no wandering.

The consequences of feeding the wrong way—of making a climb cut—are seldom dire, though they can be. I'll come back to the direness momentarily.

In some operations—and this is one of them—climb cutting has benefits. It can eliminate chipping and tearout along a long-grain edge. This is explained in the chapter "Router 101," page 29. When fed in the correct direction, the profile cutter sweeps across the wood and off the edge, sometimes splintering fibers out from the edge. The splintering can be exacerbated by gnarly, wavy grain that runs out the edge.

When fed in the climb-cut direction, the cutting edges chop into the edge and across the wood. No splintering. The upshot is that a very shallow initial pass in the climb-cut direction can be the key to eliminating tearout along an

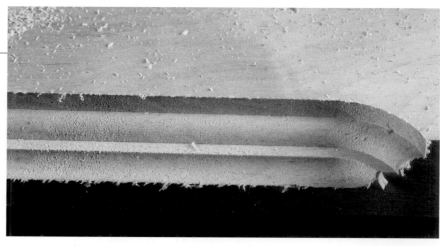

Lifting the router from the cut and seeing this can be heart-stopping. All too often, these splinters along the edges of a profiling cut extend into the wood. The fringe sands off, but the chips and cracks that scar the edge don't. Making a light pass in the climb-cut direction can prevent this, regardless of the gnarly nature of the stock.

edge. After a clean, chip-free cut has been initiated, you can expand its width with passes in the correct, controllable direction.

Now, about those dire consequences. Climbs cuts are dicey. Full of surprises. After you have some experience, you can use the technique with discretion. I would strongly advise you to use it only with a handheld router, NOT on the router table. Here's my reasoning:

When you're profiling an edge with the router in your hands, the router is shielding you from the bit. If during a climb cut it takes off, it will jerk and move away from you (depending, of course, on the movement in relation to where you are standing). Unless you are totally inattentive, it is unlikely to pull out of your grasp. The router and bit are going away from you, so the cutter isn't going to bite you.

But in a router-table setup, it's the workpiece that's between you and the cutter. In a climb cut, it's the workpiece that gets grabbed by the bit and moved. A climb cut on the router table CAN result in the workpiece being snatched from your grasp, and then your fingers can hit the spinning cutter. Let's not go there, eh? Don't climb-cut on the router table.

Where do we start (and end)? You can start a cut almost anywhere, at a corner or in the middle of a side or end. But often, it's prudent to envision the end of the cut before starting it.

If you are routing across end grain, the starting is easy; it's the ending that's tricky. You usually want to avoid routing across the end of a board and straight off because the bit blows splinters out of the long-grain edge. If you are continuing around the corner and along that long-grain edge, the splinters get milled away.

If you are routing completely around the workpiece, the starting point is established by the preferred terminus. You want to avoid finishing with that splintering across-the-end-grain exit. So start in the middle of the end grain. Then that is where you'll end. You'll avoid splinters where they can spoil the finished cut.

When you are forming a strip molding, you're routing just a single edge, generally a long-grain edge, so you rout end-to-end. Begin at one end and feed the router straight through the cut and off the opposite end of the workpiece. (On the router table, you set the piece against the fence, clear of the bit, and then slide it right to left along the fence until it clears the bit.)

How do we deal with that across-the-end-grain cut? One solution to the splintering is to clamp a scrap to the workpiece to back up the good edge. Another is to sweep off the end grain before the corner, then climb-cut in from the corner. This can take a little practice.

How do we start? As always, very carefully. You should rest the router on the work with the bit clear before switching it on. Let it ramp up to speed, and then begin the cut.

If possible, sweep into the edge as opposed to starting at a corner. If you start at a corner, there's a strong tendency for the cutter to slip back around the corner and pull you and the router down the wrong side of the work, going the wrong way, with all of the attendant adverse effects. Sweeping in allows you to ease into the cut, while developing momentum in the correct direction. It also avoids the tendency to burn where you stop or start. You can sweep back out any-time you want—to change your grip, to move the cord, or just to relax.

An alternative approach is to use an edge guide to override the pilot bearing. This doesn't work for every-one, but I've found an edge guide helpful in beginning and ending a cut along an edge. I'm able to guide the router with one hand and hold the edge guide firmly against the edge with the other. I get the guide square against the edge with the bit clear as I begin a cut, then keep the guide against the edge as the bit exits.

At the router table, the usual routine is to set up the fence tangent to the pilot bearing, then guide the workpiece along the fence to make the cut.

How fast do we go? Feed rate is a real trade-off issue. A high feed rate works the machine harder and can

Tearout and splintering (above) are likely to occur when exiting an end-grain cut, regardless of feed direction. One solution is to rout the end grain first, in the likelihood that the long-grain cuts will remove any evidence of the tearout (right).

produce wide ripples in the cut surface. Moving slower yields a smoother finish, but the bit may burn the wood if you move too slow.

There's no foot-per-second formula that will always work, because some

woods burn more quickly and some cut more easily. Push the router fast enough that the motor has to labor, but not so fast that it bogs down noticeably. If that rate produces a rippled cut, then slow down a little to

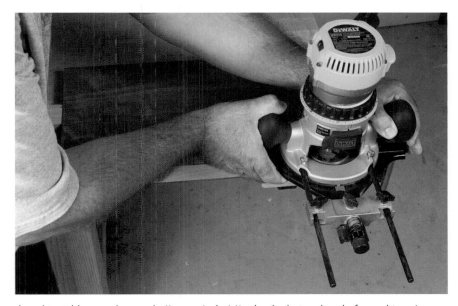

An edge guide can give you better control at the beginning and end of an edge cut, so a piloted cutter doesn't roll around the corner inadvertently. It just takes a bit of practice. A hand on the edge guide itself keeps both it and the router in contact with the workpiece as it slides into and out of the cut. Moreover, an edge guide allows you to use unpiloted cutters to make edge cuts.

get a smoother cut. If you slow down too much, you'll notice that the wood will start to burn. If you can't get a reasonably smooth cut without burning, try working in short, sweeping strokes. That will keep the bit cooler. If that doesn't do the trick, your cutter is probably dull. Sharpen or replace it.

How do we control the router? Tip and wobble are the bugbears of edge-routing. When you are routing an edge with a piloted cutter, the machine is more off the work than on. At a corner, only about a quarter of the base is supported on the work. It's all too easy to let up just a little on the inboard handle, allowing the router to tip off the work. Often, you recover and no harm is really done. But snipes and ripples and outright gouges frequently result.

Here are a couple of tricks to help.

Make and use an offset baseplate. A plan for one is in the chapter "Jigmaking," page 43. This simple teardrop-shaped jig expands the baseplate, so much more of the

A offset baseplate tames the tippiness of a router making an edge cut. Hold down on the offset knob to keep the router upright, and feed the tool along the workpiece with one of its knobs.

overall baseplate area is resting on the work. It has an extra knob so you can exert more downforce on the work, too. This jig is especially useful on plunge routers, which tend to be even more unsteady in edge-routing situations than fixed-based machines, which generally have lower centers of gravity.

Use the second trick when the workpiece is fully on the bench (as opposed to hanging off an edge of the bench). Attach a scrap of the working stock to the outboard portion of the

baseplate with carpet tape. When the router is resting on the work, with its bit hogging away at the work's edge, the support block will keep the router flat and square. It can't tumble off the work, even it you let go of it.

Routing Trim for Furniture

In terms of technique, making molding is making molding, whether it will be to embellish a piece of furniture or to trim the interior of a house. But as a general rule, the furniture molding tends to be smaller in section than architectural trim. The upshot is that it's easier to make furniture moldings with a router.

Bear in mind that you may not be able to produce the moldings you want using the router exclusively. A large-radius cove, for example, is beyond the router—do it on the table saw. Don't frustrate yourself trying to do what's not possible. Use other tools as appropriate in making your moldings.

Single-bit profiles are easiest to produce, of course. You have one setup. You may need to stage the cut if it is a heavy one, but few router operations

Stick a scrap the same thickness as the workpiece to your router's baseplate with carpet tape. You can feed the router along the edge without concern that it'll tip or wobble, compromising the cut. Here the work is shimmed above the benchtop, so a scrap of the shim is added to the support block stuck to the baseplate.

Magic on the Edge

How often do you do this? Every exposed edge on a project gets routed with a 1/4-inch round-over, your most-used bit. Is this your trademark?

If it is, *give it a rest!* It's old and tired. Take another look in the bit drawer. You've got a lot of bits, but you need a kick in the seat of your creativity. Here it comes. A few less-than-ordinary edge treatments.

A nose with a crease (top) is just a little different for a tabletop, desktop, chest top, or shelf. Use a 3/8-inch round-over to radius the upper edge, and a 3/8-inch beading bit to profile the bottom edge and introduce the

The appearance of a chest or bookcase can be altered by merely switching the orientation of the decorative edge. You can cut the main pattern into the top edge, or into the bottom edge. Though these certainly look different, both have the same edge contour.

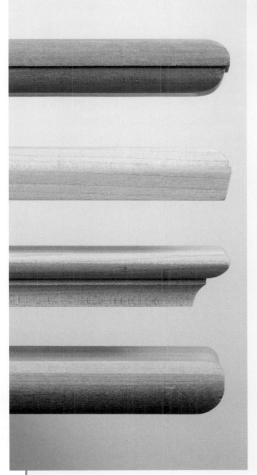

fillet between the radii. You don't even need to switch bits, since the only difference between round-over and beading bits is the pilot bearing. Swap pilot bearings between the cuts, using a 3/8-inch-diameter bearing on the bottom-edge cut instead of the standard 1/2-inch used for the top-edge cut.

The subtly beveled shelf edge (next down) was created using a 1-inch dovetail bit and a 3/8-inch round-over bit on the router table. You bevel the edge first, then round-over the acute angle along the top edge. If you don't want a distinct crease between the profiles, a little sanding is all that's needed to blend them.

The most involved of the four edge treatments is a cove-and-bead (third down). This requires three cuts

on the router table. Use a 3/8-inch round-over bit first. Make several passes, raising the bit slightly for each, until you have a 7/17-inch-wide fillet below the quarter-round profile. Switch to a 3/4-inch core-box and make a pass to create the cove profile. Leave a 1/8-inch fillet between the two forms. Finish the edge by making a pass along the top edge with a 1/8-inch round-over bit. Using the same basic approach, you can change the edge's appearance by using different-sized bits to alter the profile proportions.

Finally, we have the two-radii round-over (bottom). It's softer than the usual 1/4-inch round-over treatment top and bottom. Make one pass with a 1/2-inch round-over bit and one with a 1/4-inch bit.

are easier. As I've said, however, you ought to try at least some more-advanced work—complex forms produced through multiple cuts and built-up moldings.

The work can be done with the router handheld or mounted in a table. I usually do it at the router table. The workpieces are often hard to secure to a benchtop without hampering the router's travel, but they are manageable on the table. You can use any size bit in a table-mounted router, and some of the bits you must use are *large*.

So get started. The most understandable way, I think, is to give you some specific examples.

In analyzing the profile you need to cut, lay the bits themselves on the layout and line them up with the profile. This will help you determine which bits to use, how to orient the work for making the cuts, and in what order they have to be made.

Try This!

When routing any molding, work with a broad piece of stock if at all possible. The extra width gives you something to hold on to, something for hold-downs to bear on. And because the cut is backed up by the excess stock, the wide stock is less likely to break up as you rout it.

After completing the profile, rip it from the stock. Don't risk damaging your profile by trapping it between the saw blade and the rip fence. Instead, orient the good edge so it will be to the left of the blade, as shown.

Ogee Moldings

The ogee is a common profile, seen in a range of proportions. Look in any bit catalog, and you'll find at least one ogee bit, but more likely several. (You probably will also see "ogee" bits that cut profiles that are *not* ogees.)

What you won't see is a bit to cut a BIG ogee; only one manufacturer that I know of (Infinity) has that.

The typical furniture project that calls for an ogee profile features it on the edges of tops for tables, desks, or chests. It may be used as a modest-

Ogee Profiles

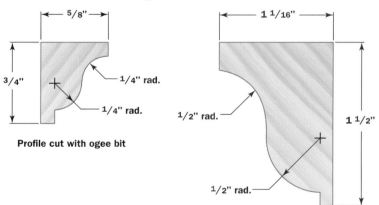

Profile cut with ogee bit

Profile cut with core-box and round-over bits.

148

scale molding at the waist or base of a case piece. These embellishments can be produced with commonplace ogee (or Roman ogee) bits. Pick the bit, chuck it in the router, and run the tool along the edges to be profiled. Done!

Once in a while, a project needs a larger-scale ogee. Here your best option is to use a round-over bit and a core-box bit to cut the molding in several steps. Working with an actual-size drawing of the profile, pick the two bits that will cut the convex and concave portions of the ogee curve. Cut a blank that's oversized in width and length, and rabbet the long edge to remove the bulk of the waste. Rout the convex cut with a round-over bit and the concave cut with a core-box. A little sanding to blend the two cuts into a continuous S-curve, and you are done.

Commonplace ogee bits profile stock that's $3/4$ inch thick or less, but if you need a large-scale ogee, you can produce it in several steps, using a large-diameter core-box bit and a large-radius round-over bit to form the curves.

Cut the cove of the ogee with a core-box bit. In positioning the fence, set it so the bit's vertical cutting edge just grazes the bottom of the rabbet. Set the bit height to round the rabbet's inside corner. Use a zero-clearance facing on the fence.

The ogee profile is completed using a round-over bit with its pilot bearing removed. As you can see, the bit must be hyperextended to make the cut. The trick is to adjust the bit to blend its cut into the previous one. The better you align the cuts, the less sanding you'll have to do. The width of the fillet is controlled by the fence position.

Cove-and-Bead Molding

Here's another commonplace profile used around the waist and the base on a case piece. Though it's complex rather than simple, you can buy single bits to cut it in one pass. But look at the photo, and compare the stock bit's profile with those produced using separate bits to form the cove and the bead.

The routine for cutting the profile with separate bits doesn't vary, regardless of the proportions. Work with a 2- to 3-inch-wide piece of stock. Keep it flat on the router table top for both cuts.

Cut the bead first, using a common round-over bit. Though the bit has a bearing, it's better to use the fence to guide the cut. The fence gives you better control of the work, and it gives you something to clamp a couple of hold-downs to. Make the cut in several passes, increasing the bit height between passes. If the radius is small, the cut is a long reach for the typical bit, but you should be able to complete it without too much difficulty.

The cove is next. Switch to a core-

A molding produced with a cove-and-bead bit is clean but bland. Using a core-box of one size to cut the cove and a round-over of a different size to make the bead requires more work, but it yields a far more dynamic profile. You can make the cove large, the bead small, or vice versa.

To cut the bead with a typical round-over bit, the bit has to be extended just about as far as it can be. Make several passes to work up to the final cutting depth.

Cove-and-Bead Profiles

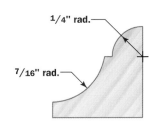

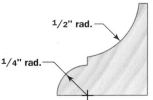

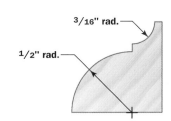

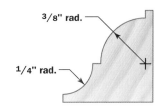

The cove is cut with a core-box bit, using the fence to guide the work over the bit. Set the bit height and the fence by sighting across the bit to the workpiece.

Bit Drawer

Cutting complex moldings like crown moldings on a single piece of solid wood is what this set is for. Router woodworkers like me usually make such moldings as built-up assemblies. We'll cut the cove on one stick, the profile above it on another stick, and the profile below on a third. Then we'll glue them together.

Lonnie Bird feels this is inappropriate. A well-known furniture-maker, teacher, and author, Bird specializes in exquisite reproductions of 18th-century furniture—highboys, tea tables, corner cabinets, slant-front desks. To him, the molding has to be a single solid piece, and he cuts it on the shaper.

A unique shaper capability is reversability. You can turn a shaper-cutter over and cut into the top of an edge by reversing the direction of rotation (a good shaper can run counterclockwise and clockwise—forward and reverse). This feature allows you to cut a profile into otherwise inaccessible edges. To adapt this capability for the router, Bird inverted the cutting heads of the bits in this set, sold by CMT. While the bead and ogee profiles aren't unusual, the inverted design and the diameter of the cutting heads enable the bits to put the profiles on the top and bottom edges of a large blank that's already been coved.

While the inverted bits are innovative, the centerpiece of the set, especially when you lift the lid on the wooden storage box, is the cove cutter. It's a heavy disk with bulky carbide cutting tips used in the table saw, and you cut coves with it in the usual way: Feed the workpiece across the blade at an angle, guided by a straightedge clamped to the saw table. The cutter reduces stress on the saw and produces an easily sanded finish.

box bit. You want a 1/16-inch-wide fillet between the bead and the cove. Set the bit elevation and the fence by sighting across the bit to the workpiece. Then rout the cove.

Rip the molding from the working stock.

Three-Part Crown

A substantial crown molding is a good example of a built-up molding. The crown often is made up of three separate pieces. The top and bottom elements are easily done using the router. The central cove has a large radius, and this element you will have to cut on the table saw.

Begin with the bull-nose molding. Cut the profile using two round-over bits. Do the top edge first, using a 1/4-inch-radius round-over bit. Then rout the bottom edge with a 5/8-inch-radius bit. Make both cuts on the router table, and guide the stock against a fence as you make the cuts.

The bead molding at the bottom is cut on the router table with an edge-beading bit that forms a 3/16-inch-radius bead. Most such bits have a shoulder on the cutter that will form the fillet below the bead on the molding. Rather than working with a flimsy strip, cut the profile on the edge of a 2- to 4-inch-wide piece of 1/2-inch stock. After routing the profile, rip the molding from the stock.

As noted, the central cove must be cut on the table saw. After the cove molding has been cut, sanded, and beveled as required, a triangular strip must be cut to back the cove and hold it at the proper cant. The three moldings—and the backup strip—can be glued up before the crown is installed.

Three-Part Crown Profile

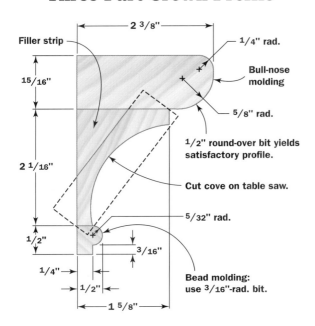

- Filler strip
- 2 3/8"
- 15/16"
- 1/4" rad.
- Bull-nose molding
- 5/8" rad.
- 1/2" round-over bit yields satisfactory profile.
- 2 1/16"
- Cut cove on table saw.
- 5/32" rad.
- 1/2"
- 3/16"
- 1/4"
- 1/2"
- Bead molding: use 3/16"-rad. bit.
- 1 5/8"

Here's a three-part crown assembly, almost ready for gluing up. The cove profile, produced on the table saw, is supported by triangular blocking cut from a secondary wood. It is flanked by a large bull-nose profile (right) and a small bead profile (left).

Picture-Frame Moldings

The leap from furniture moldings to picture-frame stock is really a short hop. Making picture-frame molding is a great way to save money and use offcut material. You can also use exotic or figured wood. Many pleasing profiles can be produced on the router table using the same bits you use on your furniture pieces—round-overs, chamfers, bull-noses, and coves (or core-boxes).

Look at existing frames in your home, and do some doodling with a bit catalog (or a few of your bits) right at hand. Start with some simple profiles. With practice, your repertoire will expand.

The only critical dimensions in a molding profile are the width and depth of the rabbet. Minimum rabbet width should be 1/4 inch. Minimum depth should be 1/2 inch. To calculate the required depth for a particular application, measure the thickness of the materials—glass, matting, and so forth—that go into the frame, and then add 1/8 inch for the fasteners.

Take advantage of your router and decorative bits to produce unique and attractive picture-frame moldings. Perhaps you'll start with simple moldings—just a strip of stock with profiled edges and a rabbet. Eventually, you'll progress to built-up moldings, milling profiles on matching or contrasting woods and gluing together two or more strips to form impressive frames.

Architectural Moldings

Those fancy strips of wood that we tack over the cracks are really designed to accent the lines of a structure by creating parallel lines of highlight and shade. The effect is obtained by creating combinations of grooves and bevels to reflect light differently. The variety of moldings available from lumberyards attests to the fact that no one molding will suffice in all applications. But when you start to work with shapes in your own custom projects, you're bound to run into a situation where you just can't find the right shape or size in just the right wood. You gotta make your own.

If it's a question of a standard profile cut into a special wood, check your catalogs. You may be able to buy a cutter that will produce exactly what you're looking for.

But if you're looking for a shape that's out of the ordinary, you'll have to go a little further. Look for cutters that will combine to make the profile you want. Consider building up a molding from several separate strips, each with its own simple or complete profile. The drawing and photo show three-part trim I've used around windows and doors.

Let me warn you up front that this can be ticklish work. It's time-consuming. Make a goof on the fourth pass, and you've wasted the time it took to do the first three.

If you're a "time is money" person, sub out the molding production to a millwork shop that has a sticking machine. Pay for the custom cutters, if that's what the profiles you want require. Chances are, though, that if the shop is a busy one, its inventory of custom profiles is extensive, and you'll be able to find something

Bits especially designed for routing architectural moldings may be worthwhile to buy, especially if your project justifies their expense. Most are simply called face-molding bits. They typically produce a 1- to 1 1/2-inch-wide, multiform profile in a single pass. Some of the contours are impossible to duplicate with commonplace single-form bits.

suitable. Moreover, the shop will probably get a better price on the trim stock than you could. Each stick will be molded in a single pass, and you won't have the chips and frustration to deal with.

On the other hand, if you're doing one room, then creating some one-of-a-kind moldings to trim it out is something you can reasonably do at the router table. Because architectural moldings tend to be far longer than anything you'd make for a furniture piece, you'll find them harder to support as you feed. Here are a few suggestions for more consistent work.

Don't try to hold a long, flexible strip down on the tabletop and firmly against the cutter while the end is swaying back and forth in

space. Support the ends of your work. Auxiliary tables or even roller stands can make your life a lot easier.

You can also use all the help you can get in holding your work against the table and cutter. You can easily make a variety of hold-downs; see the chapter "Router Table Accessories," page 101, for plans. Most of these hold-downs can be used to help guide your stock for molding work. In most situations, however, you'll find that the best setup is to use two featherboards: one holding the work to the fence, and one on the fence holding down. The greatest thing about featherboards is that if you set them steep enough, they're pretty effective at stopping kickback.

The feed rate is important. If you

Casing with Backboard

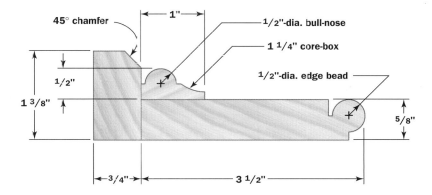

feed the stock too fast, the cut will be rippled. And each time you stop the feed—to reposition your hands—the bit will burnish a spot on the molding. Some of these defects don't show up unless the light hits them just right (meaning the light that hits them just after you've installed the molding). With a short piece, you can usually feed the stock with one continuous movement. With a long piece, get a helper. As you reach the end of your range, the helper can begin to pull the stock, keeping it moving slowly while you reposition yourself for the next push.

Relatively simple to produce with a table-mounted router, this three-part casing is a handsome step away from the trim stocked at home centers. The full bead on the foundation casing is cut in two passes with an edge-beading bit. A bed molding, produced using a small bull-nose bit and a small core-box, breaks up the expanse of the foundation casing and raises the elevation. The back-band sharply defines the perimeter of the assembled molding. It has a chamfered edge.

Architectural applications require moldings 7 feet or more long. Use featherboards to keep the stock against tabletop and fence, and outfeed stands to support the ends of the stock. That way you can concentrate on keeping the stock moving steadily across the cut.

Bit Drawer

With this one bit, the *Multiform,* you can turn out dozens of different molding profiles. Wow! Simply by adjusting the bit height and fence settings, making multiple passes, and altering the angle of attack, you can produce a welter of magnificent moldings. The bit catalog had a drawing of them.

Believe that? Then I have a bridge I'd like to sell you.

My experience with the bit is that you can mill a variety of profiles, but not nearly as many as the catalog hype implies. Few of the "almost unlimited possibilities" shown are anything but heavy, steep, and extraordinarily busy, and the hype underplays the patience and ingenuity necessary to use this bit productively.

The multiform bits range up to 2 inches in diameter. Some versions have a pilot bearing, others

don't. All should be used exclusively in router tables, with 2- (or more) horsepower routers. The larger diameter bits should be run at reduced speed. I personally would invest the $35 to $70 that this bit costs in some basic profile bits—round-overs, coreboxes, ogees and Roman ogees, beading, or bull-noses. With them, you'll be able to create far more different profiles than you can with a Multiform.

Template-Guided Work

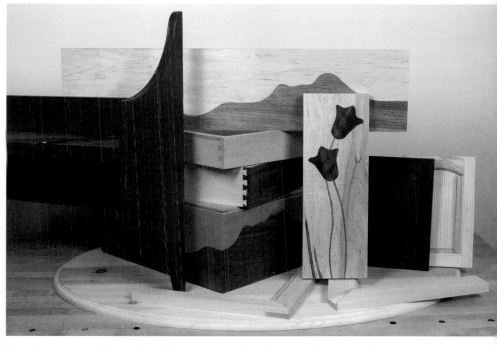

Templates play a vital role in a wide range of woodworking operations. Use them to shape parts, such as the oval tabletop, the ends of a wall shelf, or curved rails and panels for doors. Cut joints like dovetails and mitered half-laps, even complementary-curve edge joints. For inlay, templates are essential.

A template is most often thought of as a quick and easy way to duplicate shapes like circles, squares, or even letters. That's one of the uses, but there are many others.

The typical template is a durable wood or plastic or metal pattern. When the router, fitted with either a guide bushing or a pattern bit, is run along the edge of the template, the bit makes a cut in the exact contour of the template. When consistency from part to part is required, use a template.

Commercial dovetail jigs, for example, depend on guide bushings or pattern bits to guide the cuts. Every cut has to be reproduced accurately and consistently if the dovetails are to come together successfully. The template system virtually guarantees that they will.

In a production setting, templates are used to create stacks and piles of identical parts. Clamp a template to the rough-sawn part, then guide the router along the template (or feed the work past a pattern bit in a table-mounted router). The bit mills the workpiece to the same contour as the

template. And every part cut using the template will be identical.

Now you may not need *stacks* of identical parts, but if you want to make just eight identical back legs for a set of four chairs, it's worth the trouble to make a template.

Woodworkers often make patterns just for layout. Why not spend an extra half an hour, and make that layout pattern a precise template? You can even slot the template so you can use it to rout the mortises, too.

Templates can be used to guide

joinery cuts other than dovetails and mortises. You can use a template to guide dado and grooving cuts, to cut laps, and even to control a miter-gauge-like jig for cutting box joints on the router table.

Inlay is done with relative ease using a router and a template.

Once you try the technique, you'll realize how easy and reliable it is. The potential is tremendous.

Three Guidance Setups

Three common template systems are used in the home shop.

The first is designed to guide the router's base. The second uses a guide bushing attached to the base of the router. The bushing guides the tool along the edge of the template. The third system uses a ball bearing on the bit as the guide that rides along the template edge. There are pros and cons to each system.

Guiding the Base

A template that guides the router base allows the router to ride directly on the stock surface. This not only affords the best support and accuracy of depth, but it allows you to cut with the full length of your bit's cutting edges, rather than having to reach past the thickness of a template.

A less obvious advantage is that the template needn't be finely finished. The large radius of the router base can ride a neatly band-sawn edge without translating every little saw mark into the cut. But this also means it overrides fine details.

Drawbacks? The need to scale the template to the size of the router's base can be one. You can't, for example, cut an inside corner tighter than the radius of the base. The template has to be bigger or smaller than the shape you want to cut by the radius of the baseplate. This size difference can make clamping the

template to some projects difficult to impossible.

You can moderate the scale problem somewhat if you can use a laminate trimmer for your cut instead of a full-sized router. The trimmer usually has a baseplate diameter in the 3 1/2-inch range, rather than the 6- to 7-inch range.

Using Pattern or Flush-Trimming Bits

The simplest form of template-guided routing is done with either a flush-trimming bit or a pattern bit. Either has a pilot bearing matching the bit's cutting diameter. On a flush-trimming bit, the bearing is on the tip of the bit. On a pattern bit, the bearing is on the shank, right above the flutes.

Make the template (or pattern) exactly the shape you want (limited only by the bit diameter, as I'll explain

Using a template to guide the router base has its advantages. The template's edge doesn't need to be perfectly smooth, since the base tends to ride over minor irregularities without telegraphing them into the cut. Moreover, because the template is beside, rather than beneath, the router, it doesn't steal any cutting depth from the tool.

Bit Drawer

Any bit with a pilot bearing mounted on the shank is a pattern bit. The bearing rides along the edge of a pattern, while the cutting edge trims the edge of the work or plows a groove in it.

Pattern bits are available in ever-increasing variety. And it isn't surprising. All the bit maker has to do is add a bearing to the shank. The only limitation is that the cutter diameter has to be enough larger than the shank diameter to accommodate a bearing. A 3/4-inch straight bit with a 1/2-inch shank can be converted to a pattern bit with a bearing. A 1/2-inch straight on the same-sized shank cannot.

If you flip through a current catalog, you'll find all manner of groove-forming profile cutters with shank-mounted bearings: ogees, beading bits, cove-and-bead cutters, core-boxes.

When you use a pattern bit, the template is placed between the router and the workpiece (with a handheld router, this means on top of the workpiece). For the bit's shank-mounted bearing to ride along the template edge, the bit has to be fully extended. When it projects well below the work, as here, it's a hazard.

shortly). Attach the template to the workpiece with carpet tape, hot-melt glue, clamps, even nails or screws. Scoot around the template with a router and pattern bit, and the workpiece will be a duplicate of the template.

In some cases, the first of the actual parts can double as the pattern. If you expect to toss the template as soon as the actual parts are all made, this approach is sensible. All the time you invest goes into actual parts; none goes into the template making alone. And overall, the time spent is probably reduced slightly.

If you use a pattern bit—the one with the shank-mounted pilot—you orient the work with the template on top. If you use a flush-trimmer, orient the work with the template on the bottom. In either case, you should cut the workpiece to within 1/16 inch of final size before routing. Also, be aware of what is under the workpiece as you rout. Don't cut into your workbench by mistake.

The pilot bearing of a flush-trimming bit is at the tip, so the template must be under the workpiece. The template is the same size and contour as the finished workpiece. Accommodate different thicknesses of working stock by altering the bit height. Only the working portion of the bit is exposed.

Using Guide Bushings

A guide bushing, sometimes called a template guide or a guide collar, is a lot like a big washer with a short tube stuck in it. The bushing fits into the bit opening in the baseplate, and the bit projects through the tube. In use, the tube—called the collar—catches the edge of the template. The bit makes a cut that, though slightly offset from the template, matches the template perfectly. Details transfer better than with the base-guided system.

What's tricky about using guide bushings is the size difference between the collar and the cutter.

When routing with a guide bushing, the bushing rides against a template on top of the workpiece. The template must be offset by the difference between the bit and bushing diameters.

Outside Diameter (O.D.)	Inside Diameter (I.D.)	Collar Length
5/16"	1/4"	5/32"
3/8"	9/32"	5/16"
7/16"	11/32"	5/32"
1/2"	13/32"	5/16"
5/8"	17/32"	9/16"
3/4"	21/32"	9/16"
1"	25/32"	3/8"
1 1/4"	1 1/32"	7/16"

Because the collar is larger than the cutter, you must offset the template from the line of cut. The amount of offset varies with the combination of bushing size and bit diameter.

The bushing's stated size is the collar's outside diameter. The table lists some common guide bushing sizes. There *are* limits to what's available. In selecting a bushing for a job, three dimensions are significant.

Outside diameter is, of course, the diameter of the collar.

Inside diameter is that of the collar. You almost always use a bushing with an inside diameter larger than the bit diameter. (Yes, in some isolated cases, like routing dovetails with a half-blind jig, you use a collar that's smaller than the cutter.) You need clearance between the inside of the collar and the bit. Usually you'll use a collar that's at least 1/8 inch bigger than the cutter.

Collar length is the projection of the collar. Your template has to be thick enough to avoid having the collar drag on the workpiece surface. For a standard 5/8-inch bushing, for example, the template must be 5/8 inch thick because the collar length is 9/16 inch. I know from experience that your impulse is to trim the collar with a hacksaw or at the grinder to just under 1/4 inch. Then you can use thin plywood or hardboard for

templates. But the manufacturer's rationale for increasing the collar length as the bushing size increases is to provide a more stable guide surface.

Hold off on modifying your guide collars until you've got some experience. In time, you may find that you actually favor 1/2-inch and 3/4-inch material for templates.

Offset. This is the distance from the cutting edge to the guide edge. You can calculate it more easily than you can measure it. Subtract the bit diameter from the bushing diameter (yes, the collar's outside diameter) and divide by 2.

Here's an example: You are using a 3/4-inch-diameter bushing and a 3/8-inch-diameter bit. Subtracting 3/8 from 3/4 leaves 3/8. Divide by two and you have 3/16. That's the offset: 3/16 inch.

If you have laid out a line you want to cut, you must offset the line 3/16 inch to get the template contour. If it's straight, offsetting it is easy, of course. If it's curvy, offsetting it is tricker, as we'll see in the next section. If you're making an internal template—for routing a mortise, for example—add the offset to each guiding edge of your template. Thus the opening needed to make a 1-inch by 3-inch mortise must measure 1 3/8 inches by 3 3/8 inches.

Because of offset, making the template does take extra time. If you only have one or two pieces to shape, and the precise contours aren't all that important, it may not be worth the effort. But routers can do very precise work when guided by a template. When you have an especially fancy or intricate cut to make in an expensive piece of stock, it's worthwhile to make a very precise template for only one use. It's not uncommon to spend

Calculating the Offset
It's easy when you know how

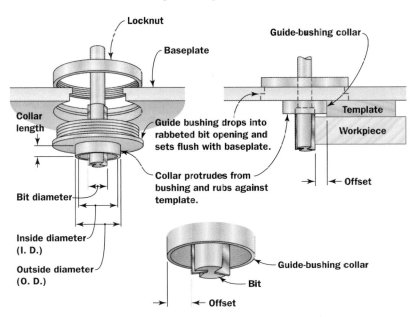

Locknut

Baseplate

Guide-bushing collar

Collar length

Guide bushing drops into rabbeted bit opening and sets flush with baseplate.

Template

Workpiece

Bit diameter

Collar protrudes from bushing and rubs against template.

Inside diameter (I. D.)

Outside diameter (O. D.)

Offset

Guide-bushing collar

Bit

Offset

plates, one of which has an opening scaled for bushings. Many dedicated plunge routers have an adapter for these bushings that closes down the base opening when it's screwed in place.

That lock ring is another drawback, at least to me. It can be difficult to get your fingers inside the router base to tighten it. I often use pliers for the job. Removing the motor from the base can help. So, too, can removing an adapter. Install the bushing in it, then reattach it to the router.

Bosch has a unique bayonet system that I really like. Push a button inside the base to mount and release the bushing. No lock rings to deal with, and no impediments to changing guides. But it only works on Bosch routers.

several hours making the template, and only a couple of minutes making the actual cut.

Bushings. While a few routers use brand-specific guide bushings, most manufacturers have simply adopted Porter-Cable's bushings. This style sets into the bit opening in the baseplate. It's secured with a lock ring threaded onto the bushing from inside the base. A big plus of this universal design, to me, is that you can buy guide bushings from a variety of sources. PC makes steel bushings, but you can buy brass ones (which are less hazardous to your bits) from many sources. In addition, you can usually get an adapter for any router that accommodates these bushings. This one style, then, can work on all your routers, regardless of brand or model.

The system does have a drawback or two. The PC-style bushing requires a 1 3/16-inch opening in the baseplate, which is small. As a consequence, many current routers come with two base-

A guide bushing is a short tube with a flange that fits into the router base. This assortment of guide bushings gives you an idea of the range of sizes available, as well as the different mounting systems. A few bushings are attached to the base with screws (lower right); these are usually required on plunge routers. Bosch uses bayonet-mount bushings that are easy to install and remove from the router (upper right). The most common "universal" system uses a threaded lock ring to secure the bushing. Most routers are designed to use these bushings, which are available in steel and brass.

Which System to Use?

Each guide system has its advantages and disadvantages. The more template work you do, the more likely it is that you'll have occasion to use them all.

The base-guided approach is useful when you don't need great accuracy or detail. You can knock out a template fairly quickly, since you don't have to worry too much about the quality of the guide edge.

Both guide bushings and pattern bits can guide far more intricate cuts. The only limit on the curves you can follow is the diameter of the bushing or the bearing.

Pattern bits (including flush-trimmers) can be used easily with table-mounted routers. This is often a big advantage with small work-

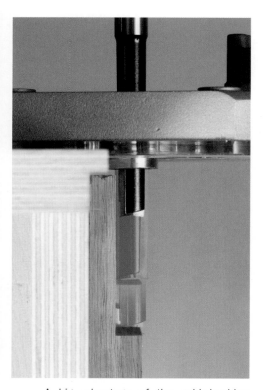

A big advantage of the guide-bushing system is that it allows you to stage a cut with a plunge router. The guide doesn't change position as you plunge the bit progressively deeper.

pieces. The template can be fitted with fences to position the blank and a toggle clamp or two to secure it. Use a starting pin to help you initiate the cut. Then rout as if you are making a cut with a piloted bit (which is really what you are doing).

With some router table setups (but not all), you can use guide bushings. You reap the same benefits as you do using pattern bits.

Guide bushings offer several advantages over piloted bits. Most important is that the guide is in a fixed position. Regardless of the depth-of-cut setting, the guide is next to the baseplate.

Thus, you can make plunge cuts. Set your plunge router on the work, guide bushing against the template edge, then plunge the bit to begin the cut. This allows you to make internal cuts guided by a template—mortises, for example. Once the cut is initiated, you can deepen it progressively, on the fly.

With flush-trimming and pattern bits, on the other hand, the guide bearing changes position with every bit-height adjustment. A pattern bit's bearing is above the cutter. Unless the cutting edges are very short or the template very thick, you can't manage a shallow cut. Staging cuts—that is, beginning with a shallow cut, then plunging deeper and then deeper still—is tricky, again because the bearing moves with the cutter.

With a flush-trimmer, the cut has to go all the way through the workpiece from the get-go. The bearing is below the cutter, remember, so the template is on the bottom of the work.

The guide-bushing system allows you to make passes around the same template with several different bits.

For example, you could run a groove around a template with a 1/2-inch straight bit. Then switch to a 1/4-inch straight, and cut slightly deeper, right in the center of the 1/2-inch groove, forming a stepped groove. Using a template enables you to position the grooves right where you want them.

Lastly, because guide bushings work in conjunction with your regular router bits, you save money. No special bits to buy. Moreover, you have a much wider variety of bits. You can use any groove-forming profile bit in a guide bushing.

The drawback of the guide-bushing system? The bit isn't always centered in the bushing. That isn't good. The error lies in the router and it can be fugitive, shifting in degree and direction as you adjust the depth-of-cut.

The problem seems most pronounced in fixed-base routers with a motor that rotates in the base to adjust the cut depth. But any router in which the motor drops into a base that's tightened around it to prevent it from moving is subject to some lateral shifting as the base clamp is opened and closed.

Alignment of the plate on the base contributes to the problem. The plates don't have registration pins, and typically they're attached with panhead screws. Loosen the screws and you can shimmy the plate.

The bushings themselves can also contribute. A few years ago, at the behest of a manufacturer's product manager, I measured about a dozen of my own guide bushings with dial calipers and discovered that their diameters varied as much as a 16th of an inch. The smallest was loose in the standard bit opening, the largest an extremely tight fit.

The motor-to-base looseness is greatly reduced in most current models, which have better, tighter depth-adjustment systems. And at least two router manufacturers provide centering cones to help you align the baseplate concentric to the bit axis. The upshot is that the accuracy possible with guide bushings is much improved.

So which system will you use? I'm betting that at one time or another you're going to use each of them.

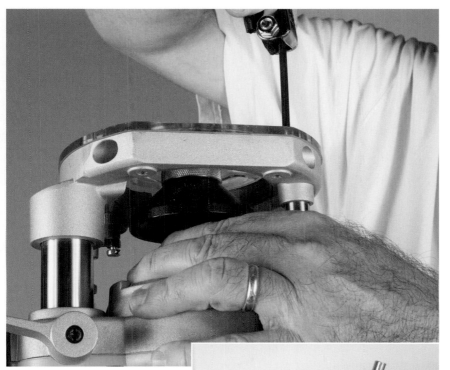

Centering mandrels, available as accessories from Bosch and DeWalt, enable you to align a guide bushing so it is concentric to the bit axis. Loosen the router baseplate's mounting screws and install the bushing. Fit the mandrel into the collet (inset), then fit the motor into the router base so the mandrel projects into the bushing. The loose baseplate will shift as the bushing centers itself on the mandrel. Tighten the screws.

Making Templates

As in other aspects of woodworking, experience makes template work easier. When you are making a template for the first time, it's beneficial to visualize the end process, the cut you'll make with the template, *before* you actually make that template.

Consider all the possibilities, including alternatives to using a template. Visualize all aspects of the process (and sure, it's tough to visualize an operation you've never done). With experience, you'll do a lot of this analysis subconsciously. You'll tackle a job quickly, without a lot of conscious planning, and it will work out perfectly. But you'll also recognize those occasional special instances that *do* require conscious planning—and perhaps some experimentation—to formulate a workable, successful approach.

Key questions:

■ What router and bit and guide system will you use?

■ How many parts will you make with the template?

■ How will you fix the template to the workpiece?

■ How will you maneuver the tool through the cut?

■ Is it an edge cut or a housed cut? Edge grain or end grain or both?

■ Can you combine several cuts in one template? Conversely, can you divide a single cut into two or more segments?

Your answers to these questions help you home in on a template configuration and design, the setup, and even your work sequence.

Making Templates

Getting to that end is a looping, not a linear, process. Sometimes you hit a snag that you can't resolve without backing up a step or two and trying a different approach. The capper is that once in a while, after your template is made and your setup is dialed in, an unexpected dynamic in cutting blows up your plan and tosses you back to the drawing board.

Following is stuff you should know, presented in the order in which you usually apply it.

Configuration. Your first consideration is whether the template will be an internal one (sometimes called a female template) or an external one (or male template). Your choice will impact on the how inside and outside corners are translated. Check out the drawing *Template Styles*.

An important distinction between internal and external templates is that inside corners on one template are

Practicality is the hallmark of a good template, as these examples show. The materials you select for flatness, stability, and workability. Cut them accurately, but don't worry about looks.

Template Styles
Choose the right one to get the corners you want

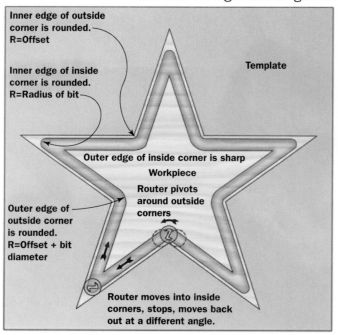

Inner edge of outside corner is rounded.
R=Offset

Inner edge of inside corner is rounded.
R=Radius of bit

Template

Outer edge of inside corner is sharp

Workpiece

Router pivots around outside corners

Outer edge of outside corner is rounded.
R=Offset + bit diameter

Router moves into inside corners, stops, moves back out at a different angle.

ROUTING AROUND AN INTERNAL TEMPLATE

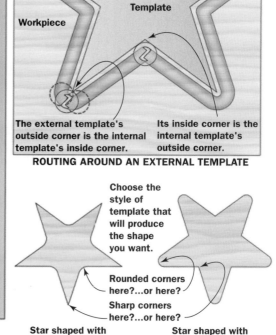

Template

Workpiece

The external template's outside corner is the internal template's inside corner.

Its inside corner is the internal template's outside corner.

ROUTING AROUND AN EXTERNAL TEMPLATE

Choose the style of template that will produce the shape you want.

Rounded corners here?...or here?

Sharp corners here?...or here?

Star shaped with internal template

Star shaped with external template

outside corners on the other, and vice versa. If you want a corner to be just as sharp as you can get it, use the template that will make it an *inside* corner. In some instances, you may actually want to use two templates, one an internal, one an external.

Template materials. A good template is flat and stable with crisp, dense edges. Why?

■ You want it to hold its size and shape, regardless of humidity and temperature.

■ You want it to just lie on the workpiece (or vice versa), making full contact, without clamping to force contact.

■ You want edges that won't dent or crush or distort as a guide bushing or bearing repeatedly rubs hard against it.

Keep these criteria in mind as you select a template material. Add to the list that the template material should be easy to work with power tools and hand tools, reasonably inexpensive, and readily available. "Jigmaking," page 43, has a rundown on materials that will be useful in this context.

Medium-density fiberboard (MDF) in various thicknesses (1/4, 1/2, and even 3/4 inch) is my preference. It's flat and dense, with crisp but easily worked edges. The cost is reasonable, as is its availability. As a bonus, MDF's color allows you see penciled layout lines and notes.

For 1/4-inch-thick templates, hardboard is a decent choice. It's cheap, yet it gives you a good edge, has no voids, and sands well. But it's so dark that penciled layout lines can be difficult to see. If the layout is intricate, try working on paper, then bonding the paper to the hardboard with spray adhesive.

A template intended for shaping dozens of pieces is worth fitting with a fence and clamps. This one, intended for router-table use, has a solid fence with a toggle clamp, a positioning pin that won't trap chips, and an extension so the pilot bearing can be engaged while the work is still clear of the cutting edges.

Quality plywood is usually good, too. Be careful about voids, splintered edges, and the like.

The place to begin looking for template material, of course, is in your stockpile of offcuts and scraps.

Design. Full-scale layout of the design comes next. Perhaps the "design" is a little rectangle for a mortise or an inlay. Maybe it's something you draw freehand. Or you use French curves or a flexible curve or a layout bow. A trammel can help you draw—and even cut—arcs.

You can do this design work on paper and transfer it to the template stock. But you may also work right on the stock. Do a good job: The accuracy of the template depends on it.

There are two important considerations here in the design phase. One is the size of the bushing or bearing that will guide the cutter. The outside diameter dictates the

minimum radius of curve you can have. If you're using a 3/4-inch-O.D. bushing, for example, your template contour can't have a curve with a 1/4-inch radius. The bushing just won't fit into it. The minimum curve radius is 3/8 inch for that bushing.

After you draw the layout, you have to calculate and scribe the offset. Set a drawing compass to the offset, and use it to draw around the original line, creating a new line parallel to the original. Pivot the compass around curves as necessary to maintain parallel. If you feel you are having difficulty doing this because the line is so curvy, try scribing little arcs, then freehanding a line that hits and connects all the high points.

This new line is the one you actually cut. And if you've done the offset correctly, the router will return you to the original layout line when you cut the good stuff.

Fixturing a template. It may seem premature to think about clamping arrangements, but often they are the most challenging problem to solve. Often, the solution is to make the template oversized so that you have space for clamps or for fences. Figure out what you are going to do *before* you cut out the template.

A template for forming a single edge is easy to deal with. Use a couple of clamps.

A template for a full-perimeter cut—decorative grooves, for example—can usually be held to the work with carpet tape or hot-melt glue. To ensure a good bond with the tape, tap the template with a wood block and hammer right where the tape is, or apply clamps to it for a few seconds. You'll be surprised at how difficult it

is to separate the template from the work. Pry with a stiff putty knife or a scraper. It'll come off. (But be very careful, if the template is going to be a keeper. Don't break it in prying it off the workpiece.)

Making multiples? You want to expedite the positioning and clamping of the template as much as possible. Solutions generally involve some sort of fixture into which you place the workpiece. Often, the template is an integral part of the fixture. Sometimes it's hinged to the fixture, or it's located with alignment pins integrated into the fixture.

If you are making the same inside cut in several pieces, you can attach fences to the underside of the pattern to help position it on the workpiece.

Cutting the template. Now it's time to cut out the template. The router ought to be your first-choice template cutter. A router bit will make a smoother cut than any saw blade, so you shouldn't have to do so

much sanding. Set up fences—or a template!—to guide the router. If there are curves with consistent radii and identifiable centerpoints, you can use a router and trammel to cut them. Just be sure you don't cut too far and screw up transitions from one arc to another. Stop short and smooth these transitions by hand. You surely will want a smooth, fair line. If the template has a tight bend or two, use a bit that's the same diameter as the outside diameter of the guide you'll be using with the template.

The band saw and the jigsaw are invaluable in cutting freehand curves. Unless the template is huge, you can quickly cut outside contours on the band saw. An easy way to cut internal shapes is with a jigsaw. Drill a starting hole in the waste area, fit the blade into the hole, and then cut.

A spindle sander is another invaluable template-making tool. So are files of various shapes. The sanding and filing can take a lot of time, but

Because a router creates such a smooth, clean cut, it's ideal for cutting out templates. Even with a fixed-base router, an inside cut can be done easily if you form inside corners by boring with a Forstner bit. Then plant a fence to guide the router.

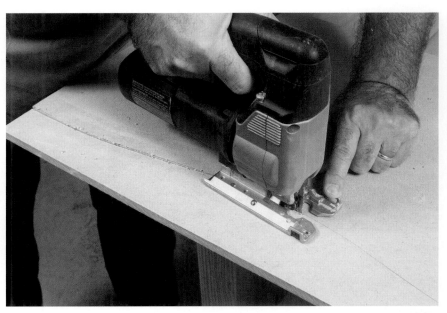

If you've laid out an undulating curve freehand, the best tools for cutting it are the band saw and the jigsaw. Don't hesitate as you cut. Move the work or the tool in a smooth, steady, continuous feed.

it's usually time well spent. The finer the edge on your template, the better your final work will be.

Regardless of the tool you choose, the goal is a smooth edge, remember. No wiggles, no bumps, no creases. Little imperfections telegraph directly into the work. Depending on the nature of the imperfection and the size of the guide, the flaw can be glaring. Any guide will transfer a *convex* bump like a ridge or a pimple into the cut. The larger the guide, the more it will magnify that bump. Conversely, a *concave* bump like a dent or dip is least likely to show up in the final cut. The smaller the guide, though, the more likely it is that the defect will transfer into the cut.

A cabinetmaker's rasp, a half-round file, and coarse sawpaper are ideal for refining the contour of a template's edge. Any of these tools will quickly remove creases and sharp corners or fair the transitions from arc to arc.

Template-Guided Routing

Guiding your router along a template to cut stock is no different than other basic routing operations. The edge guiding the router is not the edge being cut. Beyond that the techniques and the dynamics converge with general router woodworking know-how.

Clamp the template in position. Set the depth-of-cut, allowing for the template's thickness. If you are routing around the edge of the pattern and workpiece, just turn on the router and begin routing counterclockwise. If you are routing inside the pattern and workpiece, such as for a mortise, you feed the router clockwise.

You really need a plunge router for inside work. You position the router on the work with the guide bushing against the template. When you are ready, plunge the bit into the stock and guide the router clockwise around the pattern.

Splintering, tearout, and worse. This is not to say that template work doesn't harbor surprises and hazards. It's not uncommon to have tearout along an edge.

One of the most common causes of this problem is making a cut that's wider than the radius of the cutter. The cutting edge pushes out on the

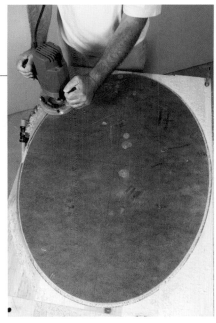

Shaping a part with a template usually is presented as an edging operation. Trim the blank close to the template with a jigsaw or on the band saw, then trim it to make the template with the router. But cutting the part from the blank with the router is often faster—one tool, one setup, instead of two tools and two setups. And the risk of problems with cut finish are diminished when you make a grooving cut rather than an edging cut.

wood as it exits the cut, and when the bit is more than half-housed in the cut, the cutting edge has leverage on the wood fibers along the edge. There's nothing behind those fibers to keep them in place, so they splinter out.

Here's a two-step way to moderate this problem.

First, reduce the width of the cut. Ideally, you shouldn't be removing more than 1/16 inch of material from around an edge.

Feed Direction

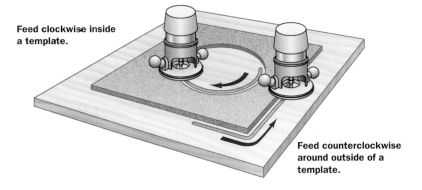

Feed clockwise inside a template.

Feed counterclockwise around outside of a template.

Template-Guided Routing

Second, use the largest-diameter cutter you can. This reduces the angle between the cut edge and the exit point, thus reducing the cutting edge's leverage.

But there's more to it when you are routing end grain, and especially when shaping curves—the stuff of template-guided work. You're guiding your router along the curved-edge template, trimming an arc across the end of your workpiece. Suddenly the router jerks and you hear a scary CRACK! You look at the cut, and there's a chunk missing from the edge. Perhaps the work has a piece split off.

The problem is the grain. When you are routing obliquely across the grain, you always want to be cutting "down" on it. It's like rubbing your hand across a rug. Move your hand one way and you raise the nap. Move it the opposite way, and you lay it down. You want to be laying down the nap, not raising it.

But you always want to feed the work against the bit rotation. Routing arcs that cross the grain presents a dilemma, because roughly half of the arc will be raising the nap. One solution is to climb-cut the latter portion of the arc, a dicey tactic.

A safer solution is to rout half the arc, then turn the work over to do the other half. On either half, you can feed against the bit rotation and cut down on the grain. Use a pattern bit for part of the arc, a flush-trimming bit for the other.

A completely different approach is to make the cut as a groove rather than an edge cut. When you cut a groove, you don't have the same issues with the grain that you do when flush-trimming. Instead of trimming the work close to the template contour, leave just over a cutter's width of waste for the bit to engage.

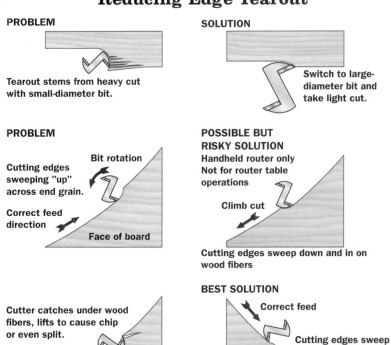

Shaping curved parts with a template requires some creative problem-solving. You want to rout "down" across the grain to avoid destructive tearout. But shaping an arc like this one forces you to rout "uphill" at least halfway. On the router table, you never want to climb-cut. Instead, rout half the arc with a pattern bit, cutting down (left). Then turn the work over, switch to a flush-trimming bit, and complete the arc, still cutting down (right).

Reducing Edge Tearout

PROBLEM

Tearout stems from heavy cut with small-diameter bit.

SOLUTION

Switch to large-diameter bit and take light cut.

PROBLEM

Cutting edges sweeping "up" across end grain.

Bit rotation

Correct feed direction

Face of board

Cutter catches under wood fibers, lifts to cause chip or even split.

POSSIBLE BUT RISKY SOLUTION

Handheld router only
Not for router table operations

Climb cut

Cutting edges sweep down and in on wood fibers

BEST SOLUTION

Correct feed

Cutting edges sweep down on wood fibers.

Turn the workpiece over.

Inlay

Inlay is the process of cutting a shallow groove or recess in a wood surface, then setting a perfectly matched strip or patch into it. It's a decorative thing. Instead of routing a profiled groove, you can inlay a strip of contrasting-colored wood. Instead of a doing a carving, inlay a colorful, geometric accent.

Nowadays, the router is the first tool you'll grab for inlay work. In some cases, perhaps *most* cases, you also need a template and guide bushings.

With one template and the right combination of bits and bushings, you rout both the recess and the insert for it. With the right technique, the insert will fit the recess perfectly no mater how often you repeat the cuts. This template technique has all sorts of applications, both practical and decorative. The primary restriction is that, without some handwork, the inlay can't have a radius in it smaller than that of the router bit.

Use any router, plunge or fixed-base. If you have a choice, a small router is most manageable. In most cases, inlays are small, and it seems silly to cut them with a big plunge router. Yes, it's easiest to begin the cut with a plunge router, but it's not all that difficult to do with a fixed-base router. Most laminate trimmers take guide bushings; consider using one.

String Inlay

Your first thought at the mention of inlay might be marquetry bands that you can buy. Rout a shallow groove and glue in a strip. You don't *really* need a template for this, but you can use one.

String inlay is a variation for which you *do* need a template, because it is sineous instead of straight.

Design your stringing. Narrow inlays have a delicate appearance, but bear in mind that the narrowest router bit you'll find is a 1/16-inch single-flute bit in high-speed steel (Bosch #85091, for example), so design your inlay with grooves no less than 1/16 inch wide.

Since it takes time to make a template, see whether you can repeat the same contour within the overall design. If you do that, you can use the template several times. Turning it over allows you to produce a mirror image of the contour.

Bear in mind that you have to fit wood into the grooves that you rout. You can bend the wood into gentle curves, but it's difficult to bend 1/16-inch-thick strips any tighter than a 1/2-inch radius. Avoid the frustration of broken inlay pieces by incorporating only "bendable" curves in your design.

Templates. As you know, when it's being guided by a template, the bit cuts a groove that's offset from the template. The distance from the centerline of the groove to the edge of the template will always be half the diameter of the template guide. So simplify your design by working with the groove centerline instead of lines for the groove edges.

To make the template, first trace the inlay design onto the template stock. Set a compass to half the guide-bushing diameter, and strike a series of arcs on the template side of the line (not the waste side). Draw a smooth curve connecting the high points of the arcs, and saw out the template. Sand the edge to assure smooth, even curves.

To use the template, clamp it to the

Inlaying bar ding doesn't usually require a template. But use of templates can take the risk out of doing string-and-shape inlays. The basic range of inlay work is displayed in this tulip: The stems represent string nlay; and the blossoms, regular template-guided inlay.

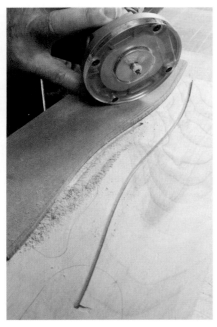

If the required undulation is modest, the template can be cut quickly on the band saw. Only a single pass is necessary to rout the inlay groove. A 1/8-inch bit is common for this sort of cut.

wood, adjust the router to cut about 1/8 inch deep, and cut the groove. Keep the template guide tight against the template as you cut. Clean out the grooves and sand lightly to get rid of any whiskers raised by the cutter.

Cutting and fitting inlay strips. Choose an inlay wood with tight, straight grain. Rip several 1/16-inch by 3/16-inch strips, and crosscut them several inches longer than the groove. If your saw leaves deep saw marks, cut the strips a bit thicker so you can sand out the saw marks and still produce a good fit in the grooves.

If you've designed an inlay with very gentle curves, you may be able to flex the strips to fit the grooves. But with most designs, you must bend the strips to the shape of the design. The easiest way to do this is using an electric soldering iron. Heat up the iron, then lay a strip of wood across the body of the iron (NOT the tip).

Press lightly to bend the strip. Start at one end of the design, bending the strip to match, and work your way from curve to curve, checking the bent strip against the design as you go. Try to be accurate with the bends. You'll be able to spring the strip a little, but the closer it is to the proper shape, the easier it will be to install. Leave the strip a bit longer than the groove.

When the strip matches the groove, place a small amount of glue in the groove and press the strip in, starting at one end. Trim the strip to length before pressing the last end into place, then set a block of wood over the strip and tap it with a hammer to seat the strip firmly into the groove.

Let the glue dry, and then sand the strip flush. Be careful not to split the strip while you are sanding. A split could easily run below the surface and show in the finished job.

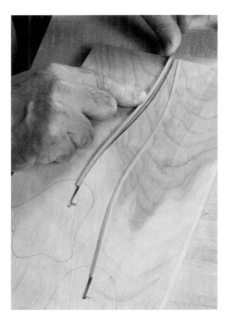

Apply a scant bead of glue to the groove, then set the bent strip into place. Start at one end, as shown, and work toward the other, flexing the strip as necessary to fit it. As you seat the strip, be especially careful not to break off its protruding ridge; you want to sand this flush and not have any splits descending into the inlay.

Inlaying Enclosed Shapes

Maybe you want a geometric shape like a diamond, a square, or an oval to accent a surface. Or hearts and flowers. Perhaps an edge-to-edge joint calls out for butterfly keys to either accent or reinforce it. Two operations are required: cutting the recess and cutting the insert. You use the same template, but with a different guide bushing for each cut.

Offset is the linchpin. Here, you work with the same offset dimension for both the recess and the insert, but you come by the measurement two different ways, depending upon whether you are calculating the offset for the recess or for the insert.

For the recess, the offset is measured from the outside edge of the bushing to the *nearest* cutting edge.

For the insert, the offset is measured from the outside edge of the bushing to the *farthest* cutting edge.

The offset dimension itself isn't important. (The sidebar on page 170 lists several bit and bushing combinations you can use.) What is important is that the recess offset be equal to the insert offset. It's also important that the cutter be of true dimension and that the bushings be concentric with the bit.

If you want to try a small inlay project without getting caught up in the math, buy an inlay kit, available from most bit retailers. The kit includes a 1/8-inch spiral cutter and a special brass guide bushing with a removable collar. The bushing is two sizes in one, prefigured to give the correct offset for the bit.

You use it just the way you would use two complete bushings of different sizes. To rout the recess, you use the bushing with the removable

Inlay Offset

SETUP FOR ROUTING RECESS

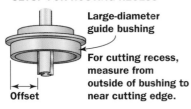

Large-diameter
guide bushing

For cutting recess,
measure from
outside of bushing to
near cutting edge.

Offset

SETUP FOR ROUTING INSERT

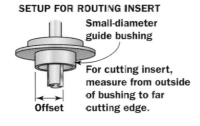

Small-diameter
guide bushing

For cutting insert,
measure from outside
of bushing to far
cutting edge.

Offset

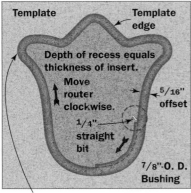

Template

Template edge

Depth of recess equals thickness of insert.

Move router clockwise.

5/16" offset

1/4" straight bit

7/8"-O. D. Bushing

No inside corner of template has radius smaller than radius of bushing.

Template

Template edge

Insert

Move router clockwise.

1/4" Straight bit

5/16" Offset

3/8"-O. D. Bushing

collar pressed onto it. To cut the insert, you pull off the extra collar.

After creating your design and determining the offset you'll use, make the template. You use the same materials and techniques for this template as you do for any other. You only make one, and you use it to cut both the recess and the insert.

Rout the recess first. Clamp, tack, or tape the template to the working stock. Remember that the actual recess will be smaller than the template, and position the template accordingly.

Set the depth-of-cut. Use scraps of the template stock and the insert stock; set the router on the workbench with the two pieces under it. Lower the bit until it just touches the bench-top, then back it up by the thickness of a couple of sheets of paper. You are going to scrape or sand the inlay flush, so your recess should be slightly less than the insert's thickness.

Typically, you cut the outline of the recess first. Keep the bushing firmly against the template. You don't want any little pimples along the edge. Vacuum or blow all the chips

out of the recess, and run the router around the edge a couple of times. Feed clockwise, remember.

Then clear the rest of the recess. If the recess is expansive, you can switch to a larger bit, set to the just-right depth-of-cut, to clean out the bulk of the recess. You can probably handle this freehand, meaning that you don't need to use a guide bushing.

Rout the insert. To get started on this phase of the operation, change to the smaller-diameter guide bushing. If you routed the recess a little less than the insert thickness, you want to use the same depth setting. That way you won't actually cut completely through the insert stock. The insert won't shift, and it won't get dinged. (It also means you won't rout into whatever the stock is clamped to—like your workbench.) The virtually paper-thin layer of wood holding the insert to the stock will be easy to cut through with a knife.

An alternative approach is to bond the insert to a piece of expendable

If you want to try an inlay project without getting caught up in the math, buy an inlay kit. It includes a 1/8-inch spiral cutter and a special brass guide bushing with a removable collar. Rout the recess with the collar pressed onto the bushing. Remove the collar to rout the insert. One bit setting takes care of both cuts.

Template-Guided Work **169**

Bit-Bushing Options

The offset measurements must be equal. If they are equal, and you have measured each correctly, then the insert will fit perfectly in the recess. To make it a little easier for you, here's a chart that lists six combinations of bushings and bits that you can use for this work. As long as you use the bit size listed with the two bushing sizes listed, you won't have to do any math. These combos will work!

Bit Diameter	Bushing for Recess	Bushing for Insert	Offset
1/8"	9/16"	5/16"	5/32"
1/8"	11/16"	7/16"	9/32"
3/16"	11/16"	5/16"	1/4"
3/16"	3/4"	3/8"	9/32"
1/4"	13/16"	5/16"	9/32"
1/4"	7/8"	3/8"	5/16"

material with carpet tape. Make sure the insert area is bonded securely. Set the bit so it cuts completely through the insert stock. The carpet tape ensures that the insert stays put. And the sacrificial scrap protects your benchtop.

In either case, position the template on the insert stock. Clamp everything securely.

Before you begin, remind yourself that you want the patch of wood inside the path formed by the cut. You can't afford to let the router drift away from the template edge, because that will ruin the insert. Be especially careful on curves and at corners. These are the most likely spots for the router to drift.

Routing the recess couldn't be more straightforward. The template is clamped to the work, and the router is set up with the bushing and bit. Set the depth-of-cut, then rout out the recess.

The insert can be cut from any piece of stock; it doesn't have to be thin. Rout what will be the insert in any stock of the right grain and color, cutting about 1/4 inch deep. At the band saw, stand the stock on edge and slice about 1/8 inch thick. As it clears the blade, the insert will fall into your hand.

The moment of truth is when you fit the insert to the recess. The fit should be snug, and you should be diffident about dry-fitting, since the insert could get stuck. Having to ease the insert with a bit of sanding isn't a bad thing. But if the insert drops into the recess and falls out as easily, you ought to try again.

Problem Solver

A knot that blemishes an otherwise excellent board can be excised and replaced with a carefully matched patch using inlay techniques. Guided by a template, rout an irregular recess that removes the defect. Using the same template, rout an insert with grain that matches the board's as closely as possible.

Can you see the already-completed patch here?

Start with the bushing against the template, but the bit above the stock surface. Turn on the router and lower the bit straight down. Feed the router around the template in a clockwise direction. This is working against the bit rotation, so it will help force the guide bushing against the template edge.

When you are done, the insert should drop right into the recess. Glue it in place, and sand it. Perfect!

Template-Guided Joinery Cuts

Template work is not just for decorative stuff. Remember that commercial dovetail jigs are all template-based units. Check out the chapter "Dovetail Joints," on page 305. You'll see that the jigs require you to use either a template guide or a pattern bit.

But cutting dovetails isn't the only template-guided joinery work you can do. You can use templates to guide mortising cuts. A template stuck to a table or chair leg so you can

finalize the contours with a router may also have a "window" in it to guide a mortise cut. See the chapter "Mortise-and-Tenon Joints," on page 273, for more details on using templates to make these joints.

And page through the chapter "Lap Joints," on page 295. A dandy variation is the mitered half-lap. Cut this one with a set of templates.

Edge-Joining along Curved Lines

Want to join two workpieces perfectly along an irregular contour? An undulating curve, for example.

Rip a board in two, and the two pieces go back together perfectly. But saw a board in two along a curved line and the two parts won't go back together perfectly. The contour on one part will be different from the contour on the other because of the saw kerf. (To visualize this more clearly, think about routing a circle: The disk removed is smaller in diameter than the hole, the difference being twice the diameter of the bit you used.)

The process of cutting the joining edges is all about putting in, then taking out that kerf. It's offset, the same offset used in doing inlay. Here you use templates and some home-brewed offset-pattern bits.

Make the master template. This is the template used to make the working templates. After you make it, you use it once, and that's it.

The essential in an offset pattern bit is having a bearing larger than the bit's cutter diameter. Having a shoulder between the cutter and the shank keeps the bearing in place. Slide it onto the shank and capture it against the shoulder with a lock collar.

Template-Guided
Joinery Cuts

What's special about this panel is obvious. Getting a good tight joint along a curving line is difficult. But a router guided by a template can do it.

Cut a blank from 1/2-inch MDF, sizing it about 6 to 8 inches wide and 3 inches longer than the workpieces you want to join. Ultimately, the working templates will allow you to begin and end your router cuts with the bit clear of the work.

Near the right edge, carefully draw the joint line. It can be a sinuous curve, a series of straight lines and arcs, or whatever contour you desire. The only restriction is that none of the curves can have a radius smaller than that of the largest bearing or guide bushing you use. In this instance, that minimum is a 5/8-inch radius.

Draw a parallel line 1/4 inch to the left of the first. This new line is the edge of the master template. To draw it, set a drawing compass to 1/4 inch and trace along the joint line with it.

Pivot the compass around curves as necessary to maintain parallel.

Cut and sand the template to this line. You can make the initial cut on the band saw or with a jigsaw. Stay just to the right of the line as you saw, then use whatever sanding tools are at your disposal to smooth and fair the contour to the line. All the template-making guidelines apply, of course.

Label the completed template "Master Template."

Edge Joining along a Curved Line

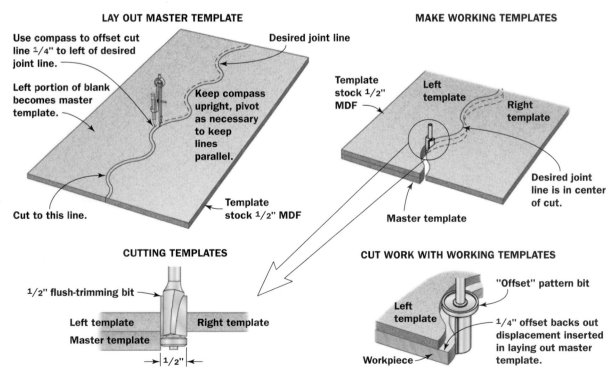

LAY OUT MASTER TEMPLATE

Use compass to offset cut line 1/4" to left of desired joint line.

Desired joint line

Left portion of blank becomes master template.

Keep compass upright, pivot as necessary to keep lines parallel.

Cut to this line.

Template stock 1/2" MDF

MAKE WORKING TEMPLATES

Template stock 1/2" MDF

Left template

Right template

Desired joint line is in center of cut.

Master template

CUTTING TEMPLATES

1/2" flush-trimming bit

Left template

Right template

Master template

1/2"

CUT WORK WITH WORKING TEMPLATES

"Offset" pattern bit

Left template

1/4" offset backs out displacement inserted in laying out master template.

Workpiece

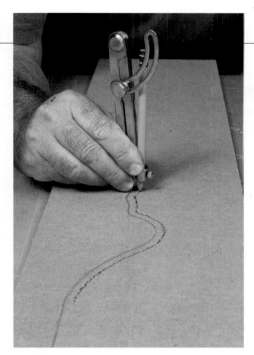

Set the legs of a drawing compass to the offset dimension. Trace along the joint line and scribe the line of the master template. Keep the compass bolt upright, and orient the compass to produce a new line parallel to the joint line. Minor deviation seldom is a problem, since the point of the joint generally is aesthetic rather than structural.

Make the working templates. The working templates are used when you rout the workpieces. Size them according to how big the work is, and whether you'll use a handheld router or the router table to shape the work. You produce both with a single cut along the master template, so dimension your blank accordingly. I recommend that you use ¹/₂-inch MDF.

Clamp, screw, or stick the master template to the blank. Use a ¹/₂-inch-diameter pattern bit or a flush-trimming bit to cut along the contour of the master. A pattern bit puts the master on top, and that makes it easier to follow the contour. You can see where the router has to go. With a flush-trimmer, the master is hidden beneath the blank and you are working blind.

What's happening here in terms of the offset? A couple of things. First,

we're holding the ¹/₄ inch of offset added to the left of the joint line when we made the master template. Cutting with a flush-trimmer ensures that. Second, we're adding ¹/₄ inch of offset to the right of the joint line by using a ¹/₂-inch cutter.

The upshot is that the joint line is offset ¹/₄ inch from either template's guiding edge. We can back that out as we shape the workpieces. Because the offset is the same for both halves of the joint, we have only one bit to set up.

But we still have to shape the working templates. Keep the pilot bearing tight to the master template throughout the cut. A sharp bit, especially one with a shear angle to the cutting edges, can plow through ¹/₂-inch MDF in a single pass.

Keeping the router steady throughout the cuts is essential. Use an offset baseplate (see "Jigmaking" on page 43) or a support block under the outboard sector of the baseplate. Better yet, use both! You don't want to risk a bobble that will ruin the cut. And *concentrate* during the cut! Don't let the router drift away from the mas-

Cut the working templates using a ¹/₂-inch pattern or flush-trimming bit guided by the master template. You can make the through cut in a single pass. Here the master template is screwed to the blank. In turn, the blank is screwed to scraps that elevate it so the bit doesn't cut into the benchtop. The work is clamped so neither working template can shift as the cut is completed.

ter edge, especially as you negotiate the curves. Use the offset baseplate's outboard knob to pull the router firmly against the master.

A goof doesn't necessarily mean

You should band-saw the rough contour of the joint line on each workpiece so that only ¹/₈ inch or so of waste must be trimmed in the template-guided cut. Use the working template to lay out the joint line. Lay the template on the work and trace the line using a washer or bearing that measures ¹/₄ inch from the rim to the bore. Saw to the outside of the line.

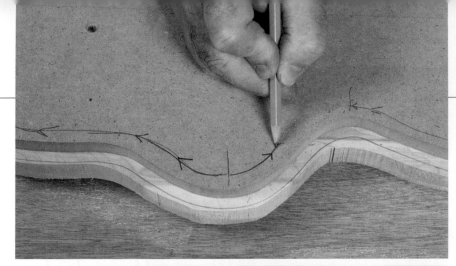

you've got to start over, since the mistake will impact both working templates simultaneously. A hiccup that gouges one template produces a complementary bump on the other.

When the working templates are done, mark them clearly left and right. On each, note the bit and bearing or bushing that must be used with it.

Rout the workpieces. This is standard template-guided work. Use the same bit and bearing for both workpieces. Any combination that produces a 1/4 inch of offset will do. I recommend a 3/4-inch straight with a 1/2-inch shank and a 1 1/4-inch bearing. The bit is large enough to produce a good cut finish without needing an excessively large bearing.

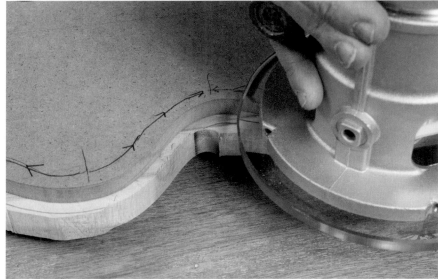

Be wary of the interplay of the joint contour with the grain of the workpiece. Refer to the information on page 166 about cross-grain cuts, and take to heart the warnings about cutting against the "nap" of end grain. You may benefit from cutting parts of the contours with a pattern bit and other parts with flush-trimmers. You may cautiously climb-cut selected stretches of the contour.

Best is to start with mild curves and get experience with the dynamics as well as the concepts. As you progress to steeper slopes and tighter curves, you'll be better prepared to deal with the difficulties that these advanced designs present.

Shaping the workpieces with the working templates requires some advance planning and a measured, methodical approach to the routing. To avoid splitting off chunks, you always want to rout "down" across the grain. Sections thus must be addressed in the climb-cut direction. Before you begin, pencil direction arrows on the template (top). Fire up the router and cut, following the arrows section by section, being especially vigilant when moving in the climb-cut direction (above).

See Also...

Templates for routing circles, page 189.

Templates for routing mortises, page 287.

Templates for cutting mitered half-laps, page 302.

Commercial dovetail jigs that use fixed and adjustable templates, page 305.

A jig for cutting box joints that's trapped on a template guide bushing, page 340.

Routing Curves and Circles

Going in circles is often considered a waste of time, but you'd be surprised how often you really need to. In fact there's been a lot of time wasted by people who couldn't figure out how to cut a good, clean circle (or arc) when they needed one.

To cut a circle—or just a part of a circle—with the router, the basic need is to get the tool to move smoothly around a given point. You'll find that there are numerous ways to accomplish this, and that each of the ways has advantages in certain applications. Almost always, you'll use a trammel of one sort or another. Occasionally, a template will guide the router.

But what about curves that aren't circles? Ovals. Arcs. Combinations of arcs. Here again, the router will do the work. To cut ovals, you use a special trammel. For those arcs and combinations of arcs, you are often best served by a template.

Basic Trammels

The most common way to cut circles or arcs with the router is to use a trammel. Your router may have one among its accessories. A trammel is often a part of the edge-guide attachment.

If you don't have one, it's easy to cut out an oversized plywood baseplate, mounting the router on one end and driving a screw for a pivot at the other. You can accomplish the same thing with a lot more flexibility by attaching a hardwood arm to the base and setting the pivot point in a sliding block on that arm. Infinite adjustment, almost.

Cutting circles is the natural turf of the plunge router. The plunger makes it easy to get the bit into the work, and to deepen the cut after each lap. My predisposition is to use the smallest router I can for such

A plain strip of plywood, attached to the router with carpet tape, with a hole for the bit at one end and a screw for a pivot at the other, makes a functional trammel. For each new job, you lay out and drill a new pivot hole for a new radius. Cheap, simple, and it works.

Safety First!

Whether you are routing a circle using a trammel or on the router table, feed the work or the tool counterclockwise. This will keep you out of trouble. With either setup, a clockwise feed yields a climb cut.

When you are using a trammel (or, on a router table, a fixed pivot) to rout a circle *as a groove-forming operation,* feed direction doesn't make much difference. The rotation of the bit probably won't help you or hurt you, so long as your pivot is secure. With a clockwise feed—the climb cut—the rotation is pulling on the pivot. With a counterclockwise feed, the rotation is pushing against the pivot.

But if the bit ever emerges from the groove to form an edge, or when the entire cut is *an edge-forming operation,* feed direction becomes a real issue. I'm talking about cutting a circle from a square, when the circle's diameter and the square's width are the same. In this situation, the bit is cutting a groove as it rounds off the corners of the square, but it's forming the edge elsewhere around the circumference. I'm also talking about routing an edge on a disk that you've roughed out on the band saw.

This is a safety issue primarily because climb cuts are such grabby, galloping cuts. The bit can dig in and jerk the router or the disk out of your control. But when routing a disk from a square, the grab that comes when the bit comes out of the groove can give you a start. If the pivot isn't set securely, it can be jerked out of position.

Feed direction becomes a quality issue because of chip-out. Chip-out occurs as the cutting edge of the bit sweeps off the wood, taking chips out of the edge. There's often a temptation to make a climb cut to avoid chip-out. In a climb cut, the cutting edge is sweeping into the wood, forcing the wood fibers in so there are no chips lifting out. A safer approach is to make a light finish cut in the proper, counterclockwise feed direction, to clean up the edge.

Feed Direction Savvy
Keep out of trouble by feeding in the correct direction

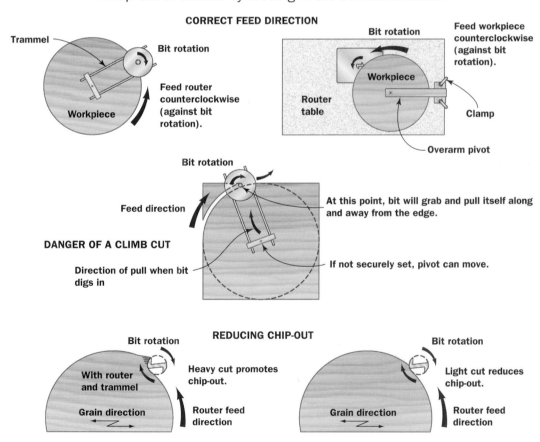

With a large trammel making a large arc, the most secure pivot is a screw driven into the work. You can use both hands to operate the router without worrying that the trammel will jump off the pivot.

operations. Manageability is a big plus in this kind of operation. With one hand on the pivot and the other on the router, you make the cut quickly and accurately.

Regardless of the router or trammel you use, you swing the apparatus on a pivot. It's best to drill a pilot for the pivot. A drilled pilot will ensure that the pivot is perpendicular. And by boring clean through the stock, you can use the same centerpoint on either side. If the stock is very thick, I'd recommend working both sides—that is, use the router and trammel to groove one side, cutting about halfway through the stock. Then flip the piece over and make a cut. Then keep going until you are through. You get a better finish on all the edges, and you don't have to cut so deeply.

Fixed Trammels

Before we delve into the trammel-making projects, you should bear in mind that you can rout circles with the most basic of trammels: a strip of plywood with the router at one end and a pivot at the other.

If you are content to be utterly down-and-dirty, bond the router to the plywood with carpet tape. This works well for me on those occasions when my project calls for an arc with a 6- or 7-foot radius (I'm not making this up). I cut a 6- or 7-inch-wide strip of cheap lauan plywood for the trammel. I stick three or four patches of carpet tape to the router base, then set the base on the plywood. I use a Quick-Grip clamp to really squeeze the base and plywood together for a few seconds. Then I rout a bit opening through the plywood, and I'm ready to measure from the bit and drive a pivot.

Of course, a lot of folks prefer a more formal, more *finished* jig than

I've just described. For them I offer a plywood teardrop, more than 3 feet long overall. With it, you can rout a 3-foot-radius arc (that's a 6-foot-diameter circle).

Here's the direct approach to making this jig. Cut a rectangle of 1/4-inch plywood as wide as your router's base and about 6 inches longer than the radius of the arc or circle you want to cut. Use your router's baseplate to lay out the trammel's head, with screw holes for mounting the router and a bit hole. Measure, mark, and drill the pivot hole you need. Attach the base to the

router and you're in business. As you use the trammel for job after job, the number of pivot holes will expand.

What is shown in the drawing and photo is the result of the quick but tidy approach. The task begins in the same way—cutting the plywood blank and laying out the head from the router baseplate. But then the trammel is cut to an elongated teardrop shape on the band saw or with a jigsaw. And a series of pivot holes are drilled. Then 1×1 stiffeners, after being bull-nosed, are glued to the edges. Finally, a finish is applied.

Teardrop Trammel
It turns your router into a compass

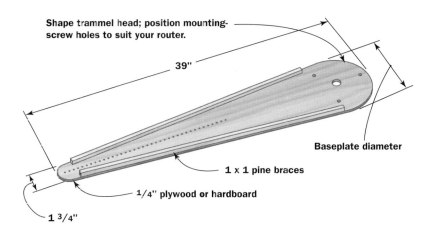

Shape trammel head; position mounting-screw holes to suit your router.

39"

Baseplate diameter

1 x 1 pine braces

1/4" plywood or hardboard

1 3/4"

Adjustable Trammel

What you will probably discover if you use the trammel often enough is that the fixed size is sometimes a nuisance. So the next step is to make an adjustable trammel, perhaps with interchangeable arms for different ranges of arc size. This way you don't have to deal with 2 or 3 feet of arm sticking out the back when you're cutting a 7-inch radius.

For routing smallish disks and holes, ranging from a 1 1/2-inch diameter up to about 16 inches in diameter, this is the ideal trammel. Change to a longer slide, and the capacity shoots up to about 3 feet in diameter. But what I like most is its ability to do those small-diameter cuts—those around 2 inches. The fact that it's got good range beyond is merely a plus.

The trammel is a roughly teardrop-shaped baseplate made of 3/4-inch plywood. A groove, extending from the bit opening out to the most distant edge, houses a slide with a pivot. Move the slide in or out to adjust the radius of the cut, then fix its position by tightening the locking knob.

Some words about the slide(s). The baseline slide is 8 inches long,

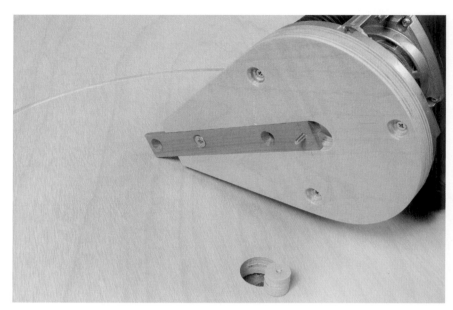

Versatility is the key attribute of this trammel. Whether you want a plug, a disk, or a hole, the mid-range trammel will serve you. The effective range of the jig is evident: The groove is the largest arc you can produce with the standard arm, while the disk (or is it a big plug?) and hole represent the smallest.

with two holes for the pivot and three for the mounting bolt. It is reversible. You can position the pivot right next to the bit for those tiny-radius cuts. Or you can have the pivot extended beyond the baseplate, about 8 inches from the bit. The extra pivot hole and mounting-bolt holes allow you to get every radius between these two extremes.

Try This!

If the circle you want to cut is smaller than the diameter of your router base, don't bother with the trammel. Drill a pivot hole in the factory baseplate. Then the baseplate is the trammel. Fit the router over the pin in the work, and turn it. Not flashy, but it works.

The secret to the small circles cut with an ordinary plunge router is the trammel's ability to position the pivot just a fraction of an inch from the bit.

Adjustable Trammel

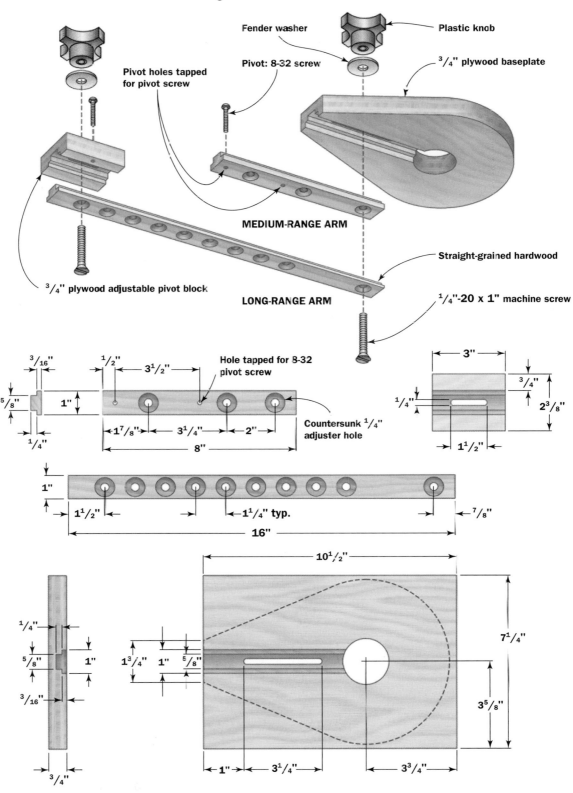

Plastic knob

Fender washer

Pivot: 8-32 screw

Pivot holes tapped for pivot screw

3/4" plywood baseplate

MEDIUM-RANGE ARM

Straight-grained hardwood

3/4" plywood adjustable pivot block

LONG-RANGE ARM

1/4"-20 x 1" machine screw

Hole tapped for 8-32 pivot screw

Countersunk 1/4" adjuster hole

3/16"

1/2"

3 1/2"

5/8"

1"

1/4"

1 7/8"

3 1/4"

2"

8"

3"

3/4"

1/4"

1 1/2"

2 3/8"

1"

1 1/2"

1 1/4" typ.

7/8"

16"

1/4"

5/8"

1"

3/16"

3/4"

1 3/4"

1"

5/8"

10 1/2"

7 1/4"

3 5/8"

1"

3 1/4"

3 3/4"

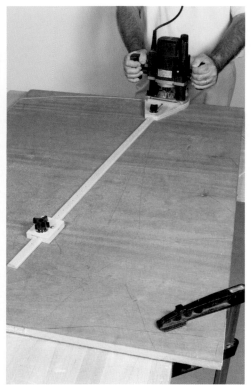

Switching to a longer arm dramatically increases the diameter of the tabletop or the radius of arc you can cut with the mid-range trammel. This one trammel may be all you ever need.

The drawing also shows a long slide and a separate pivot block. These accessories extend the range of the trammel. I don't think there's any reason why you couldn't make an even longer slide.

A small router works best on the trammel, and of course, a plunge router has the ability to initiate and deepen a cut easily. That's why I fitted my trammel baseplate to a small plunge router.

Construction is not too difficult. Lay out the baseplate contour and locate the bit hole. While the baseplate is still a rectangle, rout the grooves and adjustment slot. Drill the bit opening with a Forstner bit; bandsaw the contour and sand the edges. Make the slide(s) to fit the grooves.

Using a Trammel

Using a trammel seems pretty intuitive. It's like using a compass, isn't it? Set the compass for the desired radius, stick its pivot into the work, and spin it. But we don't usually have to account for the thickness of the pencil line it makes, or protect the surface beneath the work. Make a mistake with a compass, and you can erase the arc and redraw it. Make a mistake with a router and trammel, and you've pretty much got to toss the work and start over.

Chuck a bit in the collet. My instinct is to talk in straight-bit terms. But you may be routing a decorative profile with an unpiloted profile cutter. So choose your bit and fit it in the router.

While you are setting up the router, adjust the plunge depth, if you are using a plunge router. If you are routing completely through the stock, set the plunge depth to the stock thickness plus no more than 1/16 inch.

Set the cutting radius. On some trammels, it is a matter of locating the proper hole for the pivot nail or screw. On others, it requires moving a slide or a pivot block so the pivot is the correct distance from the bit.

Here's where you account for the diameter of the bit. If cutting a disk, *exclude* the bit from the radius; measure from the center of the pivot to the closest point on the bit. If cutting a hole, *include* the bit in the radius; measure from the pivot center to the farthest point of the bit. See the drawing.

Try This!

What if you don't *want* a pilot hole? Perhaps a pilot hole is going to mar your tabletop?

Bond a pivot plate or block to the work with everyone's favorite shop tape—the so-called double-stick stuff—carpet tape.

You can use a scrap of wood for the block. I have a small square of plastic with a hole at dead center. The trammel's pivot bolt in the trammel block projects just enough to catch in this hole, but not enough to bottom out and scratch the workpiece. The plastic plate is durable and bonds well to the tape.

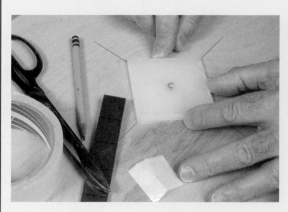

Apply carpet tape to the plate, then stick it to the work. If the location is critical, mark the point with extended crosshairs, then align the corners of the square plate on the lines.

Setting the Cutting Radius

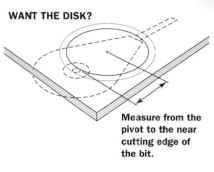

Measure from the pivot to the near cutting edge of the bit.

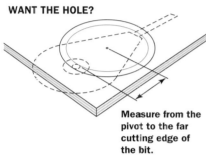

Measure from the pivot to the far cutting edge of the bit.

Cutting completely through the workpiece? Set the plunge router on the edge of the piece and bottom the bit against the bench. Drop the stop rod to the turret, slip a feeler gauge or a couple of playing cards beneath it, then lock it. Cut progressively, of course, but you're set to cut just through the work.

For best accuracy, use a metal rule, rather than a tape measure, to set the slide. If the radius is so long that a metal rule is out, a tape will have to do.

Secure the workpiece. If you are routing a through hole, you need to secure the work and, at the same time, protect the surface underneath it. You definitely don't want the pivot to move as you cut.

What do it? Bond the work to a piece of expendable material—

¼-inch plywood, for example. Use carpet tape, hot-melt glue, or—if they won't mar the work—screws or brads. Clamp the backup to the workbench, positioning the clamps where they won't interfere with the trammel's travel.

Set the cutting radius by measuring from bit to pivot. Use a metal rule for this. Turn the bit by hand to ensure that you are measuring from the cutting edge, and not the body of the bit. And measure from the center of the pivot.

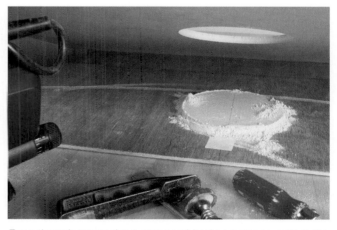

For a through trammel cut, you need backup scrap to protect the workbench. This ¼-inch plywood panel has been used repeatedly for such work. Clamp the piece to the bench. The workpiece can be stuck to the plywood with carpet tape.

Problem Solver

For really long-radius arcs, wood-workers seldom even think of the router and trammel. They'll pencil the arc, then cut it with a jigsaw or on the band saw, and refine the curve with much sanding. But swinging a router on a trammel assures you of a much smoother arc than you would get by sawing it freehand.

So what if the radius is really radical? So what indeed! Just cobble together a really long trammel. Cut a 6-inch-wide strip from the 8-foot dimension of a plywood sheet. If you have to, scab two such strips end to end. Make yourself a primitive trammel almost 16 feet long. It'll work.

Obviously, your workbench won't be long enough, but that's not an insurmountable problem. Set a pivot block on your table saw, extend your trammel through space, and have the working end—the one with the router—cutting the work that's clamped to the benchtop. Or mount a pivot on the wall. You need only be limited by the size of your shop. (And if *that's* too small for you, do the job outside!)

Drill the pivot hole. You can't get around needing a hole for the trammel's pivot. It doesn't need to be too deep, since the pivot should

When you cut just an arc—to make a template, for example—the pivot doesn't have to be on the workpiece. Attach a scrap of the stock to a piece of plywood, locate it at the right spot, at the right elevation, and clamp it.

be little more than a nubbin. Use a 1/8-inch drill bit, and bore only 1/4 inch deep. Keep the drill perpendicular to the work.

Bear in mind that the pivot point isn't necessarily on the work. If you are cutting an arc—just a *part* of the circle—the pivot may be separated from the work. Fasten a scrap to the work surface the correct distance from the desired arc, and drill the pivot hole in it. For best results, your scrap ought to be the same thickness as the work.

Rout! With everything set up, set the router on the work, and work the pivot into the pivot hole.

With a plunge router, the operation involves no more than switching on the router, plunging the bit into the work, and swinging the machine around the pivot.

Fixed-base routers are a bit more

problematic, and you may need to experiment a bit with the router you have to determine the best avenue of attack. Try setting the cutting depth to about 1/4 inch, then catching the pivot in its hole while keeping the router base tipped up from the workpiece, so the bit is clear of the work. Switch on the router and lower it to the work, plunging the bit. Uncomfortable with that? Here's a second option: Drill a starting hole the same diameter as the bit. Set the depth-of-cut, and position the router with the pivot in its pilot and the bit in its starting hole. Now switch on the router.

With the cut started, it is a simple matter to swing the router—*counterclockwise* is the correct feed direction—through a complete circle. Increase the cutting depth, and take another lap. Keep it up, and you'll get there.

For this extra-long trammel cut, the work surface is a sheet of plywood clamped to the workbench. The pivot is on a strip clamped to the plywood at right. The support in the center (a scrap) keeps the trammel strip from sagging. The workpiece is mounted on my much-used backup scrap that's clamped to the plywood.

Cutting Arcs and Circles on the Router Table

Although you can rout disks and holes on the router table, it is not the optimal setup for such work. The biggest difficulty is adjusting the cutting depth. But also, you have to set up a pivot somehow, you have to turn the work as the cut is made, and you do this without knowing exactly where the bit is.

I have done this, but not in years, frankly. Let me explain the routine, and you'll understand my lack of enthusiasm.

Place a nail, screw, or dowel in the tabletop as a pivot. Then set the stock on the pivot, and turn it to cut your circles or arcs. Undoubtedly, you aren't going to want to mess up the tabletop, so use a piece of expendable plywood or hardboard and either tape it or clamp it to the tabletop. Run the bit up through it, and install any kind of pivot you desire in this auxiliary top.

With the bit retracted, you slip the blank on the pivot. Hold the blank, switch on the router, and raise the bit enough to engage the work. Turn the blank one full rotation. Still holding the blank and with the router still running, raise the bit a little more. Turn the blank again. Eventually, following this sequence, the bit comes through.

Obviously, you must have a router table setup that allows one-handed depth-of-cut adjustments. In my experience, it works satisfactorily with a plunge router equipped with an adjusting knob or crank.

Any setup that calls for two-handed cutting-depth adjustments is out.

There are practical limits to the circle work you can do on the router

When routing out small disks on the router table, use a pusher to move the workpiece. This shop-made pusher has a dense foam-rubber sole that grips the work and won't let it slip.

An overarm pivot is a practical jig for routing disks on the router table. This one has a base with a wide, shallow dovetail groove through which the arm with the pivot slides. Use two clamps on the jig to keep it from swiveling out of position. The pivot is a pointed thumbscrew.

table. For example, too small a circle puts your fingers in jeopardy. All I can advise is that you try manipulating little disks next to a stationary bit and decide on that basis whether you want to do the actual cutting.

Another practical limit is at the other end of the size scale. Too big a circle will range beyond the capacity of the tabletop. Measure from the bit to the far corner of your router table. That's the maximum radius you can cut without resorting to a supplementary tabletop.

Oval Cutting

An oval (or ellipse) is a two-dimensional geometric shape, an enclosed curve with a continuously changing radius. It's a wonderfully plastic shape. A circle is always a circle; only the size changes. But an oval can be all-but-a-circle on the one hand, and extremely elongate on the other.

You can draw ovals using two tacks and some string. To actually cut out an elliptical form, many a woodworker will draw the ellipse, bandsaw the rough shape, then sand and sand to produce the final contour. Perhaps they'll make a template and cut the workpiece using that.

Forget all that! With this jig, you can rout a geometrically correct ellipse, directly. All you need to know is its length and width.

Oval-Cutting Trammel

The jig bears a striking resemblance to the old "BS grinder" or do-nothing machine. It's got two keys that travel back and forth in perpendicular slots. They're connected by an arm. What's interesting, and surely something you never realized when grinding a load of BS, is that the arm traces out an oval.

The adaptation for the router is a blessing when you want to make oval tabletops or oval frames. That's not BS.

The particular jig shown here was made by an old colleague of mine, Fred Matlack. You can rout dovetail slots in MDF or particleboard or even real wood, but Fred cut strips of cherry for the tracks and nailed them to a plywood base. The use of thumbscrews and T-nuts enhances the easy adjustability of the jig. The thumbscrews go through holes drilled in the trammel bar so the keys can pivot freely.

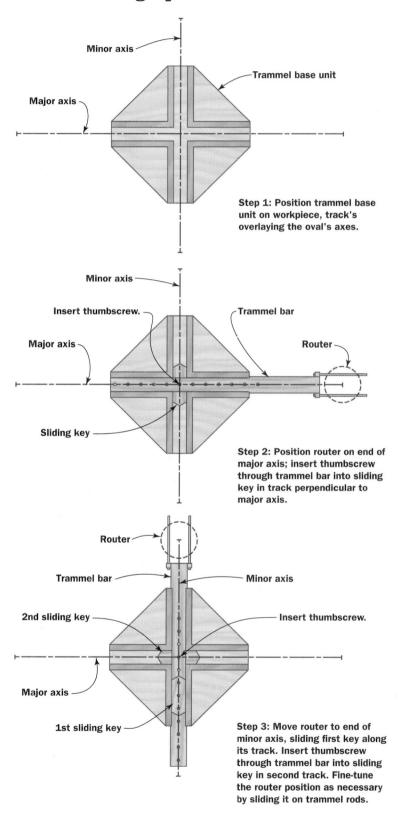

Setting Up the Trammel

Minor axis
Trammel base unit
Major axis

Step 1: Position trammel base unit on workpiece, track's overlaying the oval's axes.

Minor axis
Insert thumbscrew.
Trammel bar
Major axis
Router
Sliding key

Step 2: Position router on end of major axis; insert thumbscrew through trammel bar into sliding key in track perpendicular to major axis.

Router
Trammel bar
Minor axis
2nd sliding key
Insert thumbscrew.
Major axis
1st sliding key

Step 3: Move router to end of minor axis, sliding first key along its track. Insert thumbscrew through trammel bar into sliding key in second track. Fine-tune the router position as necessary by sliding it on trammel rods.

The structure of the oval-cutting trammel is pretty clear: the dovetail-slotted tracks formed of separate strips, the plywood base, the router mounting, the trammel bar, and the sliding keys.

The range of the jig is determined by the size of the trammel's base, the length of the tracks and the sliding keys, and the distance between the holes in the trammel bar. It is not infinitely variable. The range of proportions the jig can trace is relatively modest, though the range of sizes is wider. Let me explain.

The shortest minor axis you can cut is established by positioning the router as close to the base as you can get it. Depending on the router, you'll get the bit about 3 1/2 inches

To set up the jig, use the oval's longest dimension, called the major axis, and its shortest dimension, called the minor axis. Draw perpendicular centerlines on the stock, and measure off the major axis on one and the minor axis on the other. Position the two tracks directly over the axes and fasten it to the work. If the area to which the jig is attached is waste, you can just nail the tracks to the stock. For tabletops, you can fasten it with double-sided tape.

Fit the trammel bar to the router and park the router at one end of the major axis. Insert a sliding key in the track that's perpendicular to the major axis. Line it up at the junction of the tracks, under the trammel bar. Then run a thumbscrew through the arm into the key.

Now move the router to an end of the minor axis. Insert the second sliding key in its track, line it up at the track junction, and run a thumbscrew through the trammel bar into it. This setup establishes the *proportion* of the oval, which is to say the difference between the major and minor axes. You adjust the *size* of the oval by moving the router on the trammel rods.

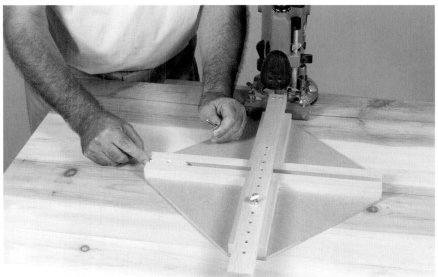

You don't need to lay out the oval's contour, only the ends of the major and minor axes. Park the router with its bit smack on the end of the major axis (top). Slide a key into the track parallel to the router and insert a thumbscrew through the trammel bar into the key. Then move the router to the end of the minor axis (bottom) and install the second slide.

Range of Sizes
Largest and smallest ellipses produced by oval-cutting trammel

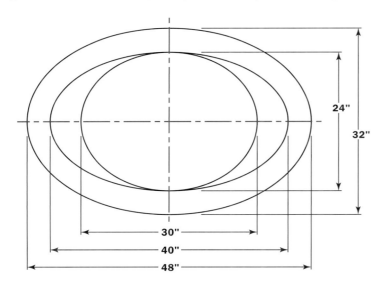

24"
32"
30"
40"
48"

from the jig base. The base is roughly 17 inches square, when measured along the tracks. This adds up to 23 or 24 inches as the shortest minor axis this jig will produce.

Given that minor axis measurement, the shortest major axis you can get is 30 inches long. The determining factor? The length of the sliding keys. If you position their pivots closer together than 3 inches, they collide at the crossing. Trimming the keys from a 3-inch length to a 2-inch length would get you a closer setting. The disparity in radii doubles, obviously, when you talk about diameters (in this case, axes), so the major axis ends up being 6 inches longer then the minor one.

Let's not leave that last factor unexplored. When you shift the pivots, you must move in 1-inch increments. The holes in the trammel bar are spaced that far apart. The 1-inch increment doubles when viewed in terms of axis length. The adjustability of the jig is in 2-inch increments.

Given that 6 inches is the smallest difference between axes you can

achieve, what's the greatest? Sixteen inches. The track length sets this figure. If you position the keys more than 8 inches apart, one will be out of its track.

Speaking in terms of oval propor-

tions, then, this jig will range in 2-inch increments, from 24 inches by 30 inches up to 32 inches by 48 inches.

You can rout larger ovals with the jig. The router can be moved out the trammel rods far enough to cut an oval with a maximum axis of 86 inches. The trammel rods are about 22 inches long, providing enough room to shift the bit position about 18 inches, so at any proportion setting, you have a 36-inch range in axis length. If you want to rout an oval frame, you would set the proportion and size to rout the outside edge, then slide the router in on the rods to cut the inner edge.

To make the trammel:

1. Cut the 14-inch square base from thin plywood.

2. Make the tracks and sliding keys. Use a hardwood, such as maple or cherry, beginning with straight-grain,

Routing an oval doesn't demand more of the operator than routing a circle does. The oval trammel's action is considerably different from a circle trammel's. As the slides move back and forth in their tracks, barely missing each other at the crossing, the router follows a much different path.

Oval-Cutting Trammel
Grind out ellipses with this shop-made device

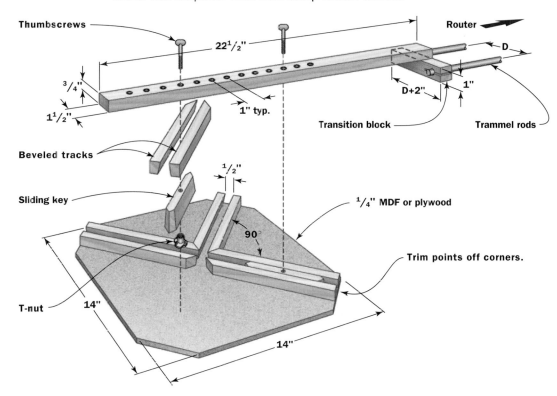

Thumbscrews

22 1/2"

Router

D

3/4"

1 1/2"

1" typ.

D+2"

1"

Beveled tracks

Transition block

Trammel rods

Sliding key

1/2"

1/4" MDF or plywood

90°

Trim points off corners.

T-nut

14"

14"

defect-free stock about 3/4 inch thick and 2 1/2 inches wide. Mark the top surface of the stock. Set the table saw to cut a 7° bevel, then rip a 3/4-inch-wide strip from the working stock. Turn the stock around, keeping the top up, and repeat the cut. The strips cut are the tracks; the "waste" will yield the two sliding keys. Joint the cut edges lightly to remove any saw marks.

3. Assemble the tracks and the base. Clamp a single strip of the waste to the base, positioning it diagonally. Miter the tracks as necessary to form the joints at the base's center. With a single sheet of paper between the waste and the rails to create sliding clearance, butt the rails to the waste and nail them in place. When the first set of tracks is set, reposition the waste across the other diagonal and

Screw the waste from the track-forming cuts temporarily to the base. Butt a piece of the track against this waste and fasten it to the base. The sheet of paper between track and waste produces clearance for the slide, which will be cut from the waste.

repeat the process to install the second set of tracks. Cut off the corners of the base assembly, as shown in the drawing.

4. Cut two keys, each about 3 inches long. Drill a hole for a thumbscrew through each, equidistant from the ends. Drive a T-nut into the bottom of the hole.

5. Make the transition block. Start by determining how big it needs to be. Fit the trammel rods into the holes for them in the router base, then measure the distance between them (labelled D on the drawing). Cut the trammel block 2 inches longer than your distance D.

The trammel rods slide through holes in the transition block that are kerfed, so the rods can be "clamped" in place. Drill holes for the rods and for the screws, then counterbore the latter holes for T-nuts. Kerf the ends of the bar, as shown. To do this on the table saw, crank up the blade to make a cut at least 1⅝ inches deep. (The kerf should extend at least ½ inch beyond the hole for the pinch to be secure.) Set the fence so the cut will pass through the center of the hole. Stand the trammel block on end to make the cut, and use a scrap block to back it up.

6. Cut the trammel bar and drill 13 holes, 1 inch apart, for the thumbscrews to pass through. Glue and screw the trammel bar to the transition block.

Template-Guided Cuts

For small arcs—including small circles—you're often better off to use a template. A template guides the cut by controlling the path of the router. You use either a pattern bit, which has a pilot bearing mounted on the shank, or a guide bushing, which is a flange surrounding the bit, with the template. The bushing's flange or the bit's bearing rides along the edge of the template, preventing the router from wandering outside the template's confines.

Templates are usually made of hardboard, plywood, or MDF. You temporarily attach the template to the workpiece—use clamps, carpet tape, hot-melt glue—then move the router over it. You can make through cuts with straight bits, or decorative cuts with groove-forming profile bits.

There are several good reasons for using templates in routing curves and circles.

■ Multiples. You need to duplicate a curve or circle again and again. A trammel will do it, but it's often faster and easier to position a template than to work with a trammel.

■ Holes. Here you confront the difficulty of holding a centerpoint if you're cutting out the area where the point is. Once it is set, the template doesn't need the centerpoint.

■ Complex curves. A trammel is great for a constant arc, but what about undulating lines? You need multiple centerpoints, different radii. Lotta setup time, and if you're cutting good stock, you don't have a margin for error. But you can fiddle with a template, trimming and sanding that curve until it is just what you want. Then you can duplicate it *perfectly* with your router.

More details on making and using templates are found in the chapter "Template-Guided Work," page 155. Suffice it to say here that you can use your various trammels and router table pivots to produce the template, then use the template to guide the cut on the good stock.

The sliding key has mitered ends and a hole with a T-nut for the mounting screw. Optimum length for the key is about 3 inches. Longer keys may collide at the track crossing. Shorter keys may not span that crossing smoothly.

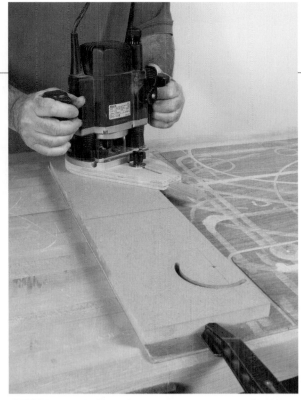

Making a template for the cutout in the base of a bookcase (bottom) involves cuts of two different radii. The ends are formed by a very short-radius arc (right). The arc connecting them has a much longer radius. Locate the pivot block carefully and, before cutting, be sure the bit begins in one short-radius cut and ends in the other (below). Thus assured, rout the arc.

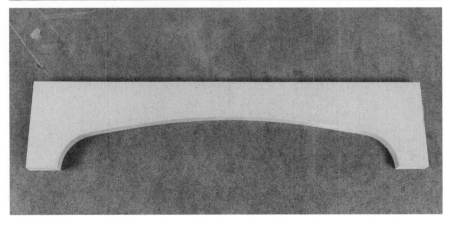

Circle-Cutting Templates

Before leaving the topic, however, here's a simple-to-make pair of templates that can demonstrate concretely how versatile and useful templates can be in routing curves and circles.

Each template has several holes cut in it, three in one, four in the other, and each corner is rounded at a different radius (eight in all). To duplicate a hole exactly, clamp the template to the work and guide a router with a pattern bit around the inside of the template hole.

Instead of a pattern bit, you can use guide bushings to offset the bit from the template edge. The diameter of the routed hole will be reduced. Using a 1/4-inch bit with a 3/4-inch-O.D. guide bushing reduces the diameter of the template hole by 1/2 inch.

The sizing chart on the next page lays it all out for you. Two different guide bushing sizes are used, in combination with three different bit sizes. If you have a broader selection of either bushings or bits, or both, you may be able to come up with some additional sizes. Just as an example, a 1/4-inch bit used in a 7/16-inch-O.D. bushing reduces the hole 3/16 inch. The 3-inch template hole would then yield a 2 13/16-inch routed hole.

Finally, you can use the templates to round off corners. No saw marks to sand away, no ripples or flat spots. Use the same template at each corner on a tabletop, for example, and you can round the corners smoothly and consistently.

The templates give you corner-round guides starting at a 3/4-inch radius and jumping in 1/4-inch increments to 3 inches.

Make the templates with a fly cutter chucked in a drill press or a

Circle Templates
Give you perfect circles without a trammel

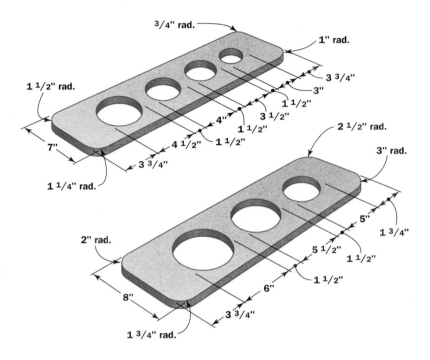

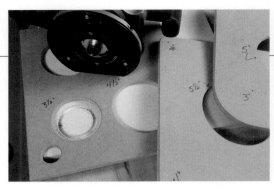

Though each template hole is labeled with the size of hole it will produce if used with a pattern bit, its range is expanded through the use of guide bushings. The bushing's offset reduces the diameter of the hole produced.

trammel to cut the holes. Lay out the corners using drafting templates (or a compass), then round them off on a stationary sander. Or use the router and trammel for them, too.

Template layouts are shown in the drawing. You *can* make individual templates—one for each size of hole—but ganging them gives you space-efficient clamping area.

Template Diameter	Guide Bushing O.D. (inches)	Bit Diameter (inches)	Hole Diameter (inches)	Template Diameter	Guide Bushing O.D. (inches)	Bit Diameter (inches)	Hole Diameter (inches)
3" hole	3/4	1/4	2 1/2	5" hole	3/4	1/4	4 1/2
	5/8	1/4	2 5/8		5/8	1/4	4 5/8
	5/8	3/8	2 3/4		5/8	3/8	4 3/4
	5/8	1/2	2 7/8		5/8	1/2	4 7/8
	none	pattern bit	3		none	pattern bit	5
3 1/2" hole	3/4	1/4	3	5 1/2" hole	3/4	1/4	5
	5/8	1/4	3 1/8		5/8	1/4	5 1/8
	5/8	3/8	3 1/4		5/8	3/8	5 1/4
	5/8	1/2	3 3/8		5/8	1/2	5 3/8
	none	pattern bit	3 1/2		none	pattern bit	5 1/2
4" hole	3/4	1/4	3 1/2	6" hole	3/4	1/4	5 1/2
	5/8	1/4	3 5/8		5/8	1/4	5 5/8
	5/8	3/8	3 3/4		5/8	3/8	5 3/4
	5/8	1/2	3 7/8		5/8	1/2	5 7/8
	none	pattern bit	4		none	pattern bit	6
4 1/2" hole	3/4	1/4	4				
	5/8	1/4	4 1/8				
	5/8	3/8	4 1/4				
	5/8	1/2	4 3/8				
	none	pattern bit	4 1/2				

Surfacing with the Router

Although the jointer, thickness-planer, and table saw are the tools of choice for preparing rough-sawed lumber for woodworking, there are occasions when the router can do a lumber-surfacing job that the other three massive, expensive shop tools can't.

■ Maybe you're on a remote job site, stuck without the shop tools.

■ Or you need to joint a batch of plywood panels, too big to balance on edge on the jointer, and with glues too hard on the jointer knives.

■ Or you have a butcher-block slab to trim. It's too heavy to maneuver on the table saw, and it's too wide for the radial arm. And your circular saw will leave an unsuitably ragged cut.

■ Perhaps you have a board to be planed that has an impossibly difficult grain, which neither the jointer nor the planer can machine satisfactorily.

■ How about hollowing out a thick board? Or planing and smoothing a convex surface? The router can do these jobs. Can the jointer or planer?

If you have the time, the router—set up with the appropriate jig or fixture—can do all of these jobs.

Flush-Trimming

Are these statements true or false: Flush-trimming is an operation only used when working with plastic laminates. Flush-trimming is an operation only done with a flush-trimming bit.

Both false, thanks to the "onlys."

Flush-trimming *is* an operation used when working with plastic laminates. But it also is done to machine edge-banding, trim plugs and keys, and level all manner of lumps and projections in otherwise flat surfaces. And, set up with the proper jigs and baseplates, you can do the job with straight bits, mortising bits, pattern bits, and bottom-cleaning bits, as well as flush-trimming bits.

Plugs covering screws that are close to an edge can easily be trimmed with a flush-trimming bit. The offset-base laminate trimmer is great for this sort of application.

Using a Flush-Trimming Bit

The least complicated flush-trimming setup is a laminate trimmer and flush-trimming bit. As explained in "Working Laminates" on page 229, the laminate trimmer is a compact router, devoid of knobs or handles, designed to fit in one hand. Despite its name, it's good for chores other than trimming plastic laminates. It has enough power to trim edge-banding and the like. And it's as perfect a package as the industry has come up with for balancing on a narrow edge.

The flushing-trimming bit, although usually listed amongst bits for laminate work, is also useful for jobs beyond that realm. Not only is it useful for trimming wooden edge-banding, screw plugs, and keys, it is often used as a pattern bit (see "Template-Guided Work" on page 155). The bit has two and some-

Try This!

One of the vexing aspects of using a flush-trimming bit is trying to keep the router—even a little laminate trimmer—square on a narrow edge. If the router wiggles one way, you get a hump, which, of course, you can remove with another pass. But wiggle the other and you get a snipe out of the material you're trying to trim flush. And you can't fix that up with another pass.

This simple brace provides bearing for a laminate trimmer on the face of the workpiece. Hold the trimmer horizontally against the edge being trimmed. Then bear down on the brace to help keep the trimmer square to the edge. (Some router manufacturers make an extra-cost trimming guide that's a lot like this one.)

The brace is easy to make from a scrap of 3/4-inch plywood and another of 1/4-inch plywood. To bring the brace's bearing surface flush with the bit's pilot bearing, mount the baseplate on the trim-

mer, and fit the bit in the collet. Set a square on the baseplate and use it to carry the plane of the bearing to the edge of the brace. Sand the nose of the brace until it's flush and square with the bearing.

If you don't have a laminate trimmer, this same concept can easily be adapted to a small router. Or attach a wooden facing to the router's edge guide and use it as a brace.

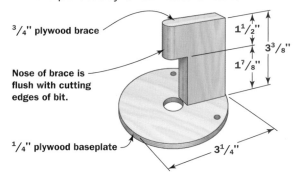

Flush-Trimming Brace
Helps steady a laminate trimmer

3/4" plywood brace

Nose of brace is flush with cutting edges of bit.

1/4" plywood baseplate

1 1/2"
3 3/8"
1 7/8"
3 1/4"

The flush-trimming brace is a simple outrigger that helps you keep the diminutive router square to the edge. Keep pressure on the brace, as shown. You particularly want to keep the trimmer from tipping down, which will gouge the edge.

times three cutting edges and a pilot bearing on the tip. To accomplish its job, it would seem that the cutting diameter should exactly match that of the bearing; but in fact, the cutting diameter is several thousandths of an inch smaller than the bearing. This so the cutting edge won't slice into the surface that the pilot references. Given the thinness of the color layer in plastic laminates, this is a capital idea.

To trim that edge-banding, set the bit height so the cutting edge not only pares the edge-banding, but also cleans away any glue that's squeezed out of the joint.

The biggest concern may be the potential for bearing tracks. These can range from outright scratches through burns marks to a burnished band that's visible only when the light strikes it at a certain angle. Before you begin, be sure the bearing is clean and that it turns freely. If it has a spur or grit on it, it can scratch. If it's frozen, it will burn the wood. When you work, be sure you don't press the bearing against the work too hard. This can lead to the burnished track. More often, though, burnishing is caused by *too little* pressure, which allows the bearing to spin with the cutter and buff the wood's surface.

Flush-Trimming Jig

Edge-banding can be trimmed with a straight bit if you use this jig. The model shown attaches to a laminate trimmer, but you should be able to adapt the design (and size) to fit any lightweight router.

Just remember that because of the router's position, the balance of the jig can be really hurt by a heavy machine. That's why a lam trimmer is nice. As you can see, the jig consists of a base-plate attached to a shoe. The side of the shoe is rabbeted and has a hole into which the bit projects. By pivoting the baseplate up and down, you adjust the position of the bit, determining how much or little it will remove from the work. At its highest setting, the bit may not even touch the work, while at its lowest setting, it'll probably cut a rabbet (a fact that might be useful to remember if you have a rabbet to cut).

To use the jig, you rest the shoe's sole on the work; the rabbet fits over the edge-banding to be trimmed. Turn on the router and slide the jig along the workpiece, almost as though you were hand-planing it. A

Bear down on the jig's front end with one hand and push it along the work with the other. You can see how a heavy router would throw the jig way out of balance and increase the work for you.

Trimming edge-banding with a router isn't without risks. A series of light cuts in the climb-cutting direction (left to right when using the flush-trimming jig) would have prevented this damage.

Flush-Trimming Jig
It works like a power planer

¹/₄" x 5" carriage bolt

¹/₄"-wide slot

Plastic knob with stud

12"

4"

Hole tapped for knob's stud

3/8"

1¹/₂"

5/8"

1"-dia. hole for bit

Hardwood shoe

13"

Plastic knob

4"

¹/₂" plywood baseplate

2"

Fender washer

feed direction note: Because of the orientation of the router, the proper feed direction is right to left. The jig, as shown, is set up to facilitate that. If tearout turns out to be a problem, you can resolve it—usually—by making a climb cut. Switching the grips can make that feed easier.

The hand-planing comparison is pertinent, too, to how you set up the jig. Turn the jig over and sight along the sole as you adjust the baseplate setting. Watch the bit's cutting edge, just as you watch the plane iron when setting it.

The jig is simple to make. The shoe is a piece of poplar 1¹/4 inches by 3 inches by 12 inches. One edge is rabbeted; the cut is ¹/2 inch wide by ¹/8 inch deep. Drill a hole for the bit into the side that will get the baseplate. Since the hole is offset and is not completely housed, we used a

1-inch-diameter Forstner bit to bore it. Drill a shallow hole for the 1-inch-diameter dowel handle, and glue the dowel in place. Finally, bore a ¹/4-inch-diameter hole for the baseplate-adjustment bolt.

The baseplate is cut from a piece of ¹/2-inch plywood. The pattern shown will accommodate a Porter-Cable laminate trimmer, and probably most other brands of laminate trimmers, too. For a regular router of

To adjust the bit in the flush-trimming jig, you swing the baseplate on its pivot to raise or lower the router in relation to the shoe. Sight along the sole as you move the baseplate, watching the bit's cutting edge, just as you watch a hand plane's iron when setting it. The cutting edge should be just flush with the sole.

light weight, you'll have to enlarge the baseplate.

Cut the shape of the baseplate, and drill the bit hole and mounting-screw holes. Cut the short slot for the adjustment bolt. Then clamp the baseplate to the side of the shoe and drive a 1-inch drywall screw pivot through the plate into the shoe. Install the washer and plastic knob, hang the router on it, and you are ready to go.

Flush-Trimming Baseplate

What do woodworkers with regular-sized 2-horse Porter-Cables or Boschs do? For trimming edge-banding, plugs, keys, and the like, this baseplate is the answer. It cantilevers the router over the edge-banding and uses a mortising or bottom-cleaning bit to do the trimming.

This baseplate is the one to use where the area to be trimmed is distant from an edge or too wide for other approaches. I use it, for

To avoid gouging the work, you need to hold the router upright by pressing down firmly at the end of the baseplate extension with one hand. Grasp the router knob with your other hand, and slide the machine along the edge to be trimmed, nibbling at the waste.

Flush-Trimming Baseplates
Easy to make, easy to use

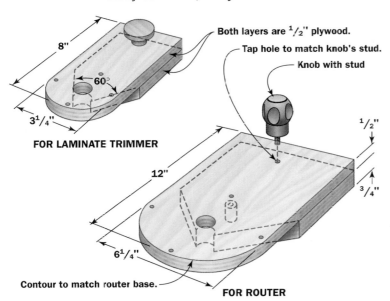

8"

60°

3¹/₄"

FOR LAMINATE TRIMMER

Both layers are ¹/₂" plywood.

Tap hole to match knob's stud.

Knob with stud

12"

¹/₂"

³/₄"

6¹/₄"

Contour to match router base.

FOR ROUTER

A router with a straight bit and flush-trimming baseplate can work in places that a piloted flush-trimming bit can't reach.

example, to trim the edge-banding on router table tops. For plugs concealing screws, this is ideal.

The drawing (page 195) shows two different-sized baseplates. One is for the laminate trimmer, the other for a regular router.

In both versions, the idea is to raise the router 1/4 to 1/2 inch above the surface so that it can clear protrusions. You set the bit so it's just clear of the surface. You advance the bit right up to the protrusion—be it a plug concealing a screw, or a strip of edge-banding—and begin nibbling at its edges. As you work, the baseplate can slide onto the newly trimmed surface, as you extend the trimmed area even further.

To make either baseplate, cut the upper layer to size, fit the router to one end, then glue the bottom layer to it. Add a knob of some sort, and you are ready to trim.

Jointing with a Router

There's a certain chicken-or-egg quality to this operation. Maybe you picked up on it. Why, you ask, would anyone joint with a router? Well, you tell yourself, because he (or she) doesn't have a jointer. He (or she) has to joint boards for edge-gluing, and the router can make a square, clean cut along the edge of a

Problem Solver

A jigsaw cut that's not square. A circular-saw cut that's too rough to the touch. A slab that's almost too beefy to move. The problem—getting a smooth, straight, *true edge*—has a lot of forms, but the solution is always the same: Use your router to trim and true the cut.

Minimize setup by using a self-positioning fence, such as the self-positioning dado guide shown in the chapter "Dadoing and Grooving" on page 235. When you make the cut with a jigsaw or circular saw, leave the line—in other words, deliberately cut well to the waste side of the line, so the cut line itself remains visible on the board. Then set your router guide *on* the line and make a pass with a straight bit. The bit will trim right to the line and leave a smooth, square edge.

Of course, if the work is thick and your bit is short, the base of the self-positioning fence may rob you of essential depth-of-cut. Go to a T-square and position it with a setup gauge, both also described in "Dadoing and Grooving" on page 235.

To prevent tearout at the end of the cut, clamp scrap to the edges of the work.

If all you are doing is truing the edge, routing away about 1/16 inch of stock, then a single pass that addresses the full thickness of the stock should do the trick. Use the largest-diameter straight bit you have to get the smoothest finish. The bit should be long enough to extend about 1/4 inch below the bottom of the stock.

If you are actually making the cut with your router, do it in a series of passes. Make the cut 1/4 inch deeper with each pass. If the stock is thick, say 8/4 oak or 10/4 maple, try cutting about halfway through, then turning the slab over to rout from the other side. When you are through, after the waste has fallen away, shift your fence 1/32 inch or so and make a last full-depth pass to really clean that edge.

A jigsaw blade seldom makes a truly square cut. Because the blade is thin and fixed at only one end, it tends to flex as it cuts, giving you a cut edge that wavers. The solution, of course, is to trim the edge with your router and a self-positioning guide.

Before edge-banding a plywood panel, you want to joint it. Standing this broad panel on edge to run it across the jointer would be venturesome, to say the least. But you can slide it across the router table's broad surface confidently, jointing it with a carbide-tipped straight bit.

Using a Handheld Router

One of the best ways to joint a board is with a handheld router. All you really need is an absolutely straight and true guide that's about a half-foot longer than the board that needs to be jointed. Plywood, particleboard, or MDF will fit the bill, certainly. The factory edge should be straight and true, and so long as you don't leave it in the rain, should remain so. Cut a 4- or 6-inch-wide strip from a new sheet, mark the factory edge, and use that edge as the guide. A strip cut across the sheet will do boards up to 3 1/2 feet long, while an 8-foot strip cut from the long dimension of the sheet will serve for boards up to about 7 1/2 feet long.

You can reference the router base against this fence, but you can also reference the pilot bearing of a flush-

board. An essential, of course, is a straight, true fence to guide either the router or the work. And how do you get that? Why you…joint…it.

Ahhh…. The sigh of recognition.

Well, recognize, first of all, that your router can do a darn good job substituting for a jointer. If you don't have a jointer, if you want to joint glue-laden materials like plywood or medium-density fiberboard (MDF), if you want to joint a board or panel that's too big to maneuver, think seriously about using the router. You can do the job on the router table with an easily made jointing fence, or using a handheld router guided by a straight edge.

And how do you get that straight edge without a jointer? Sheet goods, of course. The factory edge is going to be straight and true. Make your fence using that edge as the guide.

But remember, too, that even though you have—or have access to—a jointer, you still might want to do selected jointing with your router. *One example:* Jointing man-made panels on the jointer will dull its cutters pretty quickly. A carbide-tipped

straight bit will joint miles of MDF or plywood without losing its edge. *Others:* Jointing the freshly crosscut edge of a butcher-block panel that's much too heavy to maneuver on the jointer. Jointing a bowed board that simply can't be held against the jointer fence, though it can be clamped flat to joint with a handheld router.

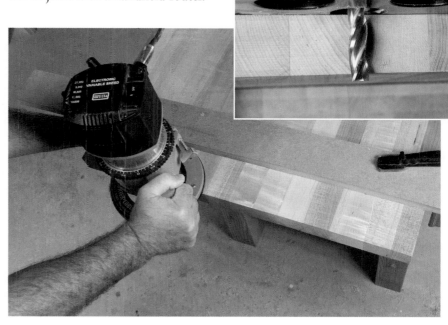

Cutting thick, hard stock, such as this butcher-block benchtop, calls for a stout bit and a powerful router, coupled with light cuts. A heavy router is actually a benefit on a cut like this. Cutting even 1/16 inch from end grain is *work* for both cutter and router.

Safety First!

The router may be the safest tool for surfacing small workpieces. Maybe the piece is small and blocky. Maybe it's thin. These are the pieces that the jointer tends to jerk around or demolish, mauling your fingers in the process. Avoid this hazard—joint the piece on the router table.

trimming bit (or a pattern bit) against the fence. It depends upon where you position the fence vis-à-vis the edge to be jointed.

As you set the fence, bear in mind that you should trim no more than ¹/₁₆ inch from the edge.

Because any bit you use must address the full thickness of the board at once, it has to be a stout one. Use is the largest-diameter ¹/₂-inch-shank bit in your collection. Its cutting edges should be ¹/₄ to ¹/₂ inch longer than the board's thickness.

■ If you're using a pattern bit, you can set the fence atop the workpiece and clamp it to the work, exposing just the amount of stock that's to be removed.

■ Using a flush-trimming bit means the fence must be clamped to the underside of the work, again, with

just the amount of stock that's to be removed standing proud of the fence edge. Because the fence is beneath the work, getting it set can be troublesome.

■ If you're guiding the router base against the fence, setup is easy. Use a gauge like the T-square setup gauge. A big brother to the self-positioning dado guide is even easier to set up. (Both of these gizmos are described in the chapter "Dadoing and Grooving" on page 235.)

In any case, the fence has to be protected from bumps and dings if you intend to maintain it as your jointing fence. Any dip or dent will be telegraphed into the workpiece edge. (A custom baseplate with a long straight edge will skim over dips and dents without telegraphing them into the cut, though it will magnify ridges, bumps, or any other *projection* on the fence edge.)

Working on the Router Table

To joint on a router table, you need a jointing fence. But it's a different sort of fence than the one used with a handheld router. Like the jointer's infeed and outfeed tables, the router

table's jointing fence needs infeed and outfeed sections, adjusted to support the work both before the bit trims away stock and after.

The most simple jointing fence is a strip of ³/₄-inch plywood or MDF with a bit notch and a strip of plastic laminate glued to it left of the bit (the outfeed half of the fence, in other words). The drawing shows a somewhat more substantial version of this, made with two strips of plywood or MDF glued face to face, thus creating a taller surface to guide the work. You can bond the laminate to the fence with contact cement, or you can use double-sided tape. The fence doesn't need to be as high as the stock being jointed, though of course the bit does.

If you've equipped your router table with a split fence, you don't need a jointing fence. All you have to do is adjust the two fence sections separately, to serve as infeed and outfeed supports. Most manufactured fences have separate infeed and outfeed facings, and you can shim out the outfeed facing. With such fences, you can vary the bite—to some extent—by varying the shim material. Use thin card stock, or slightly thicker posterboard, or thicker plastic laminate, or—if you're feeling really aggressive—¹/₈-inch hardboard.

Jointing Fence
Use it to joint on the router table

4"

Bore clearance hole for bit.

36"

Cement plastic laminate to outfeed side only.

Glue together two strips of ³/₄" MDF.

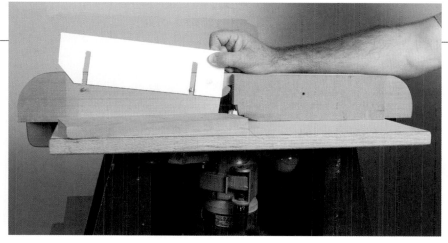

You can transform most any router-table fence with a split facing—that is, with separate infeed and outfeed halves—into a jointing fence by shimming the outfeed half. A piece of posterboard between the fence itself and the facing is all it takes.

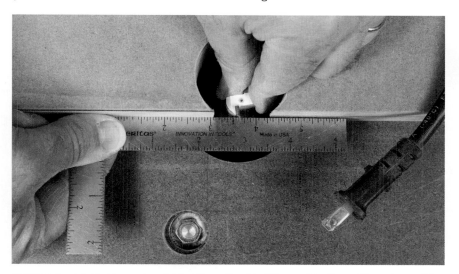

Position the jointing fence by aligning its outfeed half tangent to the cutting edges of the bit. Set a straightedge against that face and turn the bit with your fingers—unplug the router first!—to judge the alignment.

Make a test, cutting about this far. With the board held tight against the infeed side, the cut edge should also be tight against the outfeed side. If you can slip a feeler gauge of any thickness between the edge and the fence, you need to adjust the fence position. Otherwise, your edge won't be straight, and you'll get snipe at the end of the cut.

The least vexing way to set the fence is to line up the outfeed half of the fence tangent to the bit's cutting edge. Hold a straightedge against that half of the fence and, with the router unplugged, turn the bit with your fingers. You want the cutting edges to *just* brush the straightedge, not move it.

Make a partial test cut. That is, start jointing, and after cutting about 6 or 8 inches, turn off the router and assess the setup. If the board is tight against the infeed face but clear of the outfeed face, the fence must be brought for-

Bit Drawer

What bit is best for jointing? For starters, limit yourself to 1/2-inch-shank bits.

The instinctive choice is something like the 1-inch-diameter straight (right). Its 2-inch-long cutting edges can deal with stock up to 8/4. The large diameter gives the cutting edges a shallow entry angle to produce a good cut finish.

If jointing material with thin surface veneers, try a compression bit (left), a.k.a. an up-and-down spiral. It's designed to cut through sheet goods without lifting chips from either face.

Don't fret if your bit collection is small. A commonplace straight bit, such as the 3/4-inch cutter (bottom), will do fine with materials up to its 1-inch cutting capacity.

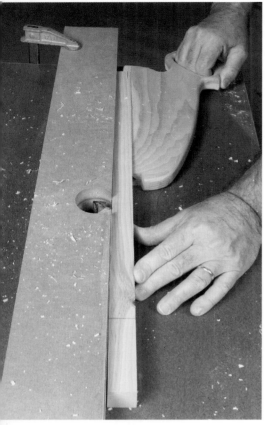

Just as you can taper legs on a jointer, you can do it on the router table. You'll probably feel safer doing it this way, too. Mark the extremity of the cutting edge on the tabletop, and mark where you want the taper to begin on the leg blank. Line up the two marks, and "joint" from that point to the end of the leg. Keep repeating this operation until you've achieved the degree of taper you want.

ward. Of course, if you don't even get that far, if the board catches on the outfeed edge of the bit notch, the fence must be moved back. The required fence adjustments are going to be tiny, so use your micro-adjuster or reference block and shims (see the chapter "Router Table Savvy" on page 119).

Once the fence is positioned, you are set up to joint your good stock.

The ideal bit, in all these cases, is a fairly heavy but well-balanced straight bit. Always use a 1/2-inch-shank bit if possible.

Thicknessing

Now we're getting to the gut of the chapter—surfacing rough stock. Yes, you can dress stock using a router.

But make no mistake here: You'd be nuts to habitually prepare lumber using the router. You can't beat the jointer-planer–table saw ensemble to dress rough-sawed boards, making the faces smooth, flat, and parallel, the edges smooth, square, and parallel. The job can be done quickly and accurately by any beginner. And even if you don't have the dough for a jointer and a planer, you usually can buy the service economically from your lumber dealer.

BUT every once in a while, there's a special project where router-thicknessing is appropriate. Maybe it is centered around a gnarly grained board—beautiful but difficult to surface without tearout. Or you've acquired a small log of some native exotic, a log you can saw into boards on your band saw. Perhaps you need a small amount of thin stock for a box or for a drawer or two. There are a lot of reasons to do it. Some day, you may have a problem, and router-thicknessing will be your solution.

Here's the basics of how to do it. What you need is a sturdy router, a large-diameter bottom-cleaning kind of bit, and a fixture that suspends the router above the stock, allowing it to move side to side and back and forth in a level plane.

We've got a surfacing platform here that's pretty flexible. It'll accommodate stock a few inches wide by a few inches long, up to 3-foot-long plank that's 2 1/4 inches thick and 11 inches wide. You can build it and, when you have a board to thickness that's in its range, pull it off the shelf. Obviously, you can change the

dimensions to revise the range. Or you can keep the concept in mind and make a job-specific fixture when the need arises.

The Surfacing Platform

The concept of the platform is this: The workpiece rests between two level tracks. A double-rail carriage that supports the router spans the tracks. The carriage is designed so the router can slide from one track to the other. And the carriage can slide from one end of the tracks to the other.

To plane a board, you set it between the tracks, with the router in

The surfacing platform has two parts: a base with tracks and a carriage for the router. You set the material to be surfaced on the base between the tracks, and you set the router that's to do the surfacing in the carriage. Work your way across the stock in a series of back-and-forth passes, smoothing and flattening it. The setup is useful for surfacing badly twisted boards, end grain, and material with particularly gnarled grain.

Cutting List

Piece	Number	Thickness	Width	Length	Material
Base	1	3/4"	19 1/2"	42"	Plywood
Sides	2	1 1/4"	2 1/2"	42"	Hardwood
Baseplate	1	6 5/16"	6 5/16"	1/4"	Plywood
Carriage rails	2	1 1/4"	2"	20"	Hardwood
Carriage guides	2	1 1/4"	2"	10 3/4"	Hardwood
Spacers	2	3/4"	12"	42"	Plywood*
Spacers	2	1/4"	12"	42"	Plywood*
Spacers	2	1/2"	12"	42"	Plywood*

Hardware

6 flathead stove bolts, 5/16" × 3"

6 T-nuts, 5/16"

4 carriage stove bolts, 1/4" × 3"

4 flat washers, 1/4"

4 wing nuts, 1/4"

*Optional

its carriage at one corner. Then you slide the carriage along the tracks, routing a strip as wide as the bit from one end of the board to the other. Move the router in its carriage in increments, and slide the carriage back, widening the machined strip. Just keep moving the router and sliding the carriage. It's a methodical, even tedious, operation, but it gets the job done.

The platform consists of a base with two sides—the tracks. One side is fixed (though it is easily removed). The second side adjusts, as the drawing makes clear. The base must be flat—plywood, particleboard, and

Surfacing Platform and Carriage
Plane problem stock with your router

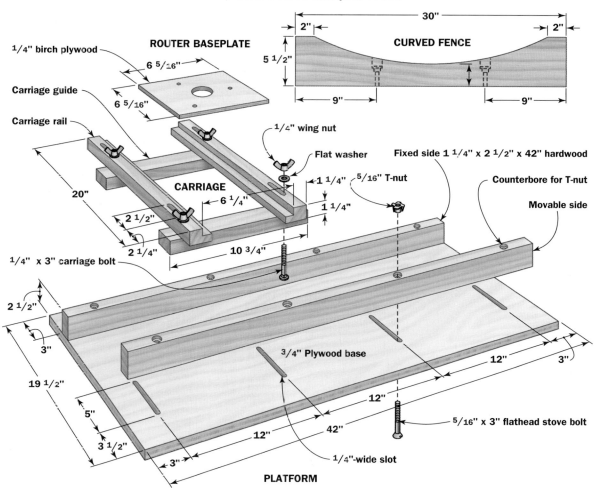

MDF are good materials for it. The sides must be straight and true. A straight-grained hardwood makes durable—as well as smooth-sliding—tracks. The carriage consists of two rails and two guides, cut from the same stock as the sides.

The real key to getting flat stock with parallel faces from the platform is accuracy in the platform itself. Each side must be straight with parallel edges, and the two must be of identical height. If one side is even 1/64 inch higher than the other, whatever you machine in the platform will have a slight taper across its faces. This important caveat aside, the platform is easy to make.

1. Cut the parts to the sizes specified by the Cutting List. You don't have to cut the spacers; but depending on the stock you are starting with and its final thickness, it may be handy to have several spacers to boost it up in the platform.

2. Position the sides 3 inches from the edges of the base and clamp them. Drill the mounting-screw holes through them. (For the adjustable side, these holes will serve as the starting points for the slots.) Countersink the holes for the fixed side. With a Forstner bit, slightly counterbore the holes on the sides so the T-nuts will be slightly recessed. Drive the T-nuts into place.

3. Use a router and straight bit to extend 5-inch-long slots from the mounting holes for the adjustable side. I used a T-square to guide the router, and eyeballed the length of the cut, which isn't that critical. After the slots are cut through, use a V-grooving bit to "countersink" each slot.

4. Bolt the sides to the base, and make sure the bolt ends don't extend above the sides' top edges (they shouldn't even be flush). They've got to be below the surface for the carriage to slide easily.

5. With the platform done, turn to the carriage. Cut a 3/4-inch by 3/4-inch rabbet into each rail. Mark and rout the 2 1/2-inch-long slots for the adjusting bolts that secure the guides to the rails. These are easiest to cut on a router table.

6. Assemble the carriage, bolting the guides to the rails.

An optional part of the rig is a square baseplate. Some routers, plungers particularly, have a flat edge or two to their bases. But most are round, and the round ones, I've found, tend to rock on the carriage. The solution is a square or rectangular baseplate. Since surfacing is a job where a good view of the bit and the workpiece is important, you might choose to make the baseplate from clear acrylic or polycarbonate instead of plywood.

Using the platform and carriage is not difficult. The workpiece has to be about 4 to 6 inches shorter than the platform, of course, so the bit can move off the edge of the work without the carriage tumbling off the ends of the tracks. (You may even want to tack stops to the ends of the tracks to prevent this from happening accidentally.)

Trapping the stock may be the hardest part. To avoid gouging the sides, you should set them so there's about a half-inch of space between each side and the workpiece. Center the workpiece, then tap wedges

Bit Drawer

The best bits for surfacing are those designed for hollowing out broad surfaces like hinge mortises and trays.

The dish at left is called a dish cutter. Its cutting edges are radiused at their outside corners. This gives you a nice radius inside a recess, but it also means you don't have a hard edge between adjacent passes. The trade-off is that you have to overlap passes a bit more than if you were using a square-cornered bit. You can find this bit in a range of sizes up to 1 1/4 inches.

Want to speed up the work and reduce the back-and-forth? Try a bottom-cleaning bit (right). Its cutting tips are short and wide, so it clears a wide swath, but can't forge deep into the stock. The bit shown has open flutes, so it has excellent chip clearance, which allows fast feed rates. Several variations on this bit are available; they're often marketed under names like mortising bit or planer bit. Diameters range up to 1 1/2 inches. Both bit types are available with a bearing on the shank.

between stock and sides to keep it from shifting.

Four-quarter stock will probably have to be elevated so the bit can reach it, and anything thinner than that surely will need a lift into the router bit's range. You should be able to mix and match the different spacers listed in the cutting list to put even the thinnest stock where you need it. Keep your roll of carpet tape handy if you are concerned that either the workpiece or the spacers will shift.

The most troublesome stock to position for machining is warped stuff. Yet this is stock that's best reserved for router-thicknessing. If it's warped enough, it can be the devil to joint flat so you can feed it through the planer. And if you plane it without flattening one face, you'll get a smooth but still warped board—smooth because the planer's feed rollers will press it flat while it's in the machine, and warped because it'll be warped when the pressure of the rollers is off. So if you can plane the board and use the router to plane one face flat, you can plane the second face in the planer or in the router-thicknessing rig.

What you need to do is set the warped stock in your platform, and shim the corners as necessary so it doesn't rock. It's like shimming cabinets to level them during installation. Try to set the board so you can get a flat surface with minimal stock removal. When the board is set, tap those wedges in place so it doesn't shift. Then you're ready to set up the router.

Set the carriage in place and adjust the guides. Chuck the bit, set the depth-of-cut to remove no more than 1/8 to 3/16 inch from the high spots, and place the router in the carriage. Then rout.

The conventional wisdom seems to be that you must make your sweeps in the direction that the grain runs. In my experience, that doesn't seem to be the case. Sweeping back and forth across the board doesn't yield a lesser finish than coursing from end to end. The router bit's cutting edges don't sweep the surface in the same way that planer and jointer

Warped stock is a challenge to set in the platform, but a little effort can save it from the woodstove. At those spots where the stock is off the base, slide shims under it. The goal is to steady the stock. Then drive wedges between the stock and the sides, as here, to keep it from shifting.

Because the cutter isn't addressing the entire width of the material in a single pass, it's natural to have some indications of overlap. The character of the material as well as the feed rate can impact the cut quality.

The surfacing platform is especially useful when you have an attractive board that doesn't plane well. Turning the cutter's angle of attack 90°, which is what you do when you switch from a thickness planer to the router and platform, can make a big difference. The routed surface (left) is free of the "chunking" caused by a planer (right).

Job-Specific Setups

The surfacing platform may represent too much of a formal commitment to suit you. A friend of mine, Fred Matlack, for years has needled me about such jigs, fixtures, and setups. The job-specific setup is Fred's approach. He'll make some ugly fixture that works for the job at hand, and not worry about whether it'll adapt to another job. When the job's done, he tosses the fixture. If he ever does another job requiring that fixture, he'll make the needed fixture then. And the one he makes then may be considerably different from the one he's making now. "Why make more of the setup than you need to?" seems to be his attitude. Very practical.

cutters do. Cut across the grain or against the grain on one of the latter machines, and you will have a choppy finish. But with the router, the bit is addressing the wood with the same motion, regardless of the direction in which you feed the tool. It is just this difference in cutting action that enables the router to plane twisted-grain woods.

Be methodical, however. Whether you work back and forth or end to end, be an automaton. Sweep on one axis, then click over a notch in the other. Sweep, then click over. Sweep, then click over.

After a first pass over the entire surface, make as many additional passes as necessary to flatten the board. Then make a final skim cut to make the surface as smooth as you can get it with the router. Scraping and sanding will then remove any remaining swirl marks.

The surfacing baseplate reflects this job-specific approach. Years and years ago, Fred made a wide plywood baseplate for one of his routers, added stiffeners along the edges, and fitted it with two hand grips (see the drawing; how to duplicate it should be evident). It didn't have stops or a dedicated platform, but it could be used to do wide lap joints and a lot of other work.

Surfacing Baseplate
For job-specific setups

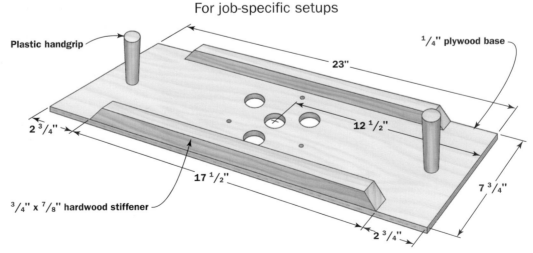

Plastic handgrip

¹/₄" plywood base

23"

12 ¹/₂"

2 ³/₄"

17 ¹/₂"

7 ³/₄"

³/₄" x ⁷/₈" hardwood stiffener

2 ³/₄"

Following Fred's lead, I've made and used such baseplates for thicknessing. To do that, all you do is set up tracks on both sides of the board. You might screw them to a base, but all you really need to do is plant a track on each side of the board, then trap the work between the vise and a bench dog, or set it all up on a couple of bar clamps. The surfacing baseplate is the carriage you use.

Everything about the operation is the same as using the surfacing platform, except that the tracks for the job-specific setup get chewed up and tossed out when the job's done, and those of the platform will see use another day. (And take up space in the shop until that day, Fred would be sure to point out.)

Shaping Surfaces

Beyond thicknessing, the router can surface stock in ways that a planer or jointer cannot. It can excavate a recess. It can taper. It can hollow out a concave depression, or cut away the edges, forming a hump. A determined and creative woodworker can probably adapt its surface-forming capabilities to produce an undulating surface.

Excavating Recesses

It's a small step from thicknessing a board to routing a recess in it. Use the surfacing platform and carriage, but plunge the bit into the stock, rather than sweeping in from an edge. This is easiest to do if you use a plunge router.

Work out a system of stops to confine the area that the router bit can

address, so you surface only the area to be relieved. You don't want to accidentally move outside the recess area. A screw driven partway into the track or rail is all you need for a stop.

A job-specific approach would be to make a template and attach it to the work. Then, with a guide bushing mounted in the surfacing baseplate, do the job as a template-guided one. See the chapter "Template-Guided Work" on page 155 for more on this.

If you have a large area to excavate—to make a piecrust tabletop, for example—the structure of the platform and carriage simply have to be reconfigured to accommodate the workpiece.

Tapered Surfaces

Tapering is accomplished two ways. You can use tapered tracks with the surfacing rig. Or you can use tracks of different heights. Which approach

you use depends upon the stock and what you are trying to achieve. Tapering a board from edge to edge? Use tracks of different heights. Tapering table legs? Use tapered tracks.

Make the appropriate tracks for the surfacing platform. Drill and

Rout a recess, forming a small tray, guided by a template. The surfacing baseplate spans the broad template window, and the dish cutter used (inset) has a shank-mounted bearing to reference the template edges.

To taper a blank, such as this one for a hand mirror, use tracks of different heights and the surfacing baseplate. Trap the blank between the tracks. When the plate rests on the tracks, it's tilted. The simplicity of the setup is evident.

keep the fences when the job's done. Unless you are going to use them again and again, just toss them.) You'll make two of these tracks, or fences; see the Curved Fence detail in the drawing on page 201 for details.

Work out your curve, laying it out directly on a piece of the track stock or laying it out on a template. A good way to find a fair curve requires two people (or just one three-handed woodworker). Use a relatively thin strip of wood, plywood, acrylic, plastic laminate, or even metal as a guide. Flex it so it bows. Have the helper trace along the strip to record the curve. You can mark starting and ending spots, as well as the deepest (or highest) part of the curve, and develop an even curve that connects them. (Check through the previous chapter, "Routing Curves and Circles" on page 175, for ideas on using your router to create the arcs that you need.)

counterbore the mounting holes, and insert the T-nuts. Depending upon your approach, remove one or both of the standard tracks, and install the tapering tracks.

Setting the stock is the same as for thicknessing, and the router operation itself is the same. Just the result is different.

The surfacing platform can be adapted to this work easily. Just change the tracks. The stock carriage should work fine. (You don't have to

Forming Convex and Concave Surfaces

If this is all a logical progression, then the next step is to machine rises and depressions, using the same basic technique. If the tracks are cut to a concave or convex curve, the router carriage will rise and fall (or fall and rise, as the case may be) as it is advanced along them. The bit will penetrate deeper at one point than at another.

If you like cabinets or other furniture pieces with curved surfaces, this is a great way to produce those surfaces.

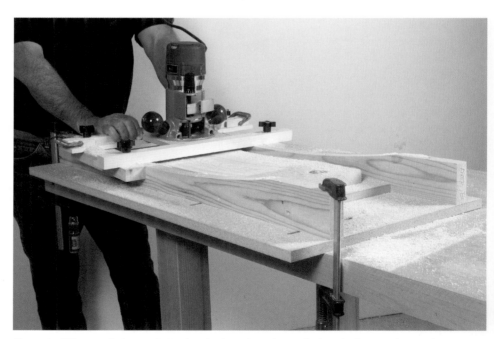

The only difference between flattening the board on the surfacing platform and scooping out a hollow with it is the contour of the tracks. And contouring surfaces is something you can't do on a jointer or planer.

Customize your surfacing platform so you can use it to hollow seats for stools. All it takes is a lazy-Susan bearing and a couple of plywood squares to make a swivel base.

To use the swivel, you mount a blank on it, then position it between the concave fences. Chuck the appropriate bit in the router, set the cutting depth, then lock the router in the center of its carriage. As you make a pass with the router, hold the blank. (The swivel spins easily, and you'll quickly discover that the bit can make it really whirl.) When the bit is free of the work, turn the blank ever so slightly. Make another pass. Turn the blank again, and make another pass. Just keep at it until the entire blank is hollowed.

Making the swivel is easy. You need a 6-inch lazy-Susan bearing. The base is an 11-inch-square

piece of 1/4-inch plywood. Scribe centerlines on it, dividing it into quarters, and then scribe diagonals. Set the bearing on it and mark where you will drive screws that will mount one of the bearing's flanges to the base; these points should be on the diagonals. On the centerlines, mark the centers of the access holes. Cut the access holes, including one at the center of the base. Now screw the bearing to the base.

Lay out and cut the turntable next. Its diameter should equal the diagonal dimension of the bearing. Drill a pilot hole at the turntable's center. Then mount the turntable on the bearing. Be sure it is centered.

To mount a blank on the turntable, drive a screw through the centerpoint of the turntable into the blank's centerpoint. One screw is all it takes to secure the work.

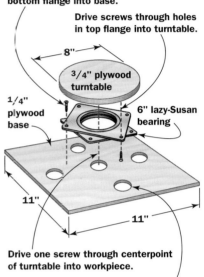

Swivel Base
Use it to hollow round seats

Drive screws through holes in bottom flange into base.

Drive screws through holes in top flange into turntable.

8"

3/4" plywood turntable

1/4" plywood base

6" lazy-Susan bearing

11"

11"

Drive one screw through centerpoint of turntable into workpiece.

Holes in base provide access to attach bearing to turntable.

Scoop out a stool seat on your surfacing platform! With the seat blank mounted on the turntable and the router pinned in the middle of the carriage, simply feed the router back and forth on the curved tracks.

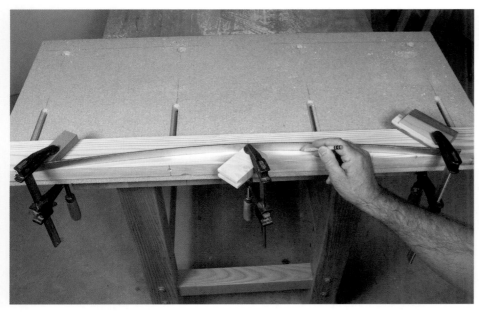

Laying out a smooth, even, "sprung" curve calls for a flexible strip of thin wood, metal, or plastic, small scraps, and clamps. Clamp a scrap at each end of the arc. With the ends of your strip against these blocks, flex it and set a third scrap to hold the curve. Trace the curve right on the work.

However you do it, lay out and then cut the curve for the tracks. Make the curve as smooth and even as you can. If you can get one good track, use a your router and a flush-trimming bit to produce a duplicate. Drill the mounting holes, install the T-nuts, and mount the tracks on your surfacing platform.

To get the curve aligned properly on the workpiece, you have to position it carefully between the tracks. Scribe centerlines across both the tracks and the workpiece. When you fit the work between the tracks, line up its centerline with those on the tracks. Fit scraps against the ends of the work and clamp them to the platform. This will prevent the work from shifting out of alignment. Then use the wedges to secure the work so it doesn't shift from side to side.

Set the carriage in place and drop the router into it. If you are using a plunge router—it will make it easier to get to the finished depth if you do—slide the carriage to position the bit at the beginning of the cut. Lower the bit until it just touches the wood, then set the depth stop so this is the deepest the bit will be able to cut.

To begin routing, raise the bit so you'll be taking off between 1/8 inch and 1/4 inch at the point of deepest penetration. Start with the carriage at one end of the track, and the router positioned at one side. Slide the carriage to the other end of the tracks, shift the router slightly, and return. Shift the router and make another pass. Work methodically in this fashion until you have completed a first pass over the entire workpiece. Plunge a little deeper and repeat the process.

Make as many additional passes as necessary to achieve the curve you've laid out. Make the final pass a skimming cut, to leave the surface as smooth as you can get it with the router. Scraping and sanding will then remove any remaining swirl marks.

Frame-and-Panel Construction

Frame-and-panel construction predates plywood and other stable man-made sheet goods. The construction system was the early woodworker's way of dealing with wood's "come and go." The rails and stiles forming the frame are relatively narrow, and the dimensional changes in it that accompany humidity changes are correspondingly modest. While the panel is much wider than the stiles, it's set into a groove or rabbet in such a way that dimensional changes are "absorbed" without damaging the structure, even cosmetically. So the frame contributes dimensional stability, and the panel (usually) contributes good looks.

The most commonplace examples of frame-and-panel construction are doors and windows. It's used in elaborate architectural paneling and in custom cabinetry and furniture. In these uses, frame-and-panel construction is styled to be attractive as well as functional. But inside casework, it can be functional, and appearance is of little consequence.

The router can be a pivotal tool in profiling and joining the frame members, and in shaping the panels.

In a well-equipped production shop, the shaper is the tool used. But the router can do the job, regardless of the joinery selected.

Making Frames

The minimal frame consists of two stiles and two rails. When the frame is displayed vertically, as in a cabinet door, the stiles are the vertical elements and the rails the horizontal elements. The rails invariably fit between the stiles. The edges are unembellished.

In more elaborate constructions, the frame can have three or more rails, as well as intermediate vertical members called mullions. The edges are embellished with beads, ogees, coves, or combinations of these shapes. A number of different joints can be used to assemble the frame: miters, laps, dowels, biscuits, and—the strongest, the most traditional—mortise-and-tenon.

One of the big challenges in frame-and-panel construction is finding practical, economical ways to meld strength and utility with beauty. The

For centuries, frame-and-panel construction has been used to moderate the impact of wood movement in furniture. Doors of all sizes and contours feature this construction, but so do cabinets and chests. Modern router techniques make it easy.

209

joinery has to be strong, especially if the unit is to be a door. The mortise-and-tenon is the traditional framing joint, but it can be time-consuming to make, especially if you are assembling a couple dozen cabinet doors. And attractive appearance is often as important as the joinery. Adding a series of operations to embellish a workpiece adds to the project's cost.

In relatively recent years, more and more of these frames—for cabinet doors in particular—have been assembled with what's known as the cope-and-stick joint (sometimes it's called a cope-and-pattern joint or a stile-and-rail joint). It's a form of the groove and stub tenon, and it's cut on the shaper or router table. At the same time that the joinery is cut, the piece is embellished. The woodworker's productivity is increased!

The router bit used has two cutters on the shank. One forms a decorative profile on the edge of the frame member and at the same time the other cuts the groove for the panel. The bit is reconfigured (by repositioning these cutters), then used to cut the ends of the rails, forming a tongue and a reverse of the decorative profile. When the cuts are properly aligned on the workpieces, the tongue fits into the groove and the rail end conforms perfectly to the profile. Bonded with a modern glue, it is a strong joint.

The terms "cope" and "stick" are carryovers from hand-tool woodworking. Cope is the more familiar term, since trim carpenters still use the technique to fit one trim piece to another at inside corners. The pertinent dictionary definition of cope is "to shape one structural member to conform to the shape of another member."

Stick, as used here, isn't in the dictionary. In the old days, a woodworker would clamp—or "stick"—a

Quickly cut with specialized router bits, the cope-and-stick joint looks great and is strong enough for cabinetry applications. The nature of the joint gives you great latitude to adjust the position of the rail along the stile.

board to his workbench, then use a profile plane to form a decorative shape on an edge. Then he'd rip the shaped edge from the wider board. The process was called sticking.

One focus of this chapter is setting up and making cope-and-stick frames. We won't go into mortise-and-tenon joinery here, because it merits its own complete chapter. Nor will we get into routing decorative edges on frame members, again because it is covered in its own chapter. Suffice it to say that cope-and-stick joinery is just one of several frame construction options available to the router woodworker.

Preparing the Stock

Cope-and-stick bits, by industry convention, are designed to work with 3/4-inch stock. This is a standard stock thickness in most areas of the United States and Canada. If you buy dressed stock, you should have no problems.

There is some leeway in the bit design, comfortably about 1/16 inch either way, but as much as 1/8 inch

Positioning the Sticking Cut

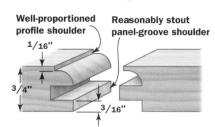

Well-proportioned profile shoulder

Reasonably stout panel-groove shoulder

1/16"

3/4"

3/16"

Typical cope-and-stick profile falls comfortably on edge of 3/4" stock.

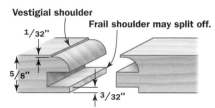

Vestigial shoulder

Frail shoulder may split off.

1/32"

5/8"

3/32"

Fitting fixed elements of profile on thinner stock requires compromising shoulder proportions.

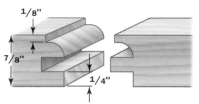

1/8"

7/8"

1/4"

Increasing stock thickness bulks one or both shoulders.

Bit Drawer

Three types of cope-and-stick cutters are (clockwise from the top) the matched pair, the stacked bit, and the assembly.

Three styles of cope-and-stick cutters are on the market: the two-bit set, the assembly, and the stacked bit.

All are available in an assortment of profiles: bead, quarter-round, ogee, cove-and-bead (sometimes called classical), and bevel (sometimes called traditional or straight). All, however, cut a groove 1/4 inch wide and 3/8 inch deep.

A 1 1/2-horsepower router has enough power to drive one of these bits, and it can be run at full speed. While some bit makers offer these

Sticking Profiles Available

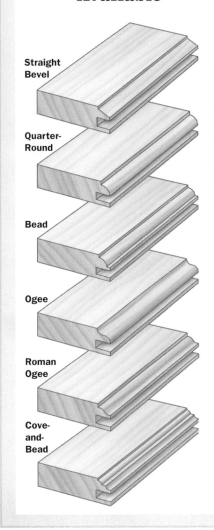

Straight Bevel

Quarter-Round

Bead

Ogee

Roman Ogee

Cove-and-Bead

sets or assemblies on 1/4-inch shanks, it's a much better proposition to buy them on 1/2-inch shanks.

Solid two-bit sets. With the two-bit sets, one of the bits makes the stick cut and the other makes the cope cut. Typically, the profile cutter is an integral part of the shank, while the bearing and the slot cutter are separate parts, secured on an arbor projecting from the bit. The stick cutter has a bearing mounted on the tip, so it can be used to make curved cuts, as is required to make arched rails. The cope bit has the bearing mounted between the profile cutter and the groover.

The overall advantage of the two-bit set is that you don't have to break down the bit to switch from one cut to the other. For those who do lots of frame-and-panel work, this means that two routers can be set up, one for each bit. This makes the switch from sticking to coping even easier.

Reversible assembly. The assembly consists of an arbor with an integral shank, two removable cutters—one for the profile, the other the slotter—a bearing, and some brass shims. When setting up the assembly for sticking cuts, you slip the profile cutter onto the arbor first, followed by the slotter, then the bearing. To set up the assembly for the cope cut, you put the slotter on the arbor first, followed by the bearing, then the profile cutter. The

shims help you tune the fit of the stub tenon in the groove.

You have to be careful when shifting the cutters that you don't turn them over. The cutting tips have to be facing the direction of rotation or they won't cut. The profile cutter is always oriented the same way, and it's obvious if you turn it over. The slot cutter is the tricky one, because it isn't always immediately obvious that it's been inverted. And when the bit smokes but doesn't cut, the cause may be a mystery unless you know to check this little detail.

The advantage of the assembly—the cost difference aside—is the perfectly matched cuts. Since you are using the same cutters to produce both the cope and the stick cuts, they're guaranteed to match. The disadvantage, of course, is that you have to dismantle the bit when you're switching from one cut to the other.

Stacked bit. A third style is the stacked bit. The one I've seen is like an assembled bit with an extended arbor and a second profile cutter. Stacked on the arbor are a profile cutter, a slot cutter, the bearing, and another profile cutter. To cut sticking, you raise the bit to its maximum height; the upper profile cutter is above the work. To switch to a cope cut, you lower the bit so that the lower profile cutter is below the router table mounting plate.

either way if you really stretch it. The typical sticking bit is designed to produce a 5/8-inch cut and leave a tongue 1/8 inch wide as the groove's panel-retaining wall. If your stock's thickness dictates it, you can shift the position of the cut slightly to either reduce the profile width and increase the groove wall's thickness or vice versa. That's the leeway.

If you find yourself with stock that's a 16th light or heavy, you'll still be okay. With 11/16-inch stock, you'll be able to finesse the bit height to produce a panel-retaining wall that's 3/32 to 1/8 inch thick without noticeably affecting the profile. And if your stock is thicker, say 13/16 inch, you can hold the width of the profile while increasing the groove-wall thickness (which might be considered a plus).

The usual wood specs apply: Use defect-free, straight-grained lumber. We usually take such provisos with a grain of salt, and you can get away with using slightly bowed or twisted stock for a frame-and-panel unit so long as it isn't a door. If the wood in a frame-and-panel unit is warped, the unit will be warped. If the unit is a structural part of case, it will be anchored to other elements that may pull it into line and hold it there. But if it is a door, it won't hang flat, and you won't be able to conceal that.

For doors, the stock *must* be flat, straight, and true.

Dress the chosen stock to whatever thickness you've settled on. Rip it to width, and crosscut at least the rails to final length.

When you cut the rails, be sure you account for the profile and stub tenon. For example, if you are making an 18-inch-wide door and using 1 3/4-inch-wide stiles, the distance between the stiles is 14 1/2 inches. But the rails must be long

Set the elevation of the cope bit with a setup block or, as here, using a small square. With 3/4-inch stock, the back shoulder of the stub tenon should be 1/8 inch-plus wide, so set the lower corner of the slot cutter 19/32 inch to 5/8 inch from the tabletop.

enough to overlap the sticking profile. If it's 3/8 inch wide (which seems to be the standard), then you need to add 3/4 inch to the length of the rails (3/8 inch for each stile, or twice the width of the profile). The easy way to measure the profile is to stick a rule into the groove and see how deep it is; the depth of the groove will match the width of the profile.

Make several extra pieces to use for testing the setups.

Cutting the Joinery

Use a table-mounted router to cut the joinery. Although you are making a one-pass cut, you don't need a big-horsepower router. And though the cope and stick bits are hefty, they aren't large-diameter, so you don't really need to reduce the router's speed.

The usual sequence is to cope the rail ends first, then stick all the stiles and rails.

Cope the rails. The cope cut is cross-grain. You need to back up the work to prevent splinters from being torn from the back edge by the cutter as it emerges from the stock. Depending on the size and number of rails, you can gang them up and

feed them as a group past the cutter. Push them along the fence with a square scrap. The second rail backs up the first, the third backs up the second, and so on. The pusher backs up the last rail in the gang.

Some woodworkers prefer to use a more formal guide, like a coping sled. They do the rails one at a time. A plan for a sled is shown opposite. One caution: A sled does impact the bit-height setting because you have to accommodate the base's thickness. This may require you to "cheat" the bit out of the collet so the cutting tips address the stock.

The first setup task, of course, is the bit. Secure it in the router's collet. Then adjust the elevation. You can do this against a rule or small square. You won't be wrong—knowing the industry standards—to measure 7/16 inch to 5/8 inch from the tabletop (or coping sled base) to the corner of the tenon cutter. You'll get a 1/8- to 3/16-inch-wide shoulder on the stub tenon.

If you've got a setup block—one that came with the bits or one you made—you can use it to set the elevation. Tuck it into the bit and adjust the bit up and down. If you're using a

Coping Sled

Butting the end of a rail against the router table fence and sliding it through a cut isn't as easy as it may sound. The rail has a tendency to "walk," angling forward or back slightly, rather than staying square against the fence. In addition, the leading corner can dip into the bit opening in the fence.

A good and popular solution to these problems is a coping sled, like the one shown here. There's no slide for a miter-gauge slot. (I don't like those slots in a router table top, remember?) Instead, the sled is used with the fence. You butt it against the fence, then slide it along the fence through the cut.

The construction is evident in the drawing.

A couple of construction notes: I recommend that the base be 1/2-inch material, because it provides a

A coping sled holds the rail securely for the cut and provides some backup against tearout. It gives you a comfortable, sure grip on the work and keeps your hand out of the bit's way. A tradeoff is that the bit has to be extended an extra 1/2 inch above the table-top, which isn't a simple matter on every router table.

better backing for the toggle clamp. You probably will want to feel some resistance and hear a *snap* as you close the clamp. Those are reassuring cues, making you feel the clamp is holding the work tight. But the clamp is pressing the workpiece with great force against the base. If the base is thin, it

will distort and you won't get consistent, accurate cuts with the sled.

The handgrip is a copy of a hand-plane tote. To make mine, I traced the tote on a scrap of wood—paying attention to grain direction—then cut the part on the band saw. Some filing and sanding smoothed and softened the edges. I cocked the tote at an angle, so when I push, I'm applying pressure toward the fence as well as along it. You don't have to do the tote: Even a block of wood or a fat dowel will serve the purpose.

A note on use: The sled's backup fence will be cut by the cope bit the first time you use it. This isn't a problem, so long as you use the sled with the same cope bit each time. In fact, that cut helps you set the bit elevation.

But an ogee profile won't properly back up a bead profile, so it behooves you to make a different sled for each different cope-and-stick set you use; otherwise you'll get tearout as the bit exits the work and cuts into the sled. And the sticking cut will remove that tearout only at one end of the rail.

An alternative is to use a separate backup strip between the sled's fence and the rail. Hold it in place with carpet tape.

Coping Sled

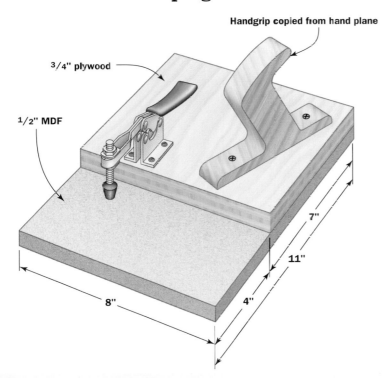

Handgrip copied from hand plane

3/4" plywood

1/2" MDF

7"

11"

4"

8"

coping sled, you have to set the block on the sled to set the bit elevation. (With a sled that's been used, you've got the cut in the backup fence to use in lieu of the setup block.)

Position the fence with its face tangent to the pilot bearing. If you like using featherboards, clamp them to the fence, locating them just fore and aft of the bit, where you need the pressure.

Make a test cut. If you've got a setup block, fit your test cut to its sticked edge. If not, look at the cut and assure yourself that it's not obviously misaligned.

The cope cuts should be completed

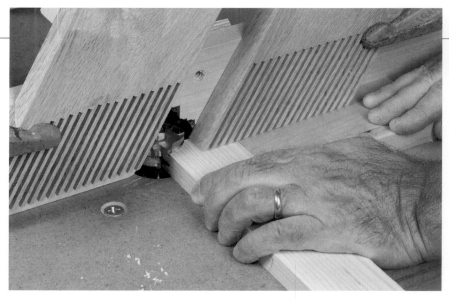

Cope the ends of rails (and muntins for a multi-panel assembly) first. Butt the end of the rail against the fence, back it up with a square-cornered scrap, and feed it through the cut. The scrap keeps the rail from "walking" along the fence, and it minimizes blowout as the cutter emerges from the rail.

Try This!

Take the guesswork out of setting up your cope-and-stick cutters by making a setup block. The block makes it easy to set the bit elevations, and it puts you in control of the appearance of the finished joints.

From an aesthetic viewpoint, the sticking cut is paramount, because it establishes the appear-ance of the joinery. But opera-tionally, it's cut after the rails have been coped. Because the cuts have to match, you take the appearance that you get. A setup block solves the problem.

Make sticking cuts on sample stock, experimenting with the bit elevation. When you have a setting that's optimum to your eye, mark it and set it aside.

Switch cutters and rout some copes, fitting them to your sample with the optimum sticking profile. When you've got the perfect fit, cope one end of the piece with the optimum sticking cut. Now you have one piece of wood with the optimum profiles, perfectly matched to each other.

Trim the block to a tidy size for storage with your bits. Next project, you can set the cope cutter quickly using the setup block, knowing you won't be disappoint-ed by the appearance of your finished assemblies.

A setup block can take the worry out of making the critical bit-height settings, especially for those who don't do the the job frequently. Some bits come with a pair of plastic setup blocks. If your bits didn't come with blocks, make your own. My model is essentially a short piece of a rail. The end is coped and the edge is sticked.

in one pass. Repeating a pass can enlarge the cut and create a loose fit. In theory, a second pass can enlarge the cut only if there's some movement in your setup. In practice, there probably *is* a skosh of movement possible, no matter how stiff your featherboards are and how firmly you grip the work.

Pay attention when you turn the rails to cope the second end. You want to turn them, not flip them. Mark the face that's supposed to be up as you make the cope cut. *Before you cut,* look for the mark.

Rout the sticking on each stile and rail after the copes are completed.

Swap bits (or with a reversible bit, switch the cutter arrangement on the arbor). Adjust the bit's elevation to align with the copes that have already been cut, or use that setup block. The overarching, aesthetic objective in setting the bit height is to position the profile for its best appearance without getting the groove too close to the back. But you've already cut the copes. Practicality intrudes. Now you just want the faces of the parts to be flush when you assemble the joints.

Adjust the bit, reposition the fence (if you've had to move it to swap bits), and make a test cut. Fit a coped rail to the test cut, and check the seam. The parts should be flush. If they aren't, adjust the bit elevation.

With the bit and fence set, (re)position your holddowns.

When everything seems to be set up properly, cut the profile and groove in the inside edges of the stiles *and* rails. If the frame has an intermediate middle rail or rails, if it has one or more mullions, these parts must be routed on both edges. One pass should be sufficient to complete each cut.

Adjust the elevation of the sticking bit, using a rail as a gauge. Align the bit's slotter with the stub tenon. Check the setting with a test cut, fitting the sample to a coped rail. But if you are careful, the setting should be right on.

The sticking cut is straightforward. The fence has a zero-clearance facing attached to it, which minimizes chipping at the edges of the cut. It is set tangent to the pilot bearing on the bit. A shop-made tandem featherboard applies downward pressure on both sides of the bit, but not at the bit itself.

Try This!

Make your frames a little oversized. In the long run, it can save you extra worry and work.

If you are making a door, for example, crosscut the rails and stiles so the assembled frame will be 1/16 to 1/8 inch longer and wider than your specs call for. The final step is to trim the door, *not* to the specified dimensions, but to *fit.* If a door opening is slightly large or slightly out-of-square, you've given yourself a margin for error. You have some room to trim the door to fit.

Making the frames slightly oversized can free you from some of the cares of woodworking, too. No more fumbling with cauls to protect the frame edges from clamp jaws. So what if you get a crease or two! The damage gets trimmed off.

Problem Solver

Chipping along the edge of a profile is demoralizing. Once it's happened, your only recourse is a do-over with new wood. But there are things you can do to prevent it.

First, look over your stock. Chipping is usually a result of susceptible wood colliding with a delicate profile and an aggressive feed. Gnarly, swirling, undulating grain that runs off the edge being worked—even fairly straight grain that happens to run out the working edge—is just prone to chipping.

Start with the fence setup. Create more of a zero-clearance opening for the bit. A little more backup for the stock, especially on the infeed side of the bit opening, can be helpful.

Stage the sticking cut, routing it in two or more passes. Working that board with a sticking profile which, when combined with the panel groove, produces something akin to a knife edge, is asking for serious chip-

ping. Move the fence forward, housing more of the bit and limiting the cut. Make a shallow first cut, then shift the fence for a deep second pass. Clean up with a very light final pass.

Don't consider a climb cut. Though climb-cutting can sometimes be a solution in a handheld router operation, it is always extremely high-risk on the router table.

Make an auxiliary facing for your router-table fence from 1/4-inch plywood. Drill a 1-inch-plus hole in it with a Forstner bit to provide clearance for the bearing and arbor nut. To cut the zero-clearance profile, you can swing one end of the fence so the bit is inside. Clamp the facing to the fence, then switch on the router and slowly swing the fence back, allowing the bit to cut through the facing. Splintering in this facing at the outfeed side of the bit is inevitable. Pick away any chips that will impede the movement of the work. The zero-clearance is needed on the infeed side.

Try This!

Loose-tenon joinery is a good way to bolster the strength of cope-and-stick. You cut mortises into both halves of the joint and, at assembly, insert a separate strip of wood as a tenon.

Rout the mortises either before or after coping the rail ends and sticking the edges. Use the mortising block and your plunge router (see "Mortise-and-Tenon Joints," page 273).

Center the mortises across the edges. They won't align with the stub tenon produced by the cope cut, but that doesn't matter. The tenon isn't going to show in the assembled joint.

While cope-and-stick joinery is satisfactory for most frame-and-panel constructions, reinforcing the joints with dowels or loose tenons (shown) is never a *bad* idea. The larger the construction, the more beneficial the reinforcement is.

Making Panels

The panel used in frame-and-panel construction ordinarily is a wood that matches the frame, but it can be a contrasting wood. The simplest panel would be a hardwood plywood matching the frame. Because plywood is stable, this panel could be glued into the panel grooves in the frame, thus reinforcing the entire assembly.

Most familiar, however, is the so-called raised panel, a natural wood panel with a beveled or shouldered band around its edge.

Whatever panel you choose can be set flush with either the front or back surface of the frame, or elevated so that it projects beyond the frame.

If you are using a natural wood for the panel, it's not unlikely that you'll have to glue up narrow boards to form the wider panels that are necessary. Even if you do have boards wide enough, it may be advantageous to rip the boards into narrow strips, then glue them back together. This is a good way to minimize cupping. See the chapter "Edge Joints" on page 259 for a variety of router techniques that can improve the strength and quality of your edge joints.

The router is the best tool in your shop to use for raising panels, unless you have a shaper. Some woodworkers use the table saw to raise panels in a straight bevel, but there are some distinct shortcomings to this. First, the saw blade can produce only a straight bevel (though the width and angle of the bevel can be varied). The blade will probably leave fairly prominent marks that take a lot of time, elbow grease, and sandpaper to eradicate. Also, you can't get the 1/4-inch-thick by 3/8-inch-long tongue around the panel that's necessary to fit it properly into the groove in the frame.

All panel-raising router bits (and shaper-cutters, too) are designed to produce a tongue of the appropriate width. They'll leave a far smoother finish to the cut than sawing would. You'll have to sand it, of course, but not nearly as much. And finally, you have a pretty interesting assortment of profiles from which to choose (see the "Bit Drawer" on page 221).

Preparing the Panel Stock

The first step in preparing stock for raised panels is to evaluate your design in terms of the cope-and-stick joinery on the frame members, as well as the profile and proportions of the available panel-raising bits.

The industry convention is to use 5/8-inch-thick stock for the panels. Nevertheless, you can satisfactorily use 3/4-inch stock, and even 1/2-inch stock. Let's look at the reasons.

As noted elsewhere, cope-and-stick cutters produce a groove for the panel that's 1/4 inch wide and 3/8 inch deep. If the frame stock is 3/4 inch thick—the industry convention— then the groove's back shoulder is between 1/8 inch and 3/16 inch from the frame member's back edge (depending upon how deep you cut the profile).

Panel-raising bits are proportioned to produce the optimum relief—not too shallow, not too deep—and the proper tongue thickness (1/4 inch) on 5/8-inch-thick stock. If you use 3/4-inch stock for the panel, you'll have to cut deeper than the optimum relief to get the 1/4-inch tongue. Or you'll have to "undercut" the back of the panel that's been raised to the optimum. The undercut, a sort of rabbet, produces a relief in the back of the panel so the tongue is 1/4 inch thick.

Horizontal bits with undercutters are available, and they are particularly popular with hobbyists. They eliminate the need to plane stock to 5/8 inch for panels. More important, the setup is less finicky. Regardless of the bit's elevation, it produces a tongue on the panel that's the perfect thickness.

Remember that the straightness and flatness of the panel is as important to the overall straightness and

Fitting Panel to Frame
How you cut it affects the fit

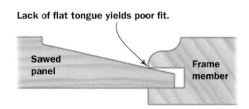

Lack of flat tongue yields poor fit.

Sawed panel

Frame member

Flat tongue formed by router bit allows panel to shrink without loosening and expand without breaking sticked member.

Routed panel

Frame member

Making Frames for Glazing

flatness of the structure as the frame is. In most circumstances, if the panel is warped, it will twist the frame. So choose the panel stock accordingly. (There are circumstances in which burled or crotch-grain wood, which is inherently unstable, is used for panels; the trick is to keep this stock thin enough that it doesn't have the strength to overpower the frame and warp it.)

Sizing the panels has to be done before you raise them. In doing this, you have to account for the relative moisture content of the wood. The length of the panel won't change over the course of time, but the width will come and go with the seasons.

You want an easy slip-fit during assembly. If the panel material (and the frame stock, too) were perfectly stable, you could measure from the bottom of one groove to the bottom of the opposite one and cut the panel to that dimension minus about 1/16 inch for assembly clearance. But of course, none of the stock is really stable. When cutting the panel to length, you need only allow that 1/16-inch assembly clearance, since wood doesn't get longer when it expands. Ripping the panel to width is a little trickier.

In the dead of a cold winter, when the relative humidity is generally low and the furnace's heat is drying the shop air even more, the panel stock is as shrunken as it will ever be. The cabinetmaker's rule of thumb is to allow about 1/8 inch per foot of width for expansion. And don't forget the assembly clearance.

In the slough of a sultry summer, on the other hand, the stock is as swollen with moisture as it will get. Cut it to fit pretty tightly in the frame; make it about 1/16 less than the groove-to-groove dimension.

Many cabinets have a mix of solid-panel and glazed doors, all with the same sticking profile. So the obvious question is: How do you make a cope-and-stick frame for glass instead of a wood panel?

Because it's so thin, glass is a bad fit in the panel groove. Moreover, it's breakable, and you want to be able to replace it without damaging the frame.

What you need is a rabbet instead of a panel groove. Transforming the groove into a rabbet is easy enough: You rip away the back shoulder on the table saw. The hitch is that you then have a gap where the rail meets the stile.

The solution is simple but perhaps not obvious. Remove the slot-cutter from the cope bit. The cut will produce the cope of your sticking project, but the stub tenon will be what's called barefaced, meaning that its cheek is flush with the surface of the rail.

The infill of the rabbeted frame need not be limited to window glass. Leaded glass could be used. A mirror. Expanded metal sheets or punched tin sheets. Caning. Use your imagination.

For a finished appearance, cut retainer strips with the same profile as the sticking. Miter the ends of the strips and install them with brads.

You can cut cope-and-stick joinery for rabbeted frames with a common pair of cabinetry bits. Remove the slotter from the cope bit and replace it on the arbor with a sleeve-type spacer or a stack of washers. A cut with it will produce a cope and a blocky tenon to fill the rabbet. After routing the sticking on all the parts, rip away the back of the panel groove, transforming it into a rabbet. The parts assemble just like a cope-and-stick joint.

Make profiled retainers for your glazing by sticking the edges of narrow strips, then ripping the profile free. Miter the ends and glue them into the frame to secure the glass panes.

Raising Panels

Panel raising is a router-table operation. In a nutshell, to work a rectilinear panel, you set the fence and bit, clamp a couple of featherboards in place, and rout. Outside of the nutshell, there's a little more to it.

Deal with the bit first. With the horizontal bit, you use a regular router table with a high-horsepower, variable-speed router. With the vertical bit, you use any router that accepts 1/2-inch-shank bits, mounted in a regular table or a horizontal table. If keeping the work flat on the tabletop is essential to you, use the vertical bit in a horizontal table.

To use a horizontal bit, first make sure your router will accommodate it. You need more than power and speed control. The router's structure has to accommodate the bit. The mounting plate's bit opening has to accept a 3 1/2-inch-diameter bit. But check the router, too. Some of the biggest plunge routers have tabs that project into the base's bit opening (template guides screw to these tabs). A big panel-raiser will hit these tabs.

This doesn't mean you can't use these routers for the job. It does mean that the mounting plate's thickness is a big part of your margin of bit-height adjustment. Even with the bit set as low as you can get it, you may still be cutting the full 1 1/2-inch width of the reveal on the first pass. More significantly, it means you will have a devil of a time installing the bit in the collet, since you have to do it with the router motor bottomed against the base, which doesn't give you much room to maneuver the wrench or wrenches.

Not all router bases have these obstructions, of course. The big fixed-base production routers from Porter-Cable and Milwaukee would

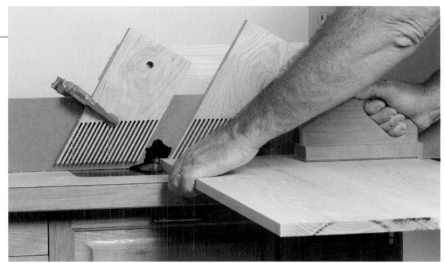

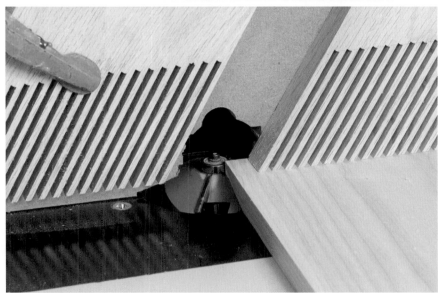

Featherboards do several jobs for you when you are raising a panel. Most obviously, they hold the panel down against the table, and given their angle, they prevent any kickback. Their downward pressure helps when the panel extends well beyond the edge of the table (top). This panel, long as it is, won't tumble off the table as long as its edge is caught under the featherboards. Finally, when properly positioned on both sides of the bit, the featherboards effectively shroud the bit (above).

accommodate an even bigger bit (if someone were foolhardy enough to make it and you were foolhardy enough to use it).

Even if the bit has a pilot, use a fence to guide and help you control straight cuts. (Obviously, you can't use the fence for making curved cuts.) The fence gives you much better control of the work than does the bit's pilot.

Moreover, use a fence to which you can clamp holddowns like feath-erboards. A basic one-board fence will guide the work, but you really need the featherboards to prevent the work from lifting off the tabletop. So use a fence with a 3- or 4-inch-high back, and clamp those featherboards to it, one on each side of the bit.

Don't forget to dial back the router speed. With a big horizontal bit, you want to set the router to run as slow as possible.

The advantage of the vertical bit is its compatibility with practically any router. High power isn't necessary to keep it spinning under load, and the bit's size allows it to be run at a router's full speed. Be sensible about such bits, though, buying and using only those with 1/2-inch shanks.

If you have a horizontal router table, the vertical bit is a natural choice. You keep the work flat on the table, rather than standing it on edge.

But truth be told, I use a vertical bit most often in a benchtop router table. I guess it's a way of asserting that even though the procedure is raising panels, the equipment isn't high-end. The table, router, and bit all are relatively low-ticket, but the results belie that.

The biggest obstacle the average woodworker sees, looming behind the vertical bit, is managing the workpiece. With the typical router table, the panel must be perched on edge, held somehow against the fence. It's common for a very tall fence to be advocated. But I've found that a medium-height fence coupled with a trap fence is the best solution.

The drawing *Trap Fence* shows the setup I use in conjunction with my regular fence. You can adapt it to work with the fences in this book, and with many commercial fences. The idea is that you have a channel between the fence and the trap fence that's just wide enough for the panel. The trap fence prevents the bottom edge of the panel from kicking away from the fence, so only modest pressure against the panel keeps it upright.

Because I don't want to have to move the trap fence and the tall fence separately, I used a hardboard base to link the two fences together *and* to the regular fence.

Setup goes like this: Install the bit in the router and adjust the elevation.

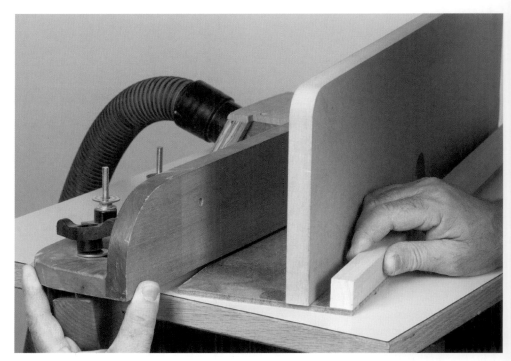

A trap fence keeps the bottom of a panel from kicking out from the fence, so even an extra tall panel is easy to maneuver through a cut. The trap is most convenient to use if it's linked to the fence. The gap between fence and trap is fixed, and when you adjust the fence position, you simultaneously shift the trap's position.

Trap Fence

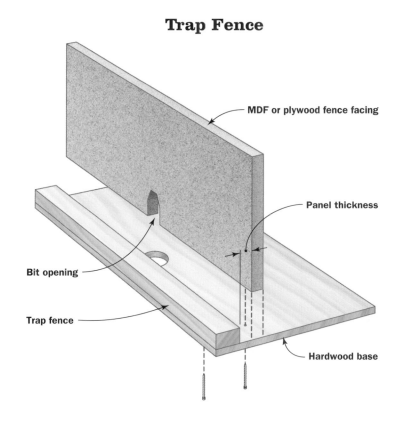

MDF or plywood fence facing

Panel thickness

Bit opening

Trap fence

Hardwood base

Bit Drawer

A panel-raising bit is serious business. It is as big a cutter as you will buy, and represents as big a cut as the router can make. It's a big investment.

Panel-raisers are available in two configurations: horizontal and vertical. The horizontal bits are more widely available than the vertical bits, and they are made in a much greater variety of sizes and profiles.

Horizontal panel-raising bits. If what you are used to is standard straight, round-over, and cove bits, the *size* is the first thing you notice about a horizontal panel-raiser. As bits go, it is huge. A typical horizontal panel-raiser is 3 1/2 inches in diameter and weighs 11 ounces. That's a lot of metal to spin.

The size of these bits is their drawback, of course. A high-horsepower router is required to drive them. A 3 1/2-inch bit spinning at 22,000 rpm is moving about 230 mph at the cutter tips. When you bend the path of that whizzing cutter around a 3-inch circle, you begin to develop centrifugal forces that put some pretty serious strain on it. Manufacturers uniformly recommend limiting the larger cutters to

10,000 rpm. To do this, obviously, you must use a variable-speed router.

The reason these bits are so big is, of course, the demand for a wide reveal. In the cabinet industry, where shapers are used to raise panels, the standard reveal (which includes the bevel and the tongue) is 1 1/2 inches. The standard reveal for horizontal router bits is 1 3/8 inches, and you need a bit 3 1/2 inches in diameter to get it. A smaller bit will suffice if you are willing to accept a narrower reveal—1 1/16 inches, for example, or 1 inch, or 13/16 inch.

Most manufacturers list three to six profiles in a couple of sizes. You need not feel limited to a beveled reveal; you can have an ogee, a cove, or any of these shapes with a bead around the panel's field.

Vertical panel-raising bits. You don't need a high-horsepower, variable-speed router to raise panels. With a vertical panel-raiser, a 1 1/2-horsepower, fixed-speed router is all you need.

That's because the vertical panel-raiser, while still pretty massive, is small in comparison to an equivalent horizontal one. Although, at a cutter

height of 1 1/2 inches, it's taller than the horizontal bit, it's usually no more than 1 1/2 inches in diameter. And that reduced diameter is the whole point. Driven at 22,000 rpm, the tip speed of the vertical bit is just under 100 mph (compared to 230 mph for the horizontal bit).

The bit shares the operating concept of architectural molding cutters. The cut's "width" is dictated by the bit height rather than its diameter. The bit designer is simply changing the angle of attack. The vertical panel-raisers currently on the market will cut a standard 1 1/2-inch reveal (but nothing less). Available patterns include ogees, coves, and standard bevels.

The typical vertical bit has two flutes. Because it has no pilot, it has to be used in conjunction with a fence, and it cannot be used to raise the edges of curved panels.

Undercutters. A subset of the horizontal panel-raisers are those with undercutters.

The undercutter is a bit that produces a recess much like a rabbet on the back of the panel. This allows you to use 3/4-inch-thick stock for panels without having to cut excessively deep with the panel-raising cutter. The undercut panel ends up being flush with both the face and back of the frame.

Most bit vendors mate an undercutter with a horizontal panel-raiser, putting both cutters on the same shank. Many sell undercutters as separate bits. You use the undercutter after raising the panels to the degree that suits your aesthetic, and relieve that panel back as necessary to size the tongue.

BIG is the enduring impression woodworkers have of panel-raising bits. But a range of sizes is available. Some, like the bit with the integral undercutter at left, really are big. In comparison, even full-sized (3 1/2-inch-diameter) raisers without the undercutter (top center) seem somewhat smaller. Horizontal bits less than 3 inches in diameter (right) really are smaller. Smallest are the vertical bits (bottom center).

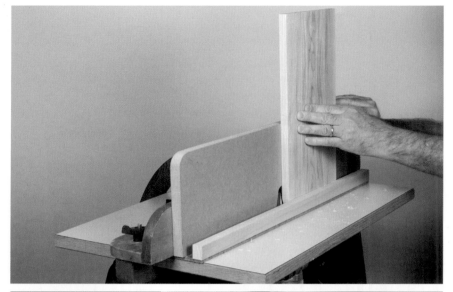

Common Panel-Raising Profiles

17° bevel

Ogee

Cove

Ogee and bead

25° bevel

Bevel and radius

Bevel and bead

Ogee and radius

Rely on the trap fence to control the panel until the final pass. On the initial pass (top), keep your hand high, forcing the panel against the tall fence and thereby levering the bottom edge against the trap. Before the final pass, take a moment to set up a featherboard (above). To ensure that the pressure is above the cut, set it on a block. This will help you maintain uniform pressure throughout each cut on the panel's four edges.

Be sure you account for the thickness of the trap-fence base. Mount the trap-fence accessory to the regular fence and drop it over the bit. Clamp one end, then measure between the cutting edges and the trap fence itself as you swing the free end of the fence. The gap width you want is 1/4 inch; when you've got it, clamp the free end of the fence. Confirm your setup with a test cut; the tongue formed should be a snug fit in the panel grooves in the rails and stiles.

Featherboards are optional with this setup. I usually stage the cuts, and before the final pass, I clamp a featherboard to the table, elevated on a block and positioned to bear against the panel above the bit.

Making the cuts. I think it is a good idea to stage the cut when raising panels. Staging means making two or more passes to cut to the full depth. Some people advocate hogging all the waste away in a single monster pass. You *can* do that, and if it suits you, fine. But staging the cut suits me.

Two approaches are possible.

With some exceptions, you can make a first pass with the bit low, then raise it for a second pass, and again for a third pass. To my mind, this approach has some drawbacks. It doesn't allow you to find the final bit elevation setting before you begin, so you are mixing setup with production. I think you can miss the ideal setting and end up cutting the panels too deep; then the panel fits loosely in the panel grooves. Moreover, this approach won't work if you are using a horizontal bit with an undercutter.

My preference—and it works with both horizontal and vertical bits—is to use test cuts to dial in the ideal bit elevation and ideal fence position, then use the fence to stage the cut. To capture the final fence position, I butt a scrap against the back of the fence on one side and clamp the scrap to the tabletop. You reduce the first-pass bite simply by swinging the fence away from that scrap. Make a pass, then move the fence closer to the reference block. Make another pass. Set the fence against the block and make that final pass. Done!

With everything set up, start making the cuts. Cut the end grain first. This cut is most likely to cause tearout, but any tearout will almost surely be routed away when you make the long-grain cuts.

Make your first cut on every workpiece, then adjust the setup to increase the cut. Make a second pass on every piece, adjust the setup, and so forth.

When you are all finished, you probably will need to sand the cuts lightly. Especially when cutting across the grain, the bit tends to lay the end grain down a little. The wood will feel smooth to the touch when you stroke one direction, but rough when you stroke the other direction. A couple of light passes with a pad sander should take care of this.

Curved-Edge Assemblies

Arch-topped doors are popular, and they represent a slightly higher level of work. More steps are involved, and the techniques for sticking the curved edge of the rails and raising the curved edge of the panels are different than for straight edges. But it is all manageable, and seldom requires specialized tools or equipment.

You have extra work at the outset, when ripping and crosscutting the frame parts and the panels to size. You have to shape the curved edges. If you are making only one door, you can do this by laying out the curve, sawing it on the band saw, then sanding the edge smooth and fair with a spindle sander or a drum sander in a drill press.

Doing several assemblies? Make templates to shape the parts. I usually cut the templates from plywood or MDF (medium-density fiberboard), using a router and trammel; see the chapter "Routing Curves and Circles" on page 175. For the rails, the template has a concave edge. For the panels, the template has a convex edge. The radii of the two curves are slightly different because the panel fits into the rail's panel groove. When you set

Raising a panel on a horizontal router table using a vertical bit is remarkably similar to doing the job on a regular router table with a horizontal bit. The panel rests flat on the table. You start with a cross-grain cut, and work your way around the panel, ending with a long-grain cut. The big difference is that you feed from left to right.

Stick a curved rail using the pilot bearing, rather than the fence, to control the cut. Here, the edge of a dust pickup serves as a starting pin. Once the bearing is engaged by the rail, you can drift off the pin without consequence. To prevent the trailing tip of the rail from breaking away, tuck a sticked scrap into the cut to support the tip (below).

up the router and trammel to cut the rail template, the bit is inside the radius. When setting up for the panel template, the radius is 5/16 to 3/8 inch longer and the bit is outside the radius.

After coping the ends of the rail to be shaped, trace the template contour on it and saw off the bulk of the waste. Then stick it to the template with carpet tape or hot-melt glue. Trim the edge flush with the template with a pattern bit or a flush-trimming bit. In like manner, shape the panel to match the panel template.

Sticking the rail requires you to use the pilot bearing on the bit, rather than the router-table fence, to guide the cut. Use the starting pin to begin the cut, then follow on through with just the bearing.

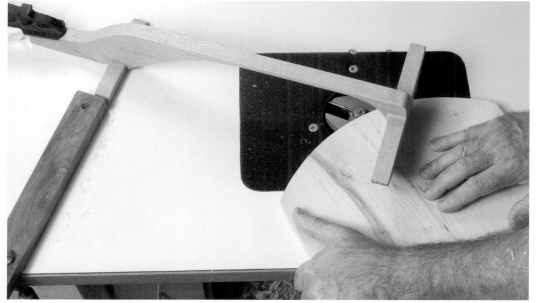

Since you can't use the fence with curved work, you can't use the usual hold-down, which clamps to the fence. The plesiosaur is the ideal alternative. Position the plesiosaur to bridge the bit itself, with the hammer-head bearing on the work, as shown. The strip butted against the side of the hold-down keeps it from twisting out of position.

Likewise, the panel-raising cut is bearing-guided. It can only be done with a horizontal bit. Use a starting pin to help you begin the cut. Obviously, you can't use featherboards, but a holddown like the plesiosaur (on page 116 in "Router Table Accessories") can help hold the work firmly to the tabletop.

Making Architectural Doors and Windows

Doors and windows for a building—your house, for example—are built using the same frame-and-panel construction as we've presented in this chapter. Usually the stock is heftier—ranging in thickness from a full inch up to 1 3/4 inches—but the same bits and techniques used for cabinetry will work for this architectural work.

Cope-and-stick joinery is probably satisfactory for interior doors, and for fixed and double-hung windows. It provides enough glue surface for contemporary glues to provide a strong, long-lasting bond, even on a door.

What makes it less than adequate for exterior doors and for awning or casement windows is exposure to weather. After a few years of baking in the sun and soaking in the rain and freezing in the snow, the wood's expansion and contraction will probably knock cope-and-stick joinery apart. Here you need full mortise-and-tenon joinery.

Making an interior door. The parts and dimensions of a fairly typical interior door are shown in the drawing. To make the door, you

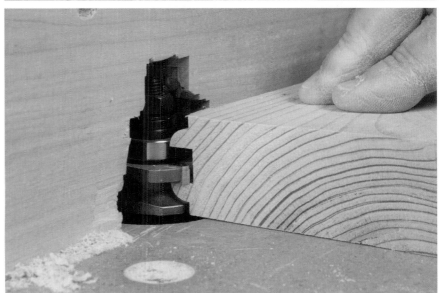

An architectural door typically has thicker rails and stiles than a cabinet door and is styled the same on both sides. You can use a regular cope-and-stick bit set or assembly to rout their frame pieces. Before making the cope cuts, remove the slot cutter from the arbor and replace it with a sleeve-type spacer (or a stack of washers). Cut across the end of the rail, roll it over, and make a second cut (top). You have the cope profile on both edges, and a nice fat stub tenon between them. Similarly, the sticking cuts are made in two passes. Adjust the bit height so the groove is centered (and the same width as the stub tenon on the rail ends), then make two passes to get the profile on both edges of the stock (above).

would cut the frame parts to size, then cope the ends of the rails and rout the sticking on the appropriate edges. You can use standard cope-and-stick bits to work heavy stock if you make two passes. Make the first pass with the workpiece face down, and the second pass with it face up. Obviously, you have to adjust the bit height so the groove (or tenon) will be centered across the stock.

Depending on the stock thickness and the sticking pattern, you may want to make the groove (and consequently the tongue) wider than 1/4 inch. When you raise the panels, do it on both faces, but don't make the tongue less thick than the sticking groove is wide.

Making an exterior door. An exterior door would be made in pretty much the same way. But after

Architectural Door Construction

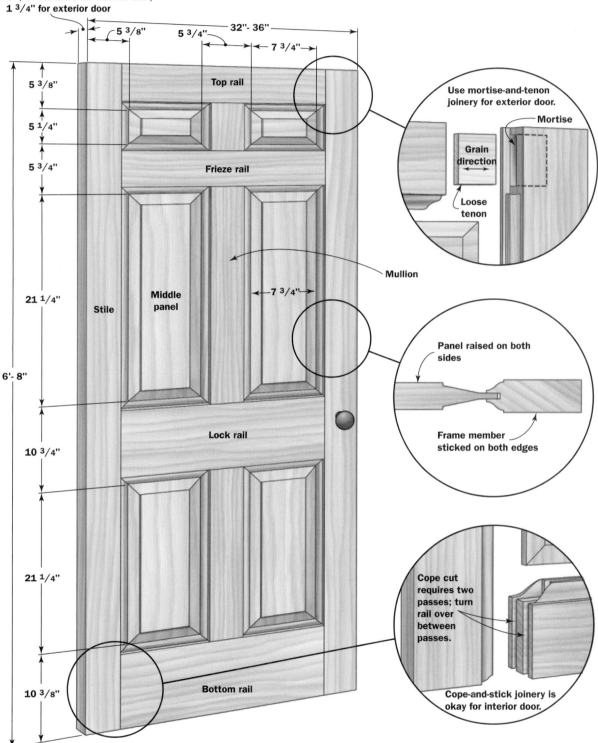

1 3/8" standard for interior door, 1 3/4" for exterior door

5 3/8"   5 3/4"   32"- 36"   7 3/4"

5 3/8"
5 1/4"
5 3/4"
21 1/4"
6'- 8"
10 3/4"
21 1/4"
10 3/8"

Top rail

Frieze rail

Mullion

Middle panel   7 3/4"

Stile

Lock rail

Bottom rail

Use mortise-and-tenon joinery for exterior door.

Mortise

Grain direction

Loose tenon

Panel raised on both sides

Frame member sticked on both edges

Cope cut requires two passes; turn rail over between passes.

Cope-and-stick joinery is okay for interior door.

Note: Locksets and hinges are proportioned to fit standard-thickness doors.

sticking all the frame parts, and coping the rails, cut mortises in both stiles and rails for long loose tenons. Use the longest bit you can to rout the mortises. Rout mortises about 3 inches deep in the stiles and 2 5/8 inches deep in the rails (the coping on the rail ends limits the bit's reach). The tenons should be cut from solid wood. Use waterproof glue to assemble the door.

Making windows. The difference between making doors and making windows is the bit. A window-sash bit (or bit set) will rout sticking with a profile and a rabbet for glass. The setups and steps are the same as with cope-and-stick bits: Cope the ends of the rails, then do the sticking cuts.

The drawing on the next page shows a 12-light fixed window.

An exterior door should have its cope-and-stick joinery reinforced with mortises and loose tenons. Cut the mortises on the mortising block or, as shown here, on the horizontal table. Use a bit at least 1/2 inch in diameter and as long as you can find. Either center the cut in the stock thickness or mark a reference face on each part so that the mortises line up.

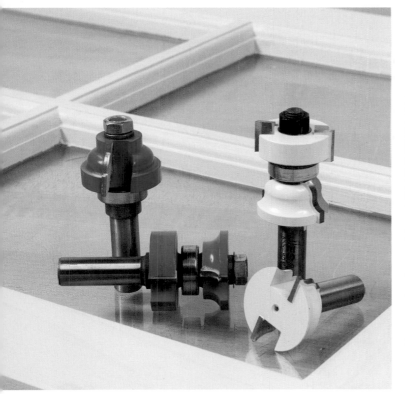

Most sash bits, such as those at left, produce a conventional rabbeted cope-and-stick joint. The pair at right work with mortise-and-tenon joinery. The inverted head on the cope cutter allows the tenon to pass over it as it cuts.

A sash bit makes window construction relatively easy. In addition to shaping the rails and stiles that frame the window, you can shape the narrow vertical mullions and horizontal muntins (often known collectively as sash bars) that divide it.

Window Sash Construction

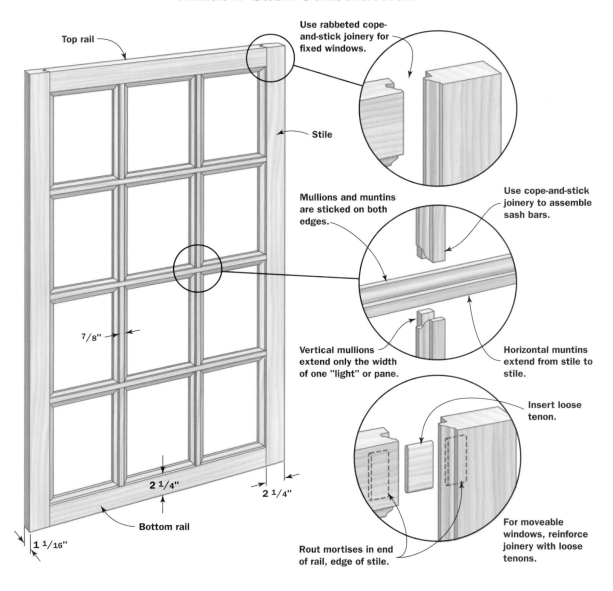

Top rail

Use rabbeted cope-and-stick joinery for fixed windows.

Stile

Mullions and muntins are sticked on both edges.

Use cope-and-stick joinery to assemble sash bars.

Vertical mullions extend only the width of one "light" or pane.

Horizontal muntins extend from stile to stile.

7/8"

Insert loose tenon.

2 1/4"

2 1/4"

Bottom rail

1 1/16"

Rout mortises in end of rail, edge of stile.

For moveable windows, reinforce joinery with loose tenons.

See also...

A number of joints other than the cope-and-stick can be used in frame-and-panel construction.

The big advantage of the cope-and-stick is the appearance of the decorative profile routed on the inside edge of the frame. Were you to assemble a frame, *then* rout the decorative profile, the profile would lack the crisp corners. Instead of being sharp and square, the transitions from rail to stile would be rounded. And any approach in which you make a stopped cut will also yield those rounded corners. The cope-and-stick seemingly is the only joinery that gives you those crisp corners. *Seemingly.*

See the splined miter joint on page 329. The miter is weak, but the splines reinforce it. And after cutting the miters, you can rout a decorative profile on the inner edges. Because of the nature of the miter, the profile cuts will meet in crisp, square corners.

See the mitered half-lap on page 295. It is inherently stronger than the miter joint, even one reinforced with splines. But you still can embellish the edges with a routed profile, and have the profiles meet clean and square at the corners.

The strongest joint that can be used, especially for doors, is the mortise-and-tenon. The explanation of how to use your router in making these joints begins on page 273. One trick you won't find

there is that of joining sticked stiles and rails in mortise-and-tenon joints.

To do this, you must trim the sticked profile and groove from the ends of the stiles, and rout mortises. In routing tenons on the rails, you remove from their ends the sticked profile and groove. Do it carefully, using a chisel to miter the ends of the profile that remains. When the joint is assembled, the miters come together, giving you the cope-and-stick's handsome appearance and the mortise-and-tenon's great strength.

This approach allows you to join beaded edges (not the quarter-round profile, but the edge-bead profile). You can't do that with cope-and-stick joinery.

Working Laminates

Here's the real reason for having those nice little one-hand-sized routers called laminate trimmers. And never was a tool so well suited for a job. The router's high-speed cutter is about the only way to cut laminate accurately without chipping it.

In a nutshell, the procedure for working with laminates is: Cut a piece of plastic laminate to a size just a few fractions of an inch larger than the plywood, particleboard, or other substrate it is to cover. Bond it to the substrate; contact cement is the most popular glue for this. The laminate is positioned so its edges overhang those of the substrate just a little. With your router or laminate trimmer and a flush-trimming bit, zip around the edges, trimming away the excess laminate, and making it flush with the substrate's edges. Perfect!

There's a little more to working with plastic laminates than that, but the router is the key tool used throughout the process. In addition to trimming the edges to finish a laminate project, you can also use the router to cut the pieces you need from the laminate sheets to start the project.

The Material

Plastic laminate is made by impregnating several layers of kraft paper with phenolic plastic resin. The color and pattern is in a separate sheet of paper, impregnated with melamine plastic resin, which covers the core. The surface can be embossed with a design or texture. The paper layers and the plastics are bonded together under high heat and pressure. The resulting material is hard and durable—scratch- and wear-resistant and easily cleaned. For all this, it isn't expensive.

The material is used to cover anything that needs a wear-resistant, easily cleaned surface. Countertops. Cabinets, inside and out. Tables. Even walls. If a stable, flat surface is needed, the laminate should be applied to both sides of the core to prevent warping. In some instances, it's appropriate to apply laminate to both surfaces; but where one will be hidden from view, money can be saved by using what's called backer on the hidden side. Backer is laminate without the color layer.

Sold in several grades, the most commonly used is the horizontal grade, which is about 1/16 inch thick. Many sheet sizes are available, ranging in width from 30 inches up to 60 inches, and in length from 8 to 12 feet. Most lumberyards sell several different brands, and will have an incredible assortment of 1×2-inch samples to choose from. Order the color and finish you want, select the sheet size, and in a few days—most likely—your plastic laminate will be ready for you to pick up, tied up in a 2- to 3-foot-diameter roll.

Safety First!

Plastic laminate is extremely hard and brittle. It chips easily, and when it's cut, razor-sharp little chips zing around. They can injure your eyes more easily and more seriously than feathery wood chips. Even if you are too tough (or stupid) to need eye protection during your wood-working sessions, don those goggles for laminate work.

229

Cutting Laminate

The table saw is a great tool for cutting plastic laminate…almost. The basic sheet is so large, and sooooo limp, it's darn near impossible for a lone woodworker to make a decent cut. Adding to this disadvantage is the fact that any saw chips the cut edge badly.

Enter the router. It allows you to lay out the sheet of laminate, then slide a tool across it that won't chip the edge as it cuts. A sheet of plywood set on a couple of sawhorses makes a good worktable. Pencil your cut line on the laminate, then slide a fairly wide, straight fence *under* the laminate, line

Although the laminate is only 1/16 inch thick, it's hard enough that this will be a pretty heavy cut. So use your regular router, rather than a laminate trimmer. The fence under the laminate guides the flush-trimming bit's pilot, ensuring that the cut will be perfectly straight.

Bit Drawer

Laminate work doesn't *require* special bits, but they are available. Any carbide or carbide-tipped bit will cut through laminate just fine. The several laminate-covered router-table tops presented in this book were actually trimmed with a standard 45° chamfering bit.

The typical flush-trimming bit—the one you get in a bit set—has two cutting edges about 1 inch long and a 1/2-inch cutting diameter. For trimming laminate, this bit has a couple of shortcomings.

■ You don't use more of the cutting edges than the 1/8 inch closest to the pilot. The risk in extending the bit too much is that it will scuff the face of the laminate, especially if the router is bobbled momentarily.

■ The two cutting edges won't give you the finest possible finish.

If you do a lot of laminate work, you may want to buy a real laminate trimmer.

Laminate trimmer

3-flute 45° bevel-trimmer

4-flute 15° bevel-trimmer

3-flute 22° bevel-trimmer

Arbor

Wrenches

2-flute flush-trimmer

Assembled 3-flute flush-trimmer

Solid-carbide combination bevel and flush-trimming bit

Assembled 4-flute flush-trimmer

Solid 2-flute flush-trimmer

Bit manufacturers with a base of commercial and industrial customers usually make an assortment of laminate-trimming bits. Most of these bits have 1/4-inch shanks, for use in laminate trimmers. The cutting-edge length is 7/16 inch or less (remember the overall caveat to always use the shortest cutting edge that will do the job). The most economical are the two-flute style. For better finishes, they also make three- and even four-flute bits. A range of bevel angles are available, ranging from flush, through 7° and 15°, to 22° and occasionally to 45°.

In some cases, the bits are assemblies, and the cutters can be interchanged. The advantage here is that you need buy only a single arbor, even though you get several cutters. It isn't likely you'll be using more than one cutter at a time.

it up right under the line, and clamp the laminate to the fence. Use wooden hand screws or cauls with metal-jawed clamps to avoid breaking the laminate. And position them so they won't interfere with the router as it makes the cut. Use a small-diameter flush-trimming bit. The pilot bearing rides along the fence and guides the cut. It should be straight and chip-free.

This technique will allow a lone woodworker to reduce the largest of sheets to whatever sizes your project calls for.

Trimming Laminates

Laminates can be trimmed flush or to one of several bevel angles, depending upon the purpose of the edge. For example, if you are applying laminate to plywood panels that will be joined together into a cabinet, you will trim the laminate flush with the plywood's edges. However, if the laminate is the top surface of a counter, you will probably bevel it.

The difficulties you have in making these cuts is influenced by the work location. If you are constructing laminate-covered cabinets in your shop, you have an easier time than if you are building them at the installation site. The same is true of laminating a countertop—it's easier to do in the shop.

The work sequence and the trim cuts you make will, of course, be affected by the edge treatment you've selected. The *self-edge* has laminate applied to it, and that laminate is applied and trimmed before the faces of the panel or counter are covered. *Edge-banding* of natural wood can be applied before or after the laminate, yielding two different appearances.

Applying the Laminate

Before you can trim the laminate, you've got to apply it to a substrate (sometimes called an underlayment). The best substrates are sheet goods—plywood, particleboard, medium-density fiberboard—because they're generally more flat and stable than natural wood panels.

Contact cement is what bonds the laminate to the substrate. It's a sophisticated rubber cement that you spread on the mating pieces and leave to dry. When you touch the dried cement on the laminate to the dried cement on the substrate, they stick. Immediately. On contact.

To avoid alignment problems that can easily arise, the standard approach is to cut the laminate about 1/2 to 3/4 inch larger in length and width than the substrate. The laminate merely has to be positioned so it overhangs on all four sides, and you're okay. The overhang doesn't have to be even, though any pattern should probably be aligned parallel with the substrate's edges to look right.

A typical application approach is to lay dowel rods or sticker strips across the substrate, and to set the laminate on them. Beginning either in the middle or at one end, you pull out spacers one at a time and press the laminate to the substrate. For a large panel, use a laminate roller to press the laminate firmly to the substrate so you get a good, uniform bond between the two. On a small panel, you can achieve the

Trimming Sequences for Three Edge Treatments

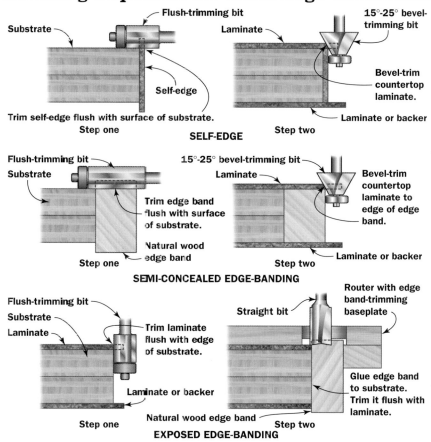

SELF-EDGE
Trim self-edge flush with surface of substrate.
Step one | Step two
Flush-trimming bit | Substrate | Self-edge | 15°-25° bevel-trimming bit | Laminate | Bevel-trim countertop laminate. | Laminate or backer

SEMI-CONCEALED EDGE-BANDING
Flush-trimming bit | Substrate | Trim edge band flush with surface of substrate. | Natural wood edge band | Step one | 15°-25° bevel-trimming bit | Laminate | Bevel-trim countertop laminate to edge of edge band. | Laminate or backer | Step two

EXPOSED EDGE-BANDING
Flush-trimming bit | Substrate | Laminate | Trim laminate flush with edge of substrate. | Laminate or backer | Natural wood edge band | Step one | Router with edge band-trimming baseplate | Straight bit | Glue edge band to substrate. Trim it flush with laminate. | Step two

Problem Solver

The contact cement you use to bond that laminate to its substrate usually turns into sticky wads of rubber when you try to cut through it. It sticks to the bit's pilot bearing and prevents it from following the edge of the stock exactly. If you don't catch it in time, it can even gum up the bearing so it spins with the cutter and burns the edge of the stock.

Many companies coat their laminate bits with some form of repellant, but these aren't 100 percent effective. There are also numerous bearing lubes on the market that are supposed to prevent the bearings from jamming. But the best remedy may be WD-40 or CRC. All it takes is a small psssst every few cuts to keep the bearings running smoothly. The amazing part is that something in the oil makes the contact cement pull up and come loose from the cutters and bearings. Double good!

Contact cement is rubbery, stretchy stuff that gums up a bit and its pilot pretty quickly. A squirt of WD-40 or the like makes it easy to pull cleanly from the bit.

same end by sliding a wood block methodically around the panel, rapping it with a hammer.

That's all there is to it. The laminate is immediately ready for trimming.

Work Sequences

Depending upon the edge treatment, your application and trimming sequences vary. If you are doing a self-edge, you apply and flush-trim the edge strips one at a time. When the edges are done, then you apply laminate to the faces and bevel-trim those pieces.

If you are applying laminate to an edge-banded substrate, you must be sure to flush-trim the wooden edge-banding so the entire surface is flat and smooth. Apply the laminate to the faces, and bevel-trim them.

The third option is to apply and flush-trim the laminate, then glue edge-banding to the panel. To complete the treatment, flush-trim the wooden edging. If desired, you can then rout a decorative edge on the wood.

Before you flush-trim laminate applied to the face of the substrate, you must check the panel's edges to make sure the pilot bearing will have a smooth, clean surface to reference. Plywood—fir plywood especially—sometimes has voids in the inner

To set the depth-of-cut, set the router or trimmer on the work and lower the bit so the cutting edge extends no more than 1/16 inch below the bottom of the layer to be trimmed. If it extends beyond that, you risk cutting into the surface that the bearing references, which in many cases is a laminated surface.

plies, and they can be exposed on the edges. If the pilot rolls into one, the bit will take a nice bite out of the laminate. Check the edges, and if necessary, fill voids with wood putty or the like, and sand it smooth.

A test cut on scrap is also in order before you trim the work. After the bit is adjusted, cut a piece of laminate-covered scrap. Lay a straightedge across the trimmed edge, and look for a whisker of light under the straightedge. Usually the cutting diameter of the bit is a mini-micron less than the diameter of the bearing. As long as the mini-micron really is small, you can shave the laminate absolutely

flush with a lick or two of a file. If, however, the bit cuts perfectly flush or scuffs the substrate, you should try a second test; but this time, apply a strip or two of masking tape for the bearing to ride on. This should pull the cutting edges away from the substrate edge and solve the problem.

Although the flush-trimmer generally leaves a satisfactory edge, sometimes you want a fit that's a little bit better than that. When you're going to lap the strips of a self-edge at an

Bevel-trim the edges of a surface that was edge-banded, then covered with laminate. On this particular job, I used a regular router and 45° chamfering bit.

232

The strips forming a self-edge are applied and trimmed one at a time. Holding a full-sized router steady against a counter edge is not easy, which is why folks who do this work regularly have and use laminate trimmers. If you can minimize the overhang, you reduce the trimmer's work and speed the cut.

At an outside corner, you flush-trim the first strip across the counter edge. Be sure it is really flush, using a file if necessary. The second strip must be long enough to overhang the corner. Trim it flush, then make a finish pass with the bevel-trimming bit to soften the edge.

outside corner, it's extremely important to get the first strip trimmed perfectly flush. Never trust the cut made by the router in this case. It's too easy for it to leave one little bump that will hold the next sheet up a little bit. File the edge just to be sure. Hold the file flat on the second surface, and push it along the edge you just routed. Any little imperfections left by the router will be quickly wiped away.

As I mentioned, you seldom flush-trim every edge. Believe it or not, laminates can be sharp enough to give you a nasty cut. To make the exposed edges look and feel just a little softer, you bevel them. A good routine is to cut all of the edges with the flush cutter, then clean up any glue-balls before making a final pass with the bevel-trimming bit. In areas of regular human contact, take a quick swipe over the very corner of the cut with a file just to be sure it's not sharp.

In many projects, there are tight corners that are inaccessible to a router, even a compact laminate trimmer. You're trimming a self-edge with an inside corner, for example, or an edge that meets a wall. So now you can't trim the last couple of inches on either side of the corner or next to the wall because the base of the router hits the adjoining edge or the wall.

Here's what to do: Nibble off the excess laminate with a pair of diago-

After the edges are trimmed, apply the laminate to the top. Your impulse may be to switch to a bevel-trimming bit and rout away the overhang. But you'll get a better job if you first flush-trim the edge, then clean up any strings and gobs of contact cement. After that's done, make a finish pass with the bevel-trimming bit.

Here's an edge the tilt-base lam trimmer was made for. You tilt the motor and thus the bit to match the angle of the edge.

Offset-Base Laminate Trimmer

If you find yourself doing a lot of counter installations, and you get tired of hand-trimming the few inches on either side of an inside corner or at the wall, use an offset-base. It's available for most trimmers.

This gem offsets the collet out on a corner of the router base. What this does is allow you to rout well within an inch of most obstructions, which really cuts down on the nibble-and-file work.

The offset is achieved using a drive belt. You replace the collet and nut on the trimmer motor with a gear. The base has a collet built in, and the belt is in place. All you do is insert the motor in the base and engage the belt on the gear.

You'll quickly discover some nifty tricks it can do for you to expedite counterwork. One of the best is trimming to a wall. If you want a counter to fit against a wall, with or without a backsplash, you usually have to set the counter in place near but not against the wall. Then you use a compass to scribe along the wall and transfer its contour to the laminate. Cutting or sanding to the line is ticklish handwork. Good results are achieved only through practice.

With the offset-base trimmer, you leave the compass in your toolbox. Instead, you guide the edge of the trimmer along the wall and trim the laminate to a perfect fit.

The offset-base trimmer is also great for normal edge-work because now the whole weight of the router is sitting securely on the counter instead of being half-off the edge. No more tipping.

After the countertop with its backsplash in place are set and screwed in place, you can run the trimmer along the top edge of the backsplash and trim the front edge. The baseplate shape and bit location even allow you to get into inside corners. Only a couple of licks with a file will be needed to square it completely.

Getting a counter to fit seamlessly to a wall is tough. The edge must be scribed, and making the cut is usually handwork. With the offset-base trimmer, however, you block the workpiece so the back edge of the laminate is about 3/4 inch from the wall. Then run the trimmer between the wall and the backsplash, feeding from left to right. The nose of the baseplate transfers every hump and hollow in the wall to the laminate.

nal cutters—the kind of wire cutters that electricians use—then carefully flush the ragged edges with a fine file.

Another sticky situation is where you have to trim an edge or an outside corner that is not 90°. The problem is that your pilot bearing runs a little below the corner, and with an off-square corner, you'll end up either leaving some overhang or gouging into the intended corner. To prevent this you can go back to the nibble-and-file technique. Or you can cut a tapered shim to stick to your router's baseplate with carpet tape. Cut the shim to the angle necessary to keep the bit shank parallel to the surface that it's following.

Dadoing and Grooving

Dadoes and grooves are funda-mental joinery cuts, and they can be decorative as well. Making these cuts is one of the operations every woodworker tackles quite early in the learning process. You tire of butt joints after a couple of beginning projects, and the dado joint and its variants (dado-and-rabbet, dado-and-spline, and so forth) are among the first improvements you try.

As router-produced joinery cuts, a dado and a groove are essentially the same thing: a flat-bottomed channel cut into the wood. (Done with hand tools, and even some power tools like a circular saw, the cutters and techniques may differ from dado to groove; with the router, however, the distinction is pretty much moot.) I think of the dado as a cut across the grain, and a groove as a cut with the grain. The distinction gets a little confusing when you talk about plywood and its layers with alternating grain directions. In the end, it's a semantical distinction, since the cutters, accessories, and basic methods are the same for either a dado or a groove.

Moreover, the term *groove* em-braces curved and decorative cuts,

along with the straight joinery cuts. The principal difference here between a joinery cut and a decorative cut is the cutter that's used. While I'll mainly stick with straight bits in the following few pages, bear in mind that a groove-forming cutter of any profile usually can be substituted.

Hand-Guided Through Cuts

The router is an excellent tool for cutting dadoes and grooves. A saw-mounted dado cutter will hog away dadoes and joinery grooves more quickly, but the router has a lot of pluses that compensate for its lower cutting speed.

One of the pluses is that the dado can be precisely sized—the diameter of the cutter determines the width of the dado. Not all saw-mounted dado cutters are so precise: They require trial-and-error adjustments to achieve a specific cutting width. Another plus is that the cut is invariably clean and square—no raggedy bottom to the cut. Routers also are particularly

good for making dadoes and grooves in plywood. Plywood splinters easily, but the router leaves a smooth cut, even in plywood.

Another plus for the router is the ability to cut stopped grooves, curved grooves, or any combination of these. Circular-saw dado sets cannot cut curves, and anytime you stop a cut, you're left with a "scoop" that matches the curve of the blade.

The primary reason I like the router for dadoing and grooving is its maneuverability. It's so much easier to maneuver a compact 5-pound router along a fence than it is guide a hefty, unwieldy board across a dado cutter. If the workpiece is bigger than a bread-box side, I don't want to dado it on my table saw. I'd rather have at it with a router. Usually a handheld router.

For some reason, I think of dadoing and grooving as handheld router operations. Clamp a fence to the work and rout. Of course, when I stop and think about it, I recall lots of dadoing and grooving operations done on the router table. I do smallish work like drawer sides on the router table, for example.

Hand-Guided Through Cuts

But I mainly think of dadoing as an operation in which I clamp a fence to the work and guide the router along it, making the cut.

Dadoing is the quintessential fence-guided router operation. But beware! Because the router follows a fence so well, you have to be careful that your fence is *straight* if you want a straight cut. You can easily make a curved groove by using a curved fence. Just don't inadvertently make that curved cut when you are expecting a straight one.

Everyone has a favorite fence setup. Some are clean, simple, and practical. Some folks are inclined to use whatever straight-and-true scrap falls to hand as a fence. Others try some pretty complicated approaches. Intoxicated by grand visions, I've made a couple of dadoing gizmos that have gathered a ton of dust since they were last used. They were simply too involved to use.

The jigs and fixtures that follow are the survivors.

T-Square

Probably the first step past the scrap-board fence every router woodworker makes is the T-square. You simply glue and screw two straight-and-true scraps together in a T-shape. One piece, called the crossbar or the head, butts against the edge of the workpiece, and the other, called the fence, guide, or blade, extends at a right angle across the workpiece surface.

The big advantage of the T-square is that it saves setup time. Instead of having to mark the full length of the dado, usually a single tick mark is sufficient. So long as the fence is perpendicular to the crossbar, you can be assured that the dado will be square to the edge.

In addition, the crossbar acts as a

A T-square is arguably the most basic router guide you use. It aligns itself perpendicular to an edge, can be secured with a single large clamp, and can guide any routers you own, not just a particular one.

brace, allowing you to secure the typical T-square with a single clamp. If you were to guide a router along an unadorned board fence secured with a single clamp, that clamp would become a pivot. With the crossbar butted firmly against the workpiece edge, that pivoting can't happen.

The common T-square has a fence between 24 and 30 inches long, and a crossbar between 6 and 12 inches long. For narrow work, a smaller guide is more manageable. If you do a lot of cabinet work, make a really big T-square, and cut both case sides at one time.

A lot of woodworkers make their T-squares like capital T's, which is to say without extensions. My T-squares have fences that extend 4 to 6 inches beyond the crossbar to steady the router as it enters or exits a cut. This is particularly useful with big routers and those with straight-edged or oversized baseplates.

You can make a T-square from straight, defect-free hardwood scrap, but I use plywood for the fence, if not for the crossbar. Plywood is strong and stable. Half-inch material is satisfactory for the typical fence, in my experience, but by all means use

Router T-Square

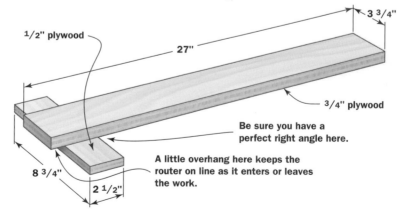

1/2" plywood

27"

3 3/4"

3/4" plywood

Be sure you have a perfect right angle here.

8 3/4"

2 1/2"

A little overhang here keeps the router on line as it enters or leaves the work.

236

3/4-inch material if you are concerned about deflection. I have made T-square-like guides with 1/4-inch MDF (medium-density fiberboard) for the fence, using a strip 6 to 10 inches wide.

The crossbar should be 5/8-inch stock, in my opinion. This thickness gives you some flexibility. You can use the square on a 3/4-inch plywood panel resting on a workbench, for example, without having to have the crossbar off the bench's edge. But of course, the crossbar can be thicker or thinner, according to your whim.

When you cut the fence and the crossbar, be sure the edges are perfectly parallel.

I usually assemble a square with three or four screws. You can use glue, but I seldom bother. Clamp the pieces together, and drive a single screw. Check to be sure the fence and crossbar are exactly square. An out-of-square T isn't a jig, it's scrap. If it is square, drive the remaining

screws. If it isn't *perfectly* square, pivot the parts on that one screw to properly align them. Then drive those other screws.

Most T-squares I've seen have notches routed in their crossbars, the result of the bit running out of the work and into the jig. There seem to be two schools here.

For those of the first school, the notches have the purpose of positioning the T-square. After assembling a T-square, you carefully rout a dado across the crossbar on each side of the fence, using the bit that will be used with the T-square. The jig can then be positioned simply by aligning the crossbar dado with the layout marks on the work. This is a useful approach, especially if you do a *lot* of dadoes of one particular width. But for some of us, it means having a different T-square for every router-and-straight-bit combination possible in our shops.

I'm frankly of the other school. To those of my ilk, the notches aren't

purposeful, they are simply consequences of routing through dadoes. I use a different technique for lining up the guide, the so-called T-Square Setup Gauge.

T-Square Setup Gauge. A scrap of thin plywood or hardboard or even plastic is all you need to make this gauge. The idea is to trim a 6- to 12-inch-long strip of material to match the distance between a bit's cutting

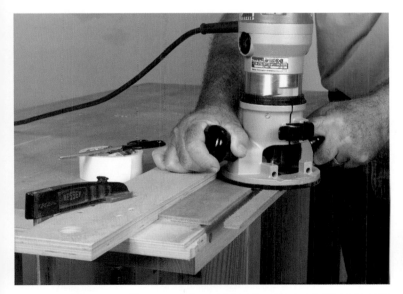

Clamp your T-square at the workbench edge, leaving just enough of a ledge to support the router. Butt a hardboard strip to the square and attach it to the benchtop with carpet tape. Run the router along the square and trim off the excess hardboard. Now you've got a setup gauge.

Using the setup gauge is as simple as aligning one of its edges with the layout mark, then butting the T-square against the other edge. The T-square's crossbar will ensure that the fence is square to the edge.

Problem Solver

edge and the router's baseplate edge. With this gauge, you can speedily and accurately position a T-square, using a mark for the dado's edge as a starting point.

To make the gauge, clamp a fence near the edge of a workbench. Butt the gauge stock to the fence and tack it down with a couple of brads or with carpet tape. Guide the router along the fence, cutting through the stock. Pry up the gauge and remove the brads or tape. You now have a gauge to position your T-square when using that router-and-bit combination.

Mark the gauge indelibly with the bit and router used. I like to drill a "hanging hole" in it, too.

To use the gauge, measure and mark one edge of each dado. You don't have to square a line across the workpiece. You don't have to mark both edges. Just a single tick mark per dado is all you need.

Align one edge of the setup gauge with the mark, and butt the T-square against the other edge. The T-square's crossbar will ensure that the fence is square to the edge. The setup gauge ensures that the fence is the proper distance from the dado location.

Quick, simple, and direct.

If you feel like being picky, make sure you have a different gauge for each dado-cutting bit in your collection. This doesn't mean simply one for each *size* bit you have, but for every *individual* straight. Your 1/2-inch-shank 3/4-inch straight may actually be slightly different in cutting diameter than your 1/4-inch-shank bit of the same size. And it should go without saying—but I'll say it anyway—that you can't use a gauge that was cut with one router to set the T-square for use with a different router.

You cut a dado, guiding the router along a fence. But when you are done, the dado isn't absolutely straight! Is there something wrong with the fence? Not necessarily. There may be something wrong with the router.

Contrary to what you might think, a round router subbase isn't always perfectly round, and it isn't always perfectly aligned—concentric to the bit—on the router base. A consequence is that the cut can wander if, as you slide the router along the fence, you also turn it.

Here's a simple solution: Paint a spot on your router's base. The spot will remind you to keep the same part of the router against the fence during the entire cut.

Self-Positioning Dado Guide

A logical extension of the fence and locating jig "co-operative" is this all-in-one jig. The setup gauge is incorporated into the fence, and the router rides on it. In the version shown, you

mark—two tick marks per dado are all you need—one edge of the dado to be cut, align the edge of the guide with the marks, and then clamp it. Moreover, it's easy to incorporate a crossbar, so you can align and square the guide on a single mark.

The self-positioning dado guide has two edges, so it can accommodate two different bits. The guide's "out-of-service" edge is the perfect place for clamping.

Self-Positioning Dado Guide
A fence and locating jig combined

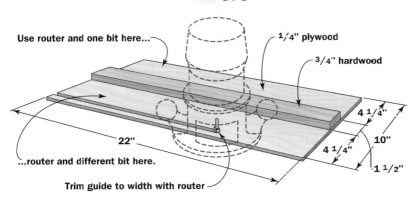

Use router and one bit here...

1/4" plywood

3/4" hardwood

...router and different bit here.

22"

4 1/4"

4 1/4"

10"

1 1/2"

Trim guide to width with router

The guide is quick and easy to make, so you can cobble up a short one for narrow work, and a long one for dadoing both of those base cabinet sides at one time.

To make the guide, glue the fence to a strip of hardboard or thin plywood. Chuck the bit that you'll use with the guide in your router, and run it along the fence, trimming off the excess plywood or hardboard. Each guide will accommodate two different bits, so mark clearly and indelibly along each edge which bit to use.

Adjustable-Width Dadoing Guide

The double-bar guide is the next logical step in the evolution. It combines the fence and crossbar with the setup gauge, and it adds a second fence as well. The fence and crossbar with the integral setup gauge make it simple to position precisely.

Its most notable feature, however, is that the two integral fences and setup gauges enable you to cut custom-width dadoes.

All you do is insert a piece of the material you want to house in the dado between the two integral setup gauges (I labeled them the fence bases in the construction drawing). Slide

the movable fence so the sample stock is pinched tight between these bases, and lock down the movable fence. Tug the sample out from between the bases, and the jig is ready to be positioned on the work.

What's at work here is that the fences trap the router. It can only cut in the gap between the bases. If the fences are just far enough apart to accommodate the router base—no side-to-side play—then the cut width will match the bit you've selected as

The One Bit you'll use with the jig. Introduce some additional space between the fences, and you get a cut—a controlled cut—that's wider than the bit.

A corollary is that, regardless of the feed direction, the router can't veer off-course. It's trapped.

As you can see in the photos and drawings, the guide consists of a fixed fence with two crossbars attached. The fence has a base layer that extends under the router. The crossbars are perfectly perpendicular to the fixed fence. When either crossbar is tight against an edge of the workpiece, then the fence will be at a right angle to that edge.

The second fence—a duplicate of the fixed one—is attached in a way that allows it to move. The distance between the fences determines the width of the dado. When they are as close together as they can be, the router baseplate will just fit between them. And when they are as far apart as they can be, the baseplate will have

The adjustable-width dadoing guide makes dadoing virtually foolproof. The router is trapped between fences and can't veer off-course, regardless of your feed direction. Reference the left fence as you push the router away; reference the right one as you pull it back, completing the cut.

Dadoing and Grooving **239**

about 1 1/4 inches of play. So, with a 1/2-inch bit, you can use this jig to cut dadoes from 1/2 to 1 3/4 inches wide.

You can set the gap between the fences with a rule, but the movable fence must be both the correct distance from the fixed fence *and* parallel to it. (You can adjust this fence to help you cut a tapered dado. While you might never want a taper dado, you might want a tapered dovetail slot. See the chapter "Sliding Dovetail Joints," page 317.) Using a piece or two of the working stock, as

The gap between the fence bases represents the cut width. Pinch scraps of the working material between them to set up the jig. The cut you make will match their thickness perfectly.

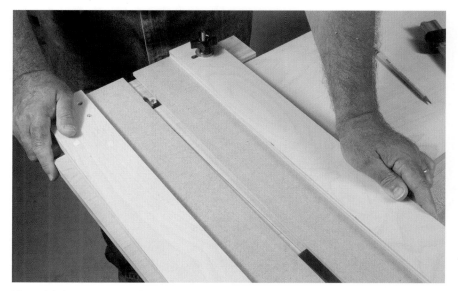

The guide is easy to align for the cut. Position it by setting the fence base edge directly on your layout line. Butting one of the crossbars against the reference edge ensures that the dado will be perpendicular to it.

Adjustable-Width Dadoing Guide

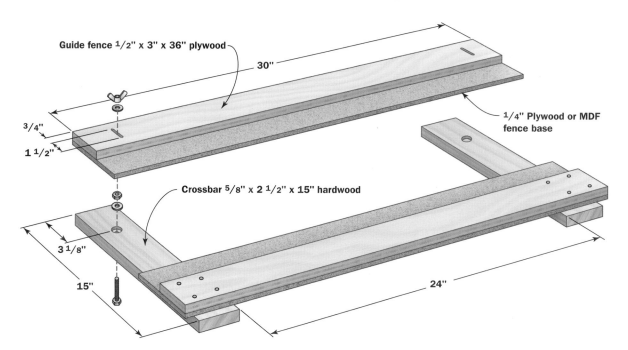

Guide fence 1/2" x 3" x 36" plywood

30"

1/4" Plywood or MDF fence base

3/4"

1 1/2"

Crossbar 5/8" x 2 1/2" x 15" hardwood

3 1/8"

15"

24"

Fred's Dadoing Baseplate

The T-square is great for a dado that's perpendicular to an edge, and the edge guide is great where a groove runs parallel to an edge. But neither will help you cut a dado or groove that skews across the work.

This jig was cooked up by an old friend, Fred Matlack—hence the name. You line up a strip of hardboard, MDF, or plywood right on the edge of the cut. This is the fence.

Attach an auxiliary baseplate to the router next. For the auxiliary baseplate, use a scrap of the same material as the fence, and attach it to the router with carpet tape. As you position the auxiliary baseplate, make sure its straight edge is tangent to the bit's cutting edge. Then burnish it down.

To make the cut, slide the auxiliary baseplate's straight edge against the hardboard fence's edge, and the cut will be just where you want it. You don't have to fret about the router tipping, because the base is fully supported—part by the auxiliary baseplate and part by the fence.

The baseplate is made in a jiffy. Bore a hole through a scrap with a 1-inch Forstner bit. The hole should be partially off the edge, as shown in the drawing. On the band saw, trim the scrap to roughly the shape of the router baseplate. It's done! Rip that fence, get out the carpet tape, and you're ready to rout.

Bit Drawer

A truism of woodworking is that the material seldom is the advertised dimension. Plywood, for example, is manufactured to a given thickness, but then finish-sanded. It ends up being a 64th or a 32nd undersized. Or it's manufactured overseas to metric dimensions.

The upshot for the router woodworker is that dadoes cut for these materials using "full-dimension" bits aren't right. The dado's exactly 3/4 inch wide, but the material rattles. A solution is to use "plywood" bits, sized at 23/32 inch for 3/4-inch plywood and 15/32 inch for 1/2-inch plywood.

A plywood panel fits loosely in a dado routed with a 3/4-inch bit (left). A piece of the same plywood fits snugly in a dado routed with a 23/32-inch bit (right).

Fred's Dadoing Baseplate
It rides a fence set at the dado's edge

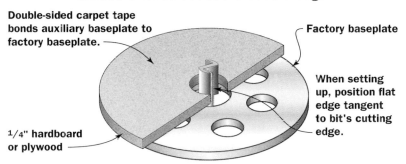

Double-sided carpet tape bonds auxiliary baseplate to factory baseplate.

Factory baseplate

When setting up, position flat edge tangent to bit's cutting edge.

1/4" hardboard or plywood

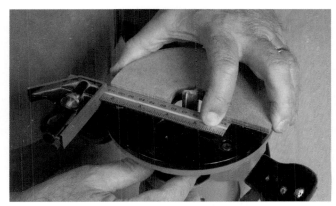

To align the auxiliary dadoing baseplate on the router's baseplate, butt a rule against its straight edge and move the baseplate until the rule just touches the cutting edge. You'll probably want to orient the baseplate so the router's handles are roughly perpendicular to the straight edge.

Using the dadoing baseplate is a lot like using a pattern bit and template, but without the router tippiness. Line up the fence directly on the edge of the dado. The bit will cut right along the fence's edge. This setup is especially good where, as here, the cut skews across the workpiece, rather than being square or parallel to an edge.

Grooving with an Edge Guide

The edge guide is a basic router accessory that's particularly useful for cutting grooves. Some manufacturers include an edge guide with the router; others charge extra for it. Some routers have good edge guides; other have lousy ones.

In the typical configuration, the edge guide is a metal and/or plastic outrigger. Mounted on one or two metal rods extending out from the router base, the guide rides along the edge of the workpiece, guiding the router in a path parallel to that edge.

The best edge-guide designs have knobs or setscrews to secure the guide body on the rods, and those knobs set the guide securely. The router's

Cutting Dentil Strips

Making dentil molding is as simple as dadoing a board, then ripping it into strips. The challenge lies in cutting crisp, evenly spaced dadoes. The router produces the crisp cuts, and this simple-to-make baseplate generates the even spacing.

The trick is the little strip on the baseplate. When you make the first cut, the strip slides along the end of the workpiece, positioning the cut. When you make the second cut, the strip slides in the first. The second dado thus is the same distance from the first as the first is from the edge. Each new cut is referenced from the previous one.

To make the baseplate, cut a scrap of 1/2-inch plywood, drill a bit hole and mounting-screw holes, and then mount it on the router base. Cut a sample dado in scrap, and cut and plane a strip to fit it. Wax the strip well so that it will slide in the dado without binding. Then attach it to the plywood baseplate with a single screw at one end. Adjust the position of the strip, the drive a second screw through the other end, fixing it in place.

A more versatile unit can be made by marking position increments on the baseplate. Then you can alter the space between dadoes without remeasuring; just pull the screw, swing the strip, and reset the screw.

Make dentil molding with your router by fitting it with a custom-made baseplate. Rout a series of closely spaced dadoes in a board, then rip thin strips from the board.

Denticulating Baseplates
Produce closely spaced dadoes and flutes

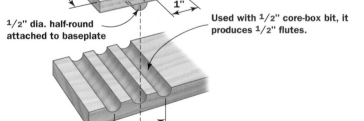

6 1/2"
Pivot screw
6 1/2"
1/2" x 1/2" hardwood
Graduations marked on baseplate
Swing guide strip to desired position; drive screw to lock it in place.
6 1/2"
6 1/2"
1"
1/2" dia. half-round attached to baseplate
Used with 1/2" core-box bit, it produces 1/2" flutes.
1"
1"

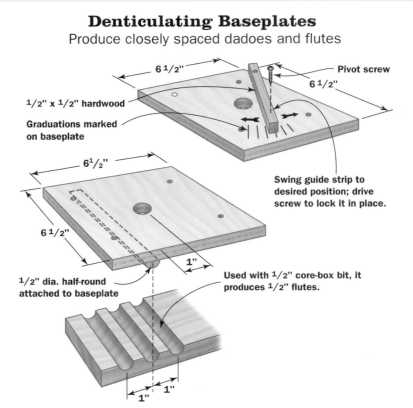

6 1/2"

6 1/2"

1"

1" 1" 1"

Try This!

A major limitation of the edge guide is its need to reference an edge.

So try this: Make a guide strip accessory that'll slide in a previously cut dado or groove, and reference that cut. This is a practical way to knock out evenly spaced dadoes for shelves in bookcase sides, or slots in a CD/DVD storage box.

The drawing shows three ways of making such guides:

- One that you make for a specific job and toss when that job is done

- An adjustable guide that mounts to an elongated baseplate

- A guide that mounts on edge-guide rods

To cut a series of closely and evenly spaced dadoes, make a jig with a strip to slide in a just-cut dado. That way, you can position each new dado in relation to the previous one. It's a lot faster than setting a T-square for each cut.

Set Up a Guide to Slide In a Dado

JOB-SPECIFIC JIG
6"
10"
1/4"
Measure from bit and attach slide to baseplate
1/4" to 1/2" plywood
Width of dado

Elongated 1/4" plywood baseplate
6"
12"
ADJUSTABLE JIG
7"
Slide matches dado; attached to moveable base
1/2" moveable baseplate

1/4" rod, 12" long
7"
1 1/2"
3/4"
1 1/2"
Thread end of edge guide rod
EDGE-GUIDE-BASED JIG

Grooving with an Edge Guide

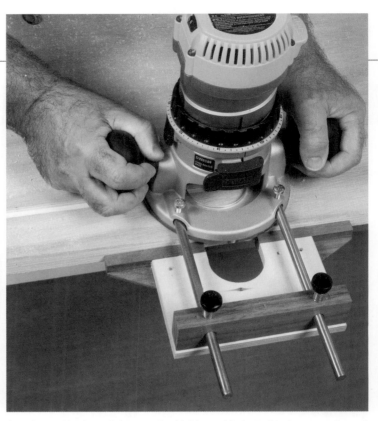

The heart of a good edge guide is its adjustment capability. This guide has a precision micrometer as its adjuster. It enables you to alter the position or width of a cut in thousanths of an inch. Sounds like overkill, but it saves time and helps you achieve better results.

An edge guide doesn't have to be highly sophisticated to be accurate and reliable. Make yourself one like this, following plans in the chapter "Jigmaking," page 43.

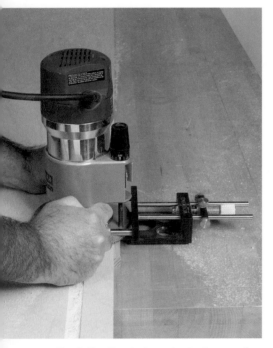

Feed direction is important when routing with an edge guide. Moving in the correct direction enlists the bit's help in pulling the guide against the reference edge as you cut.

vibrations won't shake them loose. They have provisions for you to add auxiliary faces to the guide(s). Some allow you to install two guides on those rods, one on either side of the bit. This can be useful for edge-grooving (and its kin, mortising).

The chapter "Router 101" has more information on edge guides, and the chapter "Jigmaking" has plans for a couple of edge guides. If you don't have one, and your budget is tight, you can make one.

As I mentioned, the edge guide bears against the workpiece edge to guide your cut. There's a limit to how far from the edge you can work. The apparatus can get unwieldy and difficult to maneuver. If the link between the guide body and the router is too long, the two get a fraction out of sync. The guide tends to "walk" along the edge, rather than slide smoothly. You end up with a gouge.

Router Table Through Cuts

Cutting grooves and dadoes on a router table has a lot in common with doing it on a table saw with a dado cutter. In both approaches, you have to set the fence, then slide the work across the table, keeping it squarely in contact with the fence as you do.

The biggest difference is the speed; unless it is a shallow cut—a quarter inch or less—the dado cutter is going to be faster. For large workpieces—cabinet sides, for example—the setup of your table saw may favor the dado cutter also. If you work with plywood a lot, you may have long fence rails and a table extension to the right of the blade, as well as a big outfeed table. These accessories facilitate dadoing large panels as much as they do cutting large panels. *But...* it's unlikely that your router table is set up this way.

Routing grooves for drawer bottoms and dadoes for drawer backs is a good router-table job. The cuts are close to edges, so you can guide them with the fence. And the workpiece is a maneuverable size.

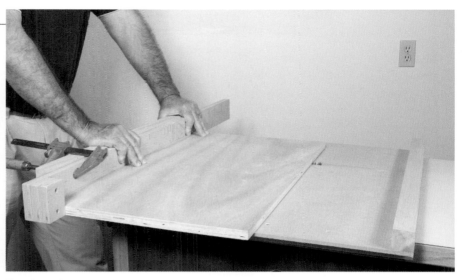

Panels as large as cabinet sides *can* be dadoed on a router table using a dadoing sled, which is similar to the sliding fence shown in the chapter "Router Table Accessories," page 101. A stop clamped to the sled fence locates the cut and immobilizes the work. Sides on the underside reference the edges of the tabletop to guide the sled.

If you have a fairly typical 2-foot by 3-foot router table and you've heeded my advice to offset the router, you have a wider support at the back of the table. This can be used to advantage in dadoing those wide panels. In addition, the sliding fence presented in the chapter "Router Table Accessories" can be a help in dadoing.

As I said before, I'd opt to use a hand-guided router for large or unwieldy workpieces. I'd just rather maneuver a compact router than a large panel. But small parts—drawer

Safety First!

Needing an 11/16-inch-wide groove in a 11/2-inch-square edge band, you decide to use a 1/2-inch straight bit and also to set the fence to center the groove across the band's width. The first pass goes fine. Then you turn the strip around and start the second pass. The cutter snatches the strip right out of your hand and shoots it across the shop. What gives here!!?

It's this: You've made a climb cut. The bit was helping you with the feed. Be glad if only the workpiece is boogered up and not your hands, too.

When cutting a groove in solid stock, the feed direction on the router table is right to left. When widening a groove, you want to cut on the side closest to you (away from the fence). The rotation of the bit will be opposing your right-to-left feed pressure, and tending to push the work against the fence.

Widening a groove by cutting on the fence side of a groove is a risky proposition. You *may* get away with a left-to-right feed, especially if you use featherboards, but there's no need to try that. Plan your cut and set it up so you can do it safely.

Page back to the chapter "Router Table Savvy," page 119, for a fuller explanation.

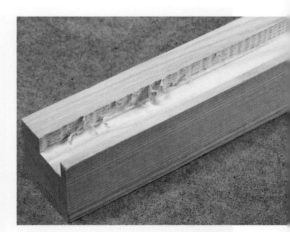

Here's the result of an unintended climb cut when widening a groove on the router table. In making a second pass to widen the groove, I fed this stock in the usual right-to-left direction. But the cutter was cutting on the fence side of the groove, rather than the far side. That's a climb cut. The bit snatched the strip from me, shot it across the shop, and in the process, butchered the cut. I'm lucky it didn't butcher my fingers.

sides and fronts, for example—I'd dado or groove on the router table.

The technique is self-evident, I think. Select the bit, chuck it in the router, and set the depth-of-cut. Adjust the fence to properly locate the cut. Make the cut. If necessary, raise the bit and make a second pass to deepen the cut.

Stopped Cuts

When a dado or groove doesn't extend completely from one edge of a board to the other, it's referred to as a stopped cut or a blind cut. It can begin at one edge and end before it reaches the other (half-blind), or it can begin and end shy of both edges (full-blind).

As I mentioned before, the router is unparalleled in its ability to cut stopped grooves. It can get into and out of the cut with relative ease. Think how you'd have to do it with a saw-mounted dado cutter.

Using a Handheld Router

Fully stopped cuts are the stuff of plunge routers and plunge cutters. You lay out the dado, indicating the cut's ends. You set your fence. Position the router, plunge the cutter, rout until the end of cut mark aligns with the bit, and retract the bit, ending the cut.

But not all of us have plunge routers. What other options are there?

Obviously, ending a stopped cut is easy, even with a fixed-base router. Turn off the router and lift it, carefully, straight up from the work. The real trick is *starting* a stopped cut with a fixed-base router.

One option is to tip in or drag in the bit. Align the cutter with the start mark. Rear the router back so that its baseplate, though not flat on the work, nevertheless *is* in contact with both the fence and the work. Turn on the router and carefully, slowly, lower the spinning bit into the work. Practice. You want the axis of the bit

aligned with the dado so that you don't create a bulb where the bit enters the work.

If the bit is not a plunging type, you can get it into the work by moving the router along the fence as you lower it into the work. The bit will cut a ramp from the surface down to full depth, and once the bit's in the work, you can carefully feed the router back along the fence to rout this ramp out to full depth.

Remember, while neither method is foolproof, either can be done. Practice! Just practice.

You may find that a double-fence guide, where the base is firmly captured between two fences, helps you keep the machine and its bit aligned with the dado.

A second, more foolproof, approach is to *drill* a starting hole for the bit. Obviously, the hole has to match the diameter of the bit. It should be the same depth as the intended depth of the dado. Set the bit in the hole, turn on the router, and cut.

Tipping in the bit to begin a stopped dado isn't difficult. Just have one end of the baseplate in contact with the work, and one edge against the fence. With the bit clear of the work, switch on the router and carefully lower the spinning bit into the work.

Using a Forstner bit of the same diameter as the router bit, bore beginning and end holes for each stopped cut. With the router bit in the starting hole, switch on the router and advance it to the end hole.

The Router-Table Approach

Stopped grooves are easily cut on the router table. Easily cut, that is, if the workpiece is of a manageable size. To make such cuts, you must lower the work onto the spinning bit, move it to make the cut, then lift it free of the bit. Obviously, if the workpiece is too big or unwieldy, you are going to have trouble maneuvering it.

To know where to begin and end a stopped cut, mark the outer edges of the bit on a piece of tape stuck on the fence or the mounting plate. With the body of a try square flat against the fence, butt the blade gingerly against the cutting edge of the bit. Scribe along the blade onto the tape. Switch the try square to the other side of the bit and repeat.

The correct feed direction for this sort of cut is right to left. Line up the mark for the beginning of the groove with the mark on the fence that's to the left of the bit. Now drop the stock onto the bit, beginning the cut, and feed the work to the left. As the end-of-cut mark on the stock comes up to the mark on the fence to the right of the bit, carefully lift the end of the workpiece off the bit. Shut off the router.

Using Stop Blocks

How about stops, you ask.

Stop blocks are good when precisely set. They're real time-savers in doing repetitive cuts, where they supplant layout markings. But a lot of times, especially for one-of-a-kind cuts, stop blocks are just extra setup work.

Nevertheless, here're a few stop block tips.

Tip One. The easiest way to set stop blocks, I've learned, is to make

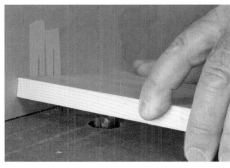
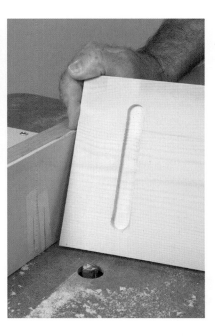

Cutting stopped or blind dadoes on the router table isn't difficult. Pencil the bit tangents on the fence (on masking tape here) and the beginning and ending points on the back of the workpiece. Tip up the work, as shown above, and advance it over the spinning bit until the appropriate marks align. Plunge the work onto the bit and cut. When the end marks align, tip the work up off the bit. You'll have a nice blind dado (right).

an initial cut mark-to-mark, *without stop blocks*. With the cut done, use *it* to set blocks for the subsequent cuts. Position the router (or the work, with a router table setup) at the beginning of the cut and attach a stop to the fence. Move the machine (or the work) to the end, and set the second block. This way, you can skip the math and the ruler work, the test cuts, and the resetting.

Tip Two. You can make rudimentary (but reusable) stops by laminating two scraps of plywood to form an end lap. Set the stops against a router T-square and drive brads or screws through the stop into the square. It may not be pretty, but it works.

Tip Three. Small hand screws make good stops to use on the router table. You can use any sort of clamp to secure little scraps to the fence, but hand screws are pretty direct. The clamp *is* the block. When you tighten them on the fence, set them just a little above the tabletop so router dust can blow under them. Then it won't collect against the stop, throwing off the accuracy of it.

Tip Four. Stop blocks you can make to use with a router table fence are shown in the chapter "Router Table Accessories," page 101.

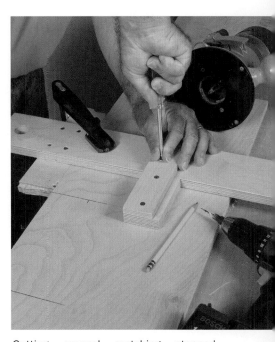

Cutting several matching stopped dadoes? Screw a stop (or two) to your T-square. When you move the square, the stop goes with it. When the job's done, back out the screws and recycle them and the stop.

Dadoing and Grooving **249**

Bit Choices

When you cut an ogee edge on a board, there really are only a couple of bits that will do—an ogee (of the appropriate size) in either a piloted or unpiloted configuration. But cutting joinery dadoes and grooves is an entirely different situation. A lot of different bits lend themselves to the job.

How do you decide what to use?

On a pragmatic level, most of us will use whatever straight bit we have that's the right diameter for the cut we want to make. Maybe you bought a set, and it included 1/4-, 1/2-, and 3/4-inch straight bits. You use those three bits for all your grooving and dadoing, because those are the bits you have.

On a more idealistic level, here's some background to help you decide what bits to buy when expanding your inventory.

Double-flute straight bit

Double-flute straight bits are THE basic router bits. Each bit has two vertical cutting edges, and thus it makes two cuts per revolution. Use a double-fluted straight when the finish is primary and the feed rate is secondary.

An enormous variety of sizes is available. Some manufacturers list 50 or more different two-flute straight bits. Cutting diameters range from 1/16 inch to 2 inches, with flute

See Also...

Grooves aren't always straight. See "Routing Curves and Circles," page 175.

Though this chapter has focused on fence-guided cuts, you can rout dadoes and grooves guided by a template. You reference the template with either a template guide or a pattern bit with a shank-mounted bearing. See the chapter "Template-Guided Work," page 155.

lengths from 1/4 inch to 2 1/2 inches. Even metric sizes are available. The typical catalog may list 1/2-inch-diameter bits with flute lengths of 3/4, 1, 1 1/4, 1 1/2, 2, and 2 1/2 inches.

So how do you choose which to buy (or use)?

Take the shortest length for work to be done. For dadoes, choose the one with the 3/4-inch-long flutes. That's plenty long for cuts that'll seldom exceed a 1/2-inch depth.

If you have a plunge router, make sure you are getting bits that have plunge-cutting ends. Most do these days, but check before you buy.

Shear-cut straight bit

Shear-cut straight bits are variants of the double-flute straights. A bit of this design is called shear-cut because the cutting edges are at a slight angle (usually about 3°) to the bit's axis. In a broad sense, the shear-cut bit shaves the work, rather than chopping it. A shear-cut bit is often recommended when the finish from a standard bit is inadequate or when the bit will be used in a relatively low-horsepower router.

Single-flute straight bit

Single-flute straight bits should be used where the cutting speed is more important than the cut finish. These bits cut once per revolution, allowing faster feed rates but yielding rougher cuts at any feed rate. Because there's only a single flute, there's extra chip clearance. The tip is generally designed for fast plunge-cutting.

Spiral bit

Spiral bits are shaped very much like twist-drill bits. Spiral-flute straights combine a shearing action in cutting with an augering action in chip clearance. The shearing action yields an especially clean, accurate cut, while the augering action clears the chips up (or down) and out of the cut. A trade-off is a reduced cutting rate.

Spirals are available in upshear and downshear designs. In a dado-cutting operation, the upshear spiral will lift the chips out of the cut. But it will also lift the wood fibers along the edges of the cut—it's paring from the bottom of the cut toward the surface, after all. The downshear spiral is a response to the latter problem. Its cutting action is from the surface down, so it leaves a smooth edge at the surface. But it is also augering the chips toward the bottom of the cut.

There is a subsidiary dynamic stemming from the shear direction. The upshear action pulls the work against the router, while the down-shear action pushes the work away from the router.

To get the twist, manufacturers make the *entire* bit from either carbide or high-speed steel (HSS). (Paso Robles spirals are carbide-tipped, but they don't have the degree of twist that other brands do; they seem more like shear-cut straights than spirals.) The HSS spiral is sharper to begin with, but it dulls quickly. The carbide spiral holds its edge a long time, but it is brittle. It is also pricey: A carbide spiral generally costs about 2 1/2 times what a comparable HSS spiral does.

Rabbeting

A rabbet is one of the joinery cuts the router does best. Essentially an edge treatment, it is done with a piloted bit.

Select the rabbet bit with the correct cutting width, chuck it in the router, set the depth-of-cut, and rout. That's all there is to it…. Until you sit down and think about rabbets and rabbeting. Then you realize there's more to the repertoire of rabbet cuts than can be executed with a rabbet bit. There are extra-deep and extra-wide rabbets. Rabbets in curved shapes, rabbets in narrow edges.

Rabbeting with a Piloted Bit

The first choice for the average rabbeting operation is the rabbet bit, which has a pilot. It minimizes setup: The only adjustments you can make are the depth-of-cut and the angle of attack. The measurement between the bit's cutting edge and its pilot governs what I call the width of the rabbet. (A lot of bit manufacturers call this the depth of the rabbet.)

Routing a rabbet is usually straightforward. Use a piloted rabbet bit, guiding it along a smooth, straight edge.

You insert the bit, adjust the depth setting, and rout. It is simple.

To alter the width of the rabbet with such bits, you can do two things. One is that you can change your angle of attack, as shown in the drawings. This can be a useful approach, since it can change the dimension over which *you* have control, while preserving the simplicity of setup and operation that piloted bits provide.

The other thing you can do is to change the pilot bearing. Every bit manufacturer sells separate bearings, and in the case of rabbet bits, they package sets that will give you many different cut widths from one bit. (See Bit Drawer on page 252.)

(There is a third thing you can do,

Bit Drawer

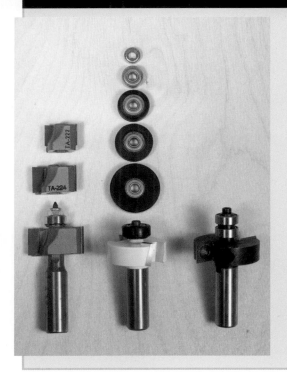

Interchangeable bearings and interchangeable cutters are two approaches to rabbet bit versatility. A number of manufacturers offer bearing sets to complement their rabbet bits. Depending on the bearing used, a standard 1/2-inch rabbet bit (center) will also give you 1/8-, 3/16-, 1/4-, 5/16-, 3/8-, and 7/16-inch cuts. That's seven different cut widths from one bit. You can find packages with fewer bearings, and with more bearings.

Paso Robles Carbide takes a different tack. You *can* change bearings, but more importantly, you can change cutters. The cutter for a 3/8-inch rabbet will fit either a 1/4-inch-shank arbor or (as shown) a 1/2-inch size. Want to make a 1/8-inch rabbet? Pull the 3/8-inch cutter off the arbor and pop the 1/8-inch cutter in place. You don't even need to take the arbor out of the router collet. Want a 3/16-inch rabbet? Switch to a different bearing.

A different sort of interchangeability is incorporated into the Amana bit on the right. It has replaceable carbide cutting tips, secured with Torx screws. Each tip is a square, and all four edges are sharpened. When your cutting edge dulls, you rotate the tip 90°. When all edges are dull, you toss the tip and install a new one.

An additional feature is that the bit has two bearings, providing a wider guide surface and ostensibly offering better stability as you rout.

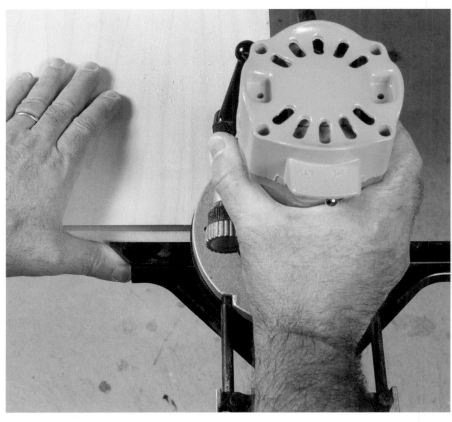

When rabbeting with a piloted bit, it's all too easy to inadvertently "dip around the corner" at the end, thus botching the cut (above). Using an edge guide helps you to slide straight out of the cut at the end, thus maintaining the square corner. Keep a hand on the trailing end of the guide to hold it against the work edge until the cutter is clear.

and that is to circumvent the pilot somehow—using an edge guide or a fence. You can only narrow the cut using this approach, but it's valid, it works. If you take this approach, though, you probably should question why you are using a rabbet bit and not a straight bit.)

The piloted bit can be used in both handheld and table-mounted routers, of course. Because the bit is piloted, you don't *have* to use the router-table fence. (You *should* use a starting pin if you don't use the fence.) If you do use the fence, set it so it lines up with the pilot. Hold a straightedge so it bridges the bit gap in your fence, and adjust the fence until the pilot just touches the straightedge (without lifting either end off the fence).

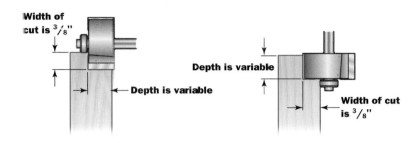

Angle of Attack
Changing it alters the cut dimension

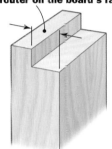

If this dimension must vary from ³/₈", rest the router on the board's face.

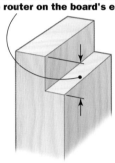

If this dimension must vary from ³/₈", rest the router on the board's end.

Thwarting Splinters

The best way to avoid splintered edges when you rout rabbets is to make the first pass what I call a scoring cut. There are two ways to make it.

With a handheld router, make the first pass a climb cut. It's usually a wavering cut, because nothing is guiding it. Rather than hitting the wood fibers head-on and driving them out from the board's edge, the cutter is sweeping in on them, creating a crisp edge to the cut. On a second pass, feed the proper direction, cutting full depth.

There's good reason to be wary in making that climb cut. The router seemingly will try to run away from you. But the cut is shallow, so the cutter can't get much traction. And of course you have a firm grip on the router, too.

The approach on the router table is different. I don't like climb cuts on the router table ever. So set the fence to allow the barest of cuts, only ¹/₃₂ inch, perhaps ¹/₁₆ inch. Feed in the correct right-to-left direction. The cutter glances across the wood fibers and doesn't get enough purchase to dig out an ugly splinter.

Reset the fence then, and cut the rabbet to whatever depth you desire.

Rabbeting with a Straight Bit

A straight bit is a very flexible rabbet-cutter. If there is a drawback, it is only that the setup can take a bit more time, especially with a hand-held router. This is because you need a fence (or edge guide) to control the cut.

On the router table, you tighten the bit in the collet, then set the fence to expose only enough of the bit to make the desired rabbet. If your router table is like mine, then it's like the table saw—the fence is always in place, and adjusting its setting before making a cut is second nature.

With a handheld router, you can either clamp a straightedge to the work, or you can break out the edge guide.

The advantage of these approaches is that you can produce an oddball rabbet, such as one to perfectly accommodate a piece of plywood.

Stopped Rabbets

A stopped rabbet, of course, is one that does not extend the full length of an edge. It can be stopped at one or both ends.

Here are two techniques for beginning and ending stopped rabbets, using a handheld router:

■ Mark the beginning and ending points on the work. Make the cut between the two marks, visually aligning the bit with the starting mark to begin, and stopping the cut when the ending mark is reached. The accuracy of this approach

In an ideal situation, the router woodworker can mark starting and stopping points on the workpiece itself and track the bit's progress visually. Setup is minimized.

depends upon the clarity of your vision and the steadiness of your hand. (It can be easier to do this if your marks reference the outer edge of the base, rather than the bit, since this relieves you of the need to sight through the baseplate's bit opening and the operation's chip storm.)

■ Clamp stops to the work. The position of the stops would correspond to the marks that reference the base. You butt the router against the stop at the starting point and rout until it hits the stop at the end point. Clamping stops to the work can be said more easily than done in many

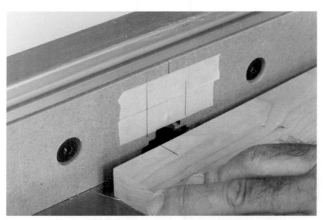

Cutting a blind rabbet on the router table is easy. Lay the work on the table. Brace its right end against the fence, and keep the left end clear of the bit. Align the start mark on the work with the mark on the outfeed side of the bit. Push the work flat against the fence, beginning the cut. Feed it to the left. When the end mark on the work aligns with the mark on the infeed side of the bit, pull the end of the work away from the fence.

Rabbeting an Assembled Box

Need to rabbet an assembled case for a back? Or a box for a lipped lid?

The problem in such operations is the narrow bearing surface. It's very difficult to prevent the router from wobbling as you move it along a surface 3/4 inch wide. The solution is a scrap of plywood stuck to the router base with carpet tape.

Spot the router at one end. Then you can perch it on one edge and have the plywood span the assembly to rest on the other side. The machine is square to the case. As you work around the case, always keep the baseplate resting on adjacent or opposite sides.

To rabbet an assembled box or case, use a baseplate that's wide enough to bridge the gap from side to side. You'll be able to keep the router bolt-upright and allow the pilot bearing to guide the cut.

cases. You might want to try using a dadoing jig with adjustable stops (see the chapter "Dadoing and Grooving," page 235, for plans for such jigs).

Doing the same cuts on the router table can be a little easier. To visually align beginning and ending marks, make marks with a pencil on the router-table fence that correspond to the edges of the bit (put a little masking tape on the fence if you don't want to mark directly on it). Obviously, your view of these marks won't be obscured.

To make the cut, you simply align the work beside the bit, push it against the fence (and thus onto the bit), make the cut, and pull the work away from the fence.

Almost easier still is to use stops. You can apply small hand screws to the router table fence as stops. The hard part is calculating the positions. The stop for the starting point will be to the right; the one for the ending point will be on the left.

■ **To set the starting block:** Add the length of the cut to the measurement from the end of the cut to the end of the work. The sum is the distance the block must be from the left of the bit.

■ **To set the ending block:** Add the length of cut to the measurement from the beginning of the work to the beginning of the cut. The sum is the distance the block must be from the right of the bit.

Example: The workpiece is 22 inches long and the rabbet is 10 inches long. The rabbet starts 7 inches from one end, and ends 5 inches from the other. The starting block will be on the right, 15 inches from the left side of the bit. The end block will be on the left, 17 inches from the right side of the bit.

Obviously, the length of your fence can pretty easily be outstripped. When this happens, you can either attach a temporary facing that's long enough for the task at hand, or revert to the visual alignment of pencil marks.

Wide Rabbets

For purposes of this discussion, a wide rabbet is one that's more than 1/2 inch wide, for that's the maximum width possible using a piloted cutter. Here you need to use a straight bit. With a handheld router, use an edge guide or fence to control the cut. Obviously, on the router table, you'll use the fence.

Most router woodworkers have a 3/4-inch straight bit. Larger straights *are* available, though not that many of us have 2-inch, 1 1/2-inch, or even 1-inch bits. Do you have a large-diameter mortising, planer, or bottom-cleaning bit? Any of these will do a great job. Use the largest-diameter bit you have, however big it is, to produce those wide rabbets.

The Dovetail Rabbet

As an alternative to the more familiar rabbet joint, you might try a dovetail rabbet. Simple to make with a router, the joint comes together neatly and squarely. It is more resistant to racking than a conventional rabbet joint.

You can cut the joint with a single setup on the router table, or you can customize it, working with the router either handheld or table-mounted. The single-setup approach is a halving process. The same volume of waste is removed from each piece, so half the joint is on one piece and half on the other. If you want to remove more from one piece than the other, you are customizing the joint—easily doable, but not with one setup.

To cut the joint on 3/4-inch stock, you need at least a 3/4-inch dovetail bit. The 1/2-inch bit, which is the most common size, won't give you a satisfactory joint because it is just a little too small. The angle of the bit is irrelevant, since you use the same bit for both cuts. The bit height is irrelevant to the fit of the joint, so set a height that looks right. The fence

setting is what makes it comes together perfectly. Take the time to cut tests on scraps of the working stock.

Cut one half of the joint with the workpiece flat on the tabletop. Stand its mate on end and slide it along the fence to cut it. The fence position is the same for both cuts. When the fence is set properly, the bit makes the same cut in both pieces. What could be simpler?

If you want to change the joint proportions, you cut half the joint, placing the shoulder where you want it. Then you adjust the fence to produce a mating cut. On the router table, no bit-height adjustment should be necessary, only a fence adjustment. You'll have to find the fit through test cuts. But even with this approach, you cut one piece flat on the tabletop, and the mate on end against the fence.

An approach to cutting the joint with a handheld router is depicted in the drawing. It's a more laborious approach because you not only have two very different setups, you also have more handling of the pieces to do.

The critical setup adjustment is the fence position. Make sample cuts and assemble them. The bottom sample indicates that you need to move the fence to house more of the bit. The middle sample indicates that you need to move the fence to expose more of the bit. The top sample is right on.

Cut the Dovetail Rabbet with a Portable Router

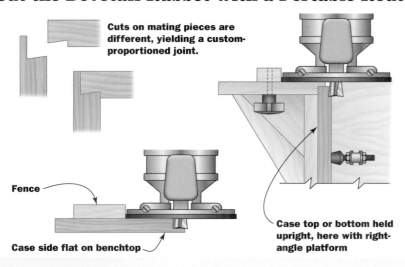

Cuts on mating pieces are different, yielding a custom-proportioned joint.

Fence

Case side flat on benchtop

Case top or bottom held upright, here with right-angle platform

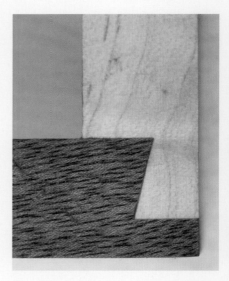

The dovetail rabbet is a "designer" joint: It looks just a little different, just a little more stylish than the rabbet joint you're used to. And that Z-shaped interlock enables a well-fitted one to resist some stresses just a little better, too.

As the cut gets wider—wide to the point that you have to make three or four passes to complete it—avoiding wobbles and dips is the challenge. On the router table, you have to keep the uncut surface of the piece tight against the table. And if the ultimate cut is wider than the remaining uncut surface, then the last pass or two can be dicey. Pressure on the wrong area of the work can cause it to tip, gouging it. Doing the cut with a handheld router isn't likely to be any easier.

One solution is to treat the rabbet as a wide dado or groove. Cut the work with some excess width or length (whichever is appropriate), and leave a ridge of unrouted stock at the outer edge of the cut. This will support the router or the work. After the router cut is done, you trim the ridge of waste away on the table saw, reducing the work to its final width and simultaneously turning the dado into a rabbet.

An alternative is to use carpet tape to stick a couple of shims to the router table at the fence after making

By using a fence instead of the pilot, you can greatly increase the width of rabbet you can cut. Though only half of this 1 1/2-inch-diameter mortising bit is engaged, the rabbet being formed is half again as wide as one cut with a piloted bit.

the first pass. The shims will support the workpiece as you make subsequent passes.

Another approach is to deal with the rabbet as a deep cut. Address the depth of the rabbet with the fence or edge-guide setting, and address the width with the router's depth-of-cut setting. On the router table, you'll set the work on edge and feed it past the bit.

Cutting a dovetail rabbet joint is easiest as a one-setup, two-pass operation. The first pass is made with the workpiece—the side of a case, for example—flat on the tabletop. To make the second cut for the joint, stand the workpiece—the case top or bottom—on end and brace it against the fence. Back up the work to keep it square and to prevent the bit from blowing out the edge.

Tricks for Cutting Wide Rabbets

To cut a wide rabbet, cut the workpiece oversized.

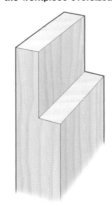

WITH A HANDHELD ROUTER

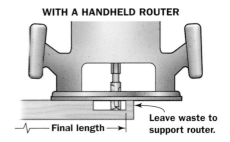

← Final length → Leave waste to support router.

After routing, saw away the excess stock, bringing the workpiece to its final length.

ON THE ROUTER TABLE

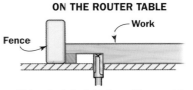

Shim stuck to tabletop with carpet tape

Deep Rabbets

What's a *deep* rabbet? Depending upon the perspective, a deep rabbet could be seen as a wide rabbet. And it could be cut like one, too. But let's look at it as a rabbet that exceeds the capacities of the standard piloted rabbet bit and, for whatever reason, needs to be attacked as a deep cut.

Before you abandon the rabbet bit, see what you can do to extend its reach. You can sometimes cheat the shank out of the collet a few fractions of an inch. Make a couple of passes to max out the bit's cutting depth, then back the bit out of the collet for another pass or two. You want to keep at least 1 inch of the shank in the collet. And it's better to be using a 1/2-inch-shank bit for this than a 1/4-inch-shank one.

Another alternative is to make the first passes to the full cutting depth of the rabbet bit, then extend the cut even deeper using a straight pattern bit. This bit has a pilot bearing on its shank. The bearing rides along the shoulder of the rabbet to guide the cut.

Finally, you can use a straight bit. With a handheld router, use a fence or edge guide. Using the latter, remember that its facing has to extend below the bit at its deepest setting so it can bear on the work. You'll probably have to attach an auxiliary facing to a commercial edge guide, which is easy enough to do. With a router table, the fence may need an auxiliary facing, extending well above the bit, to support the stock.

If you have stuck with us this far, the operation should be pretty evident. Set the fence (or guide) and make the cut. Make several passes, working down to the final depth.

Tricks for Cutting Deep Rabbets

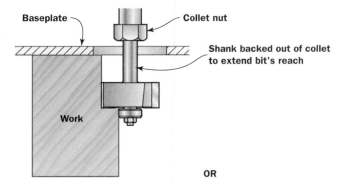

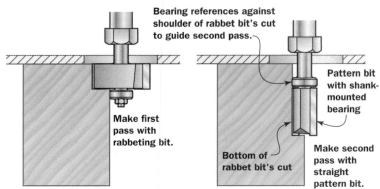

Shiplaps

A shiplap joint is formed by overlapping rabbets cut into opposite faces of adjoining boards. I'd call it a carpentry kind of thing, used in siding and natural-wood paneling. But you'll see it in the backs of centuries-old cupboards and cabinets.

The joint allows individual boards to expand and contract seasonally without opening gaps between it and its neighbors. And that's the whole point of shiplaps. The rabbets are quickly cut, precision is irrelevant, yet they serve a valid purpose.

A piloted rabbet bit and a router are all you need to make them. Lay the board across sawhorses and run the router along one edge, cutting the rabbet half the thickness (or a little more) of the stock. Roll the board onto its back and repeat. Typically, the boards are fastened with nails driven just shy of the shoulder of the "hidden" rabbet. The exposed rabbet catches under the adjacent board's hidden rabbet.

Edge Joints

If you intend to glue up stock to make large, flat panels, you will use some variation of the edge joint. In many, many instances, you simply butt two boards together to make an edge joint. A lot of woodworkers, however, prefer to work the edges a bit, to produce a means to simultaneously help align the two boards during glue-up and increase the joint's strength by interlocking the boards and expanding the glue area.

At the very least, the edges of the mating boards require surfacing to remove saw marks, dings, and chips. Traditionally this surfacing, called jointing, was done with a long-soled jointer plane. These days, it's ordinarily done on a jointer.

The router lends itself to the jointing operation, as well as to the various edge treatments that yield stronger edge joints.

■ Beyond mere jointing is routing an edge joint. It is almost imperceptible, it works with gently curving edges as well as straight edges, and you can make it only with a router.

■ A common approach is to use splines: Plow a stopped groove in the edges of the boards and insert a spline of hardwood or plywood in it. The router is the ideal tool to make the groove.

■ Biscuit joinery has become popular in recent years. A dedicated power tool, called a biscuit joiner, saws a slot into which a thin, elliptical wooden spline just fits. Thus, instead of a continuous spline reinforcing the butt joint, short splines are spaced along the joint. In some instances, particularly when joining boards edge-to-edge, you can cut the slots with your router.

■ Similar effects can be achieved by cutting tongues and grooves along the edges of the boards. Yeah, the router does it.

■ Specialty router bits cut a variety of edge shapes that provide a mechanical interlocking of the boards, while also expanding the glue area. These are covered in the last chapter, "Routed Joints."

So when tackling edge joinery, don't overlook the help that your router can offer.

If the edges are prepared so they join almost seamlessly (top), a glued butt joint is the best edge-to-edge joint. But woodworkers often want help in aligning an edge joint, so they'll use splines or biscuits in the joint (middle). The utility of the tongue-and-groove (bottom) extends beyond mere alignment. All these edge joints can be prepared with a router.

Routing an Edge Joint

The first step in preparing any edge joint is to joint the edges of the mating boards. Suffice it to say here that this is an operation you can do easily with the router. Details are found in the chapter "Surfacing with the Router," page 191. But you can joint most boards more quickly and accurately on the jointer, and there's no reason why you shouldn't use the jointer if you can.

But a router can help you do a special job of the fundamental woodworking task of edge-joining two or more boards to make a wide panel. A well-conceived and executed routed edge joint will virtually disappear—if that's what you want—because you can rout the mating edges to follow the direction of the grain, even though it meanders sinuously from one end of a board to the other. If you want the joint to stand out, you can make it do that in a special way, too.

I first ran across this technique about 25 or 30 years ago in a magazine article, and I've run across explanations of it in several places since. The concept is to rout the mating edges as positive-negative images. Doing this allows them to join much better than simply trying to give them both perfect, smooth, straight edges. And making one edge the negative image of the other is what allows you to join them along a gentle curve as well as a straight line.

In brief, the technique is this: You clamp a fence atop the first workpiece and, guiding the router base against the fence, trim about $1/16$ inch from the workpiece. Then you secure the second workpiece directly opposite the first. By guiding the router along

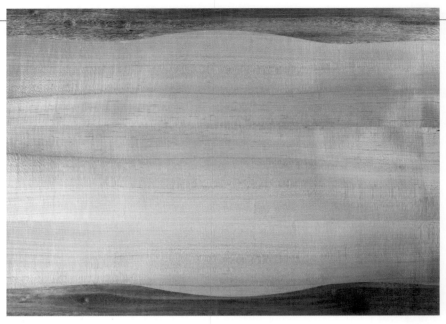

The router edge-jointing technique can enable you to produce clean, smooth, perfectly fitted edges on boards for gluing into panels. If you are adept at color- and grain-matching, your routed edge joints can virtually disappear. On the other hand, the technique enables you to produce some pretty eye-catching edge joints.

the same fence—you haven't moved it—you trim the second workpiece and produce an edge that's a negative image of the first.

To execute the technique, you should block the boards up above the work surface. Otherwise, the bit will cut a trench across it as it trims the edges of the workpieces. If you use this technique once in a blue moon, you can surely find a couple of extra boards to use as shims. If the technique becomes a frequently used part of your repertoire, you may opt to construct an edge-routing platform and matching fence. You can make it easily from a third of a sheet of good-quality $3/4$-inch plywood. I have one that's 4 feet long, sufficient for the work I've done using this technique. But you are limited only by plywood's sheet sizes.

You can use whatever router you have, although a fairly powerful fixed-base machine is probably ideal. A horse-and-a-half is probably the minimum.

By all means, use a $1/2$-inch-shank bit, which will withstand side stresses better than a $1/4$-inch-shank bit. Naturally, the bit's cutting edges must be longer than the workpiece is thick. A large-diameter cutter, $3/4$-inch or more, will probably be less prone to vibrate under load than a $1/2$-inch-diameter (or smaller) bit. Because the tip speed is higher, the large-diameter bit will give a smoother cut, too. And, of course, a shear-cut bit would be even smoother.

To make the platform, cut three 4-foot-long strips of $3/4$-inch plywood. One should be about 15 inches wide, the second about 8 inches wide, and the last about 5 inches wide. Glue the two narrower pieces atop the widest, as shown. The 2-inch-wide channel thus formed allows the bit to cut below the wood without marring the platform. It also gives all the chips and dust generated by the operation a place to go.

Router Edge-Jointing Platform
Cut perfect edge-to-edge joints

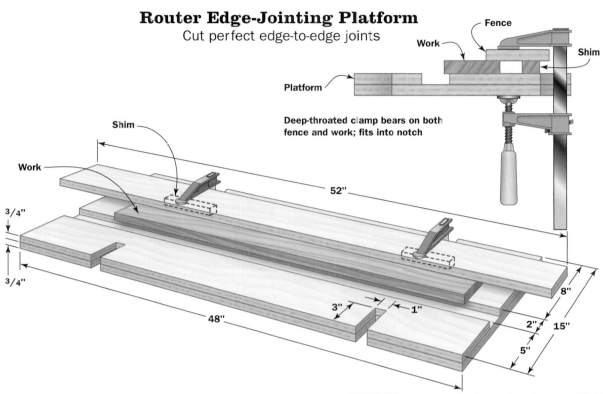

Deep-throated clamp bears on both
fence and work; fits into notch

Cut a fence about 6 inches wide and about 4 inches longer than any stock you anticipate router edge-jointing. (Although the platform shown here is only 4 feet long, you can use it to position longer boards for router edge-jointing. But regardless of the length of the platform, the fence must be longer than workpieces.)

To use the platform, you have to rest it across sawhorses or some other support(s) that permit you to clamp the work to both sides. I usually set up the jig across one end of my workbench—see the photos—so I can reach all but the shortest workpieces with deep-throated clamps.

To router edge-joint two boards, set one of the two on the wider half of the platform. Set the fence on it, and adjust its position vis-à-vis the board's edge so you'll be routing away no more than 1/16 inch of stock. Clamp the fence and the work to the

The router is an excellent tool for preparing boards for joining edge-to-edge. Using this simple rig, you can produce an almost seamless joint. Set the first board on the platform and clamp the fence on top of it. Guide your router along the fence, trimming the board's edge.

Edge Joints **261**

platform. (If the work is narrow, you may need to shim the fence; just be sure both the work and the fence are clamped so neither will move.)

Stand with the fence in front of you. Rout from right to left, pulling the router against the fence as you go. Check the edge. If it is less than smooth, square, and clean, shift the fence a tad and make a second pass.

When the first board is done, leave it right where it is. You don't move it or the fence. You simply position the second board along the the opposite side of the platform, parallel with the first piece. You need a gap between the two boards that's 1/32 to 1/16 inch less than the diameter of the bit you are using. Got the gap set? Clamp down the second board.

Now the router will rest on both boards, but the bit shouldn't fit between them (if it does, check that gap again!).

To rout the second board, stand in the same place as before. But this time, you have to feed the router left to right. Pull it against the fence as you move it. Make the cut in a single, continuous pass. If you interrupt the cut for any reason, it's likely to be botched. You can rescue the work, of course, simply by finishing the cut, then shifting the second board slightly and making another attempt.

When the second board is machined, unclamp it—NOT the first piece or the fence—and pull it against the first piece. The two should mate perfectly. You may have to juke the second piece back and forth fractionally to get the two in sync, for there's only one correct alignment. A bump on the first piece should fit into a corresponding hollow in the second piece. That's because any imperfections in the fence are telegraphed into the two

Set the second board opposite the first, with a gap between them that's just 1/32 to 1/16 inch less than the diameter of the bit. Guide the router along the fence—feeding in the reverse direction—to trim the second board. The two boards should mate perfectly.

workpieces differently—in effect, in positive form to one, in negative form to the other. When the two are in sync, they'll virtually merge together.

To help you line them up for gluing, slash a pencil line or two across the seam.

Of course, if the two pieces don't mate perfectly, it may be that you've failed to rout deeply enough. I'd try

another pass on the second board, and if that didn't cure the mismate, I'd go back to the beginning and repeat the process.

To mate two boards in a curved joint, you must first roughly cut the line on the workpieces as well as the fence. The prime caveat is that the technique won't work with tight curves,

The amount of wood that's removed in a pass is very modest, as you can see. To limit the cut, the boards have to be set very carefully. You'll easily spend more time doing that than actually routing.

because the bit is actually creating a different curve on each piece. The contour of one curve is offset from the contour of the other by the bit's diameter. When you rout along a gentle curve, however, the two pieces should be sufficiently close to fit together nicely, forming a clean joint. Using a small-diameter bit minimizes the offset.

For a good glue-up, you probably should deviate more than about 5 degrees off a straight line. Use your platform as a guide. Its channel is only 2 inches wide, so your curve can't range much more than 3/4 inch off a baseline. (See "Template-Guided Work," page 155, for a technique that allows you to join two boards perfectly along almost any curve.)

Lay out your curve, transferring it to the first workpiece and the fence. After cutting these two pieces with a saber saw or on the band saw, use one to trace the curve onto the second workpiece. Remember that this second piece must be the reverse of the first, not a duplicate.

Set up the first workpiece and the fence on the platform, much as if it were a straight joint. Rout the piece. Then position and rout the second workpiece.

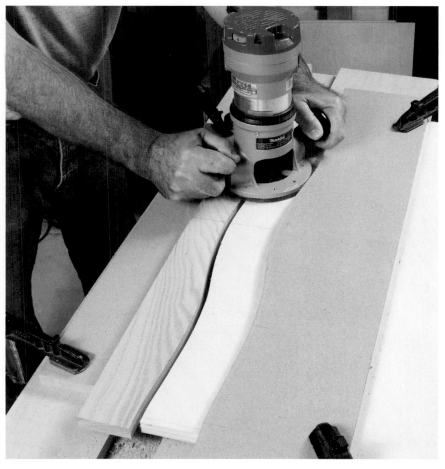

To create a mildly curved edge-to-edge joint, you use a curved fence (of course). Lay out and saw the contour on each piece, and use the router to smooth and match the mating edges. You have to position the fence with its undulations in sync with the workpiece's. To make this alignment easier to achieve, make alignment marks on both the fence and the workpiece when you lay out the curve on them.

Splined Edge Joinery

One of the best edge-joint reinforcement techniques is perfectly suited to the router. It's the spline. You cut slots (or call them grooves, if you prefer) in the adjoining edges, extending them nearly the length of the boards. Fit a strip of plywood or hardboard into the joint as you glue it up.

The spline strengthens the joint by expanding the glue area and by providing a mechanical lock. It also makes the boards a little easier to align and clamp during glue-up. If done properly, the spline will bring even slightly bowed boards into flush alignment.

The table saw might seem to be the fastest cutter of the necessary slots, and it probably is. But spline slots are usually stopped for the sake of appearance—who wants to see the spline at the edge of a tabletop, for example. A sawed slot that's stopped will have a 4- or 5-inch section at each end that won't accommodate the spline, because the slot isn't full-depth.

So do the job with a router.

Slotting for Splines

To do the job with a handheld router, use a slot cutter. You can rest the router on the face of the workpiece. Use an offset baseplate to help avoid bobbles and tips. The job can be done in a single pass.

Moreover, those slightly bowed boards can be forced flat and held that way with a few clamps. The router will have a flat surface to slide across, and the cutter will make that kerf a consistent distance from the surface.

Bit Drawer

A slot cutter is usually an assembly, consisting of an arbor, a cutter, and a pilot bearing. The arbor includes a nut that secures both cutter and bearing on the threaded end of the arbor. Often, the arbor will include a slinger or two, and several spacers.

The cutters themselves are available in two-, three-, and four-wing designs. With only two carbide cutting edges, the two-wing model is least costly, but the plate holding the carbide is smaller and thus less stiff. In general terms, the more tips a cutter has, the slower it cuts, but the better the finish of the cut is.

The size specified for a cutter is the width of the kerf it makes. The standard cutting depth, regardless of the cutter size, is 1/2 inch. In the manner typical of piloted bits, you can change pilot bearings to alter the cutting depth.

Using the spacers supplied by some vendors allows you to alter the position of the cutter on the arbor. This enables you to extend the range of your router's bit-adjustment mechanism. Remember that changing the router's bit-height setting adjusts not the cut's depth, but the cut's position.

These assemblies also allow you to put the pilot bearing either above or below the cutter, according to the job. You can even use two bearings on some long arbors, one above and one below.

Because you are dealing with an assembly, you can save by buying a single arbor, a single set of bearings, and a *selection* of cutters. Buying a single assembly as separate components never saves you money, though.

The well-equipped router woodworker has an assortment of slot cutters in various cutting widths. You can buy individual assemblies on 1/4-inch and 1/2-inch shanks. Or collect different-thickness cutters, an arbor or two, and different-sized bearings so you can make up the cutter needed for any particular job.

Jump into full-range capability with a slot-cutter set, which is conceptually like a table saw dado stack set. The typical set includes an arbor with an extra-long spindle that will accommodate four cutters along with the bearing and nut. You can use the cutters individually or in combination to rout slots between 1/8 inch and 23/32 inch.

To give an example, a 1/16-inch three-wing assembly costs $26.14 from one supplier. The cutter, arbor, and standard-diameter bearing purchased separately cost $30.72. For one cutter, the assembly is cheaper, clearly. But if you buy five different-sized cutters (1/16, 1/8, 5/32, 3/16, and 1/4 inch) as assemblies, the cost totals $131.60. Buying an arbor, a bearing, and just the cutters for those sizes brings the total to $104.18. If the convenience of having a separate arbor and bearing for each cutter is worth more than $25 to you, you know what to do.

The slot cutter is an unusual bit, in that it cuts at right angles to the bit axis. It's great for cutting slots for splines, since the router can rest squarely on the broad part of the workpiece, yet be cutting into the narrow edge (top). A handheld router can keep a slot positioned even in mildly bowed stock, since it has a relatively small contact patch that can follow the board's contour. On the other hand, the work must be absolutely flat to be slotted on the router table (middle).

Rather than get too worked up with trying to center the slot, just mark a reference face of each board. Always keep that face up—through all machining and assembly stages. The slots will all be the same distance from that face, so when the splines are inserted and the boards joined, their reference faces will be flush.

The slot cutter can also be used on the router table. The advantage of the slot cutter over a regular straight bit is that you can lay the workpiece flat on the tabletop. Save yourself the time it takes to position and clamp hold-ups

and hold-ins, not to mention hold-downs. Fit the cutter in the router, adjust the height, set the starting pin, and rout. Be consistent about whether you have the reference face up or down when you cut, and you'll get a good fit.

One or two of the boards slightly warped? Go back to the second paragraph of this section and do what it says. Bowed boards are the province of the handheld router.

A final note on the slot cutter: It's a dirt generator. If you have a dust-collector accessory, by all means use it.

Grooving for Splines

There are other approaches to use if you have a straight bit but not a slot cutter. The best of them involve the router table or the horizontal router table. In a pinch, you can do the job with a handheld router.

If your working stock is good and flat, cutting the grooves for the splines is the same as cutting any stopped groove on the router table. Mark your starting and stopping

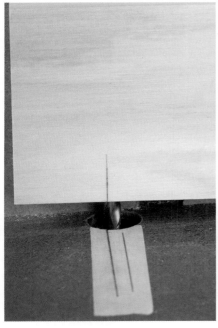

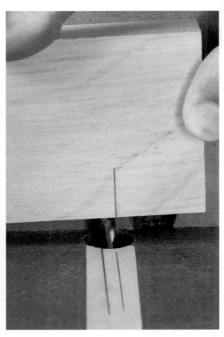

Marks on the the tabletop—on masking tape here so they'll be visible—help you begin and end a stopped groove in the right spots. With the cutting edges parallel to the fence, mark tangents on the tape, as shown. To start the cut (left), align the mark on the work-piece with the tape marking that will place the bit *inside* the groove. Then feed the work until the end mark on it aligns with the other tape mark. Tip the work up off the bit (right).

block to support the stock. As shown in the drawing, you make the pivot by gluing and screwing a support into a groove plowed down the center of a baseboard. The support projects beyond the base by a couple of inches at one end. Line up this end of the support just shy of the bit. The distance between the bit and the pivot, of course, is the distance the groove will be from the working stock's face. Clamp the pivot to the tabletop. Then set a board at right angles to the pivot, bracing it so that pressure in the proper feed direction won't force the pivot to swing out of position. Clamp the brace to the tabletop.

points on the table and the work-piece. Guide the cut with the fence.

The singular disadvantage in this approach is that you have to make two passes to get to a reasonable depth, or you have to settle for a very narrow spline. To save time, make a first pass in all the boards before resetting the bit height and doing the second cut.

If your working stock includes a board or two with some bow to them, you may need to replace the fence. It may be too difficult to press the bowed boards flat against the fence (or the horizontal table's top). The groove for the spline may end up an inconsistent distance from the reference face, a woodworking disaster.

Instead of the fence, use a pivot

A pivot block, much like support stock you would use during resawing on the band saw, also supports bowed stock for splining on the router table. And if you need to groove a workpiece that's curved by design, this is the way to do it. The brace keeps the pivot block from twisting out of position. The featherboard holds the work-piece against the pivot block's nose.

Pivot Block
Use it when edge-slotting bowed stock

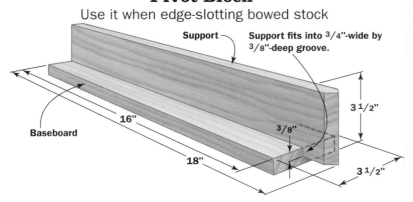

Support

Support fits into 3/4"-wide by 3/8"-deep groove.

Baseboard

16"

18"

3/8"

3 1/2"

3 1/2"

Problem Solver

Don't pull your hair over something as pointless as whether the slot cutter addresses the exact center of the workpiece. Just mark a reference face on each workpiece. Lay out the pieces as they'll be assembled. Mark the face that's up. Now rest the router on the marked face when you cut the biscuit slots. The slots will line up with one another during assembly. Perfect.

Grooving the edge of a board can be a handheld router operation if you can equip your router with two edge guides. Attach a 3- to 4-inch-wide facing to one guide. Trap the work between the guides, as shown. The facing broadens the bearing surface and keeps the router perpendicular to the workpiece's edge.

The use of this pivot is self-evident. Keep the board tight against the end of the pivot. At any time during the operation, it's irrelevant where the *ends* of the workpiece are, so long as its reference face is tight against the pivot. But you must keep the work perpendicular to the line between the bit and the pivot. Don't swivel the work, or the groove will wander.

If for any reason the job must be done using a handheld router and straight bit, you've still got an option or two.

Balancing the router on the workpiece's edge is pretty dicey, but you can trap the workpiece between two edge guides. That'll keep the router pretty much centered and upright.

However you produce the slots for the splines, completing the joint is a matter of cutting strips of spline stock, and gluing it into a slot in one board. Then bring the mating board into alignment, fit it over the spline, and clamp the joint closed.

Try This!

If you need to cut a shallow slot, make a guide from a scrap of 3/4-inch stock, and stick it to the baseplate with carpet tape. On the band saw or with a saber saw, make a cutout for the slot cutter, as shown. When you stick the block to the baseplate, set it so the cutter can cut only the depth you want.

Biscuit Joinery with a Router

Want to try biscuit joinery? For edge-to-edge biscuit joints, you can use your router and a 5/32-inch slot cutter. You won't get a perfect fit, but close enough.

Despite its seeming simplicity, biscuit joinery is pretty sophisticated, certainly more so than common spline or tongue-and-groove joinery. The biscuits are engineered. Compressed during manufacture, they swell when exposed to moisture. Apply water-based glue to the matching slots, insert the biscuits, and promptly close the joint. The biscuits are designed to expand and lock in the slots, improving the bond between the mating boards. Your standard tongues or splines won't do that.

The biscuit joiner is designed to cut slots in faces as well as edges. A router can't duplicate all its cuts, but it will do the edge slots.

If you are using a biscuit joiner, you mark the center of each biscuit slot. Align the tool on the mark and plunge its cutter. The result is an arched slot that accommodates a

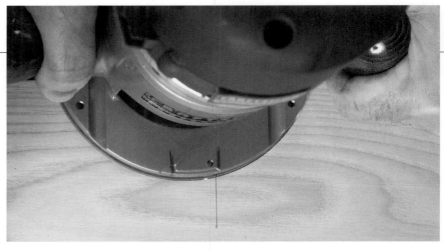

You *can* make a jig to guide slotting for biscuits, but penciling a couple of lines on the router base is all you really need do. Align the right-hand line with the mark on the work. Push the cutter into the work's edge and rout until the left-hand line squares with the work's mark.

biscuit and allows a little lateral shifting of the boards.

Here's the hitch for router-cut slots. The biscuit joiner has a 4 1/2-inch-diameter cutter. Set for a number 20 biscuit, the tool plunges that cutter about 1/2 inch into the work, producing a slot about 2 1/2 inches long.

The typical slot cutter for a router, on the other hand, is 1 5/8 inches in diameter. Plunging it to 1/2 inch yields a slot less than 1 5/8 inches long. You have to move that router laterally to extend the slot to 2 1/2 inches. In the process, you'll produce a slot that will accommodate the biscuit but won't match its shape quite as nicely as a slot cut with a biscuit joiner.

Make a test cut with your 5/32-inch slotter, just a straight plunge cut, without lateral movement. Measure the length of the cut, subtract the measurement from 2 1/2, and the difference is the distance you have to move the router. Two lines penciled on the router base are all you need.

Here's the procedure: Line up the right-hand baseplate line with the workpiece mark, push the router cutter into the work, slide the machine to the right, and pull the router when the second baseplate line reaches the workpiece mark.

The slots can also be cut on the router table using the same slot cutter. To set up, make your test cut, and determine how far you must move the work for a slot of the correct biscuit length. Put your reference lines on the fence (mark them on masking tape if you don't want to mark the fence itself), centering them on the bit.

To cut a slot, align the biscuit centerline on the work with the reference line on the infeed side of the fence. Plunge the work against the fence and onto the cutter. Advance it until the centerline aligns with the outfeed reference line. Pull the workpiece away from the fence, off the cutter.

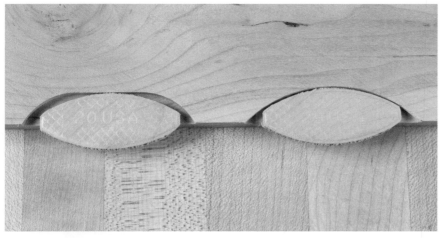

As you can see, the routed biscuit slot (left) doesn't perfectly match the biscuit's shape, while the biscuit joiner's slot does. But it is close enough for all practical purposes.

Tongue-and-Groove Joints

The tongue-and-groove joint is the older brother of the splined edge joint. Instead of a separate spline, you have a solid spline that's an integral part of the board.

Like the splined edge joint, the tongue-and-groove joint is used where surface loading might be considerable—in tabletops and the like. It's also a traditional joint used in breadboard constructions. The most familiar uses these days may be in the carpentry realm—in tongue-and-groove siding, paneling, and flooring. Here the joint provides a mechanical lock between boards that are fastened to another surface or a frame, rather than to each other. It also provides a rudimentary aesthetic—the wood can shrink with-

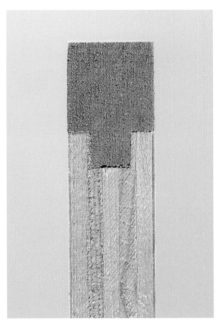

The tongue has to fit the groove properly to get the most out of the tongue-and-groove joint. Too long a tongue will bottom in the groove and prevent the joint from closing. Too thick a tongue can spread—and possibly break—the groove, giving you an uneven surface. But a perfect fit is strong and attractive.

out opening the joint enough to expose whatever is behind it.

You probably think of the tongue-and-groove as a through joint, but if cut with a router, it can easily be stopped so the interlock doesn't show on exposed edges. In addition to stopping the grooving cut, you have to trim back the tongue so the joint will close.

Typically, on 3/4-inch stock, you have a 1/4-inch-wide by 1/4-inch-deep groove, centered across the edge. The tongue thickness matches, but its width is usually 3/16 inch. The 1/16-inch difference is there to accommodate wood movement and glue. Thicker stock calls for a thicker, longer tongue. If the joint will be exposed, or if it isn't to be a glued joint (as in a breadboard-end application), the disparity between tongue width and groove depth can be narrowed.

The joint should be a firm press-fit: If you have to knock the pieces together, then struggle to pull them apart, the joint's too tight. But you don't want it to rattle, either.

You can do the job several ways, of course, depending upon your equipment, your bits, and your work preferences. Working on a router table is a lot more efficient than using a portable router, especially when the stock is narrow and the stack of it is high. Regardless of your approach, you must start with stock of uniform thickness, and you need a couple of scraps to test the setups.

On the Router Table

You can use a straight bit or a slot cutter to cut both the groove and the rabbets that form the tongue. You can also use a rabbet bit or a mortising bit for the latter operation.

Cutting the tongue-and-groove, the way I usually do it, requires only a 1/4-inch slot cutter. I set up and plow the grooves first. On the butt end of a scrap, lay out the proportions of the joint. Only mark the groove. With the scrap on the far side of the bit, set the height of the cutter above the table to match the layout.

Don't work too hard to get the cutter centered on the stock. What you'll do is center it by making two cuts. Make one cut, then flip the work and make a second. This centers the groove. It may be a tad wider than 1/4 inch, but that's usually a benefit. A tongue wider than 1/4 inch means your 1/4-inch slotter will have the capacity to cut the joint on 3/4-inch-thick stock, perhaps even 13/16-inch-thick stock.

Typically, slot cutters make a 1/2-inch cut—too deep for tongue-and-groove—so set the fence to limit the cut depth.

After the grooves are cut, lower the slotter, aligning it against a shoulder of a grooved piece. Always make the cuts on the tabletop side of the stock; otherwise you could trap the work between the bit and the tabletop. Cut one rabbet, flip the workpiece, and cut the second. Assuming your stock is 3/4 inch thick and your groove is a skosh wider than 1/4 inch, a 1/4-inch slotter will do the trick.

Particularly if your stock is thicker than 3/4 inch, you might use a rabbet bit or a mortising bit or even a straight bit to form the tongue. After switching bits, the setup routine is the same as with a slotter. Use a piece of the grooved stock to set the height. Adjust the fence as necessary, so the tongue won't be quite as long as the groove is deep. Cut a test piece and check the fit. Adjust the bit height or

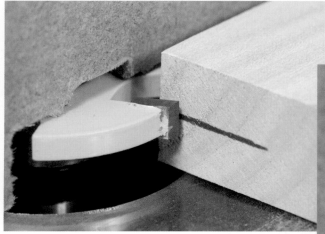

A penciled centerline—no, it doesn't have to be *spot-on*—is the starting point for plowing the groove. By eye, align the cutter against that centerline. Make a cutting pass referencing each face of the board, and the groove will be perfectly centered (photo at right).

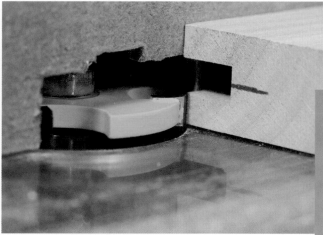

Change the setup to form the tongues by lowering the cutter to align with the groove's shoulder. The fence remains in position. Two passes will complete the tongue (photo at right).

fence if necessary. Then rout the tongues on all the stock.

If you use a straight bit, the depth of the groove is governed by the bit-height adjustment, and the placement of the groove on the stock edge is governed by the fence position. As with a slotter, you center the bit by eye on the stock for the grooving cut, then use the two-pass approach to cut and center that groove. To reposition the fence for the tongue-forming rabbet cuts, use a sample of the actual groove.

With a Handheld Router

Not surprisingly, the cutters and the setup routines aren't tremendously different if you use the router hand-held. If you have more than one router, you can set one up to cut the grooves with a slot cutter, another to form the tongues with a rabbet bit or with a straight bit and edge guide. This way allows you to maintain both setups until the job is completely done. That's often more comfortable psychologically, and that should count for something.

You won't want to cut the grooves with a straight bit, since that requires balancing the tool on the stock's edge.

As with the router table, a slot cutter is probably the best bit to use in a portable router. You don't have to

Bit Drawer

If you have a lot of tongues and grooves to cut, a special tongue-and-groove assembly may be a worthwhile investment.

The typical assembly consists of an arbor with an integral shank, two identical, removable cutters, and a couple of bearings. The bit is intended for use in a table-mounted router, and its configuration guarantees that you'll be able to keep the stock flat on the tabletop as you rout it. The bit will work on stock between 1/2 and 3/4 inch thick.

When setting up the assembly for cutting the tongues, you sandwich one bearing between the two cutters. Line up a piece of the stock next to the cutter, and adjust the cutter height to center the tongue on the stock's edge. Make a few test cuts and monkey with the setting a bit until you are happy with it. Then set up a couple of featherboards or other holddowns, and rout the tongues.

To set up for cutting slots, you mount one of the cutters between the two bearings. Don't remove the shank from the router; it's easier to do this when it's still held by the collet. Use a piece of the stock with the tongue to set the cutter height. Simply line the cutter up even with the tongue. If the tongue is slightly offset, then the groove will be equally offset. Make a test cut, and fit it on the tongue to confirm that your eye is good. Happy with the setup? Make sure the featherboards are still in the right places, then rout the grooves.

The advantage of the assembly is the perfectly matched cuts that are possible. Since you are using the same cutters to produce both the tongues and the grooves, they're guaranteed to match. And because you cut both shoulders of the tongue in one pass, you can make the tongue offset to match an offset groove (and vice versa). The disadvantage, of course, is that you have to dismantle the bit when switching from one cut to the other.

A dedicated tongue-and-groove cutter set is a worthwhile investment only if you use it a *lot*. One bit (right) cuts the groove. The other forms a matching tongue in a single pass.

Tongue-and-Groove
Joints

Clamp a board to the workbench edge when routing tongues and grooves with a portable router. Keep the clamps clear of the router's path. An offset baseplate on the router can ease the job of keeping it upright throughout the cut.

swap bits in the middle of the job. You can center the groove by making two passes. When you alter the cutter extension to form the tongues, lower it to the router, rather than jacking it away from the router so it cuts the underside of the workpiece.

As you rout, you keep the tool on the face of the work (rather than the edge) for both cuts. Swap the pilot bearing to reduce the cut from the standard 1/2 inch. The bearing will control the cut, but you must be especially careful at the beginning and end of each cut to avoid "rolling around the corner" inadvertently. Keep the router upright; more than half of the base will be unsupported.

The biggest difference between router table and handheld is in the handling. Each workpiece has to be clamped and unclamped for each *pass*. Typically, that's four times for each board. You're picking up the router and putting it down, switching it on and switching it off. While it is faster and surer on the table, don't be daunted if you don't have one. The portable router will do the work.

Mortise-and-Tenon Joints

The mortise-and-tenon is woodworking's essential frame joint. Examples of the joint that date back 5,000 years exist in museums. Even today, it's used in everything from furniture frames to post-and-beam building frames. Yet it is a joint that many woodworkers avoid, because it seems too involved and time-consuming to make and fit properly.

One of the most common applications of the mortise-and-tenon joint is in the leg-and-rail construction used in tables and chairs. It's used in all sorts of frame-and-panel construction, particularly frames for doors.

Mortise-and-tenon joints take many different forms. The basic elements are the mortise, which is a hole—round, square, or rectangular—and the tenon, which is a tongue cut on the end of the joining member to fit the mortise. Once assembled with glue or pegs, the mortise-and-tenon joint resists all four types of stress—tension, compression, shear, and racking. And it does it better than any other type of joint. The joint's strength stems from the way it

The router is an excellent tool for producing both mortises and tenons. With the assistance of different shop-made jigs and fixtures, you can rout mortise-and-tenon joints for doors, face frames, posts and rails, and other practical assemblies.

interlocks: The shoulders on either side of the tenon prevent twisting.

The router is an excellent tool for mortising, so long as the mortise isn't too narrow and deep. Its main advantages for mortising include the smoothness of its finished cuts and the accuracy of placement and sizing that's possible. The handwork can be minimized—you don't need to clean out the mortises with a chisel, as you do with those roughly formed with a drill bit. And you don't need a specialized, single-purpose tool like a hollow-chisel mortiser. A plunge router, a spiral bit, and an edge guide (or two) will handle most of the mortising you'll ever want to do. And

Mortise-and-Tenon Particulars

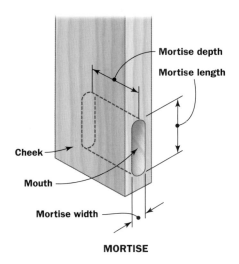

MORTISE

- Mortise depth
- Mortise length
- Cheek
- Mouth
- Mortise width

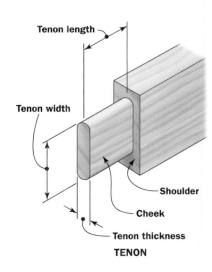

TENON

- Tenon length
- Tenon width
- Shoulder
- Cheek
- Tenon thickness

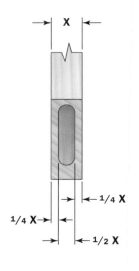

TYPICAL JOINT DIMENSIONS

- About 1/2 of stile width (deeper in narrow stiles)
- 1/8" cosmetic shoulder
- 1/4 to 1/3 total width of tenon
- 1/16" clearance

- X
- 1/4 X
- 1/4 X
- 1/2 X

they have many other woodworking applications.

The only disadvantage that comes to mind is the limited reach of the router bit. A narrow, deep mortise—1/4 inch wide by 13/4 inches or more deep, for example, or 3/8 inch wide by 21/2 inches deep—is problematic for a router, relatively easy for a hollow-chisel mortiser. With savvy project design, you can get around this limitation.

Once you try doing some mortise-and-tenon joinery using the router, you'll realize how easy it is. And your joinery universe will explode!

Mortising Setup

Here are the typical challenges in cutting a projectful of mortises with a handheld router:

- Positioning the router consistently from mortise to mortise
- Providing adequate bearing surface, so no cut is compromised by a router tip or wobble
- Minimizing workpiece handling

How well you meet these challenges will dictate how well your mortises will turn out.

This cutaway shows the difference in finish between a routed mortise (right) and a chiseled one (left). The differences are immaterial cosmetically, since the insides of the mortises are hidden. But a smooth surface yields a superior glue joint.

274

Designing the Joint

The main goal in designing a mortise-and-tenon is to maximize the glue area, especially the long-grain-to-long-grain glue surface. Choose the joint and its proportions according to the job it must do.

Here are rules of thumb for establishing the width and length of your tenons. The size of the mortise follows, obviously, from the size of the tenon. (It's much easier to match the tenon to the mortise, so when making the joint, you nearly always make the mortise first.)

The bigger the tenon, the stronger it will be, but at the possible expense of the piece with the mortise in it. You don't want the mortise walls to be too thin.

You have to keep in mind what will be required of the pieces involved. For example, aprons mortised into table legs will be under tension-compression stress, so the tenons need as much height and length as you can provide. While the tenons won't get much shear or torque stress, the legs will be heavily leveraged, so you don't want to weaken them. The upshot: Make the tenons fairly thin.

In frame-and-panel work, where the pieces are likely to be the same thickness and will be experiencing similar stresses, your tenon should be somewhere between one-third and one-half the total stock thickness. In door construction, where a panel is set in a groove inside the frame, it's common to use the haunched tenon, and to make the tenon thickness match the width of the groove. The haunch on the tenon fits in the groove, and enhances the joint's resistance to twisting—an important consideration in door construction.

When the tenon piece is narrow, there's sometimes a temptation to run the tenon across the grain. An example is the apron above or below a drawer in an occasional table. The tenon has long grain, but the mortise in the table leg will be all end grain; the result is a weak gluing situation. It's better to make two short, narrow tenons.

Occasionally, you'll need to make an angled mortise-and-tenon joint. A good example is a chair, where the seat tapers from front to back; the side rails meet the legs at an angle. The mortise can be cut square to the leg's surface and the tenon on an angle. But sometimes the resulting tenon is weakened because it doesn't have enough long grain extending from its end all the way into the rail. Better choices would be to cut the mortise on an angle and the tenon straight, or to use loose tenons. Loose tenons are a particularly good choice for router-cut joinery because the mortises can both be easily referenced perpendicular to the mating surfaces.

Design the Joint
Vary the joint configuration to suit the use

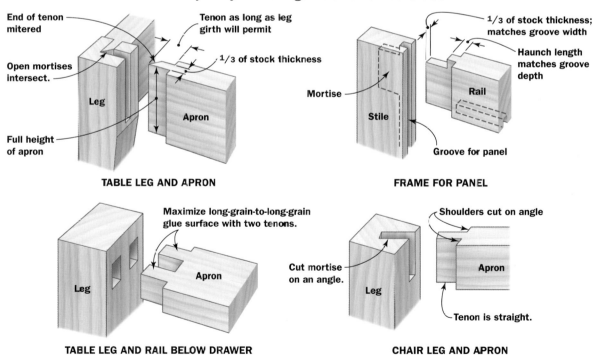

TABLE LEG AND APRON

- End of tenon mitered
- Open mortises intersect.
- Tenon as long as leg girth will permit
- 1/3 of stock thickness
- Leg
- Apron
- Full height of apron

FRAME FOR PANEL

- 1/3 of stock thickness; matches groove width
- Haunch length matches groove depth
- Mortise
- Rail
- Stile
- Groove for panel

TABLE LEG AND RAIL BELOW DRAWER

- Maximize long-grain-to-long-grain glue surface with two tenons.
- Leg
- Apron

CHAIR LEG AND APRON

- Shoulders cut on angle
- Cut mortise on an angle.
- Apron
- Leg
- Tenon is straight.

Pairing edge guides enables you to rout twin mortises. Lay out the mortise centerlines. Align the bit on one and set both edge guides. Rout the first mortise. Lift the router off the work and turn it around. The bit will be aligned with the second centerline, ready to cut the second mortise.

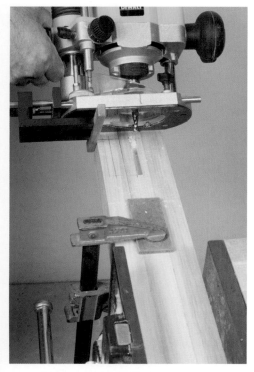

When mortising multiples, you can gang the pieces in a bench vise to provide support for the router. Your first setup should have the workpiece with the fully laid-out mortise in the middle. Set the router's edge guide to reference one of the outside pieces.

Positioning the router. The easiest way to position the router is to use an edge guide. This common router accessory slides along an edge of the work and positions the bit in relation to that edge. (You don't have to reference the work edge, of course. You could fit the work into some sort of holder and reference an edge of it.)

To set up the edge guide and cut a mortise, you first have to lay one out. Use a square and a pencil. Then transfer the extremities of the mortise to each of the other workpieces. The edge-guide setting will position the mortise laterally. But the other markings allow you to begin and end each mortise at the correct places.

Chuck the bit in the router. Set the depth-of-cut. Set the router on the marked-up workpiece and position the bit over the mortise layout. Plunge the bit into the stock so you can be sure it is aligned within the layout lines. Then slide the edge guide against the side of the work,

and cinch down its setscrews. Now you are ready to rout.

You can position the router even more positively using *two* edge guides. With one against each side of the work, the router can't drift. Not every commercial edge guide system will allow you to do this. The router may accommodate one, but not two.

Providing an adequate bearing surface. This is one of the perpetual bugbears of router woodworking. You *need* adequate support for the machine. How do you get it?

One good way is to clamp several workpieces together. If you are mortising table legs, for example, you can clamp three of them side-by-side in a bench vise. (Any more than three would be cumbersome to flush up and, later, to shift around.) Collectively, they'll provide a flat surface for the router base. If you mortise the middle leg, you'll have equal support for the router's entire base. After mortising this first leg, simply reposition the legs, with a new one in the middle position.

The approach minimizes setup time and provides excellent support for the operation. It doesn't work as well, however, when you're mortising 3/4-inch stock, since three such members don't add up to enough support. Such pieces you might better sandwich between straight, flat lengths of beefier stock.

Minimizing the workpiece handling. This is most important when you have a tall stack of parts to mortise—stiles for six or eight cabinet doors, or legs for a set of chairs. I'm willing to shuffle three-leg bundles in and out of a bench vise when four legs is the total. If the extent of the job is beyond that, I want a jig into which I can quickly clamp the workpieces.

Problem Solver

Trying to adjust your router setup so the mortise is exactly positioned on the workpiece is difficult and often frustrating. A better focus for your attention is marking each workpiece so that the mortises will be *consistently* positioned.

Example: You rout mortises in the stiles of a frame-and-panel cabinet door. The mortises aren't quite centered on the stile edges. The tenons are centered, so when assembled, the faces of the rails and stiles aren't flush. A typical solution is to sand the assembled frame to bring the faces flush.

But because you referenced the back face for one mortise, and the front face for the other, the faces of the assembly aren't parallel. One end of the rail is proud of the stile's back face, and the other end is proud of the front face. (See the drawing.) Moreover, the panel will have to be twisted slightly to fit into the groove for it. The assembly is more likely to warp, and though sanding will improve its appearance, it just won't be totally satisfactory.

If the mortises are consistently closer to one face or the other, the misalignment is a whole lot easier to cure with a little planing or sanding. The planes of the rails and stiles will be parallel, and the panel will be flat.

So mark a reference face on each of the pieces to be mortised. Lay out the pieces as they'll be assembled. Mark the face that's up. When you rout the mortises, always have the reference face oriented the same way. The mortises may not be perfectly positioned, but all of them will be the same.

Doing this will require two slightly different setups for a full frame-and-panel job. For example, if you rout the mortises on the horizontal router table, you have to shift the location of the workpiece-positioning stop. Rout one mortise on each stile, then move the stop and do the other mortise.

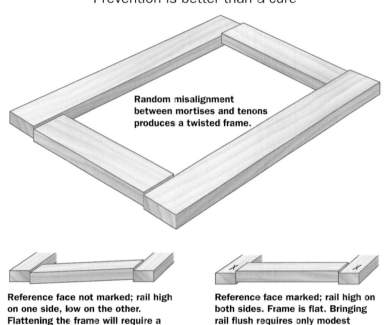

Twisted Frames
Prevention is better than a cure

Random misalignment between mortises and tenons produces a twisted frame.

Reference face not marked; rail high on one side, low on the other. Flattening the frame will require a lot of stock removal.

Reference face marked; rail high on both sides. Frame is flat. Bringing rail flush requires only modest sanding.

Mortising Fixtures

A fixture is a device for holding a workpiece so you can work on it with a tool. To do production-type mortising, where a cut of a given length and depth is made in each part in a stack, you want to minimize layout and handling of individual pieces. You want to avoid beginning and ending cuts by eye.

The right fixture can simplify the job, but there are dozens of suitable fixtures. Following are three that work. Setup and operation is essentially the same for each. You can build and use any of them, or you can treat any one as a jumping-off point for designing your own.

Let me briefly describe each one, then present a checklist for setting up.

Q & D Mortising Fixture

The first fixture is what I call the Q & D fixture. Yes, that's as in quick-and-dirty. You make it with a few small pieces (scraps, really) and assemble it with drywall screws. The dimensions are flexible—alter them to suit the scraps you have. It will likely take you longer to ferret out the right scraps than to assemble them.

Quick-and-Dirty Edge-Mortising Fixture

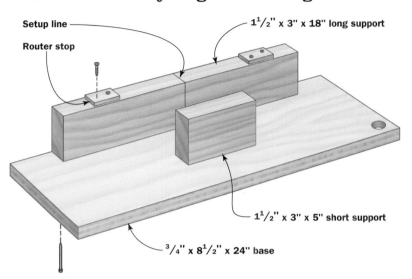

Setup line

Router stop

$1^1/2$" x 3" x 18" long support

$1^1/2$" x 3" x 5" short support

$^3/4$" x $8^1/2$" x 24" base

The Q & D fixture isn't pretty, but it does the job very well. Clamp the workpiece to the long support. The router straddles the two supports so it can't tip. Stops screwed to the long support limit the router's travel, thus controlling the length of the cut. The edge guide references the outside face of the support to ensure that the mortise is straight and properly located on the edge of the workpiece.

Try This!

A blind mortise located at the end of a stile has one distinct weakness: that 1/4 inch to 1/2 inch of end-grain stock between the end of the mortise and the stile's butt end. It's fragile, so easy to pop out if you lever the tenon during assembly.

Every woodworker has trouble with this. The traditional solution is to add extra length to the stile. The extra length bolsters that weak spot during mortising and assembly. After the glue is dry and the clamps are off the assembly, you simply trim the extensions flush with the rails. An extra 3/4 inch at each end of the stile is all that's needed.

Cut your stiles over-long so you'll have an extra inch of waste at each edge. The mortises will be easier to cut, and the extra bulk prevents the tenon from levering out the end grain during assembly. When the clamps come off, you can saw the assembly to its final size, removing these "horns."

The idea is that the workpiece is laid in the gap between the long and short supports. Line it up with the setup line, then clamp it to the long support. Set the router onto the supports and use the router's edge guide, referencing the outside face of the long support, to position the mortise. The stops screwed to the long support limit the router's travel, thus governing the mortise length. Having two supports prevents the router from tipping inadvertently, and it makes the router easier to plunge. The trade-off is that this fixture—as shown here, anyway—is usable only for edge-mortising (not for end-mortising).

The Excellent Mortising Platform

The mortising platform works like the Q & D fixture, but it has a built-in workpiece clamp. Switching workpieces is more convenient.

Pivotal to its ease of use is a pair of push-pull toggle clamps (DeStaCo model TC-605). Once the movable fence is adjusted for the thickness of stock being mortised, securing a workpiece is a matter of slipping it between the fences and pushing the two toggle clamps simultaneously to clamp it. When the mortise has been routed, pull the two toggles

This fixture holds a workpiece between two wide fences that provide good support for the router as well as a reference surface for the edge guide. Stops can be added to eliminate the need to lay out the workpieces. The fixture can be adjusted to accommodate work varying in thickness and height, too. Altogether, it's most excellent!

Cutting List

Piece	Number	Thickness	Width	Length	Material
Base	1	1/2"	15"	24"	Birch plywood
Clamp base	1	3/4"	6"	24"	Birch plywood
Fixed fence top	1	1/2"	3 1/2"	24"	Birch plywood
Fixed fence sides	2	1/2"	2 3/4"	24"	Birch plywood
Fixed fence blocks	7	1/2"	2 3/4"	3"	Birch plywood
Movable fence top	1	1/2"	2 1/2"	24"	Birch plywood
Movable fence sides	2	1/2"	2 3/4"	24"	Birch plywood
Movable fence blocks	7	1/2"	2 3/4"	2"	Birch plywood

Hardware

2 pcs. DeStaCo TC-605 push-pull toggle clamps
2 pcs. 5/16"-18 × 2 1/2" carriage bolts
2 pcs. 5/16" wing nuts
#6 × 1 1/4" drywall screws

Excellent Mortising Platform
Adjust it to suit the mortising job

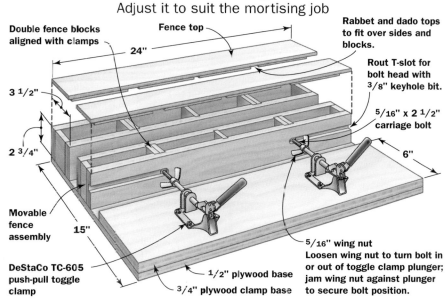

Double fence blocks aligned with clamps

Fence top

Rabbet and dado tops to fit over sides and blocks.

24"

Rout T-slot for bolt head with 3/8" keyhole bit.

3 1/2"

5/16" x 2 1/2" carriage bolt

2 3/4"

6"

Movable fence assembly

15"

DeStaCo TC-605 push-pull toggle clamp

1/2" plywood base

3/4" plywood clamp base

5/16" wing nut
Loosen wing nut to turn bolt in or out of toggle clamp plunger; jam wing nut against plunger to secure bolt position.

simultaneously to release the workpiece. Remove it and drop another in its place. The movable fence is attached to the toggle clamps, so it won't get bumped out of alignment or tumble off the workbench. No loose clamps, either.

The platform can be clamped or dogged to a workbench or the router bench. I orient the platform so the fixed fence is at the workbench edge so that I can have the router's edge guide referencing my side of the jig. It's easy to reach across to the toggle clamps.

To make the mortising platform:

1. Cut the base and the clamp base to size, and glue the two together.

2. Make the fences next. Start by cutting the fence parts to size.

Glue the doubled fence blocks together; you need three such blocks for each fence. Cut the dadoes in the fence sides, as shown in the drawing. Rabbet the sides, top, and end blocks. Assemble the fences.

3. Using a 3/8-inch keyhole bit, rout two slots in the movable fence for the heads of the carriage bolts that attach the fence to the toggle clamps. You may need to widen the slots to accommodate the bolt heads; rout them to fit.

4. Glue the fixed fence to the base. Align it flush with the edge opposite the clamp base. Drive drywall screws through the base into the fence.

5. Mount the toggle clamps on the base. To position them, turn the carriage bolts into the toggle clamp plungers as far as they will go. Roughly position the clamps, then fit the movable fence over the bolt heads. Align the fence, adjust the clamps so they are perpendicular to

Attach temporary shims and a positioning stop to the fixed fence using carpet tape. The shim lifts the work so it is flush with the top of the platform. Set the work in place, and flip the toggles to wedge the second fence against it.

Problem Solver

Mortising is a good job for a plunge router with electronic speed control. You can slow down the bit to compensate for the low feed rates that mortising generally entails. And that will prolong the life of the bit you use.

Mortising can be really hard on bits. Wood is a surprisingly good insulator. The heat generated as the bit cuts a mortise isn't dissipated through the material; it's retained in that confined pocket. The danger here isn't burning of the wood so

much as dulling the cutter. Burn marks are going to be concealed inside the joint, but a dull cutter hampers your ability to even make the joint.

Mortises aren't very long, but they usually are deep. It is hard to both plunge the bit and move it back and forth quickly. Heat builds up.

The alternative is to slow the bit down. Try running the router at about 15,000 rpm. It won't really effect the practical cutting rate, but it'll be easier on your bit.

the fence and equidistant from the edge of the base, and fasten them in place with screws.

To use the mortising platform, you must first set the fence to secure the workpiece you are routing.

The gap between the fences is adjusted by turning the carriage bolts in and out of the toggle clamp plungers. The plunger is tapped 1 inch deep, so to vary the gap more than about 1/2 inch, you need to switch bolts.

To set the fence, install bolts of the proper length for the coarse setting. When they are seated in the plungers, you should be able to push and lock the clamps and have the fence against (or almost against) the workpiece. To tighten the fence so it will in fact secure the workpiece, push and lock the clamps. Then turn the bolts as tight as you can, seating the fence against the workpiece. Pull the clamps, and give the bolts an additional fraction of a turn—about 1/8 turn.

Test the setting by pushing the clamps and locking the fence. If you can move the workpiece, you need to tighten the setting further. If you can't push the clamps completely closed, you need to loosen the setting.

Like the Q & D fixture, the platform has a setup line against which you align the workpiece. Stops on the fixed fence limit the router's travel. The stops can be attached to the top or the outer side with screws or with carpet tape.

Mortising Block

Most demanding to make, but most flexible to use, is the mortising block. The big difference, conceptually, from the other fixtures is that it allows you to do both edge mortises and end mortises. End mortises are essential to loose-tenon constructions. In addition, it enables you to do twin mortises (two mortises side-by-side).

The mortising block has the setup line and the stops (these are adjustable) like the other fixtures. It does not have support under both plunge posts, but I haven't found this to be a serious deficiency.

The major components and features of the mortising block are:

Body: This hardwood block has an extra support strip and a clamping pad glued to the back face. The block's face has keyways and mounting-bolt holes for the work-holders. It's critical that the top surface be perpendicular to the face.

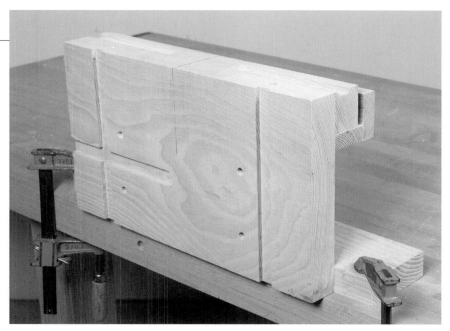

The body of the mortising block is inherently simple. It's a block of wood with the top square to the face. A strip glued to the back expands the top surface, on which the router sets. A second strip provides a means to clamp the block to a workbench. Two different supports, one horizontal, and one vertical, can be bolted to the face of the block to support the pieces being mortised.

The router stop has a slot for the mounting bolt and a key. The key keeps the stop aligned so it can't twist and throw off the setting. Drill and tap one or more holes in the body for the bolt. Set the stop with the bit lined up at the end of the mortise layout. Set the stop against the router's base and tighten its mounting bolt.

Router stops: The travel of the router on the mortising block is limited by the two stops. A key dadoed into the underside rides in a groove in the block top. The mount-ing bolt passes through a slot, which allows easy adjustability.

Edge-guide track: A facing attached to the edge guide catches in the track, and this prevents the router from drifting off course. (To do twin mortises, expand the width of the track and use a spacer next to the facing. Put the spacer on the inside, and the bit is close to the block face. Switch the spacer to the outside, and the bit shifts away from the block.)

Work-holders: Horizontal and vertical versions hold a workpiece for mortising. Mounting bolts passing through slots allow adjustability; keys keep the rest either parallel or perpendicular to the block top as you adjust its position.

To make the mortising block:

1. Mill the stock to the specified thicknesses, and rip and crosscut the main parts. Be especially careful in dressing the stock. The top and face of the body, for example, must be perpendicular if you expect to produce mortises that are properly aligned. The body and the horizontal work-holder must be exactly the same length, since you reference the ends in routing the keyways. If one

Mortising Block

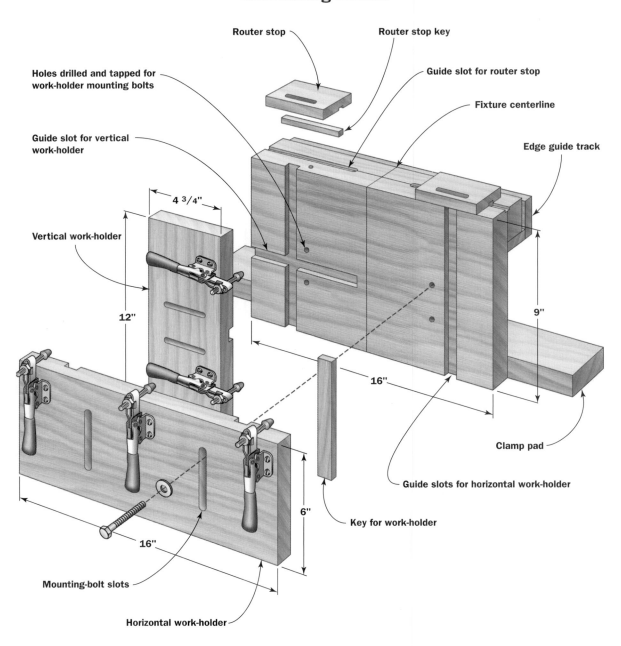

Router stop

Router stop key

Holes drilled and tapped for work-holder mounting bolts

Guide slot for router stop

Fixture centerline

Guide slot for vertical work-holder

Edge guide track

4 3/4"

Vertical work-holder

12"

9"

16"

Clamp pad

Guide slots for horizontal work-holder

6"

Key for work-holder

16"

Mounting-bolt slots

Horizontal work-holder

piece is slightly longer than the other, the keyways won't align.

2. Rout the keyways in the body and in the work-holders. Use a router and edge guide. These cuts should be 3/4 inch wide and 1/4 inch deep. The horizontal work-holder has two through dadoes 2 1/4 inches in from each end, with matching dadoes in the body. The vertical work-holder has a single through dado 5 1/8 inches below the top end, and, of course, a mate is routed into the body. The latter dado is stopped.

3. Use a plunge router and edge guide to cut two 1/2-inch-wide mounting slots in each work-holder. The slots are 4 inches from the ends of the horizontal work-holder, and 5 inches from the ends of the vertical one. Naturally, they completely penetrate the stock. If necessary, you can achieve the necessary cut depth by working from both sides of the stock.

4. Make the work-holder keys. Thickness stock to match the width of the keyways in the work-holders and the body. Rip 1/2-inch-thick strips of it, crosscut them to match the work-holder widths, and attach the keys to the work-holders.

5. Transfer the slot locations to the body and drill mounting-bolt holes. Place the vertical work-holder on the body and use a transfer punch (or just a drill bit) to mark the body at each slot location. Remove the work-holder. Line up a square with one mark, and scribe a horizontal line across the body. Repeat at the second mark. Repeat the process to mark the locations of the slots in the horizontal work-holder. Drill the mounting-bolt holes where the lines cross.

Cutting List

Piece	Number	Thickness	Width	Length	Material
Body	1	1 1/2"	9"	16"	Hardwood
Top support	1	1 1/2"	1 7/8"	16"	Hardwood
Clamp pad	1	1 1/4"	3 3/8"	22"	Hardwood
Guide track bottom	1	3/4"	1 7/8"	16"	Hardwood
Guide track side	1	3/4"	2"	16"	Hardwood
Router stops	2	5/8"	2 3/4'	4"	Hardwood
Router stop keys	2	1/4"	1/2"	4"	Hardwood
Horizontal work-holder	1	1 1/4"	6"	16"	Hardwood
Work-holder keys	2	1/2"	3/4"	6"	Hardwood
Vertical work-holder	1	1 1/4"	4 3/4'	12"	Hardwood
Work-holder key	1	1/2"	3/4"	4 3/4"	Hardwood

Hardware

6 pcs. #6 × 1" flathead wood screws fastening key in workrests
2 pcs. 1/4"–20 × 1" hex-head bolts w/washers mount stops to block
2 pcs. 1/4" I.D. fender washers
2 pcs. 3/3"–16 × 1 1/2" hex-head bolts w/washers mount workrest to block
2 pcs. 3/8" I.D. fender washers
5 pcs. DeStaCo toggle clamps (Reid Tool Co. # TC-225-U)
    3 cn horizontal workrest, 2 on vertical
20 pcs. # 10 × 1" panhead screws mount clamps on workrests (4 per clamp)

The horizontal work-holder supports work for edge-mortising. The keys attached to the work-holder slide in the vertical keyways and maintain the holder's alignment as it's adjusted up or down. Two blocks secure the holder. The toggle clamps hold the work securely, but expedite swapping one piece and the next when there're a lot of mortises to cut.

To secure the bolts, you can bore completely through the body and use T-nuts. Or you can drive threaded inserts into the hole. I cut threads in the wood itself. In any case, match the hole diameter to the size application. The bolts are 3/8-inch diameter.

6. Join the top support and the clamp pad to the body. When the clamps are off, clean off any dried glue, then joint the block to ensure that the top surface is square to the face.

7. Make and mount the guide track. Mill and crosscut the two parts. Glue the side to the bottom. Then glue the track to the underside of the top support.

8. Make and install the router stops. Instead of reducing the stops to final size first, rout the mounting-bolt slots and the keyways in oversized blanks, then trim the stops to final size. Use the same bit to cut the keyways in the block and in the stops. I used a router and edge guide to cut them in the block, but grooved the stops on the router table. I also routed the mounting-bolt slots on the router table. Make keys and attach them to the stops. Drill and tap holes in the block for the mounting bolts.

9. Mount toggle clamps to the workholders.

Setting Up for Mortising

Setup for all three of these mortising accessories is essentially the same. The steps are shown in the drawing *Setting Up Router and Stops*. Use a sample workpiece with a rudimentary mortise layout on it as an aid. The layout consists of the stock centerline (assuming I want a centered mortise), the mortise ends, and the midline between the ends.

Setting Up Router and Stops

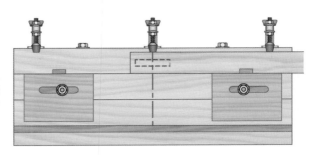

1. Set the workpiece on the workrest, lining up the centerline on it with the centerline on the jig.

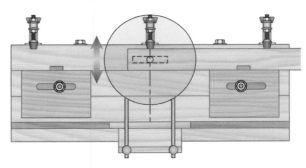

2. Move the router to position the bit exactly between the layout lines for the mortise, then lock down the edge guide.

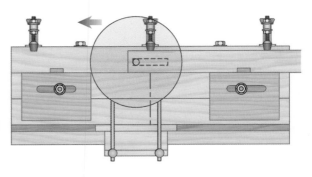

3. Move the router to position the bit just inside the layout line at one end of the mortise, and adjust the sliding stop against the edge guide's rod.

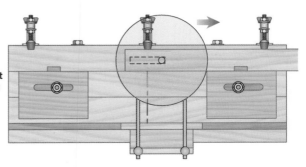

4. Move the router to position the bit just inside the layout line at the other end of the mortise, and adjust the other sliding stop against the edge guide's other rod.

Here are the setup parameters: The mortise width is set by the diameter of the bit used. The mortise depth is controlled by the plunge of the router. The length is governed by router stops on the jig. And the alignment of the mortise on the work's edge is controlled by the edge guide.

Lay out the setup mortise. Chuck the bit you are using in the router, set the plunge depth, and fit the edge guide to the router. Follow the steps shown in the drawing to complete the setup.

When you are done, the equipment will be set for all similar mortises, regardless of where they fall on the workpiece. Just mark the midline of the desired mortise on the piece, and for each cut, align the midline with the setup line.

If you are doing 50 mortises, all in the same place on each workpiece, you don't even have to mark each piece. Instead, set a stop on the fixture with a screw or with carpet tape. Butt the end of the piece against

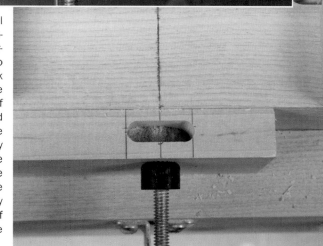

A simplified mortise layout is all you need to set up the mortising fixtures. The marked centerline splits the mortise end to end, and it is the only mark needed for every mortise. The flanking lines mark the ends of the mortise and they are used to set the router stops. Once set, the stops ensure that every mortise is the same length. The location of the cut on the edge (right) is controlled by the edge guide, which you set initially by eye. Measure the shoulders of the test cut and adjust the edge guide to center the cut.

Try This!

A common routine is to plunge the bit, and push or pull the machine to actually rout the waste. Then you return the machine to its original position and plunge a little deeper. The risk in this is that the bit will grab on the return, gouging the mortise wall. To avoid this risk, you should make the cutting pass, then retract the bit clear of the work before drawing the router back and replunging the bit for another pass.

Mortise-Routing Sequence

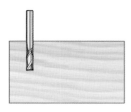

1. Plunge-bore one end of the mortise to the full depth.

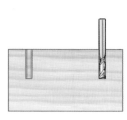

2. Plunge-bore the other end to the full depth.

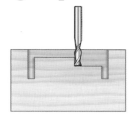

3. Rout the waste from between the two holes, nibbling about 1/4" deeper with each pass.

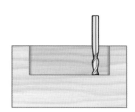

4. Continue this process until the mortise is completed.

Swapping the vertical work-holder for the horizontal one is easy, and you don't have to sacrifice your mortising setup to do it. Remove the horizontal holder. Then use a clamp to hold a workpiece in alignment with the setup line as you mount the vertical holder. Engage the keyways, then slide the holder gently against the workpiece—don't bump it out of alignment! Bolt the holder to the block.

that stop, clamp the piece, and rout the mortise.

The extra capability of the mortising block is that you can also do end mortises. The only setup difference is the work-holder. If you are routing mortises for loose-tenon joinery, you need the usual edge mortises, but you also need matching end mortises.

So set up your equipment and rout the edge mortises. Then remove the horizontal work-holder. Mark the mortise midline on the end of a workpiece, align it with the setup line on the mortising block, and clamp it to the block. Then hang the vertical work-holder on the block, slide it up against the workpiece, and tighten the mounting bolts. Now you are set up for the end mortises.

Bit Drawer

The bit of choice for excavating mortises is the upcut spiral bit. This is the router bit that looks a lot like a twist-drill bit.

There are several reasons why you want to use this bit. First of all, it's a true plunge-cutting bit. It's designed to bore straight down into the work, cutting a clean hole. In addition, it has an augering action that *moves* the chips sliced from the workpiece; the upcut configuration moves them up and out of the mortise. Finally, a spiral bit has both high hook and shear angles, so it doesn't take a lot of horses to power one. Nevertheless, it slices smoothly through wood, and cuts aggressively.

A second choice bit for mortising would be an upshear straight bit. This won't auger the chips from the cut so efficiently as a spiral, but the upshear flutes still slice the wood rather than scraping it. The cut is smooth, still without a major horsepower requirement.

The last choice—the one used more often than not, unfortunately—is the common plunge-cutting straight. It does the job, and if that's what you have, don't be deterred from mortising. It won't clear the chips, and consequently, it'll run hotter.

In selecting a bit for mortising, look for the longest one you can find. The cutting length is less important than the overall length. You'll be trimming about a quarter-inch at a time as you plunge deeper and deeper into the mortise, so the cutting is being done at the

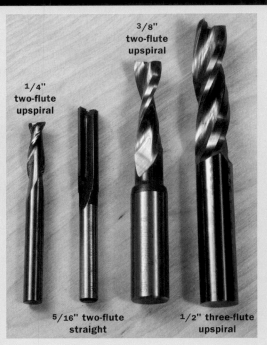

1/4"
two-flute
upspiral

3/8"
two-flute
upspiral

5/16" two-flute
straight

1/2" three-flute
upspiral

tip of the bit. A long cutting edge isn't particularly useful. A long shank, however, is essential to reach into that deep mortise.

Usually, we advise you to use the 1/2-inch-shank version of any bit. This is the exception. For mortising, try to match the shank diameter to the cutting diameter. A 1/4-inch cutter should be on a 1/4-inch shank. A 3/8-inch cutter should be on a 3/8-inch shank (assuming you have either a 3/8-inch collet or a reducer for your router). The reason is that deep reach.

A 1/4-inch cutter on a 1/2-inch shank has a transition—often an abrupt one—from the cutting diameter to the shank diameter. Usually the transition is right at the end of the cutting edges. When it contacts the work, the transition will chamfer the edges of the cut just a little and burn the wood quite a lot. You just can't get the bit to cut deeper than its cutting length.

Template Systems

Using a template to guide and control a mortising operation has several advantages. It isn't the ideal approach for every mortise, but there are occasions when it is absolutely the best.

The major disadvantage is that the template thickness steals depth from the mortise. If the maximum depth you can achieve with a particular bit is 1 1/2 inches, then using a 1/2-inch-thick template reduces the achievable depth to 1 inch. Obviously, you'll want to use the thinnest template material you can for this application.

So what are the advantages? You can cut mortises of a consistent length and width, without fiddling with edge guides. If you are mortising narrow stock, the template itself can provide support for the router, and it can serve as a clamping base for the workpiece. With a template, you can rout mortises that are wider than the bit diameter. You can rout aesthetically pleasing through mortises of the sort you'd use in a plank bench.

The chapter "Template-Guided Work" on page 155 has all the details on the best materials to use for templates, on scaling them to use with guide bushings, and so on. For mortising, given that you want to conserve as much of the depth capacity as possible, use 1/4-inch hardboard,

MDF (medium-density fiberboard), or plywood for the template. Cut the template blank so it's 3 or 4 times longer and wider than the mortise.

Work out the dimensions of the mortise you want, then bump it up to the size of the template opening that's necessary, given the bit and guide bushing you'll be using. In mortising operations, it's a good idea to use a large-diameter bushing, so the chips augered out of the mortise can escape through the gap between bit and bushing. To bump up the mortise size to the template size, subtract the diameter of the bit from the outside diameter of the bushing and add the difference to both the length and width of the mortise.

Lay out the template opening on the template blank. As you lay out the opening, scribe indelible centerlines through the length and width of the opening, extending them well beyond the opening. These will later help you align the template for a mortising cut. Routing is probably the cleanest way to make the opening. You can use a T-square with stops to control this cut.

To use the template, you simply clamp it to the work. Use a plunge router, the appropriate guide bushing, and, of course, an upcut spiral bit to make the cut.

How you position and clamp the template depends a lot on the nature of the workpiece. If you are mortising narrow frame members, glue and screw a cleat to the underside of the template to both position the template and provide a clamping surface. If you are mortising a bench seat, you can align the centerlines of the template with matching centerlines scribed on the workpiece, and simply clamp the template to the work. In most situations, double-faced tape (carpet tape) will do a good job of holding the template in place.

A through mortise can be cut with a template as a guide. Use the crossing centerlines on the template to align it with similar lines on the work. Bond the template to the work with carpet tape. Clamp the work tight to a sacrificial backing to prevent splintering as the bit breaks through the bottom surface of the work.

A template is an ideal guide for cutting multiple mortises, especially when you need several parts with matching arrays of mortises. Carefully lay out and cut the array of slots in a suitable template material. Attach a fence to the template, and clamp the workpiece to the fence and template so you can rout the mortises.

Try This!

If you need to do a mortise in a part that is shaped some way in the finished project, cut the mortise before you shape the part. A tapered leg, for example, will be easier to mortise while its faces are all still parallel.

Mortising on the Horizontal Router Table

The horizontal router table is a great choice for mortising (see page 91). Set it up with the sliding X-Y tables and the backstop appropriate to the type of mortise (edge or end) that you are cutting. Once you have the setup dialed in, cutting mortise after mortise is fast and the results are uniformly accurate.

Begin the setup by laying out the mortise on a sample workpiece. Go beyond the usual markings on the edge to be mortised; when the piece

Red setup lines on the mounting board, X table, and backstop must align with each other and with a corresponding line on the workpiece, delineating the middle of the mortise you want to cut. Trap the X table between stops to lock it on the mounting-board setup line. Align and mount the backstop. Clamp the workpiece to the table, then adjust the stops to allow just enough lateral movement to cut the desired mortise.

Set the bit in relation to the table using a setup block—the sort used by machinists. Lay the precision block on the table and lower the mounting board until the bit contacts the block. Turn the bit by hand as you fine-tune the setting. The cutting edges should graze the block without moving it.

is clamped to the tables, the layout will be largely obscured from view. Extend lines from the ends of the mortise, as well as the mortise midline (which corresponds to setup lines on the router table), across the face of the piece.

Set up the router next. Select the bit and install it in the router. Using a rule, adjust the extension to match the mortise's final depth. Finally, adjust the height of the router above the top table, the X table. You can measure between the table surface and the bit with a rule. Or you can use a precision-thickness setup block, laying it on the table and lowering the mounting board until the bit contacts the block.

Now set up the tables and stops. Park a backstop on the slides atop the X table where it can help to align, then immobilize, a workpiece for mortising.

Let me give a specific example. Making a door frame is a common mortising job. You've got a pair of stiles, each with two mortises to be routed. The ideal is a setup that enables you to do both mortises in each stile, referencing the same face for both. Here's how I set up for this:

I have marked a setup line on the mounting board, the X table, and the parallel backstop. I align the X table's setup line with that on the mounting board, then trap the table between stops on the Y-table slides. Position the work sample and the backstop, registering their setup lines with the others. Finally, reset the stops to allow the X table to move so the bit will cut the mortise.

When you mortise the actual stiles, you align the midline delineating the first mortise location with the setup lines on the router table. Rout that mortise. Then pop the toggle clamp and slide the stile right or left to align the second mortise's midline with the setup lines. Reclamp the piece and rout.

But before you do a real stile, rout your sample and evaluate the mortise's size and placement. If the setup must be adjusted, adjust it. Otherwise, rout the mortises.

Remember that on the horizontal table, the correct feed is left to right. Push the tables toward the router, plunging the bit into the work 1/4 inch or so. At the same time, slide the X table toward the right, cutting a slot. Back the work off the bit and return the X table to the starting position. Replunge the work and feed again to the right. Repeat this until the mortise is routed to the full depth.

End mortises, required for loose-tenon joinery, are routed in the same manner. The difference is in the backstop used. Line up the setup line on the work with that on the X table. Move the backstop along the X-table slides, bringing it against the left side of the workpiece; make sure it is square to the mounting board and then tighten it down.

The routing maneuvers to cut an end mortise are the same as for cutting an edge mortise.

Routing Tenons

Once you've routed the mortises, doing the tenons is relatively easy. The operation has a great deal in common with routing end-lap joints.

The difference between cutting laps and cutting tenons—and it is an important difference—is that with a tenon, you cut into both faces (and sometimes the edges). The challenge is to get the shoulders lined up all around the piece.

Because the tenons are usually cut *after* the mortises, you need to adjust the thickness of the tenons to fit the mortises. Cut a test tenon, and see

Once the workpiece is clamped to the upper sliding table, it takes only a few moments to rout a mortise. With the table against the left-hand stop, push it toward the bit, beginning the cut. Slide the table to the right until it stops. Pull the table away from the bit, return it to the left, then repeat the cut sequence, deepening the mortise. A third pass should complete the mortise (inset).

how it fits the mortise. Ideally, you'll make the tenon a bit too thick on the first pass, and subsequent bit-height adjustments will thin it to the perfect fit. Remember to trim both cheeks each time you adjust the bit, so the tenon remains centered on the work (unless your project design requires it to be off center, of course).

Easiest to cut are tenons that have the same width of shoulder all around. An offset tenon, or one with wider or narrower shoulders, takes more setups.

In any case, though, your square-cornered tenon doesn't match your routed mortise, with its rounded ends. You can resolve this problem in one of several ways. You can square the ends of the mortise with a chisel. Or you can round off the tenon's corners to roughly match the mortise; use a file or chisel to do this.

A third option is to scale the tenon width so the square-cornered tenon fits the round-ended mortise. The primary glue surfaces are the broad cheeks, and you've got the shoulders working to resist twisting and racking. If the narrow edges of the tenon aren't in contact with the ends of the mortise, it doesn't significantly impact the strength of the joint.

Loose tenons are the most easily made of all. Rip lengths of straight, defect-free stock to the width and thickness required. Round over the edges with a bullnose bit or a round-over bit. Then crosscut the tenon stock to the lengths required.

Cutting Tenons with a Handheld Router

Read through the chapter "Lap Joints," page 295. There you'll see several lap-cutting approaches that apply equally well to cutting tenons with a handheld router. You can clamp several rails together and run the cutter across all at the same time, for example.

One useful jig is designed to help you keep the shoulders square. The fixture is a T-square fastened to a base. It has a stop fence that corresponds to the T-square's crossbar, against which you butt the work. A second fence—a router guide—extends across the face of the work and serves to both clamp the work in the fixture and guide the router. A homemade toggle speeds the shifting and switching of workpieces. The guide fence is long enough that you

The tenoning fixture holds a rail so you can cut a cheek with a handheld router. You guide the tool along the guide fence, making as many sweeps as necessary to complete the cut. Pop open the homemade toggle to release pressure on the fence, freeing the rail so you can slide it out, turn it over, then replace it against the stop fence, its end against the positioning stop. Then cut the second cheek.

can clamp two or three rails at a time under it, but you may find that it's just as fast and less hassle to cut the tenons one at a time.

To use the fixture, you dog it to the workbench, then clamp the work in it. The stop fence has a dado routed in it, and so long as you always use the

Tenoning Fixture
Cut tenons with a handheld router

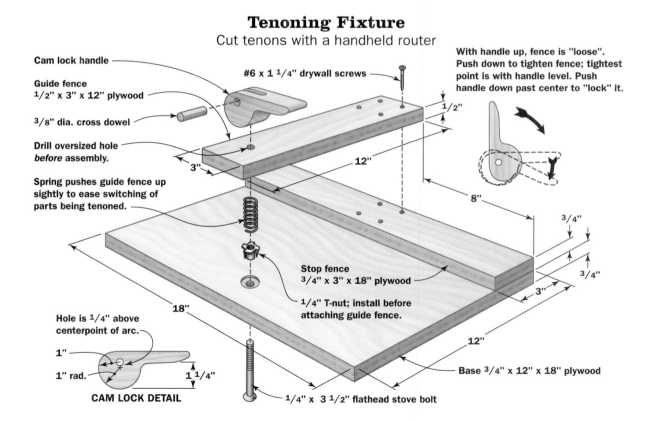

Cam lock handle

Guide fence
1/2" x 3" x 12" plywood

3/8" dia. cross dowel

Drill oversized hole *before* assembly.

Spring pushes guide fence up sightly to ease switching of parts being tenoned.

#6 x 1 1/4" drywall screws

With handle up, fence is "loose". Push down to tighten fence; tightest point is with handle level. Push handle down past center to "lock" it.

1/2"

12"

3"

8"

3/4"

3/4"

Stop fence
3/4" x 3" x 18" plywood

1/4" T-nut; install before attaching guide fence.

3"

12"

18"

Hole is 1/4" above centerpoint of arc.

1"

1" rad.

1 1/4"

CAM LOCK DETAIL

1/4" x 3 1/2" flathead stove bolt

Base 3/4" x 12" x 18" plywood

same router and bit with the fixture, you can use this dado to line up the work. The edge of the dado, of course, corresponds to the shoulder of the tenon. Guide the router along the fence, and feed toward the stop fence. It will back up the work, preventing tearout when the bit exits the cut. If the tenon is longer than you can cut in a single pass, make two or three, always feeding toward the stop fence.

Right-angle platform. As an alternative, you can use the right-angle platform, presented in the "Sliding Dovetail Joints" chapter (page 317). It holds the workpiece upright and provides both a support surface and a guide for the router. It does a great job on tenons with cheeks and shoulders across the faces but not the edges.

Clamp the platform in your bench vise to set it up and use it. The router sits on the platform and rides along the guide fence. The bit extends below the platform and cuts whatever it contacts.

The tenon length is governed by the extension of the router bit. You have to account for the platform thickness, but the typical 1- to 1 1/2-inch tenon isn't a problem to cut.

The shoulder width is governed by the position of the guide fence. The closer the fence is to the platform edge, the shallower the cut will be. A little math helps you position the fence. Subtract the radius of the bit from the radius of the router base. The difference is the distance from the cutline that the fence must be spotted.

To set up, lay out the tenon on the end of your sample. Clamp it in place. Next, choose your bit and do the math. Using a rule or small square, measure from the line on the workpiece and locate the fence. Make sure the fence is parallel to the plat-

The right-angle platform, useful for cutting laps and for cutting tails for sliding dovetails, is ideal for cutting full-width tenons. The fixture holds the work upright and supports and guides the router, so a cut with a straight bit forms a smooth cheek and a crisp, square shoulder.

form edge. If you err, try to err on the side of a too-shallow cut.

Cut both tenon cheeks, and check its fit in a mortise. Adjust the fence position if necessary. An accurate way to do this is with a reference block and shims.

Tearout along the shoulder can be pretty damaging if you feed the router in the correct direction. This is one of those instances where a climb cut is both controllable and beneficial. I generally make a shallow climbing pass, then bring the router back—cutting along the way—and finish up with a final climbing pass. The router is only fully against the fence on that final pass.

Router-Table Tenoning

On the router table, cutting tenons is a snap. Two techniques work well for me, and I'm sure there are others.

Using a long bit. By "a long bit," I mean a straight bit with cutting edges at least as long as the tenon. A tenon longer than 2 inches will outstrip the longest cutting length you'll find, but then, a tenon more than 1 1/2 inches long is unusual.

To produce a tenon this way, chuck the straight bit in your router, and adjust the extension to match the tenon length. Attach a tall facing to the fence, one that will provide good support to a workpiece that's standing on its end. The opening for the bit should be zero-clearance, in both the fence and the tabletop. Move the fence into position, housing the bit almost entirely. You want only 1/8 to 3/16 inch of it exposed. Secure the fence.

Use a flat, true, and square scrap to support and back up the workpiece. Slide the work along the fence and across the bit, routing the first cheek. Turn the rail and repeat the action, cutting across the edge. Turn the rail yet again and cut across the second face. In a fourth pass, cut across the second edge.

Your tenon will have clean, smooth cheeks with crisp, square shoulders, perfect for gluing. Obviously, the process is quick.

Tenoning sled. My favorite tenoning approach depends on a special sled. It's quirky, but to cut tenons this way, you use what's usually called a mortising bit (it's intended for routing mortises for hinge leaves). With the jig and bit you can set up in 2 or 3 minutes. No layout is needed. A typical tenon is cut in four quick passes.

Here is my method for setting up and then cutting a tenon.

Install the bit in the router, and set its elevation first. Use a rule to measure the exposure of the cutting edge above the table. Initially, I set the bit a hair under the width of the mortise's shoulder. Through test cuts, I creep up on the just-right setting. (The just-right setting is determined, of course, by fitting a test tenon in a mortise.)

Set up the sled next. The stop on the sled's fence controls the tenon length. Measure from the cut made into the fence by the bit. (You always want to use the same bit with the sled; otherwise you will get tearout at the shoulders.) If the tenon is to be 1 inch long, for example, align the 1-inch mark on the rule at the edge of the cut. Drop the stop onto the fence, and slide it gently against the end of the rule. Seat it firmly so it is square to both the fence and the tabletop. Tighten its clamping bolt.

Cut a sample. Make a pass, routing the first cheek and shoulder. Roll the workpiece over. Make a pass, cutting the second cheek and shoulder.

The router table offers a straightforward way of producing tenons. Select a straight bit that's as long as the tenon you need to cut, and chuck it in your table-mounted router. Stand the piece to be tenoned on end, brace it against the fence, then slide it across the bit with a sturdy backup block (top). One pass should produce a finished cheek. Rotate the piece a quarter-turn and repeat the action to cut an edge (bottom). Two more passes and you have a clean, uniform tenon.

Router Table Tenoning Sled

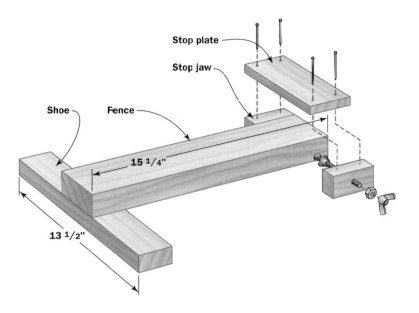

Stop plate

Stop jaw

Shoe

Fence

15 1/4"

13 1/2"

Horizontal-Table Tenoning

A final tenoning option is to use the horizontal router table with its sliding X-Y tables. Use a straight bit, and position it to cut the underside of the workpiece.

Set a backstop at the left end of the X table. Immobilize the Y table (the bottom one) between stops on one of the base slides; this is so only the X table can move. When you lock the Y table, offset it from the mounting board a distance equal to the tenon length. Set up this way, the bit cuts the underside of the workpiece without touching the X table.

Check the fit of this tenon in your mortise. You need a close fit for the joint to glue well. If you have to hammer on the tenon piece to close the joint, the fit is *too* close. Hand pressure should close it. On the other hand, the joint should stay closed until you separate the parts.

To refine the fit, raise or lower the bit. Cut another test tenon and fit it to the mortise. When you've got the settings right, cut the real work.

Hold the piece to the fence of the tenoning sled, exactly the way you'd hold a piece in a table saw's miter gauge. Butt the end against the stop. Cut the first cheek (left). Pull the sled back and roll the workpiece a quarter-turn. Cut the edge (above). Roll the piece again and cut the second cheek. Four passes, and the tenon is formed.

Routing Tenons

Adjust the bit extension and height to produce the size of tenon you want. With the X table pulled to the left of the bit, set the workpiece against the backstop and slide its end against the mounting board. Push the table through the cut. Roll the workpiece 90°, stroke the table through another cut, roll the work again, and so on, until the tenon is complete.

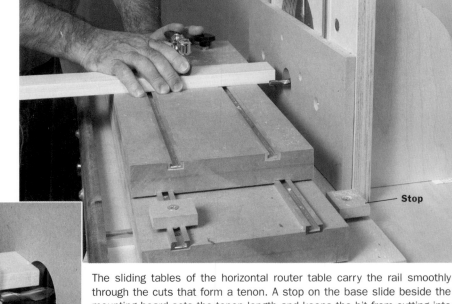

Stop

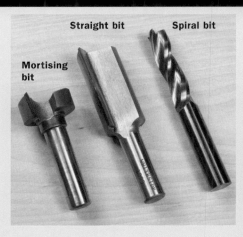

The sliding tables of the horizontal router table carry the rail smoothly through the cuts that form a tenon. A stop on the base slide beside the mounting board sets the tenon length and keeps the bit from cutting into the X table. A backstop on the X table holds the rail as you slide the table through the cut. Cutting on the underside of the workpiece (left) is the method that's generally recognized as safest.

Bit Drawer

Here are the bits of choice for cutting tenons. None of them are limited to tenoning; all are useful for other routing operations. Don't feel you need a special-purpose bit for tenoning. You don't.

With the horizontal router table: Use a spiral bit if at all possible. The configuration—upcut or downcut—is immaterial in tenoning. You aren't using the spiral for its ability to move the chips away from the cut. You are using it for its smooth cut in all sorts of wood.

A 1/2-inch cutting and shank diameter is best (while we're talking about ideal setups). For this operation, unlike for cutting mortises, the entire cutting length will be

Straight bit   Spiral bit

Mortising bit

addressing the work on each pass. You do need a cutting length that matches the length of the tenon.

Though a spiral cuts aggressively, doesn't require a lot of power to drive, and does yield that smooth

finish, the bit I use most frequently, especially for long tenons, is a 2-inch-long 1/2-inch straight cutter. What it has going for it is length: It cuts tenons a full 2 inches long.

With the regular router table: Any large-diameter straight bit will do, as will mortising bits. But my favorite is usually called a mortising bit (as in hinge-leaf mortising). Sometimes it's called a bottom-cleaning bit, other times a planer bit. The cutting flutes are very short, so it can't cut too deeply in one pass. But in a large diameter, say 1 1/2 inches, it can mill a wide swath. The finish, as you might expect from something called a planer bit, is smooooth.

See Also...

"Lap Joints" for ideas on cutting tenons, which resemble end laps (page 295).

Lap Joints

Notch one member to accommodate the full thickness of another and you have a lap joint. Notch both members, each to take half the thickness of the other, and you have a half-lap.

Within these two broad categories are many variations. End laps, cross laps, T-laps, mitered half-laps, edge laps. All of these can be cut successfully with the router.

Half-laps can be used for all sorts of flat frames. Doors, for example, but also face frames, web frames, picture frames. An intermediate rail half-lapped to the stiles "looks" right, because it visually abuts the stile, the way a mortise-and-tenon would. On the other hand, a rectangle of end grain is exposed in assembled end laps and T-laps, which can be regarded as unsightly.

The half-lap (or its kin the full lap) can be used in post-and-rail constructions, to join rails or aprons to legs. You usually see this joinery in worktables rather than fine furniture. But even in the most traditional table construction, the half-lap is used where stretchers cross (a cross lap).

T-lap

Mitered half-lap

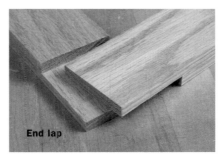
End lap

Cross lap

The joint can be very strong if properly made. The shoulder(s) of the half-lap provide resistance to twisting. In addition, the laps provide plenty of long-grain-to-long-grain gluing surface.

Be wary of using half-laps on wide boards. Wood movement can break the joint, so confine the joinery to members no more than 3 to 3 1/2 inches wide.

End Laps

The end lap is a component not only of the end lap joint, but also of the T-lap. It's the easiest lap to cut. It can be done a couple of different ways on the router table, and a couple of ways with a portable router. Choose the approach that works for the job at hand and that suits the way you work.

Router Table Sled

Use the tenoning sled shown on page 293. This shop-made device looks like an industrial-strength T-square. The stout fence is long enough to extend from the tabletop edge to well beyond the bit. The crossbar rides along the edge of the tabletop. A stop clamps to the fence to control the length of the cut.

You can use most any straight bit to cut the lap, but I prefer what's variously called a planer, mortising, or bottom-cleaning bit (see Bit Drawer on page 294).

The first time you use the sled, you'll cut into the fence. This cut is what you use to position the stop for the length of lap you want. Measure from the shoulder of the cut (include

Set the saddle-type stop on the tenoning sled with a piece of the working stock. Align the edge of the stock with the cut shoulder in the sled's fence (right), then drop the stop over the fence and slide it against the other edge of the stock.

Try This!

Before cutting good wood, test your depth-of-cut setting on scrap. Since a lap cut removes half the thickness of the stock, you need to make pairs of test cuts. Do the initial setting with a ruler. Snick the corner of your scrap, flip the scrap over, and snick a second corner so the two cuts just intersect, as shown. If the depth-of-cut is too shallow, the two cuts won't connect. If it is too deep, you'll see that. Keep adjusting and testing until the two cuts just merge.

Cut just right   Cut too deep   Cut too shallow

the cut itself in the measurement, of course). The stop prevents you from making a cut that's too long.

Be mindful of the amount of material you remove in a pass. You don't necessarily want to hog out a 3/8-inch-deep cut in a single pass, especially if you are using a 1 1/4- to 1 1/2-inch-diameter bit.

Form the full cut in small steps. The first pass should be about 1/8 inch wide, produced by holding the workpiece well clear of the stop, so only 1/8 inch of it extends over the bit. Make pass after pass, shifting the workpiece closer and closer to the stop. One last pass with the workpiece dead against the stop, and your lap is completed.

An Alternative Approach

If you are working fairly narrow stock—2 inches or less—you can use a long straight bit, and make the cuts by standing workpieces on end

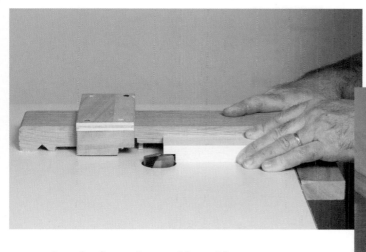

Stage a cut with the sled by making a series of narrow cuts. On the first pass, hold the workpiece well shy of the stop and cut a narrow rabbet across the end (left). Move the work closer to the stop for the second pass, then butt it against the stop for the final pass (right).

against the fence. Any end lap wider than 2 inches will outstrip the cutting length of the longest straight bits you'll find. You can stretch the reach of any bit by cheating it out of the collet, but that is done only at some risk.

Set up by chucking the straight bit in your router and adjusting the extension to match the width of the end lap. (Set a piece of the working stock on edge beside the bit, then raise the bit until its tip is flush with the stock's top edge.)

Next, attach a facing to the fence that will provide good support to a workpiece that's standing on its end. Move the fence into position, housing the bit almost entirely. You want to make only a very shallow cut, so expose just 1/8 inch of it. Lock down the fence.

Support and back up the workpiece with a scrap—one that's flat, true, and square, of course. Slide the work along the fence and across the bit, routing a shallow recess. Move the fence back slightly to expose a little more of the bit, thus increasing the depth of the cut, and make another pass. Repeat this cut-and-adjust routine until you've reached the desired depth.

If you are cutting a great number of identical laps, I'd suggest making a cut on every workpiece before shifting it to expose more of the bit. That works better—in my mind—than adjusting the fence two or three times for each individual workpiece.

Right-Angle Platform

The right-angle platform holds the workpiece upright and provides both a support surface and a guide for the router. Construction information is on page 325.

You clamp the platform in your bench vise, and the router sits on it and slides along the guide fence. The bit extends below the platform and cuts whatever it contacts, including the edge of the platform itself and the workrest fence.

The extension of the router bit governs the length of the lap. You can do 2-inch-long laps comfortably with

At the router table, a long straight bit used with the regular fence is a good alternative for cutting end laps. Use a large, square pusher to both feed the work and back up the cut. A tall fence facing can be a comfort, but isn't essential.

the setup, using a bit with 2-inch-long cutting edges. You do have to account for the platform thickness, but that doesn't rob a lot from the overall capacity.

The depth of the lap is governed by the position of the guide fence. Subtract the radius of the bit from the radius of the router base. The difference is the distance from the cut line that the fence must be spotted.

To begin setup, scribe the lap's cheek across the end of the workpiece, then clamp it in the fixture. Choose your bit and do the math. Using a rule or small square, measure from the cheek line and locate the

When cutting an end lap on the right-angle platform, you cut the full length from the outset. Make a very shallow climb cut first, to score the lap's shoulder without tearout. Then move the router back and forth, deepening the cut until the router rides against the fence throughout a pass.

Bit Drawer

Routing laps calls for bits that are a little out of the ordinary. Your lap-cutting approach dictates the sort of bit to use. No one bit does it all.

The mortising bit is designed to clear a wide, smooth recess. Perfect for laps! It's intended for cutting the hinge mortise (not the sort that takes a tenon), hence the name. The bit used to be hard to find, but versions are found these days at large home centers, evidence that it's become mainstream. It has uses far beyond hinge mortising. It cuts laps, tenons, and rabbets, and it's useful in surfacing operations.

You can buy a mortising bit with or without a shank-mounted bearing. In most instances, the bearing is secured with a collar and setscrew, so it can be removed. I find this bit perfect for lapping with a sled on the router table, as well as with a saddle jig and portable router.

Sizes range from 3/4-inch- up to 1 1/2-inch-diameter, and the vertical cutting edges range from 7/16

inch up to 7/8 inch. It's available on both 1/4- and 1/2-inch shanks.

Similar in some ways are short pattern bits. Typically, these are straights with a body that's larger in diameter than the shank, so a bearing the same diameter as the cutter can be installed on the shank. To be useful in lapping, the cutting edges must be short so you can produce a shallow cut and still be able to reference a jig's guide edge with the bearing.

The larger of the two pattern bits shown is intended for edge cuts more than bottom cuts, but it'll work. You usually are sweeping into the cut, rather than plunging into it. Most any straight bit will work.

Finally, for those end laps cut from the end of the workpiece, you need a long straight bit. Projecting from your router, such a bit can be intimidating. If you are uncomfortable with that, if you feel menaced by it, by all means opt for the mortising bit.

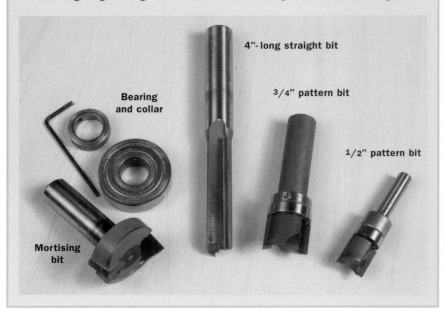

4"-long straight bit

3/4" pattern bit

1/2" pattern bit

Bearing and collar

Mortising bit

fence. A square referencing the end of the platform aligns the fence. Try to err on the side of a too-shallow cut.

Make a pair of test cuts, fit the pieces together, and check the edges and faces. Adjust the fence position as necessary. If the fence needs to be micro-adjusted, use a reference block and shims (see page 328).

The work routine is to set the workpiece against the fence, its end butted up against the underside of the platform. Secure it with the toggles. Switch on the router, and guide it along the fence, cutting the workpiece.

Tearout along the shoulder of the lap can be pretty bad. This is one of those instances where a climb cut is both controllable and beneficial. I generally make a shallow climbing pass, then bring the router back—cutting along the way—and finish up with a final climbing pass. The router is only fully against the fence on that final pass.

Cross Laps

The approaches discussed above work well for the end lap, but not for a lap in the middle of a workpiece. Ideal for the cross lap is the job-specific saddle jig, used with a handheld router. But die-hard router table users can usually do the job with the sliding fence.

Saddle Jig

The saddle jig gets its name from the way it fits over a workpiece. I called it job-specific because you make it for a particular job, fitting it to the actual workpieces. All you need are four scraps and a half-dozen or so drywall screws.

To cut laps with this jig, I use the

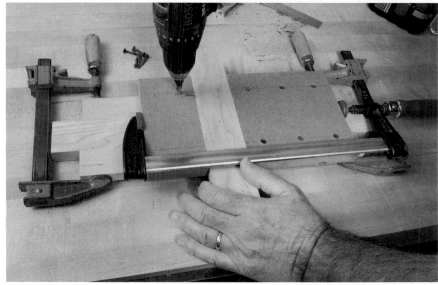

A saddle jig is easy to make. Sandwich a workpiece between the fences, and clamp these parts. Align the primary platform on them and screw it in place (top). The guide edge of the platform must be square to the work. The secondary platform completes the jig. Capture a second workpiece snugly between the main and secondary platforms, then screw the secondary platform to the fences (bottom).

mortising bit. For this application, mount a pilot bearing on the shank. I prefer to use a fixed-base router for this, rather than a plunger.

Construction of the jig should be evident from the drawing and photos. The fences need to be just under the thickness of the workpieces, and their edges need to be straight and parallel. For the platforms, use 3/4-inch MDF (medium-density fiberboard) or plywood.

The platform straddles the work-

piece, and it's easy to position: You just align the platform edges directly on your layout lines. The bearing rides along the edges of the two platforms while the bit just below it excavates the lap. The bit is trapped, so you won't get a lap that's too wide. The fences tight against the workpiece edges prevent tearout. The platforms support the router and keep it from tipping. Assuming the workpieces are equal in width, you can use one jig on both.

Saddle Jig

Width of piece to fit into lap

Main platform

Support platform

Fences

Width of piece to be lapped

You can use the jig for end laps as well as cross laps. For the end laps, add a fifth scrap as a positioning block. Attach it to the underside of the secondary platform so the workpiece end can butt against it.

Beyond the commonplace 90° cross-lap or T-lap joints, you can make versions of this jig to cut laps for any angle of joint. You need one jig for a joint angled to the left, a different one for a joint angled to the right.

The bit you use has a shank-mounted pilot bearing, and it's trapped between the platforms. So the smooth, square-shouldered cut perfectly matches the width of the gauge workpiece used to make the jig. The fences back up the cut on both sides, so splintering is eliminated.

You can also make such jigs with curved-edge platforms so you can lap curved parts. You can't use just any scraps to make such a jig, of course. Both the fences and the platforms have to have curved edges, and curved at the correct radii. Again, you'll need one jig for the right and another for the left. But you'll get tight, strong, attractive joints through a straightforward technique.

Sliding Fence Lapping

Personally, I think it's fussy to do the cross lap accurately on the router table. But if you are determined, use the sliding fence, shown in "Router Table Accessories," page 101. You need a stop to keep the work from moving as the bit cuts it; this stop helps you place and size the cut, too.

Lay out the lap on your workpieces, and extend the margins onto the edge of the stock.

Install the bit, and adjust the cut depth. You have to devise a means of staging the cut. With the end lap, you can set the bit for the final depth and make a series of narrow cuts. With a cross lap, at least the first pass has to be the full width of the bit. The only means of reducing the bite is to reduce the cutting depth. You either have to lower the bit or block up the workpiece. (Personally, I'd opt to shim the workpiece. I like to confirm my final setup through test cuts *before* I start cutting the good stuff.)

Position the stop next. Adjust it so you are cutting the left margin of the lap when the work is against the stop. Now determine the spacer dimension. Align the right margin of the lap with the bit—make sure you have the bit *inside* the cut—and measure between the end of the workpiece and the stop. That's how thick the

Routing Pocket Laps

A stopped lap, a lap that doesn't cut all the way across the face of the workpiece, is known as a pocket lap. You might use pocket laps in a face frame where you didn't want end grain showing on the sides. The lap joint between rail and stile would be hidden on the inside of the cabinet.

The easiest way to cut pocket laps is with a U-shaped jig made of a square of 1/4-inch plywood (or hardboard) for the base and several strips of 1-by stock for the fences.

To make the jig, begin with the router and bit you'll use. Make a setup gauge with them, as explained on page 237.

Cut the jig base and some strips of 1×1 material for fences. Clamp a scrap of the working stock to the base, right where you want the cutout. One side at a time, butt the gauge against the scrap, then a fence against the parallel edge of the gauge. Fasten the fence to the base.

When the three fences are attached, clamp the jig to a test piece and rout. The bit will cut through the base and the sample. And the cut should perfectly match the width of the mating piece. (If the fit isn't perfect, the best approach is to start over with new scraps.) Now you can attach a fence to the underside of the base to positively locate the jig on a workpiece.

To use the jig, first lay out the pocket lap on the workpiece. Line up the jig with the cutout on the layout lines. Clamp it to the work. Cut the lap the same way you routed the cutout in the jig.

After the pocket is routed, you will need to square the corners with a chisel.

The jig can also be used to cut through laps. Just align it across the workpiece with the back of the cutout clear of the work's edge.

The design of the pocket-lap jig allows you to position its cutout directly on the layout lines.

Pocket-Lap Jig
Here's how to make one

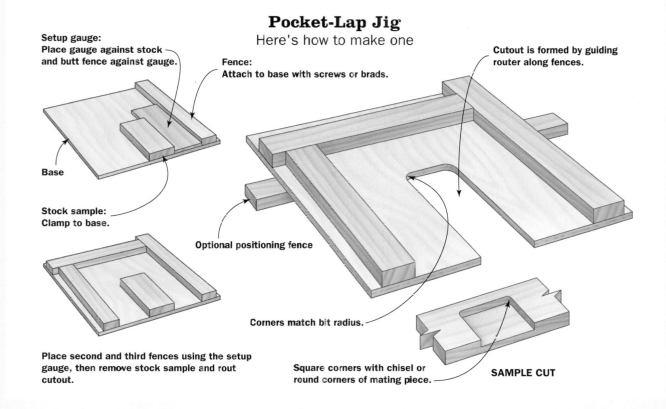

Setup gauge:
Place gauge against stock and butt fence against gauge.

Fence:
Attach to base with screws or brads.

Cutout is formed by guiding router along fences.

Base

Stock sample:
Clamp to base.

Optional positioning fence

Corners match bit radius.

Place second and third fences using the setup gauge, then remove stock sample and rout cutout.

Square corners with chisel or round corners of mating piece.

SAMPLE CUT

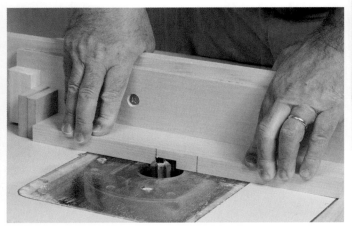

Spacers inserted between the sliding fence's stop block and the work's end shift the workpiece so the bit will align with the right shoulder of the intended lap. Make the first cut with all the spacers in place (left). Remove them one at a time and make a cut. On the final pass, the workpiece should be butted directly against the stop (right).

spacer must be. To parse the total width into three or four cuts, divide the total spacer thickness into two or three pieces.

Make a test of the full cutting sequence. Cut first with all the spacers between the stop and the work. Then remove one and make another cut. Repeat until you cut with the work directly against the stop. Check the fit of the joint. If the total cut is too wide, you must pare down the total spacer thickness.

Once you have the fit right, go ahead and cut the laps.

Mitered Half-Laps

The mitered half-lap combines the structure of the half-lap with the appearance of the miter. You can't just miter two pieces that have already been half-lapped, of course. One part of the joint could be done this way, since on the rails, the shoulder cut is square while the butt end is mitered. But on the stiles, the shoulder cut is mitered while the butt end is square.

What you need is a set of three guides. One is a right-angle guide. The others are right-hand and left-

hand miter guides. All are made using 3/4-inch MDF and strips of hardwood. They are designed to be used with a pattern bit. No pattern bit? Add router fences to the topsides and use a regular straight bit.

Make the guides following the drawings. Cut three bases to the same dimensions—7 inches by 13 inches—and be sure they are absolutely square. (The 3/4-inch thickness ensures that a pattern bit's bearing will have a reference surface without having to cut too deeply in the work; if your bit's cutting length is 1 inch, a common one, you'll be cutting 3/8 inch into the work with the bearing just barely in contact with the template.)

Use hardwood for the fences. The right-angle template has the fence attached along one 7-inch edge, as shown. For the template to be accurate, the fence has to be perfectly parallel to the base's short dimension, and square to its long dimension.

The miter templates have the fences attached along one of the long edges, also as shown. Cut a 45° miter across each template. Be sure you locate the fences and cut the miters to create right and left templates; the templates are NOT duplicates. As with the right-angle template,

accuracy is essential if the frames you make with them are to be square.

The router fences, if you add them, can be made of the same material as the other fences. The goal is to have the cutting edge of the bit grazing the guide's edge. To achieve this, position the fences so the bit will trim

If you like the look of profiled molding that meets in a crisp miter, you'll love assembling frames with mitered half-laps. The joint is strong yet easy to rout, *and* it allows you to unerringly rout a profile on the inside edge before assembly. After assembly, the profile will meet, fair and square, at the miter (upper left). A joint that must be edge-routed after assembly yields a rounded corner (lower right).

the base edge on the first pass. You can cut back on the thickness of the base material, of course. Quarter-inch plywood or hardboard is fine.

Again, because accuracy is so important, take special pains to ensure that the fences are placed at accurate angles.

Use either set of guides in the same way. Begin by machining the workpieces, cutting a groove or rabbet for a panel, if there is to be one, then routing in that profile—a bead, an ogee, whatever. Now trim the pieces to final length. In doing so, miter-cut the ends of two pieces and square-cut the other two.

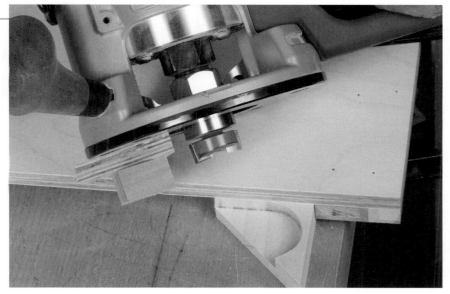

Here's how to use the right-angle guide. Align the guide exactly on the shoulder. To avoid splintering, feed the cutter into the work from all sides. Note the support block carpet-taped to the router base.

Mitered Half-Lap Templates
Use these to work with pattern bits

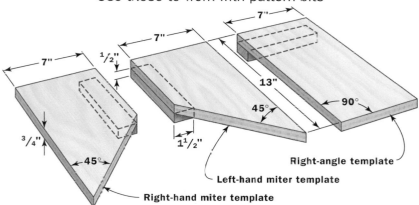

7"

7"

7"

1/2"

13"

45°

90°

3/4"

1 1/2"

45°

Right-angle template

Left-hand miter template

Right-hand miter template

Mitered Half-Lap Guides
Use these to work with straight bits

Left-hand miter guide

Right-hand miter guide

Right-angle guide

1/2"

1/4"

7"

16 1/4"

14"

45°

7"

45°

10 1/4"

1/2"

7"

3 1/4"

When routing the stiles, you can orient them as shown, so the guides together support the router.

Mitered Half-Laps

Usually the rails are mitered, the stiles square-cut.

The rails are lapped across their backs. To ensure that they're identical, lap both at the same time, using the right-angle guide. Butt them edge to edge, faces down, and clamp them together. Set the guide in place, its reference edge right on the shoulder line. Clamp it. Set the router's depth-of-cut, and have at it.

With the rails done, turn to the stiles. The stiles are lapped across their faces. Clamp the appropriate guide to each piece and, with the router setting unchanged, rout each lap. Repeat until all are cut.

Edge Laps

The edge lap is formed by notching two boards halfway across their faces, then slipping them together. It's the joint used to create egg-crate-like drawer dividers, for example. But it's also used to join stretchers for leg-and-apron assemblies.

An edge lap often requires a cutter that can produce a narrow but deep kerf. Kind of like a table-saw blade. Like the cross lap, you *can* cut it with a router, but I think there are better ways to do it. Again, if you are determined, try these approaches.

On the router table, the edge-lap notch can be cut as though it were a box-joint notch. Use a bit that matches the stock thickness. Set the bit height to half the width of the stock being notched. Stand the stock on edge and, using the sliding fence, guide the stock into the bit.

Obviously, you are limited in what you can edge-lap in this fashion. While you can find straights with up to 2 1/2 inches of cutting length, bits that long are usually about 1/2-inch-

Use the sliding fence with its adjustable stop to rout edge laps. The stop eliminates the need to lay out individual parts. Here, a thin spacer positions the workpiece for the first pass; removing it widens the lap on the second pass.

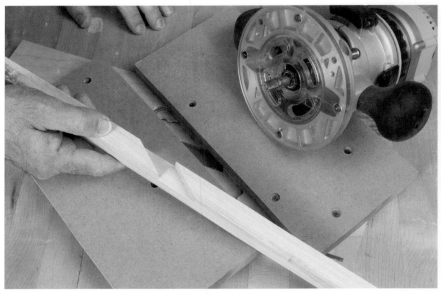

Crossing stretchers for a table are taller than their width, so an edge lap joins them. The saddle jig takes longer to make than to use, but the result is a perfect fit.

diameter. Nonetheless, where the parameters of the job permit this approach, it works well, yielding a clean, precisely sized notch. No additional handwork required.

With a handheld router, you cut the notches as if they were stopped dadoes. The advantage here is that you can deal with long cuts.

Lay out the position and length of the notch, set a fence with a stop, and make the cut with a straight bit. Because you are cutting completely through the workpiece, you need to either position it on an expendable work surface or cantilever it off the bench. A plunge router facilitates making the total cut in bites of manageable depth. Unlike the router-table approach, there's a final bit of handwork to do. The end of the cut is rounded, and you need to square the corners.

Where edge laps intersect at an angle other than 90°, a saddle-type jig makes an accurate cut easy.

Dovetail Joints

oetails. The very word elicits a sense of wonder. Any piece of woodwork that contains them is somehow special. In a way, we've come to worship this particular joint, and with good reason. But it wasn't always so. In fact, up until a relatively few years ago, dovetails were hidden when used in fine furniture.

The dovetail joint was developed (before reliable glues and cheap fasteners were available) as a very utilitarian means of holding pieces of wood together. In that it has some major advantages. The dovetail allows expansion and contraction of the wood without losing any of its structural integrity. This is extremely desirable when joining large pieces of wood, such as cabinet cases or chest sides.

The joint's strength is not dependent on glue or mechanical fasteners, so it can be used to good advantage in "natural wood" projects.

The big disadvantage in the dovetail joint has always been that it requires not only a lot of time but a lot of skill to make. Of course, that's a large part of the reason it has become so popular. In order to be considered a real woodworker, you have to cut dovetails.

Enter the router. The router doesn't eliminate the need for skill or time in cutting dovetails. But it does change the focus of skill and time you invest. Set up your router carefully, and you can cut hundreds of dovetails quickly and accurately. Just like a factory.

Wanna see how? You have to use jigs.

The Nomenclature of the Dovetail Joint

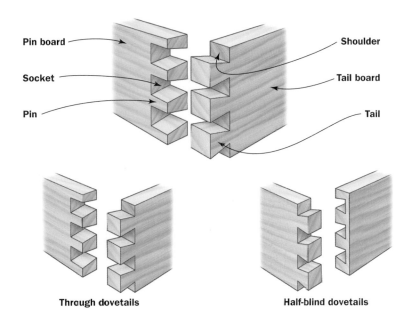

Pin board

Socket

Pin

Shoulder

Tail board

Tail

Through dovetails

Half-blind dovetails

Half-Blind Dovetail Jigs

The least expensive to buy and the easiest to set up are the many half-blind dovetail jigs. No matter how wide or thick the wood is, you clamp it into the jig, run the router through both pieces at once, and get equal-width pins and tails that are rounded to fit into each other at the back. This is the very institutional-looking joint that is often used to assemble drawers for kitchen or other production cabinets. The trickiest part of this one is to get the two parts offset just half a pin in the jig so they come out flush when you assemble them.

The worst part about this jig is the very fact that it is so foolproof and has been around long enough that macho woodworkers look down on it. Its perfectly even spacing is easy to recognize, and everyone knows that even though your dovetails fit well and perform well, you didn't work your butt off to get them that way.

All of these jigs consist of a metal base with a clamping system to hold the mating workpieces and a comb-like template to guide the router in cutting both pieces at once. The biggest difference from one brand to another, from one model to another, is the quality of the materials and hardware and the precision with which it's made and assembled. The cheapest ones have stamped parts that tend to flex and buckle, threads that strip quite easily, wing nuts that chew at your fingers. The expensive versions have basic parts that are extruded rather than stamped or diecast, big plastic knobs instead of wing nuts, and a measure of adjustability. Some even have additional templates, which let you cut 1/4-inch half-blind dovetails in addition to the standard 1/2-inch variety, and 1/4-inch and 1/2-inch box joints as well.

You have to look 'em over and decide whether you want to spend

The typical dovetail jig makes half-blind dovetails, cutting both pins and tails at the same time with the same bit. This model has a rigid extruded aluminum base and durable phenolic template. Its large clamp-knobs are easier on the hands during extended dovetailing sessions than the wing nuts found on less-costly jigs of this type.

Parts of a Typical Dovetail Jig

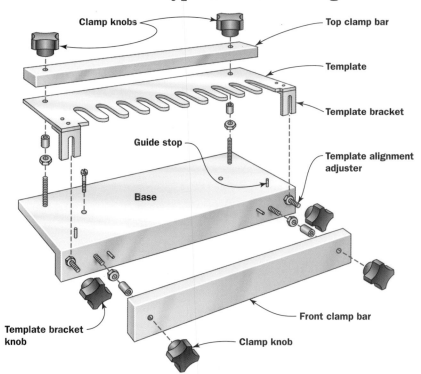

40 bucks or 3 times that for a jig that basically produces a single joint. (You can make similar jigs yourself, but be prepared to spend *a lot of time* fine-tuning the templates to get the precision required to repeatedly produce the desired results.)

shallow scoring cut across the tail piece, feeding from right to left (yes, this is a climb cut). This will help prevent the bit from pulling chips out along the tail piece's shoulder as it exits each cut.

Rout the dovetails, slot by slot, beginning on the left and working to the right. You may want to zip back through them when you are done, just to be sure you didn't pull out of a slot too soon, leaving the work only partially cut.

Don't just *lift* the router from the template—the bit will ruin both the cut and the template. Instead, cut the power and pull the router toward you, getting it well clear of the jig before lifting it. Take a good look at the work and be sure you haven't missed a spot. (If you have, rout it now, before moving anything.) Only then should you remove the template, unclamp the work, and test-assemble the joint.

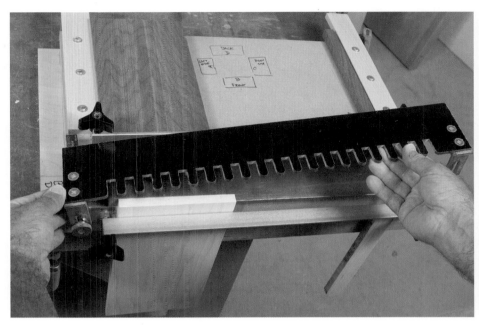

Typically, the template is screwed to a couple of L-shaped brackets. A slot in each bracket's extension fits over a stud projecting from the jig base. A stop nut serves both to adjust the fore-and-aft position of the template and as a stop against which the lock-down nut or knob jams.

Chipping along the shoulder of the tail piece can be a distinct problem with dovetail jigs. A solution is to make a shallow scoring cut, establishing the shoulder, before beginning to rout the dovetails. A climb cut—where you feed the router from right to left—is most effective here. Just be sure the router doesn't get away from you.

Actually machining the dovetails takes only a few seconds. Work along the template, feeding the router as far into each template slot as it will go. The router cuts both sockets and tails at the same time.

Fine-Tuning the Setup

Chances are, your setup needs a little fine-tuning. You slip the two test pieces together, and something's not quite right. Perhaps the fit is too loose. Or too tight. Or the sockets aren't deep enough. Or the parts are a little offset. All of these ills are cured with some fine-tuning.

Fit too tight? The bit's cutting too deep. *Reduce* the depth-of-cut slightly.

Fit too loose? The bit's not cutting deep enough. *Increase* the depth-of-cut slightly.

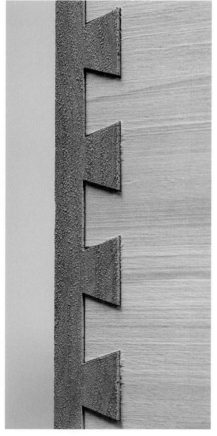

When adjusting the socket depth, you theoretically want the surfaces to come flush when the joint is assembled. But as a practical matter, it may be best to have the socket piece just proud of the tail piece. That way a pass with the belt sander will bring the joint flush, without requiring you to sand the entire side.

Are the sockets too shallow or too deep? The template is misaligned. To reduce the socket depth, move the template very slightly toward you. To increase the socket depth, move the template away from you. Your jig's instruction sheet should explain exactly how to accomplish these adjustments on your jig. Just remember that as you alter the depth of the sockets, you are also altering the thickness of the tails.

Are the two parts slightly misaligned when assembled? The top and bottom edges should be flush. If they aren't, you may not have had the workpieces snug against the alignment pins. Or the pins may be slightly misadjusted.

Any other problems you have will stem from misalignment of the workpieces in the jig. Make sure the top surface of the socket piece is flush with the top end of the tail piece, that they are at right angles to each other,

that the template is square to the workpieces, and so forth.

When you've successfully fine-tuned the setup using the alignment pins on the left, cut a test joint using the right end of the jig. Do any additional tuning needed there.

Cutting the Good Stuff

Before starting on the good wood, make sure you're organized for complete success. It doesn't matter if you are dovetailing 1 drawer or 50 drawers, it's all too easy to get mixed up and cut the dovetails in the wrong places. So label your workpieces.

Bear in mind that you must clamp the work in the jig in an orientation that seems *calculated* to befuddle. You probably noticed this when you assembled the test pieces. When the workpieces are clamped in the jig, it's the assembly's *inside* faces that are exposed. What's exposed in the con-

Labeling the Parts and the Jig

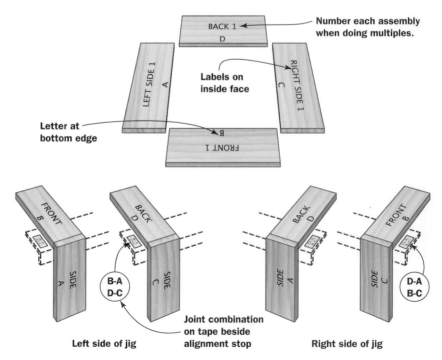

struction is hidden in the assembly. What's hidden during fabrication is exposed in the finished product. Confused now?

Do this. Label the parts on what will be their inside faces. If you can read the labels when the parts are in the jig, you've got the orientation correct. If you are doing drawers, the sides *always* go on the front, and the fronts and backs *always* go on the top.

And you need to label more than part names. Consider that each drawer or box has four joints. When you are doing machine-cut dovetails, two of the four joints must be cut on the left side of the jig and two on the right side. You don't want to get them mixed up.

The most simple organizational labeling system I've come across is shown in the drawing on the opposite page. There are few labels, but where you put them is as important as what they are. The labels indicate which is the inner face, and thus which face is up in the jig. The letters are always associated with a particular part. Each letter is placed at the bottom edge of the piece, to indicate which edge goes against the jig's alignment stops. On the jig itself, you mark two two-letter combinations beside each pair of alignment stops, as indicated in the drawing. As you clamp the parts into the jig, orient the letters toward the stops, and check the combination. If it isn't on your list of two, you are at the wrong end of the jig.

A more commonplace approach is to label each piece with its part name, to mark the bottom edge, and to number the joints in sequence around the assembly. The trick is remembering which joints get cut on which end of the jig.

Dovetailing a Lipped Drawer

More often than not, the half-blind dovetail jig is used in dovetailing drawers. Being limited to the flush version of this joint is a pretty severe design restriction, though. Very often you want to make lipped drawers, in which the drawer front has a rabbet cut around the inner face.

A few of the standard dovetail jigs have a template adjustment that makes it possible to cut this joint, and their instruction manuals lay out the procedure fairly lucidly.

But you can dovetail lipped drawers with any half-blind dovetail jig. The trick is to cut the fronts separately from the sides. What the template adjustment does, in those jigs that allow you to cut the so-called rabbeted half-blind dovetail, is to shift the template position 3/8 inch away from the operator so the sockets can be extended that 3/8 inch. (This assumes, of course, that the rabbet around the drawer front will be 3/8 inch wide.) What you do is set up the jig, clamp the boards in place, and cut the pins and tails. Then you shift the template and make a second pass, extending the sockets.

You can accomplish the same thing by positioning the drawer front forward of its usual position, then routing the sockets in one pass. And you can accommodate most any width of rabbet. Here's how.

Rough out the drawer parts, and rabbet the fronts. At the same time, cut some scraps of the drawer-front stock to use to back up the sides when routing the tails in them. And cut one scrap of the drawer-side stock to use in positioning the fronts in the jig. This scrap needs a rabbet across one end. The depth of the rabbet must be the same as the width of

To rout dovetails into a rabbeted piece, like a lipped drawer front (top), you do the sockets separately from the tails. In the front of the dovetail jig (in place of the side), clamp a rabbeted scrap. Slide the drawer front under the top clamp bar and butt it against the rabbet. Remove the scrap, set the template in place, and rout the sockets.

Problem Solver

Machine-dovetailing a drawer whose side is less wide (high) than its front need not stump you. It takes an extra setup step, but it can be done quite easily.

What you want to avoid is routing one socket too many in the drawer front. You know how it is. Routing along the fingers of the dovetail template tends to sap your attention. The router base is covering a lot of the work, and you can see there's still some uncut wood, so you kind of lose track. Then, OUCH! You've cut sockets right up to the end of the front. Just one too many!

You need to clamp a stop to arrest the router at the last template slot you intend to rout. You finish that slot and the router can't move any farther.

Setup for Cutting Rabbeted Dovetails

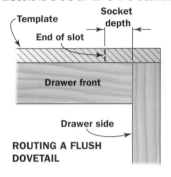

ROUTING A FLUSH DOVETAIL

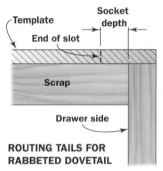

ROUTING TAILS FOR RABBETED DOVETAIL

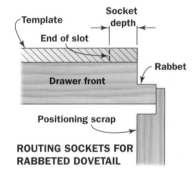

ROUTING SOCKETS FOR RABBETED DOVETAIL

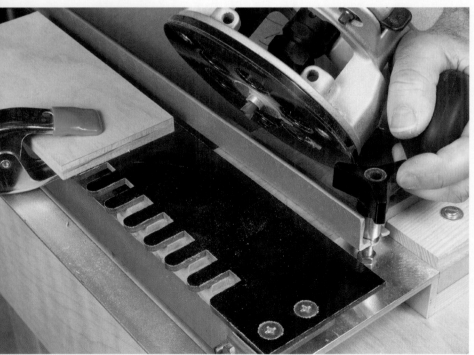

You can confidently dovetail a drawer with sides that are lower than the front (top) if you clamp a stop to the dovetail template. In a dry run, set the router on the jig with the template guide engaged with the last slot you want to cut. Lay a scrap on the template, against the router base, and secure it with a spring clamp. Now you are ready to rout.

The setup logic for routing rabbeted half-blind dovetails is evident here. When the jig is set up for routing a flush joint (top), the template overlays the front and side more or less equally. The socket depth therefore will match the tail thickness.

When you rout tails for a rabbeted joint (middle), the work is clamped in the jig as if you're routing a flush joint—but a scrap is clamped in the top position to back up the cut.

To reach beyond the rabbet and get a socket deep enough to accommodate the tail (bottom), the front must be shifted forward in the jig. The amount you shift it equals the width of the rabbet. A scrap rabbeted appropriately is clamped in place of the side to position the front.

the drawer-front rabbet. For example, if your drawer-front rabbet is the standard 3/8-inch width, then the depth of the rabbet is 3/8 inch. And if the drawer-front rabbet is wider than the drawer-side stock is thick, you need to substitute a thicker scrap so that you can cut a rabbet to the necessary depth and still have a tab left against which to butt the drawer front (as you'll see in a second).

Finally, you need a spacer to off-set the drawer front from the alignment stop so the first socket is a half-pin from the shoulder of the rabbet. To determine how thick the spacer must be, subtract the width of the drawer-front rabbet from 7/8 inch, which is the center-to-center spacing of 1/2-inch dovetails. That 3/8-inch rabbet calls for a 1/2-inch spacer.

Rout the sockets in the drawer fronts first. Clamp the positioning scrap in the jig in place of a drawer side. Set the spacer against the alignment stop, then set the drawer front in the jig, as shown in the drawing. Butt the end against the tab of the positioning scrap, and the bottom edge against the spacer. Clamp the front, then rout the sockets.

Naturally, you have to switch to the other end of the jig to rout the sockets in the other end of the drawer front.

After you've routed the sockets, fit the drawer sides in place, one by one, and rout the tails. To help you position each side, and to prevent tearout, clamp one of those scraps of drawer-front stock in place of the drawer front.

Routing Through Dovetails

A big step up the sophistication ladder you'll find a variety of jigs and templates for routing through dovetails. I have used many of them, but not all. I'm not going to tell you how to use individual jigs. Too many jigs, too many quirks.

You've got some (Leigh and Omnijig and Akeda) that resemble commonplace half-blind jigs. Others are clearly simple templates and need to be clamped to the piece being routed (Keller and Katy). Precision positioning devices (Incra and Jointech) are elaborate fences for the router table. And at least one (WoodRat) is a kind of inverted router table with a hand-cranked power feeder.

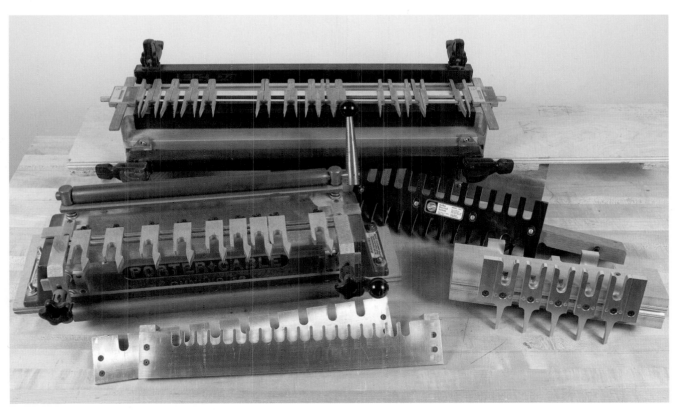

A variety of jigs and devices for routing through dovetails are on the market. This is just a sampling. Some produce only through dovetails. More elaborate jigs can do half-blinds as well as through, and a few related joints besides.

Bit Drawer

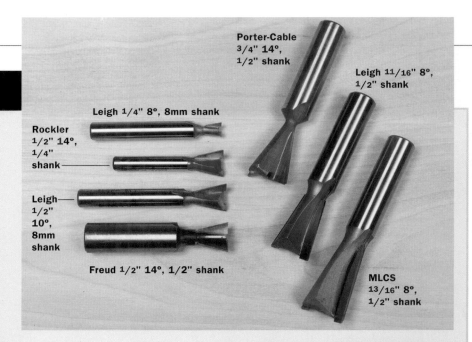

Porter-Cable
3/4" 14°,
1/2" shank

Leigh 11/16" 8°,
1/2" shank

Leigh 1/4" 8°, 8mm shank

Rockler
1/2" 14°,
1/4"
shank

Leigh
1/2"
10°,
8mm
shank

Freud 1/2" 14°, 1/2" shank

MLCS
13/16" 8°,
1/2" shank

The basic dovetail bit, the one that's in the sets of basic bits, the one that's used with the basic dovetail jigs, is the 14°, 1/2-inch-diameter, 1/2-inch-cutting-length variety.

Now, the traditional cabinet-maker's wisdom is that the optimum slope for a dovetail in softwoods is 1 in 6, and in hardwoods 1 in 8. (The difference in slope stems from the fact that softwood cells compress more easily, and so require a steeper slope.) Let's convert those traditional slope ratios to the bit maker's angles: 1 in 8 is 7°, and 1 in 6 is 9°. The standard 14° bit works out to a 1-in-4 slope. Pretty steep.

The 14° angle is one of the reasons machine-cut dovetails look different than hand-cut ones. If you have a fixed-template dovetail jig, it's likely to *require* the use of a 14° bit. (An 8° dovetail bit used with the jig, even one of the same cutting diameter and used with the same guide bushing, won't cut dovetails that'll assemble.)

By the traditional wisdom, the 14° bit should produce an unsatisfactory dovetail. Too steep a slope is supposed to yield a dovetail with weak short grain at the corners. That doesn't appear to be a problem in practice. In the context of adjusting a router bit, the 14° dovetail isn't as demanding to fit. A 7° dovetail that's a 32nd off will be a lot poorer fit than a 14° dovetail that's off the same fraction.

As it works out, you can buy bits with 7° tapers, as well as with 7 1/2°, 8°, and 9° tapers. The reason these are available, it seems, is because of the through dovetail jigs. To give their dovetails more of

a hand-cut look, the jigs' designers had bits custom-made in the 7° to 9° tapers they wanted. Most bit manufacturers include 7° to 9° dovetail bits in their catalogs.

A benefit of the more gentle taper is that it allows a deeper cut. Check out the comparative bit dimensions in the drawing. A 1/2-inch-diameter bit with a 14° taper can cut only 1/2 inch deep because, at that point, the bit has tapered to a 1/4-inch diameter. The girth at the same spot on an 8° bit is about 11/32 inch. If the bit can safely taper down to a 1/4-inch diameter, then the 8° bit can cut 13/16 inch deep. This is enough to make a through dovetail in dressed 4/4 stock.

Regardless of what's available, using a commercial dovetail jig

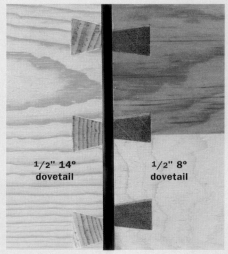

1/2" 14°
dovetail

1/2" 8°
dovetail

means you need whatever size and taper dovetail bit the jig is designed around. If, however, you are using your router to reduce the work in hand-cutting dovetails, you can use a variety of bit sizes and angles to your design advantage.

Comparing Dovetail Bit Cuts

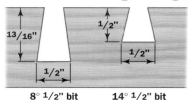

13/16"   1/2"
          1/2"
     1/2"
8° 1/2" bit   14° 1/2" bit

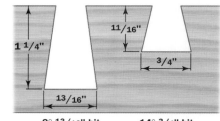

1 1/4"   11/16"
          3/4"
     13/16"
8° 13/16" bit   14° 3/4" bit

A through dovetail joint (top) is visible on both adjoining faces. Historically, it is the joint of choice for case assembly. In drawers, it is used to join backs and sides. The half-blind, in contrast, is visible on only one face. Its most common use is to join drawer fronts to sides.

Dive in, if you dare. But here's an alternative approach that doesn't require an investment of several hundred dollars.

Hand-Cut Router Dovetails

Now and again, you'll hear of a woodworker who starts dovetails with the router, then finishes them by hand. Most of the projects they do are one-off, special, even oddball ones that don't lend themselves well to mass-production-type jigs. They'll start by cutting either the pins or the tails with the router. Sometimes

A box-joint type of jig can aid you in cutting tails, preparatory to hand-cutting the pins. If you use the key with it, you can evenly space the tails. But you can also lay out oddly spaced or sized tails and use the jig only to hold and guide the workpiece while you eyeball the positions of the cuts.

After the tails are cut, use the tail board to lay out the pins. Clamp the tail board at the edge of the bench, and position and clamp the pin board, as shown. Scribe along the edges of the tails with a knife to lay out all the pins. Mark each piece with the joint number so you don't get them mixed up.

Depending on the spacing of pins and tails, you can use a router to rough out the gaps between pins. Here, the pin board is secured in a shop-made holder so the router has more support. Rout close to the knife lines, as close as you can. Then pare the pins to fit.

they'll use a simple T-square type of guide, other times a box-joint jig (see "Box Joints" on page 337). They've even been known to work freehand. With one element of a joint cut, they'll trace those onto the mating piece and cut it to fit with saw and chisel, the old-fashioned way. For a single, oddball job, that's usually quicker than setting up a jig.

The moment of truth comes when you try assembling the joint for the first time. You should get to this point a lot quicker, thanks to the router. Yet the handwork you've done should enhance the appearance of the joint, and make the achievement of a good fit more satisfying to you.

See Also...

Page 337 for jigs for cutting dovetail and box joints on the router table.

Sliding Dovetail Joint

The sliding dovetail joint is a hybrid of the dado and the dovetail joints. One mating piece has a groove, and the other has a tongue; the tongue fits in the groove. Because both the groove walls and the tongue sides are angled like the dovetail, the joint has to be assembled by sliding the tongue into the groove.

The joint's advantage is its mechanical strength. Even without glue, the mating pieces stay linked together. Only if the wood breaks or crushes will the two pieces separate. As a consequence, assembly routines are simplified. The parts won't collapse while you're fumbling with clamps or fasteners. Slightly bowed panels can sometimes be pulled into line without elaborate clamping configurations. Two hands are usually sufficient.

Another advantage of the joint is that it allows the parts to move without separating. A breadboard end is a good example: You apply a narrow strip of wood across the end of a glued-up panel to conceal its end grain and to keep it flat. The joint allows the tabletop to expand and shrink across its width, even though the end strip isn't elongating and shrinking.

To take the thread a little further, this characteristic makes the sliding dovetail excellent where movement is needed—drawer slides, extension-table slides, and the like. It's used in a number of our router jigs.

Cutting the Joint

Cutting a dovetail groove in the face of the work is usually done with a handheld router, while grooving an edge is easiest to do on a router table. Tails are almost always easiest to cut on a router table, most difficult with a handheld router.

The inward-slanting walls of the dovetail groove prevent the tail from pulling straight out. This is the primary benefit of this joinery. To assemble the joint, you slide the tail into the groove from the end.

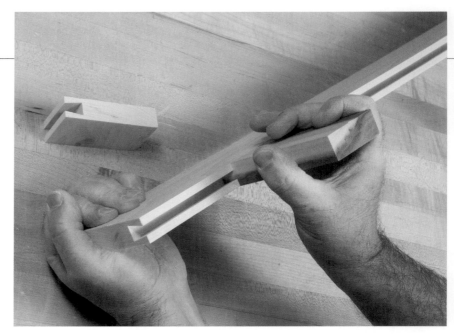

You can cut the slots for case joinery with a handheld router, then do the tails on the router table. For the breadboard end on a chest lid, you probably should do both the slot and the tail on the router table.

The joint's disadvantage is that fitting the two pieces is a trial-and-error process. Ideally, you want the fit tight, but not so tight that friction stalls the tail as it slides into the slot. On the other hand, you don't want the fit to be too sloppy—however easy that makes the joint to assemble.

The usual fitting technique is to plow the groove, then creep up on a tail dimension that fits that slot. If the actual groove is more than 3 inches long, you ought to make a short "fitting" sample of it. You can slide this across the full-length tail to determine whether you have wide spots that will make assembly of the joint difficult. Similarly, you should make a short "fitting" sample of the tail, which you slide through the groove.

To get the groove as right as possible, try making two passes through it, making a special effort to keep the work against the fence on both passes. If you do get a bump on the first pass, you may trim off the high spot on the second. The same is true of the tail.

Assembling a long tail in a long groove is risky. Too tight, and the parts may seize halfway home. To check the joint before final assembly, cut "fitting" samples of both the groove and the tail with the final setup. Use the appropriate sample to check the mating part.

Problem Solver

We all know that the router is a trimmer, that the full depth of every cut has to be achieved by making a series of trimming passes. Well, try cutting a sliding dovetail slot in three passes! Doesn't work, does it?

As a practical matter, most sliding dovetails aren't all that deep. Just 1/4 inch or so. But what about those 3/8-inch-deep cuts? Those 1/2-inch-deep cuts? Especially in dense hardwoods. In situations where you're limited to a 1/4-inch-shank bit. What then?

Make a pass or two with a straight bit. This will clean out the bulk of the material, leaving only the walls of the cut to be formed by the dovetail bit. Use a straight whose diameter matches (or is slightly smaller than) that of the dovetail bit's waist, which is usually about three-quarters of the bit's stated diameter. Set the bit to cut just shy of the groove's bottom, so that when you do make the dovetail cut, you'll get a good bottom finish.

Don't get lazy. Plowing a 5/8-inch-deep groove in a 23-inch-long breadboard end—without first wasting the channel with a straight bit—overtaxed this dovetail bit. The cutter twisted off the shank. No physical danger involved, but the bit is now scrap and the job remained uncompleted until I could get a new bit.

Routing Dovetail Grooves

The basic grooving operation is a lot like cutting dadoes. Clamp a straight-edge to the work to guide the router, and make the cut. Depending on your setup, the straightedge can guide the router base, a template guide, or a pattern bit's bearing.

If the cut is more than 3/16 inch deep, it's a good idea to rough out the groove with a straight bit no larger than the waist of the dovetail bit. Switching bits again and again can be aggravating, but having two routers with the same-diameter base allows you to set a straightedge and use it to guide the roughing cut with one router and the dovetail cut with the other. If the base sizes are different, using template guides or pattern bits to reference the straightedge will accomplish the same thing.

Stopped Grooves

Consider this common situation. You are making a chest of drawers, and your plans call for stopped slid-ing dovetails to join the drawer dividers to the chest sides. This presents a feed-direction problem. Because of the dovetail profile, you want to make all the cuts—in both chest sides—by feeding in from the edge. But that's the correct feed on only one of the two chest sides. On the other chest side, the correct feed is from the endpoint of the groove out to the edge.

Remember that when you feed in the correct direction, the spinning bit's rotational forces help keep the tool against the guide. When you feed in the wrong direction—when you make a climb cut, in other

Routing a through dovetail groove is as straightforward as routing a dado. Clamp a straightedge to the workpiece, and guide the router along it, cutting from one edge of the work through to the opposite edge.

words—those forces want to pull the tool *away* from the guide. There's a risk of the bit grabbing somewhere along the cut and pulling the router off the fence. That would ruin the cut.

You *can* just rout, maintaining enough force to keep the tool against the fence. You may even have success with it. But the risk is that you'll relax your guard, and *that's* when the bit will grab.

I prefer to make stopped cuts with the router trapped, either between a pair of fences or with a template. If the router's trapped, it can't wander, regardless of the feed direction. With either guide system, I can plow into the cut, then back out, with the router running all the while.

You can make a twin-fence guide in 15 minutes to a half-hour. All you need is four strips of plywood or MDF (medium-density fiberboard) and a few drywall screws. Attach a

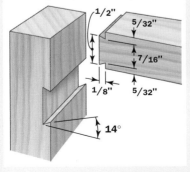

Twin-Fence Guide
For routing both through and stopped sliding dovetails

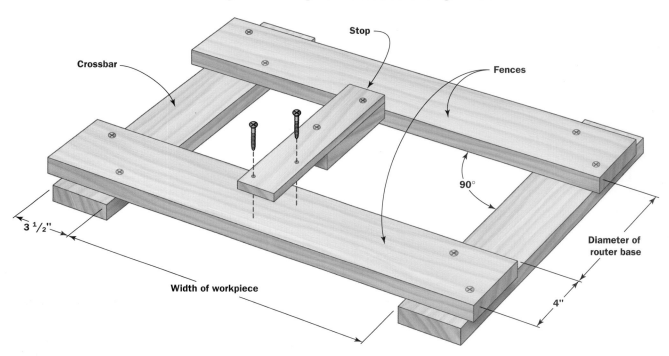

Crossbar · Stop · Fences · 90° · Diameter of router base · 4" · 3 ¹/₂" · Width of workpiece

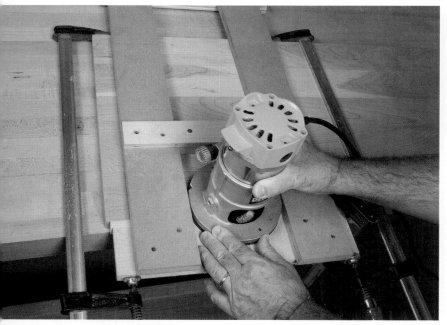

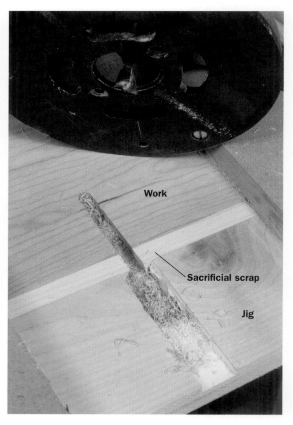

Work · Sacrificial scrap · Jig

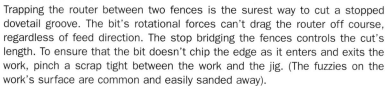

Trapping the router between two fences is the surest way to cut a stopped dovetail groove. The bit's rotational forces can't drag the router off course, regardless of feed direction. The stop bridging the fences controls the cut's length. To ensure that the bit doesn't chip the edge as it enters and exits the work, pinch a scrap tight between the work and the jig. (The fuzzies on the work's surface are common and easily sanded away).

Use a template to produce uniform stopped cuts. To ensure that the template guide is captured in the guide slot while the bit is still clear of the work, scale the template with some overhang. Clamp a scrap strip to the front edge of the work to prevent chipping.

stop to one or both fences to limit the length of the cut. The cut will be centered between the fences, of course, and you'll cut the crossbar on the very first use. That cut can be used to align the guide on your layout marks.

A template can be made from a piece of 1/4-inch hardboard or plywood. Simply rout a slot in from one edge. Make the slot the width of the template guide you'll use. Extend it no longer than necessary to get the length of slot you want.

An advantage of the template is that you can use any two routers, since the template guide is the registration device, not the router base.

Edge Grooves

Making an edge groove on the router table makes the most sense, as far as I'm concerned. First, you plow a groove with a straight bit. Then you finish the groove with a dovetail bit. The work is guided along the fence for both cuts.

The setup is probably obvious. The fence is positioned to roughly center the cut on the edge; the position is, of course, the same for both cuts.

It's good procedure to reduce the size of the bit opening in the tabletop as much as possible. If your router mounting doesn't have reducers for the opening, use thin hardboard as an auxiliary top. Bore a zero-clearance hole by raising the spinning bit through it.

You surely want the groove centered on the edge. To center it, you simply make a pass in each direction. That is, cut the groove, then turn the piece around and make a second pass. The shoulders will be the same width, and the cut will be centered.

Be sure, on the second pass, that you are cutting on the side of the groove closest to you, not the side closest to the fence. This is a safety

Try This!

The dovetail shape is a joinery detail that you want to showcase in your furniture. The last thing you want is a chip or three out of the dovetail seam. But those chips are awfully common. Be certain to clamp a scrap strip to the edge of your workpiece whenever you cut a dovetail groove. That way, it's the scrap that yields the chips, not the good wood.

issue. The latter situation represents a climb cut (assuming you feed the work in the standard right-to-left direction). The work *could* be snatched from your hand and fired in the direction you are feeding it. If the work disappears unexpectedly, your fingers *could* go into the bit. (See page 125 for a fuller explanation.)

Naturally, you should do your setup and make at least one test cut to ensure that you're content with the result before cutting the real workpieces. Save the test cut for fitting the tail (or make a separate piece for this purpose).

Using a handheld router to groove an edge is a tricky balancing act. If

Center a dovetail groove across an edge simply by routing it in two passes. But pay attention to the fence position to avoid a feed-direction mishap. The first pass is never a problem. But be sure the bit is cutting the groove wall farthest from the fence on the second pass—as shown here—so the pass can be safely made right to left, as usual.

Try This!

If you have to move the fence to change bits—some router tables are like that—you can "save" its position by setting reference blocks against its front edge at both ends. You'll be able to move the fence, change the bits, then return the fence to the same spot.

you *must* do the cut this way, you obviously must use an edge guide to control where the groove will be on the edge. But the guide hanging off one side makes the router even more difficult to balance on a narrow edge. Try fitting the guide with a wide facing, and keep a hand on the facing, pressing it against the side of the workpiece. Even better, see if you can equip your router with two edge guides to trap the workpiece.

The work is the same: Plow a groove with a straight bit, feeding the router first in one direction, then in the other, so the groove is centered. Switch cutters and repeat the process.

Routing Tails

Tails for sliding dovetails are commonly cut on the router table. There are some alternatives, but on the router table, the work is fast and easy.

It should go without saying (but I'll say it anyway), you use the same bit for the tails and the grooves. That guarantees that the geometry of the mating parts matches.

If you are shifting the router table from cutting grooves to cutting tails, the changeover is elementary. Reset the fence. That's all. Leave the bit height right where it was when you cut the groove.

If you are starting a completely new setup, begin by closing down the bit openings in the tabletop and fence as much as possible. Set the height of the bit above the table to match the depth of the groove.

Bring the fence into position, housing all but the very edge of the bit in the fence. Depending upon the size and proportions of the workpiece, you may want to add a tall facing to the fence. This may be worthwhile to you if you're working something like a tabletop or chest lid, but I've found that a well-placed featherboard (and my regular fence) is all I need for even these big pieces.

The most common approach to actually cutting the tail? Make it fat initially, and in a series of adjustments, work to thin it down just enough to fit the slot. Remember as you adjust the fence after the first cutting that you'll be doubling what-

Cut a tail on a narrow piece by standing it on end and sliding it along the fence. Cut across one face, then spin the piece and cut the second face. The backup block—just a square scrap—helps stabilize the work, reducing its tendency to "walk" along the fence. It also minimizes "blowout," in which the bit splinters the edge as it emerges from the cut.

Conceal the end of a stopped groove by trimming the tail on the mating part. The easiest way to do it is to snick off the end, as shown, at the same time you cut the tail.

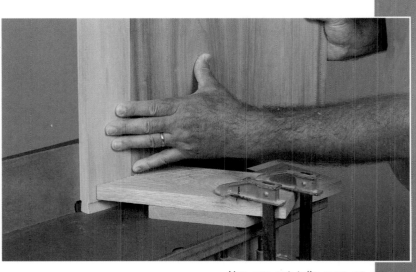

ever amount you move it, because you make two passes to form the tail. And since moving only one end of the fence halves the change at the bit, you should move one end of the fence the amount you want to change the cut. Confusing, huh? Here's an example. If the tail is 1/16 inch too wide, move one end of the fence 1/16

You can cut tails even on large panels on the router table. It *looks* precarious, perhaps, but it isn't. One well-placed featherboard is the secret. The featherboard (top) is aligned just ahead of the bit, and it is elevated with a block underneath so it's pressing above the cut. A tall fence isn't necessary.

Breadboard Ends

The sliding dovetail is ideal for joining a breadboard end to a glued-up panel, like a tabletop or chest lid.

The breadboard end, which is simply a narrow strip of wood, is a traditional method for preventing wide, glued-up panels from cupping. It is attached across the panel's end, concealing the end grain. The breadboard end keeps the panel flat, but because its grain direction is perpendicular to that of the panel, it introduces a new problem. It has to be attached in a way that allows the panel to expand and contract, as wood is wont to do.

The sliding dovetail does this. You plow a dovetail groove in the bread-board's edge, and cut a tail across the end of the panel. Slide the breadboard end onto the tail, and drive a nail or dowel through the assembly, roughly at the center, locking the two pieces together. The breadboard end can't pop off the tail, but the panel can expand and contract.

The truth is, the ends of the breadboard and the edges of the panel will seldom be perfectly flush. When the season is dry, the panel will be less wide than the end is long. When it's humid, the panel edges will be proud of the breadboard's ends.

The tough part is achieving the appropriate fit. Glue can tighten a loose sliding dovetail in a lot of situations, but not this one. If you glue the parts together, you'll defeat the purpose of the joint. Be as precise as you can in the fit, and before assembly, rub some paste wax on the tail.

inch. This changes the cut by 1/32 inch at the bit. Taking 1/32 inch off each side of the tail will reduce its width 1/16 inch.

How you hold and maneuver the work depends on its size. You can stand a relatively narrow workpiece on end, back it up with a square-edged piece of scrap (both for support and to prevent tearout), and slide it along the fence through the cut. Keep your fingers above the cutter. If the piece is headed for a stopped groove, you can cut an edge along with the faces. A larger panel—a chest lid, for example—may require a featherboard or two to jam the work against the fence.

Horizontal Table

As good as the router table is, the horizontal router table is even better. Consider that you can rest the work flat on the table to cut the tails or to slot an edge.

Even better, tails especially can be routed using the accessory sliding tables. You set the workpiece against the fixed fence, snap the toggle clamp to hold it, and slide it through the cut. While this capability won't help much for a chest lid, it will when you are cutting tails on both ends of a half-dozen drawer dividers.

The process doesn't change significantly. The bit-height adjustment has the same effect on either router table. But on the horizontal router table, you adjust the router height rather than adjusting the fence. Again, for safety's sake, the cut should be made between the work and the tabletop so you don't trap the work between the bit and the table.

When you make the cuts, remember to feed left to right on the horizontal table.

Groove an edge on the horizontal router table. The work rests flat on the table, and a featherboard keeps it there. The proper feed direction on this table is left to right, remember. Here a dovetail bit is poised to shape a groove that's been wasted with a straight bit.

The sliding table accessory for the horizontal table holds the workpiece securely for a tail cut. Use stops on the X-axis tracks to keep the tables clear of the bit and to prevent any front-to-back movement. Lay the work against the fixed fence, slide its end against the router mounting board, and secure it with the toggle clamp. The bit engages the underside of the work as you slide the table along the Y axis.

Using a Handheld Router

Routing a tail with a handheld router is as dicey as routing a dovetail groove with the tool. But the consequences of a bobble in mid-cut aren't as disastrous. The cutter is grazing the outer surface of the board, not trapped inside it. If you tip the tool away from the work, you get a bump in the cut, which a second pass removes. Tip the other way, and you get a gouge. It'll be hidden inside the groove. Not a calamity.

But you do have that business of balancing a large, dynamic tool with a sharp, high-speed cutter sticking out of one end on a bitty, narrow edge. To control the cut, you need an edge guide—or two. The smaller the router, the better. The cut isn't heavy and thus doesn't require brute power. I'd use a laminate trimmer.

But I'd only use this approach with a reasonably wide workpiece. A chest lid. A bookshelf. Not a 3-inch-wide drawer divider for a chest of drawers.

Right-Angle Routing Platform

For that drawer divider, the platform shown in the drawing is what I'd use. It provides a way to rout a tail across the end of a board by providing a wide, solid base for the router. It helps you avoid tipping the router as you work.

Obviously, this platform serves you in working relatively narrow stock. Once your workpiece exceeds a foot in width, the platform required becomes awkwardly wide. If you are working with a deep cabinet or a

The right-angle platform makes it possible to balance a portable router on the end of a board, so you can make a precise tail cut. The fixture's vertical fence and toggle clamps hold the workpiece, and the platform provides solid bearing for the router.

Right-Angle Platform

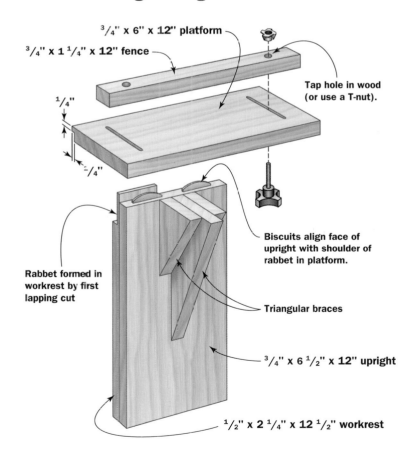

3/4" x 6" x 12" platform

3/4" x 1 1/4" x 12" fence

Tap hole in wood (or use a T-nut).

1/4"

3/4"

Biscuits align face of upright with shoulder of rabbet in platform.

Rabbet formed in workrest by first lapping cut

Triangular braces

3/4" x 6 1/2" x 12" upright

1/2" x 2 1/4" x 12 1/2" workrest

A laminate trimmer has enough power for a tail cut, and it's the right size for balancing on the edge of a panel. Fit it with an edge guide with a wide facing, and you'll be able to cut the tail with a handheld router.

French-Dovetailed Drawers

Dovetails are the traditional joint for drawers, but they're time-consuming to cut.

So how about a French dovetail? It's nothing more than a sliding dovetail, which gives you the mechanical strength of the dovetail without the "overhead" of setting up a jig, clamping and unclamping each part, and so on. You cut all the joinery on the router table.

Look first at the illustration of the drawer. It has sliding dovetails joining the back to the sides, as well as the sides to the front. The bottom passes under the back and rides in grooves in the sides and front. Obviously, you can modify the construction, for example, using dadoes or a dovetail rabbet for the back.

Each slot in the drawer front has to be inset about a half-inch so its shoulder has enough meat to resist splitting out. If you need to provide space for drawer slides, you've got it. Use the same offset in cutting the slots for the back.

Fit a 1/2-inch dovetail bit in the table-mounted router. This bit will work whether the drawer sides are 3/4-inch stock or 1/2-inch stock. It's the most common size of dovetail bit, too, being the size any router bit set includes. Adjust the cut depth to 1/4 inch. Set the fence so the slot's centerline will be 3/4 inch from the end of the drawer front. Test it by slotting some scraps of the working stock.

To cut the slots, butt the workpiece end against the fence, back it up with a pusher scavenged from your scrap bin, and feed the work from right to left, cutting the slot. In this manner, you cut slots in the drawer sides for the back, and in the drawer front for the sides.

You may want to stop the dovetail

The assembled drawer is clean and functional. The sliding dovetail joint is a natural for this application, since its shape mechanically resists the tendency of the front to separate from the sides. And assembly is quick—no fasteners or clamps required.

slots shy of the front's top edge so the joint is concealed, or so the front can extend a bit above the sides. This can be done, but for best, safest results, make and use a sliding fence to guide these stopped cuts. Plans for the fence are on page 111.

The problem is feed direction. You can do the left end of each drawer front feeding right to left, as is proper. To slot a front's right end, though, you either have to set the fence far from the cutter, which makes the feed and cut very dicey, or you have to make a climb cut, feeding from left to right, which is equally dicey.

I've done it the latter way, and it's a white-knuckler. Even though you're anticipating it, the moment when the bit grabs the work and jerks it and tries to help the feed is always startling. Sometimes the work gets trashed.

The sliding fence allows you to make both cuts in the proper feed direction, and without changing the basic setup.

The key is the stop on the fence. You locate it to the right of the bit, because the cutter wants to pull the work that direction, and the stop resists that pull.

Position the stop for the cut on the drawer front's left end. With the front's right end against the stop, you advance the fence and make the cut near the front's left end. To reposition the workpiece for the second cut, you place a spacer between it and the stop. The length of the spacer matches the distance between the two cuts.

To govern the *length* of the cut—to prevent you from the inadvertent through cut—you clamp a stop to the tabletop to arrest the movement of the sliding fence.

Let me be clear that withdrawing the work from the cutter constitutes a climb cut. There is a bit of risk as you pull the fence and workpiece back, so hold the work tight to the fence as you pull it back at the cut's end.

With all the slots cut, including a few in scraps, put the regular fence back on the table and position it to cut the tails. Don't touch the bit setting, of course, just the fence. If you cut stopped slots, you need to trim the tails on the sides with a chisel.

With the sliding dovetails cut, change bits and cut slots for the drawer bottom.

To assemble the drawer, apply a bit of glue to the leading edges of the tails and slide them into their slots. The glue will be spread along the tail and slot as the two slide against one another. Slide the bottom into its grooves, which should act to square the drawer.

French-Dovetailed Drawer

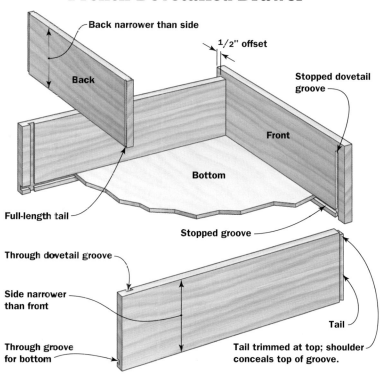

- Back narrower than side
- Back
- 1/2" offset
- Stopped dovetail groove
- Front
- Bottom
- Full-length tail
- Stopped groove
- Through dovetail groove
- Side narrower than front
- Tail
- Through groove for bottom
- Tail trimmed at top; shoulder conceals top of groove.

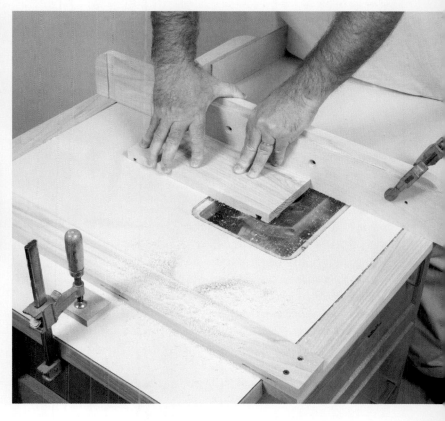

The sliding-fence accessory takes the worry out of making the joinery cuts for French-dovetailed drawers. Cutting both stopped grooves in a drawer front can be done in the proper feed direction. A stop block clamped to the tabletop controls the length of the cut. The fence's stop holds the work in position. One groove is cut with the front directly against the stop (right). The other groove is cut with a spacer between the stop and the front (above). Note the clamping strip bradded to the spacer.

wide tabletop, consider some form of the double edge-guide approach, explained above.

The platform, I should point out, can be used in cutting elements for some other joints, such as tenons and half-laps. It's not a one-use jig.

The dimensions and the construction are shown on page 325. The choice of materials isn't critical, though you do want the parts to be flat and true. I used scraps of Baltic Birch plywood for the body and a hardwood off-cut for the fence. You can use carriage bolts and wing nuts to mount the fence, though I tapped holes in the fence and threaded shop-brewed studded plastic knobs into them. (Cut threaded rod to length and "glue" it into a plastic knob with Loctite.)

What is critical is to have the platform square, the upright perpen-

dicular to the platform, and the edge of the platform parallel to the face of the upright. If these aspects of the fixture are imprecise, your cuts also will be imprecise.

To use the platform, you clamp it in a vise. The workpiece is, of course, tucked against the fence and up against the underside of the platform, then secured with the toggle clamps. Adjust the bit extension and the guide fence position, and rout.

A tail is cut in two passes. Cut across one face, turn the workpiece around, and cut across the second face. Test-fit the resulting dovetail in one of the dovetail grooves. If you need to adjust the size of the tail, loosen the fence and move it. Always keep the fence parallel to the edge, of course. When the fit is right, rout the tails on the workpieces.

The initial pass should be a shallow climb cut to score the shoulder and eliminate chipping. Then work the router back and forth until it is tight against the fence throughout a pass. Unclamp, turn, and reclamp the work. Cut the second face in the same way, completing the tail.

Try This!

A basic trick can make platform-fence adjustments easy as well as precise. Use a reference block.

The reference block is a strip exactly like the fence; it is mounted to the platform behind the fence. You can clamp it to the platform only when you need to use it, or you can use bolts to mount it to the platform, using the same slots as the fence.

To move the fence a specific distance, use shims or spacers between the reference block and the fence. Using things like thin hardboard, plastic laminate, business cards, playing cards, even paper money as spacers allows you to literally micro-adjust the fence. It's essential when you need to skim just a whisker from the tail to achieve the perfect fit. And remember that the distance you move the fence will be doubled in the

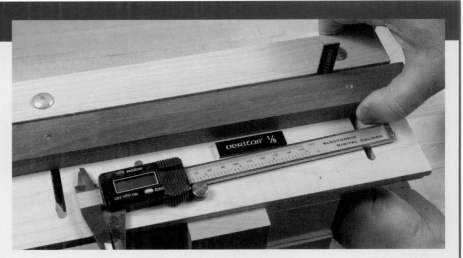

Need to adjust the tail width by a few thousandths? Use shims between the guide fence and a reference block. This low-tech method enables you to adjust the fence in or out in micro-fine increments.

cut, since you are cutting both sides of the tail after an adjustment.

To increase the cut (thus reducing the width of the tail), you must move the fence back. Put the spacer behind the fence, set the reference block against the spacer, and clamp it.

Then loosen the fence, remove the spacer, slide the fence back against the block, and relock the fence.

To reduce the cut (thus producing a wider tail), set the block tight against the fence. Then loosen the fence, insert the spacers, and reset the fence.

Splined Miter Joint

The miter joint represents the best and worst in joinery.

Tightly crafted, it is almost totally hidden: There's a barely discernible seam and *right there,* the figure of the wood changes direction sharply. You don't see any end grain. That's the best of it.

The worst is that the simple miter joint is, structurally, a terrible joint. It's sissy-weak. If you glue it, you're trying to glue end grain to end grain, a hopeless cause. Run some fasteners into it, and you're running them into end grain, where they won't hold very well. Moreover (when things go bad, they go *really* bad), the joint is vexing to assemble. Because of the angles involved, a mitered corner always wants to slide out of line when you apply clamping pressure to it.

The solution to all the problems, a solution that doesn't affect the pure, pristine appearance of the miter in any way, is a spline.

A spline is a separate piece of wood, often plywood, that reinforces a joint. Usually, the spline is set into slots in the mating surfaces in such a way that the grain of the spline will run across

the main joint to resist splitting along that joint. This placement just happens to be ideal for holding the pieces in place for gluing, too.

The question is how to cut the slots in the right places. There are several answers, and all involve the router as the cutting tool. The main reason that there are several answers, which are spread out on these pages, is that there's fair variety to the miter. How many can you list? Here are three main groups:

- Flat miters, in which the angled cuts run across the faces of the pieces

- Edge miters, in which the pieces to be joined are actually beveled rather than mitered

- Compound miters, in which the pieces are cut with combination miter and bevel cuts.

Each kind of miter joint requires a slightly different approach to cutting the grooves for the splines—a different router table fence, perhaps, or a different router fixture. Within each group, it's possible to isolate variations that require a change of approach.

Flat Miters

Routing slots for splines in a flat miter joint (sometimes called a frame miter joint) can be done with a straight bit or a slot cutter. You want to use common sense in matching the router and bit and setup to the particulars of the job. Assuming the workpieces aren't totally unwieldy, I think these slots are cut most easily and safely on the router table.

To begin, cut the miters as accurately as possible, of course. Mark a reference face on each piece, too. By *always* orienting the reference face the same way as you cut, you can ensure that the joints will line up properly at assembly time.

As a handheld operation, cutting spline grooves—especially stopped ones—in flat miters is problematic. The work doesn't provide a lot of bearing for the router. With a slot cutter, you should be able to do through cuts because the router rests on the face of the work, while the cutter slots its end.

Stopped grooves are another matter. When you make a stopped groove with a slot cutter, it has a somewhat

For cutting through grooves in the ends of relatively narrow stock, a small, easy-to-maneuver router, like this offset-base laminate trimmer, is ideal. When it's fitted with a slotting cutter, you can plow from edge-to-edge.

oval section—a lot like a biscuit-joiner cut. This is okay if you are using biscuits (see "Biscuit Joinery with a Router" on page 268), but if you are making splines from wood or plywood scraps, shaping the splines to fit the grooves creates extra work.

To make a stopped groove with a straight bit, you'd need a plunge router. But moving that tool over the area to be worked is nigh unto impossible.

Safety First!

A throat opening that's substantially larger than the bit can be a hazard when feeding the narrow end of a board across the router table. The leading and trailing points can dip into the throat and hang up, startling you, trashing your work, and maybe even leading to an injury.

If you don't have reducers for the bit opening, you can lay an auxiliary top on your router table, as detailed in the chapter "Router Table Savvy," page 119.

After all, a mitered surface may be small enough to fit into the bit opening in the router base. Yes, you *can* add an auxiliary baseplate to the router to close down the opening, then fit the machine with two edge guides to trap the workpiece. But that's transforming an operation that's fundamentally easy into one that's difficult.

Save yourself some time. Avoid the exasperation. Do it on the router table instead.

Through groove. If you don't mind having the spline be a visible part of the joint, cut through slots. This is a "zzzppp zzzppp" operation. (Because, as a friend of mine says, you just take the router and, zzzppp zzzppp, the job's done.)

The easiest approach on the router table is to cut a through groove with a slot cutter. Raising and lowering the cutter locates the cut on the workpiece, while fence adjustments control the depth of the slot. The router table offers good support for the work. Use a triangular pusher, as shown in the photo, to guide the work along the fence and to back up the cut.

The advantage to the slot cutter is that you can cut a 1/2-inch-deep groove in one pass, while the use of a straight bit would dictate making three or more passes to complete a similar cut.

To make the grooves with a straight bit, you have more setup work. Close down the baseplate's throat as much as possible, and use a tall fence. You'll be standing your work on end and sliding it over the bit, so you must be sure that the work surface is as free of snags as possible, and that the work is well supported as it slides over the bit.

Set the bit elevation, and position the fence. Holding the marked face of the workpiece against the fence, feed it from right to left, cutting through the piece from edge to edge. Here again, the use of a triangular pusher is advisable.

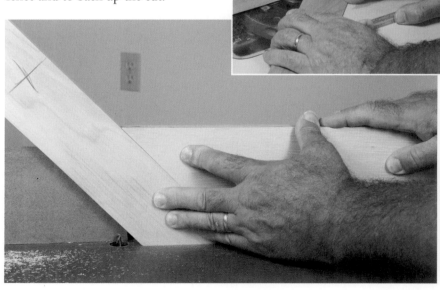

On the router table, either a slot cutter (inset) or a straight bit will cut through slots in flat miters. The difference between the cutters is in the orientation of the work. Use a pusher made from scrap, mitered so that it fits tightly against the trailing edge.

Stopped groove. For a stopped groove, use a straight bit and the same basic setup that you'd use to cut a through groove with it. What you need to add are a couple of erasable markings on the router table (or on

masking tape applied to the router table) indicating the diameter of the bit. (Set a square against the fence and slide its blade against the bit; scribe along the blade on the tabletop. Move the square to the other side of the bit

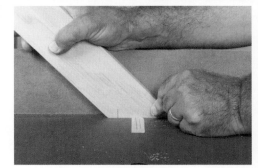

Try This!

It's possible to accurately slot work for splines without laying out each slot on each piece. You can save a bit of layout time, especially if there's a need to slot a lot of pieces.

Because the alignment of the slot will undoubtedly be different in one end of each piece than in the other, you actually have to do two setups. Do the setup for the left end, then cut all the slots in the left ends of the workpieces. Then redo the setup for the right end, and cut all those slots.

To set up your router table, lay out the slots on both ends of a test workpiece. Cut the two slots. Now, with the router switched off, slip

one end of the slotted piece over the bit and, on the tabletop, mark the position of the workpiece's leading edge at the start of the cut. Move the piece to the end-of-cut position, and mark where the trailing edge is.

To cut duplicate slots in that end of the other pieces, you now need only align the leading edge with the starting mark on the tabletop. Plunge the work onto the bit, and feed it right to left. Stop the cut when the trailing end of the work aligns with the appropriate mark.

After all the lefts are cut, redo the setup in the same way for the rights. Then cut all of them.

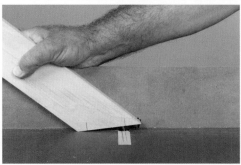

Rout Spline Slots
No layout required

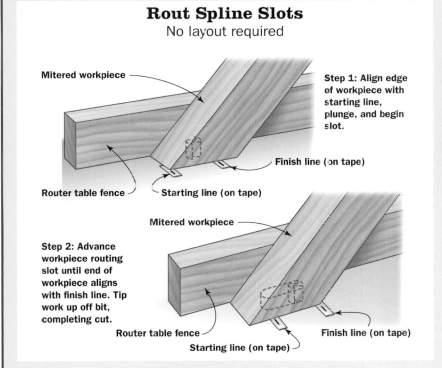

Mitered workpiece

Step 1: Align edge of workpiece with starting line, plunge, and begin slot.

Finish line (on tape)

Router table fence

Starting line (on tape)

Mitered workpiece

Step 2: Advance workpiece routing slot until end of workpiece aligns with finish line. Tip work up off bit, completing cut.

Router table fence

Finish line (on tape)

Starting line (on tape)

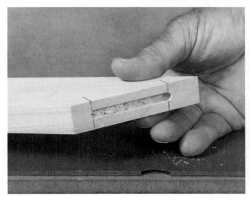

The sequence for cutting a stopped slot in a flat miter is straightforward. With the workpiece tipped up so it clears the bit (top), align the mark on the work with the appropriate mark by the bit. Lower the work onto the bit and advance it right to left (second from top). As the end-of-cut mark comes into alignment with the mark by the bit, tip the work up off the bit (third from top). The cut is clean and straight, with its ends rounded on the same radius as the bit (bottom).

Splined Miter Joint   **331**

and repeat.) On the face of the workpiece that will be visible as you rout, mark the ends of the desired slot.

When you cut the slot, always move the work from right to left. And always keep the reference face against the fence. Brace it against the fence and slide it to the bit. Tip the leading edge up and over the bit, aligning the starting mark on the workpiece with the left bit mark on the table. When the marks line up, plunge the work onto the bit and feed the work to the left. When the end mark on the workpiece aligns with the right bit mark on the table, tip the trailing edge up off the bit, thus ending the cut.

Quick and simple.

Each piece can be cut in the same way, regardless of angle of the miter, regardless of whether it leans to the right or to the left. Just mark the ends of each slot.

Edge Miters

Edge miters, a.k.a. case miters, lend themselves to a greater range of applications than do flat miters. You might find them in casework as well as framework. The scale of casework—the size of the individual parts—makes it worthwhile to find some practical ways of cutting spline slots with a handheld router. Muscling a cabinet side along an angled router table fence may not be as easy as sliding a lightweight router and jig along the cabinet side. So, here are several options, beginning with the router table.

Router Table Fence

To cut spline slots in edge miters on the router table, you need a fence that's canted at the same angle as the edge miter. This allows you to keep the reference face of the workpiece flat against the fence and have the cut surface flat on the router table.

There are two directions, of course, in which the fence can be angled. In one direction, the fence forms an acute angle with the tabletop. In the other, it forms an obtuse angle. The acute angle fence is great, simply because it traps the work, ensuring that the groove will be where you want it. I see possibilities in both, largely because I can envision workpieces that would be difficult to maneuver along almost any acutely angled fence. Let's take a look.

The acute-angle fence: Make a fence canted to 45° from a straight, flat 2×4, and you'll have the fence you'll use 90 percent of the time. Tilt your table saw to 45° and, with the broad face flat on the saw table, rip one edge off the 2×4. (Obviously, if you are splining edge miters of some angle other than 45°—the sides of a hexagonal or octagonal case, for example—your fence needs to be beveled at that angle.) On the band saw, cut the ends to form clamping ears on the ends of the fence, as shown in *Acute-Angle Fence*. Set up and clamp this fence as you would a conventional one.

Cutting through slots with this setup is as simple as trapping the

Use the workpiece—or a beveled scrap of the working stock—to set the acute-angle fence. Adjust the bit to the desired height first. With one end of the fence clamped and the setup scrap trapped behind the bit, you can sight along the tabletop and fence and see exactly where the bit is going to cut.

Acute-Angle Fence
Cut spline grooves in edge miters

3 1/2"
3/4"
3/4"
45°
Width of router table
Shape "clamping ears" on band saw.

Use the same setup scrap to mark the bit size on tape applied to the tabletop. You can butt the wood against the cutting edge without damaging it, then scribe along the edge of the scrap on the tape.

To make the cut, push one end of the work into the V formed by the fence and tabletop, and hold the work firmly against the fence. Line up the marks and tip the work onto the bit. Feed the work to the end of the cut, and tip it off the bit. The key is keeping the work up against the fence.

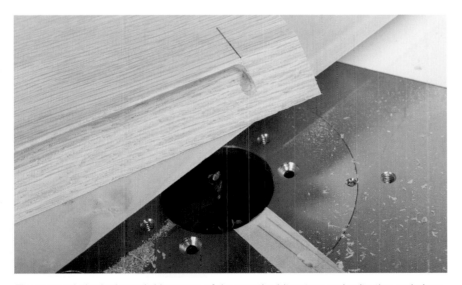

The stopped slot looks weird because of the way the bit enters and exits the workpiece. As long as the bit doesn't penetrate the work completely, you're okay—the joint will be secure.

work in the crotch formed by the fence and the tabletop, then feeding it into the bit. As with the flat miters, an expendable pusher can help prevent tearout that often comes when the bit exits the work, so long as it fits tightly against the edge of the work.

To cut stopped slots, mimic the flat miter slotting operation. That is, mark parallel tangents to the bit on the tabletop. Mark the ends of the desired slot on the work. Hold the work against the fence, tip the leading edge over the bit, align the mark on the work with the appropriate mark on the tabletop, and plunge the work onto the bit. Feed the work from right to left, cutting the slot. When the cut is done, tip the work up off the bit. The routine is easier to do than to describe.

The obtuse-angle fence: Once in a while you have a workpiece that's a little too unwieldy for the acute-angle fence. That fence traps the bevel well enough, but you have to support the stock as well as feed along the fence. Here's one that helps you with your burden.

What's more, it can be used with a straight bit or with a slot cutter.

Make it from 3/4-inch plywood. The drawing gives the dimensions of the fence shown in the photos, but you can modify them to suit your router table and the job you have to do.

Cut the fence to size and rip a bevel along one edge. The bevel, naturally, matches that of the work you are going to spline; a 22$\frac{1}{2}$° angle is shown. That angle is half of a 45, so the braces are easily made by cutting on a diagonal any rectangular piece that's twice as long as it is wide. The base has to be long enough that it can be clamped—at the back or side of the tabletop.

Splined Miter Joint **333**

The obtuse-angle fence will support the workpiece for you, but you've got to clamp a trap fence opposite it (and parallel to it) to prevent the work from skidding down the fence, across the tabletop, and onto the floor.

Assemble the pieces with drywall screws.

To use this fence with a straight bit, position it so the slot will be where you want it in the edge of the workpiece. Clamp it to the table. To keep the work in place, use a trap fence, as shown. Lean the workpiece on the fence and let it go. The trap fence will keep it from skidding across the tabletop and onto the floor. All you have to do is slide the piece across the fence. A stopped slot is created through the typical tip-rout-and-tip sequence.

To use it with a slot cutter, you pair it with the regular fence. The workpiece is laid on the angled fence, back up, with the bevel against the regular fence. To set up, you adjust the height of the cutter to locate the slot where you want it in the bevel. Move the regular fence around the cutter so you get the desired depth-of-slot. Then position and clamp the angled fence, as shown.

Obtuse-Angle Fence
Supports the stock as it guides the cut

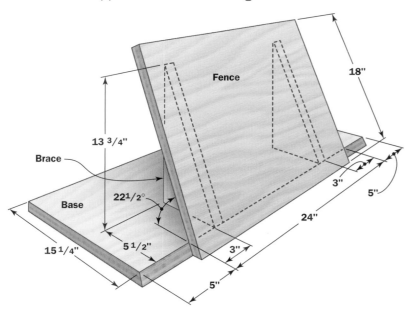

If you have a small router, you might try grooving casework miters for splines with a modified slotting cutter. There are two tricks involved in this approach, and the cutter modification is one of them. The other is how you clamp the work.

To prepare the cutter, switch the positions of the cutter and the pilot bearing. You simply have to remove the arbor nut, switch the cutter and bearing, and then reinstall the nut. (You can't do this on *all* slot cutters.)

To prepare the stock, you lay two pieces together, face to face, and line up the miters as shown. Clamp them securely. The router rides on one mitered surface while the cutter grooves the other. Your bearing surface will be a tad wider than 3/4 inch, and the piloted bit will give the tool bearing on a second edge. A lightweight router enhances your control.

As you can see, by switching the bearing and cutter, the pilot has sure contact with the miter edge, while the cutting edge is in the meaty part of the miter.

Edge-Miter Slotting Fixture

Though simple, this fixture for slotting an edge miter is quite versatile. To work large pieces like the side of a cabinet, attach it to the router as an auxiliary base, and run the unit over the clamped-down work. With smaller work, you can clamp the router and fixture to a bench to make it convenient to pass the stock through it. You can even make a custom version to clamp to a router table.

The fixture consists of a plywood base and two fences, canted to 45°. The model shown was made from scraps of 3/4-inch MDF (medium-density fiberboard). (The thickness of the base does limit the depth-of-cut somewhat, but you're not going much deeper than 3/8 inch in edge-mitered 3/4-inch stock.) If you foresee a need to clamp down the fixture to feed work through it, or if you want a router-table version,

adjust the dimensions of the base accordingly.

Construction is simple.

1. Glue and screw the main fence and its braces to the base.

2. Position the catch fence to fit the thickness of the mitered stock that you want to spline. Attach this fence to the base with screws only, so you can reposition it to accommodate stock of a different thickness.

3. Bore a 1-inch hole where the cutter will pass through the base. You'll be cutting a groove in a captured piece of stock, and you need lots of space for the chips to escape if you don't want them to jam up in the cut.

4. Mount the router to the base. With the bit you'll be using to cut the spline slots in the collet, set the router on the fixture. Adjust its position, setting the bit well into the stock area. Be sure the cutter doesn't come too

close to the catch fence; you don't want to weaken the stock you are splining. With the position set, scribe around the router base and, if possible, tick-mark both the baseplate and the fixture.

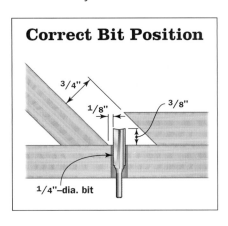

Downsize the jig to mount directly to router base

Edge-Miter Slotting Jig

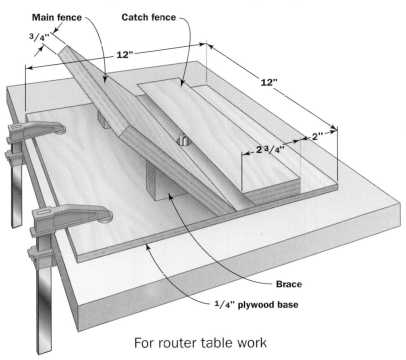

Main fence
Catch fence
3/4"
12"
12"
2"
2 3/4"
Brace
1/4" plywood base

For router table work

Correct Bit Position

3/4"
1/8"
3/8"
1/4"–dia. bit

The edge-miter slotting jig allows you to use a standard straight bit in a table-mounted router to slot beveled edges. The jig has two fences that trap the work. You just slip the workpiece, beveled edge down, into the channel and push it through.

Remove the router from the fixture, and unfasten its baseplate. Return the baseplate to the fixture, aligning the tick marks. Now mark the locations of the mounting-screw holes. With a long bit, drill the holes, penetrating the fences as well as the base. Turn the fixture over and drill counterbores so you can get the mounting screws into the holes to mount the fixture on the router.

5. Screw the fixture to the router. Catch the edge of the clamped-down stock in the chute formed by the two fences. The main fence should be beneath the work. Switch on the router and feed it over the stock from left to right. The rotation of the cutter will tend to push the stock against the catch fence and keep it accurately placed. If you must feed the opposite way, you'll need to exert plenty of pressure to be sure that the cutter doesn't push away from the stock. If that happens, the groove will be shallow and be in the wrong place.

For this operation, you may want to use an upshear or spiral bit, which will tend to eject the chips. Depending on the job, you'll want a 1/8- to 1/4-inch cutter.

It is possible to plunge, stop, and exit with this jig by simply attaching it to a plunge router.

Box Joints

The box joint is a sort of square-cut through dovetail. It's used in the same situations as the dovetail—assembling boxes, and drawers, and casework. It has pretty fair mechanical strength, but what it does is generate long-grain–to–long-grain glue area (the sort of glue area that yields the strongest bonding).

The box joint is a machine-cut one (as opposed to something like a dovetail, which, although it is easily machine-cut, is nonetheless regarded generally as a hand-cut joint).

A lot of woodworkers think that the only way to cut the slots is on a table saw with a dado cutter. Make a little jig to attach to the miter gauge, and go to town. Well, I'm here to tell you the table-mounted router does a cleaner job in the same amount of time. You make a little sled-like jig, but once that's done, it is strictly repetitive cutting.

The router bit yields a cut that's not only square, but also flat-bottomed and clean all around. The cuts are fast, too. If your router has enough moxie, you should be able to cut the full depth in one pass.

(You may know this joint as a finger joint. I use that name for an interlocking edge-to-edge joint that's cut with a special bit.)

The Box-Joint Jig

The box-joint jig is simply an adaptation of the one you'd make and attach to your table saw's miter gauge. It's a specialized miter gauge for your router table, one that's guided by a couple of fences rather than a slot in the table. (It is easy enough to accessorize the sliding fence so it is guided by the edges of the table. The sliding fence is shown on page 111 in the chapter "Router Table Accessories"; the box-joint attachment for it is shown in the drawing on the next page.)

The critical element of any box-joint jig is the adjustable facing and

A dado cutter cuts slots quickly but often leaves an uneven, ridged bottom. The router-cut slot, on the other hand, is square and clean all around. Which would you prefer for your box joints?

The Box-Joint Jig

its key. The key is sized to match the pins, or fingers, of the joint. Its position relative to the bit is adjusted by shifting the facing side to side.

The jig itself can be any old scrappy thing, so long as it is accurate, with the back perpendicular to the base and the base edges square to the back. The adjustable facing and key are interchangeable. You make a different facing for each size pin you cut. (By sliding the facing fully right for one job, then fully left for another, and then rotating it 180° and repeating, you should be able to use a single facing for at least four jobs. Then you can trim it down and drill new mounting holes and use it for a couple more.)

Pin size refers not only to the width of the cut, but also the depth-of-cut. The router bit establishes the width of the cut, and thus the width of the pins. The cut depth is dictated by the thickness of the working stock. If you are joining 3/4-inch-thick parts, the slots and pins need to be 3/4 inch deep. If it's 1/2-inch stock, then the depth is 1/2 inch.

While you probably can get acceptable results cutting 1/2-inch-deep slots on a jig set up for a 3/4-inch depth-of-cut, splintering or "blowout" is likely to occur as the bit exits a cut. The backing is 1/4 inch above where the tip of the bit cuts through the workpiece, which is as good as no backing at all.

But the facings are so easy to make, there's no good reason not to make a fresh one for each project. (You can cut, drill, and countersink a stack of them to stash with the basic jig. All you need to do at joint-cutting time is cut the key slot and craft the key.)

To make the jig, select suitable materials from your scrap pile. I used

The basic box-joint jig is generic. Use it to cut different widths of slots in stock of many thicknesses. The job-specific part of the jig is the facing and key, which are shown in the center and at left. You mount a facing to the jig with the bolts and plastic knobs.

Try This!

The sliding fence is an excellent alternative to the dedicated box-joint jig. You can cobble a facing lickety-split and be routing joints in no time. No trap fences to set, no extra jig to store.

The Sliding Fence Alternative
Add a facing to make it a box-joint jig

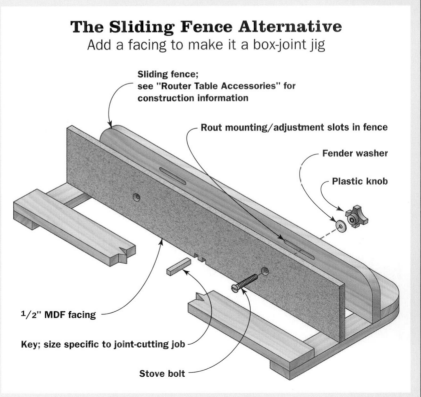

Sliding fence; see "Router Table Accessories" for construction information

Rout mounting/adjustment slots in fence

Fender washer

Plastic knob

1/2" MDF facing

Key; size specific to joint-cutting job

Stove bolt

sheet goods (primarily plywood and MDF—medium-density fiberboard) for most parts because they're stable, and because I always seem to have odd scraps around. The key is the one part that should always be a hard wood. It's subjected to a lot of wear, and if it's too soft, it will deform and throw off the accuracy of your cuts. The pins won't mesh, in other words. The key should be replaced if it gets worn, dented, or deformed.

Building the Jig

1. Cut the parts—except the back—to the sizes indicated in the Cutting List. The handle is reduced in size as it is shaped, but you'll need the extra size to cut the shape. The back must be slotted, and that job is easier to do if the blank is oversized. Trim it to final size after routing those slots.

2. Cut the adjustment slots in the back. While the screws used in the slots will be 1/4-inch, it's a good idea to make the slots somewhat oversized, perhaps 5/16 inch or as much as 3/8 inch. You want the slots centered between the top and bottom edges.

The cut is best made with a plunge router. Cut the back to final size after the slots are routed.

3. Assemble the base, support, and back. Glue the support to the base, then glue the back in place. Drill pilot holes and drive two drywall screws through the base into the back. Be

Cutting List

Piece	Number	Thickness	Width	Length	Material
Base	1	1/4"	8"	9 1/4"	MDF
Support	1	3/4"	8"	4 1/2"	Plywood
Back	1	3/4"	8"	5 1/4"	Plywood
Handle	1	1"	6"	6"	Plywood*
Facing	1	1/2"	8"	5 1/4"	Plywood
Key	1	1/2"	3/4"	10"	Hardwood

Hardware

4 to 8 drywall screws, #6 × 1 5/8"

2 flathead stove bolts, 1/4" × 2"

2 fender washers, 1/4" I.D.

2 plastic wing nuts, 1/4"–20 thread

*Start with a piece this size; cutting the profile reduces its size.

A Simple Box-Joint Jig

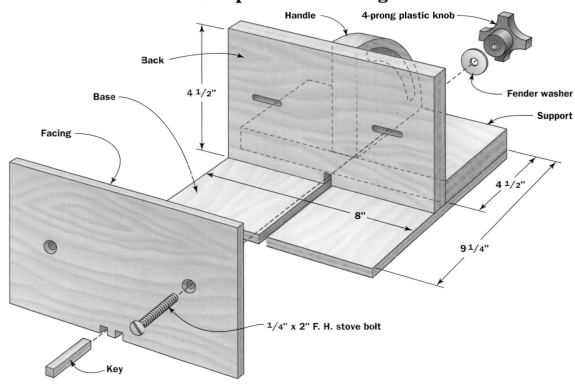

Handle

4-prong plastic knob

Back

Fender washer

Base

4 1/2"

Support

Facing

4 1/2"

8"

9 1/4"

1/4" x 2" F. H. stove bolt

Key

sure you position the screws toward the outer edges, so the bit won't hit them.

4. Make the handle. On the handle blank, scribe two lines, each 1 inch in from an edge and parallel to it. The lines should be along adjacent sides so they cross, forming a 1-inch square. Drill a 1/8-inch-diameter hole in the center of that square. This is the pivot hole for routing the arc profile.

I cut the arc with the adjustable trammel (see page 178 in the chapter "Routing Curves and Circles"). To do this, stick the blank to an expendable piece of plywood with carpet tape. Clamp the plywood to the bench. Set the trammel and plunge router to the correct radius and rout the arc in three to five passes.

While you could use the same general procedure to rout a hand hole, I drilled a series of overlapping holes with a 1-inch Forstner bit. Then I routed the curved handle edge, as well as the hand-hole edges, with a 1/4-inch round-over bit.

Finally, cut along the two lines you marked first on the handle blank, reducing it to its final size.

5. Attach the handle to the jig with glue and a couple of drywall screws. Be sure to position the screws where they'll not be hit by the bit.

6. Rout a slot in the base, from the leading edge into the back. It doesn't have to be any specific width, since it merely provides clearance for the bit. Set the bit height to a hair more than the base thickness. Position the fence so the slot will be centered in the base, and make the cut.

7. Stand the facing against the back and transfer the slot locations from the back to the facing. Drill and countersink a 1/4-inch hole roughly in the middle of each slot for the mounting bolts.

Install the facing using the stove bolts. Use fender washers rather than regular flat washers, since they are less prone to dent the back in a way that will make minute adjustments difficult. Plastic wing nuts are easier on the fingers.

Template-Guide Centered Jig

You don't have to use a fence to cut box joints, so long as you make it to fit over a template guide bushing. And so long as your table's router mounting allows you to use template guides.

As you know, the guide bushing is a metal fitting that mounts in the router baseplate. It has a low collar that surrounds the bit. If you cut a stopped slot in the jig's base, and if you make it the correct width, it will drop over the collar. The jig's trapped! It can slide back and forth as far as the slot will allow. It'll pivot around the collar. But unless you lift the jig, it is in the control of that collar.

If this way of guiding your box-joint jig is appealing, it's easy to accommodate when constructing the jig. When you cut the jig parts, make the base about 3 or 4 inches longer than specified in the cutting list; make the parts and assemble them as specified.

When routing the cutting slot, use a bit whose diameter matches that of the outside diameter of the template guide's collar. (I used a 1-inch template guide, so the jig could be used to cut fingers as wide as 7/8 inch.) Adjust the bit height to a hair over 1/4 inch—just enough to cut through the base. Plunge-cut into the base, beginning about 2 inches in from the front edge. Don't break through that front edge; you need a stopped slot.

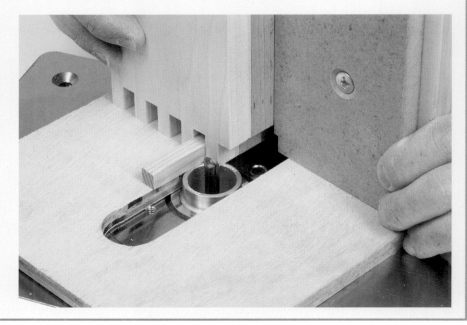

8. Fashion the key from a hard wood, making it the same width as the cutting diameter of the bit. You can establish the dimension either by measuring with dial calipers, or by making a sample cut with the bit in some scrap, then hand-planing the key to fit the cut snugly.

Crosscut two pieces of the key, both about 4 inches long. One will be the key, the other a gauge.

Getting the depth-of-cut just right isn't difficult. The ideal is to set the bit to cut a slot whose depth exactly matches the thickness of the working stock. If the slot is too shallow (bottom sample), you'll either have to replane the stock or recut the slots. The better alternative is to knowingly cut the slot a tad too deep (third from top), and plan to sand the projecting fingers.

Using the Jig

The initial step is to reconcile the bit diameter and the width of the workpieces. You really want to begin and end each array of pins with a full pin or slot. For you to accomplish this, the width of the boards should be evenly divisible by the bit diameter. If this isn't the case, then it's best to change either the bit size or the joint width.

A corollary is that a joint layout that begins with a full pin and ends with a full slot mates two identical pieces. You can cut both at the same time. All four parts of a box can be cut simultaneously.

If the layout begins and ends with a full pin, you must cut the sides and ends in sequence. I'll explain this in just a few more paragraphs.

It's worth pointing out that the stock thickness has no bearing on the pin thickness. You can use 1/4-inch pins on 3/4-inch stock, for example, or 1/2-inch pins on 3/8-inch stock.

But it does impact the pin length. The bit elevation must equal the stock thickness (plus the jig base thickness, of course).

Set up the router table and jig. Install the bit in the router and adjust the height. The easiest way to set this is to lay a scrap of the working stock on the jig base, park it beside the bit, and raise the bit to that height.

Use a fence no higher (thicker) than the jig's base on each side. The double fences prevent the jig from drifting and ruining your cuts. It moves back in forth as if on a track.

The fence thickness allows the workpieces to extend beyond the jig's edge. You can cut joints on very wide stock as easily as on narrow boards. Use strips of plywood, hardboard, or MDF. Set the fences so the jig is roughly centered on the bit.

With the jig captured between the fences, mount and set up the adjustable facings and key. It's

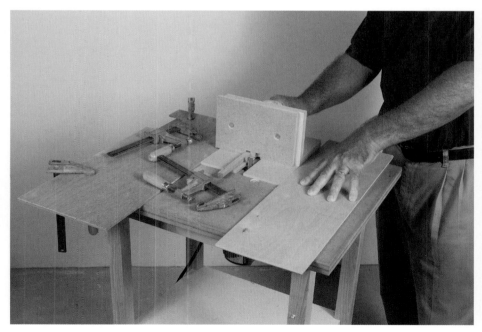

Trap the jig between two strips of 1/4-inch-thick material. You can be sure it won't drift while you're concentrating on holding the workpiece and watching your fingers and the bit. Equally important, the work can extend beyond the edges of the jig without interference.

Dovetail Splice

Dovetails joining two boards end-to-end are pretty glitzy, but it turns out they're also pretty easy to do.

The box-joint jig is the router aid that produces these dovetail splices. You use a dovetail bit instead of a straight.

Because of the nature of the joint, the stock thickness has no particular bearing on the length of the tails (or depth of the slots). Neither does the diameter of the cutter or the angle of the bit. Use whatever dovetail bit you have.

The first thing to do is shift the box-joint jig's facing to expose a fresh,

uncut segment at the cutter slot. Clamp the trap fences to the router table on either side of the jig. Install the bit in the router and set the height arbitrarily. Make a cut into the facing.

Use this cut to size the key and the slot you'll cut for the key. The narrowest part of the dovetail cut is the "waist diameter." The widest part is the "bit diameter," which is, of course, the stated diameter of the dovetail bit.

The waist diameter is the width of the key slot, and thus the width of the key. Use a straight bit of the correct diameter to cut it. Correctly positioned, the key slot must be a

"bit diameter" from the bottom of the dovetail cut in the facing.

Cut your key slot, make and fit the key, then remount the facing on the jig.

Using the dovetail-splice jig is like using the box-joint jig. You make the first cut in the first piece with the edge against the key. Then lift the stock to fit the slot over the key, and cut the next slot.

The second piece begins with a slot, so you must align the edge of the stock with the edge of the cutting slot. Then just step and cut your way across the wood.

The dovetail splice jig is used as you would the box-joint jig. Cutting mitered stock is no different than straight-cut stock.

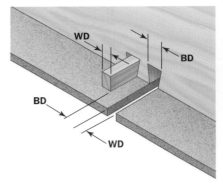

Dovetail-Splice Jig

The dovetail bit has two diameters that affect the design of the dovetail splice jig. The bit diameter (BD), which is the stated cutter size, is the distance from the slot to the key. The waist diameter (WD), which is the cutter's smallest diameter, is the width of the key.

possible to reuse a facing, of course, but unless the stock thickness and pin size is duplicated exactly, it may be better to use a fresh pair of slots—not necessarily a fresh facing—for each new job.

The first cut creates a slot in the facing for the key. What I do is offset the facing to the left

to begin. Lock the facing and cut a slot. Loosen the facing and slide it right slightly. Fit a key in the slot.

To adjust the facing position for the joinery cuts, set the loose key against the bit and slide the facing toward it until its key touches the loose one. The gap between the

cutter and the key now equals the bit diameter.

Cut a test joint. Stand a stacked pair of samples in the jig, edges snug against the key. Cut a slot. Move the stack, fitting the slot over the key. Cut another slot. Repeat the process until all the pins are formed.

Fit the joint together (offset them

if need be to align pins with slots). If the pins won't go into the slots, the key is too far from the bit. If the pins are loose in the slots, the key is too close to the bit.

Rather than slide the facing left or right a "hair," or a "tad," or a "skosh," use your dial calipers. Measure a pin and a slot. The amount you move the facing is HALF the difference between the pin width and the slot width. You can use a feeler gauge to make precisely what's most likely a minute adjustment.

■ If the pin is bigger than the slot, move the key closer to the bit. Set a block against the key and clamp it. Loosen the facing, slip the feeler gauge between the block and the key, and relock the facing. Remove the block.

■ If the slot is bigger than the pin, move the key away from the bit. Clamp the block to the jig with the feeler gauge between it and the key. Loosen the facing, remove the gauge, and reset the facing with the key tight against the block. Then remove the block.

A second set of cuts will confirm the accuracy of your adjustment.

Cutting the Joints

There's no reason to cut the parts one at a time. It's repetitive, tedious work, so you'll appreciate anything you can do to expedite it.

As I already mentioned, if your joint layout begins with a pin and ends with a slot, you can cut sides and ends simultaneously. Four parts in a stack.

As with the test cut, you first align the parts in the stack and stand them on the jig base, upright against the back. Butt the edges against the key. Cut. Step the stack

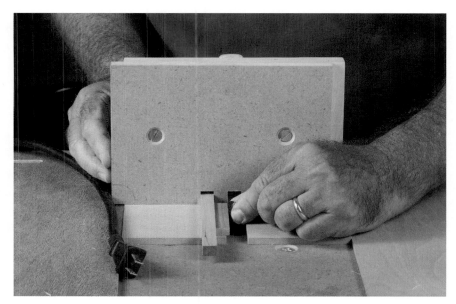

Hold the loose key against the router bit as you slide the facing and key up to it. You want the keys to just kiss, rather than jamming them together.

The first cut is made with the work standing on end, back against the jig, edge against the key. Push the jig into the bit. You'll be able to tell when it's penetrated the work into the jig; when it has, pull the jig back, clearing the work from the bit.

Step the work to the right, dropping the newly cut slot onto the key. Make another cut. Step the work right again, and cut again. That's all there is to it.

over the key and cut. Step again and cut again. Repeat and repeat until the last slot is cut.

If one piece begins *and* ends with pins, the mate will begin and end with slots. They must be cut in sequence. You can, of course, pair up parts of a box, but you can't cut all four of these parts at once.

Start with the piece that begins and ends with pins. Cut the slots in it. After the last slot has been cut, step that slot over the key. Stand the mating piece beside it. Cut. Remove the first piece and slide its mate to the right, the slot over the key. Cut again. Step and cut until all the slots are completed.

It's possible to slot several parts at the same time. The base of the jig can support quite a stack. This can expedite production. Note that if your joint's layout begins with a pin and ends with a slot, both sides and ends are alike, so you can rout all four parts of a box at the same time.

When the work widths are such that one half of the joint begins and ends with a pin, you need to use it to begin cutting its mate, which begins and ends with slots. Step the last slot of the first workpiece over the key. Butt the mating workpiece against it and cut. Then set the first piece aside and continue slotting the second.

Swinging Fingers

Turning the box joint into a hinge is surprisingly easy. Before cutting the slots for the joint, round-over the ends of the workpieces. Because you won't have a square edge for a pilot bearing to reference after the first pass, you need to do this on the router table. The radius of the round-over must equal half the thickness of the working stock. (A bull-nose bit will do the job in a single pass; its cutting diameter must equal the stock's thickness.)

Before you actually round-over the edges, use a square and pencil to lay out the centerpoint for the hinge-pin.

Cut the box joint. This is a case where a slightly loose fit is desirable. Assemble it, and bore the hole for a hinge-pin. Insert the pin, and test the action.

Box joints can be turned into wooden hinges. Round-over the ends of the workpieces before cutting the slots. Drive a nail or dowel into each end of the assembly to act as a hinge-pin.

Spline and Dovetail Keys

What we're looking at here is one of the paradoxes of woodworking. Fitting spline keys or dovetail keys is an operation that gussies up one of woodworking's really elegant joints, the miter joint. Why would we want to do this?

The miter joint, after all, is the one you use when you *don't want the end grain to show*. We go to a lot of trouble to conceal the end grain, then we rout grooves in the corner and glue keys in them so their end grain shows. Looks like dovetails, you know?

Why we do this is not entirely a mystery. The miter is a lousy joint structurally. The keys are just another way to spline the joint for added strength. The router is the tool to use to cut the key slots. You need to make a jig. Here's how.

Making the Jig

The jig is in effect a V-block that helps you to cut easily and consistently through a corner of a box. The jig's supports embrace the box's sides, and the base provides a firm work surface that perfectly bisects the planes of the corner.

A key in the jig helps you position the slots consistently. For the first cut, the work is butted against the key. But for the second and subsequent cuts, the previous cut is indexed over the key.

You use the jig on a router table, and the box to be worked rests in it. And that's the limitation. The jig, and thus the joinery, is best for smallish work.

You can, of course, enlarge the plan, building a larger jig that will support a much larger box. But it can't exceed your capacity to lift it into the jig and to maneuver it on the router table.

If you are determined, I'm sure you can find a way to clamp the jig to the casework and to trap the router on the jig so it can make precise, controlled cuts. I'm not at all convinced it would be worth the effort, though.

Keys, whether square or dovetail-shaped, add a visual embellishment to mitered assemblies like boxes and frames. Beyond that, the keys reinforce the joints.

Making the Jig

The key jig is a large V-block to hold an assembled box so that cuts can be made through its corners. Thin trap fences position the jig but allow the box to protrude from the jig without interference. The strip of wood visible beside the bit (above) is the secret behind cutting uniformly spaced slots. A newly cut slot in the work fits over that key, positioning the work for the next slot.

Construction

1. Cut the plywood parts, which is everything except the key. The base is simply a rectangle. The supports are beveled at 45° along one edge, as are the braces.

Plywood is the material of choice because it is stable and because it accepts screws driven into its edges. MDF (medium-density fiberboard), a logical alternative, tends to split when screws are driven into its edges, even when pilot holes are drilled first. Use pneumatically driven fasteners, and either material will work fine.

2. Glue and screw the supports to the base, as shown in the drawing.

This can be a vexing task. I had a lot of trouble making the first jig, but the second took maybe 20 minutes. Try this: Use the two braces to trap the supports, so they don't slide out of alignment as you try to drill pilots and drive the screws. To protect them from glue, wrap the bevels of the braces with common packing tape during this phase of assembly.

Scribe a line across the middle of the base with a try square. Clamp a brace flat against the base along the line. The brace's miter should form an acute angle to the base. Stand one of the supports on its mitered edge and push it under the brace's miter, as shown in the construction detail to the drawing. Lay the second brace on the base and slide it in behind the support, trapping it. Clamp the second brace. You should now be able to extract the support, apply glue to it, and return it to its position.

Drill pilot holes and drive two 1-inch screws. And unclamp the braces.

Now clamp a brace to the face of the support you just installed. With one of its square edges down, this brace forms an acute angle with the base, allowing you to trap the second support in place. Complete the trap with the second brace, and glue and screw the second support to the base. Unclamp the braces.

(It is entirely likely that the points of the screws are jutting through the faces of the supports. If so, file these points off after the braces are installed.)

3. Install the braces next. To ensure that the two supports form a right angle, rest a square (or a square scrap of wood) in the V. Apply glue to the brace edges and slip one into position. Push it further under the support until you see that the V is at a right angle. Hold the brace in place while you drill pilot holes and drive two 1 5/8-inch screws through the support into the brace.

Repeat the process to position the second brace.

When both are glued and screwed to their supports, turn the jig over and drill pilots and drive the remaining screws through the base into the braces.

4. What remains is to cut the slots in the jig and to fit the key to one of them. The first slot is what I would call the "cutting slot," since it's the one the cutter is in when the jig is being used. It should be equidistant from the two sides.

Set the fence on the router table 4 inches from the center of the bit (whatever bit you're using). With the jig tight against the fence, rear it back and plunge it onto the spinning bit, punching a hole in the base between the forward brace and support. Slide the jig forward, cutting a slot clear through both supports. Lift the back end of the jig up off the bit and switch off the router.

5. Determine next what spacing you want between the slots. Following the same procedure as in the previous step, set the fence and cut a slot to one side (or the other) of the cutting slot. Then make a key from a hardwood—maple, cherry, what-have-you—and plane it to a tight press-fit in the key slot.

Now you are ready to put the jig to work.

It's worth noting that you can add a second (and possibly a third and a fourth) key slot to your jig. If you have a second spacing you plan to use with *the same bit,* mark off its key slot on the other side of the cutting slot from the first. Work additional slots out on paper before trying to cut them. It may be that, if the

increment is large enough, you can set up your jig for three or four alternative spacings for a particular bit.

You need to resist the temptation to use different bits with one jig. I took a jig already slotted by a big cutter, and tried using it with a small bit. As I suspected it would, the bit blew splinters out of the work when exiting the cut. There was nothing backing up the cut, so it was bound to happen.

So, if you want to do dovetails *and* splines, you should have two jigs. If you want to do 1/4-inch splines *and* 1/2-inch splines, you should have two jigs. If you want the two sizes of splines, plus two sizes of dovetails, that's four jigs.

Cutting List

Piece	Number	Thickness	Width	Length	Material
Fences	2	1/2"	3"	36"	Plywood
Base	1	1/4"	8"	15"	Plywood
Supports	2	3/4"	8"	8"	Plywood
Braces	2	3/4"	8"	4 3/4"	Plywood
Key	1	3/8"	5/8"	4"	Hardwood
Hardware					

8 wood screws, 1" × #8
2 flathead machine screws, 1 1/2" × 1/4", with washers and nuts
2 plastic wing knobs, 1/4" I.D.

Slotting on the Table

Because it's likely that your work will extend beyond the periphery of the jig, you can't use your standard router table fence. What works best is to trap the jig between two fences. Then the jig can't drift away from the fence, regardless of the feed direction.

Use strips of hardboard or plywood that are the same thickness as the jig's base. That way, the work can overhang on either side.

To set the fence, you first need to get the jig set up over the bit. Chuck the correct bit in the router. Set the jig over it, and position it so the bit is in the center of the V. Adjust the height of the cutter, and turn it so the cutting edges are aligned across the jig. To establish the correct position of the jig on the tabletop, slide the jig so the cutter is housed in one of the supports. Slide the fence against the edge of the jig's base and clamp it. The jig should slide back and forth along the fence without catching on the bit as it passes through the slots in the supports.

To cut the slots, rest the assembled box in the jig, with one edge butted against the key. With the router switched on, push and pull the jig, cutting the first slot. Lift the work slightly, shift it toward the key, and lower it

Dovetail/Spline Key Jig

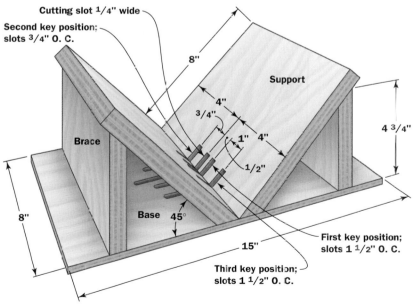

Cutting slot 1/4" wide

Second key position;
slots 3/4" O. C.

8"

Support

Brace

4"

3/4"

1" 4"

1/2"

4 3/4"

8"

Base 45°

15"

First key position;
slots 1 1/2" O. C.

Third key position;
slots 1 1/2" O. C.

again into the jig, dropping the cut over the key. Make another cut, lift and shift the work, and make a third cut.

You just repeat this process over and over until the job is done.

In the ideal situation, one of your pre-established spacings will suit the work at hand. But you may need to make the first cut without the key in place, so you can alter the space from the work's edge to the first key. If this is the case, you can use carpet tape to stick a temporary stop in the jig for the first cut. I'd suggest making that first cut on all four corners of the box before pulling out the temporary stop and reinserting the key to finish out the job.

Routing key slots is simple and repetitive. Pull the jig clear of the bit and set the assembled box in place. One edge must be tight against the key. Push the jig across the bit, cutting the first slot. Step the newly cut slot onto the key (above) and make the next cut. Repeat and repeat and repeat until all the slots are cut in one corner. Then rotate the box a quarter-turn and start over.

Swinging on a Template Guide

You can eliminate the need for fences for the keying jig if you modify it to catch on a template guide bushing. This jig swivels around the guide's collar, but it's always in the correct alignment with the cutter.

Build the jig following the directions. You *do* need to use a fence to cut both the cutting and the key slots. Having done that, line up the fence so the cutter resides in the cutting slot.

Pick the template guide, and measure the outside diameter of its collar. Fit a straight bit that matches that measurement in the router. Set the depth-of-cut to equal the height of the collar. Now enlarge the cutting slot only. Butt the jig against the fence, tip it back, and start the router. Plunge the jig, feed it through the cut, then lift the back end of the jig off the cutter.

The new slot should accommodate the guide collar without interfering with the cutting of slots for your chosen keys.

To use this jig, install the template guide in the mounting plate. Chuck the correct bit in the router. Set the jig over the template, and adjust the height of the cutter. Cuts are made just as if you were using the fence.

You'll notice, however, that the template guide provides positive stops at the extremes of a cutting stroke. You never have to wonder whether the cutter is housed in the work, or whether it's free of the work and you're extending the slot in the base. Pull the jig toward you until it stops. Push it away from you until it stops. No doubts.

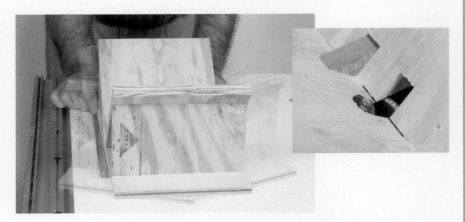

With the slotting jig's movement regulated by the template guide (inset), you need never worry about the jig—and the work it carries—drifting away from a fence and ruining both the jig and the work. The template guide allows the jig to swivel—giving you freedom of motion—without compromising the cut placement.

Splining a Frame

The miter joint is very commonly used in light frames—picture frames, face frames. A spline key in each corner strengthens the joint, and it adds a subtle embellishment, too.

While you might be able to clamp temporary support blocks in the key jig to hold a frame over the cutting slot, you can make a jig just for frames almost as easily. It works on a router table two ways. You can slide it along the L-shaped fence to cut the slot with a straight bit. And you can lay it flat on the tabletop, sliding it along a low fence, and cut the slot with a slot cutter.

The construction is evident from the drawing. Miter the ends of the two frame supports, then glue and screw them to the plywood back. The supports must be at a 45° angle to the baseline, and at right angles to each other. Having done this, you have the jig to use with the slot cutter.

You *can* use the same jig upright, braced against the L-shaped fence, too. But you'll have better support if you make the fence hook, consisting of a spacer that's about 1/32 inch thicker than the fence stock and a plywood flange. If you simply clamp this accessory to the jig when you need it, then the jig can serve you both ways. If you glue it on, you're stuck using it always with the fence and straight cutter.

Obviously, to use the jig, you set the frame in the V formed by the supports. Snap a spring clamp on each side of the jig to hold the frame. Hit the switch and push the jig and frame through the cutter.

With the frame-splining jig riding the router-table fence, you can use a straight bit or a dovetail bit to cut slots for splines or keys. To keep the frame from tipping away from the fence, attach a fence hook to the jig.

If you rest the frame-splining jig flat on the tabletop, as shown, you need to use a slot cutter. Use the fence to control the depth of the slot.

Frame-Splining Jig
Use keys or spline to reinforce your picture frames

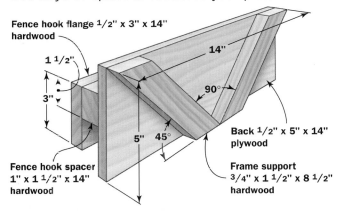

Fence hook flange 1/2" x 3" x 14" hardwood

1 1/2"

3"

14"

90°

Fence hook spacer 1" x 1 1/2" x 14" hardwood

5"   45°

Back 1/2" x 5" x 14" plywood

Frame support 3/4" x 1 1/2" x 8 1/2" hardwood

Fitting the Keys

Once the slots are cut, the keys must be made.

Cutting splines (keys for slots cut with a straight bit) is a table-saw task. Rip strips of stock to the appropriate thickness, and if necessary, plane them to fit. Crosscut the strips into bits and glue a bit into each slot. The project will look pretty ratty until the glue dries and you can trim the keys.

Cutting dovetail keys is a router-table chore. Use the same bit that cut the slots. First, cut a sample slot in a short piece of scrap.

Then cut a tail along the edge of a board. House most of the bit in the fence, and feed the stock along the fence, scoring the side. Turn the board around and score the other side. Viewed from the end, the result is a tail.

Dovetail keys are cut on the router table, usually using stock that contrasts with the box. Cut the key strips parallel to the grain of the stock.

In a trial-and-error process, start with an oversized tail and methodically trim it down. Move the fence back to expose a little more of the bit and recut both sides of the board. Fit the tail to the slot in the scrap. Adjust the fence again, if necessary, and recut.

When you've got a good fit, rip the tail from the board. Then cut another tail and rip it from the board.

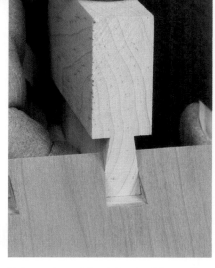

Cut your key strips into short keys, then glue a key into each slot. Clamping isn't necessary.

Try This!

Use your router to trim the keys. A laminate trimmer or other *small* router, fitted with a flush-trimming baseplate, will make quick work of this job. The baseplate holds the router about $^1/_4$ inch above the working surface, so it can clear the material to be trimmed away. The bit is set flush with the work surface.

To use this technique, trim the keys as short as possible with a saw. Then trim the remaining projections with the lam trimmer with the special baseplate, as shown.

Plans for the baseplate are on page 195 in the chapter "Surfacing with the Router."

Repeat the process until you have enough key stock. Next, cut the stock into short keys, and glue a key into each slot.

When the glue dries, the keys must be trimmed flush. The usual technique is to saw off the keys as close to the surface of the workpiece as possible without scuffing it. Then trim the remaining stubs flush with a chisel—work from the corner in, so you don't tear out splinters of the keys—or sand the stubs flush using a belt sander. Or use coarse sandpaper wrapped around a block of wood. A file also works well.

Routed Joints

The router makes quick work of cutting many traditional joints. But there are a few industrial-era joints that the router cuts very efficiently, too.

For most of these industrial joints, a single cutter and setup produces both halves of the joint. Most commonly, the shaper was the tool originally used. But now economical cutters designed for use in the table-mounted router are available.

This chapter focuses on three such joints.

Routed Glue Joint

This industrial joint was developed for high-volume production glue-ups. In that setting, the stock is propelled across a shaper with a power feeder, and the cutter simultaneously joints and profiles the edge in a single pass. One edge is milled with the face up, the other edge with the face down. Literally miles of stock is processed this way to produce panel after panel for factory-produced cabinets and furniture.

Long ago, the cutter was scaled down for router table use. Because it's typically under 2 inches in diameter, it can be run at full tilt (22,000 rpm). But it's a substantial bit, and it removes a major amount of stock, so lots of horsepower is a requisite.

The concept is, of course, that you have a single setup of bit height and fence position. One board is routed face up, the other face down. If the setup is just right, the two boards will

The router cuts a variety of specialized industrial joints quickly and efficiently. You can use them to assemble panels, casework, and drawers.

come together with their faces flush. The zigzag profile of the joint is centered in the edges, meaning the top and bottom shoulders are of equal width.

Gluing up is a cinch. Because of the interlock, the boards can't shift up or down. The gluing surface is expanded, too.

Preliminaries

You have to prepare your stock well. It is especially important for it to be flat and of a consistent thickness. If the thickness varies from board to board, the faces won't come flush when you assemble the joint. Any bowing can lead to a misaligned cut.

It *is* possible, using featherboards or a power feeder, to machine the profile evenly on the edges of slightly bowed stock. In theory, the profile could then be used to force a bowed board into a glue-up with other flat boards, thus yielding a flat panel.

Bit Drawer

Two configurations of the glue-joint bit are available. The most common has the small diameter at the shank and the large diameter at the tip. This will cut edge-to-edge joints only. The other form has the large diameter at the shank, the small at the tip. With this bit, you can rout both edge-to-edge and edge-to-face joints.

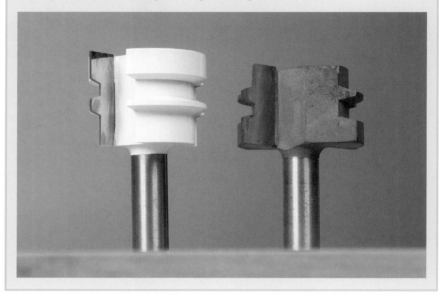

I think it's a dicey proposition. I certainly wouldn't recommend it as your first experience with the joint.

If you are tackling this joint, it's likely you've already done some panel glue-ups. You've dealt with setting the boards side-by-side, finding the best-looking arrangement, then marking them for assembly. What may be new is marking them for the joinery cuts.

All but two of the boards in a glue-up must be routed on both edges. (The outermost boards are routed only on one edge.) The routine usually is to rout one edge with the face down, the second edge with the face up. To prevent mix-ups—routing both edges with the face down, for example—you should mark one end of each board so you are reminded of which face goes against the table for a cut. Arrowheads are all you should need: an up arrow at

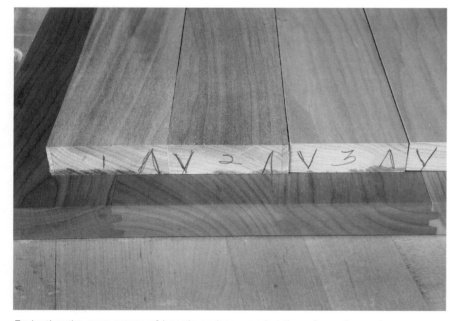

Evaluating the appearance of boards and sequencing them for a glue-up is a common procedure. When you are planning to machine them with a glue-joint bit, extra marking is helpful. On the ends, number them in sequence and mark up and down arrows at each edge. This will indicate to you which face should be up for machining an edge. Usually, you rout an edge, then roll the board over before routing the second edge.

one edge, a down arrow at the other. Number the boards' sequence to supplement your triangle on the face of the panel.

Cutting the Joint

Here's the setup sequence for the standard routed glue joint.

1. Eyeball a bit-height setting. Do this by marking the stock centerline on a setup sample and setting it beside the bit. Then raise and lower the bit to visually align its centerpoint as best you can with the mark. The center of the bit profile is indicated in the drawing.

2. Set up your router table fence for jointing. The glue-joint bit cuts the full edge of the stock, not just a portion of it. You have to set up your router table fence as if you were jointing, with the outfeed half of the fence offset from the infeed half.

The easiest way to accomplish this

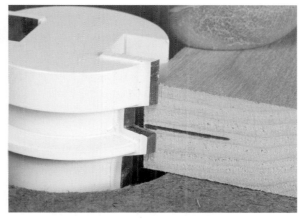

Set the glue-joint bit height by eye initially, then refine the setting based on test cuts. To start, mark the center of the work, and align the sweet spot on the glue-joint bit with your mark. It probably won't be perfect, but it'll get the setup process started.

Align the outfeed side of the fence tangent to the cutting edges of the bit's smallest diameter. Use a straightedge and turn the bit by hand—unplug the router first, of course!—to find the correct alignment. You want the cutting edge to graze the rule without actually moving it.

is with a special jointing fence. There's a plan for one in the "Edge Joints" chapter, page 259.

Many commercial and shop-made fences have separate infeed and outfeed facings. Usually, you can offset the outfeed facing by inserting a shim of some sort between it and the fence body. A variety of materials can be used, from plastic laminate to cardboard to true shim stock.

3. Align the fence. The outfeed half of the fence must be tangent to the small-diameter cutting edge. Lock down one end of the fence and move the free end to establish the precise alignment. Sight across the outfeed facing to the cutting edge for the initial position. Then check it with a straightedge held against the outfeed side and across the cutting edge (see the photo). Clamp the free end.

Glue Joint

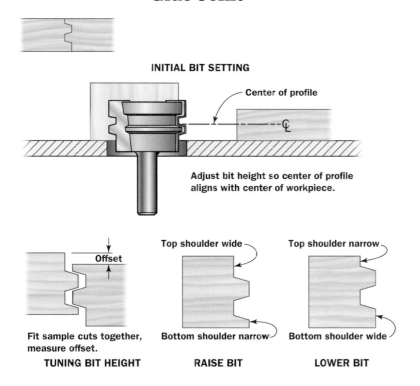

INITIAL BIT SETTING

Center of profile

Adjust bit height so center of profile aligns with center of workpiece.

Offset

Fit sample cuts together, measure offset.
TUNING BIT HEIGHT

Top shoulder wide
Bottom shoulder narrow
RAISE BIT

Top shoulder narrow
Bottom shoulder wide
LOWER BIT

If you have a small number of boards to work—say, three or four for a single panel—you may opt to use an off-center glue joint.

You cut half the joint at whatever your initial bit-height setting is. Then you make an adjustment to produce a cut that complements the first, and cut the second half of each joint. You end up with an off-center joint.

The final, infinitesimal bit-height adjustment, which can be frustrating to dial in with some router table setups, is what tips some woodworkers toward the off-center joint. If you are really good at the initial setup, you could be trying to move the bit a 64th or even a 128th because the faces of your test joint are offset only 1/32 inch or 1/64 inch.

It is a whole lot easier to dial in a movement of 1/16 inch or 1/8 inch. So the thinking is, if your initial setting yields an offset of 1/16 inch, leave well enough alone. Cut half of each joint at that setup; in other words, mill all the up-arrow edges at that setting.

Having done that, raise (or lower) the bit that 1/16 inch. Make a test cut and see how it fits with one of the workpieces. If the faces are flush, machine the second half of each joint (i.e., all the down-arrow edges).

The logic of the standard approach is that of fast production. You take a bit of extra time at the outset, tuning the bit height, then you just go. Typically, you use the joint where you are gluing relatively narrow boards into wide panels. Each board is milled on both edges. The first edge is done with the face down on the router tabletop, and the second with that face up. So you pick up a board, mill one edge, roll it over and mill the second, then set the board aside.

The logic of the second approach is aimed at simplifying (somewhat)

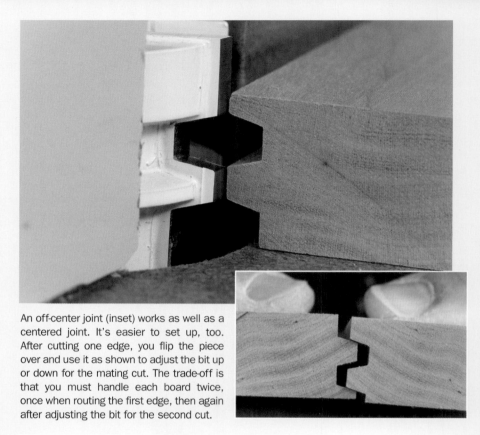

An off-center joint (inset) works as well as a centered joint. It's easier to set up, too. After cutting one edge, you flip the piece over and use it as shown to adjust the bit up or down for the mating cut. The trade-off is that you must handle each board twice, once when routing the first edge, then again after adjusting the bit for the second cut.

Off-Center Joint
For small jobs, faster setup but more work handling

Cut half the joint.

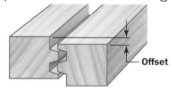

Fit samples together and measure offset.

Offset

Raise bit the full offset and rout second half of joint.

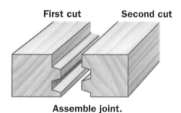

First cut Second cut

Assemble joint.

the setup. The adjustment you make between the first half of the joint and the second is more coarse and, presumably, easier to hit without trial-and-error micro-adjusting. But it can also be seen as doubling the

work handling, since each board must be picked up, milled, then set aside two times.

Either approach is legit; either yields a strong joint. Take the one that works for you.

Check the fit of the test joint to fine-tune the bit height. You want the faces to be flush. If there's a step, measure it with the depth bar of a dial caliper. The adjustment is *half* the measurement.

4. Confirm the fence setting with a partial test cut. Begin the cut and feed several inches of the piece beyond the bit. If the stock hits the edge of the outfeed facing, clearly the fence isn't aligned properly. Adjust it and try again.

Once you've cut several inches and the stock extends past the bit and along the outfeed facing, switch off the router. Check whether the routed edge is in contact with the outfeed side of the fence. If there's a gap between the stock and the fence—if you can slip a piece of paper or a feeler gauge between the stock and the fence—then you need to move the fence forward that amount.

Get the fence positioned precisely before moving to the next phase of the setup.

5. Fine-tune the bit height. Make a test cut on a short piece of the working stock. Cut the piece in half and fit

the parts together to assess the fit. If the faces are not flush, you need to change the bit height by half the offset.

This is where the operation can get ticklish. Measure the offset with a dial caliper. The offset is often some tiny fraction, and you've got to raise or lower the bit by half of that tiny fraction. The better your vertical adjustment system, the more easily you can make this adjustment.

How do you know whether to raise or lower the bit?

Look at the cut as it comes off the bit. If the shoulder at the bottom is wider than the shoulder at the top, the bit must be lowered. If it is the opposite—wide shoulder at the top, narrow shoulder at the bottom— then raise the bit.

6. Make a final test cut to confirm the setup, then rout the joinery.

Lock-Miter Joint

The lock-miter joint—the one we call the lock miter today—is created by a special router bit.

The original lock-miter joint was a table-saw product. Each half of this lock miter is different, and producing it on the saw requires several setups and some finicky fitting.

Today's lock miter is descended from the original by way of a shaper adaptation. As the joint profile was adapted to the shaper, it was transformed to permit a single cutter and setup to produce both halves of the joint.

The joint itself, when assembled, looks like a miter. But the two routed edges (or ends) have cogs that interlock when the joint is assembled. You get a mechanical strength that no plain miter joint has. To me, that interlock is the primary benefit of the joint. You do get expanded glue surface, but I think that's less significant.

Try this with an ordinary case miter! The lock miters hold together on their own, freeing both your hands to handle the workpieces or apply clamps. The pieces will probably seat square. But don't assume that; always check and monitor as you clamp.

In its most common configuration, the bit used is very big—as much as 3 inches in diameter. It needs to be run at reduced rpm and be powered by a high-horsepower motor, and it requires the use of a fence since it has no pilot bearing. Bit manufacturers recommend that you use it only in a table-mounted router. I wouldn't argue with that.

The lock miter is one of those trick bits. The trick is that one setup suffices for cuts on both pieces to be joined. When you have the bit adjusted spot-on, and the fence perfectly positioned, you are golden. You lay one panel flat on the tabletop, and

Lock-Miter Bonus

The lock miter is a great corner joint for casework; everyone knows that. But did you know it's equally good as an edge-to-edge joint? The setup is exactly the same as for the corner joint, but you rout one board with its face down, the other face up. The two should go together perfectly.

Lock-Miter Bonus

An interlocking edge-to-edge joint for flat panels

EDGE-TO-EDGE JOINT

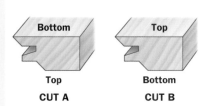

CUT A   CUT B

Bit Drawer

The common lock-miter bit (right) is a big hunk of metal that will machine stock between 5/8 and 1 1/8 inches thick. Use it for casework being built of sheet goods—plywood, MDF, and the like—as well as solid wood. Run it at reduced speed—between 12,000 and 14,000 rpm—in a high-horsepower router. For thinner stock—between 3/8 inch and 11/16 inch—the junior-sized version (left) can be run faster and with less horsepower.

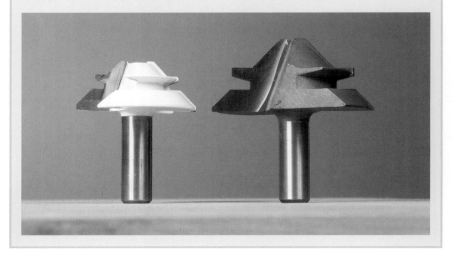

slide it along the fence to rout it. The mating panel you stand on edge, face against the fence, to make the cut.

The resulting cuts interlock, giving you a right-angle joint that's easy to assemble and clamp. The joint itself is invisible.

Setting Up

Now the $64,000 Question: How do you get the blamed thing set up properly? Two parts to the process: setting the bit height, and setting the fence. Both steps are shown in the drawing. You have to make gross settings of both the height and the fence position before cutting *anything*. Through a series of test cuts, you home in on the optimum settings, first of the bit height, then of the fence position.

Frustration will be the only fruit of fiddling with both settings at once. Get out your fluorescent high-

lighter and mark these words: Do the bit height, get it right. Then do the fence.

Good stock preparation is critical. The joint is sensitive to thickness. All the stock must be the same thickness, and it must be flat and true. Be wary when working plywood, since the thickness can vary from sheet to sheet, as can flatness.

Before you actually begin the setup process, prepare all your stock, including extra material to use for test cuts. It's far better, at least the first couple of times you use the bit, to set aside more scrap than you think you can possibly need for setup. Once you've successfully worked through the setup process—and really understand how you got the setting you did (don't discount beginner's luck!)—then you can get by with only three or four setup samples.

As you size the project parts, it's a good idea to leave them an inch or so

Lock-Miter Joint

TUNING BIT HEIGHT

Faces offset — Obtuse shoulder wider than acute one — Bit too high

Faces offset — Acute shoulder wider than obtuse one — Bit too low

Faces flush — Shoulders equal — Just right

SETTING UP BIT

Midpoint of profile
Centerline of stock

1. Set bit height, aligning midpoint of profile with centerline of stock.

Tabletop
Workpiece

Fence
Workpiece

2. Set the fence back from bottom of profile by thickness of working stock.

Bottom edge of profile

TUNING FENCE POSITION

Flat indicates fence is too far forward.

Knife edge flush with end of stock indicates fence position is perfect.

Notch indicates fence is too far back.

wider than the final dimensions. Narrow pieces can be left united in a single wide panel. A wider panel will be easier to rout. After the lock miters are routed, you can trim the parts to final width, and at the same time remove any blown-out splinters.

Setting the bit height: The key in setting the bit height is lining up the midpoint of the bit with the center of the stock. The midpoint of the bit is on the very slightly angled edge of the interlock. (It's labeled in the drawing.)

The best thing you can do is to mark the centerline on a scrap piece of the working stock, set it right beside the bit, hunker down and squint across the tabletop, and line them up by eye. Maybe you'll nail the alignment, but probably it'll take a test cut and an adjustment (maybe two) to get it just right.

Set the initial height of the bit with the fence backed out of the way. Mark the center of the stock thickness and, by eye, raise or lower the bit to align the sweet spot on the bit profile with the mark. The mark may be slightly off, and the bit elevation as well, but it's a good starting point.

Having set an approximate bit height, move the fence into position to guide your first test cut. I stand a piece of the working stock "behind" the bit and sight along the fence to the bit. My objective is to have the stock aligned with the profile's bottom edge (see the drawing on page 357). If I'm going to err, then I want the fence too far forward, rather than too far back. (Remember that this is just an approximate fence setting and that we aren't going to touch it until after the final bit height is established.)

Make a test cut with the sample flat on the table. Cut it in half, turn one of the pieces over, and join the two. If you are a true magician, the faces will be flush. The bit setting will be perfect.

More likely you are like me, and the faces will be offset. An adjustment will be needed.

First, measure the offset. Use the depth-bar of a dial caliper to measure it and give you a reading on the dial. Raise or lower the bit half the measurement. (Having a good depth-adjustment system on your router and table is a boon here.)

How do you know whether to raise the bit or lower it? Read the sample joint, as shown in the Tuning Bit Height detail of the drawing on page 357.

- If the "obtuse shoulder," formed where the bit meets the tabletop, is wider than the acute shoulder, then the bit's too high and you must lower it. The amount you lower it is half the offset.

- If that shoulder is narrower than the acute shoulder, the bit is too low, and you must raise it. Again, the adjustment distance is half the offset.

Note that when the bit is properly centered, the "shoulders" above and below the "cog" will be equal.

Don't get distracted by the profile as you assess the sample cut. You may not have the full bevel, but that's a function of the fence position. It doesn't affect the vertical adjustment, so ignore it at this time.

But once the bit setting is established, focus on the fence.

Setting the fence: Before you move the fence into final position, trick it out to help you achieve those clean, chip-free cuts I'm sure you want. This is especially helpful if you are working plywood or veneered MDF (medium-density fiberboard). Make sure the bit opening in the fence is as close to zero-clearance as you can make it.

If your fence has a split facing, you can slide each half into the bit as it spins, cutting the profile into the end. If not, an add-on facing works fine. Cut a strip of MDF or hardboard as high and as long as your fence. After roughing out an undersized bit opening, mount the strip to the fence (use double-sided tape or hot-melt glue), and use the

bit to create a zero-clearance opening in the facing.

In cutting the joint, you are dealing with a 45° bevel. The exposure of the cutting edge above the table and in front of the fence must match the thickness of the working stock. The bit is set, and that's no longer a variable.

If the fence is set too far back, a cut will remove too much stock and alter the length or width of the workpiece. If it is too far forward, you won't get the full miter. You already have a gross setting. Here's how to refine it.

Cut a scrap of the working stock, feeding only a few inches into the cut. Examine your cut (see the photo).

- If the tip is square, the fence must be moved back to expose more of the bit.

- If the cut is shortening the material, the fence must be pulled forward to house more of the bit.

- If the tip comes to an acute angle whose tip is flush with the square, unrouted edge of the stock, the fence position is just right.

With the final fence position set, you can proceed to the real workpieces.

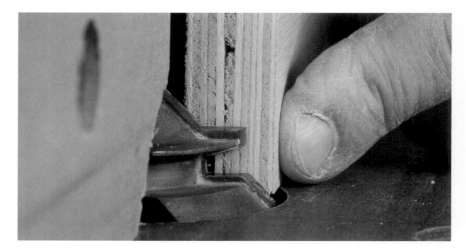

Eyeball the initial fence setting. Stand a piece of the working stock against the fence and sight across the bit to it. With the far end of the fence locked down, swing the free end to align the bottom edge of the stock with the lower end of the bit's cutting edge.

Cutting the Joints

Cutting the joint is relatively easy, once the router table is set up. The typical right-angle joint is produced by routing one part flat on the table-top, and the mating piece standing on edge against the fence.

These cuts, first of all, are pretty heavy, since each addresses the full width of the stock. Two measures can be taken to reduce your router's workload.

You can chamfer the edges to be routed to reduce the waste. Just don't saw a full bevel, because that will throw off your dimensions (see the photos).

An alternative is to stage the cuts. The lock miter is not a profile that must be hogged out in a single pass. You can work progressively to the final cut depth. Here's how:

You've got the final fence position. Capture it with a pair of stops clamped to the tabletop behind the fence. Tuck them against the fence's back edge and clamp them securely. Then pull the fence forward, off the blocks. Make a cut on each work-piece. Push the fence back against the stops, and make a second and final pass on each workpiece.

A decision I make concurrently is whether or not to use feather-boards. With relatively small parts, I usually don't use featherboards. Cabinet parts will prompt me to get out and set featherboards.

Here's how the two matters—workload and featherboard use—come together. If I'm using feather-board because the parts are big, I'll chamfer the parts to reduce the necessary bite (rather than subject myself to twice setting the feather-boards for the on-end cuts).

Bear in mind that featherboards aren't a reliable means of compensating

A common "tip" advises you to saw a bevel on the edge of your work to reduce the cutting load on your router and bit. Be wary. The lock-miter bit will groove a beveled work-piece but won't produce the mating cog (bottom sample). That's no good! If the workpiece is chamfered, on the other hand, you'll get both the groove and the cog (top sample).

Half of each lock-miter joint is cut with the work flat on the router tabletop. A pusher holds the work down while it advances it across the bit.

Stand the work on end, flat against the fence, to rout the other half of the joint. A featherboard keeps the workpiece against the fence, obviating the need for a tall fence facing.

for slightly unflat workpieces. If you apply enough pressure with a featherboard to straighten a slight bow in the stock, you are probably applying enough pressure to make feeding the stock very difficult.

Assembling the Joint

Assembly time is when the lock miter pays off. You've assembled—or tried to, anyway—a case miter. Keeping the parts in alignment is maddening. The glue acts as a lubricant, and the parts want to squirm and slide. There's no easy way to apply clamping pressure perpendicular to the glue surfaces. You've got to glue or clamp

blocks to the parts so you can apply clamps to the assembly.

The lock miter joint closes easily and the mating parts don't squirm or slide. The effect of the joint's interlock is also miraculous. Clamping is easy and direct—no extra blocks or jigs are needed.

Drawer-Lock Joint

Drawers take a lot of abuse. Not at first, of course. At first we lay a few items in a newly made drawer, and gently slide it closed, admiring our craftsmanship. Day in and day out, we pull that drawer open and slide it closed.

But eventually, the bloom passes from the rose. Little by little, we get that drawer loaded up. All right, maybe *over*loaded. And we begin to *YANK* it open. And we take to *SLAMMING* it shut. Give'er the ole

hip bump. *WHAM!!* Over and over and over again.

It's no wonder drawer joints need to be extra-strong.

A couple hundred years ago, drawers were assembled with dovetails. Half-blind dovetails up front, through dovetails at the back. Such construction is still the benchmark.

But it's the 21st century now. We don't have *time* to hand-cut dovetails. We don't even have time to *rout* dovetails. We need something that can be cut fast and assembled quickly. Of course, we *know* it has to be strong.

The drawer-lock joint is just the ticket. It has an interlock that holds the front and sides together (and/or the back and sides), and it resists the main stresses administered to a drawer—tension and compression and racking. The finished drawer won't have the pizzazz of one assembled with dovetails, but depending upon how we cut the joint, it can go together a whole lot faster.

You work on a router table, and

You needn't limit your use of the drawer lock to utilitarian constructions. The joint works for lipped as well as flush drawers, constructed with all sorts of materials and in a wide range of stock thicknesses.

use the fence to guide the work-pieces. Because the bit is small, you can use it in a low-power router and run it at full speed. One height setting is used for all the cuts. The fence is used in one position for the ends (drawer fronts and backs, in other words), and a slightly different one for the sides.

Setup

I like to set up the router table and fence with zero-clearance overlays made from pieces of 1/8- or 1/4-inch hardboard. The layer on the table-top I position before mounting the fence. If you have your router hanging from a mounting plate, and it has reducers for the bit opening, you probably don't need the auxiliary tabletop.

The piece on the fence will minimize chipping and eliminate feed hangups, however. It can be held with a couple of spring clamps. Put it in place with the bit running, and you'll have your zero-clearance cutout.

Bit Drawer

Two different bits can produce the drawer-lock joint.

One bit is about 1 3/4 inches in diameter with a low body (about 1/2 inch high). Each cutting edge has a protruding tab, so it cuts a single dado. This is probably the more familiar bit, and I'd be inclined to label this the drawer-lock bit, since that's what it cuts.

The other form of bit is smaller in diameter (a little more than 1 inch), and the body is taller, up to about 3/4 inch. If you think it resembles the glue-joint bit, you are

correct. It is a miniature of that bit, and it can, in fact, produce a routed glue joint on thin stock. (Page back to the beginning of this chapter, and follow the general directions for setting up the bit for that application.)

Set up and used as a drawer-lock bit, it produces a tapered tongue with a slant-walled dado on one side, a slant-shouldered rabbet on the other.

How do the two bit forms compare?

The joint produced by the mini-glue-joint bit is stronger, I'd say, thanks to that extra shoulder. And it will cut a glue joint on your solid-wood drawer stock (assuming it isn't too thick).

But the drawer-lock bit is easier to set up, and it will cut all the joinery you need for making a drawer, including the groove for the bottom. That's a significant time-saver.

Which joint looks stronger to you? Both provide a mechanical lock and both conceal the end grain of the side.

Drawer-Lock Joint

Flush

3/8" rabbet

3/4" front, 1/2" side

3/4" front and side

1/2" front and side

1" front, 1/2" side

SETTING THE FENCE

Fence

Side thickness + overhang width

Mounting plate

FOR DRAWER FRONT

Fence

Fence flush with cutting edge; only tab protrudes.

Mounting plate

FOR DRAWER SIDE

TUNING BIT HEIGHT

Gap here means bit is too low.

Won't close; bit is too high.

As a starting point, set the bit about 3/8 inch to 7/16 inch above the tabletop. Slide the fence into position and adjust it so it is tangent to the small cutting diameter. Just the tab should protrude from the fence.

Make cuts in the edges of two pieces of the working stock, turn one over, and fit them together. While the pieces won't be flush, the interlock should be nice and tight (see the photo). If it is, you've got the setup just right.

- If the fit is loose, raise the bit to tighten it.

- If the fit is too tight, lower the bit to loosen it.

If necessary, adjust the bit and make a couple of additional cuts to check the fit. But once you have the setting, you are ready to make drawers.

The only subsequent alteration you'll need to make to the setup is to shift the fence back when you do the fronts and backs to expose more of the bit. Assuming you want flush-fitting drawer boxes, use a piece of the side stock as a gauge. Hold it against the fence and move the fence until the protruding tab is flush with the exposed face of the stock sample.

One upshot is that it is easy to move back and forth between cutting sides and cutting fronts and backs. For the sides, the fence must be tangent to the small diameter of the

You've got to start somewhere. Use a rule to set the initial height of the drawer-lock bit, then refine the setting through test cuts. The setting shown is a good starting point.

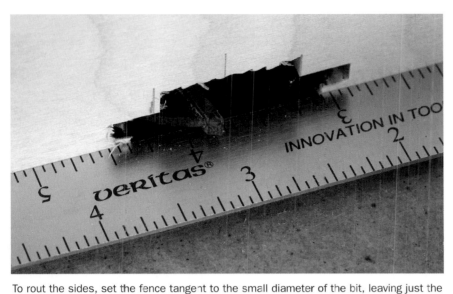

To rout the sides, set the fence tangent to the small diameter of the bit, leaving just the tab protruding. Check the setting with a rule. You want the cutting edge to graze the rule without actually moving it.

A practical workaround is to leave the parts (except the bottom) slightly wide. After cutting the lock joints, rip them to the final widths. In some situations, you may opt to work with wide blanks and rip two or three sides from each after the joinery is routed.

I advise against grooving the parts for the bottom until *after* both halves of the corner joints are cut. You'll be dismayed to see the damage done to the bottom grooves by the bit as it cuts the modified rabbet across the fronts and backs. The bit is emerging from the work into the groove, and you have no backup material in there. The result is splintering (see the photo).

cutting edge. (You'll also use this fence position to rout the bottom groove and to mill the underside of the bottoms.) For the fronts/backs, the fence is set to expose a portion of the bit equal to the sides' thickness.

Cutting the Joinery

Before cutting the joinery, you should mill your stock to the final thicknesses and crosscut the parts the final lengths. To determine how long to cut the parts, the sides especially, you can make sample cuts in scraps of the working stock.

The thickness of your stock *will* have an impact on this. If you are using 1/2-inch stock, for example, the sides generally will be about 1/8 inch shorter than the desired drawer length (front to back). With 5/8-inch stock or with a front that's thicker than the back, the adjustment will be different. Figure out what it is going to be before crosscutting the parts and routing the joinery.

Because you are making cross-grain cuts, blowout is a common woe.

Stand a side on end, braced against the fence, and feed it across the bit. The zero-clearance tabletop and fence surfaces minimize chip-out and prevent catches in the work's movement through the cut. To help stabilize the stock as you slide it (and further minimize tearout), back up the work with a square scrap.

A workable routine is this:

■ Rout the sides first. To do a side, you stand it on end, inside face against the fence, and slide it across the bit. Cut one end, then the other. I've never found a tall fence to be necessary, even with long sides, nor do I bother with featherboards. If you are more comfortable with either accessory (or with both), use them. I do use a square scrap as a pusher.

■ Do the fronts and back next. Adjust the fence position first. The workpiece rests flat on the tabletop, its end butted against the fence. Again, a square scrap used as a pusher helps me keep the work moving evenly—and squarely—along the fence.

Bear in mind here that the thickness of the workpieces will not impact the fit of the joints. You can mix 3/4-inch-thick fronts with 1/2-inch-thick backs, routing all with the same setup.

■ Rip the parts to their final widths.

■ Rout the groove for the bottom next. Return the fence to the position used to cut the sides. Reference the inside face of each part against the fence, and cut from end to end with the drawer-lock bit, just as it is set. Because of the way the joints go together, the groove won't be visible.

■ Finally, mill the bottom to fit the groove. You keep the bit and fence setting as they are. The 1/4-inch plywood bottom should be face down on the tabletop. Mill all four edges.

Use a scrap of the stock used for the sides to reposition the fence for the joinery cuts in the ends. The tip of the cutting edge must be flush with the scrap's surface. This ensures that the nose of the end piece will overlap the end grain of the side piece when the joint is assembled.

Lay a drawer end—either the front or the back—flat on the tabletop, its end butted against the fence. Feed it across the bit. Use a backup block to keep the workpiece square to the fence throughout the cut and to minimize tearout.

Assembling the Drawer

Assembly of a drawer is straightforward. First, of course, make sure all the parts are finish-sanded. Then apply glue to the joints and put the parts together. I glue a plywood bottom into place, regardless of the stock used for the sides, front, and back.

In keeping with the "make 'em fast!" mindset, I've taken to shooting two or three brads into each joint. Glue holds the parts together, of course, but the brads eliminate the

Get a rattle-free fit of bottom to groove by routing both the groove and the bottom with the drawer-lock bit. After the corner joinery is cut, return the fence to the setting for the side cuts. Rout bottom grooves in both sides and ends. Then lay the bottom, face down, on the table and rout all four edges to form a chamfer that matches the groove profile.

The Other Bit

The mini-glue-joint bit requires a slightly different setup routine. Cutting the corner joinery and assembling the drawer is exactly the same. But sorry, you can't rout the bottom groove with this bit.

Setting up the bit requires a series of test cuts. Because the thickness of the stock has no bearing on the fit of the joint, you can use scraps to zero in on the setting up. (And of course, after you have the setup, you can make yourself a setup block to use the next time you use the bit.)

What works for me during the setup process is to position the fence a little farther back than I want to have it for routing the drawer sides. This compromise position will allow you to make two cuts quickly—that is, without having to jockey the fence back and forth—and assess the fit. One of your test cuts is made with a scrap in the drawer-side orientation—that is, on end, braced against the fence—and the other with a scrap in the drawer-front orientation, which is flat on the table, end against the fence.

Fit the cut pieces together (see the photo). You'll easily be able to evaluate the fit. If you have a gap between the end of the "side" and the overlapping shoulder of the "front," you must raise the bit. If you can't close

need to clamp up each drawer, saving a lot of time.

The bottom *should* ensure that the assembly will be square, but I check with a try square, just in case. Likewise, the parts *should* go together without a hitch, and a dry run *does* take some time, but I think the dry run is worth the few moments it takes. Saves your bacon when you've been a little sloppy with a cut or a measurement.

Start your assembly sequence with a side. Apply glue to the end grain and the dadoes, as well as to the bottom groove. Next, apply glue to a front/back, and connect it to the side. It'll stand up all by itself. Fit the bottom in place. Apply glue to the second front/back, then fit it in place. Finally, apply glue to the second side and set it in place. You've got an assembled drawer box.

With your try square, check a couple of inside corners. You can measure the diagonals, too.

Assured that the drawer is square and the joints are seated, shoot a couple of brads into each joint, directing them through the side into the front/back.

If you don't have a pneumatic brad nailer, you can use masking tape to "clamp" small drawers. Larger drawers ought to be clamped. Use parallel-jaw clamps or bar clamps. All you need to do is apply pressure from side to side. Front-to-back clamping is unnecessary.

Alternate Drawer-Lock Joint

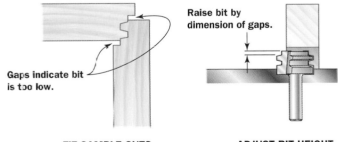

Gaps indicate bit is too low.

Raise bit by dimension of gaps.

FIT SAMPLE CUTS

ADJUST BIT HEIGHT

the joint, you must lower the bit. There is no "halving" going on here: If the gap is 1/8 inch, then raise the bit 1/8 inch.

With the bit height set, you are ready to make drawers. First, move the fence into proper position for routing the sides, and do them. Shift it back and rout the fronts and backs.

You will have to saw the bottom grooves or switch bits to make them on the router table. But once that's done, assembling the drawers proceeds as if you're doing all the cuts with the drawer-lock bit.

In the end, when the drawer's fitted to the case, shellacked, and loaded up with your…eh…*stuff*, it'll perform as well as the ones you devoted hours to crafting with dovetails. And the proof is in the performance, right?

Establish the height setting of the miniature glue-joint bit through test cuts made with the fence in a compromise position. The key criterion is the fit at the ends of the two pieces. The seam where the walnut "front" overlaps the maple "side" must be tight.

Sources

Here are addresses of selected router, bit, and accessory manufacturers and retailers.

As a general rule, router manufacturers sell through dealers, including direct-mail retailers that advertise in woodworking magazines. Several of the bit manufacturers and importers listed below sell only through dealers, though many of them sell directly to retail customers.

If you can't find a dealer for a particular brand of router or bits in your area, call the manufacturer or importer.

Amana Tool
120 Carolyn Boulevard
Farmingdale, NY 11735
800-445-0077
www.amanatool.com
High-quality saw blades, router bits, and shaper-cutters. Sells through dealers.

Bench Dog
3310 Fifth Street NE
Minneapolis, MN 55418
800-786-8902
www.benchdog.com
Router tables, router lifts, and associated products.

Bosch Tool Corp.
4300 W. Peterson Avenue
Chicago, IL 60646-5999
877-267-2499
www.boschtools.com
Manufacturer of full range of portable power tools, including routers, bits, and accessories. Sells through dealers.

CMT USA, Inc.
307-F Pomona Drive
Greensboro, NC 27407
888-268-2487
www.cmtusa.com
High-quality router bits. Sells through dealers.

Craftsman Tools
Your local Sears or Sears Hardware
800-549-4505
www.sears.com/craftsman
Retailer of full range of portable power tools, including routers, bits, and accessories.

DeWalt Industrial Tool Co.
701 E. Joppa Road, TW425
Baltimore, MD 21286
800-433-9258
www.dewalt.com
Manufacturer of full range of portable power tools, including routers and accessories. Sells through dealers.

Fein Power Tools
1030 Alcon Street
Pittsburgh, PA 15220
800-441-9878
www.feinus.com
Manufacturer of portable power tools, including routers and accessories. Sells through dealers.

Festool USA
Tooltechnic Systems, LLC
140 Los Carneros Way
Goleta, CA 93117
888-337-8600
www.festoolusa.com
Manufacturer of portable power tools, including routers, bits, and accessories. Sells through dealers.

Freud, Inc.
218 Feld Avenue
High Point, NC 27263
800-334-4107
www.freudtools.com
Routers and other portable power tools, high-quality saw blades, router bits, and shaper-cutters. Sells through dealers.

Highland Hardware
1045 North Highland Avenue NE
Atlanta, GA 30306
800-241-6748
www.tools-for-woodworking.com
Retailer of tools, accessories, and supplies.

Hitachi Power Tools
3950 Steve Reynolds Boulevard
Norcross, GA 30093
800-706-7337
www.hitachipowertools.com
Manufacturer of full range of portable power tools, including routers and accessories. Sells through dealers.

Infinity Cutting Tools
2762 Summerdale Drive
Clearwater, FL 33761
877-872-2487
www.infinitytools.com
High-quality saw blades, router bits, and shaper-cutters. Sells direct.

JessEm Tool Co.
124 Big Bay Point Road
Barrie, ON L4N 9B4
Canada
866-272-7492
www.jessem.com
Router lifts, tabletops, fences, and related accessories.

Jointech, Inc.
11811 Warfield
San Antonio, TX 78216
800-619-1288
www.jointech.com
Router lifts, tabletops, fences, and related accessories. Sells direct.

Lee Valley
in the U.S.:
P.O. Box 1780
Ogdensburg, NY 13669-6780
800-267-8735
in Canada:
P.O. Box 6295, Station J
Ottawa, ON K2A 1T4
800-267-8761
www.leevalley.com
Woodworking tool manufacturer (Veritas) and supercatalog retailer of tools, accessories, supplies, hardware, and books.

Leigh Industries
P.O. Box 357
Port Coquitlan, BC U3C 4K6
Canada
800-663-8932
www.leighjigs.com
Manufacturer of Leigh dovetail and
mortising jigs.

Magnate
20639 Lycoming Street, #B-6
Walnut, CA 91789
800-827-2316
www.magnate.net
Router bits. Sells direct.

Makita USA, Inc.
14930 Northam Street
La Mirada, CA 90638
800-462-5482
www.makitatools.com
Manufacturer of full range of portable
power tools, including routers, bits, and
accessories. Sells through dealers.

MicroFence
13160 Saticoy Street
North Hollywood, CA 91605
818-982-4367
800-480-6427
www.microfence.com
Finest router edge guide (and kindred
accessories) known to woodworking.

Milwaukee Electric Tool Corp.
13135 W. Lisbon Road
Brookfield, WI 53005
800-729-3878
www.milwaukeetool.com
Manufacturer of full range of portable
power tools, including routers and
accessories. Sells through dealers.

Paso Robles Carbide
731-C Paso Robles Street
Paso Robles, CA 93446
800-238-6144
[no website]
Router bits. Sells through dealers.

Porter-Cable
4825 Highway 45 North
P.O. Box 2468
Jackson, TN 38302-2468
800-487-8665
www.porter-cable.com
Manufacturer of full range of portable
power tools, including routers, bits, and
accessories. Sells through dealers.

Reid Supply Company
(formerly Reid Tool Supply)
2265 Black Creek Road
Muskegon, MI 49444
800-253-0421
www.reidtool.com
Extensive catalog of machinists' tools,
hardware, and fascinating widgets. First
place to look for toggle clamps, plastic
knobs, and other jigmaking hardware.

Ridge Carbide Tool Corp.
595 New York Avenue
Lyndhurst, NJ 07071
800-443-0992
www.ridgecarbidetool.com
Router bits and other carbide-tipped
cutters; makes custom router bits for
special jobs; sharpening.

Rockler Woodworking and Hardware
4365 Willow Drive
Medina, MN 55340
800-279-4441
www.rockler.com
Supercatalog retailer of tools, accessories,
supplies, hardware, and books.

Sommerfeld's Tools for Wood
1408 Celebrity Road
Remsen, IA 51050
888-228-9268
www.sommerfeldtools.com
Source for CMT cutters, plus router tables,
cabinetmaking accessories and supplies.

Triton Workshop Systems
2107 Second Street
West Cornwall, ON K6H 5R6
Canada
888-874-8661
www.tritonwoodworking.com
Manufacturer of routers and woodworking
equipment.

Pat Warner
1427 Kenora Street
Escondido, CA 92027-3940
760-747-2623
www.patwarner.com
High-quality router accessories, jigs and
fixtures, and sound router-woodworking
information.

Whiteside Machine Co.
4506 Shook Road
Claremont, NC 28610
800-225-3982
www.whitesiderouterbits.com
Router bits. Sells through dealers.

Woodcraft
P.O. Box 1686
Parkersburg, WV 26102-1686
800-225-1153
www.woodcraft.com
Supercatalog retailer of tools, accessories,
supplies, hardware, and books.

Woodhaven
501 West First Avenue
Durant, IA 52747-9729
800-344-6657
www.woodhaven.com
Router tables, woodworking jigs and
fixtures, router bits, and more.
Sells direct.

Woodline
111 Wheeler Street
La Vergne, TN 37086
800-472-6950
www.woodline.com
Extensive catalog of affordable router
bits and shaper-cutters, plus accessories.
Sells direct.

Woodpeckers
11050 Industrial First
North Royalton, OH 44133
800-752-0725
www.woodpeck.com
Router lifts, tables, fences, and related
accessories. Sells direct.

Index

Half-lap joints, 295. *See also*
    Mitered half-lap joints
Handheld routers. *See also specific*
    cuts or techniques
        cutting techniques for
            making cut, 37–42
            setting up, 33–37
        feed direction for, 37–40
        main parts of, 1–7
        selection criteria for, 7–16
Handles, *6, 7*
Hardboard, for templates, 163
Hardware, for jigmaking, 49–51
Hearing protection, 29–30
Hinges, from box joints, 344
Hold-downs. *See also* Control, of
    workpiece
        plesiosaur, 116–117, *224*
        types of, 36–37
Horizontal router tables. *See also*
    Router tables
        building, 93–100
        cutting joinery with
            sliding dovetails, 324
            tenons, 293–294
        described, 91–93
        feed direction for, 99
        setting up, 99
Horsepower
    ratings of, 1–4
    router size and, 8–9

I
Index cards, as shims, 128
Induction motors, 2
Inlay, 167–171
Insert plates
    described, 62–63
    installing, 78–79
Inserts, for inlay, 169–171
Inspection, of bits and collets, 34
Internal templates, 162–163
Inverted bits, 151

J
Jigs and fixtures. *See also* Baseplates;
    Edge guides
        baseplates, 242–244

box-joint, 337–343
building, 53–54
circle-cutting, 177–181
coping, 213
dadoing and grooving
    dado guides, 238–241, 245
    T-square, 236–238, 245
defined, 43, 277
designing, 44–46
dovetailing, 305–307, 313
dovetail-splice, 342
edge-jointing, 260–261
edge-miter slotting, 335–336
for end-grain cuts, 117
flush-trimming, 192–195
versus job-specific setups, 204
keying, 345–347, 349
lap-cutting, 299–301, *304*
materials for, 46–51
mortising
    mortising block, 281–284
    mortising platform,
        279–281
    quick-and-dirty mortising
        fixture, 277–278
oval-cutting, 184–185
overarm pivot, *183*
pivot block, 266–267
pocket-lap jig, 301
saddle jig, *304*
safety of, 46
tenoning, 290–293, 296, *297*
thicknessing, 200–205
Job-specific setups, 204
Joinery, bits for, 22. *See also specific*
    joints
Jointing
    with handheld routers,
        197–198
    routers versus jointers for,
        196–197
    on router tables, 198–200

K
Keys. *See* Dovetail keys; Spline keys
Kickback, 23
Knobs, for jigmaking, *50*
Knots, replacing with inlay, 171

L
Labeling parts, 310–311
Laminate
    applying to substrate, 231
    cutting, 230–231
    described, 229
    for jigmaking, 48
    safety with, 229
    for tabletops, 77–80
    trimming, 231–233
Laminate trimmers
    cutting sliding dovetails with,
        325
    described, 10–11
    flush-trimming with, 192–195
    offset-base, 234, *330*
    trimming keys with, 350
Laminate-trimming bits, 230
Lap joints
    cross laps, 299–302
    edge laps, 304
    end laps, 295–299
    half-laps, 295
    mitered half-laps, 228, 302–304
    pocket laps, 301
Layout
    in jigmaking, 54
    tools for, 33
Lock-miter bits, 356
Lock-miter joints, 355–360
Loose-tenon joints, 216, 289
Lubrication of bits, 27–28

M
Machine screws
    for jigmaking, *50*
    as starting pins, 102
Manageability of routers, 9–11
Marking techniques
    for glue-joint cuts, 352–353
    for identifying parts, 310–311
MDF (medium-density fiberboard)
    for jigmaking, 46–47
    for tabletops, 77
    for templates, 163
Measuring and layout
    in jigmaking, 54
    tools for, 33

Screw covers, trimming, *191*
Seats, hollowing, 207
Self-feeding, 136
Self-positioning dado guide, 238–239
Self-releasing collets, 4–5
Setup blocks
    for cope-and-stick joints, 214
    described, *53*
    for horizontal table setup, 99
    for setting bit height, 121
Setup gauges, 99, 120, 237–238
Setup routines
    for handheld routers, 33–37
    for router tables, 119–123
Shaping surfaces
    curves, 206–208
    recesses, 205
    tapers, 205–206
Sharpening bits, 28
Shear-cut straight bits, 250
Sheet goods, for jigmaking, 46–48
Shims
    for fence micro-adjustments, 128
    for staging cuts, 134–135
Shiplap joints, 258
Single-flute straight bits, *21,* 250
Sizes of routers, 8–9
Sleds
    coping, 213
    for end-grain cuts, 117
    tenoning, 292–293, 296, *297*
Sliding dovetail joints
    bits for, 318
    cutting
        grooves, 319–322
        tails, 322–328
    described, 317, 319
    fitting, 318
    French, 326–327
    tools for, 317–318
Sliding fences
    building, 111–112
    cutting joinery with
        box joints, 338
        cross laps, 300–302, *304*

Sliding tables, in horizontal router table, 97–98
Slot cutters
    described, *22,* 264, 265
    modifying, 334
    using, 263–265, 267
Small pieces
    cutting, 137–138
    surfacing, 198
Smoothness
    of plunge router operation, 16
    of router tables, 59
Soft start, 3
Speed
    bit longevity and, 280
    bit size and, 26–27
    in pacing cuts, 137
    variable control for, 3, 280
Spiral bits
    for dadoes and grooves, 250
    described, *21*
    for joinery, *22*
    for jointing, 199
    for mortises, 286
    for tenons, 294
Splined edge joints, 259, 263–267
Splined miter joints
    described, 329
    edge miters, 332–336
    flat miters, 329–332
    for frame-and-panel construction, 228
Spline keys
    cutting, 347–348
    described, 345
    fitting, 350
    jig for, 345–347
Spline slots, duplicating, 331
Splintered edges, avoiding
    in circle-cutting, 176
    with handheld routers, 38–40, *41,* 144–145
    in joinery
        cope-and-stick joints, 216
        dovetail joints, 321, *322*
        drawer-lock joints, *363*
        rabbet joints, 253

on router tables, 126–127, 136–137
    in template work, 165–166
Split-arbor collets, 5
Springboards, 115
Stacked bits, 211
Staged cuts
    with piloted bits, 160
    with sled, 297
    techniques for, 133–134, 222–223
Stand-type router tables, 65, 71–73. *See also* Router tables
Starting pins, 101–102, 131–132
Step-and-repeat process, *54*
Stiles, defined, 209
Stock
    for accurate cuts, 30–31
    for frame-and-panel construction, 210–212, 217–218
    warped, 203, 263–265
Stop blocks
    custom-tailored, 106
    for staged cuts, 135
    for stopped cuts, 133, 249
Stopped cuts
    dadoes and grooves, *241,* 248–249
    rabbets, 254–255
    techniques for, 132–133
Storage, of bits, 27, *28,* 56
Straight bits, *21, 22. See also specific types or applications*
Straightedges, *45*
String inlay, 167–168
Surfacing
    flush-trimming, 191–196
    jointing, 196–200
    router advantages in, 191
    shaping surfaces, 205–208
    small pieces, 198
    thicknessing, 200–205
Surfacing baseplates, 204–205
Surfacing platform
    building, 200–202
    using, 202–204